Equity and the Law of Trusts

Centuries in the Making

Steven Gallagher

GALLAGHER
& BLAKE
PUBLISHING

First published in 2013 by Gallagher and Blake

Gallagher and Blake
12 Sandiland Crescent
Hayes
Bromley
Kent BR2 7DR

www.gallagherandblake.co.uk

British Library cataloguing in Publication Data.
A Catalogue record for this book is available from the British Library.

ISBN 978-0-9926278-0-5

Printed and bound by Intype Libra Ltd, UK

Cover design by Nicky Sayers - Madeyoulook
Edited by A.Brown
Typeset in Palatino by PABPS, London

FSC
Mixed Sources
Product group from well-managed
forests and recycled wood or fiber
Cert no. SGS-COC-004311
www.fsc.org
© 1996 Forest Stewardship Council

CONTENTS

UK Cases

Oughtred v IRC [1960] AC 206, [1959] 3 All ER 623, HL: 5.2.2
Oxley v Hiscock [2004] EWCA Civ 546; 3 All ER 703; [2005] Fam 211: 11.6.4
Pallant v Morgan [1953] Ch 43: 10.7.7
Palmer v Simmonds (1854) 2 Drew 221: 6.2.2; 10.5
Paradise Motor Co. Ltd. [1968] 1 WLR 1125.*GREY v. IRC Re* [1960] AC 1 (HL): 5.2.2
Paragon Finance plc v DB Thakerar (a firm) [1999] 1 ITELR 735, CA: 10.7.7
Partington, re (1887) 57 LT 654: 13.12; 13.13
Pascoe v Turner [1979] 1 WLR 431: 11.8.4
Paton v Trustees of British Pregnancy Advisory Service [1979] QB 276: 2.3; 3.6
Patten and Edmonton Union Poor Guardians, re (1883) 52 LJ Ch 787: 13.6.1
Paul v Constance [1977] 1 WLR 527; 1 All ER 195, CA: 5.4; 6.1.1; 9.3; 10.1
Pauling's ST, re [1963] Ch 576; [1964] Ch 303: 13.11; 13.13
Peffer v. Rigg [1977] 1 WLR 285: 10.7.3
Penn v Lord Baltimore (1750) 1Ves Sen 444: 2.3; 3.2
Pennington v. Waine [2002] EWCA Civ 227; [2002] 1 WLR 2075: 9.4; 9.5.1
Percival v Wright [1902] 2 Ch 421: 14.1
Pettingall v. Pettingall (1842) 11 LJ Ch 176: 7.3.1
Pettitt v Pettitt [1970] AC 777: 10.4.3: 11.6.1
Phillips v Lamdin [1949] 1 All ER 770: 3.7
Pickton v Littlecote (1579-1580) Cary 93, 21 ER 49: 3.5
Pilkington v. IRC [1964] AC 612: 13.7; 13.11
Pinion, re (Westminster Bank Ltd v Pinion) [1965] Ch 85, CA: 8.8
Pinnel's Case [1558-1774] All ER Rep 612: 2.6
Pirbright v Salwey [1896] WN 86: 7.3.1; 7.3.2
Pitt v Holt [2011] 3 WLR 19, EWCA : 13.5
Plumptre's Marriage Settlement, re [1910] 1 Ch 609: 9.6.2
Portman Building Society v Dusangh, [2000] 2 All ER 221: 2.5.1
Prendiville v Prendiville [1989] No 597 Sp Ct 5: 12.5
Pryce, re [1917] 1 Ch 234: 9.6.1
Pullan v. Koe [1913] 1 Ch 9: 9.6.2
Queensland Mines v Hudson (1978) 18 ALR 1, PC: 14.4
R (Beer (trading as Hammer trout farm) v Hampshire Farmers Markets Ltd [2003] EWCA Civ 1056: 8.2
R v Clowes (No 2) [1994] 2 All ER 316: 10.5.2; 16.5.1; 16.5.2
R v Ghosh [1999] 1 Cr App Rep (S) 225: 17.7
R v Price (1884) 12 QBD 247: 6.1
R v. District Auditor ex parte West Yorkshire Metropolitan County Council [1986] RVR 24: 6.3.2
R. Griggs Group Ltd v Evans [2005] Ch 153: 3.2
R. v. Beddoe [1893]1 Ch 547: 13.4
R. v. Radio Authority ex parte Bull [1997] 3 WLR 1094: 8.10
R. v. Registrar General ex parte Segerdal [1970] 2 QB 697: 8.6
Rabaiotti's Settlements, re [2000] WTLR 953: 13.9
Radmacher (formerly Granatino) v Granatino [2010] UKSC 42: 11.3
Ralli's WT, re [1964] Ch 288 Ch D: 9.5.1
Ramsden v Dyson (1865) LR 1 HL 129: 11.8.4
Ramskill v Edwards (1885) 31 Ch D 10: 13.12; 13.13

Foreign Cases

Brown v Brown (1993) 31 NSWLR 582: 10.4.6

Chan Chui Mee v Mak Chi Choi [2009] 1 HKLRD 343: 11.6.1

Chan Chun Chung v PBM (Hong Kong) Ltd [2004] HKEC 630; [2005] 1 HKLRD 565, CFA: 16.5.5

Cheung Pui Yuen v Worldcup Investments Inc [2008] HKCU 1669; HKEC 1808 (CFA): 10.4.6; 11.2

Cheung, Lily v Commissioner of Estate Duty [1987] 3 HKC 307: 10.4.4

CY Foundation Group v Cheng Chee Tock [2011] HKEC 1629; [2012] 1 HKLRD 532: 16.5.4; 16.6

Dagle v Dagle Estate (1990) 70 DLR (4th) 201: 10.4.6

Ebraham Sadick, re [2009] HKEC 1983 (CFI): 3.3

Eiders Pastoral Ltdv Bank of New Zealand (1989) 2 NZLR 180: 16.6

Evans v European Bank Ltd [2004] NSWCA 82: 16.6

First Laser Ltd v Fujian Enterprises (Holdings) Co Ltd [2003] HKEC 7: 16.6

Gillies v Keogh [1989] 2 N.Z.L.R. 327: 10.2; 11.6.1

Hang Seng Bank Ltd v Lau Ching Che [2007] HKEC 2255: 16.6

Harry Talbot v Mrs Lam [1946] HKLR 17: 16.3

Hartigan Nominees Pty Ltd v Rydge (1992) 29 NSWLR 405: 15.2

Hiranand v Harilela [2004] 4 HKC 231: 15.4

Ip Man Shan, Henry v Ching Hing Construction Company Ltd (No 2) [2003] 1 HKC 256: 10.4.4; 12.2.2

Joint and Several Trustees of the Property of Karson Otto Fan, Karno (In Bankruptcy) v Kong Suk Chun [2012] HKCU 324: 16.6

Ledgerwood v Perpetual Trustee [1997] 41 NSWLR532: 12.5

Lee Tso Fong v Kwok Wai Sun [2008] 4 HKC 36: 10.4.6

Leung Chi Man v Mok Sau Lim [2005] HKCU 761: 12.3.1

Leung Mui v Hong Kong and Shanghai Banking Corporation (1923) 18 HKLR 56 1: 6.5.5

Li Hung Chan v Wong Woon Heung (alias Wong Yuen) (1950) 34 HKLR 213: 10.4.6

Lui Kam Lau v Leung Ming Fai [1994] 3 HKC 477: 10.1; 11.2

Luo Xing Juan Angela v Estate of Hui Shui See Willy (Deceased) [2008] HKCU 918: 2.6; 11.8.4; 11.9

McMahon v McMahon [1996] 3 N.Z.L.R. 334: 11.6.1

Ng Jack Fong v Ng Chan Ning [2008] 2 HKC 527 (HKCA): 12.2.4

Pecore v Pecore [2007] 1 SCR 795; (2007) SCC 17: 10.4.6

Peter v Beblow [1993] 1 SCR 980: 11.6.1

Pettkus v Becker (1980) 117 D.L.R. (3d) 257; [1980] 2 S.C.R. 834: 10.2: 11.6.1

Re Larkin, 9 N.Y. 2d 88, 211, N.Y.S. 2 d 175, 172 N.E. 2d 555 (1961): 5.6.2

Royal Brunei Airlines v Tan (Kok Ming) [1995] 2 AC 378; 2 HKC 409: 17.7

Tam Mei Kam v HSBC International Trustee Ltd [2011] HKCU 964: 15.2

Terkild Johan Terkildsen v Barber Asia Ltd [2007] HKCU 399 (CFI): 16.6

Tingler v Chamberlain 71 Conn. 466: 2.1

Foreign Legislation

International Conventions

UK statutes and foreign statutes

Preface

After teaching students from both common law and civil jurisdictions I wanted to write a text which aimed to explain the difficult concepts and principles of equity and the law of trusts to students from either background. This work is intended to be an introductory and intermediary level text for students studying the required courses for a qualifying law degree in the UK. The text also introduces some issues that may be of interest for further study and contains references for those who wish to examine these issues in more depth.

Equity is the most responsive and flexible part of the common law. To understand the modern legal principles of equity the text considers how these principles were developed in the Court of Chancery in response to changing social needs.

I hope that the text is readable and explains the most important concepts and issues in equity. It would be wonderful if it sparked in any reader an interest in equity and the law of trusts. There may be a little too much history in this work for some readers- especially in the first and fourth chapters- my excuse is this provides necessary context for the development of modern equity, but really it reflects my interest and love of the history of the Court of Chancery. It may be that after reading this work you can point out its errors or how to improve it, please share any criticism with me at the email below.

I would like to thank colleagues in the United Kingdom and Hong Kong for their help and criticism- in particular Greg Allan and Mark Hsiao and Alan Brown for his editing expertise in the United Kingdom and Michael Lower at the Faculty of Law at CUHK. I would also like to thank those who taught me equity and inspired my love for the subject- in particular Richard Royle, Chris Turner and Professor Roger Gregory for the two-year tutorial while sharing his office. I am quite sure they would not agree with all the views in this text, but that is the beauty of equity. I would also like to thank all the students I have taught in Hong Kong for their questions and for their patience in listening to me getting excited about uses and conscience, especially those who attempted my equity crossword puzzles!

All errors remain my own.

Steven Brian Gallagher
stevegallagher@cuhk.edu.hk
The Chinese University of Hong Kong,
Hong Kong

Driney,
Eire,
2 July 2013

PART I
EQUITY

CHAPTER 1
WHAT IS EQUITY?

1.1 Why Study Equity?

Most of the world studies equity because of historical accident. The world has two major systems of law based upon the customs of European peoples.[1] The two systems are Roman law, which has to a greater or lesser extent been developed into the civil codes,[2] and the common law of England. Equity is part of the common law of England. The common law was exported from England by the British Empire as a means to enforce British rule and because there was a genuine belief that the common law was the most just system of law. Although the British Empire has been subject to many criticisms, one of the legacies of the British Empire is that many widespread parts of the world have a common law system. Although many of these former colonies and dominions have long been politically independent of England, their legal systems are still based upon the English common law.[3] The common law is a system of law developed over a millennium in response to the changing customs and needs of the people of England, and subsequently of the Empire. Of course, the legacy of the common law has been developed in these individual jurisdictions in response to the changing customs and needs particular to their society. The flexibility of the common law is aided by the ability of judges in each common law jurisdiction to take note of decisions by courts in other

---

[1] 'It has happened twice only that the customs of European peoples were worked up into intellectual systems of law; and much of the world today is governed by laws derived from the one or the other.' S.F.C.Milsom, *Historical Foundations of the Common Law*, (London: Butterworths, 2nd edition, 1981) p.1.

[2] For example, the civil jurisdictions of France, Germany, the People's Republic of China, etc.

[3] For example, the United States of America declared independence in 1776, but retained the common law and thus remains a common law jurisdiction where many of the principles of law are similar to those in other common law jurisdictions including its former political master.

common law jurisdictions as "persuasive" precedents. This has allowed many areas of the common law to develop in line with the best jurisprudence in each jurisdiction. This interaction between the different common law jurisdictions means that there remains a remarkable degree of similarity between them. In later chapters, when we consider different areas of equity, such as resulting trusts, the presumption of advancement and constructive trusts, we will emphasise the interaction between the jurisdictions and examine how the flexibility of the common law, and especially equity, enables the law in countries with common law legal systems to take note of decisions in other jurisdictions, or to develop in line with the unique needs of a state's own jurisdiction.

It is also important to study equity, as it is a prescribed subject for most professional courses leading to practice as a lawyer in common law jurisdictions. When students of equity are told, as they usually are, that the law of equity and the trust is amongst the most difficult areas they will study in their degree, students may wonder if the direction by professional bodies to study such a complicated and seemingly archaic topic may simply be revenge by professionals who had to study the area themselves; however, although equity was developed many centuries ago, the principles, processes and remedies of equity have continued to be adapted and developed to serve modern financial and commercial needs. In fact, as England developed into a financial and commercial power, it was the flexibility of the common law and the power of equitable remedies that aided its success alongside the gunboats and merchant princes. The common law and equity were exported with an Empire which eventually covered almost a third of the globe.[4] The principles and remedies that were originally designed to protect the individual in England from injustice were rapidly tailored to finance and commerce. Indeed many modern financial and commercial concepts would not exist without equity, and equitable principles are still important in their application. The injunction, remedies other than damages for breach of contract, fiduciary obligations and remedies, commercial securities and the trust are vital today to international finance and trade. All have their roots in equity and equitable principles, and these principles and remedies are still being developed to meet changing needs.[5]

Equity was and is a vital part of the common law. Equity is the body of principles and remedies developed by the English Chancellor in his own

---

4   In 1924 it was estimated to cover between a quarter and a third of the globe and represented an area of over one hundred and fifty times the size of Great Britain itself. http://www.britishempire.co.uk/ accessed 24/10/11.

5   For example, the development of new forms of injunction and trust to suit modern commercial needs, see the Anton Pillar order and the Mareva injunction in chapter 3, and the *Quistclose* trust in chapter 10.

Court, the Court of Chancery, to deal with injustice and unconscionable behaviour. As equity is usually taught as a separate subject towards the end of a qualifying law degree, the law student will probably already have come across many equitable remedies and principles before studying equity itself. The importance of equity lies in its unique ability to provide solutions to legal disputes by means of its institutions, the most important of which are trusts, and the range of remedies at its disposal. To understand the common law, especially the most powerful remedies available for actions in civil cases, it is vital to study equity. In fact equity developed to provide remedies when the common law could not, or when the rigid application of the common law itself would cause injustice.[6] The equitable jurisdiction, equitable principles and equitable remedies permeate through almost all areas of the common law. Today the remarkable range of flexible and powerful institutions and remedies in equity's arsenal remains vital to the success of the common law itself.

Example

1. I have agreed to purchase a flat in London, contracts have been exchanged, but another party has offered the vendor more money. The vendor is willing to breach our contract and to pay damages for the breach as he can obtain a much larger amount from the new purchaser. What can I do? [7]
2. I am selling my old flat to finance the new purchase. Although I am the sole legal owner, an old partner who cohabited with me in the flat for some years is claiming that she has an interest because she made some mortgage payments and paid for the redecoration of the flat. Does she have an interest? [8]
3. My neighbours' teenage son is playing loud music late into the night. No one will buy my flat if this disturbance continues. How may I stop him? [9]

---

6   For example, Chancery was the first court to redress the discrimination against women's ownership of property and protected the wife against abuse of her property by her husband. See the comments of Jessel MR in *Re Ridley (Buckton v Hay)* (1879) 11 Ch D 645, at 648-649 and Montague Crackanthorpe, 'The Uses of Legal History' (1896) 19 *Annu. Rep. A.B.A.* 343, 358.
7   The equitable remedy of specific performance is usually available for contracts for the sale and purchase of land. See chapter 3.
8   She may have an interest by way of resulting or constructive trust, or proprietary or even promissory estoppel. See chapter 13.
9   It may be possible to obtain an injunction forbidding the playing of the loud music as a nuisance. See chapter 3.

4.   I want to call witnesses to provide evidence at any hearings. Some of those I wish to call may refuse to appear. How can I ensure they appear? [10]

5.   I want to plan for the protection of my family when I die. I want my wife to enjoy living in my flat until she dies and then pass it on to my son. If she remarries I do not want her new husband to gain any interest in the flat, or any children they might have together. How can I achieve this?[11]

6.   I am also concerned my son might inherit the flat before he is sensible enough to look after his own finances. I want to make it a condition of his inheritance that he must become a solicitor; otherwise, I want the flat to be given to the Ealing Home for the Elderly. How can I do this?[12]

7.   I also want to make provision for my mistress and illegitimate son in my will; however, I do not want my wife or legitimate son to find out about them, as this might hurt their feelings. How can I do this? [13]

8.   My company has advanced money to a supply company that is in financial trouble. The money is to purchase raw materials which the supplier needs to fulfil its obligations to us. It has placed the money in a separate account. Before the materials are supplied the supplier goes into liquidation. Can my company recover the money or will it form part of the fund for liquidation? [14]

Equity may provide potential answers to all of these problems. They are based upon principles and remedies developed by equity. Although some of these remedies may now have a statutory basis,[15] equitable principles are still important in deciding whether they should be granted.

Thus, equity is a vital part of the common law, aiding its flexibility and responsiveness to the changing needs of society, and providing powerful remedies. The international nature of the common law thus provides that equity has an important role in many areas of law that are vital for the success of international finance and trade. This is recognised by professional bodies in most common law jurisdictions and is why it is considered necessary for those studying the common law to study equity. Equity is an integral part of the common law.

We should now consider how equity is defined in law.

---

10   It may be possible to issue a subpoena, an order under penalty to appear in front of the court.

11   A life interest trust, allowing the wife the property for life and then passing it to the son after the wife's death in remainder. See chapter 5.

12   A simple condition can be inserted into the trust making the son's interest contingent on his becoming a solicitor. See chapter 5.

13   By using a secret trust. See chapter 12.

14   This may give rise to a *Quistclose* trust. See chapter 10.

15   For example the injunction is now subject to the Senior Courts Act 1981.

1.2 What is Equity?

Asked to consider what the word "equity" means, most people would think of "fairness" and "justice", and these are good indications of the original motivations for the development of equity in the common law. Most legal systems seem to have had a concept of equity.[16] Aristotle talked of equity correcting the inflexibility of the law.[17] He noted that it was impossible to develop a system of laws to cover every eventuality. Thus, cases would arise where the law did not cover the circumstances of the case, or the rigid application of the law itself would be unjust. In these cases the law needed a concept of fairness and justice to prevent injustice. This was equity.[18]

The principles of natural justice, for example that the other side must be allowed to respond to a case against them,[19] were very much part of the original reason for the development of equity. The common law would often not hear a defendant's argument, perhaps because he had not complied with some formality the common law required, or just because for many centuries the common law did not allow a defendant to give evidence. In these cases justice was only to be found in front of the Chancellor who would examine the conscience of both parties, hear both sides of the argument and decide which was most just. This was 'justice pure and simple'.[20]

Equity is therefore a 'correction of legal justice';[21] it exists to correct injustices of the law, to be fair and just. It fills in the gaps in the law and

---

16 Roman law had the concept of *aequitas* from which we derive the English word 'equity': H.F. Jollowicz, *Roman Foundations of Modern Law* (Oxford, 1957), p.56. In ancient China the concept of Quing was a concept of human feeling and social norms used to supplement the rigidity of the law, or gaps in the law.

17 Considered in Aristotle's *Nichomachean Ethics*.

18 See, for example, S.F.C.Milsom, Historical Foundations of the Common Law, (London: Butterworths, 2nd edition, 1981) p.6; Mike Mcnair, 'Equity and Conscience' (2007) 27(4) *Oxford Journal of Legal Studies* 659, 660.

19 Known by the Latin maxim *audi alteram partem*, the other side must be heard. In early editions of *Snell's Principles of Equity*, a leading practitioners' text, equity was said to be, 'in its popular sense it is practically equivalent to natural justice'.

20 Stuart E. Prall, 'The Development of Equity in Tudor England' (1964) 8(1) The American Journal of Legal History 1, 1.

21 Stuart E. Prall, 'The Development of Equity in Tudor England' (1964) 8(1) *The American Journal of Legal History* 1, 2. Even when equity was considered the jurisdiction of the Court of Chancery, English common law continued to consider the equity of statutory interpretation and the law generally. See Thomas Ashe, *Epieikeia* (London, 1609), considered in D.R Klinck, *Conscience, Equity and the Court of Chancery in Early Modern England*, Farnham: Ashgate Publishing Limited, 2010, at p. 150.

moderates the harshness or unfairness of rigid application of the law. Thus, equity is part of the law and acts within the law. It is the discretion afforded those administering the law to develop the law to cover new circumstances that the law makers could not have foreseen, or to mitigate the harshness of the rigid application of the law which would cause injustice that, again, the law makers could not have foreseen or wished to happen.

Equity as part of the common law has developed beyond these general principles into a body of law that has at times been considered as separate from the common law. Only the Chancellor in his own court, the Court of Chancery, administered this body of law. The principles and remedies that were developed here became known as equity; however, although separately administered from the rules of the common law, equity was a part of the common law as it worked alongside it dealing with the injustice of the common law.

To understand equity we must therefore consider the common law. The term 'common law' is used in three main ways:

1   The common law as compared to civil law: this refers to common law jurisdictions as opposed to civil law jurisdictions; for example the legal systems of England, Australia and the United States of America as opposed to the legal systems of France , Germany and China;
2   The common law as opposed to legislation: this refers to its judge made law as opposed to Acts of Parliament; and,
3   The common law as opposed to equity: this is the body of principles and rules developed by the courts of common law as opposed to the body of principles and rules developed by the courts of equity (the Court of Chancery).

Equity is part of the common law for the purposes of the first and second meanings but is separate from the common law in the third meaning. This may seem confusing, but equity is fairness and justice within the common law but acting upon the common law. It tries to overcome the rigidity of the common law, the dogmatic application of the law, and the upholding of legal rights when it would be "unconscionable" to do so. In trying to achieve this, the Chancellors developed their own body of rules, a series of principles, doctrines and remedies, which were separate from those administered by the courts of common law but acting upon the common law.[22]

---

22   Maitland, a famous 19th century legal historian, in his series of lectures titled "Equity", described equity as 'that body of rules administered by our English courts of justice which, were it not for the operation of the Judicature Acts, would be administered only by those courts which would be known as Courts of Equity.'

To understand how equity can be part of the common law but also distinct from the common law it is necessary to consider the origins of equity within the common law.

1.3 The Establishment of the Common Law and the Need for an Equitable Jurisdiction

In this section we shall discuss briefly the development of the common law and equity.

A large area of what is now England and Wales was conquered in 1066 by an army of mercenaries under the command of Duke William of Normandy, who thus became King William I, [23] or William the Conqueror. Renowned for his cruelty, he famously considered the death penalty too lenient and ordered blinding and emasculation instead.[24] William is still perceived by many in England as a cruel and tyrannical "foreign" King. This may seem strange, as England suffered several subsequent invasions and replacements of the monarchy, but few still arouse such wide hostility as this invasion almost 1000 years ago. William considered that, 'since the English landowners had denied his right to the Crown of England, and had compelled him to assert it by force, their landed possessions became his to dispose of as he chose.'[25] Thus, all land in his new kingdom was his by right of conquest. To ease William's control and administration of this kingdom he granted land to his loyal knights in return for service. In addition those English landowners that wished to keep their land had to convince the King of their loyalty and were made to pay a fee to him for this privilege. Thus all held land 'of the King' owing loyalty and service to the King in return. [26]

The King's knights and the English lords who had pledged loyalty to the King administered the land for their own benefit in return for this pledge of service, usually to provide themselves and men at arms for the King when he waged war or needed to protect his new realm. The knight or lord would allow others to cultivate and live on the land in return for their pledge of service and provision of goods such as armour, grain or livestock. Each grant of ownership of the land was a grant of an "estate" in the land. This was the basis of the English feudal system, a 'series of

---

23   Reigned 1066- 1087.
24   R.C. Van Caenegem, *The Birth of the English Common Law* (London: Cambridge University Press, 1973) p. 9.
25   Burn, E.H., 'Cheshire & Burn's Modern Law of Real Property, 16th edition (London: Butterworths, 2000), p.12. Referring to Stenton, *William the Conqueror*.
26   The Crown was acknowledged subsequently as liege lord under the feudal system to all citizens: *Calvin's Case* (1608) 7 Co. Rep. 1a at 5a.

bargains',[27] and a pyramid of obligations and service with the King at the top retaining ultimate control and ownership of the land.[28] This differed from the feudal system as it developed in other European countries at the same time, as there the feudal obligations were limited to the lord directly granting the right to use land. In England the obligations always included recognition that '[e]very acre of land in the country was held of the King'.[29]

At first all tenants would only hold the land for their lifetime. The King would want to ensure that the new tenant when the landholder died was also loyal. Thus the landholder's eldest son would only receive his father's lands if he pledged loyalty to the King and the King trusted him. Otherwise the King would give the land to someone he did trust. Those below the knight in the feudal pyramid might thus find themselves with a new overlord to whom they also had to pledge loyalty. The interests in land were therefore similar to a modern life interest only. Loyalty to the King, the pledge of support, whether in warfare or in goods, would be renewed with each new tenant, in time this was represented by a fee being paid, a "relief", on the accession of each new tenant- a form of transfer tax. In time it was accepted that the land would pass to the eldest son and he would pay a fee at the passing to his lord, and part of the fee would be paid up the feudal pyramid; a form of death duty. If there was no legal heir then the estate passed to the landholder's immediate lord by way of the feudal principle of *escheat*, a valuable feudal right, and a fee was payable from this lord to those above in the feudal pyramid, including the King.[30]

---

27. S.F.C.Milsom, *Historical Foundations of the Common Law*, (London: Butterworths, 2nd edition, 1981) p.19.
28. It has long been argued that the 'Norman Conquest, in imposing feudalism on England, did but accelerate a process that was already begun." Henry E. Davis, Paper before the American Bar Association (1898) 6 *American Lawyer* 205, 207. The concept of land for service, "*servitia debita*", was introduced by William throughout England and this became the English feudal system: R.C. Van Caenegem, *The Birth of the English Common Law* (London: Cambridge University Press, 1973) p. 6.
29. Burn, E.H., *Cheshire & Burn's Modern Law of Real Property*, 16th edition (London: Butterworths, 2000), p.13. "The person whom we may call the owner, the person who has the right to use and abuse the land, to cultivate it or leave it uncultivated, to keep all other off it, holds the land of the King either immediately or mediately": Pollock & Maitland, *History of English Law*, 2nd ed. Vol. 1 p.237.
30. Most land in England is still ultimately 'owned' by the Crown, even 'freehold' land ultimately belongs to the Crown, which is why when any property is without a legally recognised owner it returns to the crown by the feudal principle of *escheat* (the principle of *bona vacantia*, literally 'to the good of no one', replaced the feudal principle of *escheat* in the Administration of Estates Act 1925).

Tenants could still not freely alienate their land, that is transfer their land to another, without the permission of their overlord and without the original tenant still retaining his feudal obligations. [31]

Although the Conquest of 1066 has been described as "a cataclysm of the first magnitude", [32] it did not sweep away all the pre-Conquest administration and government. William was cruel but he was not a fool. William realised that any conquered state was easier to run if the pre-existing administration reflecting the laws and customs of the people were preserved as much as possible. [33] This also reflected William's wish to be seen as a 'legitimate' ruler according to the laws and customs of England. [34] As Maitland stated:

'To all seeming, the Conqueror meant that his English subjects should keep their old laws. Merely Duke of the Normans, he was going to be King in England, and he was not dissatisfied with those royal rights which, according to his version of the story, had descended to him from King Edward.' [35]

Thus the new Norman rulers, whilst imposing their rule, preserved the pre-conquest fiscal institutions that had made Anglo-Saxon England 'the best organized monarchy in all Europe'. [36] This included the royal Chancery, an administrative office overseen by the Chancellor. Thus, '[t]he Conqueror took over a going concern, one to which he claimed lawful title; and he expressly confirmed the laws of his predecessors.' This attempt to legitimise his reign by maintaining existing useful institutions coupled with an undoubted Norman gift for administration, was the driving force behind the development of the common law. The English could keep their laws but the Normans could also keep theirs. A two-part system of old English land law existed with the new feudal principles. The old English courts of the Shires and Hundreds coexisted with the new feudal courts. At the top remained the King and his council, the *curia regis*. [37]

---

31   The statute *Quia Emptores* (1289-90) eventually provided for freedom of transfer of land and transfer of obligations, again a fee would be paid.

32   R.C. Van Caenegem, *The Birth of the English Common Law* (London: Cambridge University Press, 1973) p. 12.

33   William Lindsay Carne, 'A Sketch of the History of the High Court of Chancery from its Origin to the Chancellorship of Wolsey' (1927) 13(7) (Nov.) *The Virginia Law Review* 391, 395.

34   William was careful to attempt to show he was King of the English as well as the Normans. He was crowned in Westminster according to English tradition and maintained that he was the rightful heir to the throne: R.C. Van Caenegem, *The Birth of the English Common Law*, (London: Cambridge University Press, 1973) p. 4-18.

35   F.W. Maitland & F.C. Montague, *A Sketch of English Legal History*, 1850-1906. Charleston, SC: Bibliolife, 2010, at p.27.

36   R.C. Van Caenegem, *The Birth of the English Common Law* (London: Cambridge University Press, 1973) p. 9.

37   William Lindsay Carne, 'A Sketch of the History of the High Court of Chancery from its Origin to the Chancellorship of Wolsey' (1927) 13(7) (Nov.) *The Virginia Law Review* 391, 391.

In addition, William ordered an administrative account to be taken of all land in England, it's wealth, and who owned it. This was recorded in the Domesday Book, a record of what the King owned and what was due to the King by way of feudal dues and obligations. The collection of revenue requires a certain amount of 'judicial business' and so laws were developed to aid this administration.[38] Gradually these laws were standardised by use across the country by a centralised fiscal administration.[39] Eventually this centralised fiscal administration and the administration of the King's courts meant these laws became "common" to the whole of England.

It required the influence and insight of another great King, Henry II,[40] to ensure that the common law would take the path it did. Variously described as 'that subtle inventor of new judicial forms' and a man who was 'by instinct a lawyer',[41] Henry realised that by drawing all litigants into the royal courts he could 'greatly strengthen and extend the royal influence' and at the same time charge a fee.[42] Henry also needed to clarify the common law as to property rights, settling disputes that had arisen over land during the civil war between Stephen and Matilda, known as "the Anarchy",[43] which was only settled by Stephen's acceptance of Henry as his heir. Thus the year 1189, which marks the end of Henry's reign and the accession of his son Richard I,[44] also known as Richard the Lion Heart, is referred to as 'time immemorial' or 'the limit of legal memory', as it represents the certainty of property interests established by Henry after the anarchy of the civil war between Matilda and Stephen and the birth of the common law.[45] Thus the law was made more accessible to everyone in the King's courts and so by the reign of Henry II it was possible to speak of a common law.

---

38 William Lindsay Carne, 'A Sketch of the History of the High Court of Chancery from its Origin to the Chancellorship of Wolsey' (1927) 13(7) (Nov.) *The Virginia Law Review* 391, 393.

39 Thus the common law has been called, 'the by-product of an administrative triumph': S.F.C.Milsom, Historical Foundations of the Common Law, (London: Butterworths, 2nd edition, 1981) pp 11-12.

40 Reigned 1154- 1189.

41 R.C. Van Caenegem, *The Birth of the English Common Law*, (London: Cambridge University Press, 1973) p. 3 & 100.

42 William Lindsay Carne, 'A Sketch of the History of the High Court of Chancery from its Origin to the Chancellorship of Wolsey' (1927) 13(7) (Nov.) *The Virginia Law Review* 391, 396.

43 1135- 1153.

44 Reigned 1189- 1199.

45 F.W. Maitland & F.C. Montague, *A Sketch of English Legal History*, 1850-1906. Charleston, SC: Bibliolife, 2010, at p.201 in the Appendix II an extract from Jenks, Edward, *Law and Politics in the Middle Ages*.

The common law continued to develop, taking note of accepted usage and custom in the newly created King's Courts of Common Pleas and King's Bench. Records were kept of the claims before the courts and the judgments and principles used by the courts to reach these judgments. Thus the doctrine of precedent and certainty in the common law was developed and a body of precedent developed to deal with all the problems of the King's subjects; however, if there was a dispute that could not be settled by recourse to the common law, or a lord was ignoring the law, or a plaintiff could not obtain justice from the royal courts, then a petition could be made to the King asking for his royal justice as the ultimate authority in the land.[46] The King was the 'fountain of justice'; all justice flowed from the King.[47] Thus, if there was a dispute between a lord and his tenant and the lord ignored the law, the tenant could ultimately ask the King to intervene to enforce justice.[48] Furthermore, the common law did not cover every eventuality and certainty in the law did not always ensure justice. At times, it would be obvious that a legal right was being enforced when it was unjust to do so. At such times the person suffering the injustice had no recourse except to go to the King. The King could use his prerogative powers, literally his power to speak above the law, to order that justice be done and the legal right not enforced. This was "extraordinary" justice. It was not available generally and was dispensed at the discretion of the King.

The common law also placed an overwhelming emphasis on formality. For example, a debtor who had repaid his debt but failed to have his bond of debt released by his creditor could be made to pay the debt again because the deed was proof he owed the sum. Baker states this was because the judges would not compromise legal rules with exceptions, as 'the law did not bend to protect fools'.[49] This obsession with formality meant that the common law did not recognise the use or trust. Thus the beneficiary under a use or trust, an institution formed when a person transferred legal title to their property to another to be held for the benefit of the original owner or other beneficiaries he had indicated,[50] had no rights at common law, as the common law was only

---

46 R.C. Van Caenegem, *The Birth of the English Common Law* (London: Cambridge University Press, 1973) p. 17.

47 R.C. Van Caenegem, *The Birth of the English Common Law* (London: Cambridge University Press, 1973) p. 35.

48 Ultimate appeal had been to the King and his Witenagemont in Saxon England: William Lindsay Carne, 'A Sketch of the History of the High Court of Chancery from its Origin to the Chancellorship of Wolsey' (1927) 13(7) (Nov.) *The Virginia Law Review* 391, 395.

49 J. Baker, *An Introduction to Legal History*, (London: Butterworths, 1990, 3rd edition), p.118.

50 The trust is examined in detail in chapter 4.

concerned with the legal owner of property and did not acknowledge the existence of the beneficiary's (equitable) interest. Again, the only way to deal with this rigidity of the common law was to apply to the King.

Although the common law had developed to reflect the needs of the King's subjects, further development was stifled by the 'writ' system. To bring an action at common law the plaintiff needed to obtain a writ, a written statement of his claim, asking the sheriff to bring the defendant to answer the claim.[51] Writs were prepared in Latin and, at a time when many were illiterate, the plaintiff went to the royal secretariat, the Chancery, to obtain the writ he needed to bring his case.[52] The Chancery was the office of the Lord Chancellor and staffed by clerks, who were usually clerics, religious men trained to read and write Latin. The plaintiff would pay a clerk in the Chancery to draw up his writ. The writ had to be in an accepted form and in the exact wording necessary for the claim otherwise the plaintiff would not be able to bring his claim. As time passed plaintiffs were faced with new actions that were based on circumstances not covered by previous common law writs. Thus the range of writs available was not always adequate for their purposes. As the clerks in Chancery were only paid for the writs they wrote, they began slightly changing existing forms of writ to cover these new circumstances. Thus the clerks in Chancery developed new writs and new causes of action; however, there were obvious concerns about the Chancery clerks literally taking the law into their own hands when they wrote these new writs. New writs were needed but not just at the behest of Chancery. Legislation prohibited the creation of new writs unless they were "*in consimili casu*", or 'of a similar case' to the writs already in existence.[53] This was very narrowly interpreted and thus severely restricted by the King's Council and parliament and so the common law did not develop to deal with the new problems it's customers faced.[54] By the end of the thirteenth century the common law was rigid and stagnating, limited by the existing form of writs. Unless there was a 'writ to fit' the circumstances of your case there was no remedy at common law.[55] Even if you were successful

---

51 S.F.C.Milsom, *Historical Foundations of the Common Law* (London: Butterworths, 2nd edition, 1981) p.34.

52 For a history of the writ see R.C. Van Caenegem, *The Birth of the English Common Law*, (London: Cambridge University Press, 1973) chapter 2.

53 The Provisions of Oxford 1258 prohibited the creation of new writs unless by the King's Council. This was followed by the Statute of Westminster the Second 1258 which introduced the 'consimili casu' clause.

54 S.F.C.Milsom, *Historical Foundations of the Common Law* (London: Butterworths, 2nd edition, 1981) p.36.

55 'Thenceforward the cycle of writs must be regarded as a closed cycle; no one can bring his cause before the king's courts unless he can bring it within the

in obtaining a writ and winning your case, the common law suffered from a very limited range of remedies available for the successful plaintiff. The only recourse available to the plaintiff without a cause of action because of the writ system, or an appropriate remedy at common law, or the defendant unjustly penalised by the common law, was thus a direct petition to the King. The King could intervene and decide the matter because his would be a personal remedy, only involving the parties to the litigation and not setting a precedent for the law. The King's justice was extraordinary justice, not to be used in every case but only when justice and conscience demanded. As the King was often engaged with the business of princes', such as defending his lands, waging war against his fellow princes or engaging in holy crusades, the King's deputy, the Lord Chancellor usually heard these petitions and administered the King's personal justice, according to the King's conscience, to combat the injustice or inadequacy of the common law.

1.4 The Chancellor

In early mediaeval England the office of Lord Chancellor was second only in importance to that of the King himself. The Chancellor was usually Keeper of the Great Seal, the King's confessor, the keeper of the King's conscience and the King's secretary. In addition his office, the Chancery, ran the administration of justice on behalf of the King.[56] As mentioned above, the Chancery was also the office from which common law writs were issued. There have been many famous and notable Chancellors, for example, St Thomas Beckett,[57] Cardinal Wolsey[58] and Sir Thomas More.[59] The Chancellor was, until the 17th century, generally a holder of religious office with knowledge of both civil and canon (Church) law. As the King's confessor, he would hear the King's confession and prescribe his religious penance to safeguard the King's conscience and soul. Thus the Chancellor was eminently suited to decide matters of conscience affecting the King's subjects.[60]

---

scope of one of those formulas which the Chancery has in stock and ready for sale. We may argue if there is no writ there is no remedy, and if there is no remedy there is no wrong; and thus the register of writs in the Chancery becomes the test of rights and the measure of the law.' F.W. Maitland & F.C. Montague, *A Sketch of English Legal History*, 1850-1906. Charleston, SC: Bibliolife, 2010, at p.98 & p101.

56 William Lindsay Carne, 'A Sketch of the History of the High Court of Chancery from its Origin to the Chancellorship of Wolsey' (1927) 13(7) (Nov.) *The Virginia Law Review* 391, 393-400.
57 Lord Chancellor 1155- 1162.
58 Lord Chancellor 1515- 1529
59 Lord Chancellor 1529- 1532.
60 S.F.C.Milsom, Historical Foundations of the Common Law, (London: Butterworths, 2nd edition, 1981) p.25.

Using the prerogative power of the King and the Great Seal, the Chancellor could order, in the King's name, that parties and witnesses attend the Chancery to give evidence of the case. These orders were *subpoena*, subject to penalty if they were not obeyed, the usual penalty being imprisonment.[61] The Chancellor also, in a similar manner to ecclesiastical courts, could order examination *viva voce*, he could examine witnesses, including the plaintiff and defendant, under oath, to establish the truth of a case. This developed into the process of 'discovery', the requirement of revealing evidence that was important to the Chancellor's consideration of the matter. If relevant evidence was not disclosed it might result in the party responsible not being granted an equitable remedy or being in contempt. Thus subpoena and discovery became important processes of the Court of Chancery.[62]

Chancellors developed the Chancery jurisdiction until they could stop the prosecution of an unfair case in the common law courts, as these were 'matters of grace affecting the King's conscience as *parens patriae*'.[63] Similarly, the defendant could petition the Chancellor to forbid the enforcement of a judgement using the King's prerogative power. These orders developed into the injunction, *in personam* orders directed against the conscience of the person involved in the litigation. They were not actions *in rem*, against the thing that was the subject matter of the litigation; however, an order from the Chancellor to hand back property, although termed an order against the conscience of the person holding the property was in reality an order affecting the property itself because, if not obeyed, contempt was being shown, not just for the Chancellor, but also for the King. Severe penalties could follow, again usually imprisonment. Today equity is still said to act *in personam*, against the conscience of the individual, not *in rem*.

Beginning an action in Chancery was much easier than at common law as you did not have to acquire a writ but made a simple statement of your problem, a 'bill', which had no 'set or crystallized form', could be verbally amended, and could also be in French or, from the end of the fourteenth century, in English rather than Latin.[64] The other side to your petition need only make a simple reply of their case.

---

61 William Lindsay Carne, 'A Sketch of the History of the High Court of Chancery from its Origin to the Chancellorship of Wolsey' (1927) 13(7) (Nov.) *The Virginia Law Review* 391, 407.

62 These processes are similar to those available to the inquisitorial courts of civilian jurisdictions.

63 *Parens patriae*, literally father of the country. See William Lindsay Carne, 'A Sketch of the History of the High Court of Chancery from its Origin to the Chancellorship of Wolsey' (1927) 13(7) (Nov.) *The Virginia Law Review* 391, 400.

64 William Lindsay Carne, 'A Sketch of the History of the High Court of Chancery from its Origin to the Chancellorship of Wolsey' (1927) 13(7) (Nov.) *The Virginia Law Review* 391, 405.

By the reign of Edward I[65] petitions were being addressed to the 'Chancellor and the Council' and by the end of the fourteenth century to the Chancellor alone. [66] The Chancery increased in power after the near anarchy of the Wars of the Roses[67] because of 'the urgent need to restore law and order to the realm, unhindered by the formal procedures of the common law and the unreliability of juries.'[68] Eventually, by the reign of Elizabeth I,[69] the decisions of the Chancellor in the Court of Chancery became known as equity,[70] the role of the Chancellor's justice being 'to temper and mitigate the law' with the 'sweetness of mercy' when the law did not deal with the wrong or would prove harsh in its rigid application.[71] The Court of Chancery thus developed alongside other courts, such as Star Chamber,[72] using the bill procedure, to deal with the 'failure of juystice [sic] and by the appeal from the King's *potestas ordinata* or regulated power to his *potestas absoluta* or absolute power.' [73]

The jurisdiction of the Chancellor and equity was therefore over matters that the common law did not deal with, whether that was in not recognising a cause of action or providing an appropriate remedy, or cases where the common law was obsessed with formality or unduly rigid and its application produced injustice. Of particular importance in the growth of the Chancery jurisdiction was the enforcement of the use and trust which brought money into the coffers of the Lord Chancellor and into the pockets of lawyers practising in Chancery.[74]The continued use of

---

65 Reigned 1272- 1307.
66 The statute of 22 Edw. III directs that matters of 'grace' be should be referred to the Chancellor, however the principle is generally considered to be older than the statute. The first recorded decree made upon a Chancellor's own authority was not until 1474.
67 1455- 1485.
68 Stuart E. Prall, 'The Development of Equity in Tudor England' (1964) 8(1) *The American Journal of Legal History* 1, 10.
69 Reigned 1558- 1603.
70 Stuart E. Prall, 'The Development of Equity in Tudor England' (1964) 8(1) *The American Journal of Legal History* 1, 15. Referring to Edward Hake, *Epieikeia, A Dialogue on Equity in Three parts*, ed. D.E.C. Yale (New Haven, 1953).
71 Christopher St. Germain, *Doctor and Student* 1528-31 (18th ed., Dublin, 1792). A purported dialogue between a doctor of divinity and a law student concerning the basic principles of the common law.
72 A court which has been described as a court of "criminal equity" and, which should be remembered, was, before its association with tyrannical and unjust practices, described by Bacon as "one of the sagest and noblest institutions of this Kingdom": Robert L. Munger, 'A Glance at Equity' (1915) 25(1) (Nov.) *The Yale Law Journal* 42, 51.
73 Mike Mcnair, 'Equity and Conscience' (2007) 27(4) *Oxford Journal of Legal Studies* 659, 668.
74 William Lindsay Carne, 'A Sketch of the History of the High Court of Chancery from its Origin to the Chancellorship of Wolsey' (1927) 13(7) (Nov.) *The Virginia Law Review* 391, 404.

injunctions to prevent the enforcement of the judgements of the common law courts also seriously affected the revenue of common law judges and lawyers. Common lawyers became increasingly critical of equity as their anger grew at the loss of revenue and undermining of the authority of the common law courts. A bitter dispute developed between the two jurisdictions.

1.5 The Fight for Fees: Common Law or Equity?

The main source of dispute between the two competing jurisdictions and the lawyers who practised in them, as might be expected between professionals, was money.[75] Common lawyers were losing business to their Chancery rivals. Plaintiffs who knew they had no 'writ to fit' available at common law would come straight to Chancery for a remedy. Defendants who lost their case at common law would rush to Chancery for an injunction preventing the winning plaintiff from enforcing his judgment. It has been said that even the judges of the common law, whose fees depended on the number of cases they heard, were watching 'with longing eyes the stream of gold which was flowing into the coffers of their rival, the Chancery, and constantly casting about for some means to divert a portion of it into their own hands.'[76] They could not redirect this revenue without revolutionary changes to the common law, for example by recognising the interest of the *cestui que use* (the beneficiary) or by adopting the bill system to begin actions. The common law did fight back with concepts such as consideration allowing them to reach into the law of promises, an area that had been controlled centuries before by the Church courts and which might otherwise have been subsumed into the court of conscience of the Chancellor. It has also been argued that the connivance of lawyers in the enacting of the Statute of Uses for Henry VIII was designed to wrest the control of property back from Chancery by abolishing the use or making it subject to the common law.[77] The use was the forerunner of the trust and brought a large revenue stream to Chancery as it was an extremely popular device to avoid feudal incidents and allow testamentary disposition of land, something the common law did not permit.

The main criticisms of equity were:

75 Berman considers this a continuation of the jurisdictional battle between the courts originating in the battle between secular authority and the ecclesiastical courts in the reign of Henry II between the King and Thomas Beckett: Harold J. Berman, *Law and Revolution: The Formation of the Western Legal Tradition*(Harvard University Press, 1983), p.260.

76 William Lindsay Carne, 'A Sketch of the History of the High Court of Chancery from its Origin to the Chancellorship of Wolsey' (1927) 13(7) (Nov.) *The Virginia Law Review* 391, 412.

77 Robert L. Munger, 'A Glance at Equity' (1915) 25(1) (Nov.) *The Yale Law Journal* 42, 53. See discussion on the development of the trust in Chapter 4.

- The Chancellor was trained in the canon or civil law not the common law;
- Chancery was slow and corrupt; and,
- There was no certainty in equity as the decisions of the Chancellor were discretionary and based on conscience.

1.5.1 The Chancellors and the Canon and Roman law

Common lawyers claimed that Chancellors were religious, untrained in the common law, and even worse, trained in the law of the Catholic Church, the canon law, which was closely linked to Roman law.[78]

There was some justification in the claim that Chancellors were usually religious men untrained in the common law, at least until the end of the 16th century (with the notable exception of Sir Thomas More).[79] Also from earliest times there have undoubtedly been elements of canon and Roman law introduced into equity.[80] Thus the Chancellor would sometimes adopt principles of Roman law to decide on matters before his extraordinary jurisdiction,[81] and the procedure of the Court of Chancery was based upon the procedure of ecclesiastical courts.[82] In fact it has been claimed that equity in England was far more similar to the Roman law concept of *aequitas* than the Greek concept of equity.[83]

---

78 'For it should never be forgotten that the Canon law was the medium through which the Christian Church aided the preservation of Roman Civil law to modern times.' Charles P. Sherman, 'A Brief History of the Canon Law' (1918-1919) 7 *Cal. L. Rev.* 93, 94. 'The Laws of Justinian have been woven into the fabric of the Canon law and in that form ...obtained the sanction of the Church.' William Carey Morey, 'Outlines of Roman law: comprising its historical growth and general principles' (G.P. Putnam's Sons, 1896), p.206: available on Google Books: accessed 24/10/11.

79 '...for most commonly the chancellors of England have been spiritual men, that have had but superficial knowledge in the laws of the realm.' Stuart E. Prall, 'The Development of Equity in Tudor England' (1964) 8(1) *The American Journal of Legal History* 1, 6. Quoting from Anon, *Replication of a Serjeant at the Laws of England*, p.347, a reply to St Germain's *Doctor and Student* published shortly thereafter.

80 From 1390 there had been complaints of the Chancellor, a religious man 'enamoured' of the Roman law, interfering with the common law. William Lindsay Carne, 'A Sketch of the History of the High Court of Chancery from its Origin to the Chancellorship of Wolsey' (1927) 13(7) (Nov.) *The Virginia Law Review* 391, 419.

81 Robert L. Munger, 'A Glance at Equity' (1915) 25(1) (Nov.) *The Yale Law Journal* 42, 45.

82 F.W. Maitland & F.C. Montague, *A Sketch of English Legal History*, 1850-1906. Charleston, SC: Bibliolife, 2010, at p.125.

83 Stuart E. Prall, 'The Development of Equity in Tudor England' (1964) 8(1) *The American Journal of Legal History* 1, 2. As Roman *aequitas* 'remains closely connected with law; it is a criterion of the correctness of the law and a

Although such noted 'anti-Romanists'[84] as Maitland, Pollock and Oliver Wendell Holmes might claim that there was no direct Roman influence on the common law, the common law is not itself untainted by Roman law.[85] It should be remembered that for more than three centuries Britain was a Roman province and was occupied by Roman legions for five centuries. Thus it would be strange if there was no Roman influence on the customs that became the common law.[86] Furthermore, the Church in the 8th and 9th centuries and the Norman invaders themselves exerted subsequent Roman influence indirectly on the development of the common law.[87] Thus, the common law was also not immune from Roman contamination. Furthermore, it should be noted that, although a fear of canon and Roman law influence on the common law was cited as a reason for disapproval of equity and the Chancellors interfering with the common law, for much of this early period men would consider nothing wrong with ecclesiastical principles being considered in the administration of justice. The Church was an intrinsic part of everyday life. Furthermore, the judges of the common law often consulted the Chancellors, as some of the best-educated men in the land, when there were difficult questions of law to determine,[88] and the Chancellors themselves might ask for help from common law judges. As late as the end of the seventeenth century, Lord Nottingham,[89] one of the most famous Chancellors, asked his common law brothers to sit with him in *Howard v Duke of Norfolk*,[90] one the most important cases he decided;[91] however, it should be noted that having requested their advice he chose to ignore it and decide the matter as he thought best, providing the Rule Against Perpetuities and headaches for generations of lawyers.

---

principle of construction not a contrasting principle.' H.F. Jollowicz, *Roman Foundations of Modern Law* (Oxford, 1957), p.56.

84 Montague Crackanthorpe, 'The Uses of Legal History' (1896) 19 Annu. Rep. A.B.A. 343, 354.

85 Thus '...the Roman law of charities has entered the Anglo-American common law via the Canon law.' Charles P. Sherman, 'A Brief History of the Canon Law' (1918-1919) 7 *Cal. L. Rev.* 93, 94.

86 Papinian, one of the most famous of Roman Jurisconsults, dispensed justice in the forum of York. Montague Crackanthorpe, 'The Uses of Legal History' (1896) 19 Annu. Rep. A.B.A. 343, 350.

87 Even Maitland and Pollock were willing to accept this indirect influence. Montague Crackanthorpe, 'The Uses of Legal History' (1896) 19 Annu. Rep. A.B.A. 343, 350.

88 A practice that continued as late as 1315 according to William Lindsay Carne, 'A Sketch of the History of the High Court of Chancery from its Origin to the Chancellorship of Wolsey' (1927) 13(7) (Nov.) *The Virginia Law Review* 391, 397.

89 Lord Chancellor 1673- 1682.

90 (1681-5) 3 Ch Cas 1: 22 ER 931; 2 Swans 454; 36 ER 690; 1 Vern 163; 23 ER 388.

91 William Lindsay Carne, 'A Sketch of the History of the High Court of Chancery from its Origin to the Chancellorship of Wolsey' (1927) 13(7) (Nov.) *The Virginia Law Review* 391, 412.

Thus the influence of the Roman law on early equity is a criticism that is well founded, although whether this was a problem is open to debate, and equity has subsequently developed in sympathy to the needs of the common law rather than Roman principles.[92]

1.5.2 Delay and corruption in Chancery

As Chancery became more successful there was undoubtedly a problem with long delay in bringing your case before the Chancellor, and indications that the court of conscience had been corrupted. The very success of the injunction and the relative ease of bringing an action in equity made the Court very popular, but there was only one judge, the Chancellor. Furthermore, Cardinal Wolsey, Chancellor to Henry VIII[93] and one of the most infamous Chancellors, brought the office into disrepute by his arbitrary exercise of the authority of the Chancellor and willingness to issue injunctions more for the fee than for justice.[94] In fact Wolsey fitted the stereotype that common lawyers despised, as he had no legal background whatsoever and was directly hostile to lawyers.[95] He has been described as the last Chancellor who ruled England.[96]

The depths to which Chancery had sunk under Wolsey were best indicated by the praise given to his successor, Sir Thomas More, described as one of the great figures in legal tradition.[97] He was famous for dealing expeditiously and conscientiously with cases so that there was no appreciable delay for litigants in Chancery during his Chancellorship.[98] Following More's removal from office and subsequent execution, the reputation of Chancery suffered further. Allegations of delay and corruption would haunt equity well into the nineteenth century. The most stinging criticism of equity by common lawyers was reserved for the

---

92   It has been argued that England nearly suffered a Reception of Roman law in the 16th and 17th century and as has been noted many areas of the common law were originally and continue to be influenced by Roman law.

93   Reigned 1509- 1547.

94   Stuart E. Prall, 'The Development of Equity in Tudor England' (1964) 8(1) *The American Journal of Legal History* 1, 6.

95   Mike Mcnair, 'Equity and Conscience' (2007) 27(4) *Oxford Journal of Legal Studies* 659, 670.

96   F.W. Maitland & F.C. Montague, *A Sketch of English Legal History*, 1850-1906. Charleston, SC: Bibliolife, 2010, at p.126

97   This despite not authoring any legal texts or 'fathering' leading cases: Richard J. Schoeck, 'The Place of Sir Thomas More in Legal History and Tradition: Some Notes and Observations' (1978) 23 *American Journal of Jurisprudence* 212, 212.

98   More was Chancellor from October 1529 to May 16, 1532 and was well educated in Canon and common law. Richard J. Schoeck, 'The Place of Sir Thomas More in Legal History and Tradition: Some Notes and Observations' (1978) 23 *American Journal of Jurisprudence* 212, 215.

uncertainty created by the fundamental principles of 'conscience' and 'discretion'.

1.5.3 Court of Chancery or court of conscience

It has often been stated that central to the rule of law is the concept of certainty. Common lawyers would thus criticise the use of discretion and conscience by priests to decide commercial disputes, claiming that introducing uncertainty was fatal to the rule of law.[99] The criticisms of common lawyers over the administration of equity in the 16th century were similar to those raised by commercial lawyers today. Common lawyers, especially those involved with commerce, have always stressed the need for certainty in the law. Just as in the present day, business in the 16th and 17th centuries relied on the parties to a transaction being sure of their legal rights, of what obligations the law would enforce for them. The law needed to be certain so that merchants could depend on their contractual obligations being honoured. Indeed the common law had just come up with a novel solution to one problem of certainty over which contracts would be upheld by the law, the doctrine of consideration, which had seen an influx of business into the common law courts.

Equity's use of the terms 'conscience' and 'discretion' sat uncomfortably with the concept of legal certainty, and still does. Thus a 12th century maxim of the common law was *iudex secundam allegata et probata non secundam conscientiam iudicat* (the judge should decide according to what is alleged and proved, not according to conscience).[100]

Common lawyers would ask: how can anyone know what the law is if it depends on the discretionary decision of the Chancellor according to how he thinks his conscience or the conscience of the defendant directs? This criticism was voiced in a famous comment ascribed to the noted common lawyer, John Selden:

'Equity is a roguish thing. For law we have a measure... equity is according to the conscience of him that is chancellor, and as that is longer or narrower, so is equity. 'Tis all one as if they should make the standard for the measure the length of the chancellor's foot.'[101]

Selden's criticism of equity was all to do with uncertainty. Law was certain, it had a 'measure', but equity could vary according to the conscience of the Chancellor administering it, and he might not even be a lawyer!

---

99 For an interesting consideration of the falsity of the claim that the common law is both flexible and subject to the rule of law see Professor Lutz-Christian Wolff, 'Law and Flexibility- Rule of Law Limits of a Rhetorical Silver Bullet' (2011) (11) (October) *The Journal Jurisprudence* 549-568.

100 Mike Mcnair, 'Equity and Conscience' (2007) 27(4) *Oxford Journal of Legal Studies* 659, 672.

101 John Selden (sometimes Seldon), *Table Talk* (1689).

It was true that equity was founded upon conscience which was that divine spark that is, 'in the midst of every reasonable soul, as a light whereby he may discern and know what he ought to do, and what he ought not to do.'[102] Lord Ellesmere[103] considered this the advantage of equity: "…the judges of the common law shall determine questions in Law, and *Pares & Iurors* to try matters in fact, so the *Chancery* is to order and decree matters of Conscience and Equitie, which cannot be remedied by the strict rules of the common law."[104]

Of course common lawyers would ask. What is conscience? To which a Chancery lawyer might reply that it is that divine spark that is 'in the midst of every reasonable soul, as a light whereby he may discern and know what he ought to do, and what he ought not to do.'[105] Not very helpful for a common lawyer seeking certainty in the law! There was a need for Chancery to clarify the concept of conscience and, at the beginning of the seventeenth century, when the dispute between equity and the common law was at its height, Sir Francis Bacon, before he became Chancellor,[106] attempted this. Bacon noted that there was a distinction between 'private conscience' and 'the general conscience of the realm, which is Chancery.'[107] This had sometimes been equated with the King's conscience, which was to uphold the justice of his realm; however, in the seventeenth century when the King's use of prerogative powers was increasingly criticised and challenged this was not a satisfactory answer. 'Conscience' had no certain meaning within equity, and some would say it still does not.

Thus, undoubtedly the Chancellor was influenced by canon and Roman law, and guided by a mysterious concept of conscience; also his Court suffered from problems of delay and corruption. But what was perhaps worse, the Court of Chancery was becoming ever more successful taking fees from the common lawyers and undermining the authority of the common law courts. A resolution of the conflict between equity and the common law was needed.

---

102 Stuart E. Prall, 'The Development of Equity in Tudor England' (1964) 8(1) *The American Journal of Legal History* 1, 4. Quoting from St Germain's *Doctor and Student* p.44.

103 Lord Chancellor 1603-1617.

104 Thomas Egerton (Lord Ellesmere), *The Privileges and Prerogatives of the High Court of Chancery* (London 1641). See Klinck, D.R., *Conscience, Equity and the Court of Chancery in Early Modern England*, Farnham: Ashgate Publishing Limited, 2010, p. 158.

105 Stuart E. Prall, 'The Development of Equity in Tudor England' (1964) 8(1) *The American Journal of Legal History* 1, 4. Quoting from St Germain's *Doctor and Student* p.44.

106 Lord Chancellor 1603-1617.

107 Francis Bacon, *Reading of the Statute of Uses*, in J. Spedding, R.L. Ellis and D.D. Heath (eds), *The Works of Francis Bacon* (14 vols, London, 1857-74), vol. 7 p.401.

1.5.4 Equity Prevails

This dispute between the jurisdictions simmered throughout the 16th century and came to the boil in the 17th century, although some would claim it has continued until the present day.[108] There had been a peaceful interlude when Sir Thomas More became Chancellor. More was the learned lawyer who replaced the much-hated Cardinal Wolsey under whom Chancery had been said to fall to its lowest level.[109] More attempted to placate his common law colleagues whilst Chancellor, inviting them to explain their opposition to the Chancery jurisdiction and to aid in reforming the law to avoid the need for injunctions; however, when the common lawyers 'refused to condescend',[110] he had to admit defeat and simply attempted to administer his office and equity in as fair and just a manner as he could.[111] He is supposed to have addressed his common law critics with these words: 'Forasmuch as yourselves my lords, drive me to the necessity for awarding our injunctions to relieve the people's injury, you cannot hereafter any more justly blame me'.[112]

At the beginning of the seventeenth century the dispute between the common law and equity centred on three leading legal personalities: Lord Coke,[113] Lord Ellesmere and Sir Francis Bacon. In the *Earl of Oxford's Case*,[114] the dispute became so heated that the King had to intervene. Lord Chief Justice Coke was furious that the Chancellor, Lord Ellesmere, was issuing injunctions preventing successful parties at common law from enforcing their judgements. Coke claimed this was illegal meddling with the workings of the common law and its courts. Ellesmere claimed that there was no meddling in the common law, as equity acted only on the conscience of the individual and an equitable injunction was an order only against the conscience of the individual. It did not affect the common law and so was not an interference with the jurisdiction of the common law courts.[115]

---

108 See below 1.9, The fusion fallacy.
109 Mike Mcnair, 'Equity and Conscience' (2007) 27(4) *Oxford Journal of Legal Studies* 659, 670. Stuart E. Prall, 'The Development of Equity in Tudor England' (1964) 8(1) *The American Journal of Legal History* 1, 6.
110 Robert L. Munger, 'A Glance at Equity' (1915) 25(1) (Nov.) *The Yale Law Journal* 42, 54
111 Mike Mcnair, 'Equity and Conscience' (2007) 27(4) *Oxford Journal of Legal Studies* 659, 678. referring to William Roper, *The Life of Sir Thomas More*, in Richard S. Sylvester and Davis P. Harding (eds), *Two Early Tudor Lives* (New Haven, CT: Yale University Press, 1962) at 221-2.
112 Quoted by Robert L. Munger, 'A Glance at Equity' (1915) 25(1) (Nov.) *The Yale Law Journal* 42, 54.
113 Sir Edward Coke was Lord Chief Justice between 1613 and 1616.
114 (1615) 1 Ch. Rep. 1.
115 Klinck, D.R., *Conscience, Equity and the Court of Chancery in Early Modern England*, Farnham: Ashgate Publishing Limited, 2010, p. 158.

A litigant was imprisoned for contempt for refusing to obey the Chancellor's injunction. Coke used *habeus corpus* to free him. Unfortunately the litigant concerned was an extremely unpleasant and unworthy recipient of Coke's help. The King, James I, asked a team of 'law officers' to respond to the question about Chancery's power to hear cases after a judgment at law. In fact the question itself was so framed as to make it difficult to decide otherwise than for equity. Is there any statute which so restrains Chancery that 'Conscience and Equity [are] excluded, banished and damn'd'?

As Sir Francis Bacon, later Lord Chancellor, headed the law officers, and the question involved the power of the Chancellor, itself at least initially based upon the King's prerogative powers,[116] it is not surprising that the officers answered 'No'.[117] Bacon's justification was similar to that given by Ellesmere for his injunctions: Chancery never reverses the judgment itself, but 'leaves in peace and only meddleth with the corrupt Conscience of the Party'.[118]

The King, James I, asked to rule on Bacon's judgment, having to choose which area of law should prevail, followed Bacon and decided that if there was a conflict between the rules of equity and the rules of the common law then the rules of equity would prevail.[119]

In his speech to the Star Chamber in 1616, James repeatedly refers to his own conscience, acknowledges the supremacy of God's law and describes Chancery as 'the dispenser of the King's Conscience.'[120]

Note

The principle from the *Earl of Oxford's Case* was confirmed in the Judicature Acts 1873-5. This was re-enacted as s.49 of the Supreme Court Act 1981, now renamed as the Senior Courts Act 1981, which provides: 'wherever there is any conflict or variance between the rules of equity and the rules of the common law with reference to the same matter, the rules of equity shall prevail.'

---

116 It has also been noted that Coke's anger at equity was also fuelled by personal animosity towards Bacon and jealousy at his rapid rise to power. Robert L. Munger, 'A Glance at Equity' (1915) 25(1) (Nov.) *The Yale Law Journal* 42, 45.

117 Klinck, D.R., *Conscience, Equity and the Court of Chancery in Early Modern Eng* Reproduced in 'The Jurisdiction of the Court of Chancery Vindicated', in *Reports of Cases taken and Adjudged in the Court of Chancery* (London, 1693). see Klinck, D.R., *Conscience, Equity and the Court of Chancery in Early Modern England*, Farnham: Ashgate Publishing Limited, 2010, p.167.

119 This may seem unsurprising as the jurisdiction of the Chancellor and equity originally stemmed from the royal prerogative and the king's conscience. See Robert L. Munger, 'A Glance at Equity' (1915) 25(1) (Nov.) *The Yale Law Journal* 42, 46.

120 Klinck equates this with the public conscience. Klinck, D.R., *Conscience, Equity and the Court of Chancery in Early Modern England*, Farnham: Ashgate Publishing Limited, 2010, pp.167-168.

1.5.5 Lord Nottingham and the defence of equity

Within 50 years of the *Earl of Oxford's case* equity would enter its golden age, but in the following century it would fall into its darkest times. Although the dispute over jurisdiction between equity and the common law had seemingly been settled, the criticisms of the common lawyers had not been addressed; however the greatest of the Chancellors was about to deal with some of the problems associated with equity.

At the time Selden made his criticism of equity and the use of conscience many of the issues were already being dealt with.[121] Thus, by the beginning of the seventeenth century it became usual for the Chancellor to be a lawyer. This was important because the role was now more judicial than executive or ceremonial.[122] Furthermore with the reporting and publication of Chancery cases, such as the *Earl of Oxford's Case* in the Chancery Reports,[123] the Court of Chancery and equity developed respectively as a court and jurisdiction of record and precedent.[124] Perhaps this precedent was not as rigidly followed as at common law, equity is discretionary after all, but still it provided guidance on what equity would do in certain circumstances.

The term conscience had also become more settled and clear. Thus the 'rapid increase in the number of causes that [the Chancellor] had to decide began to make his conscience a technical conscience.'[125] This technical conscience would be subject to precedent and thus certain principles or rules were developed to help the Chancellors exercise their equity. These principles are called the maxims of equity. It is generally considered that the development of these principles owes much to Heneage Finch, later Earl of Nottingham and referred to as Lord Nottingham. Nottingham is known as the 'Father of Equity',[126] and became Chancellor shortly after the Restoration of the monarchy,[127] at a time when land rights were muddled

---

121 Seldon was a contemporary of Lord Nottingham. Robert L. Munger, 'A Glance at Equity' (1915) 25(1) (Nov.) *The Yale Law Journal* 42, 42.

122 F.W. Maitland & F.C. Montague, *A Sketch of English Legal History*, 1850-1906. Charleston, SC: Bibliolife, 2010, at p.126.

123 (1615) 1 Ch. Rep. 1.

124 Lawyers reported Chancery decisions from the 1450s but only regularly reported from the 1590s. Mike Mcnair, 'Equity and Conscience' (2007) 27(4) *Oxford Journal of Legal Studies* 659, 667 & 671.

125 F.W. Maitland & F.C. Montague, *A Sketch of English Legal History*, 1850-1906. Charleston, SC : Bibliolife, 2010, at p.126.

126 See, for example, Robert L. Munger, 'A Glance at Equity' (1915) 25(1) (Nov.) *The Yale Law Journal* 42 at 47, and Lord Denning in *Re Downshire's Settled Estates* [1953] 1 All ER 103 at 133.

127 Lord Chancellor 1673–1682. He was also Lord Keeper to 1675.

and needed to be settled.[128] He was a religious man,[129] and 'perhaps the first important lawyer to try to bring intellectual order to the trust institution and to the learning then available on it.' [130] Maitland and Montague described Nottingham as:

'A jurist first, and a public man afterwards, he owes his high place among the chancellors of England solely to his transcendent merits as a judge. He is the first in that series of great magistrates by whom equity was reduced to a system almost as precise and as little dependent upon individual opinion as the common law itself, the first to take away the reproach that equity had no measure but the chancellor's foot.'[131]

During his chancellorship he tried to clarify the equitable principles, or maxims, which should be applied by Chancellors when deciding cases at equity and the concept of conscience. Thus Nottingham famously stated with regard to conscience:

'With such a conscience as is only *naturalis et interna* this Court has nothing to do; the conscience by which I am to proceed is merely *civilis et politica* and tied to certain measures; and it is infinitely better for the public that a trust, security, or agreement, which is wholly secret, should miscarry, than that men should lose their estates by the mere fancy and imagination of a chancellor.'[132]

The conscience of equity was thus the conscience of the state, a concept of the right behaviour required of the individual by society. After Nottingham 'the rules of equity begin to take a very definite shape, comparable in rigour to the rules of the common law.'[133] Thus, by the end

---

128 During the 'convulsions' of the Civil War and the Interregnum, 'all documents of a constitutional and legal nature were industriously sought after, in order to be destroyed.' Thus after the Restoration, 'the best security which any man could have for an estate of which he was in possession, would be the certainty that there were no title-deeds in existence.' S.R. Maitland, *The Dark Ages; A Series of Essays, Intended to Illustrate the State of religion and Literature in the Ninth, Tenth, Eleventh and Twelfth Centuries*, (London: Francis & John Rivington, 3rd edition, 1853), p.288.

129 Nottingham was said to have instilled in his son, Daniel Finch, later Earl of Nottingham, 'a special relationship with the Anglican church and clergy.' Grant Tapsell,'Laurence Hyde and the Politics of Religion in Later Stuart England' [2010] CXXV (517) *English Historical Review* 1414, 1423.

130 Paul Mathews, 'The Words Which Are Not There: A Partial History of the Constructive Trust', in Charles Mitchell (ed), *Constructive and Resulting Trusts* (Hart Publishing, 2009), 5.

131 F.W. Maitland & F.C. Montague, *A Sketch of English Legal History*, 1850-1906. Charleston, SC: Bibliolife, 2010, at p.135-136.

132 Coke v Fountain 3 Swanst. 585 at 600, 73 Selden Soc. 362 at 371.

133 F.W. Maitland & F.C. Montague, *A Sketch of English Legal History*, 1850-1906. Charleston, SC: Bibliolife, 2010, at p.126.

of the 17th century, there was a distinct body of relatively certain law known as 'equity' and 'modern equity' began.[134]

In the eighteenth century Lord Hardwicke,[135] one of the longest serving Chancellors, helped establish these principles so that by the beginning of the nineteenth century Lord Eldon was able to say:[136] 'Nothing would inflict on me greater pain in quitting this place than the recollection that I had done anything to justify the reproach that the equity of this court varies like the Chancellor's foot'.[137] Lord Eldon further explained that equity was a body of law that should lay down 'fixed principles, but taking care that they are to be applied according to the circumstances of each case'. Therefore the criticism of uncertainty in equity levelled by common lawyers against equity had, by the end of the seventeenth century and certainly by the beginning of the nineteenth century been eradicated. Similarly the Chancellors were unlikely to resort to the Roman law for guidance in the Court of Chancery;[138] however the criticisms of delay and corruption remained, and unfortunately the very certainty that had been required of equity now made equity as unjust as the common law it had been formulated to alleviate. Chancery would enter its darkest and bleakest time.

1.6 Chancery's Bleak House

By the beginning of the nineteenth century equity had developed its own rules and principles of precedent to such an extent that, anyone who has read *Bleak House*, the novel by the famous 19th century novelist Charles Dickens, will be familiar with the Court of Chancery as an inflexible, inefficient, slow and unjust court in its dealings with the case of *Jarndyce v Jarndyce*. This fictitious case, based upon many true cases that Dickens knew of from his time at the Inns of Court, concerned the administration of a deceased estate. Eventually the case was concluded with all of the property of the estate being consumed by the costs of the actions in Chancery and so nothing was left for the beneficiaries. How could this happen in a court based on justice and fairness?

---

134 Maitland states that, 'The history of modern equity begins with the reign of Charles II. Not only was the Court of Chancery more recent in its origins than the Courts of Common Law, but it was remarkably slow to form a definite jurisprudence…The rules of equity could not be methodized until the chancellor should regard the dispensation of equity as his principal function and the office of chancellor should be given only to men who made the law their profession.' F.W. Maitland & F.C. Montague, *A Sketch of English Legal History*, 1850-1906. Charleston, SC: Bibliolife, 2010, at p.134-135.

135 Lord Chancellor 1737-1756.

136 Chancellor 1801-1806, 1806-1827.

137 *Gee v Pritchard* (1818) 2 Swans. 402, 414.

138 Although for a recent Chancery recommendation of Roman law principles see *Re Knapton (Knapton v Hindle)* [1941] Ch 428. Referred to below in Chapter 6.

Inflexibility developed from the reporting of cases, the consequential use of precedent, and the development of equitable principles by Chancellors like Nottingham and Eldon.

Thus, 'Born in protest of precedent, proceeding in defiance of it, it now embraces it.'[139] The very crystallisation of the principles of equity in the late 17th century, from the time of Lord Nottingham, through the early 19th century and Lord Eldon, had made equity as inflexible and hidebound as the common law had been. It was now claimed that equity was no better than the common law it had originally sought to remedy.

The delay of equity was mainly due to the success of equity. Equity offered more flexibility in the claims that could be pursued and in the remedies available for the successful suitor, thus many suitors came to the Court of Chancery for their claim. Also, by the eighteenth century equity had vastly expanded its jurisdiction to encompass almost all law affecting property;[140] however there were very few judges. Originally there was only one judge, the Chancellor. In 1729 the Master of the Rolls was appointed to aid the Chancellor, [141] and then, in 1813, the office of Vice Chancellor (VC) was created. Two further judges were appointed to Chancery in 1841. By 1851 there was a Court of Appeal in Chancery, with two Lords Justices of Appeal in Chancery, but in 1873, when the jurisdictions of common law and equity fused, there were still only seven judges to deal with all the cases before Chancery.

---

139 Robert L. Munger, 'A Glance at Equity' (1915) 25(1) (Nov.) *The Yale Law Journal* 42, 47.

140 Swift wrote: '...it has directly or indirectly claimed cognisance of almost every other matter that resects property, so as to become the most important tribunal in England': Swift's Digest, Vol. II. Quoted in Robert L. Munger, 'A Glance at Equity' (1915) 25(1) (Nov.) *The Yale Law Journal* 42, 49.

141 The office had existed with judicial authority from the time of Edward I and he was sometimes referred to as "Vice-Chancellor" in the reign of Henry VIII. The Master of the Rolls had assisted the Chancellor from the reign of Elizabeth I but it was only in 1729 that his authority was officially confirmed by Sta. 3 Geo. II c.20. See William Lindsay Carne, 'A Sketch of the History of the High Court of Chancery from its Origin to the Chancellorship of Wolsey' (1927) 13(7) (Nov.) *The Virginia Law Review* 391, 416.

Judges in Chancery [142]

Year	Judge	Note	Total Number
Until 1729	Chancellor	Consider this was the period in which the principles of equity developed.	1
1729	Master of the Rolls	Originally sat with the Chancellor but gradually gained independent status.	2
1813	Vice-Chancellor		3
1841	Two more Vice-Chancellors		5
1851			
	Two Lords Justices of Appeal in Chancery	They, and the Chancellor, did not hear first instance cases.	7

Therefore there were far too few judges to deal efficiently with the number of cases being brought before the Court. The backlog and delay in cases was such that it has been estimated that by 1824 there were assets worth £39 million tied up in cases waiting to be heard by the Chancery Court, a huge sum at the time. Furthermore, judgments of the Court of Chancery were praised for their learning and considered nature; this was because they were long and thus took a long time to write. This added to the delay in hearing cases. Added to the normal delays in Chancery, the 19th century saw massive industrial expansion in England and colonial expansion in the formation of the British Empire. Many of the new businesses and the business organisations, such as partnership and the registered company, relied on equitable principles for their commercial success. When they had business problems that required litigation the judgment needed to be fast and efficient, but they was heard in Chancery.

There were also complaints of corruption in Chancery in the seventeenth and eighteenth centuries. For example, injunctions were easily obtainable because of the fees they generated. Also the clerks in Chancery had a monopoly on copying documents for litigants and were paid to copy documents by the page. It was claimed that they used huge handwriting and very wide margins when they copied documents so increasing the page count and their fee.[143]

The final criticism of the Court of Chancery, and the common law generally, was the traditional problem of 'bouncing claims'. Plaintiffs could

---

142 Compiled from information in F.W. Maitland, *Equity* (2nd edition 1936).
143 There had been complaints of 'graft and corruption' amongst the lesser officials in Chancery in Tudor times: Stuart E. Prall, 'The Development of Equity in Tudor England' (1964) 8(1) *The American Journal of Legal History* 1, 7.

either claim at law or in equity, they could not claim in both jurisdictions. Similarly a defendant asserting an equitable defence could only do so before the Court of Chancery.

Example
If a defendant to a common law action had an equitable defence then he had to obtain an injunction to stay the common law proceedings. Once he had done this he would begin his case before the Court of Chancery to establish his equitable defence and rights.

Thus, cases would roll on for years, much as the fictional case of *Jarndyce v Jarndyce*, bouncing between the common law courts and the Court of Chancery. Often, as with *Jarndyce v Jarndyce*, when the case was eventually concluded there would be no assets to divide as they had been eaten by the costs of litigation.

The Court of Chancery was therefore criticised for being inefficient and slow at a time of massive commercial expansion and demand for its services. It had become as inflexible and unjust as the common law it was meant to supplement, and was subject to corrupt practices by its clerks. The continued practice of referring cases between the jurisdictions exacerbated these problems. It was time to reform the Court of Chancery and the common law generally.

1.7 Reform and the Judicature acts 1873-75

Reform of Chancery and equity had been promised centuries before. In the mid-seventeenth century the Civil War[144] and the interregnum of the Commonwealth[145] found the Court of Chancery under attack. The Commonwealth had considered revising the procedural rules of the Court of Chancery because of the delays already encountered, its growing jurisdiction and the 'uncertainty of its decisions'. Oliver Cromwell and the Rump parliament considered abolishing Chancery for these reasons and it's association with 'royal' justice. [146] The reform of Chancery was overtaken by other events and it survived for the Restoration and the golden age of Nottingham.[147]

---

144 In effect three wars between 1642- 1651.
145 1649- 1660.
146 Robert L. Munger, 'A Glance at Equity' (1915) 25(1) (Nov.) *The Yale Law Journal* 42, 56.
147 As Maitland wrote, '[t]ired of change and confusion, men were glad to return to the institutions of their forefathers. Satisfied to be rid forever of the Court of Star Chamber, and the Court of High Commission, they regarded little the barbarity of the criminal law, or the vexatious expense and delay of proceedings in Chancery.' F.W. Maitland & F.C. Montague, *A Sketch of English Legal History*, 1850-1906. Charleston, SC: Bibliolife, 2010, at p.132.

More than 200 years later, the Supreme Court of Judicature Acts 1873-75 fused the administration of the common law and equity in a single unified High Court. The Chancery Court became the Chancery division of the High Court. The High Court would administer both law and equity. Any judge of the High Court or the Court of Appeal was free to deal with cases that had previously been considered exclusively the province of the common law or equity. The judges were also free to award legal or equitable remedies according to accepted principles. The Judicature Acts were replicated almost universally throughout the common law world.[148] Today s.49 of the Senior Courts Act 1981 provides: 'wherever there is any conflict or variance between the rules of equity and the rules of the common law with reference to the same matter, the rules of equity shall prevail.'

The principle of fusion of the jurisdictions of the common law and equity was tested shortly after the Judicature Acts with the case of *Walsh v. Lonsdale.*[149] The Court had to consider a case where the formalities necessary for the creation of a legal lease had not been followed and there was question of whether the Court could rely on equitable principles and defences. Jessel MR stated, 'since the Judicature Act…There are not two estates as there were formerly…there is only one court and the equity rules prevail in it.' This case has been criticised for giving rise to what is termed the 'fusion fallacy'. That is that the two bodies of law, the common law and equity, have actually become one. The Master of the Rolls' statement that 'there is only one court and the equity rules prevail in it' is probably incontrovertible, the previous distinctions between the courts which could administer the common law and equity having been abolished by the Judicature Acts, there is only one High Court in each common law jurisdiction; however his comment about there being 'not two estates as there were formerly' is more controversial. This implied that there was no distinction between the common law and equitable estates and would seem to support the view that there was, and is, one single body of law. These comments have probably been taken out of context as the Master of the Rolls was probably noting that, prior to the Judicature Acts, on the facts of Walsh v Lonsdale, there would have been a periodic tenancy (one estate) recognised in the common law courts and an equitable lease (the other estate) recognised in the Court of Chancery, but that since the Judicature Acts, as there was a conflict and equity prevailed, the equitable lease or estate was the only one that would be recognised by the newly formed court with jurisdiction in both law and equity.[150] It is unlikely that the Master of the Rolls

---

148 Although the fusion of administration did not happen until late in the 20th century in the Chancery Court in New South Wales, Australia: Keith Mason, Keith, 'Fusion: Fallacy, Future Or Finished?' 2004 (16 December) paper delivered at the Fusion Conference.

149 (1882) 21 Ch D 9

150 I am grateful to Gregory Allan, Senior Lecturer in Law at the University of Wolverhampton for clarification of this point.

was commenting in any general way on any notion that law and equity, or legal and equitable estates, was fused; however, these comments excited debate shortly after the judgment,[151] which has continued for well over a century.[152]

1.8 The Fusion Fallacy

No one would really argue with the proposition that the common law and equity are now administratively fused. [153] A plaintiff no longer has to consider which jurisdiction to bring his claim in. The High Court is a 'one-stop shop' whether your claim is based on the common law or equity; however there has been a continued dispute between jurists and academics regarding whether the two bodies of law that comprise the common law and equity have actually fused and become one. Usually, the debate centres on whether the Judicature Acts fused the two bodies of law or merely joined their administration. Thus the question is posed; is there a single body of rules which now makes up the common law?

The fusion supporters would argue that the effect of the Judicature Acts, and the administrative fusion of the jurisdictions, was to develop a single body of common law and equity comprising the principles of both. Those supporting this view would argue it is irrelevant if a cause of action, principle or remedy is legal or equitable; it is part of the common law and can be applied by the common law courts without regard to its jurisdictional origin. Those arguing that this fusion argument is a fallacy would explain that the Judicature Acts were merely an administrative measure allowing plaintiffs to bring an equitable or legal claim in any court, the Acts did not fuse the bodies of the law, and so it is still important to consider whether causes of action and remedies are legal or equitable, and the principles that apply to them, to decide if they are available to the parties, or if the court has the authority to grant them. There has also developed a third argument. This is that the dispute is really irrelevant, as equity and the common law had always been part of the common law, and, if the jurisdictions were not fused

---

151 See, for example, F. Tudsbury, 'Equity and the common law", (1913) 29 *Law Quarterly Review* 154, and S. Holdsworth, 'Relation of the equity administered by the common law judges to the equity administered by the Chancellor' (1916) 26 *Yale Law Journal* 1

152 See, for example, Jill Martin, 'Fusion, fallacy and confusion: a comparative study', [1994] *Conveyancer and Property Lawyer* 13, and Andrew Burrows, 'We do this in common law but that at equity', (2002) 22 *Oxford Journal of Legal Studies* 1.

153 See Lord Justice Munby's discussion of the false notion that there are separate courts within the High Court and so different laws for each division: 'An unconscionable time a-dying: reports from a traveller in a foreign country' (2011) 17 (9) *Trusts & Trustees* 809-828.

originally, fusion of the common law and equity had taken place long before the Judicature Acts.

Those in the fusion camp would argue that the common law and equity have already 'fused' to form just one single system. This is not a new theory and was proposed in articles at the beginning of the 19th century in England and the USA, relying on cases such as *Walsh v Lonsdale* and the comments of Jessel MR. The more modern supporters of this argument would point to judicial comment such as that of Lord Diplock in *United Scientific Holdings v Burnley Borough Council*:[154]

'The innate conservatism of English lawyers may have made them slow to recognise that by the Supreme Court of Judicature Act 1873, the two systems of substantive and adjectival law formerly administered by the courts of law and the Courts of Chancery...were fused.'

They would further point to statements such as that of Lord Denning, when he wrote that the 'fusion is complete'.[155] Similarly, Lord Browne-Wilkinson said in *Tinsley v Milligan*:[156] 'More than 100 years has elapsed since the fusion of the administration of law and equity. The reality of the matter is that, in 1993, English law has one single law of property made up of legal estates and equitable interests.'

The orthodox view has been that law and equity are only administratively fused. Those supporting this view would claim that the Judicature Acts, and their colonial counterparts, merely allowed for the administration of the two systems to be carried out by all courts. They did not actually join the common law and equity into one single body of law. Those in favour of the view that the systems have not fused would point to judicial comment such as that made by Mummery L.J in *MCC Proceeds Inc v Lehman Bros International (Europe)*,[157] that the Judicature Acts, 'were intended to achieve procedural improvements in the administration of law and equity in all courts, not to transform equitable interests into legal titles or to sweep away altogether the rules of the common law...'

Supporters of this view would also point to s.49 of the Senior Courts Act 1981, where provision is made for equity to prevail if there is a conflict between the principles of equity and the law, as evidence that there must be two systems of law, although they are administered by one court. Thus academics such as Pettit state there are two systems not one.[158]

---

154 [1977] 2 WLR 806.
155 Writing extra-judicially: Alfred Denning, *Landmarks in the Law* (LexisNexis UK: 1998)
156 [1993] 3 All ER 65.
157 [1998] 4 All ER 675, 691.
158 Philip H. Pettit, *Equity and the Law of Trusts* (Oxford: Oxford University Press: 2009).

A compromise from the "orthodox" school of thought might be that proposed by Jill Martin, 'more than a century of fused jurisdiction has seen the two systems working more closely together… They are coming closer together. But they are not yet fused'.[159] Similarly, Burrows puts forward areas where fusion, if not already having happened, is, in his view, imminent.[160]

The third school of thought is that there is really no question regarding the fusion of equity and the law after the Judicature Acts because they were already fused. This is probably best represented by Mason when he states: '[t]he fusing of law and equity has been going on for centuries. It has generally been encouraged by all branches of government since the time that Chancery began behaving like a court of law. It reflects the law's striving for coherence and consistency.'[161] Mason points to the *Earl of Oxford's Case*, back in 1615, as a time when fusion at least began between the law and equity. The decision of the King that equity would prevail over the common law is, he argues, evidence that the two systems were working together even then. It is submitted that, extending from this, the very fact that equity has traditionally been considered a 'gloss' on the common law, and, in the *Earl of Oxford's Case* was described by Ellesmere, the Lord Chancellor, as serving to "soften and mollify the extremity of the law" is evidence that equity has always been a part of the common law. Similarly, in the United States, Benjamin Cardozo stated that "Equity works as a supplement for law and does not supersede the prevailing law."[162] Furthermore, the Chancellor was always seen as one of the foremost experts in law in the country, this was the case even before the appointed Chancellor was usually a lawyer. This was because the Chancellor would be a cleric versed in the civil and canon laws. Often the Chancellor was invited to sit on King's Bench to aid in a particularly difficult point of law, [163] and as late as Nottingham's time the Chancellor

---

159 Jill E. Martin, *Modern Equity* (London: Sweet & Maxwell: 18th edition, 2009).

160 Andrew Burrows, 'We do this in common law but that at equity', (2002) 22 *Oxford Journal of Legal Studies* 1.

161 Mason, Keith, 'Fusion: Fallacy, Future Or Finished?', 2004 (16 December) paper delivered at the Fusion Conference. Available at http://www.lawlink.nsw.gov.au/lawlink/Supreme_Court/ll_sc.nsf/pages/ SCO_mason161204 : last accessed 24/10/11.

162 *G Graf v Hope Building Corporation* (1930) 254 N.Y. 1 at 9. Benjamin Cardozo (May 24, 1870 – July 9, 1938) was an eminent American jurist and associate Supreme Court Justice famous for his influence on the development of the common law in the United States

163 A practice that continued as late as 1315 according to William Lindsay Carne, 'A Sketch of the History of the High Court of Chancery from its Origin to the Chancellorship of Wolsey' (1927) 13(7) (Nov.) *The Virginia Law Review* 391, 397.

would invite common law judges to sit with him to decide difficult cases in Chancery, even if he ignored their advice![164]

Thus it may be helpful to consider that there is a single body of common law in the wider sense of the common law, which is made up of common law and equitable principles, doctrines, defences and remedies. Although this single body of common law is administered by all common law courts, it may still be necessary to consider the original jurisdictional nature of the claim before the court to determine what principle, doctrine, defence or remedy, should be accepted or applied to maintain certainty and consistency in the law. It is the nature of the common law to develop in response to social and commercial needs, and in doing so for the different areas of the law to borrow concepts that have proven useful and fair in the interests of justice. This happened long before the Judicature Acts, for example when the common law borrowed equitable principles on evidence, and equity constructed its principles of compensation in consideration of common law damages. Thus, although it may be necessary to determine a fiduciary relationship before an equitable remedy is granted, because the remedy was traditionally based upon such a relationship, it is submitted that the law may develop the fiduciary categories to reflect changing needs and encompass relationships previously only recognised at common law. Lord Millett, writing extra-judicially, commented that, 'neither law nor equity is now stifled by its origin and the fact that both are administered by one court has inevitably meant that each has borrowed from the other in furthering the harmonious development of the law as a whole.'[165] Thus, as Keith Mason has said, questions about the 'institutional bifurcation of law and equity are becoming increasingly irrelevant, if not distracting.'

Although the Judicature Acts may have been the most significant identifiable event in the development of the equity jurisdiction, there is still a way to go before the 'absolute wiping out of all distinction between law and equity' occurs, as was predicted in 1915,[166] and it is still debateable whether this would be desirable. Equity is, and long has been, a vital part of the common law. To understand how important equity is to the common law the next two chapters will consider equitable principles, doctrines, defences and remedies.

---

164 E.g. *Howard v Duke of Norfolk* (1681-5) 3 Ch Cas 1. See William Lindsay Carne, 'A Sketch of the History of the High Court of Chancery from its Origin to the Chancellorship of Wolsey' (1927) 13(7) (Nov.) *The Virginia Law Review* 391, 412.
165 Peter Millett, 'Equity – the road ahead' (1995) 9 *TLI* 35.
166 Robert L. Munger, 'A Glance at Equity' (1915) 25(1) (Nov.) *The Yale Law Journal* 42, 42.

1.9 Summary

Equity began as a remedy for the inadequacies and injustice of the common law. The Chancellor administered his special justice, which became known as "equity", in his Court of Chancery. The Lord Chancellor's authority derived from the prerogative power of the King to "talk over" the judgment of his courts and the religious principles of the mainly clerical Chancellors. The Chancellor's jurisdiction was over the conscience of the parties before him. He could order the parties to act according to "good" conscience or to stop acting in "bad" conscience. This developed into the equitable remedy of the injunction, an order to do or to stop doing something. Originally the Chancellor would order a plaintiff who had succeeded in a common law court not to enforce his judgement because it would be unconscionable to do so. The jurisdiction of the Chancellor was greatly extended when he recognised that those who had promised to hold land for the use, trust or confidence of another, and to whom the land had been conveyed as required by the common law, should be made to keep their promise in good conscience. The injunction and the recognition and enforcement of the use, trust and confidence, undermined the authority of the common law courts. This resulted in a battle for jurisdiction between equity and the common law. The King eventually ruled that whenever there is a conflict between equity and the common law equity will prevail. The Court of Chancery became immensely successful but eventually suffered from the same problems of the common law which it had been developed to overcome, becoming renowned as slow, corrupt and inflexible, and causing injustice to those who appeared before it. To combat this inefficiency and injustice, legislation was enacted to fuse the administration of the principles and remedies of equity and the common law in one court. Today equity remains an intrinsic part of the common law although there is dispute about whether equity and the common law are a single body of principles and remedies or equity remains a separate body of principles and remedies within the common law.

CHAPTER 2
MAXIMS AND DOCTRINES

2.1 Discretion and Conscience

From the sixteenth century the most consistent criticism of equity had been its discretion. Common lawyers, especially those involved in commercial law, are cautious and critical of equity's discretion. It is generally agreed that to foster a successful business climate the law should be certain. The parties to a contract must know what rights and obligations the contract confers, and that the law will enforce those rights and obligations. Lord Browne-Wilkinson said, in *Westdeutsche Landesbank Girozentrale v Islington London Borough Council*:[1] 'Wise judges have often warned against the wholesale importation into commercial law of equitable principles inconsistent with the certainty and speed which are essential requirements for the orderly conduct of business affairs.'

On top of this at times equity relies on the concept of 'conscience' to apportion liability. The discretionary nature of equity and its emphasis on conscience as a guiding principle in deciding liability is the cause of much concern to common law judges, practitioners and students. However, equitable discretion is highlighted not in Chancery judges being able to make up the law, but in being able to decide whether a party who had established their case is still deserving of a remedy. Of course, there is some discretion in the common law, for example a judge may not award nominal damages because the case involves a minor technical breach of contract or duty and perhaps should not have been brought, or because of some other element of the conduct of a party. However, remedies in equity are completely discretionary. A party may bring a suit in equity, prove every part of his claim and yet still not be given the remedy he has asked for. The 'winning' party may not *deserve* the remedy claimed because they have not acted in 'good conscience'. To common lawyers this smacks too much of judges making judgments not by applying the law but by deciding what is 'right'. The common law has consistently refused to accept that judgments should be teleological. However, judges in Chancery seem to have made their decisions applying equitable principles based on how the conscience of the party should have directed that party to act and what the just outcome would be. For a common lawyer this seems wrong, even if the outcome is unjust it is the law and should be applied and upheld. However, it should be noted that judges have criticised the slavish

---

1 [1996] AC 669; 2 W.L.R. 802 (HL).

following of precedent. As Hamersley J. noted in the United States, referring to the rule against perpetuities in a dissenting judgment:

'The rule of "*stare decisis*" is wise and salutary, it is based upon the supreme importance of certainty in the law, but there are instances where the necessities of truth and justice demand a modification of former decisions...I must accept my share of responsibility for a passive concurrence in some cases...It is an evil to be compelled to acknowledge a mistake in recent decisions, but it is a greater evil to be compelled to repeat time after time a statement which we, in common with all the profession, know is not true...'[2]

Of course, this was one of the reasons equity developed. As Milsom has noted, although certainty in the law is often called for, 'The more explicitly law is stated, the less readily it can respond to changing circumstances...'[3] The big problem for common lawyers, as we have seen, is that equity's discretion and conscience works and is still popular today, especially with litigants to commercial transactions who wish for remedies the common law cannot give them, but are amongst the panoply of remedies available in equity (these will be discussed in the next chapter). To understand how equity did work and why these decisions are not teleological but are based upon principles of law, it is necessary to consider the concept of conscience in equity.

The concept of conscience is only applied in equity subject to guiding principles or maxims and is not an arbitrary judicial tool. Of course the application of these principles means that equity is not as straightforward as the common law at times and requires more of an overall knowledge of equity to understand some of the judgments. This chapter is intended to introduce the guiding principles or maxims of equity and their development into doctrines, again guiding principles, which help judges to decide cases.

'Conscience' is a term that was mentioned in chapter 1. The first decisions in equity to soften the common law were those taken by the king according to conscience. The king was the spiritual guardian of his people and, at a time when religious principles were inextricably interwoven with the law,[4] the king was concerned with the immortal souls of his subjects and so was concerned that his subjects should act in 'good conscience'.

If there is a single unified thread running through the law and rules of equity, and some have argued that there is not (including Maitland), it is the concept of conscience. As Lord Browne-Wilkinson has noted with

---

2   *Tingler v Chamberlain* 71 Conn. 466.

3   S.F.C. Milsom, *Historical Foundations of the Common Law*, 2nd edition, London, Butterworth's, 1981, p6.

4   Harold J. Berman, *Law and Revolution: The Formation of the Western Legal Tradition*(Harvard University Press, 1983).

regard to trusts, equity's greatest creation,[5] 'Equity operates on the conscience of the owner of the legal interest. In the case of a trust, the conscience of the legal owner requires him to carry out the purposes for which the trust was vested in him ...'

Of course the problem is; what is good conscience? This was the reason for John Selden's reproach:

'Equity is a roguish thing. For law we have a measure... equity is according to the conscience of him that is chancellor, and as that is longer or narrower, so is equity. 'Tis all one as if they should make the standard for the measure the length of the chancellor's foot.'[6]

Selden's criticism was that the guiding principle of equity was conscience and this was a personal thing, personal to the Chancellor, so judgment sin equity would depend on the personal conscience of the Chancellor and different Chancellors might decide cases differently. This is a good point, and originally the King and the first Chancellors would have decided what the conscience of the defendant should have made him do by recourse to religious thought and their own moral standards. However, by the time Selden's words were published Chancery was entering the golden age of Lord Nottingham's Chancellorship.[7] Nottingham took time to explain in his judgments that the Court of Chancery did not proceed according to conscience *'naturalis et interna'* but by conscience *'civilis et politica'*.[8] Thus the conscience of equity was not a man's own natural and internal conscience but the conscience of the state and policy- a public conscience. This would reflect the predominant moral standards of the time, well at least as much as the Chancellor understood them. Thus a man before equity was being judged on the standards of society and should have known these.

Today a Judge deciding an equitable matter would be careful before ascribing his decision to a particular religious teaching or his own moral standards. Nottingham's public conscience is still probably the most accurate way to describe conscience in equity. In deciding whether to grant equitable relief or refuse to enforce a legal right, the court must decide whether the plaintiff or defendant's actions have affected their conscience, this is particularly important when implied trusts are considered and strangers are made liable as trustees.[9] Thus, if the defendant's conduct has been 'unconscionable', against good conscience, then the plaintiff may be

---

5   *Westdeutsche Landesbank Girozentrale v Islington London Borough Council* [1996] AC 669, 705.

6   John Selden (sometimes Seldon), *Table Talk* (1689).

7   Lord Chancellor 1673- 1682.

8   *Cook v Fountain*, 3 Swanst. 600. See Robert L. Munger, 'A Glance at Equity' (1915) 25(1) (Nov.) *The Yale Law Journal* 42, 47.

9   These are discussed in later chapters; see particularly chapters 10, 11, 12 & 17.

granted equity's aid, the defendant may be liable. However, if the plaintiff has acted unconscionably then he may not be awarded a remedy, as this would be inequitable. At this point the court has to weigh the conduct of both parties to see where the balance of justice lies, who has acted conscionably, or even who has acted least unconscionably. The judge is helped in deciding whether a party's actions are in good conscience by the 'maxims of equity'. A maxim is a principle and the maxims of equity are a series of principles that have developed to guide judges in deciding whether to grant equitable relief. Lord Nottingham responded to criticism of the arbitrary nature of equity by standardising certain principles of equity and explaining when these principles should be used to help a Chancellor decide if the party had acted in good conscience. In the 18th century these principles were collected and printed as the 'maxims of equity'. As considered in chapter 1, during the 18th and 19th century these principles and the use of precedent in the Chancery Courts led to criticism that equity was as rigid as the common law. Lord Denning stated that, 'the Courts of Chancery are no longer courts of equity...they are as fixed and immutable as the courts of law ever were.'[10] This was a complaint because he was one of the foremost advocates of discretionary justice in every area of law, including the use of constructive trusts.[11] Lord Denning was referring to the restrictions that have been placed on the use of equitable discretion by the courts themselves. The remedies are still awarded at the discretion of the court but the courts have developed recognised situations where they will or will not be awarded. To do otherwise would be to provide 'palm tree justice' and even the Courts of Chancery have realised the importance of certainty. As famously stated by Bagnall J in *Cowcher v. Cowcher*:[12]

'I am convinced that in determining rights, particularly property rights, the only justice that can be attained by mortals, who are fallible and are not omniscient, is justice according to law; the justice which flows from the application of sure and settled principles to proved or admitted facts. So in the field of equity the length of the Chancellor's foot has been measured or is capable of measurement. This does not mean that equity is past child-bearing, simply that its progeny must be legitimate - by precedent out of principle. It is well that this should be so; otherwise no lawyer could safely advise on his client's title and every quarrel would lead to a law suit.'

---

10   Denning (1952) 5 CLP 8. Pollock the legal historian had said in 1905 that the court of chancery was no longer a court of conscience: see Robert L. Munger, 'A Glance at Equity' (1915) 25(1) (Nov.) *The Yale Law Journal* 42, 47.

11   See chapter 12 , *Equity and the family home.*

12   [1972] 1 WLR 425, 430.

Thus equity is still able to develop new principles and new law but this must be based upon accepted principles. These principles are the maxims of equity.

2.2 The Maxims as Guidance

The Concise Oxford English Dictionary defines a maxim as 'a general principle, serving as a rule or guide'. Maxims occur in the common law as well as in equity, for example *nemo dat quod non habet* is a well known common law maxim meaning 'no one can give what they do not have'. The use of maxims is as a guide for the application of the law and, even at common law, as with most legal principles, maxims are rules that can have exceptions. Therefore, when considering the use of maxims in equity it is important to remember that they are not fixed and firm rules; they are merely guides for the court to decide whether a party has acted in good conscience and should receive the help of equity.

To understand how modern equity works it is necessary to consider these principles because they form the basis of equitable relationships, e.g. the trust, and the basis on which the doctrines of equity operate and remedies are awarded. However, there may be times when a judge will justify his decision in terms of one or more of the maxims, but at other times similar decisions will be made by reference to other maxims, or no reference will be made to the maxims at all.

At this point it is also important to introduce the concept of equity's darling. If a plaintiff seeks a remedy against a defendant who is equity's darling then the court may refuse to award the remedy. Following on from the concept of conscience is the sanctity accorded by equity to the *bona fide* purchaser of property for value without knowledge of a prior equitable interest, otherwise known as 'equity's darling'. An early example was **Bassett v Nosworthy**,[13] where Lord Nottingham specified that where a purchaser could defend his purchase at law then 'his adversary shall never be aided in a Court of Equity'. Of course this depended on the purchaser being "a Purchaser, bona fide, without Notice of any defect in his Title at the Time of the Purchase made..."[14] Thus if a purchaser, someone who has given value for property, has no knowledge of a prior equitable interest, thus their conscience is not affected by it, equity will not enforce the prior equitable interest against the purchaser. Of course if they have knowledge of the prior equitable interest then their conscience is affected and equity will enforce the prior equitable interest against them.[15] Equity will also

---

13   (1673) Rep. Temp. Finch 102. Lord Nottingham was Lord Keeper at the time.
14   (1673) Rep. Temp. Finch 102, 103.
15   As early as 1465 it was held that a person who bought land from a trustee with notice that the land was subject to the trust obligation was bound by the trust: YB 5 Ed IV, Mich pl 16, fo. 7.

enforce the prior equitable interest against someone who is not a purchaser, has not given value and so is a volunteer, because, as explained below, *equity will not assist a volunteer*.[16]

It should also be noted that equity has developed its own evidential presumptions, tools of evidence, from which the court may presume a fact in issue from other evidence. The most important of these are the presumption of resulting trust, that a transfer of property for no consideration or a gratuitous contribution to the purchase price of property will raise a presumption that the donor or contributor retains a beneficial interest in the property, and the presumption of advancement, that gratuitous transfers of property to near family (such as from husband to wife or father to child) will raise a presumption that a gift was intended. These are mentioned below but discussed in detail in the chapter on implied trusts. The most important thing to remember with these two presumptions is that they only come into play when there is no evidence regarding the transfer of property or the evidence is tainted with illegality or so self-serving as to be unreliable.

2.3 The Maxims of Equity

In reading through the many textbooks available in the common law world dealing with equity it will be found that there is some disagreement over how many maxims there are. The same maxim may also be expressed in different terms, for example *equity assists the diligent and not the tardy* is often more intelligibly rendered *delay defeats equity*.

Academic disagreement is not unusual in equity or any area of the common law, but disagreeing on the number of rules of equity may seem quite fundamental. Some texts claim there are only 12 maxims of equity and some many more, Osborn's Concise Law Dictionary lists 20![17] The confusion seems to lie in some authors regarding only the traditional maxims, as printed in the 18th century as being 'truly' maxims of equity. Of course, the Courts of Chancery were not static, however inefficient they became in the 18th and 19th century they still developed new principles to deal with new problems. This is the basis of equity (one of the maxims provides that *equity will not suffer a wrong without a remedy*). These new developments may seem to some authors to be no more than interpretative devices; a claim made against the maxim *equity will not permit a statute to be used as an instrument for fraud*. However, they are still important guides for the application of equity.

---

16   By 1595 those who received trust property without knowledge but provided no consideration- volunteers- were held to hold trust property subject to the trust obligation: *Chudleigh's Case* 1 Co Rep 113b, 122b.

17   Mick Woodley, *Osborne's Concise Law Dictionary* (London: Sweet & Maxwell, 2005).

Some of the most important are listed below:

1   Equity will not suffer a wrong to be without a remedy
2   Equity follows the law
3   He who comes to equity must come with clean hands
4   He who seeks equity must do equity
5   Where the equities are equal the law prevails
6   Where the equities are equal the first in time prevails
7   Equity imputes an intention to fulfil an obligation
8   Equity regards as done that which ought to be done
9   Equity is equality
10 Equity looks to the substance rather than the form (sometimes, equity looks to the intent rather than the form)
11 Delay defeats equity (sometimes, equity assists the diligent and not the tardy).
12 Equity acts *in personam*
13 Equity will not permit a statute to be used as an instrument of fraud
14 Equity will not assist a volunteer
15 Equity will not perfect an imperfect gift
16 Equity will not construe a valid power out of an invalid trust
17 Equity will not permit a trust to fail for want of a trustee
18 Equity, like nature, does nothing in vain.

The most important will be discussed below and others discussed as they are referred to in the text.

• *Equity will not suffer a wrong to be without a remedy*
As previously stated this maxim underlies the very reason for the emergence of equity. Equity developed to mitigate the harshness of the common law and because the common law had no remedy available to correct an obvious wrong. The most important example of this is the trust. The common law does not recognise the existence of the trust and is only interested in legal ownership; therefore to enforce beneficial interests under a trust the beneficiary must rely on equity. However, equity will not merely provide a remedy in order to do 'justice'. As Lindley L.J. stated in **Holmes v Millage**,[18] 'It is an old mistake to suppose that, because there is no effectual remedy at law, there must be one in equity'. In order for an equitable remedy to be awarded there must be a recognised equitable cause of action or one must be capable of being asserted by analogy. For example, Sir George Baker P, when refusing to grant a husband an order to prevent his wife aborting their child, in **Paton v Trustees of British**

---

18   [1893] 1 QB 551, 555

Pregnancy Advisory Service,[19] noted that the husband had 'no legal right enforceable in law or equity to stop his wife having this abortion or to stop the doctors from carrying out the abortion'.

• *Equity follows the law*

This maxim is support for the view that equity is part of the common law. Unless there are special circumstances (e.g. equitable fraud) equity will follow the law. Equity has always been a 'gloss' on the common law and so should only come into effect when the common law cannot provide justice, or when strict application of the common law would be unjust. Otherwise equity should follow the law. Equity always follows statutes and generally follows the common law unless to do so would be unconscionable. An early example was ***Bassett v Nosworthy,***[20] where Lord Nottingham specified that where a purchaser could defend his purchase at law then 'his adversary shall never be aided in a Court of Equity'. Of course this depended on the purchaser being equity's darling- 'a Purchaser, bona fide, without Notice of any defect in his Title at the Time of the Purchase made...'[21]

• *He who comes to equity must come with clean hands*

This maxim is linked to the maxim *He who seeks equity must do equity* (considered next). This maxim applies to conduct before the trial, whereas 'doing equity' refers to future conduct. This maxim means that equity will not assist a plaintiff who has acted unconscionably or illegally in connection with the matter before the court. A party seeking equitable relief, based on good conscience, cannot rely on their illegal actions or intent. For example, in ***Re Emery's Investments Trusts,***[22] the British husband wished to purchase American Savings Bonds but was unable to do so at the time because of American tax law. The husband used his money to buy the bonds but registered them in the wife's name with the husband named as the beneficiary. The Bonds were later swapped for common stock but still registered in the wife's name. There was evidence the intent was for an equal beneficial interest in the stock, but that the husband wished to avoid paying U.S. tax as an alien. The wife sold the stock and the husband claimed half. In giving judgment that the wife held all of the interest in the stock, because of the presumption of advancement, Wynn-Parry J. refused to accept the husband's evidence as it was tainted with an illegal purpose, to evade tax:

'The husband...satisfied me by his evidence that his intention was that

---

19   [1979] QB 276, 281.
20   (1673) Rep. Temp. Finch 102. Lord Nottingham was Lord Keeper at the time.
21   (1673) Rep. Temp. Finch 102, 103.
22   *Emery v Emery* [1959] Ch 410, [1959] 1 All ER 577.

the beneficial interest should be shared, and there are various indications to support that, such as the retention of control and payment of dividends into the joint account. But matters such as the retention of control and the payment into the joint account cannot be decisive when once the equitable presumption of advancement has arisen, and it is necessary for the husband, in his endeavour to rebut that presumption, to assert that the property in question was put into his wife's name in order to avoid the payment on his beneficial interest of tax which would otherwise have been payable… He comes to this court seeking the aid of equity…it is impossible for this court to help him". [23]

Similarly, in *Tinker v Tinker*, [24] Salmon L.J. opined:

'It is trite law that anyone coming to equity to be relieved against his own act must come with clean hands. If, in a case such as the present, he were to put forward, as a reason for being relieved against his own act, a dishonest plot on his part, for example, to defraud his creditors, the court would refuse him relief and would say: let the estate lie where it falls.' [25]

If a plaintiff has performed illegal or improper actions they may still be able to obtain relief provided that they do not have to rely upon their illegality in order to establish their claim, or if they have rectified their unconscionable conduct. [26]

In considering 'clean hands' it must be remembered that 'equity does not demand that its suitors shall have led "blameless lives".' If the unconscionable conduct is not material to the matter before the court then it will not be a problem. Thus, in the case of *Argyll v Argyll*, [27] the adultery of the Duchess of Argyll was irrelevant to the matter before the court, even though that matter was an application by the Duchess to obtain an injunction preventing the Duke publishing details of her adultery.

• *He who seeks equity must do equity*

This maxim applies to conduct after the hearing. Thus, a plaintiff who seeks equity must be prepared to comply with the rules of equity and act fairly towards the defendant if they are granted a remedy. In *Re Diplock*, [28] the Court of Appeal held that some tracing claims could be defeated if it would be inequitable to allow the plaintiff to trace. The mistakenly paid parties had used the disputed funds to improve their properties and, if the Court had granted the claims, the only way the plaintiffs could enforce the

---

23   *Emery v Emery* [1959] Ch 410, 420-422, per Wynn-Parry J.
24   [1970] P 136.
25   [1970] P 136, at p.143 per Salmon L.J.
26   See *Tinsley v. Milligan* [1994] 1 AC 340 and the concept of illegality and resulting trusts discussed in the chapter on implied trusts.
27   [1965] 1 All ER 611.
28   [1951] AC 251.

judgment that the defendants' property represented their property, would be to force the innocent parties to sell their properties. In seeking such an order the plaintiffs would not therefore be acting equitably. The doctrine of election owes its origins to this maxim.

• *Where the equities are equal the law prevails*
This maxim is the foundation of the doctrine of notice and the source of the *bona fide* purchaser without notice rule. The *bona fide* purchaser for value of a legal interest without notice of an equitable interest is known as 'equity's darling'. An equitable claim will not prevail against equity's darling because the equity's darling and the holder of an equitable interest both have equitable rights (interests in the property). However, as the equities are equal, but the *bona fide* purchaser has a legal right also, he is the owner in law, the law prevails. An early example was the previously mentioned **Bassett v Nosworthy**,[29] where Lord Nottingham specified that where a purchaser could defend his purchase at law then 'his adversary shall never be aided in a Court of Equity'. Of course this depended on the purchaser being 'a Purchaser, bona fide, without Notice of any defect in his Title at the Time of the Purchase made...'[30]

• *Where the equities are equal the first in time prevails*
This maxim, in Latin *'qui prior est tempore, potior est jure'*, also explains the doctrine of notice. A purchaser with notice of another's prior beneficial interest takes their legal title subject to the other's equitable interest. Both the purchaser and the beneficial interest owner have equitable interests. As the purchaser's equity is newer, the prior beneficial interest wins.

• *Equity imputes an intention to fulfil an obligation*
This maxim provides the foundation for the doctrines of satisfaction and performance. It is therefore the reason for the rule in **Strong v. Bird**,[31] that if an imperfect gift is made during the donor's lifetime, and the intended donee is made executor/administrator of the donor's estate, then the vesting of the property in the donee as executor/administrator perfects the gift. It fulfils the intention of the donor. Similarly, if a testator leaves a legacy to a creditor it will be assumed this was done to aid in satisfying the debt. If the amount satisfies the debt the creditor has no further claim against the testator's estate.

• *Equity regards as done that which ought to be done*

---

29   (1673) Rep. Temp. Finch 102. Lord Nottingham was Lord Keeper at the time.
30   (1673) Rep. Temp. Finch 102, 103.
31   (1874) LR 18 Eq 315.

This maxim is used mostly in contract cases and is the reason for the remedy of specific performance and the rule in **Walsh v. Lonsdale**.[32] Thus, when a contract is specifically enforceable, equity regards the promisor as already having done what he promised to do. In **Walsh v Lonsdale** a contract to grant a legal lease that did not comply with the required formalities was still seen as giving rise to an equitable lease. The maxim also applies when a party has acted unconscionably in a fiduciary position. So, in **Attorney General of Hong Kong v Reid**,[33] where a fiduciary received a bribe in breach of his fiduciary duty, it was held that the fiduciary 'ought' to have paid the money instantly to their principal. As equity would regard that this had been done, the fiduciary was therefore regarded as holding the money for the benefit of his principal, he was a constructive trustee. The maxim is also the basis of the equitable doctrine of conversion.

• *Equity is equality*
This maxim is often a rule of last resort. If there is no evidence to the contrary, then the default position in an equitable division of property will be in equal proportions. This is important in division of property in social or familial relationships and was reconfirmed by the English House of Lords in **Stack v Dowden**.[34]

• *Equity looks to the substance rather than the form* (sometimes *equity looks to the intent rather than the form*)
Equity is not obsessed with formality as the common law is. Thus, at common law if a receipt is given for full payment of a price but only part-payment has been made, the law presumes the full payment has been made. The form is all. In equity the true state of affairs is more important. In other words, it does not matter how an agreement is worded or recorded, it is the effect of the agreement that matters. For example a covenant can be worded, 'not to allow a property to fall into disrepair'. This would seem to be a negative covenant but its substance is positive, as its effect is to make the person bound by the covenant spend money. Therefore, equity regards this as a positive covenant.

• *Delay defeats equity (equity assists the diligent and not the tardy)*
A plaintiff must not delay for too long before seeking the assistance of equity. This maxim explains the doctrine of laches.[35] A plaintiff will be bound by his laches if the delay in initiating proceedings would cause

---

32   (1882) 21 Ch D 9.
33   [1994] 1 AC 324.
34   [2007] UKHL 17; 2 AC 432.
35   see *Nelson v. Rye* [1996] 2 All ER 186.
36   [1950] 2 K.B. 86.

injustice or prejudice the defendant. In *Leaf v. International Galleries*,[36] an oil painting had been bought by the plaintiff from the defendant gallery five years before. The painting was represented as being by the English landscape artist John Constable. However, when the plaintiff tried to sell the painting at the auctioneers, Christies, it was discovered to be a work by another artist. The plaintiff brought an action for rescission of the contract and the repayment of the purchase price.[37] The court held that the plaintiff had suffered from the defendant's innocent misrepresentation of the identity of the artist who had painted the painting, but could not avail himself of the equitable remedy of rescission of the contract, because of the delay of five years in bringing the action:[38]

'...the attribution of works of art to particular artists is often a matter of great controversy and increasing difficulty as time goes on. If the plaintiff is right in saying that he is entitled, perhaps years after the purchase, to raise the question whether in truth a particular painting was rightly attributed to a particular artist, most costly and difficult litigation may result.'

The basis of this maxim is the consideration that equitable remedies are so powerful that they can affect third party interests. If there was no cut off point then there could potentially be inequitable consequences for other parties. Therefore, they are available at the discretion of the court only if brought swiftly. The statutes of limitations originally had no application for claims in respect of uses or trusts.[39] Today, however, provisions in the Limitations Act 1980 will apply. However, if the claim involves an equitable remedy and the Limitations Act 1980 does not apply then the doctrine of laches will still apply.

• *Equity acts in personam*
This is one of the most important principles of equity and has been accepted since early in the equity jurisdiction. Equity is 'compulsory *ad personam* and not *ad rem*, as at the common law it is...It bindeth not the right but bindeth the person to obedyence.' [40] Equity acts upon the conscience of the parties. It acts in order to prevent unconscionable behaviour. Thus, prior equitable interests do not bind equity's darling because he has no notice of them, he has no knowledge of them and so his

---

37 Of course this action predates the Misrepresentation Act 1967 and so damages were not available for innocent misrepresentation.

38 [1950] 2 K.B. 86, 94, per Evershed M.R.

39 Paul Mathews, 'The Words Which Are Not There: A Partial History of the Constructive Trust', in Charles Mitchell (ed), *Constructive and Resulting Trusts* (Hart Publishing, 2009), 22.

40 Stuart E. Prall, 'The Development of Equity in Tudor England' (1964) 8(1) *The American Journal of Legal History* 1, 18. Quoting Edward Hake, *Epieikeia, A Dialogue on Equity in Three parts*, ed. D.E.C. Yale (New Haven, 1953), p.123.

conscience is not affected. It is also the basis of equitable remedies such as the injunction and specific performance. Equitable remedies are personal remedies; they are directed at the conscience of the individual. Thus an order for specific performance can be made even if the property the action concerns is out of the court's jurisdiction;[41] for an equitable remedy the relevant factor is whether the defendant's conscience is within the jurisdiction. Equity's orders are personal. If the order is not followed then the party is in contempt of court and can be imprisoned, fined or have property sequestered (if a corporation).

• *Equity will not permit a statute to be used as an instrument of fraud*
Though not one of the original maxims, and not listed as a maxim in *Snell's Equity*, this maxim is now one of the most frequently invoked. It is sometimes considered to be more an aid to statutory interpretation than a maxim. It is the reason for the rule in **Rochefoucauld v. Boustead**,[42] and has also been used to justify secret trusts. Some legislation provides formalities in the creation of instruments such as those for the declaration of a trust of land,[43] and the writing of a will.[44] These provisions are intended to prevent fraud by ensuring there is full documentation of the intents of the parties. If the fact that these provision have not been complied with, for example that a declaration of a trust of land is not in writing, is being used to perpetrate a fraud then equity will look to the true intent of the parties even though the formalities were not observed. However, there have been questions about the constitutional significance of a court using an equitable principle to ignore a statute.

• *Equity will not assist a volunteer*
A volunteer is one who has given no consideration for a transfer of property. Equity generally dislikes interfering with the rights of a third party, especially if they have no notice of prior equitable interests. Thus equity's darling will defeat a tracing action because he has given consideration, value, for the transfer. However, an innocent volunteer, i.e. a party without notice but who has not given value, will not receive equity's aid. The only real exception to this is the beneficiary who usually has not given any consideration for his beneficial interest but upon whose behalf equity will enforce the trust.

• *Equity will not perfect an imperfect gift*
This principle follows on from the previous maxim that *equity will not aid*

---

a volunteer, and is the principle that was used to justify the decision in *Milroy v Lord.*[45] A donee of a gift does not give value for it. At law, to perfect a gift there must usually be intent by the donor to allow the donee to enjoy the property the donee's own and this is 'perfected' or finished by the donor delivering the gift to the donee. Some forms of property, such as land and shares, require certain formalities in their transfer. If the donor or their agent does not follow these formalities then equity will not step in to perfect the gift. The logic behind this maxim seems to be that the law requires delivery of the property to perfect the gift to allow the donor to realise the significance of their actions and the chance to change their minds. This is especially true of important property such as land, which is why formalities are required. Equity here follows the law and will not step in to perfect an imperfect gift.

• *Equity will not permit a trust to fail for want of a trustee*
Once a trust is constituted then it will be enforced by equity. If a trustee resigns, retires or is removed from his position equity will not allow the absence of a trustee to defeat the valid trust. The court will appoint a new trustee and at times make decisions on behalf of the trust itself.

These are a selection of the maxims of equity. It should be remembered that the maxims are there to help the court decide whether it should exercise its equitable discretion. A case may involve the consideration of one of the maxims or more than one. Sometimes the maxims can seem contradictory and would be inappropriate if applied to the facts of a case. However, they serve to guide the court in assessing the actions of the parties and whether their conscience has been affected. The maxims of equity have given rise to the doctrines, defences and remedies of equity.

2.4 The Doctrines of Equity

A doctrine is a principle of belief. In equity doctrines are principles of belief built on the maxims. However, they are more rigid than the maxims and intended to be followed in certain circumstances. They were of more significance historically than today but may still apply.

The doctrines of equity are conversion, election, satisfaction and performance.

• *Conversion:* The doctrine of conversion is based upon the maxim that *'equity regards as done that which ought to be done'.* Thus, if a settlor or testator directed trustees to convert realty into personality, or personality into realty, the doctrine of conversion would treat the property as the intended species of property even if the conversion had not taken place. The principle was

---

45 (1862) 4 De GF & J 264.
46 (1779) 1 Bro CC 497.

explained in *Fletcher v Ashburner*,[46] where Sir Thomas Sewell MR stated:[47] '...money directed to be employed in the purchase of land, and land directed to be sold and turned into money, are to be considered as that species of property into which they are to be converted...' This doctrine had more significance when the different species of property were subject to restrictions on inheritance. In England the Trusts of Land and Trustees Act 1996 has abolished the doctrine for trusts of land.

• *Election*: the doctrine of election is all to do with choice. It usually arises when a testator has provided legacies in his will to a party but has also left the legatee's, the party receiving the legacy, own property to another. For example, Gary dies and in his validly executed will he leaves his flat to his eldest son, Michael. He also leaves Michael's flat, even though Gary does not own it, to Gary's younger son, Peter. For Michael to take his father's flat he must elect, or choose, to accept the whole of the will and so give his flat to Peter. The doctrine also applies if a party has a choice of mutually exclusive remedies after successful prosecution of a claim. An example would be as explained by Lord Millett in *Foskett v McKeown*,[48] the right to choose between a proprietary interest and a lien in traced property after a successful equitable tracing process. The party cannot have both remedies; he must elect which he wishes to have.

• *Satisfaction*: the doctrine of satisfaction is based upon the maxim that *equity imputes an intention to fulfil an obligation*. It relies on the imputation that an act has been done in substitution for the performance of an obligation. Thus, if Gary dies owing Paul £10,000, but in Gary's valid will he has left Paul £10,000, equity will consider that it was Gary's intention to leave Paul the money to satisfy the debt. Paul cannot claim that the legacy is merely a gift and he is still owed the £10,000 by Gary's estate.

• *Performance*: the doctrine of performance is also based upon the maxim that '*equity imputes an intention to fulfil an obligation*'. Thus, in *Tubbs v Broadwood*,[49] Lord Brougham stated, '...a person is to be presumed to do that which he is bound to do, and if he has done anything, that he has done it in pursuit of his obligation'. The doctrine is very similar to satisfaction although satisfaction deals with a person's presumed intention to fulfil an obligation by performing a substitute act, whereas performance deals with the presumption that an act was carried out to further performance of the obligation. The doctrine was formerly most often invoked when there had been a covenant, an enforceable promise, to settle property. If the

---

47   (1779) 1 Bro CC 497, 499.
48   [2001] 1 AC 102.
49   (1831) 2 Russ & M 487.

covenanter had bought the property but the settlement had not been made, then equity would impute an intention that the act had been done to help the settlement.

Although not considered traditional doctrines of equity, the doctrines of undue influence and estoppel have become increasingly important in recent years, especially in regulating commercial transactions involving parties having unequal bargaining power. Equity has developed these doctrines for fairness and justice to protect non-commercial parties in particular.

2.5 Undue Influence

The doctrine of undue influence is concerned with consent- in particular the doctrine applies when pressure has been applied by one party in a position of power or trust over another so that the party who has seemingly agreed has not validly given consent. In this case equity will set aside the agreement between the parties. There will be a weaker and a stronger party and the weaker party must be subject to some pressure by the stronger party to perform the transaction which they cannot resist. As Lord Nicholls stated in *Royal Bank of Scotland plc v Etridge (No 2)*,[50] '... undue influence is one of the grounds of relief adopted by the courts of equity as a court of conscience. The objective is to ensure that the influence of one person over another is not abused...'[51]

The courts have been reluctant to define undue influence because the circumstances in which it will be recognised vary depending on the nature of the relationship and they are concerned not to unduly fetter their discretion.[52] Thus, rather than limit the circumstances in which it can arise, the courts have left themselves room to recognise relationships and circumstances as giving rise to undue influence.

The doctrine may also be useful when the common law doctrine of *non est factum*, 'this is not my deed', cannot be used. The central principle of the doctrine comes from the idea of free consent; the weaker party must have been subject to such influence from the stronger party that their consent to the transaction is vitiated. The remedy that may be available for undue influence is rescission, the contract is terminated such that the parties are returned to the state they would have been in if there had been no contract. Cases of undue influence also usually involve claims for misrepresentation, that the consenting party has not been given the true facts and so has not validly consented to the transaction; however, undue

---

50   [2001] UKHL 44; [2002] 2 AC 773.
51   [2002] 2 AC 773, at 749G per Lord Nicholls.
52   See, for example, Evershed M.R. in *Re Downshire's Settled Estates* [1953] 1 All ER 103 at 109, and Lord Chelmsford LC in *Tate v Williamson* 2 Ch App 60.

influence may be easier to establish as it does not rely on the misled party being able to show they would have acted differently just that they were not able to consider the matter as they should.[53]

Thus the doctrine of undue influence will be used to set aside a transaction if the court is satisfied the party did not validly consent because they were subject to some abuse of position by the other. However, such claims will not always be successful and the burden of proof is upon the party alleging that consent was not valid.

The most important development of the doctrine of undue influence is that it may be used to set aside a transaction between the weaker party and a third party, a party who did not exert the undue influence, but knew or should have known of the likelihood that the other party to a transaction had been subject to undue influence and so had not validly consented to the transaction.

Thus there are two applications of undue influence:

1   To set aside the transaction between the party who exerted the undue influence and the party who was unduly influenced; and,
2   To set aside a transaction between a lender and party who has been unduly influenced to act as surety.

The second category is obviously particularly important for banks and other lenders as they will lose their guarantee even though they have not exerted any undue influence.

Before considering this second application of the doctrine it is necessary to consider the categories of undue influence that the courts have identified. The examples considered above have involved actual undue influence, where a party has established they were subject to undue influence, but in some cases the courts have held that a relationship or set of circumstances raises the presumption of undue influence.

2.5.1 Actual or presumed undue influence

In *Barclays Bank Plc v O'Brien*,[54] the House of Lords identified two classes of undue influence.[55]

*   **Class 1:** actual (or express) undue influence: this is the traditional type of undue influence where the parties have no special relationship and the party claiming undue influence has the burden of proving it;
*   **Class 2:** presumed undue influence: this is the situation where a special relationship exists.

---

53   *UCB Corporate Services Ltd v Williams* (2003) 1 P & C.R. 12.
54   [1994] 1 AC 180
55   Relying on a categorisation of cases originally made in *Bank of Credit and Commerce International SA v Aboody* [1990] 1 QB 923.

Actual undue influence
Actual undue influence (Class 1) was first defined in **Allcard v Skinner**, [56] as 'some unfair and improper conduct, some coercion from outside, some overreaching, some form of cheating...' The plaintiff had made a gift of property to the leader of her religious order. The Court held she had placed trust and confidence in the leader. This trust had been exploited and so the gift could be avoided.

Slade L.J. broke down the elements of establishing actual undue influence, in **Bank of Credit and Commerce SA v Aboody**:[57]

a) the other party to the transaction (or someone who induced the transaction for his own benefit) had the capacity to influence the complainant;
b) the influence was exercised;
c) its exercise was undue;
d) that its exercise brought about the transaction.

Thus the burden of proof is on the party seeking to establish undue influence has vitiated his consent to the transaction.

Presumed undue influence
The nature of a transaction may be such that it gives rise to the presumption that there has been undue influence and the party relying on the transaction will have the burden of establishing undue influence was not exerted. In **Allcard v Skinner**,[58] Lindley L.J. pointed out that where a gift of a small amount is made to a person standing in a confidential relationship to the donor, some proof of the exercise of the influence of the donee must be given to procure the transaction. The mere existence of the influence is not enough. However, Lindley L.J. continued: 'But if the gift is so large as not to be reasonably accounted for on the ground of friendship, relationship, charity, or other ordinary motives on which ordinary men act, the burden is upon the donee to support the gift.'[59] Thus an 'immoderate or irrational' gift gives rise to a presumption which the defendant must rebut with evidence that it was not unreasonable or that there was no undue influence exerted upon the donor.[60]

The importance of the decision of the House of Lords in **Barclays Bank Plc v O'Brien**,[61] was in identifying presumed undue influence as arising

---

56 (1887) 36 CH D 145; [1886-1890] All ER Rep.
57 [1990] 1 QB 923, 967.
58 *Allcard v Skinner* (1887) 36 CH D 145.
59 *Allcard v Skinner* (1887) 36 Ch D 145 at 185, [1886-1890] All ER Rep at 100-101. Cited with approval by Lord Nicholls of Birkenhead in *Royal Bank of Scotland plc v Etridge (No 2)* [2001] UKHL 44 at [22]; [2002] 2 AC 773, 842 at [159].
60 *Bank of Montreal v Stuart* [1911] AC 120, 137, per Lord MacNaughten.
61 [1994] 1 AC 180

from certain relationships. Thus O'Brien Class 2 undue influence involves indentifying categories of relationships or relationships of trust and confidence which give rise to a presumption of undue influence.

If the presumption is raised then the party relying on the transaction must establish there was no undue influence. If they are a third party they must establish they had no knowledge of the undue influence. Class 2 relationships thus give rise to an evidential presumption. Class 2 is further divided into:

- Class 2A: relationships automatically raising the presumption: this includes all fiduciaries including trustee and beneficiary; solicitor and client; medical adviser and patient; parent and child (but not *vice versa*).
- Class 2B: the presumption arises if the relationship does not fall under Class 2A but the defendant proves the de facto existence of a relationship under which the defendant generally reposed trust and confidence in the wrongdoer. This may apply to spouses, cohabitants, banker and client etc. if the defendant can establish that they generally reposed trust and confidence in the other party and the transaction cannot be readily justified by the relationship.

Thus for a party claiming there has been undue influence involving a Class 2A relationship it is only necessary for them to establish they are in the required relationship and that the transaction is not readily explicable by the relationship or ordinary motives, in which case a separate presumption will arise to the effect that the transaction is the result of the abuse of the influence, unless the presumption is rebutted. The effect of the presumption is that the evidential burden then shift to the other party to show that the transaction was entered into with an independent mind and free of any undue influence.

Of course parties may be within a Class2A relationship and participate in an unusual transaction without there being undue influence.

The relationship of husband and wife has been expressly excluded from Class 2. Lord Browne-Wilkinson rejected the theory from some older authorities that a wife had a 'special equity' in **Barclays Bank Plc v O'Brien**.[62] In **Royal Bank of Scotland plc v Etridge (No 2)**,[63]Lord Scott of Foscote said of a wife acting as surety for her husband:

'Rather I would regard her support as a natural and admirable consequence of the relationship of a mutually loyal loving couple. The proposition that if a wife, who generally reposes trust and confidence in her husband, agrees to become surety to support his debts or his business enterprises a presumption of undue influence arises is one that I am unable

---

62 [1994] 1 AC 180
63 [2002] 2 AC 773, 842, at [159].

to accept. To regard the husband in such a case as a 'presumed' wrongdoer does not seem to me consistent with the relationship of trust and confidence that is a part of every healthy marriage.'

This does not mean that a wife can never be subject to her husband's undue influence, just that she will have to establish actual undue influence or that their relationship came under Class 2B. To raise the presumption of undue influence under Class 2B the party seeking to establish undue influence must prove that they were in a relationship where they generally reposed trust and confidence in the party alleged to have exerted undue influence and the transaction is one that calls for explanation. At this point the evidential burden shifts to the party relying on the transaction to establish undue influence was not exerted.

Class 2A and 2B relationships therefore give rise to a rebuttable presumption of undue influence. Therefore once a Class 2 relationship is established then the burden of proving the relationship was not one of undue influence is on the party asserting their legal right.

More recently the usefulness of the O'Brien categories has been doubted.

Concerns have been raised over Lord Browne-Wilkinson's comments, in *Barclays Bank Plc v O'Brien*,[64] that the complainant (or donee) in a Class 2B case would succeed in a claim if they merely proved that they reposed trust and confidence in the wrongdoer without the need to prove the wrongdoer had exerted actual undue influence or otherwise abused such trust and confidence. It has been suggested that the approach should be that in *Royal Bank of Scotland v Etridge (No. 2)*,[65] and that the use of the term 'presumed undue influence' particularly in relation to Class 2 B cases and the utility of the classifications overall was in doubt. In *Etridge* it had been noted that the presumption in Class 2B cases was doing no more than recognizing that evidence of relationships between the dominant and subservient parties, coupled with whatever other evidence is for the time being available, may be sufficient to justify a finding of undue influence on the balance of probabilities.

The use of Class 2B has continued, although *Etridge* confirmed that where there was no Class 2A relationship there would need to be more than just a relationship of trust and confidence, there would have to be a transaction that was 'manifestly disadvantageous' to the party seeking to set it aside that could not be reasonably explained on the grounds of friendship, relationship, charity of some other motive on which ordinary people act. Thus although Class 2A relationships may still be used to establish a presumption of undue influence, in other cases the party alleging undue influence must show they placed trust and confidence in

---

64   [1994] 1 AC 180 at 189-190.
65   [2002] 2 AC 773.

the other party in relation to the management of their affairs and the transaction in question is one that calls for an explanation. At this point the burden will shift to the other party to show there was no undue influence. As the test for rationality of the transaction is objective, even if a motive is identified for the transaction, the court may decide that the benefit conferred is out of proportion to the motive.

The correct approach now seems to be for the court to ignore Class 2B and follow Lord Scott's guidance and simply consider whether the evidence as a whole justifies the inference that, on a balance of probabilities, the impugned transactions were procured by undue influence- that is by an abuse of the trust and confidence reposed in the allegedly dominant party by the allegedly subservient party.

A relationship of trust and confidence and a disadvantageous transaction will not always give rise to a finding of undue influence. In *Portman Building Society v Dusangh*,[66] a father mortgaged his house to secure finance for his son's business. The father knew of his son's business liabilities but received no independent legal advice as the same solicitor acted for the building society, the son and the father. The son's business failed and the building society sought to enforce the mortgage against the father and his property. The father claimed he had not received any independent legal advice and thus, as in *Credit Lyonnais v Burch*, the building society should have been put on notice of possible undue influence. The Court held that the building society was entitled to enforce the mortgage. There was no actual undue influence and this was not a Class 2A situation, as that would only apply to a parent presumed to be exerting undue influence over a child. Furthermore the presumptions only succeeded if there was no evidence to the contrary. Here there was evidence that the father had known exactly what he was doing and had entered the agreement without any undue influence.

Similarly a relationship of trust and confidence between unrelated parties and a valuable transaction does not mean the court will hold the transaction was procured by undue influence.

Karsten v Markham:[67]

A solicitor had formed a relationship with a man who had come to the Citizens' Advice Centre where she volunteered. The man had been seeking advice on his indebtedness and the attempted foreclosures by banks on his properties. The solicitor, who was married to a circuit judge at the time, suggested he instruct her through her firm. He did so and over the next few years as their relationship blossomed, she lent him in excess of £1million.

---

66   [2000] 2 All ER 221.
67   [2010] 1 FCR 523.

The relationship ended and she began an action for the return of the money. The issue of undue influence arose because the solicitor had a deed of trust and indebtedness signed by the defendant against one of his properties. However, he claimed the money had been advanced to him as a gift or for services rendered, for instance looking after the solicitor's children, and that the deed had been procured by undue influence and should be set aside as manifestly against his interests. Judge Raynor QC considered the law of undue influence as it applied in this case quoting with approval Lord Nicholls of Birkenhead in *Royal Bank of Scotland v Etridge (No 2)*.[68]

'...there are two prerequisites to the evidential shift in the burden of proof from the complainant to the other party. First, that the complainant reposed trust and confidence in the other party, or the other party acquired ascendancy over the complainant. Second, that the transaction is not readily explicable by the relationship of the parties.'[69]

Judge Raynor QC thus concluded that although there was a relationship of trust and confidence, as the claimant had been the defendant's solicitor, the transaction was readily explicable as the claimant had wanted to secure the debts.[70] It was not necessary for the defendant to have received independent advice. There was no undue influence.

Judge Raynor QC may have been influenced here by finding that the defendant had consistently fabricated and lied in his evidence and was undoubtedly a "confidence trickster". The Judge ordered the securing of the amount claimed against the property.

The most interesting application of the doctrine of undue influence is its use to set aside a transaction between a party who has been subject to undue influence and another party who has NOT been the party exerting undue influence. This usually involves the suffering party standing surety for the party exerting undue influence and the transaction set aside is the guarantee.

2.5.2 Notice of undue influence

In *Barclays Bank Plc v O'Brien*,[71] Lord Browne-Wilkinson noted that the doctrine of notice 'lies at the heart of equity' and it certainly lies at the heart of undue influence as applied to parties not guilty of exerting the undue influence themselves. Undue influence is often raised as a plea in defence of an action by a bank or other creditor for possession of property pledged in guarantee by the defendant for the benefit of another's debt. Thus, most of the leading cases involve banks taking action where a party has agreed

---

68   [2001] UKHL 44; [2002] 2 AC 773.
69   [2001] UKHL 44, at [21] per Lord Nicholls of Birkenhead.
70   [2010] 1 FCR 523 at [135] & [136], per Judge Raynor QC.
71   [1994] 1 AC 180 at 195.

to a loan secured on their property, but there is a question of whether there was undue influence by another party, for example a spouse or a boss, who forced them to agree to the loan and vitiated their consent. To decide if the guarantee will be set aside the court must first consider whether there has been actual or presumed undue influence. Once actual undue influence is established or a presumption of undue influence is raised the surety must next establish the creditor had notice or should have had notice of the undue influence. This may involve the creditor being put on notice so that they should have made inquiries. Of course this has caused concern for banks and other lenders. If the bank is held to have had notice of the undue influence then the transaction is set aside as between the surety and the bank. If the bank is held not to have notice then it may enforce its rights under the transaction and the party who suffered the undue influence may only seek a personal remedy against the party who exerted the undue influence, which is usually futile.

Probably the most worrying aspect of this for banks is O'Brien Class 2 undue influence- presumed undue influence. In particular Class 2B relationships that are based on trust and confidence and may give rise to the problem and especially husband and wife. We have already noted that the modern approach is to consider Class 2B not as useful as it once was and to focus more on establishing undue influence on a balance of probabilities, but banks may still fall foul of husband and wife sureties if they do not inquire as to the knowledge of the surety of the nature and extent of their guarantee.

In *Barclays Bank Plc v O'Brien*,[72] a husband and wife took out a second mortgage on the family home. The mortgage was to secure the husband's business debts. Mrs O'Brien went to the bank to sign the mortgage documents, but there was evidence that her husband had misled her as to the amount and duration of the mortgage. The husband's business deteriorated and he defaulted on the mortgage. The bank sought possession. The House of Lords held that the husband's misleading statements based on their relationship amounted to actual undue influence over the wife. The undue influence made her agree to the mortgage and therefore she had not freely consented. The bank should have made enquiries as the transaction was to the benefit of the husband but not obviously to the benefit of the wife. As the bank made no enquiries of her it had constructive notice of the undue influence and so could not enforce possession of the house as against the wife.

Of course, this instantly raises problems for banks and other lenders regarding whether they will be able to enforce their rights or whether they will have been fixed with notice of some undue influence from another

---

72   [1994] 1 AC 180.

party. Should banks just refuse to lend to anyone who might be within a recognised category (2A) or even be wary of anyone who might be subject to undue influence (2B)?

In O'Brien some guidance was given to banks and other lenders as to the steps they should take to protect themselves (and the vulnerable party) and when they should be put on notice.

- Banks should be on notice if the transaction is on its face not to the financial advantage of the party making it.
- Banks should further enquire as to the rights in the property of the party agreeing to the loan, make sure the parties know the risks they are taking and advise all parties that they should take independent legal advice.

It should be noted that in the near contemporaneous House of Lords decision in **CIBC Mortgages Plc v Pitt**,[73] the bank succeeded in recovering the property from the wife. The husband and wife remortgaged their house to finance the husband's share speculation. It was established that the husband had exerted actual undue influence over the wife to secure her agreement to the remortgage- he had not shown her the documentation and she had not received independent advice. Thus the wife could succeed in setting the transaction aside as between her and the husband. However, the bank was not affected as it had no notice of the actual undue influence. There was nothing in the transaction to indicate that this was anything other than a loan for joint benefit of the husband and wife. This was unlike the guarantee cases as it seemed to be for the benefit of the wife as well. The emphasis was on this being a joint loan not a guarantee by one party for another. The court noted that otherwise loans to husband and wife would become almost impossible.

O'Brien was applied by the English Court of Appeal in **Credit Lyonnais v Burch**.[74] Mr P employed Miss Burch in a tour operating company of which P was the alter ego. The company needed to extend its credit and needed security for this. Miss Burch agreed to give a mortgage over her flat as security for the company's debts. The bank did not explain the amount of the company's indebtedness or the intended increase in indebtedness (this was an unlimited all moneys guarantee). However, the bank's solicitors wrote to Miss Burch advising her that this was an unlimited guarantee and that she should obtain independent legal advice. She did not. Miss Burch signed the document at the offices of the bank's solicitors with P present. The company went into liquidation and the bank claimed some £60,000 from Miss Burch. When she did not pay the bank

---

73   [1994] 1 A.C. 200; [1993] 3 W.L.R. 802, H.L.
74   [1997] 1 All ER 144.

issued proceedings in the County Court for possession of her flat. The County Court judge found there was a relationship of trust and confidence between the defendant and P and that this had given rise to a presumption of undue influence (Class 2B), which the bank had not rebutted. He dismissed the action and set aside the bank's charge over her property. The bank appealed to the English Court of Appeal on the grounds that it had discharged its duty to Miss Burch by urging her to take independent legal advice and was not responsible if she chose not to.

The Court of Appeal held that the transaction was so manifestly to Miss Burch's disadvantage, because she had risked her home for a business in which she had no personal interest and the terms of the loan were so harsh, that the presumption of undue influence on the part of P was 'irresistible'. It was not enough in the circumstances to inform her that the guarantee was unlimited without telling her how much the company already owed. Also the bank should have ensured she sought independent legal advice. The relationship of employer and employee was one that could give rise to trust and confidence and her failure to seek independent legal advice was evidence of undue influence. The transaction had properly been set aside and the appeal was dismissed.

As Millett L.J. said: 'The transaction … was one which, in the traditional phrase, shocks the conscience of the court … The transaction gives rise to grave suspicion. It cries aloud for an explanation.' Millett L.J. continued, stressing the need for banks to consider the circumstances of the transaction even if independent legal advice had been sought:

'The cases show that it is not sufficient that she should have received independent advice unless she acted on that advice. If this were not so, the same influence that produced her desire to enter into the transaction would cause her to disregard any advice not to do so …'[75]

The circumstances surrounding this transaction gave notice to the bank that there must have been undue influence on Miss Burch to enter into the guarantee, as the bank 'must have known that no competent solicitor could advise her to enter into a guarantee in the terms she did.'

The House of Lords revisited the question of when a lender should be put on notice of possible undue influence, and what steps it should take to avoid liability, in *Royal Bank of Scotland plc v Etridge (No 2).*[76] Probably the most worrying guidance for banks given in *Etridge* is that: 'In future, banks should regulate their affairs on the basis that they are put on inquiry in every case where the relationship between the surety and the debtor is non-commercial.' The justification for this is that banks can deal with the burden because it is their business to make loans and part of that business

---

75   [1997] 1 All ER 144 at 156.
76   [2002] 2 AC 773.

should be responsible lending- please note this was some years before the banking crisis over irresponsible lending. In contrast the non-commercial surety was usually not in a position of financial knowledge and the consequences for them were catastrophic. Therefore, the bank should be on inquiry whenever there was a relationship of trust and confidence or a transaction that calls for explanation. This translates to a bank should make enquiries whenever a wife gives guarantees for her husband's debts. However, in establishing undue influence it was not to be presumed that a wife's guarantee is ordinarily to her manifest disadvantage, as supporting her husband's business could often be to her advantage, and so a wife would have to prove that it was to her manifest disadvantage.

Thus, following *Etridge*:

- A bank should arrange a private meeting between the bank and the wife where she would be informed of the extent of her liability, warned of the risk and urged to take legal advice;
- If the bank has any further concerns they should advise the wife that she take separate legal advice (from her husband and the bank);
- The bank needs to take reasonable steps to satisfy itself that the wife has had brought home to her, in a meaningful way, the practical implications of the proposed transaction;
- If the bank does involve a solicitor then it has to explain that it does so to protect itself from a possible undue influence defence by the wife;
- Finally, having ensured all of this, the bank needs to ensure that the wife then knows she has a choice about whether to proceed.

To succeed in setting aside the guarantee against the bank the surety must show that the bank had knowledge of the relationship between the surety and the party which exerted undue influence and that the nature of the transaction is such as to be apparently disadvantageous to the surety. Such knowledge could be constructive because the bank had not made enquiry.[77]

Of course the problem is that to consider any transaction involving the matrimonial home a non-commercial relationship neglects the fact that it is usually the married couple's major financial investment and asset, which is usually apparent to both husband and wife.

2.6 Estoppel

Estoppel simply means 'stop'. Estoppel is a rule of evidence that in certain circumstances a person is stopped from denying the truth of something because of his own actions. Equity has developed the rule into principles

---

77 *Royal Bank of Scotland plc v Etridge (No 2)* [2002] 2 AC 773, 841 [158] per Lord Scott of Foscote.

preventing people asserting legal rights when it would be unconscionable for them to do so.

For example, if Gerald has induced a belief in Simon, or allowed Simon to continue in a mistaken belief, about Simon's legal rights, and Simon has relied on this mistaken belief to his detriment, then it would be unconscionable for Gerald to now assert the true state of affairs. Even though Gerald has legal rights and Simon has no legal rights, equity will stop Gerald from asserting his legal rights against Simon as it would be unconscionable for him to do so.

The two most important doctrines of estoppels are proprietary estoppel and promissory estoppel. Both of these doctrines are considered in the chapter on informal interests in the family home. Simply, proprietary estoppel applies to prevent the legal owner of property asserting his legal rights when it would be unconscionable to do so. Thus if Gerald is the legal owner of property and allows Simon to believe that Simon will have an interest in the property, and Simon relies on this belief and this causes him to act to his detriment, then Gerald will be 'estopped' from denying Simon's interest in the property as it would be unconscionable for him to assert his legal rights.

Promissory estoppel deals with contractual situations and can be an exception to the common law principle that part-payment is never good consideration or satisfaction for the whole of a debt.[78] Lord Denning developed promissory estoppel in **Central London Properties Trust Co. Ltd v High Trees House Ltd**,[79] creatively basing his doctrine on *obiter dicta* of Lord Cairns L.C. in **Hughes v Metropolitan Railway Co.**[80]

Denning J (as he then was) said that these cases were, '...cases of promises which were intended to be binding, which the parties making them knew would be acted on and which the parties they were made to did act on...If one party promises to forego or not to rely in the strict sense upon his strict legal rights and the other party, in reliance on that promise, acts upon it, then the promisor is estopped from asserting his full legal rights.'

Lord Denning further clarified the necessary ingredients of promissory estoppel in the decision of **Coombe v Coombe**:[81]

- there must be a pre-existing contractual relationship;
- one party within that relationship agrees to waive their contractual rights;
- they do this knowing that the other party will rely on this in deciding their future actions; and,

---

78   The rule in *Pinnel's Case* [1558-1774] All ER Rep 612.
79   [1947] 1 KB 130.
80   (1877) 2 AC 439, 448.
81   [1951] 2 KB 215.

• the other party does rely upon this promise in their future acts.

If all these four elements are satisfied then the party making the promise is stopped from going back on the promise. In **High Trees** the landlord had promised to accept a lower rent whilst war continued. When the war finished he was allowed to increase the rent back to the original contractual amount. However, he was stopped from taking action to recover the agreed reduction in rent that had accrued during wartime.

There are some differences between the application of promissory and proprietary estoppel:

• In promissory estoppel there is some debate about whether the party relying on the promise has to have acted to their detriment. For proprietary estoppel detriment is usually required.
• In *Coombe v Coombe*,[82] it was said that promissory estoppel is 'a shield not a sword'. It can be used to defend an action against a person who is trying to enforce their legal rights but not to bring an action against them. In contrast proprietary estoppel often forms the basis of an action to claim an interest and so can be a sword as well as a shield.

It should be noted that promissory estoppel has been developed in Australia and in Hong Kong to such an extent that it may be used as a cause of action and may also be applied when there is no formal contractual relationship between the parties. [83]

2.7 Summary

Criticism of equity has traditionally focused on its discretionary nature and the use of conscience in deciding if parties are liable. However, these concepts are not applied arbitrarily but are subject to the maxims and doctrines of equity. The maxims are a series of guiding principles of equity which are aids for judges in deciding whether to award remedies. A particular case may involve the use of one or more maxims, or may involve no consideration of the maxims at all. It should be remembered that the maxims are merely guiding principles not hard and fast rules. The doctrines of equity are principles of belief. The most important doctrines of equity are undue influence and promissory estoppel. Promissory estoppel involves the legal owner of property being stopped from denying the belief of another party that they have an interest in that property if it would be unconscionable for them to do so. Undue influence is a doctrine which sets aside transactions between parties because one of the parties

---

82   [1951] 2 KB 215.
83   For Australia see *Waltons Stores (Interstate) Ltd v Maher* (1988) 164 CLR 387; 62 ALJR 110; 76 ALR 513; for Hong Kong see *Luo Xing Juan Angela v Estate of Hui Shui See Willy (Deceased)* [2008] HKCU 918.

has exploited their control over the other to such an extent that the unduly influenced party has not validly consented to the transaction. The doctrine has been extended to set aside transactions where the unduly influenced party has been influenced to act as surety for the party exerting the undue influence. If the lender in such a transaction has knowledge of the undue influence or should have known of the undue influence then the transaction may be set aside between the surety and the lender.

CHAPTER 3
DEFENCES AND REMEDIES

3.1 Defences Available in Equity

Before considering the actions and remedies available in equity it is useful to consider the defences that may be available. A defendant may be able to avoid the award of an equitable remedy against him because of the principles of equity; in effect this amounts to a defence to an equitable action. Thus, a plaintiff may not be awarded a remedy because it would be inequitable to do so or because the effect of enforcing the remedy would be inequitable, for example:

- If the plaintiff has come to equity without clean hands, that is, he has acted unconscionably with regard to the matter at hand;
- If the plaintiff would not be doing equity if he enforced his remedy;[1]
- If the plaintiff has inequitably delayed in seeking his remedy: 'delay defeats equity' and the equitable doctrine of laches; but note that if there is a prescribed limitation period for action under the Limitation Act then this will take priority over the doctrine. Thus in *Leaf v. International Galleries*,[2] the plaintiff purchaser brought an action for rescission based upon misrepresentation as the painting had not been painted by the artist the gallery claimed. However, although the plaintiff had only recently discovered the misrepresentation, the English Court of Appeal held that, as the painting had been purchased some five years before, the remedy had not been applied for within a reasonable time.
- If the action is against 'equity's darling', the *bona fide* purchaser for value of a legal interest without notice of a prior equitable interest. Equity's darling has the best chance of avoiding an equitable remedy because, having no knowledge of the prior equitable interest, 'Equity cannot touch him, because, to use the old phrase, his conscience is unaffected by the trust.'[3]

All of these defences rely on the maxims of equity, discussed in the last chapter, and the concepts of conscience and knowledge. Of course, the decision to award a remedy or accept a defence is discretionary and will involve the judge considering all of the relevant actions of all parties to the litigation.

---

1   *Re Diplock's Estate* [1948] Ch 465, EWCA.
2   [1950] 2 K.B. 86.
3   F.W. Maitland, *Equity*, 2nd edition, (London, 1936).

3.2 Equitable Remedies

Equity is remedy. Equity developed as a series of remedies because the common law did not provide a remedy for a wrong,[4] for example the enforcement of the beneficiary's interest in trust property as against the legal owner, the trustee. It is a maxim of equity that *'equity will not suffer a wrong to be without a remedy'*. However, this does not mean that equity will provide a remedy whenever the common law cannot, just whenever there is a recognised cause of action which cannot be adequately remedied by the common law or when it would be unconscionable to allow legal rights to be enforced.

The strength of equity is in the flexibility, power and variety of its remedies. The continued debate over the fusion of the common law and equity has been driven in part by common lawyers' frustration that they cannot make use of the panoply of equitable remedies. The variety of equitable remedies is best shown by comparison with the remedies available at common law.

Common law remedies and aids to a remedy	Equitable remedies and aids to a remedy
Damages	Declaration
Money had and received	Compensation
Common law tracing	Account
Common law lien	Equitable tracing
	Injunction
	Specific performance
	Rescission
	Rectification
	Equitable lien
	Resulting trust
	Constructive trust

It should be noted that a benefit of an action at common law over equity is that the plaintiff at common law will receive their remedy as of right if they win their case, whereas the plaintiff in equity will know that the award of his remedy is at the discretion of the court. The exercise of this discretion has been the main criticism of the equitable jurisdiction for 400 years as it sits uncomfortably with certainty in the law. However, as Jessel MR noted equitable discretion is exercised, 'not by the caprice of the judge,

---

4   A.K.R. Kiralfy, 'Law Reform by Legal Fictions, Equity and Legislation in English Legal History' (1966) 10(1) (Jan.) *The American Journal of Legal History* 3, 12.

but according to sufficient legal reasons or on settled principles'.[5] The 'legal reasons' and 'settled principles' are precedent, and the maxims of equity take into account relevant actions and conduct of all parties.[6] Of course equity is quite capable of developing its existing remedies and creating new remedies following these equitable principles.[7]

The strength of equitable remedies is also apparent when comparing the limits set on the application of equitable processes in aid of a remedy and the limits set on their common law counterparts. For example, tracing is the process of seeking the conversion or substitution of assets for misappropriated assets. Common law tracing is generally limited by not being able to trace through a mixture of the misappropriated asset with other assets. Equitable tracing has no such limit.[8] Similarly, the lien is a security right to require the fulfilling of an obligation, usually the payment of a sum of money, before the security over an asset is released. A common law lien will only be available if the party seeking fulfilment of the obligation still retains possession of the property, for example a solicitor retains a lien over his client's papers in his possession and may hold them until his account has been paid. An equitable lien does not require possession of the property as equity acts *in personam*, against the person not against the property itself. Equity acts on the conscience of the person who has possession of the property.

The power and flexibility of equitable remedies derives from the principle that *'equity acts in personam'*. The power of actions against the conscience of the individual was recognized at the beginning of the equity jurisdiction as equity acts, 'compulsory *ad personam* and not *ad rem*, as at the common law it is...It bindeth not the right but bindeth the person to obedyence.'[9] Thus equity is not concerned with legal rights as the common law is, but with the conscience of the individual and may order that individual to act in good conscience with regard to virtually any property: 'compelling the wrongdoing litigant himself to comply with the rule prescribed by equity.'[10] Thus the jurisdiction of the equitable remedy is very wide as it is not limited to the jurisdiction of the court or state, but the conscience of the individual it is directed against. This means that an equitable remedy, if granted, may have effect outside the normal

5   *Beddow v Beddow* (1878) 9 Ch D 89 at 93.

6   *Cowcher v Cowcher* [1972] 1 WLR 425.

7   Y.BB. 20 and 21 Edw. 1 (R.S.) 374. See A.K.R. Kiralfy, 'Law Reform by Legal Fictions, Equity and Legislation in English Legal History' (1966) 10(1) (Jan.) *The American Journal of Legal History* 3, 10.

8   *Foskett v McKeown [2001] 1 AC 102*. Tracing is discussed in chapter 16.

9   Stuart E. Prall, 'The Development of Equity in Tudor England' (1964) 8(1) *The American Journal of Legal History* 1, 18. Quoting Edward Hake, *Epieikeia, A Dialogue on Equity in Three parts*, ed. D.E.C. Yale (New Haven, 1953), p.123.

10   *R. Griggs Group Ltd v Evans* [2005] Ch 153 at 164, *per* Peter Prescott QC.

geographical jurisdiction of the court. As noted in **Carron Iron Co v Maclaran**,[11] 'the court acts *in personam*, and will not suffer anyone within its reach to do what is contrary to the notions of equity, merely because the act to be done may be, in point of locality, beyond its jurisdiction.' Thus, in **Penn v Lord Baltimore**,[12] there was a dispute concerning the boundaries between Maryland and Pennsylvania in what was shortly to become the United States of America. Penn sought specific performance of an agreement concerning the boundaries. The question for the English Court of Chancery was; did it have jurisdiction to order the equitable remedy of specific performance outside the geographical jurisdiction of the English Court of Chancery? The Court held that it had jurisdiction even though it would not be able to enforce its decision *in rem*, against the land itself. This was because *in personam* remedies such as specific performance are within its jurisdiction because the conscience of the defendant was within its jurisdiction: 'The conscience of the party was bound by this agreement; and being within the jurisdiction of this court, which acts *in personam*, the court may properly decree it as an agreement, if a foundation for it.'

Of course equity has placed its own limits on the exercise of its jurisdiction and, although injunctions and other remedies are often granted for personal property outside the court's usual jurisdiction, generally injunctions will not be granted in respect of title to, or possession of, land outside the jurisdiction.

The power of equitable remedies also lies in the penalty for non-compliance with them.

Failing to comply with an order of the court for specific performance or an injunction is a contempt of court. The penalty for contempt can be a fine, sequestration of assets if the defendant is a company, or even imprisonment. Thus, in **Shalson v Russo**,[13] a fraudster was imprisoned for two years for breaching a *Mareva* injunction freezing his assets.

Thus the almost limitless jurisdiction and grave penalties that may be faced for non-compliance make equitable remedies very powerful and, consequently, very popular. Of course, the power and variety of equitable remedies is the main reason the law of equity developed as it did. Equitable remedies are also constantly evolving to meet modern commercial needs, thus relatively recently special injunctions were developed for commercial purposes: the *Anton Piller* order and the *Mareva* injunction. These are often described as the 'nuclear weapons' of the law's arsenal of remedies,[14] as they are so powerful and can have potentially

---

11   (1855) 5 HL Cas 416.
12   (1750) 1Ves Sen 444.
13   [2003] EWHC 1637 (Ch).
14   See, for example, Fiona Loughrey, Gareth Hughes, & Jose-Antonion Maurellet, 'How to curb a headstart using the springboard doctrine', (2010) *Hong Kong Lawyer*, 24 at 30.

enormous consequences for the plaintiff, defendant and third parties. Their existence is proof that equity will still develop remedies to deal with novel commercial problems using the principle of unconscionability.

It should be noted that many equitable remedies, such as the injunction, are now awarded on a statutory base, but they are still subject to equitable principles in their application and effect.

3.3 Declaration

The inclusion of the declaration as a remedy may be controversial as a declaration merely clarifies beneficial interests and obligations, but its importance cannot be overstated. At common law or in equity the court will only consider claims or suits based upon a recognised cause of action at law or in equity. A court will not answer hypothetical questions because, as Lord Bridge explained in *Ainsbury v Millington*:[15] "[I]t has always been a fundamental feature of our judicial system that the courts decide disputes between the parties before them; they do not pronounce on abstract questions of law where there is no dispute to be resolved." Thus, in *Glasgow Navigation Company v Iron Ore Company*,[16] the House of Lords dismissed an appeal as the parties had withdrawn the questions of fact from the jurisdiction of the House and simply desired to take the opinion of the House upon a question of law. As was stated at the time, 'Our law makes no provision for the issue of *decreta*.'[17] So parties cannot go to the court to ask questions in the abstract about what might happen if a party carries out an action or to clarify a state of affairs. However, limited power to declare interests and rights in the absence of a dispute was recognized in the Courts of Chancery in the 19th century (and may have been available earlier). This is the basis of declarations in equity today. A declaration is usually sought about the existence of rights and obligations under a trust or by reason of a contract. Thus a declaration takes the form of an outline of the circumstances of the parties' relationship and a question about their obligations; for example, is there a trust? Or, is a remainder interest vested immediately or contingent on, and so only vested, upon the death of the life tenant?[18]

A declaration states what the parties' rights and obligations are, and will usually be cheaper and easier to obtain than pursuing an action for a substantive remedy. In *Re Diplock*,[19] the executors of the deceased's will believed there to be valid charitable bequests in the will; they distributed

---

15   [1987] 1 WLR 379, HL.
16   [1910] AC 293.
17   Notes (1910) 26 *Law Quarterly Review* 193.
18   *Re Ebraham Sadick* [2009] HKEC 1983 (CFI).
19   [1951] AC 251.

funds as directed in the will. The next of kin of the deceased challenged the bequests. The Court held the bequests were not validly charitable. The executors were personally liable for all funds wrongly paid out. The executors would have saved themselves a considerable amount of expense and worry if they had sought a declaration regarding the validity of the bequests.

The declaration was included in remedies as once the parties' rights and obligations are clarified it may take effect as a remedy ensuring that all perform their obligations as clarified by the declaration.

3.4 Account

The duty to account is a duty of trustees. Account will be further dealt with when we consider trustees' liabilities but a short summary here would start with the duty of the trustee to account for his conduct of the trust and the assets of the trust. The trustee is under an obligation of good faith to protect the trust fund for the benefit of the beneficiary; this is often referred to as stewardship. The beneficiaries or parties acting on their behalf can call the trustee to account to ensure that he is fulfilling his obligations to the trust by clarifying the state of the trust investments and justifying any disbursements. The duty to account has been summarised as the trustee must: 'keep accounts, provide them when required, and provide to the beneficiaries all reasonable information as to the manner in which the trust estate has been dealt with.'[20]

If the trustee has made a profit from his position as trustee, which, as will be discussed later, is strictly forbidden, whether by way of taking advantage of a business opportunity, self-dealing or accepting a bribe, the trustee must account for the profit he has made from his position as trustee. That is he must pay the profit to the trust. Indeed it may be argued that the profits are not his but are considered those of the trust, and that he is merely holding them on constructive trust until he pays them into the trust account.[21]

If the call for account reveals that the trustee has negligently caused the trust fund to decrease then the beneficiaries can call for the trustee to compensate the trust fund.

---

20 *Walker v Walker* [2007] EWHC 597 (Ch), per Deputy Judge Roger Kaye Q.C.
21 *AG of Hong Kong v Reid* [1994] 1 AC 324, P.C. Although this has recently been doubted by the English Court of Appeal in *Sinclair Investments (UK) Ltd v Versailles Trade Finance Ltd (in administrative receivership)*[2011] EWCA Civ 347. See later discussion in chapter on implied trusts.

3.5 Equitable Compensation and Damages

If a trustee negligently causes the trust fund to decrease or makes an unauthorised distribution of trust funds then the beneficiaries can call for the trustee to account for the loss and then to compensate the trust. The trustee must make good the loss to the trust fund.

A trustee has powers of investment with regard to the trust fund but must not act beyond those powers otherwise he will be in breach of his duty to the trust. However, the trustee is not liable for every loss to the trust fund attributable to a breach of duty. In **Target Holdings Ltd v Redferns**,[22] the House of Lords held that a trustee should only be made to compensate for those losses which, in light of hindsight and common sense are seen to have been caused by the breach of duty. Thus, in *Target Holdings* itself, solicitors, acting on behalf of Target Holdings (a mortgage lender) paid funds, in breach of trust, to a company that they were not authorised to. There was a breach of trust. However, the transaction was completed as intended and target Holdings received security over the property it had intended. Unfortunately the valuation of this property had been inflated. When Target Holdings sold the property it received only £500,000 as against the £2 million secured against it. Target Holdings brought proceedings against the solicitors, and the English Court of Appeal finding that there had been a breach of trust, ordered the solicitors to compensate Target Holdings for the loss. The House of Lords reversed this judgment. The breach of trust had not caused the loss; the lender had received the security it required, it was not the solicitor's fault that it was not worth the required amount.

The award of damages in equity has caused some debate. Of course, equitable compensation looks very much like damages, and some academics have called it equity's damages. However, although equitable remedies were developed because common law damages were not adequate, for example the injunction and specific performance were developed where money damages would not be good enough to compensate the loss, and the development of equity was to aid where the common law could not, it seems that equity has long had jurisdiction to award damages.[23] The jurisdictional debate was ended by Lord Cairn's Act 1858,[24] which expressly provided that the Court of Chancery might award damages. Damages can be awarded in lieu or in addition to other equitable remedies as will be seen below.

---

22   [1996] 1 AC 421
23   *Pickton v Littlecote* (1579-1580) Cary 93, 21 ER 49.
24   The Chancery Amendment Act 1858 (21 & 22 Vict c27).

3.6 Injunction

The injunction is possibly the most important creation of equity after the law of trusts and injunctions have been granted by the Court of Chancery since the fourteenth century.[25]

An injunction is, 'An order directing a person or persons to refrain from doing some particular thing or to do some particular act or thing.'[26] Injunctions are particularly important in a commercial context. For example, interlocutory injunctions can be awarded before a case is heard, so an order can be obtained in disputes over copyright to prevent parties from continuing to exploit a design before trial. In a contractual situation they may be required to enforce the terms of the contract. For example, a contract of employment contains a restraint of trade clause which prohibits the employee from setting up business in competition with the employer for one year after leaving their employment and within one square mile of the employer's business premises. As long as the court considers this clause fair and reasonable in duration and affect it can be enforced, therefore if the employee leaves the employment and, within a week of leaving, sets up in competition in premises next door to his former employer's premises, the employer could seek an injunction forcing the ex-employee to stop trading. If they did not comply with this they would be in contempt of court and could then be fined or imprisoned.

Lord Brandon stated, in *South Carolina Insurance Co v Assurantie Maatschappij de Zeven Provincien NV*,[27] that an injunction might be granted in two basic situations:

- 'Situation (1) is when one party to an action can show that the other party has either invaded, or threatens to invade, a legal or equitable right of the former for the enforcement of which the latter is amenable to the jurisdiction of the court
- Situation (2) is where one party to an action has behaved, or threatens to behave, in a manner which is unconscionable.'

Therefore, injunctions are available where the plaintiff would suffer damage if the complained action is not carried out, is carried out or is repeated. However, it has already been explained that injunctions are very flexible and Lord Goff, in the same case was, 'reluctant to accept that the

---

25   A.K.R. Kiralfy, 'Law Reform by Legal Fictions, Equity and Legislation in English Legal History' (1966) 10(1) (Jan.) *The American Journal of Legal History* 3, 12.

26   Philip H. Pettit, *Equity and the Law of Trusts*, 11th edition (Oxford: Oxford University Press, 2009) at 567.

27   [1986] 3 All ER 487.

power to grant injunctions is restricted to certain exclusive categories. That power is unfettered by statute; and it is impossible to foresee every circumstance in which it may be thought right to make the remedy available.' Thus, injunction may be used in a wide variety of circumstances and for a multitude of purposes, as long as there is a recognised cause of action.[28]

Although the injunction was originally a creature of equity, it is now awarded on a statutory basis subject to equitable principles. Section 37(1) of the Senior Courts Act 1981 provides that the High Court may grant an injunction when it is 'just and convenient to do so'.[29] As granting an injunction interferes with another's rights, injunctions are only awarded if damages or another remedy would not be adequate (this also applies to orders for specific performance). Damages may be awarded instead of an injunction. Damages may be appropriate if the interference is *de minimis*, for example, if an ex-employee is contractually bound not to set up in competition with his former employer for a year after leaving the employment, but has set up in competition 350 days after leaving the employment, and the application for an injunction to prohibit the new business was then made after the expiry of the year, it would be unjust to then prohibit the new business. A small amount of damages would probably be more appropriate.

The principle that a court may award damages instead of an injunction has led to the court's determining question once it has decided that a remedy should be awarded. The court should ask itself whether is it more just to grant an injunction than to award damages? If it is not then damages should be awarded. This test also applies when the court has to decide whether to award specific performance or damages.

Injunctions are powerful because they can be phrased in very wide terms. For example it is now possible to grant an injunction:

- Against anyone who is not a party to the action but who knowingly acts in breach of the injunction resulting in impedance to or interference with the administration of justice;[30]
- *Contra mundum*, against the world;[31]
- Against unnamed defendants.[32]

Injunctions are categorised as follows:

- They can be prohibitory or mandatory: that is they can order a party to stop doing something (prohibit) or to do something (mandate);

---

28 See Sir George Baker in *Paton v Trustees of British Pregnancy Advisory Service* [1979] QB 276 at 281.
29 Renamed from he Supreme Court Act 1981.
30 *AG v Times Newspapers* [1992] 1 AC 191.
31 *Venables v News Group Newspapers Ltd* [2001] 1 All ER 908.
32 *Bloomsbury Publishing Group plc v News Group Newspapers Ltd* [2003] 1 WLR 1633.

- They can be interlocutory (Interim) or perpetual (final or permanent): that is they can be awarded before the final hearing of the dispute between the parties to prevent interim damage or they can be awarded as a final remedy for the wrong proved;
- They can be issued *quia timet:* literally 'because it is feared'. This is an order sought because the plaintiff fears that the defendant is about to do something that will harm the plaintiff.

A very important factor in the award of an injunction is that they can awarded *ex parte,* that is without notice to, or the presence of, the party against whom they are to be phrased. This may be very important if it is thought notice of the order would alert the other party and cause them to do something that would prevent the plaintiff obtaining justice at the final hearing. For example, freezing orders (formerly *Mareva* orders), an order freezing the assets of a defendant, are often sought when it is thought the defendant would move his assets out of the jurisdiction if he had notice of the claim. If notice of the order were given to the defendant he might move his assets before the hearing and so defeat the order. Of course, the court has to be careful about awarding an *ex parte* injunction as, 'no order should be made to the prejudice of a party unless he has the opportunity of being heard in defence'.[33] The principle of awarding a powerful remedy such as injunction against a party without giving them the right to defend themselves should only be used in very limited circumstances as it goes against the principle of natural justice that the other side must be heard - *audi alterem partem.*[34] Thus *ex parte* injunctions are usually only awarded as an interlocutory measure and are subject to challenge by the defendant at any time.

An applicant for any injunction is always under a duty to disclose all relevant information to the court, especially if the application is ex parte, this is based upon the maxim *he who comes to equity must come with clean hands.* If the applicant does not disclose all relevant information then he may find the application dismissed on the discovery of concealed relevant information, or the injunction removed, or liability in costs. In fact the whole basis of the equitable relief of the injunction is based upon good faith and the maxim *he who comes to equity must come with clean hands.*

As injunctions are so powerful, equity has developed rules to guide the court in the circumstances of their grant. There are different rules applicable to the award of interim as to perpetual injunctions.

---

33   *Thomas A. Edison Ltd v Bullock* (1912) 15 CLR 681.
34   See *Re First Express Ltd* [1991] BCC 782, 785 *per* Hoffmann LJ (as he then was).

3.6.1 Interim and interlocutory injunctions

Interim injunctions and interlocutory injunctions are varieties of the same type of injunction as they are both intended to be temporary orders of the court until the matter is next or finally dealt with. In England the term interlocutory injunction has been replaced by interim injunction in the civil procedure reforms. Interim injunctions are awarded after an application by the plaintiff for an urgent order to prevent damage or harm that might occur to the plaintiff because of some act of the defendant. The main difference between interim injunctions and interlocutory injunctions is that the interim injunction is designed to finish on a certain date or after a certain event, whereas the interlocutory injunction lasts until the next hearing of the case between the parties to the injunction. These injunctions are applied for at the beginning or in the course of proceedings and are intended to take immediate effect because the plaintiff cannot wait for the full hearing. Lord Wilberforce, in *Hoffman-La Roche & Co v Secretary for State for Trade and Industry*,[35] stated that they are, 'to prevent a litigant, who must necessarily suffer the law's delay, from losing by that delay the fruit of his litigation'. Of course, as stated above, the award of such a powerful remedy before the court has heard all the evidence is not without potential problems. As Lord Diplock famously said in the leading case of *American Cyanamid Co v Ethicon Ltd*:[36]

'...the decision has to be taken at a time when *ex hypothesi* the existence of the right or the violation of it, or both, is uncertain and will remain uncertain until final judgment is given in the action ... The object of the interlocutory injunction is to protect the plaintiff against injury by violation of his right for which he could not be adequately compensated in damages recoverable in the action if the uncertainty were resolved in his favour at the trial.'

The case of *American Cyanamid Co v Ethicon Ltd*,[37] gave guidelines for the court to follow when deciding whether to award an interim injunction. The plaintiffs owned a patent for artificial catgut sutures. The defendants, Ethicon, were about to launch their own artificial catgut suture in Britain. The plaintiff claimed that this infringed their patent. The House of Lords granted an interim injunction indicating the test that should be applied was: unless there is no real prospect of succeeding, the court should consider whether the balance of convenience lies in favour of granting or refusing the injunction.

Therefore, the court must consider two factors when deciding whether to grant an interim injunction:

---

35   [1975] AC 295 at 355.
36   [1975] AC 396.
37   [1975] AC 396.

1   There must be a serious issue to be tried; the plaintiff must have a prima facie case.
2   If there is a case to be answered then the court moves on to consider the question, which way does the balance of convenience fall?

Thus the court must consider whether there is a triable issue and then whether the injunction should be awarded because the award of damages at final hearing to the plaintiff would not be good enough. They must balance the potential damage to the plaintiff from refusing an injunction against the damage caused to the defendant by the award of the injunction. The court must also consider whether an undertaking from the plaintiff to pay damages if he does not win at final hearing could adequately compensate any damage to the defendant caused by the injunction.

Thus the principles governing the award of an interim injunction are:

1   Is there a triable issue?
2   Are damages for interim harm to the plaintiff good enough?
3   If not, could the defendant be compensated by damages if the interim injunction is granted?
4   Can the plaintiff make an undertaking as to damages, and can he meet it?
5   If the decision is still unclear the court must decide what is the balance of convenience?
6   If this is evenly balanced then the court will try to preserve the status quo.
7   The court must consider which party will lose most because of the grant (or otherwise) of the interim injunction, if that party succeeds at the final trial?
8   Are there any special factors that need to be taken into consideration?

Although the court considers whether the plaintiff has a triable case there has been some debate over how far the court should look into the strength of the parties' cases. It has been suggested that the court should consider who has the stronger case as a final part of the balancing exercise. However, the question of who has the stronger case is really best left to the final hearing because the interim hearing will not be able to consider all of the evidence.

As the injunction is an equitable remedy the usual principles of equity will apply to its grant. The most common factors militating against the grant of an interim injunction are:

•   Delay or acquiescence on the part of the plaintiff: for example the plaintiff has known about the defendant's complained act for some time and has done nothing about it, or even aided in its execution;
•   The plaintiff lacks 'clean hands': some act of the plaintiff relevant to the complained action would make it unconscionable to award an injunction;

- The effect of the injunction on third parties: the award of the injunction would in some way infringe or damage the rights of third parties.

Examples of special interim injunctions are the relatively new search orders and freezing orders.

3.6.2 Search orders or *Anton Piller* orders

The *Anton Piller* order is a special type of interim injunction named after the case of **Anton Piller KG v Manufacturing Processes Ltd.**[38] In England this is now referred to as a 'search order'. These orders are usually awarded *ex parte*, as giving notice to the defendant would 'tip them off' and allow them to hide the material being sought. An *Anton Piller* order allows the plaintiff's representatives to search the defendant's premises and copy or retain material relevant to the issue between the parties found there for safekeeping. It can include electronic records. The order may also require the defendant to provide information or an article relevant to the issue between the parties. Because of the infringement of the rights of the defendant there must be a strong prima facie case that the plaintiff will suffer actual or potential serious damage if the material is not provided or is destroyed. There must also be evidence that the defendant has these incriminating documents or things and that there is a real possibility they may be destroyed. Judges are very wary of being asked for these orders as a 'fishing trip' and will require cogent evidence of the need for the order. The applicant is required to give an undertaking in damages. The order works because it orders the defendant to allow the other party to search for the material. Failing to comply with the order will be contempt of court. These orders are most commonly used in disputes over intellectual property rights.

3.6.3 Freezing orders or *Mareva* injunctions

The *Mareva* injunction, named after the case of **Mareva Compania Naviera SA v International Bulkcarriers SA,**[39] is now referred to in England as a 'freezing' injunction or order because it freezes the designated assets of a litigant. The purpose of the order is to restrain the defendant from disposing of, or removing, his assets from the jurisdiction where there is a risk that any judgment will go unsatisfied by reason of that disposal or removal. Thus the order freezes the assets of the defendant if there is likelihood he will get rid of them and frustrate the plaintiff in successfully enforcing judgment. As with Anton Pillar orders, Mareva Injunctions are usually awarded *ex parte* because of the likelihood that notice of the

---

38   [1974] CH 55.
39   [1975] 2 Lloyds Rep 509.

application for the order would allow the defendant to move his assets. The injunction also covers the bank or other party holding the assets as long as they have notice of the order. The ease with which assets may be moved around the world using modern financial instruments and institutions has necessitated the development of the 'Worldwide' Mareva injunction to freeze assets wherever they are.[40] Because of the draconian nature of the *Mareva* injunction the court has laid down guidelines as to when they should be used. The applicant for a *Mareva* injunction must:[41]

- Make full and frank disclosure of all material matters: applicants must not hide anything from the judge that is relevant to the grant of the injunction;
- Give particulars of the case against the defendant: again this does not mean the application is prejudging the outcome of the case but the applicant must provide a good arguable case;
- Give grounds for believing the assets which may be subject to the final order are in the jurisdiction: the applicant must, for example, give details of bank accounts or property title to form the basis of the order: of course, the worldwide *Mareva* injunction may not require such precision;
- Give grounds for believing there is a risk of assets being removed from the jurisdiction before judgment is satisfied: thus an application cannot be based on a 'hunch'. There must be evidence that the defendant will move assets before final judgment, this can be in the form of statements made by the defendant to the applicant;
- Give an undertaking in damages.

The undertaking in damages for any interim injunction is a promise to the court to pay for the damage suffered by the defendant if the injunction is granted but the applicant later loses the final case. It is usual for a court to require such an undertaking from the applicant although in some circumstances the undertaking can be dispensed with. For example, if the applicant does not have the funds to make the undertaking but justice would still demand the injunction was granted. The undertaking is to the court and so cannot be used as a cause of action by the defendant. The court must enforce it.

3.6.4 Perpetual and final injunctions

The perpetual injunction is sometimes referred to as the final or permanent injunction. This does not mean that the injunction will go on indefinitely,

---

40   *BCCI SA (No 9)* [1994] 3 All ER 764.
41   *Third Chandris Shipping Corpn v Unimarine SA* [1979] 2 All ER 972, *per* Lord Denning.

although this may be ordered,[42] just that it is intended to end the dispute between the parties and is granted at the final hearing. The injunction is a discretionary remedy granted when the legal remedy available for a wrong is inadequate. The question for the court then, when deciding whether to award a final injunction is: 'whether this is a case in which the remedy at law is so inadequate that the court ought to interfere, having regard to the legal remedy, the rights of the parties, and the consequence of the court's interference.'[43] Again, the court must consider the usual equitable principles when deciding whether to exercise its discretion. The court must also consider whether it is in the public interest to award the injunction. Thus, in the case of **Miller v Jackson**,[44] Lord Denning refused to award an injunction to stop cricket being played in a cricket ground, even though cricket balls were causing damage to a neighbouring house. Lord Denning said that there was a greater public interest in, 'protecting the environment by preserving our playing fields in the face of mounting development and by enabling our youth to enjoy all the benefits of outdoor games.'[45] Thus an injunction should not be granted as, 'I am of the opinion that the public interest should prevail over the private interest.'[46] However, the public interest is not always a sufficient reason to deny an injunction.[47]

The *quia timet* injunction is unusual because no harm or infringement has yet been suffered by the applicant. It is based on an immediate threatened action of the defendant. However, there must be a real likelihood that the action will be carried out and the harm or infringement suffered as, 'a mere vague apprehension is not sufficient.'[48]

As stated above, s.37(1) of the Senior Courts Act 1981 provides that the court can grant an injunction when it is 'just and convenient to do so' and that damages may be awarded instead of the injunction. Therefore the question a court must ask itself today when deciding whether to award a final injunction should be, is it more just to grant an injunction than to award damages?

The courts discretion to award damages instead of the injunction has been considered in numerous cases. In **Shelfer v City of London Electric Lighting Co.**,[49] A.L. Smith L.J. laid down what he referred to as 'a good

42 *Venables v News Group Newspapers Ltd [2001] 1 All ER 908.*

43 *AG v Sheffield Gas Consumers Co* (1853) 3 De G M & G 304 at 321, per Turner L.J.

44 [1977] QB 966.

45 [1977] QB 966 at 981.

46 [1977] QB 966 at 982.

47 *Kennaway v Thomson* [1981] QB 88.

48 *Graigola Merthyr C Ltd v Swansea Corp.* [1929] AC 344 at 353, *per* Lord Buckmaster.

49 [1895] 1 CH 287 at 322. Approved by the English Court of Appeal in *Jaggard v Sawyer* [1995] 1 WLR 269, per Millett L.J

working rule' on when damages should be awarded instead of an injunction:

- When the injury to the applicant is small;
- When the injury is one that is capable of being estimated in money;
- When the injury is one which can be adequately compensated by a small money payment, and;
- When the case is one in which it would be oppressive to the defendant to grant an injunction against him.

However, it was noted, in *Regan v Paul Properties*,[50] that, although the court should consider awarding damages instead of the injunction, the burden of proof is not on the applicant to show why an injunction should be awarded rather than damages.

The strength of the injunction is then in its flexibility and the development of new commercial uses for the injunction. There may be development of further varieties of injunction because, as Lord Nicholls noted in *Mercedes Benz v Leiduck*:[51]

'As circumstances in the world change, so must the situations in which the courts must properly exercise their jurisdiction to grant injunctions. The exercise of the jurisdiction must be principled, but the criterion is injustice. Injustice is to be viewed and decided in the light of today's conditions and standards, not those of yester-year.'

A recent development in the UK has been the so-called 'super' injunction. This is an injunction which has been awarded to celebrities and sports stars wishing to prevent public exposure of their private lives. It has been described as a 'super' injunction because the order is phrased so that the existence of the order itself cannot be reported.

3.7 Specific Performance

Specific performance is an old remedy of equity encountered as a far back as the fifteenth century.[52] It is an order by the court directing a party to a contract to perform his obligations under the contract according to its terms. The order may seem to be an injunction and its effect and application are very similar; however, specific performance can only be

---

50   [2006] 3 WLR 1131.
51   [1996] AC 284 at 308.
52   Lady Audley's case 1 Pomeroy Eq. Juris. 37 n2. See William Lindsay Carne, 'A Sketch of the History of the High Court of Chancery from its Origin to the Chancellorship of Wolsey' (1927) 13(7) (Nov.) *The Virginia Law Review* 391, 399. A.K.R. Kiralfy, 'Law Reform by Legal Fictions, Equity and Legislation in English Legal History' (1966) 10(1) (Jan.) *The American Journal of Legal History* 3, 12

awarded where there is an executory agreement. Thus, there must be a contract to perform some future promise. It is an order of the court to carry out what has been promised for the bargain. If it is not followed the party may be in contempt of court and fined or imprisoned. Specific performance, as with an injunction, is only granted when it is 'just and equitable' to do so. The subject matter of the contract must usually be so special or 'unique' that damages would not be an adequate remedy for the bargain not being fulfilled.[53] For example the remedy is often sought when the vendor to a contract for the sale and purchase of land refuses to convey the land. The breach of contract could be remedied with the payment of damages but, because land is considered unique,[54] the injured party can claim damages would not be a good enough remedy. Only the conveyance of the land would be a fair and just remedy and put him in the position he would be in if the contract were completed.

Specific performance will generally not be granted for personal property unless the subject matter of the contract is rare or unique, such as a rare painting or antique, or something made to order and not readily available.[55] Specific performance may also be ordered if the subject matter of the contract is not readily available, for example, shares in a private company as they are not available on the open market. As shares in a public company can be obtained relatively easily on the open market specific performance will not be ordered if they are the subject matter of the bargain.

Specific performance may be granted to prevent the court having to deal with multiple actions if there is a situation that involves a continuing obligation that may be breached in the future.

Beswick v Beswick[56]

The plaintiff's late husband, Peter, had entered into an agreement with his nephew that he would transfer his business to the nephew in consideration of the nephew employing Peter as a consultant for the rest of his life, and thereafter paying an annuity of £5 per week to Peter's widow for her lifetime. After Peter's death the nephew made only a single payment to the widow. The widow brought a claim against the nephew both personally and in her capacity as administratrix of the estate. She sued for specific performance although this was not the type of contract for which specific performance was usually granted. The problem was she had no

---

53 *Marks v Lilley* [1959] 1 WLR 749.
54 Land was of such importance in the development of the common law and equity that it is always considered 'unique' and so a contract for the sale of land will usually be capable of specific performance.
55 *Phillips v Lamdin* [1949] 1 All ER 770.
56 [1968] AC 58, HL.
57 [1968] AC 58 at 102.

direct cause of action because, although she had suffered loss, she was not a party to the contract. As administratrix she could sue for only nominal damages because the estate had suffered no loss. The defendant argued that as she had no right of action and the estate had suffered no loss, how could it be argued that nominal damages were inadequate?

Judgment: the House of Lords held that the very fact that there was no available legal remedy except nominal damages meant that justice demanded an equitable remedy. Lord Upjohn said, 'the court ought to grant a specific performance order all the more because damages are nominal'. [57] Lord Pearce noted the fact that the nephew had received the whole benefit of the bargain but refused to fulfil his obligations was, 'wholly repugnant to justice and commonsense'.[58] The Lords ordered specific performance of the nephew's obligations.

As with an application for an injunction, the court can award damages instead of awarding specific performance. The parties may also contract out of this discretion to award specific performance. Thus, a liquidated damages clause, an agreement to pay damages in certain circumstances actually inserted into the contract by the parties, may effectively stop the court issuing an order. This will depend on the actions of the parties and whether the court considers the clause truly does cover the circumstances.

As with all equitable remedies the award of specific performance is at the discretion of the court. Thus in *Re Scott v Alvarez's Contract*,[59] the application by the vendor of land for specific performance of the purchaser's obligation to buy was refused by the English Court of Appeal because of the unconscionable behaviour of the vendor. This was much to the consternation of Lopes L.J. a common law judge, who found it difficult to accept that the vendor could prove his case and yet still not be awarded the remedy applied for. Rigby L.J. explained why the Court did not award the equitable remedy:

'From the very first, when specific performance was introduced, it has been treated as a question of discretion whether it is better to interfere and give a remedy which the common law knows nothing at all about, or to leave the parties to their rights in a Court of Law.'

Some circumstances in which the court may refuse an application are:

- When the contract involves personal property (personalty), unless it is unique or not readily available;
- When the conduct of the applicant is contrary to equitable principles;
- When the applicant has delayed in his application (the doctrine of laches);
- When the contract is for personal work or services;[60]

---

58   [1968] AC 58 at 89.
59   [1895] 2 Ch 603, EWCA.
60   *Rigby v Connol* (1880) 14 Ch. D. 482.

- When there is no valid contract or there is a contract that is illegal or contrary to public policy;[61]
- When the order would require constant supervision by the court. This includes cases where the court is asked for an order compelling the defendant to carry on business indefinitely;[62]
- When the order would unfairly benefit the claimant or unfairly prejudice the defendant.[63]

The whole basis of the remedy is that damages would not be an adequate alternative. If the subject matter of the contract is personalty then it can usually be replaced and so damages, covering the cost of substitute property would be adequate.

The grant of specific performance is also subject to a restriction that it will not be granted to enforce a personal contract, such as a contract of employment. For example, a contract is made between a shopping centre and a movie star for the movie star to appear at the shopping centre for its opening. The movie star refuses to attend. The shopping centre can sue for breach of contract and receive damages. The shopping centre cannot sue for specific performance of the contract. It is considered contrary to public policy to enforce personal relations between people. As Jessel M.R. noted in *Rigby v Connol*:[64]

'...the courts, as such, have never dreamed of enforcing agreements strictly personal in nature whether they are agreements of hiring or service, being the common relation of master and servant, or whether they are agreements for the purpose of pleasure, or for the purpose of scientific pursuits or for the purpose of charity and philanthropy.'

If there is no contract then obviously no one can be made to perform the supposed obligations. Thus, if the purported contract is for an illegal purpose, it will not be enforced.

An order will not be granted if enforcement would require constant supervision. Thus, an order will not be granted forcing a party to carry on a business.

Co-Operative Insurance Society Ltd v Argyll Stores (Holdings) Ltd[65]

The defendant, Argyll Stores, was granted the lease of large supermarket premises in the plaintiff's shopping centre. The premises were the 'anchor unit', the main premises designed to attract shoppers. The presence of the defendant affected trade for the rest of the shops in the centre. As any

---

61 *Waring and Gillow Ltd v Thompson* (1912) 29 TLR 154, EWCA.
62 *Co-operative Insurance Society Ltd v Argyll Stores (Holdings) Ltd* [1998] AC 1, HL.
63 *Co-operative Insurance Society Ltd v Argyll Stores (Holdings) Ltd* [1998] AC 1, HL.
64 (1880) 14 Ch. D. 482 at 487.
65 [1998] AC 1, HL.

closure of the defendant's business would be disastrous to the other shops and the plaintiff's centre, a 'keep open' covenant was inserted into the lease. The clause provided that the defendant's business would be kept open for retail trade during the usual hours of business in the locality. However, the defendant suffered severe financial loss in keeping the business open and decided to close the business down. This was therefore a breach of the lease and the plaintiff applied for an order for specific performance of the defendant's contractual obligations arguing that the damage incurred could not be compensated in damages.

Judgment: at first instance the court awarded damages only. On appeal by the plaintiff the English Court of Appeal,[66] by a majority decision, awarded specific performance. The Court justified its award because it would be inequitable to allow the defendant to deliberately breach its contractual obligations. Leggatt L.J. said that the defendant should not profit from its 'gross commercial cynicism'.[67] Roch L.J. described the circumstances of the case as the 'unedifying spectacle of a large commercial company seeking to rely on its own wanton and unreasonable conduct'. [68]

The defendant appealed to the House of Lords, which awarded damages only. Lord Hoffman gave the leading judgment and gave some guidance on this difficult area. His Lordship stated that orders requiring a party to continue running a business would be denied. It would be impracticable to write such an order, as it would have to be exact in its specification of the amount of the premises to be kept open, the amount of stock kept in the premises, and so on. The order needed to be exact because the defendant would have to know what would be a breach of the order, as this would carry potentially harsh sanctions (fine, sequestration or even imprisonment). There were problems for any court to enforce such an order as it was, in effect, indefinite, and, if it were made, it would require constant supervision. It was also contrary to public policy to order a business to stay open when it was losing money. The House of Lords also held that specific performance would unfairly benefit the plaintiff as it secured more expenditure in money terms by the defendant than was due to the plaintiff. It was therefore unjust.

The defendant may raise the usual equitable defences of laches and inequitable conduct by the plaintiff as grounds for refusal of the remedy. Other defences available to an application are that the contract was obtained by misrepresentation or mistake, or that specific performance would impact unfairly on a third party. The party applying for specific performance must be ready to perform their side of the bargain when they make the application.

---

66 [1996] Ch 286.
67 [1996] Ch 286 at 294.
68 [1996] Ch 286 at 296.

3.8 Rescission

Rescission is the revocation or termination of a contract. It allows a party to a contract to consider the contract as no longer existing in certain circumstances, i.e. that the party is no longer bound by its promise to carry out its side of the bargain. Rescission is available in a number of circumstances when there is some inherent invalidity in the contract. This usually involves a lack of consent by one of the parties or a serious breach of a condition. Thus, it may be available when there has been misrepresentation by one side to a bargain,[69] or mistake as to the nature of the bargain. In a case of mistake, it is available if it would be unconscionable to allow one party to take advantage of the mistake by insisting on the completion of the contract.[70] In the previous chapter we considered rescission being awarded when a party to a contract has not validly consented to it because they have had undue influence exerted upon them.

If a contract is illegal then it cannot be enforced but an order of rescission can be granted to clarify that the parties have no obligations. In all but the case of an illegal contract, the contract is valid until the innocent party rescinds it. Thus the court grants the order to confirm that the parties are no longer bound by their obligations. Rescission is very important in commercial contracts, as sometimes businesses do not want damages. They may just want to be released from their side of the bargain.

The award of rescission is subject to the usual equitable principles. The right to rescission may be lost in the following circumstances:

* If *restitutio in integrum* is not possible: if the parties cannot be restored to their pre-contract positions because of the use of some of the subject matter, which cannot be restored, rescission will not be awarded;
* If the innocent party affirms the contract: for example, if the party who has relied on the misrepresentation has found out about it and then decided to continue with the contract he cannot later rescind the contract;
* If there is excessive delay: the principle in **Leaf v International Galleries**[71] and the maxim *delay defeats equity* apply. Therefore, rescission will only be permitted if it is claimed in reasonable time;
* If a third party's rights would be adversely affected: for example, if an innocent third party who has given value for property involved in the disputed contract would have their property rights affected then rescission will not be granted;
* If the court feels damages under the Misrepresentation Act 1967 would be more appropriate.

---

69   *Derry v Peek* (1889) 14 App Cas 337.
70   *Solle v Butcher* [1950] 1 KB 671.
71   [1950] 2 KB 86.

3.9 Rectification

A court can use the equitable remedy of rectification to rewrite a contract to fulfil the original intentions of the parties. This is obviously a drastic remedy as the usual policy is for courts not to interfere and to allow parties to be bound by their written contracts.[72] Thus it is a remedy that the courts use sparingly. Rectification can occur only when the party seeking rectification can prove:[73]

- A complete and certain agreement was reached; and,
- This remained unchanged until the time the written contract was executed; and,
- This is not reflected in the written contract.

The usual equitable principles apply.

The court may even change a trust instrument to reflect the intentions of the settlor if there is convincing proof of the intentions of the relevant parties;[74] for example, to add beneficiaries to a discretionary trust.[75]

3.10 Lien

The lien is a security right to require the fulfilling of an obligation, usually the payment of a sum of money, before the security over an asset is released.[76] A common law lien will only be available if the party seeking fulfilment of the obligation still retains possession of the property.[77] For example, Michael takes his car to the garage for repair. He agrees the repair price. At common law, if the garage has not released the car to Michael, the garage can retain possession of the car until Michael pays the agreed repair price. Law students would do well to remember that a lien could arise in favour of a solicitor over his client's documents or other personal property in the possession of the solicitor if the solicitor's fees have not been paid.

An equitable lien, or equitable charge, does not require possession of the property. The equitable lien does not give the plaintiff a share in the property but it gives him an interest secured by the property to fulfil the obligation. Thus an equitable lien gives the plaintiff the right to have the property sold to satisfy his debt (or part of it). It takes priority in the event of the defendant's insolvency.[78] It is therefore a very powerful aid to

---

72   *L'Estrange v Graucob* [1934] 2 KB 394.
73   *Craddock Bros. v Hunt* [1923] 2 Ch 136.
74   *Joscelyne v Nissen* [1970] 2 Q.B. 86, EWCA.
75   *Lawie v Lawie* [2012] EWHC 2940 (Ch).
76   *Hall v Richards* (1961) 108 CLR 84.
77   *Re Vital Learning Aids Pty Ltd* [1979] 2 NSWLR 442.
78   *Re Hallett's Estate* (1880) LR 13 Ch D 696, EWCA.

achieving the desired remedy.

As discussed later in the chapter on tracing, the lien and the proprietary nature of a beneficiary's interest under a trust were compared in *Foskett v McKeown*.[79] Lord Millett explained that such interests could arise concurrently but that the plaintiff would have to elect which to take; he could not have a lien over the property and assert a beneficial proprietary interest at the same time. If the interest was a lien then the plaintiff could call for the property to be sold to satisfy the obligation, if the interest were proprietary then the plaintiff was asserting that the property was his and could call for the transfer of the property to him from the legal owner. The importance of choosing between these interests will often be due to the value of the asset, as was confirmed in *Foskett*, the lien only entitles the plaintiff to the proceeds of sale of the property in satisfaction of the debt, any surplus above this would not be the plaintiff's. If the plaintiff asserted a proprietary interest in the property then any subsequent increase in value of the asset would also be the plaintiff's. An equitable lien would thus be suitable for a plaintiff claiming against a rogue who has misappropriated assets which have decreased in value, the plaintiff could sell the assets and recover some of the debt and maintain a personal claim against the rogue for the balance. Although there has been some confusion over whether equitable liens can only be enforced against real property, the comments of Lord Millet, in *Foskett v McKeown*,[80] seem conclusive that an equitable lien can exist in any property, including a mixture of misappropriated assets with those of the misappropriating rogue or innocent volunteers.

3.11 Resulting and Constructive Trusts

Resulting and constructive trusts are not expressly created by the parties involved but are implied by the courts. They are inferred from the circumstances of the case. They will be covered in some detail in chapters 10 and 11. There is some dispute (however,) over whether they are remedies. Certainly both resulting and constructive trusts undoubtedly act as remedies, either by returning property to beneficial owners or preventing legal owners acting unconscionably, however, the courts in England have restricted their use, particularly the use of the constructive trust, to recognised circumstances, and have been adamant that they are not available, as they may be in other jurisdictions, notably Australia, to be used by the courts as remedies whenever it would seem just to do so. Thus constructive trusts are referred to as 'institutional' in England and 'remedial' in Australia.

---

79   [2001] 1 AC 102.
80   [2001] 1 AC 102 at 131.

3.12 Summary

Equity has a vast array of remedies available to right wrongs and prevent parties acting unconscionably. These remedies are not available as of right but are available at the discretion of the court in consideration of the usual equitable principles espoused in the maxims of equity. Equitable remedies are powerful and flexible because of the penalties for non-compliance, these are the penalties for contempt of court, and because equity acts in, it acts against the conscience of the individual.

PART II
THE LAW OF TRUSTS

CHAPTER 4
WHAT ARE TRUSTS?

Maitland, a scholar not given to the use of hyperbole, described the trust as 'the greatest and most distinctive achievement performed by Englishmen in the field of jurisprudence'.[1] Furthermore it has been claimed that, 'The trust is as much of an institution in English culture as is soccer and tea parties.'[2] Perhaps the latter is not such a good thing considering how well the English fare at soccer and the adverse affects of tea parties on the British Empire. However, it is true that the English trust has spread around the world, as 'Wherever the British went, the trust went with them.'[3]

Maitland's statement may seem a huge overstatement of the importance of the common law trust. A colleague of the author's who was brought up in the common law but practised in the civil law of Germany and Italy once told the author, "there is nothing special about the trust". He was explaining that the financial and commercial benefits of the trust can be replicated using other financial arrangements and the law of contract. However, the author would counter that there is something very special about the trust and that is the fiduciary nature of trusteeship, from which all other principles of the law of trusts flow. The civil law had and has its own versions of the trust but they are pale comparisons. The proof of the importance of common law trusts is the adoption of principles of the law of trusts for commercial and financial transactions by international commercial and financial corporations. The world of commerce requires certainty but appreciates the flexibility of trusts and the wealth of remedies available from equity if there is a fiduciary relationship. The importance of trusts are such that those civil jurisdictions which do not have a residual trust have adopted legislation to

1   F.W. Maitland, *Equity* (Cambridge: Cambridge University Press, 1949 (first published 1909)).
2   Dante Figueroa, 'Is the Lack of Trusts an Impediment for Expanding Business Opportunities in Latin America?' (January 26, 2007) *bepress Legal Series.* Working Paper 1962. http://law.bepress.com/expresso/eps/1962
3   Donovan Waters Q.C., 'The Future of the Trust from a Worldwide Perspective', in *The International Trust* (John Glasson, ed. 2002), at 625.

create trusts, these will be briefly considered at the end of this chapter; however, these civil trusts cannot incorporate the strength of the fiduciary obligation on the trustee or the ability of equity to imply a trust. Still, imitation is the only sincere form of flattery!

4.1 The Problem with Trusts

Many textbooks will seek to explain the trust and its origins. However, there are many difficulties in explaining the trust and giving a concise definition of a trust. There are also many different theories as to the origin of the trust. The main problem with attempting to explain, define or tell the origin of the trust is that the trust is not a singular phenomenon; there are many different types of trust and these originated from different models to suit different needs. The common factor with trusts was their eventual enforcement by the Chancellor in his Court of Chancery using the principles of equity. In developing the law of trusts equity has tried to homogenise the principles of trusts as if they were the same for all trusts, but has had to accept that sometimes the common principles of the law of trusts should not be applied to a particular trust.

Having said that there is no single trust to define we need to accept that man and the law has a need for definitions. The common law has required a definition of the trust to permit the law of trusts to be applied to new developments and, in this time of international trade and finance, civil law jurisdictions have come to recognise the common law trust in certain situations and so an international definition of the trust has also been required.

The 'classic' common law definition of a trust comes from Professor Underhill:[4]

'A trust is an obligation, binding on a person (called a trustee) to deal with property over which he has control (which is called the trust property) for the benefit of persons (who are called the beneficiaries or *cestuis que trust*) of whom he may himself be one, and any one of whom may enforce the obligation'.

So, 57 words to explain the trust concept. Of course this definition is really only applicable to express private trusts and may not cover all institutions which we refer to as trust, for example the public or private trust, the private purpose trust or implied trusts.[5]

---

4   David Hayton (general editor) with Paul Matthews, Charles Mitchell, *Underhill and Hayton, law relating to trusts and trustees* (London : LexisNexis Butterworths, 2007) 17th ed.

5   Thus other academics have attempted to expand on Underhill's definition see Simon Gardner, An introduction to the law of trusts (Oxford ; New York : Oxford University Press, 2011) 3rd ed; and P.H. Pettit, Equity and the law of trusts (Oxford ; New York : Oxford University Press, 2009) 11th ed.

International law, perhaps because civil jurisdictions do not have the flexibility of common law jurisdictions, requires a substantially more exhaustive definition. The Hague Convention on the Law Applicable to Trusts and their Recognition, 1985,[6] article 2, provides:

"the term 'trust' refers to the legal relationship created-inter vivos or on death-by a person, the settlor, when assets have been placed under the control of a trustee for the benefit of a beneficiary or for a specified purpose...

A trust has the following characteristics:

* The assets constitute a separate fund and are not a part of the trustee's own estate;
* Title to the trust assets stands in the name of the trustee or in the name of another person on behalf of the trustee;
* The trustee has the power and the duty, in respect of which he is accountable, to manage, employ, or dispose of the assets in accordance with the terms of the trust and the special duties imposed on him by law.
* The reservation by the settlor of certain rights and powers and the fact that the trustee may himself have rights as a beneficiary, are not necessarily inconsistent with the existence of a trust."

In this definition 161 words are used to try to cover as many types of trust as possible. This has been included to make the reader realise that the law of trusts is not 'one size fits all', as with many areas of the common law there are recognised trust law principles but these will usually be subject to exceptions that have developed over the centuries.

Perhaps a simple explanation of the basic principle behind the trust is that it is a device of equity that allows the ownership of any property to be split into legal and equitable title. Thus a trust occurs when the legal and equitable title to property has been split between a legal owner (the trustee) and an equitable owner (the beneficiary). A trust may be created expressly either by the absolute owner of property transferring property to a third party, the trustee, under an obligation of trust, or the absolute owner declaring themselves trustee of their own property. The trustee is under fiduciary obligations, obligations of good faith, to hold the property for the benefit of the beneficiaries. Trusts may also be implied by the court or arise by operation of the law in which case the parties to the trust may never realise there is a trust until the court informs them.

To understand what trusts are it is necessary to consider how they originated, compare them to other legal relationships and then look at the different types of trust that have developed.

---

6   The Convention has to be incorporated into each member state's legislation
      to be effective, e.g. the UK has incorporated the Convention by means of the
      Recognition of Trusts Act 1987.

4.2 The Origins of the Law of Trusts

All societies have developed their own notions of trust. From the first time a primitive human gave an item of value to a friend to be passed onto another, there was trust. However, the common law has elevated the notion of trust to a legal institution with guiding principles of trusteeship which are enforced by the law.

The common law trust developed from the mediaeval institution of the 'use. This was a simple device which existed before the Norman Conquest and allowed property to be transferred to another *ad opus*, 'to the use of', another. The word 'use' is said to derive from the Norman-French *oes*, which is itself derived from the Latin *opus* meaning 'benefit'.[7] Thus *ad opus* meant 'to the benefit of' not 'to use' as we understand it today. In this context land was conveyed to another to be held for the benefit of the original transferor or another party. Thus A would transfer property to B to hold for the use of A and/or C. The monumental accounts book known as Domesday, compiled in 1086 shortly after the Conquest, refers to instances of land being held *ad opus* another and prior to that there are records of land being held *ad opus* religious organisations. Possibly this may have been because of Christianity's ideal that the religious should undertake the poverty of Christ, or an attempt to conceal religious ownership, as Kings became concerned at the wealth of the Church. At this point we have a simple concept, a legal owner of property transfers this property to hold for the use of himself or another; he entrusts it to that other party. What makes the use special is the enforcement of the obligation of trust by the Court of Chancery. We do not have enough clear evidence to give a detailed account of the development of the enforceable use, but we have a number of speculative theories. To consider these theories we need to consider the origins of the use, which is usually ascribed to what could almost be described as a legal myth.

4.2.1 The mythical origins of the use

Most textbooks will give a brief account of this theory of the development of the enforceable use. The author has been researching the origins of the law of trust and approached this story with a degree of scepticism, as will be noted from the reference to 'mythical'; however, the more research that is made into the origins of development of the enforceable use the more it seems the myth is, at least partly, true.

As previously noted, the transfer of property *ad opus* another was known before the Conquest. The origin of the use itself may have been

---

7   For a discussion of the derivation of the term see "Cestui Que Use': Cestui Que Trust' (1910) 26 *Law Quarterly Review* 196, 196.

influenced by Roman law, by such institutions as the *fideicommissum* or *pia causa*, or the law of the Salian Franks, by way of the *salmannus*, as many areas of England had been subject to Germanic control. It is not clear whether the early law was enforceable in the courts. The transfer of your property to another 'to the use' of another may have been seen as just bringing moral obligations on the transferee, but it has been speculated that the local customary courts in England before the Norman conquest may have enforced these moral obligations. This would have been especially true of any court subject to Church supervision as they would have made the transferee keep his word. Local courts would often have recourse to the local monk or priest for advice on what should be done when a new problem faced them, as religious men might be the only ones in the area who could read. They were also versed in ecclesiastical law and concerned with men carrying out their moral obligations. All we do know is that after the Conquest the use continued to be employed, and so was recorded in Domesday, although it is not clear if it was enforced in courts.

Shortly after the Conquest the Western Christian world was called by the head of the Church, the Pope, to take part in a holy war to regain Jerusalem, the site of the Temple of Solomon and Christ's execution. This call was for the first of the Crusades. Jerusalem had been subject to Islamic rule for some time, but Christians had been permitted to visit their holy sites in the city. However, the local ruler had recently refused entry to Christian pilgrims and had ordered the destruction of the Church of the Holy Sepulchre. It may seem strange that the barbaric primitive European races would react so strongly to events that occurred thousands of miles from home, however it must be considered in the context of Christianity being the only accepted religion in western Europe at this time, all others being at best tolerated if not persecuted, and consequently immensely powerful. The concentration of Christianity's religious sites in Jerusalem made it the centre of the Christian world, and in fact many world maps of the period show Jerusalem at their centre. Also the Pope promised some absolution from the suffering you would receive after death for your earthly sins if you took part in pilgrimage. Thus kings and knights from all over Europe, often having lived 'sinful' lives of violence and debauchery, left their homes for a long and perilous journey, from which they might not return, in the hope of salvation. While he was away there was a need for someone to look after the crusader's lands, and at the time, women and children were not permitted to do this. If the crusader did try to transfer his property to an heir who was a minor then the feudal right of wardship arose, the land would be under the control of his feudal lord until he was of majority and the lord would be entitled to all dues on the land until then. The lord would also have the right arrange a marriage for the heir and might take advantage of the heir's value, because of the land they were to receive, and sell them into marriage. Therefore the crusader needed a 'trusted' friend to transfer the property to, one who would hold the land for the 'use' of the crusader, his wife and his children. He had to be trusted because to effectively manage the land it had to be conveyed to him; he would have legal title to the land and the common law would consider him the owner. If the crusader returned he had to trust his friend to return the property to him. If the crusader did not return he had to be trusted to use the income from the land to look after the crusader's family and then transfer the property to the heir when he was of age.

The problem was that often the trusted friend was not worthy of that trust. If the crusader died the friend would forget his obligation and treat the land as his own. If the crusader returned the friend would refuse to return the property. The crusader could not get any help in the common law courts because the common law was interested only in the formalities of the transaction; if the property had been transferred to the friend with all necessary formalities then the friend was the legal owner. This must have become a problem for crusader recruitment because, in the early to mid-twelfth century, the Pope began to include in his calls to crusade an order that all should recognise and enforce the property rights of crusaders. Thus the returning crusader would petition the King and, wanting to be seen as a staunch supporter of the crusades and the Church, he would make the friend return the property. Similarly, if the crusader did not return, his family could petition the King, who would make the friend fulfil his obligations. As the use developed the petitions were made directly to the Chancellor,[8] in his role as the king's deputy and because of his ecclesiastical background. Thus the use (and eventually the trust) was not recognised at common law and could only be enforced in equity in the Court of Chancery.

The influence of the crusades and the subsequent and concurrent medieval wars against the French were instrumental in the evolution and development of enforceable uses. The influences responsible for subsequent development of uses have been the subject of some debate.

Speculation on influences on the development of the use

It has been postulated that the use was subject to the influence of other jurisdictions such as Roman law, the *Fideicommissum* , the law of the Salian Franks, the *Salmannus*, and Islamic law, the *Waqf or Wakf*. It has also been suggested the use developed because of the need for an institution that avoided those tasked with living lives of poverty to be considered to own property, in particular Franciscan monks.

---

8   From circa 1400 petitions were made directly to the Chancellor.

Fideicommissum

The *fideicommissum* of Roman law was an executor or heir of the deceased who was charged, subject to good faith (*'fidei'*) with certain responsibilities with regard to the deceased's property.[9] Although at first not enforceable, this was merely a moral obligation, eventually Roman law would enforce these obligations under the jurisdiction of the magistracy of the praetor *fideicommissarius*.[10] The heir had an obligation to carry out the wishes of the deceased, which were usually just to give certain property to certain people. It was an important institution because, as discussed in the chapter on secret trusts, Roman law did not originally recognise the right to leave property as you wished after death but just passed it to your heirs.[11] The *fideicommissum* would fail if the heir refused the inheritance, although later developments in this area meant that once the heir consented to the vesting of the inheritance in the beneficiary, the beneficiary was considered in the position of the heir.[12] The later Institutes of Justinian combined reforms and regarded the beneficiary as in the position of the heir, recognising a proprietary right of the beneficiary in the property and a personal right against the heir. It has been suggested the fideicommissum was the forerunner of the ecclesiastical (canonical) trust.[13]

Salmannus

The *salmannus* or the *saleman* from the Lex Salica, law of the Salian Franks, possibly originating in the fifth century C.E.,[14] was very similar to the *fideicommissum*, although he may have had an *intervivos* role as well. He was also an executor or heir of the deceased who was charged with certain responsibilities with regard to the deceased's property. He had an obligation to carry out the wishes of the deceased, which, again, were usually just to give property to certain people. Oliver Wendell Holmes also ascribed to him an *intervivos* role as a third party, a steward, who was charged with handing over property, although such transfers were usually only to take effect after death.[15]

---

9   See F. Sanders, 'Essay on Uses and Trusts' (1792).
10   Mike Mcnair, 'Equity and Conscience' (2007) 27(4) *Oxford Journal of Legal Studies* 659, pp.663-664. William Lindsay Carne, 'A Sketch of the History of the High Court of Chancery from its Origin to the Chancellorship of Wolsey' (1927) 13(7) (Nov.) *The Virginia Law Review* 391, 404.
11   Henry E. Davis, Paper before the American Bar Association (1898) 6 *American Lawyer* 205, 209.
12   Reforms of Ad Senatus Consultum Trebellianum AD 56.
13   Shael Herman, '*Utilitas Ecclesiae*: The Canonical Conception of the Trust (1995-1996) *Tul. L. Rev.* 2240-2278.
14   see Oliver Wendell Holmes, 'Law in Science and Science in Law' (1898-1899) 12 *Harv. L. Rev.* 443-463, 445-6.
15   Montague Crackanthorpe, 'The Uses of Legal History' (1896) 19 Annu. Rep. A.B.A. 343, 354.

Holmes placed a lot of emphasis on his link of the *salmannus* to the use because the *salmannus* would carry a staff of office presented to him by the land owner, which he surrendered as a signal that he was transferring ownership and ending his office.[16] Holmes claimed this was the origin of the *feoffee to uses*, the trustee as we would call them today, and that executors of wills were originally nothing more than *feoffee to uses*.[17] This also seems to be based upon the common law's requirements for the transfer of property, the concept of seizing, when property was conveyed the purchaser would be given a handful of the soil or a twig from a tree on the property to symbolise transfer of ownership, when feudal estates were passed the transfer of seizing would sometimes be accomplished by a steward of a lord taking a staff of ownership from his lord and giving it to the new owner. Holmes believed this had developed from the *salmannus* and then had been incorporated as symbol of the obligations of stewardship of the trustee. [18]

Holmes' view was criticised by his contemporaries who referred to the use developing from 'a still older foster-parent' in the *fideicommissum*, noting that the *salmannus* might also be derived from this.[19]

Maitland seemed to support Holmes' view, although it should be noted that both have been described as 'anti-Romanists',[20] as they could not see any direct influence of Roman law on the development of the common law. Of course the truth of the origin of uses is probably a blend of both Roman and Salian law with a touch of early Christian principle thrown in. The common law has always proved adept at adopting and adapting ideas from different jurisdictions to its own uses and it seems decidedly improbable that both concepts did not impact on the development of the use. The closeness of England to its continental neighbours, their shared ancestry, and the overarching influence of the Catholic Church in Europe would have been important factors in developing economic and financial principles in international trade and law.[21] These influences could not

---

16   Oliver Wendell Holmes, 'Law in Science and Science in Law' (1898-1899) 12 *Harv. L. Rev.* 443, 446.

17   See also Oliver Wendell Holmes, 'Early English Equity' (1885) 1 *LQR* 162; William Lindsay Carne, 'A Sketch of the History of the High Court of Chancery from its Origin to the Chancellorship of Wolsey' (1927) 13(7) (Nov.) *The Virginia Law Review* 391, 404.

18   See Richard Helmholz & Reinhard Zimmermann (eds), *Itinera Fiduciae* (Dunker & Humblot: Berlin, 1998.

19   Montague Crackanthorpe, 'The Uses of Legal History' (1896) 19 *Annu. Rep. A.B.A.* 343, 355.

20   Montague Crackanthorpe, 'The Uses of Legal History' (1896) 19 *Annu. Rep. A.B.A.* 343, 354.

21   Gaillard Lapsley, 'Some Recent Advances in English Constitutional History (before 1485)' (1936) 5(2) *Cambridge Historical Journal* 119, 147.

always have been quarantined from domestic law, however much the English might have wished, and would have been stronger than today 'when national separation has developed to excess'. [22]

Waqf

The use may have been subject to the influence of Islamic law because of the crusades. The *waqf or wakf*, authorities differ on the spelling, comes from Islamic law.[23] This was also an obligation on the deceased's representatives to hold and use property for the benefit of others, usually the family of the deceased, although there also had to be an end purpose which was charitable as understood by Islam.[24] Another difference between the *waqf* and the Roman or Germanic obligation was that the *waqf* could not only be established by the wishes of the deceased but could be established by the living.

There are many differences between early uses and *waqfs*, primarily the requirement of an end charitable purpose, but also the obligations were subject to control by a third party, usually a religious man appointed by the *waqf* creator in a similar manner to the enforcer or protector of certain private purpose trusts today. However, there are also similarities, a trustee would hold the property for the benefit of beneficiaries, the obligation was to maintain the property for the *waqf* and to keep the property separate from the trustee's own. The proponents of the theory that the *waqf* was instrumental in the development of the use point to early charitable uses, such as the establishment of Oxford University's Merton College.[25] The theory is that returning crusaders brought back the idea of the charitable trust and used it to create their own charitable trusts by endowing schools, hospitals and perhaps even the Inns of Court. Of course charitable endowments had been known before the crusades, indeed the church had encouraged donations *pia causa* for pious or charitable causes, which were

---

22   Charles V. Langlois, 'The Comparative History of England and France during the Middles Ages' (1890) 5(18) (April) *The English Historical Review* 259, 262. Langlois noted (at 261) that the origins of England and France 'are partly common, because on a primitive Celtic base combined Roman and Germanic forces have been imposed under the influence of Christianity.'

23   See Ann Van Wynen Thomas, 'Note on the Origin of Uses' (1949) 3 *S.W.L.J.* 162- 166, and Avisheh Avini, 'The Origin of the Modern English Trust Revisited' (1995-1996) 70 *Tulane Law Review* 1139-1163. Frederik van Tuyll, 'The emergence of the Islamic trust' (2006) 12(9) Trusts & Trustees 7- 9.

24   George Makdisi, 'Legal History of Islamic Law and the English Common Law: Origins and Metamorphoses', (1985-1986) 34 *Cleveland State Law Review* 3-18.

25   Merton was founded in 1264 by Walter de Merton, who had been Chancellor. See Monica M. Gaudiosi, 'The Influence of the Islamic law of WAQF on the Development of the Trust in England: The Case of Merton College', (1987-1988) 136 *University of Pennsylvania Law Review* 1231-1261.

later adopted by the civil law. The charitable *waqf*/use was then adapted for private needs and became the use.

Franciscan monks

Another theory has the use being developed by Franciscan monks. The Franciscan order of monks followed the teachings of their founder, Saint Francis of Assisi (1181-1226). He had instructed them to follow the teachings of Christ and live in poverty. Thus the Franciscan monks could not own property. To enable them to protect their property they appointed a layman, a non-religious member, as their representative, transferring all property to him to hold for the benefit of them all. Maitland claimed that the year 1230 was the earliest record of one man holding land permanently and generally to the use of another and that this was directly influenced by the Franciscans.[26] Thus the development of the use and its protection by the Chancellor, even though it may have been used to avoid mortmain provisions,[27] which prevented religious orders receiving gifts of property, has been described as 'the Chancellor, being a clergyman, protected his own.'[28]

The theory has also been promulgated that St. Francis may have picked up the idea of the *waqf* on his travels in the Holy Land during the years 1219-1220 and adopted it as the use.

It is probable that all these institutions and arrangements influenced the development of the use and it is unlikely we will ever have a certain idea of the origins of the use,[29] but we can trace some of the development of the rights and obligations of those involved in early uses.

4.2.3 The development of the use

When a crusader conveyed his land to his friend to hold to the use of the crusader and his family, the common law was only interested in the conveyance giving good title and did not consider any other party. The

26 F.W. Maitland, *Equity* (Cambridg

25 see E.H. Burn, 'Cheshire & Burn's Modern Law of Real Property, 16th edition (London: Butterworths, 2000), 43, which mentions a Papal Bull ordained in 1279 that a use was not property.

27 William Lindsay Carne, 'A Sketch of the History of the High Court of Chancery from its Origin to the Chancellorship of Wolsey' (1927) 13(7) (Nov.) *The Virginia Law Review* 391, 404.

28 Mike Mcnair, 'Equity and Conscience' (2007) 27(4) *Oxford Journal of Legal Studies* 659, 664, referring to the example of Gilbert, *The Law of Uses* (London: W. Reed & P. Phelan, 3rd edn, 1811) at 3-4.

29 See William F. Fratcher, 'Uses of Uses', (1969) 34 *Missouri Law Review* 39-66; Brendan F. Brown, 'The Ecclesiastical Origin of the Use', (1934-1935) 10 *Notre Dame Lawyer* 353- 366.

common law was only interested in clear ownership of property because, at this time, holding land not only gave rewards it incurred obligations under the feudal system. Thus the holder of legal title to property was responsible for paying feudal dues on that land. The crusader or his family could petition the King to enforce the friend's obligations, but, from circa 1400, the Chancellor began to intervene and enforce the obligations of the friend and enforce the use. The Chancellor could not counteract or contradict the common law directly, he could not make an order against the land, but he could direct the conscience of the friend, ordering them to perform the use. Equity acts *in personam*, against the conscience of the parties, and the conscience of the friend who had promised to hold the land to the use of another was within the jurisdiction of the Chancellor.

The terms used for the parties to a use were derived from common law conveyancing of land. At common law the conveyance of the free inheritance of land, the fee simple, to a man and his heirs was known as *feoffment*, the transferor of land was known as the *feoffer*, and the transferee was known as the *feoffee*. The delivery of possession, the livery of *seisin*, was a public event,[30] carried out on the land by the *feoffer* symbolically handing over a handful of earth or a twig to the *feoffee*. The event was public because written conveyances were rare so everyone needed to know who had lawful ownership and possession of the land.[31] The use involved three parties: the *feoffer* to use, the *feoffee* to use and the *cestui que use*;[32] although often, as today with trusts, one person would carry out more than one role. A simple use would be as follows: the *feoffer* to use would transfer the legal title of property to the *feoffee* to use to be held for the use of the *cestui que use*. This is usually symbolised as follows:

Feoffor to use   →   <u>Feoffee to use</u>
                        Cestui que use

Often the *feoffer to use* was also the *cestui que use* or one of them and Maitland postulated that, 'in the first stage of the development [of the trust] the *cestui que trust* is a trustor who has placed trust in a feoffee; he is the author of the trust as well as sole beneficiary. This makes further confusion possible.'[33] So our crusader would transfer his land to his *feofee to use* who would hold it for the benefit of the crusader and his family as

---

30   F.W. Maitland & F.C. Montague, *A Sketch of English Legal History*, 1850-1906. Charleston, SC : Bibliolife, 2010, at p.56-57.

31   Written conveyances of land, although more common as literacy increased, were only compulsory after the Statute of Frauds 1677.

32   A letter from Maitland dated 23 January 1904, extracts published in "Cestui Que Use': Cestui Que Trust' (1910) 26 *Law Quarterly Review* 196, 197.

33   "Cestui Que Use': Cestui Que Trust' (1910) 26 *Law Quarterly Review* 196, 196.

cestuis que use. Today we would refer to the crusader being a settlor, his friend being a trustee, and the crusader and his family being the beneficiaries.

As well as the problems of war and crusade, uses were developed to deal with other contemporary problems. These included evading feudal dues and obligations, avoiding the forfeiture of property for treason, allowing the owner of property to leave it to whom he wished when he died,[34] creating family settlements and evading restrictions on gifts to the Church.[35] We have already discussed the feudal system, which relied on the paying of fees and fulfilling of obligations between the parties. Feudal dues and obligations came with the privilege of owning land and were payable by those at the bottom of the feudal pyramid to those above them. Fees were payable whenever legal title to land was transferred to a new owner. A larger sum was payable if the heir was a child because the lord would be the child's protector. This right of wardship of heirs who were underage was often exploited by lords.[36] The lord was also entitled to a division of property on the death of a tenant and the heir would also have to pay a fee to his lord on entering into his inheritance. If there was no heir the lord was entitled to the land by the law of escheat. To avoid this, the owner of land would convey the land to a *feoffee to use* who would hold the property to the use of the *feoffer to use* and his family. A fee might be payable on the transfer here but not as large as that payable on the death of the landowner. The *feoffee to use* would, on the death of the feoffer, either transfer the property to the designated family member or continue holding the property for the benefit of the family. Thus there was no problem with fees for death and no chance of wardship. Thus one of the main reasons for the development of the use was the purpose the trust is still used for today, minimising liability to taxation. Of course the use had another benefit, as it looked just like a conveyance of property and the reasons behind it would not have to be made public, thus, this secret trust could avoid the necessary publicity of the times.[37]

---

34 See Stuart E. Prall, 'The Development of Equity in Tudor England' (1964) 8(1) *The American Journal of Legal History* 1, 10.

35 R.H. Helmholz, 'The Early Enforcement of Uses' [1979] 79 *Colum. Law Rev.* 1503-1513.

36 Of course at this time minority continued until the ward attained 21.

37 'In the twelfth century ...men really knew far more of the doings of their neighbours than we know nowadays. It was expected that all legal transactions would take place in public; the conveyance of land was made in open court, the wife was endowed at the church-door, the man who bought cattle in secret ran a great but just risk of being treated as a thief; every three weeks a court was held in the village, and all the affairs of every villager discussed.' F.W. Maitland & F.C. Montague, *A Sketch of English Legal History*, 1850-1906. Charleston, SC : Bibliolife, 2010, at p.56-57.

Another important early employment of the use was to avoid the forfeiture of property upon conviction of treason. Times were very unsure and Kings were notoriously fickle. If you were convicted of treason then your property became forfeit to the King. Of course, if you were a wealthy landowner it might be worth the King or one of his loyal servants concocting a charge of treason against you to gain your property. Once accused of treason it was very hard to establish your innocence, as, although no one could be tried by jury unless they gave their consent to be tried, the *peine forte et dure* could be used to elicit that consent. This was a mixture of punishments which were, as the name suggests, harsh and slow. Starvation and pressing under heavy stones were common methods used to elicit the consent of the accused to be tried by a jury, which would usually find him guilty of treason and order his execution and forfeiture of his property to the King as recompense for the treason. Many preferred to die under the torture rather than condemn their family to poverty.[38] Of course, if you had conveyed your property to a *feoffee to use* you had nothing to lose and your family might be protected.[39]

A further reason for creating a use was the restriction on leaving land by will. Today we take it for granted that we may leave our property in a will to whomsoever we choose; however this is a relatively recent right.[40] Land could not be left in a will; it could only be transferred whilst the legal owner was alive. This was to ensure the lord could consent, and so control, who was to receive the land. Usually the eldest son, through the principle of primogeniture, inherited the land. To avoid the restriction on testamentary disposition of land and the payment of more fees than necessary, the property might be transferred to more than one *feoffee* during the life of the feoffer. If any of the *feoffees* died the others would still own the land through the principle of *ius accrescendi*, survivorship, without the need for a transfer which involved a fee paid to the feudal lord.[41] The use of more than one *feoffee* meant that they could watch each other and new *feoffees* could be appointed without the need for a legal transfer. The transfer could also be made well before the feoffer was likely to die, as the feoffer could make himself the *cestui que use*. Thus the *feoffees* would hold

---

38 F.W. Maitland & F. C. Montague, *A Sketch of English Legal History*, 1850-1906. Charleston, SC : Bibliolife, 2010, at p.60-61. Until 1772 men might still be pressed to death (12 Geo III., c.20).

39 Of course this depended on the friend being truly trustworthy or the king or the Chancellor enforcing this agreement which had been intended to thwart the king.

40 Henry E. Davis, Paper before the American Bar Association (1898) 6 *American Lawyer* 205, 209.

41 E.H. Burn, *Cheshire & Burn's Modern Law of Real Property*, 16th edition (London: Butterworths, 2000), 47.

the property for the use of the feoffer until he died and then for the person named in the feoffer's will. Such a use could be used to avoid property going to an eldest son who was incompetent or did not deserve the land. Thus the use avoided the restriction on testamentary disposition of land and reduced the fees payable to the feudal lord. In all these examples the *cestui que use* did not have to pay any fee because the lord could not look behind the legal owners, the *feoffees to use*, they were his tenants; it did not matter that they were holding the property to the benefit of another.[42]

Although uses and their avoidance of testamentary restrictions were not recognised at common law, the Chancellor would enforce them by issuing an order directed against the person of the *feoffee* to act according to their conscience and carry out the instructions of the feoffer. Landowners could therefore direct who should inherit their property, avoiding escheat and the fees due on transfer.

Example

Gerald has a son and a daughter, Barry and Anne. Barry is gambler and alcoholic. Gerald is worried that when he dies Barry will inherit his land through the principle of primogeniture and lose it all. Gerald does not want to leave Anne penniless, but his lord will not allow him to transfer the property to a woman. He also hopes that his son will mend his ways. Gerald (the *feoffer* to use) transfers legal title to the property to Paul, Gary and Charles (the *feoffees to use*) for the use of Gerald himself (the *cestui que use*) until he dies, and then for Anne. He has also told his *feoffees* that they can use the property to benefit Barry if he mends his ways. If one of the *feoffees* dies then the others can continue as legal owners. If Barry does become more responsible the *feoffees* can look after him. Otherwise the *feoffees* will hold the property for the benefit of Anne.

The overarching influence of the Roman Catholic Church in society at this time has already been mentioned. The Church taught of purgatory and hell for those who had sinned. As men neared the end of their lives they became more concerned about their fate. The Church did, however, provide a remedy in the form of absolution on the payment of a fee or on the saying of masses after death. Both could be achieved by giving property to the Church. Of course this meant that more property entered the dead-hand, mortmain, of that Church and was not subject to the same feudal dues and obligations as other land. The King and his lords were losing out and the King was concerned at the wealth and power of the church. To prevent men giving land to the Church various mortmain provisions were enacted, the first in Magna Carta, requiring such gifts to be subject to a licence from the

---

42 Paraphrasing F.W. Maitland, *Equity* (Cambridge: Cambridge University Press, 1949 (first published 1909)), 27.

King. The use became a useful tool in evading mortmain provisions as the property could be passed to the *feoffee* for the use of a religious institution. This became such a common practice that a mortmain provision of 1392 attempted to outlaw uses for mortmain.[43]

For these various purposes the use became more popular, but it was only the enforcement of the use by the Chancellor that made it so helpful an institution. The Chancellor's jurisdiction seemed virtually unlimited, so the Chancellor's development of the use was 'as clay in the hands of the potter'.[44] However, Chancellors began to develop their own rules to control the enforcement of the use, and the most important of these, probably in recognition of the importance of a settled common law of property, was that equity would follow the law.[45] Thus even though the use was enforced against the strict rules of the common law, Chancellors would, most of the time, try to keep as close to the common law as possible.[46]

Probably the most important development of the trust by Chancellors was the recognition that, although the trustees were the legal owners of the property, the beneficiaries were the owners of the property in equity. This proprietary right of the beneficiaries was eventually extended to be good against anyone except the bona fide purchaser of the trust property without notice of the prior equitable interest (equity's darling).

Maitland describes the development of the use in Chancery as the saviour of the Chancellor's jurisdiction and thus equity. The Chancellor was willing 'to enforce these honourable understandings, these "uses, trusts, or confidences," as they were called, to send to prison the trustee who would not keep faith,'[47] and this made the use and consequently equity very successful. Thus by 1450 it has been estimated that 90% of the work of Chancery was concerned with uses,[48] by the beginning of the sixteenth century it has been stated that most land in England was held in 'use'.[49] Most feudal lords were gaining, because, although their revenue from feudal dues had decreased, they did not have to pay dues to those

---

43   15 Ric. 2, c.5. E.H. Burn, *Cheshire & Burn's Modern Law of Real Property*, 16th edition (London: Butterworths, 2000), 48.

44   Brent's Case (1583) 2 Leon 14, 16, per Manwood J.

45   '...there scarcely is a rule of law or equity of more ancient origin, or which admits of fewer exceptions, than the rule that Equity followeth the law." Butler's note to Co Litt 250b, xvi.

46   E.H. Burn, 'Cheshire & Burn's Modern Law of Real Property, 16th edition (London: Butterworths, 2000), 48.

47   F. W. Maitland & F.C. Montague, *A Sketch of English Legal History*, 1850-1906. Charleston, SC : Bibliolife, 2010, 122-123.

48   Margaret E Avery, 'Evaluation of the Effectiveness of the Court of Chancery under the Lancastrian Kings' (1970) 86 *Law Quarterly Review* 84.

49   Y.B. Mich 15 Hen VII 13 pl 1, *per* Frowike C.J.

above them, and could use the use to leave their property to whomsoever they wished and avoid forfeiture. [50] Of course the one feudal lord who did not gain was the King as the head of the feudal pyramid. Thus successive Kings attempted to restrict the use by legislation. The first of the few pieces of legislation in the short reign of Richard III was headed, 'All acts made by or against *cestui que use* shall be good against him, his heirs and *feoffees in trust*.'[51] Thus the use was under attack to prevent the evasion of the claims of creditors and of the Statute of Mortmain, the reduction of royal revenues by avoiding feudal dues, and to ensure certainty of title to land. [52] However, the King was still losing, and he had no benefit as he had no lord to pay dues to, he just lost any revenue or escheated land from those below him. It needed a powerful and ruthless King to deal with the problem, and who better than Henry VIII and his introduction of the Statute of Uses.

4.2.4 The Statute of Uses

At times the effect of the use on crown revenues has been downplayed but it should be remembered that the overthrow of feudal duties by way of the use was only obtained in other European states by violent insurrection.[53]

The popular view of Henry VIII as an obese much-married despoiler of the Church neglects the intelligence of the man and his clever reorganisation of property law.[54] Thus when Henry needed more money to fortify England and wage wars he questioned the low returns from feudal dues. The crown no longer received large amounts from 'escheat, forfeiture, wardship, and marriage.' [55] Thus the main motive force behind

---

50 For example, many noble men had their land conveyed to use to avoid forfeit for treason in the Wars of the Roses. Montague Crackanthorpe, 'The Uses of Legal History' (1896) 19 *Annu. Rep. A.B.A.* 343, 357.

51 H.G. Hanbury, 'The Legislation of Richard III' (1962) 6(2) *The American Journal of Legal History* 95, 98.

52 Ibid, 98-99.

53 Percy Bordwell, 'The Repeal of the Statute of Uses' (1926) 39(4) *Harvard Law Review* 466, 468.

54 'We owe to Henry VIII – much rather to him than his Parliament- not a few innovations in the law of property...' F.W. Maitland & F.C. Montague, *A Sketch of English Legal History*, 1850-1906. Charleston, SC : Bibliolife, 2010, at 108.

55 Stuart E. Prall, 'The Development of Equity in Tudor England' (1964) 8(1) *The American Journal of Legal History* 1, 10. W.S. Holdsworth, 'The Political Causes Which Shaped The Statute Of Uses' (1912-1913) 26 Harvard Law Review 108-127.

the Statute of Uses was the revival of the King's revenue.[56] Of course it was not easy to get such legislation from a parliament packed with wealthy land owners and lawyers, all of whom benefitted from the use. The enacting of the Statute of Uses has been characterised as a battle of a strong willed king against an extremely unwilling parliament, as the 'King was the one person who had all to gain and nothing to lose by the abolition of uses.'[57] However, there was support in parliament from common lawyers jealous of Chancery's success with the use and anxious to regain control of land.[58]

The Statute of Uses was enacted in 1535;[59] however, because of parliamentary support for some uses of the use, it was not abolished completely. It provided that where one person was 'seised' of any land to the 'use, trust or confidence' of another person in any estate, that second person would be deemed to hold an estate at law equal to that previously held for him in use. Thus the use was 'executed'.

Example
If Stephen conveys property to Terry for the use of Ben then the use will be executed, it will be carried out, and the legal title will automatically pass to Ben. Any feudal dues would have to be paid.

The Statute did not apply to active uses, these were uses that were not just a sham to avoid feudal dues, but were necessary because the *cestui que use* required the protection of the *feoffee*.[60] An active use involved real management duties and responsibilities for the *feoffee*, not just passing the property onto the *cestui que use*.

The immediate effect of the Statute was to fuel an uprising of the people in the North of England, the Pilgrimage of Grace.[61] People had grown accustomed to being able to devise property in their wills and felt that the Statute was interfering with their property rights and thus 'prejudicial to the common wealth.'[62] The uprising was crushed but in recognition of

---

56 Percy Bordwell, 'The Repeal of the Statute of Uses' (1926) 39(4) *Harvard Law Review* 466, 468. See also E.W. Ives, 'The Genesis of the Statute of Uses' (1967) 82 HER 676.

57 F.W. Maitland, *Equity* (Cambridge: Cambridge University Press, 1949 (first published 1909)), 34; and see Froude, History of England, vol.iii pp.91,105,158.

58 Robert L. Munger, 'A Glance at Equity' (1915) 25(1) (Nov.) *The Yale Law Journal* 42, 53. Stuart E. Prall, 'The Development of Equity in Tudor England' (1964) 8(1) *The American Journal of Legal History* 1, 10.

59 27 Hen VIII cap 10.

60 For a consideration of the difference between trust and uses see N.G. Jones, 'Uses, Trusts and a Path to Privity', (1997) 56 *Cambridge Law Journal* 175-200.

61 F.W. Maitland, *Equity* (Cambridge: Cambridge University Press, 1949 (first published 1909)), 34; and see Froude, History of England, vol.iii pp.91,105,158.

62 *Letters and Papers, Foreign and Domestic, of the Reign of Henry VIII*, XII, part 1 (1537), 497.

some of the concerns the Statute of Wills was enacted in 1540,[63] which allowed testamentary dispositions of land subject to the Crown receiving a share, in a similar way to modern inheritance tax.

Of course the Statute of Uses was also a threat to the jurisdiction of equity as it removed a sizeable body of work from Chancery,[64] and, although feudal obligations were becoming less burdensome because of the replacement of work obligations with money payments, the use was still missed by many landowners attempting to provide for their families. [65] Thus over the next 140 years the trust was developed.

4.2.4 The use upon a use and the trust[66]

The Statute of Uses was interpreted as only executing passive uses (similar to a bare trust today), whilst permitting the continued existence of active uses.[67] Thus, if the *feoffees to uses* had active duties to perform the use was not executed by the Statute. The use had become such an important tool for conveying and protecting property that lawyers began experimenting with the wording of the use to see if they could avoid the effect of the Statute (very similar to the practices of lawyers today). A simple method was to insert another use into the instrument, a 'use upon a use'. For example, Stephen conveys his property to Terry to the use of Trevor to the use of Ben. When such a use was first created the courts considered that the first use was executed and so Trevor received the property. The use to Ben was void as it was repugnant to Trevor's interest.[68] Therefore Trevor took the property. The debate on the use upon a use was to continue for over a century until it was accepted that, in certain circumstances and for certain property, the use upon the use was valid and Trevor would actually hold the property to the use of Ben.[69]

---

63 32 Hen VIII cap 1.
64 Stuart E. Prall, 'The Development of Equity in Tudor England' (1964) 8(1) *The American Journal of Legal History* 1, 10.
65 Lawrence Sone & J.C. Fawtier Stone, *An Open Elite? England 1540-1880* (Oxford: Clarendon Press 1986), 69-70.
66 See James Barr Ames, 'The Origin of Uses and Trusts', (1908) 21 *Harvard Law Review* 261-274.
67 N.G. Jones, 'Trusts Litigation in Chancery after the Statute of Uses: the First Fifty Years'.
68 Tyrrel's Case (1557) 2 Dyer 155a. This has been described as the lawyers throwing away the victory of the Statute by "timid and narrow construction". Robert L. Munger, 'A Glance at Equity' (1915) 25(1) (Nov.) *The Yale Law Journal* 42, 53, quoting Hallam, *English Constitution*, p.197.
69 Gradually they became accepted and enforced by the Court of Chancery, e.g. *Sambach v Daston* (1634). see D.E.C.Yale, 'The Revival of Equitable Estates in the Seventeenth Century: An Explanation by Lord Nottingham' (1957) *Cambridge Law Journal* 72-86.

The major political changes after the English Civil War of the mid-seventeenth century led to the abolition of most feudal dues and obligations.[70] Thus the main reason for the Statute and for executing the use, to prevent landholders avoiding their feudal obligations, was removed. Therefore, the Court of Chancery began regularly enforcing the second use. The use of the second 'use' was dropped and the term 'trust' inserted instead. The *feoffer* became the settlor or testator, the *feoffee* became the trustee, and the *cestui que use* became the *cestui que trust* and then the beneficiary. Thus the use upon the use was no longer a 'repugnant' creature and was employed more in its modern form, the trust.[71]

The Chancellorship of Lord Nottingham, 1673-1682, saw the blossoming of the trust. This was at a time when land rights were in disarray. The Civil war had left title to property uncertain, and for any man in possession of property, his best security was the lack of title deeds !.[72] Nottingham promoted the trust as a method of protecting property rights, for example the desire of landowners for a family settlement trust as a method of preventing their families losing the land in the future,[73] a desire of landowners that had been thwarted for centuries, was permitted to a limited extent by Nottingham's development of the rule against perpetuities.[74] Nottingham sanctioned the trust as permitting a whole range of future interests in land that had been consistently rejected at common law.

The development of the modern trust was such that the eighteenth century Chancellor Lord Harwicke was able to famously comment on the Statute of Uses that, 'a statute made upon great consideration, introduced in a solemn and pompous manner, by this strict construction, has no other effect than to add at most three words to a conveyance.'[75]

---

70 The Tenures Abolition Act 1660 (12 Car 2 c 24).
71 Although it should be noted that this is a simplified version of the development of the trust and the true story of its development is not known. D.E.C. Yale has researched Lord Nottingham's writings on the development of the modern trust and points out that Nottingham, writing when the 'modern' trust was young, comments that 'a trust is and always was a thing quite different from a use.' D.E.C.Yale, 'The Revival of Equitable Estates in the Seventeenth Century: An Explanation by Lord Nottingham' (1957) *Cambridge Law Journal* 79.
72 S.R. Maitland, *The Dark Ages; A Series of Essays, Intended to Illustrate the State of religion and Literature in the Ninth, Tenth, Eleventh and Twelfth Centuries*, (London: Francis & John Rivington, 3rd edition, 1853), p.288.
73 Lawrence Sone & J.C. Fawtier Stone, *An Open Elite? England 1540-1880* (Oxford: Clarendon Press 1986) p. 73.
74 *The Duke of Norfolk's Case* (1682) 3 Ch. Cas. 1; 22 Eng. Rep. 931.
75 *Hopkins v Hopkins* (1738) 1 Atk 581, 591. Although Cheshire and Burns describe this remark as "picturesque and arresting" but "scarcely accurate", as the Statute had a "vital and lasting" effect as it enabled "a class of future interests

4.3 Classification of trusts

It may seem that we now have a very simple concept to consider. The trust as a development of the use, whether influenced by Roman, Germanic or Islamic law, seems to be just a device whereby the settler transfers legal title to the trust property to the trustee to be held subject to fiduciary obligations for the benefit of the beneficiary. However, as stated earlier, the major problem with defining the trust is that this simple but effective instrument had been developed by equity into many different varieties. In trying to understand the law of trusts it is necessary to identify what type of trust has been created.

Trusts can be classified in a number of ways:

- By how they are created;
- By the type of beneficiary;
- By the discretion afforded the trustee;
- By the trustee's duties.

4.3.1 Express or implied?

All trusts are either express or implied.[76] Trusts can be created expressly by a settler or testator or implied from the circumstances or the law.

Express trusts
An express trust is created by the settlor 'expressly' intending to create a trust.

Settlor   →   <u>Trustee</u>   (<u>legal owner)</u>
                                 Beneficiary   (equitable/beneficial owner)

The settlor transfers the legal title of the property to the trustee (or trustees) subject to the obligation to hold it on trust for the beneficiary (or beneficiaries). The settlor is the absolute owner of the property before he transfers the property to the trustee, but after transfer he has no interest in the property unless he declared himself the trustee (a self-declaration of trust) or made himself a beneficiary. Unless he has retained such an interest he has no interest in the trust property after a valid trust is constituted.[77]

The trustee and beneficiary are shown above and below a dividing line respectively. This is to exemplify that the trustee is the legal owner, he has

---

(springing and shifting uses), hitherto unknown to the common law, to be carved out of the legal estate." E.H. Burn, 'Cheshire & Burn's Modern Law of Real Property, 16th edition (London: Butterworths, 2000), 54.

76   Cook v Fountain (1676) 3 Swans 585, 591-592. per Lord Nottingham
77   *Re Bowden (Hulbert v Bowden)* [1936] Ch 71.

legal title and his ownership will be apparent or visible to the world. If the property is of a type which requires ownership to be registered, for instance land or shares, then the trustee will be the registered owner. He has control of the property and may sell it or do with it as he will, although he is subject to possible penalties if he does not obey the instructions given him by the settler when the trust was created, or if he does not do his best to protect the property for the benefit of the beneficiary. The beneficiary is shown below the line as his interest is usually hidden from the world. Unless there are special provisions to do with property which allow for equitable ownership to be registered there will be no easy to access registration of equitable (beneficial) interests.

Thus, in the trust we have a simple instrument of equity, where an absolute owner has transferred property to a trustee under a trust obligation, at which point equity divides ownership of this property between the legal owner (trustee) and equitable owner (the beneficiary). Equity then places the trustee under a fiduciary obligation to protect the property and hold it for the benefit of the equitable owner in good faith. Equity also recognises the independent equitable interest of the beneficiary in the trust property.

A settlor may also declare himself trustee of his own property for the benefit of beneficiaries (including himself). If there is a self declaration of trust the settlor does not need to transfer the legal title to the property as the settlor already has legal title. He merely declares that he holds it subject to the self-imposed obligation to use it for the benefit of the beneficiary.

Before declaring himself trustee the settlor owns the property absolutely. He has both legal and equitable title to the property.

<u>Settlor</u>	<u>legal owner</u>
Settlor	equitable owner

The diagram above is meant to show the absolute ownership of the settlor before declaring a trust. However, we do not usually speak of the settlor having both legal and equitable title because the equitable interest does not come into being until the trust is created.[78] Thus we just refer to absolute ownership.

After the settlor had declared himself a trustee the trust may be represented as follows:

<u>Settlor now trustee</u>	<u>legal owner</u>
Beneficiary	equitable owner

---

78   See the comments of Lord Browne Wilkinson in *Westdeutsche Landesbank Girozentrale v Islington LBC* [1996] AC 699 (HL).

The settlor may transfer property to another to hold on trust but make himself the beneficiary of the trust, either alone or with other beneficiaries.

| Settlor → | Trustee | legal owner |
| | Beneficiary (was settlor) | equitable owner |

If a settlor attempts to declare himself sole trustee of property with himself as sole beneficiary then there will be no trust as he is still the absolute owner with legal and equitable title vested in him. Similarly if the trustee transfers property to another to hold on trust but with that other being sole beneficiary there will not be a trust, the purported trustee will just be the absolute owner, and this will be a gift.

Of course the settlor can declare himself to be one of the trustees and one of the beneficiaries.

Settlor →	Trustee A + Trustee B (was the settlor)	legal owners
	Beneficiary A + Beneficiary B	equitable
	(was the settlor)	owners

A settlor may make his express declaration of trust to come into effect whilst he is alive, an *inter vivos* trust, or include it in his will to come into effect after he is dead, a testamentary trust.

The trustee is under the trust obligation. He holds the legal title to the trust property and must protect it and use it for the benefit of the trust beneficiaries or the trust purpose. The trustee must keep the property separate from his own, e.g. usually trust money would be kept in a separate bank account from the trustee's own money.

A trustee can be a beneficiary of the trust as well.

Settlor →	Trustee	legal owner
	Beneficiary A (the trustee)	equitable owners
	+ Beneficiary B	

The beneficiaries are the parties who benefit from the trust. They receive an equitable interest in the trust and may be regarded as the owners of the trust property in equity. However, although the trust is a device which separates ownership, the settlor does not transfer the different interests to the trustee and beneficiary. Before the creation of the trust the property is owned absolutely by the settlor, there are no separate legal and equitable interests. The settlor transfers the whole ownership of the trust property to the trustee subject to the trust obligation at which point equity creates the equitable interest for the beneficiaries.[79]

---

79   See the comments of Lord Browne Wilkinson in *Westdeutsche Landesbank Girozentrale v Islington LBC* [1996] AC 699 (HL).

Implied trusts

Trusts that are not created expressly are implied trusts. These are sometimes referred to as trusts that arise by operation of law. These may arise because a statutory provision declares that a trust arises in the circumstances,[80] or because they are implied from the circumstances. It is very hard to give an exhaustive all encompassing definition of implied trusts, as with equity generally they have developed piecemeal in response to the needs of equity. Thus it is easier to understand implied trust when examples are considered. Implied trusts are considered in detail in a later chapter, this is just a brief introduction. In certain circumstances the law will recognise a trust as being in existence although the parties may not have intended to create a trust, and sometimes when the parties have deliberately tried not to create a trust. Implied trusts include resulting and constructive trusts, although some texts prefer not to refer to the resulting trust as implied. Implied trusts usually arise because the legal owner (usually the defendant) has done something unconscionable or the non-legal owner (usually the plaintiff) has done something by mistake, or on reliance of some undertaking of the legal owner, or has failed to do something, e.g. failed to validly create a trust when he has transferred legal title of the property to the defendant.

The court will declare a resulting trust exists when legal title has been vested in another but the beneficial interest in property still remains with the former absolute owner. Resulting trusts are usually categorised as presumed resulting trusts (PRT) and automatic resulting trusts (ART).

A resulting trust can arise because of an evidential presumption, the presumption of resulting trust, this arises when property is transferred to another and no consideration is given for the transfer. If there is no evidence of the reason behind the transfer equity presumes that the original owner always wanted to retain an interest in the property or have it returned to him unless there is evidence to the contrary.[81]

An automatic resulting trust can arise because the parties have intended to create an express trust but some vital requirement has not been complied with. For example, a settlor may intend to create a trust by transferring property to the trustee subject to the trust obligation but not complying with the requirement to identify the beneficiaries with the required certainty.

Settlor →   Trustee   legal owner
                Beneficiary ?   equitable owners

---

80   e.g. Intestates' Estates Act 1952 s.47.
81   *Dyer v Dyer* (1788) 2 Cox Eq Cas 92.

The beneficiaries must be ascertainable (see chapters 5 & 6 as to the three certainties and the beneficiary principle), as the trustee must know in whose favour he must carry out the trust obligations. The settlor has therefore transferred legal ownership to the trustee. The trustee knows the property is not a gift but is subject to trust obligations. The trustee cannot therefore keep the property, it would be unconscionable for him to do so, but he does not know in whose favour he holds the property. In these circumstances a resulting trust automatically arises. The trustee holds the property on resulting trust for the settlor who may call for its return or settle it on a new trust with the trustee, this time making sure he identifies the beneficiaries. If the trust has been created in a will obviously the testator cannot be given the property back. It will be held on resulting trust for the testator's estate and distributed as provided in the will or, if it was the last provision, the residuary estate or residue, it will be distributed on the rules of intestacy.

Constructive trusts arise in certain set circumstances usually to prevent fraud or unconscionable behaviour, e.g. if a murderer is an heir of his victim it would be unconscionable for him to inherit the victim's estate and so equity considers that he holds his inheritance on constructive trust for his victim's estate to be distributed to all other heirs *per* the victim's will or the rules of intestacy. Constructive trusts can also arise because the conscience of the legal owner is affected by some knowledge of the plaintiff's interest in the trust property.[82] For example, if a purchaser of trust property from a trustee knows that the trustee should not have sold the property he will hold the property subject to the interests of the beneficiaries; the court will construct a trust and enforce it against his conscience. He will hold the property on constructive trust for the beneficiaries and, again, they may call for its return.

In England constructive trusts are said to be 'institutional'; they arise in certain recognised situations. The courts in England refuse to classify constructive trusts as 'remedial'. They are not available as a general equitable remedy. This is not the situation in Australia where the courts have been more realistic in their recognition of their use of constructive trusts. However, as will be seen, the courts in England may claim that the constructive trust is not remedial, but its use in these jurisdictions at times verges on the remedial.[83]

There are academic and judicial disagreements on the classification of implied trusts. At times a relationship may be categorised as a resulting trust and sometimes as a constructive trust even though the circumstances giving rise to both are very similar (see, for example, later consideration

---

82 See chapter 10, implied trusts, and chapter 17, the liability of strangers to the trust.
83 See chapters 10 & 11.

of *Quistclose* trusts). There is also an important ongoing debate about the time when a constructive trust arises and the duties of constructive trustees. This is important because trustees owe duties towards the trust fund and the beneficiaries; however the trustee of a constructive trust may not even know he is a trustee until the court declares him one. The question then arises; will his previous actions towards the trust be judged subject to fiduciary trust obligations?

4.3.2 Private or public?

Trusts can be classified by the type of beneficiary; they can be for private individuals or public purposes. A private trust is set up to benefit private individuals usually because of their relationship with the settlor, for example a trust to benefit the settlor's family and friends. Private express trusts are by far the most common trusts. Public trusts are charitable trusts. The general rule is that a trust must have ascertainable beneficiaries (the beneficiary principle), so that the court knows in whose favour they may order the trustees to act.[84] Thus private purpose trusts are generally void.[85] However, charitable trusts do not have to comply with the beneficiary principle as equity recognises they benefit the public as a whole and anyone may enforce them.

4.3.3 Fixed or discretionary?

Trusts can also be categorised by the discretion afforded the trustee.

Fixed trust
A fixed trust is where property is transferred by the settlor to the trustee subject to 'fixed' instructions as to who shall benefit and what they are to receive.

Example
Stephen's will provides as follows: I leave £30,000 to Terry and Trevor to hold on trust for my two good friends, Bella and Ben, in equal shares.

Stephen → <u>Terry (Trustee 1) + Trevor (Trustee 2)</u>   legal Owners
(Testator)   Bella (Beneficiary 1) + Ben (Beneficiary 2)   beneficial Owners

When the executors carry out the instructions in the will and the property is passed to Terry and Trevor, they will become the legal owners subject to a trust obligation, they will become the trustees. They will hold the

---

84   *Morice v The Bishop of Durham* (1804) 9 Ves 399; (1805) 10 Ves 522.
85   *Re Astor's Settlement Trusts* [1952] Ch 534.

property for the benefit of Bella and Ben in equal shares. They have no discretion as to who shall be a beneficiary or how much they are to get. They have exact instructions as to who is to benefit and how much they are to get. Bella and Ben each have a beneficial interest in the trust fund to the extent of £15,000 at the point when it is created. The fixed trust could also specify that the beneficiaries are to get different proportions e.g. Ben is to receive 80% and Bella 20%. The trustees must carry out the division as directed. They have no discretion.

Once the trust is constituted, the trust property is passed to the trustees; the settlor has no further interest in the trust unless he has made himself a trustee or beneficiary. The trustees are under the mandatory trust obligation and must carry out their instructions. If they do not they will be in breach of trust and the beneficiaries can take action against them.[86] The beneficiaries have a fixed interest in the trust. They can sue the trustees for breach of trust if they do not carry out their trust obligations. They can ask the court to make the trustees carry out their obligations. If the trustees misappropriate funds the beneficiaries can take personal action against them to account for any loss to the trust and make it good. They can also trace the trust property into substitutions or into the hands of others because they have a proprietary interest in the trust property.

Discretionary trust

A discretionary trust is where property is transferred to the trustees but they have the ability to choose who is to benefit or how much they are to get. They have discretion. The trustee's duty is 'to select from among a class of beneficiaries those who are to receive, and the proportions in which they are to receive, income or capital of the trust property.'[87]

Example

Stephen's will also provides as follows: I leave £100,000 to Terry and Trevor to hold on trust for any of my first cousins as they shall in their absolute discretion think fit and in the proportions they decide.

Here the trust will come into being (will be constituted) when the executors transfer the £100,000 to Terry and Trevor. They will then be the legal owners of the £100,000 subject to the trust obligation. They have the duty to distribute the fund but they have the discretion to choose which members of a class, 'any of my first cousins', shall receive any of the trust fund. They must choose at least one of the first cousins but they do not have to choose more than one. None of the cousins has the right to insist on being a beneficiary. The trustees also have discretion to decide how

---

86   Sometimes the settlor can take action for breach of contract.
87   *Mettoy Pensions Trustees Ltd v Evans* [1991] 2 All ER 513, *per* Warner J.

much each cousin shall get. If there were four cousins and the trustees chose two to receive trust funds they could give them £50,000 each or £10,000 and £90,000 respectively, or any proportion they wished.

Discretionary trusts are often used to maintain control over beneficiaries. The settlor appoints trustees who use their discretion to ensure the beneficiaries behave as the settlor wished. Potential beneficiaries do not have an interest in trust property until they are selected as beneficiaries, until then they only have a *spes*, a hope of an interest. Potential beneficiaries may only sue the trustees if they misappropriate assets, this would be to return the assets to the trust fund not the potential beneficiaries, or if the trustees select beneficiaries from outside the class specified in the trust. A discretionary trust may have hundreds or thousands of possible beneficiaries. The problem for trustees is what consideration must be given to selecting from the class of potential beneficiaries. This will be considered later when we examine certainty of objects for a private express trust. This may create a problem for the trustees as to what duty they may have to consider all the potential beneficiaries.[88]

At times it can be very difficult to distinguish a discretionary trust from a fiduciary power. A power is another method by which equity allows property to be distributed. Powers are often couple with trusts, but a power is purely discretionary, the donee of a power is under no obligation to use his power, whereas a trust is mandatory, it must be carried out. Therefore it is important to distinguish between the two in order to understand the party's obligations. Distinguishing powers and trusts will be considered in the next chapter.

4.3.4 Bare or special trust?

Trusts can also be categorised by reference to the trustee's duties. An express trust can be a bare trust or a special trust. A bare trust is often referred to as a 'simple' trust because the trustee has no duty to perform other than holding the property to transfer it to the beneficiary in the future. The trustee has no special duties to perform. An example would be a nominee who is given legal title to property such as shares but has no active management duties with regard to the trust.

A special trust is an express trust where the trustee has duties to perform. Thus a trustee who has to manage trust property, invest it and retain it for a number of years until beneficiaries are of a certain age or another event happens will be subject to a special trust. There are many other special forms of trust such as the secret and half-secret trust, the life-interest, the trust of imperfect obligation and the *Quistclose* trust. These will be dealt with as they are met in the text.

---

88   See the comments of Megarry V-C in *Re Hay's ST* [1980] 1WLR 202 considered later.

4.4 Characteristics of a trust

Although there are many different types of trust there are some characteristics which they share. Generally trusts:

- Are mandatory;
- Are fiduciary;
- Are non-revocable;
- Create a separate equitable interest in property which gives the beneficiaries enforceable rights.

Trust are mandatory, the obligation on the trustee is exactly that, an obligation. The trustee must perform the trust instructions subject to the fiduciary obligations of a trustee. He must carry out the trust in good faith towards the beneficiaries. Thus, as mentioned above, a trust may be discretionary because the trustees have discretion as to how to carry out the trust, but they have to use that discretion, they cannot ignore it. For example, a discretionary trust may be exhaustive or non-exhaustive. If the discretionary trust is exhaustive they must use all of the funds over which they have discretion to distribute to the beneficiaries they choose. If the trust is non-exhaustive they may retain some of the fund for investment and later distribution for trust beneficiaries. Of course, they can never take the fund themselves unless they are also beneficiaries.

Once a settlor creates a trust he loses all interest in the trust unless he is a beneficiary or trustee. The trust exists independently of the settlor. Therefore, the settlor cannot revoke the trust, he cannot call for the return of the trust assets. Once he has established the trust he cannot change his mind.

Re Bowden (Hulbert v Bowden)[89]
The settlor had decided to enter a religious order which required her to divest herself of all property. She settled her property and any future property she might receive on trust. Many years later she changed her mind and instructed the trustees to return the trust property to her. There was an issue over the validity of a trust created including future interests in property, but the court was emphatic that she had no interest in the trust property once the trust was constituted. Since it had been constituted and existed, she no longer had any interest in the property and could not call for its return.

One of the most powerful aspects of the trust is the creation of the separate equitable interest of the beneficiaries. The trustees may have legal ownership of the property but the beneficiaries have equitable ownership and ultimate control over the property. Their interests are enforceable as

---

89   [1936] Ch 71.

against the trustees. As the trust is mandatory they can go to court to make the trustees perform their duties. If the trust property is lost the beneficiaries may have a personal right of action against the trustees. However, the rights of the beneficiaries as regards the trust property depend on the type of trust. Thus beneficiaries under a discretionary trust have fewer rights than under a fixed trust because their interests are not identified until and unless they are selected. However, the beneficiaries of a discretionary trust together own the trust property and can take action against a trustee. An individual beneficiary can also go to court to compel a trustee to exercise his discretion if that is his instruction in the trust instrument.[90]

The most important aspect of the beneficial interest is its proprietary nature. The beneficiaries have a proprietary interest in the trust property, an ownership right that is good against third parties, except equity's darling. It even prevails on the insolvency of the trustees.[91]

Example
Stephen is trustee of a trust in favour of Ben. The assets of the trust are a flat in Chester and £100,000 in a separate bank account. Both the flat and bank account are in Stephen's name as he is the legal owner. Stephen's business has been in trouble for some time and his creditors, including his bank have taken an order in bankruptcy against him. His trustee in bankruptcy has taken charge of his assets. The bank wants to offset the £100,000 against money owed by Stephen to the bank. The trustee in bankruptcy and the bank cannot touch the flat or £100,000 because although Stephen is the legal owner, they are trust assets and are not part of his own assets. Ben's equitable ownership can be asserted over any other claim.

The proprietary interest is important as it can be exercised if the trustee is not in a position to pay if a personal action against him were successful. For example, if he is bankrupt there is no point in suing him. The proprietary action allows the beneficiary to trace the trust property and assert the proprietary interest against third parties except equity's darling.

Equity acts *in personam*, which explains the personal action available to the beneficiary against the trustee. However, the proprietary interest of the beneficiaries equitable interest in trust property has been likened to a right *in rem*, as it seems to be a right in the thing itself.[92] This is because it can

---

90   *Vestey v IRC (No 2)* [1980] AC 1148.
91   As early as 1465 it was held that a person who bought land from a trustee with notice that the land was subject to the trust obligation was bound by the trust: YB 5 Ed IV, Mich pl 16, fo. 7. This was extended in 1595 to cover those who received trust property without knowledge but provided no consideration- volunteers: *Chudleigh's Case* 1 Co Rep 113b, 122b.
92   Ross Grantham, 'Doctrinal Bases for the Recognition of Proprietary Rights' (1996) Oxford Journal of Legal Studies 561- 585.

be enforced against third party recipients and substitutions for the trust property can be claimed.[93] Generally, however, the proprietary interest of a beneficiary is regarded not as a right *in rem*, but as a personal right enforceable against the trustee or anyone whose conscience is affected by knowledge of the beneficiary's interest (as '*equity acts in personam*').[94]

It is important to distinguish between the equitable interest and 'mere equities'. Mere equities are rights to take action which have not yet been enforced. They are purely personal rights. For example the right to rescission on the grounds of fraud or undue influence is a mere equity. It is not enforceable against the purchaser of the equitable estate without notice of the equity (equity's darling). The mere equity is therefore not as powerful as the equitable interest. However, the mere equity may give rise, after its exercise to an equitable interest.

4.5 Distinguishing trusts from other concepts

At times the trust may resemble other legal concepts, for example:

- Contract;
- Bailment;
- Agency;
- Personal representatives;
- Powers of appointment.

It is necessary to distinguish between trusts and these other concepts because of the fiduciary and proprietary nature of the trust.

4.5.1 The trust *v.* contract

There are times when a transaction may be designed as a trust or a contract. For example, Michael agrees that he will transfer legal ownership of his shop in Central to James, and James agrees that he will pay the rent from the shop to Stephen for Stephen's lifetime. When Stephen dies James will

---

93   See the chapters on tracing and strangers to the trust.

94   Academics have debated whether the equitable interest is a right in rem. Salmond claimed they were rights *in rem* (P.J. Fitzgerald, Salmond on Jurisprudence (London : Sweet & Maxwell, 1966) 12th ed.). Maitland said that the equitable interest in a trust were not *in rem* but that, "by and by they have come to look very like' *in rem* interest." However, he said they were essentially "not rights against the world at large, but rights against certain persons". See also R. A Reid, 'The Place of Trust in Jurisprudence' [1912] The Canadian Law Times 767-775. Milsom noted that '...equity has proved that from the materials of obligation you can counterfeit the phenomena of property.' S.F.C.Milsom, Historical Foundations of the Common Law, (London: Butterworths, 2nd edition, 1981) p.1

be entitled to the rent. What has been created? Is this a contract or a trust? It is important to know which because of the differing duties and obligations of the parties and the remedies available to the parties for breach of contract and breach of trust. The agreement may be a contract between Michael and James for the transfer of the property, subject to the condition that James pays the rent to Stephen for his lifetime. James is purely under an obligation to pay the rent. If he does not pay the rent then an action for breach of contract would be available to Michael, but he will suffer very little loss so nominal damages may be all he can recover for the breach. Stephen will suffer loss but he has no privity of contract with James and so may have difficulty enforcing the contract (specific performance may be available following the principle in *Beswick v Beswick*[95]).

The agreement may also be structured as a trust by way of a life interest. Michael may have transferred the property to James subject to a life interest for Stephen. James is the legal owner, he is the trustee, but he is also a beneficiary with Stephen. James is the beneficiary of the ultimate interest or the 'remainder', thus he is the 'remainder man', and Stephen is a beneficiary of the life interest. Therefore, James must protect the trust property for both Stephen and James himself. When Stephen dies James takes the property absolutely. Unless Michael has retained an interest in the property by making himself a trustee or beneficiary he has no interest in the property. If James breaches the trust in any way Michael has no standing to bring an action for breach of trust. However, Stephen has standing as a beneficiary to take action against James, this can be personal, i.e. Stephen can sue James for any loss, or the action can be proprietary, Stephen can trace any misappropriated trust assets into the hands of third parties (except equity's darling). James has fiduciary duties towards the trust and Stephen, he must act in good faith, these duties are far more onerous, that is they are of a higher standard than most contractual duties.

Thus it is important to distinguish between the contract and the trust because of the more onerous duties and obligations imposed on the trustee and the ability to take personal and proprietary action to remedy breach of these obligations.

One of the most important differences between contracts and trusts is that contracts are formed by negotiation and informed agreement whereas trusts do not require negotiation and may be formed without agreement. For example, Gerald writes a will in which he leaves £100,000 to Omar to hold on trust for Cheryl. Omar may never have discussed the trust with Gerald and may only find out about it when Gerald's executors tell him of the provision. The only agreement required is Omar's acceptance of the role of trustee. However, even if Omar does not agree the trust will still be

---

95   [1968] AC 58(HL), see chapter 3.

formed because 'equity will not allow a trust to fail for want of a trustee', the executors will have to find another trustee, they may even go to court to ask that they appoint a trustee. Similarly, Cheryl may know nothing about the trust until the executors inform her she is the beneficiary.

Although trusts may be formed on the basis of a contract,[96] that is an enforceable agreement with consideration passing between the parties may be made to create a trust,[97] generally trusts are not formed with any consideration.[98] The trustee and beneficiary do not usually provide any consideration for the creation of the trust. It may be thought that the trustee deserves some consideration for the onerous nature of his role; however, a principle of trusteeship is that the trustee must not profit from the trust, therefore trustees should not be paid.[99]

Confusion between trusts and contracts may also occur when the contract involves the transfer of money, for example a loan. The transfer of money usually only creates a debt. The money becomes the property of the debtor and he merely agrees to pay a sum of money to the transferor, the creditor.[100] For example, bankers are merely debtors of their clients when their clients' accounts are in credit. There is merely a contractual relationship; the bank does not hold the client's money on trust. Generally, an action for recovery of a debt will be purely a personal action, and, if successful, will result in a monetary award. However, equity has developed what are referred to as *Quistclose* trusts.[101] These are loans which have been advanced for a specific commercial purpose. If the loan is not used for this purpose and the debtor becomes insolvent, then equity has held that a trust exists with the debtor holding the money on trust for the lender. This, of course, gives the lender a proprietary interest in the money and defeats any action by other creditors of the debtor on liquidation.

Therefore contracts differ from trusts in the nature of the relationship between the parties, the remedies available for breach, and the parties that may enforce actions to obtain these remedies.

---

96 See John H. Langbein, 'The Contractarian Basis of the Law of Trusts', (1995-6) 105 *Yale Law Journal* 625-675

97 For example see 'covenants to settle' in the chapter on constitution of trusts.

98 See Lon L. Fuller, 'Consideration and Form' (1941) 41 *Colum. L. Rev.* 799- 824.

99 It has been noted that this rule may be considered "obsolete" today because of the number and extent of the exceptions to the rule: Lawrence Ma & Michael Lower, *Principles of Equity & Trusts Law in Hong Kong* (Hong Kong: LexisNexis, 2009). See the later chapter on trustees for details of the exceptions to this rule.

100 See Lord Millet in *Twinsectra Ltd v Yardley* [2002] 2 All ER 377.

101 From the case of *Barclays Bank v Quistclose Investments Ltd* [1968] 3 All ER 651. *Quistclose* trusts will be considered in chapter 10.

4.5.2 The trust *v.* bailment

Bailment occurs when property is passed to a party, the bailee, for a particular purpose after which the property is returned to the bailor. Again, this may seem similar to a trust but there are important differences. For example, if Stephen's car is damaged in an accident and he delivers his car to Peter, a car mechanic, for repair, Peter may retain the car until Stephen pays for the repair. Peter is the bailee of Stephen's car, he can hold it until he is paid, and he must look after the car whilst it is in his care. Peter is not a trustee of the car because Stephen does not transfer legal ownership to Peter. Peter's lack of legal ownership is a very important difference as the trustee may transfer the property to third parties, who may obtain good title from the trustee (equity's darling). The bailee cannot give a third party good title to Stephen's goods. Peter's only interest in the car may be a lien on the car, which will allow him to prevent Stephen taking the car before he is paid, and to seek a court order for the sale of the car to satisfy the debt. This is not a property interest as such. Another important difference is that bailment only applies to personal property, whereas a trust can be created involving any property.

4.5.3 The trust *v.* agency

Agents are people who have authority to act on behalf of another, their principal. They may enter into contracts on behalf of their principal if so authorised. Agency is based on the law of contract but the agent is a fiduciary of the principal. However, an agency relationship is not a trust relationship. There are important differences, for example agents do not usually have legal title to their principal's property, and thus actions against an agent who has become bankrupt are limited to personal actions, remedied by the award of damages. Also the agent represents his principal in transactions and enters contracts on their behalf, but the trustee does not represent the beneficiaries, although he performs his duties for their benefit, and the trustee does not enter contracts on behalf of the beneficiaries but on behalf of himself as a trustee.

4.5.4 The trust *v.* personal representatives' responsibilities

Personal representatives are those who carry out the administration of the estate of the deceased; they are either executors or administrators. If the deceased has left a will he has died testate and his representatives are the executors of the will appointed by the testator in the will. If the deceased has not left a will he has died intestate and his representatives are the administrators of the deceased, these are those who have applied to the High Court for letters of administration to administer the deceased's estate. There is some confusion over the nature of the role of the personal representative as it may be that of a fiduciary for some of the role but may become that of a trustee.

Personal representatives are subject to fiduciary obligations to the heirs of the deceased (the legatees in the will or those entitled to benefit by the rules of intestacy if there is no will). The personal representatives also hold the property for the benefit of others.

The main difference between personal representatives and trustees is in the rights and interest of the potential beneficiaries of the estate and the beneficiaries of the trust. Potential beneficiaries under an administration of an estate have no rights in the estate property while it is being administered, whereas beneficiaries under a trust have a proprietary interest in the trust property. The beneficiaries under an estate may take action against the personal representatives for breach of their fiduciary duties but they do not have the proprietary action available to the beneficiary under a trust.

The nature of personal representation is further confused because Testators often appoint their executors as trustees of the trusts in their wills. If this occurs the question may arise as to at which point the executor become the trustee, because at this point the beneficiaries have a proprietary interest on the trust property. Usually this is thought to occur when the assets have all been gathered in and the debts of the estate paid. The importance of deciding when the trusteeship arises is to determine when the proprietary interest of the beneficiaries commences.

4.5.5 The trust *v.* powers of appointment

A power of appointment is a further way that equity allows a party to control the distribution of another's property. Powers of appointment are powers given by the legal owner of property to another to decide who shall receive his property. An example would be; I give Cheryl the power to choose whichever of my nephews and nieces shall receive my shares in the Hong Kong and Shanghai Banking Corporation (HSBC). Here the legal owner of the shares has given Cheryl, the donee of the power of appointment, the authority to select from a class of potential appointees, the nephews and nieces, whom shall receive the shares. Cheryl has a bare power of appointment because she is not given legal ownership of the shares. A power is discretionary and so does not have to be exercised. Cheryl does not have to select any of the nephews and nieces to receive the shares. If she does not exercise her power then the property will be dealt with by any other relevant provision, e.g. if Cheryl does not select any of my nephews and nieces to receive the shares they shall be divided equally between them. If there is no alternative provision then the property will remain with the settlor or, if the power is testamentary, the property will remain with the testator's estate to be applied as per any residuary legacy, or if the power is over the residue it should be divided under the rules of intestacy.

Powers often occur alongside trusts and are often given to trustees. For example, I leave all of my shares in HSBC to Cheryl to hold on trust for my children until they are 18 years old. In the meantime Cheryl may apply the income from the shares to support any of my children as she thinks fit. Here Cheryl is a trustee and has a power of appointment. Because she is a trustee under a mandatory trust obligation, she must hold the shares and give them to the children when they are 18. She also has a power of appointment, discretion to distribute the income from the shares, the dividends, to any of the children. She does not have to do this. As a trustee she has fiduciary duties towards the trust property and beneficiaries, therefore she has a fiduciary power of appointment.

The most important difference between trusts and powers of appointment is that trusts are mandatory, they must be carried out, whereas powers are discretionary, and do not have to be exercised.

Powers are usually identified by considering the words used in the provision and its construction. The court will look for discretionary words such as 'may' and 'discretion' to evidence a power and mandatory words such as 'must' and 'shall' to evidence a trust. The main problem is differentiating between fiduciary powers and discretionary trusts as provisions creating both may contain similar words such as "may" and "discretion". Trusts and powers are dealt with in detail in the next chapter.

Thus, there are other concepts that may seem similar to trusts but have important differences. The most important differences are the onerous fiduciary duties and obligations placed by the trust on the trustee, the rights and interests of beneficiaries of a trust, and the remedies available for breach of trust as against the trustee and third parties who may obtain trust property. Because of these important duties, rights, interests and remedies, equity requires a clear certainty of intention by the settlor to create a trust by his actions and not another concept.

4.6 International Recognition of Trusts

To a certain extent the common law trust is and always has been international because no matter where formed, if the jurisdiction in which it is sought to enforce the trust recognises the arrangement as a trust then it will be open to that court to enforce it. If the defendant's (trustee's) conscience is within the court's jurisdiction he may be made to fulfil his obligations, and the defendant's conscience is nearly always within the court's jurisdiction. Of course any common law court today would be careful about ordering enforcement of an agreement involving land in a jurisdiction which did not recognise the trust because of the political fallout of such an order.

As discussed below, most civil jurisdictions have no comparable institution to the trust. However, it is widely used in commerce and succession planning and may involve assets in many jurisdictions. Therefore, with the growth in international trade and consequent international litigation it has been recognised that there needs to be a basis for ensuring jurisdictions recognise and enforce the trust. The previously mentioned Hague Convention on the Law Applicable to Trusts and their Recognition was created to allow trusts to be used in international commerce and finance between jurisdictions which were not always subject to the common law.[102] Any civil law state that signs the Convention must recognise the trust concept, as described in Article 2 in the section dealing with definition of trusts. This does not mean that signatories must accept the trust into their legal system but only that they recognise a trust created in any jurisdiction which corresponds to the detailed definition in article 2. In addition to this international recognition many civil jurisdictions are trying to create their own version of the trust.

4.7 Trusts in Civil Jurisdictions

The value of trusts to commerce and finance is most apparent because of the rush of civil law jurisdictions to create their own versions of the trust. In Asia,[103] many civil law jurisdictions have their own trust law. For example, Japan has used trusts since the early part of the twentieth century. Other jurisdictions including Taiwan,[104] South Korea,[105] and, of course, the People's Republic of China,[106] have introduced their own version of the trust more recently.

These trusts are statutory and their main purpose is commercial. In China the main purposes of these trusts are for asset management, financial planning and charitable activities.[107] Most investment funds in China are now structured as trusts, the main benefit being mandatory separation of the trust fund from the trustee's own funds and priority on

---

102 Common law jurisdictions have also become parties to the Convention e.g. the UK incorporated the Convention by way of the Recognition of Trusts Act 1987.

103 For consideration of other civil jurisdictions which have developed their own trust see for example David Hayton, 'The Development of the Trust Concept in Civil Law Jurisdictions' (2000) (Sep) *Journal of International Trust and Corporate Planning* 159; Maurizio Lupoi, 'The Civil Law Trust' (1999) 32 *Vanderbilt Journal of Transnational Law* 1-24.

104 Trust Law, 1996, amended by the Trust Enterprise Act of Taiwan, 2008.

105 Trust Act, No. 900, 1961.

106 Trust Law, 2001.

107 Rebecca Lee, 'Conceptualizing the Chinese Trust' (2009) *International Comparative Law Quarterly* 58 (July), 665-669.

bankruptcy. China's Trust Law was introduced in 2001 and defines a trust in article 2 as:

'For the purposes of this Law, trust refers to that the settlor, based on his faith in trustee, entrusts his property rights to the trustee and allows the trustee to, according to the will of the settlor and in the name of the trustee, administer or dispose of such property in the interest of a beneficiary or for any intended purpose.'

Other civil trust legislation refers to the trustee managing and disposing of the trust property in the interests of a specified person or object,[108] or administering or disposing of the trust property for the benefit of a beneficiary or specified purpose.[109] These descriptions imply more of a management role than the fiduciary duty of a trustee at common law and this has much to do with the fact that trusts in civil law jurisdictions are being created in completely the opposite way to trusts at common law. The common law trust was created for family protection, between trusted friends, developed by equity according to principles of good faith and conscience. The instruments aping the common law trust being created by legislation in civil law jurisdictions are created purely for commercial reasons, they are creatures of commerce. Thus they are more similar to a mandate or a contract conferring benefits on third parties than the fiduciary instrument of equity. They are often restricted in the way that they can be created, for example, in China the trust must be created by a written contract between the settlor and trustee, or by will.[110] They may also be restricted to the use of professionals in the role of trustees.

Of course one of the most important uses of trust in common law jurisdiction is not available to courts in civil jurisdictions, as they have no implied trusts, such as the constructive trust, to remedy wrongs. However, the construction of trustlike devices in civil law jurisdictions exemplifies the usefulness of the trust for international commerce and finance.

4.8 The Value of Trusts

Many of the major financial and commercial centres in the world are common law jurisdictions. One of the reasons these centres flourish is the

---

108 Trust Act of Korea, 1961, article 2.
109 Trust Law of Taiwan, 1996, article 1.
110 See Lusina Ho, 'China: trust law and practice since 2001' (2010) 16 (3)(April) *Trusts & Trustees*, 124-127; Lusina Ho, 'The Reception of Trust in Asia: Emerging Asian Principles of Trust' (2004) *Singapore Journal of Legal Studies*, 287-304.Lusina Ho, *Trust Law in China* (Sweet & Maxwell Asia, Hong Kong 2003); W. Hutchens, 'The PRC's First Trust Law: Trusts Without Chinese Characteristics' (2001) 15 *China Law & Practice*; Stephen M. Nelson & Daniel L.F. Terry, 'New Trust Law in China' (2001) (September) *Trusts & Trustees* 12-14.

flexibility of the trust and the protection the trust affords beneficiaries on bankruptcy of the trustee or other misappropriation. Other benefits include the ability to create trusts quite informally and even in secret, and, of course, the reasons that trusts probably originated; asset protection and tax benefits.

Trusts may be of social, financial and commercial benefit. Trusts can be used for many socially important purposes, for example many charities are based on trusts and trust principles may allow unincorporated associations to hold property. Trusts may also be used as they were originally intended; to manage the family estate and protect dependants, and to hold property for incompetent persons. A special type of family trust is the protective trust. This is a type of trust by which property is transferred to trustees in order to prevent a beneficiary from squandering the trust property or losing it to his creditors. The protective trust works by giving the principal beneficiary a life interest which determines upon the happening of any event which would lead to him not being entitled to the income (e.g. bankruptcy). If the life interest determines the interest in remainder is accelerated and the remaindermen become entitled. For example, Simon's will contains the following provision: 'I leave my flat in London to my eldest son Larry on protective trust for life and then to my grandson Richard. If Larry shall be declared bankrupt then Larry will lose his life interest and the property shall immediately vest in Richard.' In this scenario Larry is the life tenant of the property and Richard is the remainderman, Richard will only receive the property when Larry dies. However, if Larry is declared bankrupt then he loses his life interest and Richard is accelerated into his interest.[111]

Trusts can be used to minimise liability to taxation as may any legal means, as 'No one may act in contravention of the law. But no one is bound to leave his property at the mercy of the revenue authorities if he can legally escape their grasp.'[112] However, although the avoidance of tax may be lawful, 'it is not yet a virtue',[113] and there is an important difference between tax avoidance, the rearrangement of one's affairs so as to minimise the liability to tax, which is legal, and tax evasion, non-payment of tax that one is under a legal obligation to pay, which is illegal. Trusts are important financial vehicles to avoid taxation. Other financial uses of trusts involve investment in unit trusts and pension funds.

---

111 For an example of a protective trust involving the English aristocracy see *Hambro v. Duke of Marlborough* [1994] Ch 158.
112 *Commissioner of Stamp Duties v Byrnes* [1911] AC 386, at p. 392 per Lord Macnaghten discussing the presumption of advancement.
113 *Re Weston's Settlements* [1969] 1 CH 223, 245.

In modern commerce the value of trusts is exemplified by their longevity, a testament to their flexibility, adaptability and versatility. Trusts are used to promote commercial arrangements, protect lenders, protect customers and provide an incentive to the workforce. These trusts often benefit from management by professional trustees. New trusts, such as the *Quistclose* trust, and more inventive ways of using the constructive trust by the courts have ensured the trust an important place in modern commerce and finance. In fact, rather than being an instrument for family protection or succession, it has been estimated that 90 % of wealth held in trust in America was there incident to business.[114] However, there are problems using trusts in modern commerce. As Lord Browne-Wilkinson has noted:[115]

'In the modern world the trust has become a valuable device in commercial and financial dealings. The fundamental principles of equity apply as much to such trusts as they do to the traditional trusts in relation to which those principles were originally formulated. But...it is important, if the trust is not to be rendered commercially useless to distinguish between the basic principles of trust law and those specialist rules developed in relation to traditional trusts which are applicable only to such trusts and the rationale of which has no application to trusts of quite a different kind.'

Thus it must be remembered that trusts were developed for familial or quasi-familial purposes, rather than commercial purposes, and the principles of equity may not always suit commercial needs. For example, it has already been noted in preceding chapters that commercial lawyers have criticised the discretionary nature of equity and the uncertain concept of conscience. Problems associated with the use of the trust for commerce are linked to its benefits. The trust can be created without formality and so there is no record of its creation, thus it is ideal for those who wish to hide the existence of a commercial relationship, for example tax evaders, money launderers and even terrorists. Also the trust is under no obligation to prepare accounts as the registered company is. Thus it is ideal for illegal or improper purposes generally. However, the fiduciary nature of the trust and the proprietary protection afforded beneficiaries will ensure its continued use in commerce and finance, as the proprietary nature of the trust and equitable tracing practices can be used to recover assets or their substitutions that wrongdoers have tried to hide with trusts.

New developments in the commercial and financial use of trusts include non-charitable purpose trusts which have been developed in some jurisdictions, mostly associated with tax avoidance.[116] They do not require

---

114 John H. Langbein, 'The Secret Life of the Trust: The Trust as an Instrument of Commerce' (1997-1998) 107 *Yale Law Journal* 166-189.

115 *Target Holdings v Redfern* [1996] AC421.

116 For example, the STAR (Special Trusts Alternative Regime) trusts of the Cayman Islands.

identification of human beneficiaries and so can confuse issues of beneficial ownership thus avoiding or delaying taxation. These trusts are statutory and cannot be created in common law jurisdictions that do not have the relevant enabling legislation as they offend the beneficiary principle. [117] However, jurisdictions which are parties to the Hague Convention on the Law Applicable to Trusts and their Recognition, 1985, may have to recognise them.

The trust is continuously developing to facilitate modern commerce and finance and will always be useful. The attempts by civil law jurisdictions to create their own versions of the commercial trust and the international moves to recognise the common law trust are further evidence of the long term value of trusts.

4.9 Summary

It is very difficult to give a short all encompassing definition of the trust because there are so many different types of trust which are used in very different circumstances and have developed for different purposes. Perhaps the nearest that can be attempted to a short definition of trusts is to say that they are instruments of equity which separate the legal and beneficial interests in property. Thus the separate legal and beneficial interests in property only arise on the creation of a trust. Trusts share some common characteristics, for example once constituted they are mandatory, they must be carried, they are fiduciary, the trustees owe fiduciary duties to the trust and the beneficiaries, they are non-revocable, thus once constituted the settlor cannot usually revoke the trust and call for his property to be returned, and, probably the most important characteristic, the trust separates the legal and equitable interest in property creating the beneficial interest of the beneficiaries. This last characteristic, the beneficial interest, is the most important aspect of the development of the trust as it is enforceable against all except equity's darling. Thus it may defeat claims of the creditors of a bankrupt trustee and may be used to recover property that has been transferred to a third party in breach of trust. The future of trusts is very positive with increased use of trusts for commercial and financial transactions and international recognition being promoted. The next chapters will deal with the creation of the express private trust, still by far the most popular and numerous of trusts.

---

117   see Matthews, 'Shooting STAR' (1997) 11 *TLI* 67; Duckworth, 'STAR WARS: The colony strikes back' (1998) 12 *TLI* 16; Matthews, 'STAR: Big Bang or Red Dwarf?' (1998) 12 *TLI* 98; Duckworth, 'STAR WARS: Smiting the bull' (1999) 13 *TLI* 158.

CHAPTER 5

CREATING AN EXPRESS TRUST

5.1 How is an Express Trust Created?

A valid express trust is created when a settlor makes a valid declaration of trust and the trust property is transferred to the trustee. The transfer of legal title to the trust property to the trustee is referred to as the constitution of the trust. The trustee must have legal title to the trust property for a trust to come into being. Different types of property require different methods of transfer, for example land must be conveyed to the trustee, and shares must be transferred according to the restrictions placed on share transfer. Generally personal property is transferred by delivering the property to the trustee, for example a trust of £1,000 could be constituted by delivery of bank notes to the value of £1,000 to the trustee.[1]

Declaration and constitution of the trust may occur at the same time or at different times. Thus a settlor may hand over £1,000 to a friend whilst at the same time telling that friend that they are to hold the property on trust. The settlor may also tell his friend that he will be giving him £1,000 in the future and that when he receives it the friend is to hold it on trust. The trust is only constituted and so valid when the property is transferred to the friend/trustee. A settlor may also transfer property to a friend and subsequently inform the friend that the property is to be held on trust; however, this method of formation of a trust may cause evidential problems as the friend may have believed the initial transfer was a gift. Thus the transferee must know he is not receiving the property as a gift. If there is evidence that the property has been transferred as a gift then any subsequent attempt to declare a trust over the property by the transferor will fail as the gift to the transferee takes effect; the common law does not acknowledge a gift for a limited time, a gift is a gift.[2] A settlor may also declare himself trustee of his own property, in which case he does not have to transfer the property as he already has legal title. For example "I now hold this £1,000 on trust for Sarah."

---

1   Methods of transferring property to constitute a trust and perfect a gift will be considered in the subsequent chapter on constitution of trusts.
2   If there is no evidence of the intention of a transferor of property then equity presumes that they would wish their property returned to them at some point and so presumes a resulting trust- the transferee holds the property on trust for the transferor. See chapter on resulting trusts.

Until the trust is constituted the settlor can change his mind and decide not to create the trust.[3]

The declaration of trust can also be in a will and the constitution of the trust occurs when the executors transfer the property to the trustee as they administer the will; "I am leaving Michael my copy of Maitland's *Equity*, Michael will hold it on trust for my nephew until he is a qualified lawyer." When the executors of my estate pass the copy of the book to Michael then the trust is constituted and Michael will hold the book on trust for my nephew to receive when he is a qualified lawyer. Later chapters will explain what happens if Michael refuses to take the book or my nephew does not become a lawyer.

The process of creating a trust thus seems quite straightforward: to create an express trust there must be:

- A valid declaration of trust; and,
- Valid constitution of the trust.

However, because the trust obligation is such an onerous or heavy burden for the trustee, and the rights of a beneficiary of a trust are so powerful, equity requires that for a trust to be recognised and enforceable the declaration of trust must contain certain elements, and the constitution of the trust must be complete. Thus a more detailed explanation of what equity requires for a valid express declaration of trust would be:

- a valid express trust is created when a **capable settlor** makes a **declaration of trust**, complying with required **formalities** and the **law**, imposing a **certain trust obligation** on a **capable trustee** to hold legal title to **certain property** for the benefit of **certain beneficiaries**, **constituted by the transfer of legal title** of the certain property to the trustee.

Thus the elements of a valid express trust are:

- **Declaration:** a declaration of trust;
- **Formalities**: complying with required formalities (if any);
- **Capacity**: by a capable settlor imposing the obligation on a capable trustee;
- **Certainty of intention**: imposing a certain trust obligation;
- **Certainty of subject**: concerning certain property;

---

3   This is because generally the beneficiary and trustee are volunteers, they have not provided valuable consideration for the creation of the trust, and, as equity will not assist a volunteer, they cannot enforce the trust until it is constituted. If consideration has been given, so there is a contract to create the trust then it may be possible to force the settlor to create the trust. These issues are considered in the chapter on constitution.

- **Certainty of object and beneficiary principle**: in favour of certain human beneficiaries
- **Legality**: complying with the law and not being against public policy;
- **Constitution**: constituted by the transfer of legal title to the trustee.

5.2 Declaration of Trust and Formalities

An express trust may be created with very little formality. A trust may be created by spoken words or in writing. A written declaration of trust is referred to as the trust instrument. Trust instruments may be *intervivos*, written by a settlor to give effect to a trust between the living, or testamentary, written in a will to create a trust after the testator's death. Trust instruments may thus be in simple written form, on a scrap of paper, or in a more formal form such as a deed, when they are usually referred to as 'deed trusts' (DT).[4] Trusts may also be declared in a settlement of property, a 'settlement trust' (ST) or in a will, a 'will trust' (WT).

In rare circumstances a trust may be implied from the actions of the settlor. For example in *Re Kayford Ltd*,[5] the court implied a trust from the actions of the insolvent company. The company had created a separate account for its customer pre-payments which it called the "customers' trust deposit account" and only transferred money from this account to its main account when it had sent the goods. The court held that the segregation of the money in a customer account with this title implied a declaration of trust evidencing an intention to place itself under a trust obligation.

The declaration of trust must evidence the three certainties:

1. **certainty of intention** that the settlor intended the recipient of the property to receive the property under a trust obligation and nothing else;
2. **certainty of subject matter**: the declaration must identify the property to be subject to the trust obligation;
3. **certainty of object**: the declaration must identify, or provide the means to identify the beneficiaries of the trust.

There are also negative requirements for the declaration as it must not evidence any illegal purpose or purpose contrary to public policy, e.g. a trust that is to encourage crime or that will continue forever.

---

4   A deed is a document that states it is a deed and must be signed by all parties, witnessed and delivered. The Law of Property (Miscellaneous Provisions) Act 1989, s1, requires that a deed must be signed, delivered and witnessed by at least one person. Any conveyance of land must comply with the Law of Property Act 1925, s.52, which requires a conveyance of land to be by deed.

5   [1975] 1 WLR 279.

The declaration of trust may also have to comply with formalities to be valid. Formalities are requirements as to the method or manner of an action which must be complied with for the action to be valid and enforceable. Thus formalities of declaration are the specified requirements that must be complied with to make the declaration recognised as effective. The constitution of a trust may also be subject to formality requirements depending on the type of property forming the subject matter of the trust.[6]

At common law no formalities are required for the valid declaration of a trust. Formalities are only required by statute and usually involve, that most precious of commodities, land.[7] Formalities are required for declarations of trusts of land because land is so important to society. Formalities are also required because it is so easy to create a trust society considers it necessary to focus the settlor's mind on the consequence of his actions.[8] Formalities also provide evidence that a trust has been declared if there is a subsequent dispute. [9]

For *intervivos* declarations of trust formalities are only required for declarations of trusts of land or equitable interests in land. Formalities are not required for *intervivos* declarations of trust of personal property. All testamentary trusts, of any property, are subject to the formalities required for the creation of a valid will.

Formalities for the declaration of trusts thus apply to:[10]

---

6 For example legal title in land must be conveyed by deed: s. 52 Law of Property Act 1925. Formalities for constituting a trust will be dealt with in the chapter on constitution.

7 Formalities were only introduced for declarations of trusts of land in the Statute of Frauds 1677, 'which distinguished sharply between express and constructive trusts': Paul Mathews, 'The Words Which Are Not There: A Partial History of the Constructive Trust', in Charles Mitchell (end), *Constructive and Resulting Trusts* (Hart Publishing, 2009), 8. Land is defined in s.205(1) LPA 1925: 'Land' includes land of any tenure, and mines and minerals, whether or not held apart from the surface, buildings or parts of buildings (whether the division is horizontal, vertical or made in any other way) and other corporeal hereditaments; also a manor, an advowson, and a rent and other incorporeal hereditaments, and an easement, right, privilege, or benefit in, over, or derived from land'.

8 Fuller considers formalities a cautionary factor making sure people do not rush into legal relationships without thinking of the consequences: Lon L. Fuller, "Consideration and Form (1941) 41 *Columbia Law Review* 799.

9 Austin noted that formalities perform many functions at law but the most important are as evidence that the relationship exists: Austin, "Fragments- On Contracts", in 2 *Lectures on Jurisprudence* (4th edition, 1879), 939-944.

10 Further important formalities requirements are also contained in the Law of Property Act 1925, s.52,which requires a conveyance of land to be by deed, and the Law of Property (Miscellaneous Provisions) Act 1989, s1, which requires that a deed must be signed, delivered and witnessed by at least one person.

- Declarations of trusts of land: section 53(1)(b) LPA 1925;
- Dispositions of the equitable interest in a trust: section 53(1)(c) LPA 1925;
- A testamentary declaration of trust: section 9 of the Wills Act 1837;

5.2.1 Formalities for the declaration of an *intervivos* trust of land

To declare a valid trust of land the declaration must comply with section 53(1)(b) of the Law of Property Act 1925: "a declaration of trust respecting land or any interest therein **must be manifested and proved** by some writing signed by some person who is able to declare such a trust or by his will." (Emphasis added).

Thus the formality requirement:

- Applies only to a declaration of a trust of land;
- Does not have to be declared in writing but "must be manifested and proved" in writing. Thus later writing could satisfy this.
- Requires that the settlor must sign the proving document himself. An agent cannot.

The formality requirement will apply to any declaration of a trust or sub-trust of land. A trust may involve the legal owner transferring legal ownership to the trustee subject to the trust obligation to hold the property on trust for the beneficiary. It can also involve the legal owner declaring himself trustee of his own property, which he then holds subject to the trust obligation for the benefit of the beneficiary. In both cases if the property is land then s.53(1)(b) LPA 1925 applies.

S → **T**   Settlor transfers property to trustee to hold for
    B   beneficiary.

S → **T(S)**   Settlor declares himself trustee and then holds his
    B   property for the beneficiary.

A declaration of sub-trust involves the beneficiary of a trust of declaring a trust of his beneficial interest in favour of another. The first beneficial owner now holds the equitable interest on trust for the new beneficiary. Thus there is already a trust and the beneficiary (B1) now declares he holds his beneficial interest on trust for someone else (B2).

T   T
B1   →   B1
           B2

The trustee of the original trust is still the same but the beneficiary of this original trust (B1) is now trustee of his beneficial interest for the benefit of B2. Again, if the property is land then s.53(1)(b) LPA 1925 applies. To be enforceable the declaration of sub-trust must be manifested and proved in writing. It is important to distinguish the declaration of a sub-trust from a disposition of the equitable interest. The disposition of an equitable interest is the disposal, usually by sale or gift, of the beneficiary's beneficial interest in a trust; this is considered below as it may be subject to different, more stringent formality requirements.

If a declaration of a trust or sub-trust of land is made without complying with the formalities in s.53(1)(b), i.e. it is not evidenced in writing, the trust is valid but unenforceable.[11] Thus, if the trustee carries out his obligations he will be fulfilling a valid trust and no one may challenge his actions,[12] but if he does not the beneficiary cannot enforce the trust. However, the formality requirements do not apply to resulting, implied or constructive trusts because of s.53(2) LPA, which provides: 'This section does not affect the creation or operation of resulting, implied or constructive trusts'. Thus a court may recognise an implied trust even though it does not comply with the formalities required in the preceding provisions.[13]

The problem with formalities is that not everyone is aware of them and so insisting on formalities may cause injustice, as a settlor may have transferred land to a trustee making an oral declaration of trust which is unenforceable. The common law regards the transfer of legal title as transfer of ownership, thus the trustee is looked on as the legal owner. If the beneficiary cannot enforce the trust against the trustee because of the lack of formality in the declaration then the trustee will enjoy the property without the trust obligations. Of course, equity has always had more regard to the intentions of the parties than formality, *equity looks to the intent rather than the form,* and this was one of the reasons for the emergence of equity and the divergence of equity from the common law's insistence on formality. A maxim or method of statutory interpretation was thus developed by equity to deal with such situations; equity *will not permit a statute to be used as an instrument of fraud.*[14] Thus if a defendant seeks to rely (or hide behind) on formality requirements in a statute to perpetuate a fraud, equity will not permit the fraud to be achieved by the use of the statutory provision.

---

11   *Gardner v Rowe* (1828) 5 Russ 258.
12   This may seem of little value, but, as we shall see in the chapter on trustees, it is very important that a trustee has the power to carry out an action as he may attract personal liability if he carries out an action which is not valid.
13   See *Hodgson v Marks* [1971] 1 Ch 933, discussed subsequently.
14   Sometimes phrased as equity will not be used as an engine of fraud: *Wong Wing Tao v Wong Wai Keung* [2003] HKCU 244 at 11.

Rochefoucauld v Boustead [15]

The *Comtesse de la Rochefoucauld* owned the Delmar Estates, which were large coffee plantations in Ceylon, subject to mortgage. She agreed that Boustead would purchase the plantations from the mortgagee and that he would hold the plantations on trust for her. Boustead did purchase the plantations, but rather than act as trustee he treated them as his own. He mortgaged them and was eventually declared bankrupt. The *Comtesse* had not paid particular attention to the plantations or the trust, but was now sufficiently aware to seek recognition of the trust so that the plantations would not be used to settle Boustead's obligations in bankruptcy. However, the declaration of trust was oral only and did not comply with section 7 of the Statute of Frauds, the predecessor to s.53 (1)(b) Law of Property Act, which required that any trust of land must be evidenced in writing. There was no written evidence of the trust and so Boustead argued that the trust was unenforceable.

Judgment: the court held that the Statute of Frauds was intended to prevent fraud when trusts of land were created. To allow the defendant to use a statute that had been intended to prevent fraud to perpetuate a fraud was unconscionable. Applying the maxim *equity will not permit a statute to be used as an instrument of fraud* the court allowed oral evidence to be admitted to prove the existence of the trust. The plantations were held by Boustead on trust for the *Comtesse* and did not form part of his property on bankruptcy.

Lindley L.J. said:[16]

"It is further established by a series of cases, the propriety of which cannot now be questioned, that the Statute of Frauds does not prevent the proof of a fraud; and that it is a fraud on the part of a person to whom land is conveyed as a trustee, and who knows that it was so conveyed to deny the trust and claim the land himself. Consequently, notwithstanding the statute, it is competent for a person claiming the land conveyed to another to prove by parol evidence that it was so conveyed upon trust for the claimant, and that the grantee, knowing the facts, is denying the trust and relying upon the form of conveyance and the statute, in order to keep the land himself."

The court clearly enforced the express trust which had been declared informally by the *Comtesse* thus ignoring the statutory provision. This was undoubtedly just, as the rogue Boustead should not have been allowed to profit from his fraud however foolish the *Comtesse's* actions, but this does not sit comfortably with the constitutional principle of parliamentary sovereignty in Britain. The common law has generally developed in the

---

15   [1897] 1 Ch 196 (subnom **De La Rochefoucauld v Boustead**).
16   [1897] 1 Ch 196 at 206.

eighteenth and nineteenth centuries to accept that courts must follow statute above the common law. Thus there are constitutional problems whenever a court 'ignores' a statute and this is in effect what the court was doing when it gave justice to the *Comtesse*.[17] This problem was faced again when similar circumstances arose in the case of **Hodgson v Marks**.[18]

Hodgson v Marks[19]

Mrs Hodgson, an 83 years-old lady, had taken E as a lodger. Eventually she looked on E as a 'man of substance'; she trusted him and allowed him to manage her business affairs. She had a nephew who was to inherit her house but the nephew did not like E. Mrs Hodgson and E were concerned that the nephew would eject E from the house. Therefore Mrs Hodgson agreed to transfer the legal interest in the property to E and E agreed to look after the house for her benefit. The house was to be held on trust for Mrs Hodgson by the lodger E but there was no evidence of this in writing. Sometime after the house was conveyed to E he sold the house to Mr Marks. Marks had seen Mrs Hodgson when he visited the house and knew that a woman lived in one bedroom. Marks mortgaged the house and the mortgagee registered a charge against the property. After almost a year Mrs Hodgson eventually discovered that the house had been sold and mortgaged. She sought an order from the court that E had held the house on trust for her and that her interests overrode the sale of the house and the subsequent charge. The purchaser and mortgage company argued that if there were a trust it did not comply with s53(1)(b) LPA 1925 and thus was unenforceable.

Judgment: the Court of Appeal held that there was a trust and that Mrs Hodgson's interests overrode the purchaser's and the mortgagee's. Although the Court approved the decision in **Rochefoucauld v Boustead**, the reasoning of the present decision was quite different. In **Rochefoucauld v Boustead** the court had stated, 'the trust which the plaintiff has established is clearly an express trust…' In *Hodgson* the Court said that the

---

17 See R P Meagher, J D Heydon and M J Leeming, *Meagher, Gummow and Lehane's Equity Doctrines & Remedies* (LexisNexis Butterworths, 4th ed, 2002) [12–130], where the authors conclude that the doctrine in *Rochefoucauld v Boustead* involves 'a blunt refusal to follow legislation which in its terms applies to the facts at hand; this is no less than the exercise by equity of a suspending or dispensing power denied the executive branch of government since the Bill of Rights 1689'. For argument against a resulting trust being available in this context see William Swadling, 'A Hard Look at *Hodgson v Marks*' in Peter Birks and Francis Rose (eds), *Restitution and Equity Volume One: Resulting Trusts and Equitable Compensation* (Mansfield Press, 2000).

18 [1971] 1 Ch 892 (CA).

19 [1971] 1 Ch 892 (CA).

trust was a resulting trust, as the transfer of legal title had been gratuitous and it should always be presumed that Mrs Hodgson had intended that the equitable interest remain with her. As this was a resulting trust, s53(2) LPA1925 expressly provided that resulting, implied and constructive trusts need not comply with the formality requirements in s53(1). Thus the Court avoided the unfortunate constitutional implications of ignoring a statute.

Confusingly, an earlier decision, that of *Bannister v Bannister*,[20] had dealt with a similar problem by declaring that there was a constructive trust.

Bannister v Bannister[21]

When the defendant's husband died she inherited two cottages from him, one of which they had lived in. The deceased husband's brother, the plaintiff, negotiated with her to sell him the two cottages. The cottages were worth about £400 but the defendant sold them to her brother-in law for £250 because he agreed to let her stay rent free in one of the cottages for life. When the sale was complete, the plaintiff sought possession of both cottages. The defendant claimed there was a trust but there was no writing evidencing this.

Judgment: although there was no question of fraud, the brother-in-law had not intended to take possession but had fallen out with his sister-in-law after the purchase, the court held that the plaintiff's conscience was affected by his promise and so he held the cottage on constructive trust for the defendant for her life. Again this neatly sidestepped the statutory requirements because of s.53(2) LPA 1925.

Thus courts will not allow the formalities required by statute to prevent fraud to be used for the purposes of fraud. However, although the decision in *Rochefoucauld* is still good law it seems more likely that a court would consider either a resulting or constructive trust interpretation and s.53(2) LPA 1925 as preferable to just ignoring s.53(1)(b) LPA 1925.

5.2.2 Formalities for the disposal of an equitable interest

Formality is also required if the beneficial interest of a beneficiary is disposed of. As mentioned above the commonest dispositions are the sale or gift of the beneficial interest. This should be distinguished from the declaration of a sub-trust of a beneficial interest as described above. Thus, if a trust has been created the beneficiary may sell or gift his beneficial interest.

$$\underline{T} \quad \longrightarrow \quad \underline{T}$$
$$B1 \qquad\qquad B2$$

20   [1948] 2 All ER 133.
21   [1948] 2 All ER 133.

In this example the beneficiary of the original trust (B1) may sell or give his beneficial interest in the trust to another (B2). The trustee remains the same, all that changes is the identity of the beneficiary on whose behalf the trustee holds the property, the original beneficiary should instruct the trustee that he now holds the property on behalf of B2. Sale may happen because a beneficiary's interest will not realise for some time and he wishes to sell his interest and so receive funds now. Gifts of beneficial interest often happen because parents are beneficiaries of family trusts and wish to give the interest to their children or grandchildren.

In England and Wales any disposition of an equitable interest in any trust must comply with s.53(1)(c) LPA 1925: "a disposition of an equitable interest or trust subsisting at the time of the disposition, **must be in writing** signed by the person disposing of the same, or by his agent thereto lawfully authorised in writing or by will." (Emphasis added).

Thus the formality requirement:

- applies to the disposition of any equitable interest no matter what the subject matter;
- provides that the disposition must be in writing. Later writing cannot effect the transfer retrospectively;
- can be signed by the owner or by an authorised agent (with written authority).

If there is a failure to comply with the formality requirement the disposition is void, it has not happened.[22]

The reasoning behind s.53(1)(c) LPA 1925 is to allow the trustee, the court and the tax authorities to easily trace who is the beneficial owner of the trust property. If dispositions of equitable interests could be made informally it would be very difficult to establish the identity of the beneficial owner and consequently who the trustee held the trust property for, whose rights the court could enforce, and who the taxman could tax.

A beneficiary may refuse to accept his beneficial interest in a trust; this is known as disclaiming his interest. If a beneficiary disclaims his interest before he has accepted it then this will not be a disposition of the interest;[23] however if he accepts the interest and then attempts to disclaim it this will be a disposition.

The tax authorities have been most concerned about dispositions of the equitable interest in trusts, as transfers of ownership of certain property may attract taxation by stamp duty. Of particular importance here are shares, and most of the cases involve attempts to avoid stamp duty on transfer of the beneficial interest in shares. Stamp duty is charged on

---

22   S.53(1)(C) LPA 1925 is based upon s.9 of the Statute of Frauds 1677 s9, which stated that unwritten dispositions "shall be utterly void and of no effect."
23   *Re Paradise Motor Co. Ltd.* [1968] 1 WLR 1125.

written instruments in certain cases, therefore the writing requirements of s.53(1)(c) may attract taxation. These cases are useful for considering what constitutes a disposition for the purposes of s.53(1)(C) LPA 1925, and normally involve complicated financial transactions, as they are undertaken by wealthy people with expert financial advice, intended to confuse the tax authorities.

GREY v. IRC[24]

Grey was a nominee of 18,000 shares, he held legal title to the shares on behalf of Mr Hunter. Hunter wished to transfer his beneficial interest to his six grandchildren; however if he complied with s.53(1)(c) LPA 1925 and did this in writing then the written instrument would be liable to *ad valorem* stamp duty. Therefore Hunter orally directed Grey to divide the beneficial interest into six parts of 3,000 shares each and hold these on separate trusts for his six grandchildren. Deeds of transfer were only completed subsequent to the oral direction by Grey and the other nominees. H claimed that the oral direction had transferred the equitable interest and so the transfer did not attract stamp duty. The Inland Revenue claimed that the oral declaration was not effective as it did not comply with s53(1)(c). Therefore the disposition took effect only when the deeds were executed and these were liable to stamp duty.

Judgment: as the oral direction did not comply with s.53(1)(c) LPA 1925 it was void. The transfer only occurred when the deeds were executed and so these were liable to stamp duty.

Grey seems quite straightforward, an oral direction to transfer the beneficial interests will be void because it does not comply with s.53(1)(C) and so does not take effect, but a deed executed to transfer the beneficial interests will satisfy s.53(1)(c) and be effective. More complicated is the case where parties attempt to take advantage of s.53(2) by claiming a resulting, implied or constructive trust.

Oughtred v IRC[25]

This was another attempt to avoid stamp duty. Mrs Oughtred held 72,000 shares in a private company absolutely. There was also a trust in which trustees held 200,000 shares in the company for Mrs Oughtred for life, with remainder to her son, Peter. Mrs Oughtred and her son entered into an oral contract by which Peter would forfeit his remainder interest in the 200,000 shares so that Mrs Oughtred would be absolutely entitled to them. In return Mrs Oughtred would transfer her 72,000 shares to the trustees to hold on bare trust for Peter. Thus Mrs Oughtred would have 200,000 shares

---

24 [1960] AC 1 (HL).
25 [1960] AC 206, [1959] 3 All ER 623 (HL).

absolutely and Peter would have 72,000 shares absolutely, the arrangement was beneficial for both. The problem was that *ad valorem* stamp duty was payable on "transfer on sale" of shares.[26]

Subsequently a deed releasing Peter's life interest in the 200,000 shares and transferring legal title to the 200,000 shares to Mrs Oughtred was executed. The Inland Revenue argued that the oral contract could not transfer the beneficial interest in the shares because of s.53(1)(c) LPA 1925. Any transfer of the beneficial interest by this oral contract was void, thus the deed transferred the beneficial interest and attracted stamp duty. Mrs Oughtred argued that as the oral contract was for the transfer of shares in a private company, shares which are not available on the open market, it was specifically enforceable. With a specifically enforceable contract the transferor holds the beneficial interest in the property on constructive trust for the transferee. If the interest was held on constructive trust then s.53(2) LPA 1925 provides that the preceding formality requirements do not apply and the transfer did not have to be in writing. Thus there was no document to attract stamp duty. The later deed merely transferred bare legal title and so had little value for stamp duty.

Judgment: the House of Lords held, by a majority of three against two,[27] that the oral contract was void because it did not comply with the formality requirements. Thus the purchaser of the shares would only get the beneficial interest when the formal transfer took place and so stamp duty was payable on the full value of the transfer.

The argument in favour of the constructive trust was quite strong and was later applied in *Neville v Wilson*,[28] discussed subsequently, although the circumstances of that case differ from those of *Oughtred*.

The situation is also complicated if the beneficial interest is in a bare trust, this is a trust where the trustees are merely nominees for the beneficiary and have few trust duties apart from holding the property for the beneficiary. In effect the beneficiary may have control over the legal as well as beneficial interest.

Vandervell v IRC[29]

Vandervell wanted to donate £150,000 to the Royal College of Surgeons (RCS) to endow a professorship in pharmacology. His bank held 100,000

---

26 Stamp duty was payable on a transfer on sale of property: Stamp Act 1891 (c 39) s 54.

27 Lord Radcliffe giving a particularly persuasive dissenting judgment, arguing that the beneficial interest in shares in a private company passed if there was a specifically enforceable contract. This was followed by the Court of Appeal *Neville v. Wilson* [1997] Ch 144.

28 [1997] Ch 144.

29 [1967] 2 AC 291, [1967] 1 All ER 1, (HL).

shares in his company for him on bare trust as nominees. Vandervell decided to pay the money to the RCS in dividends and also avoid tax. Vandervell orally directed his bank (trustees) to transfer to the RCS both the legal estate (held by the bank) and the beneficial interest in the shares (held by Vandervell). The proposal was that subsequently a dividend of £150,000 would be declared on the shares, and no tax would be payable as the RCS is a charity. To ensure that the RCS would return the shares an option to re-purchase the shares once the dividend had been granted was included in the agreement in favour of Vandervell Trustees Ltd (VTL). VTL was intended to hold the shares on trust for beneficiaries to be nominated by Vandervell in the future- but he did not nominate beneficiaries at this time. Vandervell hoped to divest himself of any beneficial interest in the shares and therefore avoid surtax on the dividends. The Inland Revenue claimed that Vandervell was liable to pay the tax as the oral direction to transfer legal and equitable title to the shares was a disposition for the purposes of s.53(1)(c) LPA 1925 and so void. Thus Vandervell still held the beneficial interest in the shares and was liable to the surtax on the dividend.

Judgment: the House of Lords held that, as V was the solely entitled beneficial owner under a bare trust, he was entitled to direct the trustees to divest both the legal and equitable interest in the shares. When this was done the equitable interest was extinguished and so s.53(1)(c) did not apply. However, the option to buy back the shares was held by VTL and, as no beneficiary had been elected for this interest, the beneficial interest in the shares remained with Vandervell by way of resulting trust. Thus Vandervell still had an interest in the shares and was liable to surtax. As noted by Lord Wilberforce:

"The conclusion on the facts found, is simply that the option was vested in the trustee company as a trustee on trusts, not defined at the time, possibly to be defined later. But the equitable, or beneficial interest, cannot remain in the air: the consequence in law must be that it remains in the settlor."

Mr Vandervell's interests were subject to oral disposition but the resulting trust of the option meant that he had not completely divested himself of all interest in the shares. He tried to exercise the option in favour of his children to get rid of any interest but this again resulted in litigation.

Re Vandervell's Trusts (No 2)[30]

Vandervell was still trying to divest himself of his beneficial interest in the shares. In 1961 Vandervell ordered the trustees of Vandervell Trustees Limited (VTL) to exercise the option on the shares and buy them back from

---

30   Subnom *White v Vandervell Trustees Ltd* [1974] Ch 269, [1974] 3 All ER 205 (EWCA).

the Royal College of Surgeons using money held on trust for Vandervell's children. This should have ensured that the beneficial interest in the shares would be held by the children and the legal title held by VTL. Therefore Vandervell could have no interest in the shares. VTL's solicitors wrote to the Inland Revenue informing them that the shares were held beneficially for the children's trusts. Between 1962 and 1964 the company paid dividends on the shares which Vandervell allowed to be added to the children's settlements. The Revenue still claimed that Vandervell had not divested himself of the interest on the shares and so in 1965 Vandervell executed a deed transferring any interest he may have had in the shares to the children's trusts. Vandervell died in 1967 and his executors took action against VTL to recover the dividends paid between 1962 and 1964 as part of his estate.

Judgment: the executors failed in their action as the transfer to the children's trust had occurred when Vandervell directed the trustees to exercise the option as this was under his direction and used the children's funds. The resulting trust of the option in his favour had come to an end at this point. Lord Denning MR noted:

"A resulting trust for the settlor is born and dies without any writing at all. It comes into existence whenever there is a gap in the beneficial ownership. It ceases to exist whenever that gap is filled by someone becoming beneficially entitled. As soon as the gap is filled by the creation or declaration of a valid trust, the resulting trust comes to an end."

s.53(1)(c) LPA did not apply as this was a new declaration of trust and involved shares not land, therefore it was also not covered by s.53(1(b) LPA.

More recently the Court of Appeal has had to consider the issue of specifically enforceable contracts and constructive trusts as regards s.53(1)(c).

Neville v Wilson[31]

Trustees (nominees) held shares in U Ltd on trust for N Ltd (beneficiary). N Ltd was liquidated. The shareholders of N Ltd orally agreed to distribute the beneficial interests in the shares in U Ltd, which N Ltd owned beneficially, amongst each other. The court had to decide whether s.53(1)(c) invalidated the oral agreement to distribute the beneficial interest in the shares in U Ltd. If it did invalidate the agreement, the shares would have no beneficial owner, and would thus pass to the Crown on the principle of *bona vacantia*.

Judgement: the oral agreement gave rise to a constructive trust in favour of the shareholders of N Ltd. Therefore s.53(1)(c) did not apply because of

---

31 [1997] Ch 144, [1996] 3 All ER 171 (EWCA).

s.53(2). Therefore the disposition of the equitable interest did not have to be in writing and the agreement was valid. This follows the argument put forward on behalf of Mrs Oughtred, in **Oughtred v IRC**,[32] that her oral agreement with her son to exchange interests in shares in a private company was specifically enforceable and thus gave rise to a constructive trust. This had been the dissenting judgment of Lord Radcliffe in *Oughtred*. Of course the circumstances of Oughtred are very different to Neville, as in the former the court was asked to decide whether Mrs Oughtred and her son had avoided taxation, whereas in the latter the court had to decide between the shareholders receiving the benefit or it going *bona vacantia* to the state.

Whatever the outcome of a case however, the legal principles should be consistent.

These decisions have been much criticised by academics as showing little coherent reasoning about the nature of a disposition. This may because they are tax cases and there is a tendency for the courts to interpret legislation in favour of the tax authorities on the principle that the legislature would not intend its legislation to be used to avoid taxation.

Thus whenever a transaction occurs which involves a beneficial interest the parties should be wary of falling foul of s.53(1)(C), unless of course it is a deliberate attempt to avoid the writing requirement in order to avoid taxation.

5.2.3 Formalities for the creation of a valid testamentary trust

All declarations of testamentary trusts must comply with the Wills Act 1837, s9, which provides:

No will shall be valid unless–

(a) it is in **writing**, and signed by the testator, or by some other person in his presence and by his direction; and
(b) it appears that the testator intended by his signature to give effect to the will; and
(c) the signature is made or acknowledged by the testator in the presence of 2 or more witnesses present at the same time; and
(d) each witness either–
    (i)   attests and signs the will; or
    (ii) acknowledges his signature,
in the presence of the testator (but not necessarily in the presence of any other witness),
but no form of attestation shall be necessary.

---

32   [1960] AC 206, [1959] 3 All ER 623 (HL).

Thus this formality requirement:

- applies to all property;
- provides that all testamentary dispositions must be in writing in the will;
- provides that the will must be signed by the testator, or by someone in his presence under his direction;
- provides that the will must be witnessed by at least 2 persons

If a testamentary disposition does not comply with these formalities, for example it is not in writing or is not witnessed, it will be void. However, as we shall see in the chapter on secret trusts and mutual wills, equity will sometimes enforce testamentary trusts known as secret trusts even though they are not in writing in the will.

5.3 Capacity of Settlors, Trustees and Beneficiaries

Capacity here refers to legal capacity, being legally able to do something. Some people are not recognised as having legal capacity, for example the mentally ill or minors, and is for their protection. The law will not automatically recognise some actions of these people so that they do not enter into transactions that they do not understand or do not intend. These restrictions on capacity are usually provided in statute. Minors are those under the age of 18 years. Minors may not hold the legal estate of land.[33] When a minor attempts to settle personalty, then the trust will be voidable at the instance of the minor at any time within a reasonable time of his attaining majority. A minor may not make a will;[34] therefore a minor cannot create a trust by will.

Those adjudged to be suffering from a mental illness or suffering from some other form of mental incapacity, which means they are incapable of understanding what they are doing, are considered to have no capacity to contract, execute deeds, make dispositions or manage their affairs. The court may administer the affairs of the mentally ill and make wills for them.

However, everyone is presumed to be capable unless it is established otherwise. Thus it is the burden of the party seeking to establish they were not capable, or those they are acting for were not capable, to establish they were minors at the time of the transaction or acting under some legal incapacity.

The parties to a trust have varying requirements as to capacity:

Settlor: only a capable settlor or testator can make a valid declaration of trust. Generally anyone who is capable of owning property may settle it.

---

33   s.1(6) Law of Property Act 1925.
34   The Wills Act 1837, s.7.

Challenges to wills are often made on the grounds that the testator was not of sound mind when they made the will, thus they did not know what they were doing, and so were incapable of creating a valid will. An artificial person, e.g. a company, has legal capacity and so can be a settlor.

Trustee: only a capable trustee can administer a trust. The trustee must be capable of holding the legal estate and dealing with the property otherwise the trust cannot be carried out. If a trustee becomes incapable of dealing with the property, perhaps through mental or physical illness, a new trustee can be appointed to aid or replace the original trustee. An artificial person, e.g. a company, has legal capacity and so can be a trustee. In fact companies that are formed especially for trust management administer many trusts; these are referred to as 'trust corporations'.

Beneficiaries: anyone can be the beneficiary of a trust and trusts are often set up to protect those who are incompetent and so incapable of owning or dealing with property, e.g. the mentally ill and children. A company can be the beneficiary of a trust. A trust may even be created which, for a time, has no beneficiaries; for example, I leave the residue of my estate to my grandchildren (yet to be born).

5.4 The Three Certainties Required to Create a Valid Private Trust

The three certainties required to create a valid private trust are often ascribed to Lord Langdale's judgment in *Knight v. Knight*,[35] but had been recognised and required for some years before this judgment. To create a valid express private trust the declaration of trust must evidence the three certainties:

1 **certainty of intention-** the certainty of the intention of the settlor to place the transferee of property under a trust obligation;
2 **certainty of subject-** the certainty of what property is the subject matter of the trust; and,
3 **certainty of object-** the certainty or means of ascertaining who the beneficiaries of the trust are.

The three certainties will be dealt with in some detail in the next chapter but a brief overview will clarify the requirements for a valid declaration of an express private trust.

The declaration must be a declaration of the intention to create a trust and nothing else. The obligation of trust upon the trustee is so onerous that

---

35   (1840) 3 Beav 148.

a court will only uphold the trust and impose the obligation if it is certain the transferor of property intended the transferee to be under this trust obligation and the transfer was nothing else. We have already seen that other arrangements may appear similar to a trust, for example a contract; however the obligations and rights of the parties are very different. Therefore, the court will need evidence that a trust was intended when property was transferred and nothing else.

Property can be transferred for various reasons:

- It can be sold or swapped- that is transferred for consideration;
- It can be a gift;
- It can be a trust;
- It can be a transfer subject to a power to allocate.

To uphold the creation of a valid express trust the court must be satisfied that the transferor did not transfer the property for another reason. To do this the court will look at the circumstances surrounding the transfer and the construction of the instrument purported to be the trust instrument. If consideration were given for the transfer then the court will probably construe the transfer as a contract, although it may be a contract to create a trust. If no consideration is given then it is more likely to be a gift, trust or power. If a written instrument was used to transfer the property then the instrument's construction will be considered. If words were spoken the court will hear evidence of the words spoken; did the transferor say "I give you this property" or "I give you this property to hold on trust"? However, as we will see, there is no need to refer to a 'trust' in the trust instrument to create a trust but there must be evidence that a trust obligation was intended.[36]

A transfer of property without consideration in return may be a gift or property transferred on trust. A gift is a gratuitous transfer of property. Gifts are valid and upheld at common law and in equity. Generally all that is necessary for the valid gift of property is an intention by the transferor to 'give' the property to the transferee coupled with the transfer of the property. With chattels transfer is usually by delivery. With land certain formalities have to be complied with; a conveyance of land must be in writing in the form of a deed.

Equity presumes that a gratuitous transfer of property with no evidence of the reason behind the transfer will create a resulting trust (the presumed resulting trust[37]). Equity presumes that the absolute owner of property will not transfer it to another without consideration in return. Thus the transferee holds the property on a resulting trust for the transferor.

---

36   *Paul v Constance* [1977] 1 WLR 54.
37   *Dyer v Dyer* (1788) 2 Cox Eq Cas 92, and see *Hodgson v Marks*, above.

However, transfers of property between certain classes of persons are subject to the equitable presumption that they are gifts. This usually involves close family members and is known as the presumption of advancement: if a transfer of property occurs between these classes of persons then the transferor will have to provide evidence to rebut the presumption that a gift was intended and that a resulting trust was established.[38]

When establishing an express private trust the settlor must make a declaration of trust which evidences an intention to create a trust and nothing else. The certainty of intention is sometimes referred to as the "certainty of words", as the words used whether written or spoken, must evidence this certainty. The courts are particularly wary of precatory words; these are words that evidence a wish or hope. If precatory words are used when property is transferred then the transferee will not be under a trust obligation but just a moral obligation, which the court will not enforce as a trust. Thus in *Re Snowden* [1979] Ch 528 the testatrix had left all her property to her brother Bert, but had said in front of her solicitor that she hoped he would divide it as appropriate between her nephews and nieces. On Bert's death in quick succession to her own the court held that Bert had not been under a trust obligation as the words were merely precatory and not certain enough.

The legacy was an absolute gift to Bert.

The subject matter of the trust must also be certain or capable of being ascertained by the trustee. The trustees must know what property they hold subject to the trust obligation and the beneficiaries must be able to find out what property they have an interest in.

Certainty of subject matter divides into two parts:

- Certainty of the subject matter itself; and,
- Certainty of the beneficial interest.

Therefore the trust must be over certain specified property, the property must be identifiable. Thus a trust of the residue of an estate is certain as it is the amount left after all expenses of administering the estate and all other bequests and legacies have been settled and is capable of being ascertained. Although it may not be a certain amount until the estate is administered it is certain because it is whatever is left.

The beneficial interests of a trust are the amount of the trust property that each beneficiary is to get. Usually this must be specified, for example I leave £100,000 to my brother Bert to hold on trust on equal amounts for my two sons. This is a simple fixed trust with the beneficiaries and their beneficial interests clearly identified. Here the subject matter is certain,

---

38   This is considered in detail in the chapter on resulting trusts.

£100,000 and the beneficial interest, the shares of the beneficiaries is also certain, it is an equal share of the fund, £50,000 each.

Sometimes the beneficial interest is not specified but is left to be decided by the trustee or another. These trusts are known as discretionary trusts and do not fall foul of the requirement for clear beneficial interests because someone has been given the power to decide these interests.

Example

I leave £100,000 to Bert to hold on trust for whichever of my children he regards as deserving in such amounts as he shall decide at his absolute discretion.

With this trust Bert has the discretion to decide who the beneficiaries are and how much they will get; their beneficial interest. The subject matter is £100,000 and so is certain and Bert can decide on their beneficial interests.

To be valid an express trust must also identify the beneficiaries or provide the means to identify the beneficiaries. The beneficiaries of a trust are known as its 'objects'; thus there must be certainty of objects. In a fixed trust it must be possible to literally write a list of the beneficiaries; this is known as the list certainty test.[39] As we shall see, if the trustees of a discretionary trust have been given discretion to identify the objects the trust will not fail for want of certainty of objects if a clear class of potential beneficiaries has been identified to the trustee. The problems of identifying whether a class of objects is certain, and the tests the courts have adopted to decide on certainty of objects, will be considered in the next chapter.

In addition to the requirement of certainty of objects an express private (non-charitable) trust must generally be for human beneficiaries or legally recognised entities, e.g. a limited company. This is because of the beneficiary principle.

5.5 The Beneficiary Principle

The beneficiary principle is linked to the certainty of objects and was effectively espoused by William Grant the Master of the Rolls in *Morice v The Bishop of Durham*,[40] as 'there must be somebody in whose favour the court can decree performance'.[41] Once the trust is formed, there must be a beneficiary of the trust who is able to ask the court to enforce the obligations of the trust against the trustee. The beneficiary controls the trust and acquires property rights in the trust. This beneficiary may be

---

39   *Inland Revenue Commissioners v. Broadway Cottages Trust* [1955] Ch. 20.
40   (1805) 10 Ves 522.
41   Although it is possible to have a trust for the benefit of an unborn or unformed beneficiary as long as the trustees are certain who they owe the obligation to, for example, a not yet incorporated company: *Town Bright Industries Ltd v Bermuda Trust (Hong Kong) Ltd* [1998] 2 HKC 445.

human or a legally recognised entity (a registered company). If there is no identifiable beneficiary then the trust is a purpose trust, and trusts for private purposes (non-charitable purposes) are generally void.[42] However, as with any legal rule there are exceptions, thus charitable trusts, also referred to as public trusts do not have to comply with the beneficiary principle. These are also the trusts of imperfect obligation, very limited categories of non-charitable or private purpose trusts.[43]

The beneficiary principle also causes problems for trusts in favour of unincorporated organisations, these are groups of people who have joined together for a common purpose but have not become a separate body in law from their constituent members. Unincorporated associations should be contrasted with corporations such as the registered company which has a separate legal personality. The problem is that a trust in favour of an unincorporated organisation seems to be a trust for the purposes of the organisation and so should be void as a private purpose trust. We will see how the courts have attempted to clarify such trusts and gifts in favour of unincorporated organisations in the chapter dealing with the beneficiary principle.

5.6 Vitiating Factors: Legality and Public Policy

A vitiating factor is a factor which makes an agreement faulty, it invalidates an agreement. In contract law misrepresentation or duress may be vitiating factors. In equity we have already considered the doctrine of undue influence which may vitiate or invalidate a contract. In trust law factors that may invalidate trusts are trust purposes which are illegal or against public policy. Such factors can be divided into:

- Trusts for illegal purposes: trusts which are for illegal purposes or encourage illegal purposes;
- Trusts that are against public policy, for example they prevent or break up marriage, or have a capricious purpose;
- Trusts may also be against public policy if they offend the trust principles of perpetuity, alienation and accumulation.

5.6.1 Trusts for illegal purposes

It is not possible to have a trust for an illegal purpose or a purpose contrary to public policy. Trusts are built on conscience and so it should be impossible for equity to recognise a trust which furthered an illegal

---

42   *Re Astor's ST, Astor v Scholfield* [1952] Ch 534.
43   Charitable trusts are dealt with in their own chapter and trusts of imperfect obligation are dealt with in the chapter on the beneficiary principle.

purpose or one which was against public policy.[44] Trusts for illegal purposes may be to encourage others to do something illegal or to affect an illegal purpose. Trusts that are set up to encourage illegal purposes are void. For example, a trust to pay the fines of convicted poachers was declared void as it would take away the penalty of the law and encourage poaching.[45]

The most common illegal purpose behind creating a trust is to commit fraud. When equity considers fraud it is not considering the same sense of deceit as at common law. In equity fraud takes a more general meaning such as, 'any breach of the sort of obligation which is enforced by a court that from the beginning regarded itself as a court of conscience.'[46] Thus equitable fraud would include obtaining an advantage by any behaviour which equity would consider unconscionable, as equity must 'correct men's consciences for frauds, breach of trusts, wrongs and oppressions'.[47] If a court believes a trust has been set up to defeat the claims of creditors then it will be declared void as a sham.[48]

Midland Bank plc v Wyatt [49]

Mr and Mrs Wyatt were joint owners of the family home, subject to mortgage. They both signed a declaration of trust of the beneficial interest of the house in favour of Mrs Wyatt and their daughters. At this point, if the trust were in existence, Mr Wyatt held only bare legal title and no beneficial interest. Mr Wyatt took out loans with his bank on the understanding that he still had a beneficial interest in the property. His business went into receivership and the bank attempted to effect security against the house. Mr Wyatt claimed that he was only a trustee of the house for his wife and daughters and therefore it could not be used to satisfy his creditors.

Judgment: the court held that the arrangement was purely a sham; Mr Wyatt had never intended to create a trust. He had never intended to give his beneficial interest in the property to his wife and daughters he had merely set up the arrangement to defeat his creditors. Therefore the trust did not exist and the bank could take action against the house.

---

44 However, the origin of the doctrine of secret trusts may be closely associated with fast changing political regimes in 16th and 17th century England where secret trusts were created for purposes illegal under the existing regime but legal and so recognised and enforced by the succeeding regime.

45 *Thrupp v Collett* (1858) 26 Beav 14.

46 *Nocton v Lord Ashburton* [1914] AC 932, 954, *per* Viscount Haldane L.C.

47 *Earl of Oxford's Case* (1615) 1 Ch Rep 1, *per* Lord Ellesmere.

48 Trusts cannot be set up to avoid statutory obligations – for example to avoid obligations on divorce in matrimonial legislation and making provision for dependents in your will (the Inheritance (Provision for Family and Dependants) Act 1975.

49 [1995] 3 FCR 11.

Equity will also not consider evidence of an illegal purpose to rebut a trust or an equitable presumption such as the presumption of advancement.

Example
A gratuitous transfer of property from Tim to Robert creates a presumption that Robert holds the property on resulting trust for Tim.[50] However, if Robert is Tim's son then there is also a presumption of advancement; it is presumed that Tim wished to help his son, that this is purely a gift. This presumption can be rebutted with evidence that a gift was not intended, that Tim intended the property to be held on trust for him and eventually returned. However, if the property were transferred for an illegal purpose, for example, if Tim were insolvent and had creditors demanding payment, he may have transferred the property to Robert to avoid the property becoming part of his assets on bankruptcy to be divided between his creditors. If this is the case then Tim cannot plead his own illegal motives in transferring the property to rebut the presumption of advancement. Equity will not listen to his illegal motives and will see the transfer as a gift to Robert. (That is unless it can be set aside by the creditors as an illegal transaction anyway.)

Generally if property is transferred for an illegal purpose then the transferor cannot rely on that illegal purpose to establish that there is a trust.[51] As will be discussed later, a more relaxed approach has recently been taken by the courts if the party seeking to rely on the illegal purpose has not carried this purpose out, or has repented and retreated from the illegal purpose, or if the party with an illegal purpose does not have to plead that illegal purpose.[52]

5.6.2 Trusts which are against public policy

Trusts are against public policy:

1 If they are intended to prevent or break up marriage;
2 If they are for capricious purposes; and,
3 If they offend the principles of perpetuity, alienation and accumulation.

(As the last category is so important it will be dealt with under a separate sub-heading.)

---

50 The presumed resulting trust: see **Hodgson v Marks**, above, and the chapter on resulting trusts.
51 See *Gascoigne v Gascoigne* [1918] 1 KB 223 and *Tinker v Tinker* [1970] P 136 discussed in more detail in the chapter on resulting trusts.
52 *Tinsley v Milligan* [1994] 1 A.C. 340 (HL). *Tribe v Tribe* [1996] Ch. 107 (EWCA).

Trusts are against public policy if they are intended to prevent marriage or induce the separation of a married couple. This is because it is considered good for society generally for people to marry; therefore any trust against marriage is contrary to public policy and therefore void. Thus in **Westmeath (Earl) v Countess of Westmeath,**[53] Lord Eldon queried an agreement to pay an annuity to a wife whilst the couple was separated as it might prevent the future reconciliation of the couple. Although trusts preventing marriage are usually void it has been possible to create a trust preventing marriage to a particular person or class of persons, for example, **Re Tuck's ST,**[54] involved a trust of money for issue who married into the Jewish faith, the requirement was not challenged. However, in **Re Remnant's Settlement Trusts,** [55] the term of a trust which prevented any interest for any beneficiary if they married a Roman Catholic was removed to prevent family discord.

At common law the court may also declare any trust void for being capricious. Capricious purposes are those based upon a whim or without reason.[56] This follows from the general common law principle that the court will not compel the carrying out of purposes that are "absurd, abhorrent or a waste of the assets of an estate".[57]

This rule is important when we look at the exceptions to the beneficiary principle and the limited categories of non-charitable purpose trusts, the trusts of imperfect obligation, as it may render such trusts void. Thus, a trust to board up a house for 20 years was deemed capricious, without reason and so contrary to public policy and void.[58] Similarly, a trust to erect bronze statues of the testatrix and her parents was "a sheer waste of money,[59] and a trust for the erection of artistic towers was also deemed capricious and void.[60] A trust which directed the destruction of property

---

53 (1821) Jac 126.

54 [1978] Ch 49.

55 *Re Remnant's Settlement Trusts (Hooper v Wenhaston)* [1970] Ch. 560.

56 The Law Commission of England described this power as the "court's jurisdiction to strike down grossly unreasonable testamentary provisions… "The Law Commission of England and Wales, Item 7 of the Sixth Programme of Law Reform: The Law of Trusts, *The Rules Against Perpetuities and Excessive Accumulations*, p.21.

57 This principle exists throughout the common law world: for example see the U.S. cases of *Re Larkin*, 9 N.Y. 2d 88, 211, N.Y.S. 2 d 175, 172 N.E. 2d 555 (1961), and *Eyerman v Mercantile Trust Co. Nat'l Assoc.* 524 S.W. 2d 210 (Mo. App., D.St. L. 1975) where, in the latter, the testatrix's wish to have her house 'razed' was considered to violate public policy and not followed.

58 *Brown v Burdett* (1882) 21 Ch D 667.

59 *M'Caig's Trustees v Kirk-Session of United Free Church of Lismore* (1915) 52 SLR 347.

60 *M'Caig v University of Glasgow* (1907) 44 SLR 198.

might also be deemed capricious.[61] A court might also be able to use statutory powers or its inherent jurisdiction to vary the terms of a trust and so exclude or ignore a capricious element if it did not wish to void the whole trust.[62]

5.6.3 Perpetuity, alienation and accumulation

Many centuries ago the state and the common law recognised that arrangements of land which removed or alienated land from the open market could lead to economic stagnation. In mediaeval England when men neared death they sought salvation by passing their property to the Church in return for forgiveness for their sins. However, the Church was a corporation which did not die, therefore, as it was not subject to normal feudal dues and was unlikely to sell land, so also ensuring no fees would be payable to the crown on transfer of land, the King and feudal lords were in genuine fear that all land would eventually end up in the 'dead hand' of the Church.[63] Thus the Statutes of Mortmain (literally 'dead hand') were introduced in 1279[64] to prevent gifts or trusts in favour of corporations, which could have perpetual existence and alienate property from the market forever. However, the general principle from the Acts, that property should not be alienated from general circulation, as this adversely affects commercial progress (and the state's revenue), was developed into the rules against perpetuities. These rules developed because landowners attempted to found dynasties by creating family settlement trusts that restricted land to pass to their children and their children's children, and so on. If such settlements were allowed then these descendants would not be able to deal with the land as an absolute owner, they would not be able to sell or dispose of the land, in effect they would be life tenants forced to look after the land for succeeding generations. This was again considered

---

61   Although ownership usually includes the right to destroy property this is only possible if it does not harm others or their interests. Thus a trust which specified the destruction of property might be seen as harming other possible interests and thus against public policy. See J. H. Langbein,'Burn the Rembrandt? Trust Law's limits on the settlor's power to direct investments' (2010) *Boston University Law Review*.

62   See the chapter on beneficiaries and variation of trusts.

63   The increasing wealth of the Church also made kings nervous of the Church as a powerful political rival.

64   Such restrictions were originally included in the Great Charter of 1217. Halsbury's states that the principle that a perpetuity is forbidden was a principle of the common law and may have been introduced after *Quia Emptores* (18 Edw 1, 1289-90): *Halsbury's Laws of England*, 13, Perpetuities (1) [230.0855]. Some of the provisions of the Acts were not repealed until the 20th century.

to tie up land in a way that would adversely affect the economy and society. As Jekyll M.R. stated in *Stanley v Leigh*:[65]

'the mischief that would arise to the public from estates remaining for ever or for a long time inalienable or untransferable from one hand to another, being a damp to industry and prejudice to trade, to which may be added the inconvenience and distress that would be brought on families whose estates are so fettered'. [66]

Thus perpetuities were not accepted at common law. It was only in the late seventeenth century that Lord Nottingham developed the rule against perpetuities, in **Howard v Duke of Norfolk**,[67] and so equity permitted restrictions on future disposition for a certain period.

Perpetuities represent one of the most confused areas of the common law and have been described as having 'superfluous technicalities and complexities'.[68] The rule against perpetuities is further complicated by its confusion with other rules. There are three rules which deal with issues of restricting future enjoyment of property. These are:

- The rule against perpetuities;
- The rule against excessive accumulation of income; and,
- The rule against inalienability.

These three rules are distinct but interrelated.[69] Although the rules against perpetuities and excessive accumulation are the most commonly met today the rule against inalienability must be considered first.

The rule against inalienability

The rule against inalienability has also been referred to as the rule against perpetual trusts (or perpetual purpose trusts), the rule against excessive duration, the rule on duration,[70] and the rule against prolonged indestructibility.[71] The rule against inalienability is a rule preventing

---

65   (1732) 2 P Wms 686 at 688
66   As Emery asks, 'why should the dead rather than the living prescribe indefinitely who should be entitled to the use and enjoyment of property...?' C. Emery, 'Do We Need a Rule Against Perpetuities?' (1994) 57 *MLR* 602, at 603.
67   (1681-5) 3 Ch Cas 1: 22 ER 931; 2 Swans 454; 36 ER 690; 1 Vern 163; 23 ER 388.
68   W. Barton Leach, 'Perpetuities in Perspective: Ending the Rule's Reign of Terror', (1952) 65(5) *Harvard Law Review* 721, at p. 723.
69   The rule against inalienability and rule against perpetuities have long been confused. '[I]t is natural that there has been some confusion between these two rules. The public policies they serve are identical': Joseph P. Morray, 'The Rule Against Prolonged Indestructibility of Private Trusts' (1949-1950) 44 *Ill. L. Rev.* 467, at p.468.
70   See PAA 2009, section 18.
71   Joseph P. Morray, 'The Rule Against Prolonged Indestructibility of Private Trusts' (1949-1950) 44 *Ill. L. Rev.* 467, at pp.468 & 470.

settlors from devising property subject to conditions that it cannot be sold or transferred by the recipient.[72] Although, this is a separate rule from the rule against perpetuities, and it has sometimes been said that this rule has nothing to do with the rule against perpetuities, it is a corollary of the rule against perpetuities that property must not be rendered inalienable.[73] This rule is economic based and 'reflects the policy that property, particularly land, should not be tied up indefinitely'.[74] Thus restraints on the disposal of property placed upon the recipient of that property should be void.[75] The rule has been divided into two further rules, the first prohibited, the second subject to time limits:

1 the rule against trusts for a beneficiary absolutely subject to provisions purporting to restrain the beneficiary from alienating or disposing of the beneficial interest; and,
2 the rule against the restriction of alienability of property for longer than the perpetuity period: the rule against excessive duration.

The first rule will render any provision void that tries to restrict a beneficiary under a trust in which property is held for the beneficiary absolutely from disposing of the property. For example, a devise of property to a beneficiary subject to a provision that if he became bankrupt the transfer to the beneficiary should be declared void and the property pass to another. The 'conditional' provision would itself be void for being repugnant to the absolute interest and the property remains an absolute gift to the original devisee.[76] Such void provisions should not be confused with protective trusts, which are provisions made for the maintenance of a beneficiary for their lifetime subject to disentitling events. Thus there may be determinable interests but not conditional gifts.[77] For example a

---

72 The rule derives from the principle that 'a restraint on alienation being contradictory to the grant is repugnant thereto and void.' Jack J. Rappeport, 'The Equitable Separate Estate and Restraints on Anticipation: its Modern Significance' (1956-1957) 11 *Miami Law Quarterly* 85, at p.85.
73 See *Carne v Long* (1860) 2 De GF & J 75, at p.80. See also Oakley, A. J., *Parker and Mellows: the modern law of trusts*, 9th ed. (London: Sweet & Maxwell, 2009) p. 269.
74 Haley, M. & McMurtry, L. *Equity and Trusts*, 2nd edition (London: Sweet & Maxwell, 2009) p.119.
75 Halsbury's refers to this as 'the rule which invalidates limitations and trusts that impose restrictions upon the future alienation of property, which extend beyond the [perpetuity period]'. Halsbury's Laws of Hong Kong, 13, Perpetuities (1) [230.0854]. Jessel MR stated, in *Re Ridley* (1879) LR 11 Ch D 645, 648, 'the law of this country says that all property shall be alienable...' and then listed the exceptions to the rule.
76 *Re Machu* (1882) 21 ChD 838, 843.
77 *Hatton v May* (1876) 3 CH D 148.

settlor may provide that his land will pass to A for his life but be forfeit to B if A becomes bankrupt. A has a life interest as long as the determining event, his bankruptcy, does not occur. B's interest only comes into being if the determining event happens. If the property were given to A then it is his and no condition may be set on it.

The rule against inalienability provides justification for the rule in *Saunders v Vautier*.[78] This rule provides that, if all the beneficiaries of a trust are *sui juris*, of full age and legally capable, and absolutely entitled to the trust property, they may unanimously call for the transfer of the trust property or its resettlement upon terms they decide.

The first rule against inalienability is not referred to in any perpetuities legislation and so is still subject to the common law, but is rarely invoked.

The second rule against inalienability is the rule against excessive duration. This restricts the amount of time for which property can be rendered inalienable by preventing certain trusts from continuing indefinitely. If a private trust is set up which places property in the trust forever, then it will make that property inalienable. This rule predates the rule against perpetuities, but the rule against inalienability has limited importance for private trusts today because, as we shall see, the rule against perpetuities makes it impossible today to have a private (non-charitable) trust in favour of human beneficiaries which will last forever, as the property must vest absolutely with a human beneficiary within the relevant perpetuity period who can alienate it. Thus its application is limited to non-charitable purpose trusts (also referred to as trusts of imperfect obligation or private purpose trusts) and gifts in favour of unincorporated associations. Non-charitable purpose trusts are exceptions to the rule that private (non-charitable) trusts must have an identifiable human beneficiary or a non-human legal entity capable of holding property in its own right (the beneficiary principle[79]). Generally, if there is no human beneficiary to enforce a trust then it is a trust for a purpose and trusts for non-charitable purposes are void.[80] However there are three

---

78 (1841) 4 Beav 115,49 ER 282. See Paul Matthews, 'The Comparative Importance of the Rule in *Saunders v Vautier*' (2006) 122(APR) *Law Quarterly Review* 266-294.

79 Espoused by Sir William Grant MR, in *Morice v. Bishop of Durham* (1805) 10 Ves 522, as, "there must be somebody in whose favour the court can decree performance."

80 E.g. *Re Shaw* [1957] 1 WLR 729; *Re Astor's Settlement Trusts (Astor v Scholfield)* [1952] Ch 534. The principle does not apply to charitable trusts (also known as public purpose trusts): *Chamberlayne v Brockett* (1872) 8 Ch App 206, at 211; Thompson v Shakespeare [1859] Johnson's Reports 612; [1860] 1 De G.F. & J. 399. This is because they confer public benefit and do not require an ascertainable human beneficiary as the Secretary for Justice can enforce the

categories of non-charitable purpose trust which are accepted as exceptions to this:[81] trusts for the erection of tombs and monuments, trusts for saying masses in private,[82] trusts for the maintenance of specific animals.[83] The rule against excessive duration for non-charitable purpose trusts is expressly excluded from the legislation relating to perpetuities.[84] Therefore if a trust is intended to take advantage of one of the exceptions it must be restricted to the common law period of 21 years.[85] Non-charitable purpose trusts may continue for no more than 21 years, if there is a possibility it may continue for longer than 21 years it will be void. Non-charitable purpose trusts are also subject to the rule against perpetuities discussed below, any such trust interest must vest within 21 years otherwise it is void. As the perpetuities statutes do not apply to these trusts the period for consideration will always be 21 years. If non-charitable purpose trusts infringe the rules against inalienability or perpetuities, they will fail and the putative trust properties would be held on a resulting trust for the settlor or his estate.

The rule against perpetuities

John Chipman Gray gave the classic statement of the rule against perpetuities: 'No interest is good unless it must vest, if at all, no later than twenty-one years after some life in being at the creation of the interest.'[86] However, as Maureen Markey noted, 'Gray may have been able to distil

---

trust on behalf of the public. The beneficiary principle was said not to apply to charitable trusts by Sir William Grant MR, in *Morice v. Bishop of Durham* (1805) 10 Ves 522: '...it is now settled, upon authority, which it is too late to controvert, that where a charitable purpose is expressed, however general, the bequest shall not fail on account of the uncertainty of the object...'

81 These are referred to as trusts of imperfect obligation, as they are valid but unenforceable. Lord Evershed identified the three categories in *Re Endacott* [1960] Ch. 232, at p. 246. He doubted the inclusion of unincorporated associations as a separate category and stated that the inclusion of a category of 'miscellaneous cases' should not be encouraged, as the categories of these non-charitable purposes 'ought not to be extended'.

82 These are special prayers said for the souls of the dead.

83 Trusts which are for masses in public or the maintenance of animals generally may be charitable: see the chapter on charitable trusts.

84 The Perpetuities and Accumulations Act 2009 (c.18), s.18 provides (to the same effect as the Perpetuities and Accumulations Act 1964, s.15 (4)): 'This Act does not affect the rule of law which limits the duration of non-charitable purpose trusts.'

85 A traditional period of the common law which represents the time that a newly born human infant beneficiary would take to reach majority and then take the interest from the non-charitable purpose trust.

86 J.C. Gray, The Rule Against Perpetuities (4th ed. 1942), known as *Gray on Perpetuities*.

the Rule into twenty-seven words, but it took an eight-hundred-plus-page treatise for him to explain it.'[87] Although it has been stated that law teachers delight to make a 'mystery' of the rule against perpetuities,[88] the mystification of students, practitioners and settlors probably has more to do with the rule also being known as the rule against remoteness, [89] the rule against remoteness of vesting, [90] and the rule limiting perpetuities,[91] and with establishing the perpetuity period and confusion surrounding when the rule applies.

The rule against perpetuities prevents an interest in trust property vesting too far in the future and thus ensures property must be vested in someone within the perpetuity period who can deal with it as an absolute owner. A vested interest is an interest that is with the beneficiary now or will definitely be with the beneficiary in the future. Vested interests are considered in the chapter on beneficiaries where they are contrasted with contingent interests, those relying on an occurrence to vest the interest. Thus a trust may provide for A for life with remainder to B. In such a case A has an interest vested in possession, he enjoys the property now, and B has a vested interest but it is a future vested interest, he does not enjoy the property now but he definitely will because A must die. If a condition were attached to B's receiving the interest, for example if the clause read 'B shall receive the property if he has passed a law degree before A's death otherwise it is to go to C on A's death', then both B and C would have future contingent interests, their interests depend on whether or not B passes his law degree before A dies. If B passes the degree his interest is vested and C's fails, if B does not pass the degree before A dies then B's interest fails and C's interest vests. Obviously C's interest would actually vest in possession in this last circumstance as A has died and C will now take possession of the property.

---

87   Maureen E. Markey, 'Ariadne's Thread: Leading Students into and out of the Labyrinth of the Rule Against Perpetuities' (2006) 54 *Cleveland State Law Review* 337, 354 f.n. 52. Referring to *Gray on Perpetuities*.

88   W. Barton Leach, 'Perpetuities in a Nutshell', (1938) 51(4) *Harvard Law Review* 638, at p.638.

89   *Gray on Perpetuities* states: 'The Rule against Perpetuities should have been called the Rule against Remoteness.' It is aimed at the control of future interests; it has nothing to do, save incidentally, with present interests. But its name is a constant temptation to treat it as aimed against restraints on the alienation of present interests': J.C. Gray, J.C., *Gray on Perpetuities* (4th ed. 1942) p.x, quoting the preface to the first edition (1886).

90   Lawrence Ma, *Equity and Trusts Law in Hong Kong*, 2nd ed. (Hong Kong, Lexis Nexis, 2009) p.397.

91   A.W.B. Simpson, "Entails and Perpetuities", (1979) 24 *Jur Rev* 1, 17.

The common law rule against perpetuities is very strict;[92] if there is a possibility that any interest that may occur will vest outside the perpetuity period then the trust is void. The perpetuity period at common law is a life in being and 21 years.[93] Therefore, if a trust is subject to future contingencies that might not occur within 21 years of the death of a designated person in the trust then the trust will be void.[94] The rule was applied with such rigidity that a trust would be invalidated not only when it was certain the rule would be broken but even when there were a possibility that it might offend the rule. This produced results which did not reflect the testator's wishes and were extremely unfair to potential beneficiaries.[95] The strictness of the common law rule led to the introduction of the Perpetuities and Accumulations Act 1964 (PAA), which introduced a more relaxed application of the rule by providing a statutory "wait and see" approach to the application of the rule,[96] guidance on who would be the relevant life in being, and an alternative 80 year perpetuity period, although the period is still 21 years if no human lives are associated with the trust.

Thus the PAA 1964 clarifies that a trust can be created which specifies its vesting and duration as long as this is not more than 80 years from the creation of the trust. However, if there is no human life relevant to the trust then the perpetuity period is 21 years. If the trust instrument does not specify a period then the court may adopt a "wait and see" approach,

---

92   Lord Nottingham created the rule against perpetuities in *Howard v Duke of Norfolk* (1681-5) 3 Ch Cas 1.

93   Originally it had been a life in being, but 21 years was later added to ensure the beneficiary would be at the age of majority and able to take his interest when it vested: the period was settled by the House of Lords in *Cadell v Palmer* (1833) 1 Cl & F 372; 6 ER 956; see also Jessel MR in *Re Ridley* (1879) 11 Ch D 645, 649. "Lives in being" refers to a life associated with the disposition or named in the trust instrument. A life may be specified as the life for reference, e.g. "after the death of my youngest grandchild alive today", in which case the trust will be valid for 21 years after the death of that grandchild. If no life has been specified then the reference is to any life in the trust provision relevant to the trust. If children are born posthumously to the settlor (children *en ventre sa mère* at the date of the death of the settlor) then the gestation period is added to the 21 years. If there are no human lives associated with the trust then the perpetuity period is 21 years thus non-charitable private purpose trusts must vest within 21 years: *Mussett v. Bingle* [1876] WN 170 (HC).

94   *Cadell v Palmer* (1883) 6 ER 956, 1 Cl & F 372.

95   See *Re Dawson, (sub nom Johnston v Hill)* (1888) 39 Ch D 155

96   A disposition is to be treated as valid even though it might vest outside the perpetuity period. It only infringes the rule against perpetuities when it becomes established that the power will not be exercisable within the perpetuity period. This is the so called "wait and see" provision.

which allows the trust to be administered until it is apparent that it will offend perpetuity,at which time it will be void.

Unfortunately the statutory changes did not provide a unified rule against perpetuities and only served to further complicate the law of perpetuities. The introduction of the "wait and see" approach meant that, as the PAA 1964 only applies to dispositions made after its commencement, the rule effectively became two rules as:

Any disposition which was effected before the PAA 1964 was implemented is subject to the rule that a future interest in any type of property will be void from the date that the instrument which attempts to create it takes effect, if there is any possibility that the instrument may vest or commence outside the perpetuity period.

Any disposition which was effected after the PAA 1964 was implemented is subject to the rule that a future interest in any type of property will only be void if it must vest outside the perpetuity period.

If a private trust is declared void for offending perpetuity then, if the trust is created *intervivos* the property is held on resulting trust for the settlor, he may do as he wishes with the property, which may include resettling the property and complying with the rule. However, if the gift or trust is testamentary then it is held on resulting trust for the testator's estate to be applied as per the will or, if a trust of the residue, by way of the rules of intestacy, which often will involve a disposition in no way intended by the testator.

The UK has now implemented the Perpetuities and Accumulations Act 2009 which has increased the statutory perpetuity period to 125 years for trusts after the implementation date of the statute, April 6, 2010.[97]

The rule against excessive accumulations of income
The rule against accumulations is the only purely statutory rule. Accumulation has been described as 'the addition of income to capital, thus increasing the state in favour of those entitled to capital and against the interests of those entitled to income.'[98] Most trusts provide power for trustees to accumulate income until some specified event when it is to be distributed. The common law restricted accumulation of income without distribution to the beneficiaries of a trust to the perpetuity period by means of the rule against perpetuities.[99] Thus the rule against perpetuities ensured that the trust would have to vest with a human beneficiary who could

---

97   PAA 2009, s.5.

98   *Re Earl of Berkeley, dec'd* [1968] Ch 744, 772, per Harman L.J.

99   *Thellusson v Woodford* (1799) 4 Ves 227, 338; 31 ER 117, 171; (1805) 11 Ves 112, 147; 32 ER 1030, 1044. This does not apply to income retained to meet potential obligations or liabilities, although this income must be applied to the extent it is not needed to meet these eventualities.

enjoy the accumulated fund within the common law perpetuity period of a life in being.[100]

The *Thellusson*[101] case was an extreme case where the testator directed the income from his real estate to be accumulated and reinvested in real estate during the lives of his son, grandson and the great grandchildren living at his death, with division amongst his next of kin at the death of the survivor of this class. This provision was held valid as it restricted the accumulation to lives in being at the time of the testator's death. Agitation in the popular press and undue political concerns resulted in the legislation, which limited the period of accumulation even further than the common law perpetuity period to certain statutory periods. The reasons for this statutory restriction were political rather than social, as Lord Eldon LC noted in the *Thellusson* case that there was no economic reason for restricting accumulation of income further than that provided by the perpetuity period.[102] The original legislative restriction[103] was reformed and specified in the UK Law of Property Act 1925 (c. 20) and the Perpetuities and Accumulations Act 1964.

These provide statutory accumulation periods and that no accumulation can be directed to just purchasing land.

The original legislation has often been described as an overreaction,[104] and the UK has now implemented the Perpetuities and Accumulations Act 2009 which has abolished the restrictions on accumulation for trusts created after April 6, 2010.[105] However, charitable trusts may not accumulate income for more than 21 years to ensure that such trusts, which are for public benefit, do not indefinitely accumulate income but use it for that public benefit.

5.7 Constitution of the trust

A trust must be completely constituted or supported by valuable consideration before it is enforceable. Constitution here refers to· the

---

100 Morray notes the rule against accumulation may also be linked to the rule against prolonged indestructibility of the trust (the rule against inalienability): Joseph P. Morray, 'The Rule Against Prolonged Indestructibility of Private Trusts' (1949-1950) 44 *Ill. L. Rev.* 467, at p.476.

101 *Thellusson v Woodford* (1799) 4 Ves 227, 338; 31 ER 117, 171; (1805) 11 Ves 112, 147; 32 ER 1030, 1044.

102 The Law Commission of England and Wales, Item 7 of the Sixth Programme of Law Reform: The Law of Trusts, *The Rules Against Perpetuities and Excessive Accumulations*, p. 6.

103 The Accumulation Act 1800 enacted after *Thellusson v Woodford* (1799) 4 Ves 227; (1805) 11 Ves 112.

104 R.H. Maudsley, *The Modern Law of Perpetuities* (1979) p.201.

105 PAA 2009 s.13.

transfer of the trust property to the trustee subject to the trust obligation. Generally property subject to a trust obligation will be effectively transferred to the trustee by delivery.

Example

I declare a trust of my copy of Maitland's *Equity* in favour of my nephew with my brother Tim as trustee. When I hand the book to Tim the trust is constituted, it is in effect and enforceable.

Some property is subject to statutory formality requirements when it is transferred, e.g. land and shares. These formalities must be complied with otherwise the property is not effectively transferred and equity will not consider the trust constituted and enforceable.[106] Problems occur when property is not transferred as intended or in the correct way and the beneficiaries seek to enforce the trust. If the trust is not constituted then it does not exist and cannot be enforced and the beneficiaries, who generally have not given consideration for the creation of the trust, are volunteers-*equity will not assist a volunteer*. Similarly, gifts require delivery of the property to be constituted- that is effective and recognised at law and in equity. If the property is not transferred as required by statute then again, *equity will not assist a volunteer* and *equity will not perfect an imperfect gift*. Generally a trust will not be constituted and a gift will not be perfected unless the settlor/donor has done everything necessary to effect the transfer of the property to the trustee/donee. [107] However, equity has relaxed this rule so that equity will consider a trust constituted and a gift perfected when the settlor/donor has done everything within their power to transfer the property to the trustee/donee.[108]

A trust that is supported by consideration, for example a contract to create a trust, can be enforced by the parties to the contract.

5.8 Summary

An express trust is created when a capable settlor/testator makes a declaration, orally or in writing, which complies with the legal formalities required, identifying certain property and transferring its legal title to a capable trustee subjecting him to the certainty of the fiduciary obligation to hold the property for the benefit of certain others as long as this is not contrary to law or public policy.

The declaration of trust must evidence the three certainties required to create an express trust: the certainty of intention, the certainty of subject

---

106 *Milroy v Lord* (1862) 4 De GF & J 264. These principles are considered in the chapter on constitution of trusts.

107 *Milroy v Lord* (1862) 4 De GF & J 264.

108 *Re Rose* [1952] Ch 499.

matter, and; the certainty of objects. The objects of a private trust must usually be ascertainable human beneficiaries (the beneficiary principle) or a non-living legal entity, a corporation, as the beneficiaries must be able to ask the court to decree performance of the trust. Declaration of an *intervivos* trust of land must also comply with statutory formalities, thus there must be some writing evidencing the declaration signed by the settlor. Testamentary trusts, trusts created in wills, must comply with the formalities required in the legislation concerning wills. Any disposition of a beneficiary's equitable interest in a trust must also comply with statutory formalities and so must be made in writing. Settlors and trustees must be legally capable of creating the trust and administering the trust respectively. Minors and the mentally incapacitated may not create trusts, either *intervivos* or in a will, and may not be trustees. Anyone may be a beneficiary, as providing property for the legally incompetent was the reason equity enforced the trust.

A trust must not be for an illegal purpose or promote an illegal purpose otherwise it will be void. A trust must not be against public policy, for example it must not prevent marriage or indefinitely prevent property being alienated. Any beneficial interest must vest within the relevant perpetuity period. Trusts must not indefinitely accumulate income.

The next chapter will consider how equity has required certainty of intention, subject matter and objects and the tests it has developed to decide if the required certainty is present in a trust instrument.

CHAPTER 6
THE THREE CERTAINTIES

The three certainties are often ascribed to Lord Langdale's judgment in *Knight v. Knight*,[1] but had been recognised some years before this judgment.

To create a valid express private trust the declaration of trust must evidence the three certainties:

1 Certainty of intention- the certainty of the intention of the settlor to place the transferee of property under a trust obligation;
2 Certainty of subject- the certainty of what property is the subject matter of the trust and what interest each beneficiary is to receive; and,
3 Certainty of object- the certainty of who the beneficiaries of the trust are.

If any of the three certainties is not present then there is no express trust and the property may be an absolute gift to the transferee or held on resulting trust for the transferor or his estate (if testamentary).

6.1 Certainty of intention: gift, trust or power?

To create an express trust there must be certainty that the settlor or testator transferred the property to the recipient with the intention that the recipient would be under a trust obligation and for no other reason. Equity imposes the need for this certainty because of the onerous duties and obligations that the trustee is under and because of the rights in the trust property that the beneficiaries have. The obligation on a trustee is onerous because a trust is mandatory, it must be carried out by the trustee, he is under an obligation to perform the wishes of the settlor with regard to the trust property and the beneficiaries. If the trustee does not perform his mandatory trust obligations he is in breach of trust and may face penalties.

There may be uncertainty over the intent behind a transfer because the common law and equity recognise different types of transfer. The common law regards the absolute owner of property, i.e. an owner who does not hold the property subject to the interests of anyone else, as free to do what he will with that property as long as his use of that property is not contrary

---

1   (1840) 3 Beav 148.

to the law and does not injure another. An absolute owner may lend his property to anyone, in which case it will be returned to him or he may dispose of his property by selling it, giving it away, or creating a trust of the property. The absolute owner may even dispose of the property by destroying it as long as the destruction is not contrary to common law or in a manner which is an actionable nuisance.[2]

Thus we have to consider three main types of right of disposal of property:

- Sale
- Gift
- Trust

The absolute owner may also give someone else the right to decide who his property is to be given to. This is referred to as a power of appointment, as the owner gives the donee of the power the right to pick who shall receive his property.

For our purposes the law of sale is subject to the common law of contract and so outside the scope of this work, unless the common law requires the assistance of equity to set aside the bargain, rescission, or remedy an actionable defect of the bargain.[3] A bargain here requires consideration to be enforceable at common law and equity follows the common law here as equity will not assist a volunteer, i.e. someone who has not provided valuable consideration.[4]

In deciding whether there is certainty of intention it is most often the gift, trust and power that are confused as all may involve a transfer of property for no consideration. The gift, trust and power need to be distinguished:

---

2   For the celebrated but unusual case which gives this principle , albeit for a very strange category of property, involving the cremation of the defendant's infant son's corpse, see *R v Price* (1884) 12 QBD 247. As already noted it may be considered against public policy to direct the destruction of property in a will: see *Eyerman v Mercantile Trust Co. Nat'l Assoc.* 524 S.W. 2d 210 (Mo. App., D.St. L. 1975), where the testatrix's wish to have her house 'razed' was considered to violate public policy and not followed; and *Brown v Burdett* (1882) 21 Ch D 667, where a trust to board up a house for 20 years was deemed capricious, without reason and so contrary to public policy and void.

3   See the chapter on remedies.

4   We shall consider this maxim when we consider the constitution of trusts and the perfection of gifts The most important exception to the principle that equity will not assist a volunteer is the beneficiary. Beneficiaries usually do not give consideration to be made beneficiaries, but receive equity's assistance in enforcing the trust against the trustee and those who have knowledge of the trust.

Gift: if a transferor has intended to give the beneficial interest in property to the person he transfers legal title to then this is a gift not a trust. The transferor is called the donor and the transferee is called the donee.

Trust: if a transferor transfers legal title of the property to the recipient with the intention that such recipient hold the property for the benefit of someone else then that is a trust. The transferor is a settlor (or testator if the transfer is in a will), the transferee is the trustee and the ultimate recipient is the beneficiary.

Power: if the transferor has transferred property to another and has instructed that other that they may select who is to receive it, either from the world or from an identified group of possible recipients, but they do not have to select anyone, then the person who may select the ultimate recipient is the donee of a power of appointment. Those who may receive the property are possible appointees under the power.

If there is no reliable evidence of the intent behind a gratuitous transfer of property equity will presume that the transferor intended the property to be returned to him or held on trust for him: this is the presumption of resulting trust.[5] To be any other sort of transfer, such as a gift, express trust or power, there must be evidence of the intention of the transferor to transfer the property for this purpose.

6.1.1 Gift or trust?

From the outside the gift and trust seem very similar as both involve a transfer of legal title to property from the transferor to the transferee without consideration;[6] the difference is the intent of the transferor. Thus to be a gift the property must be delivered to the donee with the intention of the donor that the donee receives beneficial interest in the property as well as legal title. The donor must intend to abandon all interest in the property. For testamentary devises of land there is a very important statutory presumption, in s.28 of the Wills Act 1837 that any devise of real estate without words of limitation shall pass the whole interest the testator had in the estate unless a contrary intention shall appear in the will.[7] To be an express trust all the requirements for the establishment of an express trust must be complied with, including transfer of the property to the trustee, coupled with certainty of the intention of the settlor to subject the trustee to the trust obligation.

---

5   *Dyer v Dyer* (1788) 2 Cox Eq Cas 92.
6   Consideration may be given as part of a contract to create a trust: see chapter on constitution of trusts.
7   This provision means the presumption of resulting trust will rarely arise regarding dispositions of land in a will unless there is an attempt to create a testamentary trust which fails because, for example, the beneficiary is not identified, in which case a resulting trust will arise automatically in favour of the estate rather than as a presumption.

Equity decides if there is sufficient intention for a gift or trust by considering the words used to effect the transfer, the construction of the trust instrument and the circumstances of the transfer. The words used before or at the time of transfer of the property are very important so that the certainty of intention is sometimes referred to as the certainty of words. Of course a trust may be created with very little formality, so no set words are necessary, unless it is a trust of land, because *equity looks to the intent (or substance) rather than the form.* Therefore the settlor 'need not use the words, "I declare myself a trustee', but he must do something that is equivalent to it'. Of course the words 'trust' or 'trustee' may indicate that the transfer was subject to a certain trust obligation; however, it is not necessary to use these words.

Paul v Constance[8]

Mrs Paul and Mr Constance co-habited, Mr Constance was still married and had not bothered to get a divorce. Mr Constance received £950 as an award for an industrial injury. He and Mrs Paul went to the bank to open a joint bank account to place this award and some of their savings in. As this was a time when cohabiting was not generally socially acceptable, the bank manager advised that they open the account in Mr Constance's sole name. The couple subsequently placed some joint bingo winnings in the account. Mrs Paul was concerned about the money, but Mr Constance told her that 'the money is as much yours as mine'. Mr Constance died and Mrs Constance, his estranged wife, reappeared and demanded the contents of the bank account as his widow. Mrs Paul's lawyers argued that Mr Constance had held the money on trust for himself and Mrs Paul.

Judgment: the English Court of Appeal held that Mr Constance's repeated reassurance of Mrs Paul that the money was as much hers as his, the attempt to create a joint bank account and their dealings with the account as if it were joint, showed a clear intention by Mr Constance to hold the money on trust for them both. The Court ordered the money divided between Mrs Paul and the widow. The Court stressed that due to Mr Constance's 'unsophisticated character' he would not have used terms such as 'trust' and 'trustee'. However, his words and actions were equivalent to declaring himself trustee of his own account.

An intention to create a trust may also be found from the actions of the settlor.

Re Kayford Ltd [9]

The company was a mail order business that received money from customers before posting products to them. The company got into financial

---

8   [1977] 1 All ER 195 (CA).
9   [1975] 1 WLR 279.

difficulties and was in danger of liquidation. In what may be considered an unusually honourable action for many businesses, the company created a separate account for its customer pre-payments which it called the 'customers' trust deposit account'. The company only transferred money from this account to its main account when it had sent the goods. The company went into liquidation and the liquidator attempted to claim the money in the account for the general distribution on liquidation. The court was asked to decide whether placing the money into a separate account was enough to evidence that the company had certainty of intention to create a trust in favour of its customers.

Judgment: the court held that the action of placing the money in a separate designated customer account showed sufficient intention to create a trust. All the express trust requirements were complied with. The money belonged to the customers who had paid for goods but not received them; it could not be used for the liquidation and did not belong to the general creditors.

Some academics have questioned the legitimacy of inferring a trust from such actions and in such circumstances, as when a company is liquidated or a person declared bankrupt the assets available to meet the debts is usually not enough, therefore someone must lose. In those circumstances it has been argued it is unfair to recognise a trust over assets of the bankrupt unless the three certainties are clearly present. This argument will be considered again when we consider certainty of subject matter in insolvency/bankruptcy cases.

As will be seen when we consider certainty of subject matter the segregation of the fund is usually vital for the creation of the express trust even if there is clear certainty of intention. Thus in ***Moriarty v Atkinson***,[10] the English Court of Appeal held that funds designated for a client account were not subject to a trust if they were not placed there, even though the failure to place them in the account was in consequence of a breach of trust by the company. Thus the client had no beneficial interest in the misplaced funds and so no proprietary right and consequent right to trace.

If the word 'trust' is not used then the court will look for other words which import a mandatory obligation, e.g. 'shall' and 'must',[11] as trusts are mandatory, they must be carried out by the trustees. Of particular concern for a court when deciding whether there is sufficient certainty of intention to create a trust are precatory words. Precatory words are words that merely evidence a wish or hope rather than a mandatory obligation. Up until the mid-nineteenth century in England precatory words could be held to evidence an intention to create a trust, sometimes termed a 'precatory

---

10   [2009] All ER (D) 154 (Feb); The Times, January 12, 2009.
11   *Re Sayer* [1956] 3 All ER 600; *Re Saxone Ltd's Trust Deed* [1962] 2 All ER 904; *McPhail v. Doulton* [1971] AC 424.

trust'. For example in *Palmer v Simmonds*,[12] the phrase 'in full confidence' was used and the Vice-Chancellor held that: 'In most of the cases of this class the Court is called upon to do what it is persuaded was never the intention of the testator; for when a testator expresses his *confidence* that the devisee will do so and so, what he really means is to say that he expresses the *confidence*, because he does not mean to create a *trust*. He gives absolutely, because he has confidence. But then this Court has said that is a reason why the Court should create a trust.'[13]

Therefore, even though the court was sure there was no intention to create a trust it upheld a trust. However, in this particular case, as there was uncertainty of subject matter, discussed below, there was no trust but an absolute gift. The tide turned in *Lambe v Eames*.[14] The Court of Appeal held that such words were not enough on their own to evidence certainty of intention to place the transferee under a trust obligation. The testator had left his estate to his wife, 'to be at her disposal in any way she may think best, for the benefit of herself and her family'. The Court held that the words used were insufficient to evidence a certainty to place the wife under a trust obligation. The legacy thus took effect as an absolute gift to the wife, which might be subject to a moral obligation to benefit her family, but no more. The previous acceptance of Chancery of precatory words creating trusts was described by Sir W.M. James L.J. as 'officious kindness'. However, he was 'unable to spell out of the word "*wish*" any such thing as an imperative command'.[15] Subsequently, Chancery was reluctant to find a trust obligation if words such as 'hope', 'desire',[16] 'wish' or 'confidence' without some other mandatory word. Thus, in **Re Adams and the Kensington Vestry**,[17] the testator left his estate 'unto and to the absolute use of my dear wife, Harriet… in full confidence that she will do what is right as to the disposal thereof between my children, either in her lifetime or by will after her decease.' The court held that the precatory word 'confidence' was not enough to place the wife under a trust obligation. Again the wife took the property as an absolute gift with merely a moral obligation to 'do what's right' by the children. The Court also held that the whole trust instrument should be considered to detect sufficient certainty. Cotton LJ said:

'we must not extend the old cases in any way, or rely upon the mere use of any particular words, but, considering all the words which are used, we

---

12   *Palmer v. Simmonds* (1854) 2 Drew 221.
13   *Palmer v. Simmonds* (1854) 2 Drew 221, at 225.
14   [1871] 6 Ch App 597.
15   [1871] 6 Ch App 597, at 599 per Sir W. M. James, L.J.
16   In *Re Diggles* (1888) 39 Ch D 253 no trust was created by the words, 'it is my desire that she allows [X] an annuity of £25.'
17   [1884] 27 ChD 394.

have to see what is their true effect, and what was the intention of the testator as expressed in his will.'

Thus the whole of the trust instrument must be considered when the court looks for sufficient certainty of intention to create a trust. Although this certainty was not present in *Adams*, similar wording coupled with mandatory words in the instrument can provide certainty that a trust was intended. This is exemplified by the case of **Comisky v. Bowring–Hanbury**,[18] where the testator left property to his wife:

'in full confidence that … at her death she will devise it to such one or more of my nieces as she may think fit and in default of any disposition by her thereof by will… I hereby direct that all my estate and property acquired by her under this my will shall at her death be equally divided among the surviving said nieces.'

The House of Lords held that the precatory words 'in full confidence' should be considered in the light of the whole instrument which also contained the mandatory word 'shall'. Thus although 'in full confidence' had failed to evidence certainty of intention to create a trust in Adams, the word 'shall' imputed a mandatory obligation upon the wife. Thus she was under a trust obligation.

Today precatory words on their own do not evidence sufficient certainty of intention to create a trust, but they are also not fatal to the transfer being a trust. The court should take a benignant approach. Therefore, the court should not unduly strive to find a trust but should be willing to consider the overall construction of the instrument to see if there was a trust obligation intended. If the transfer of property is in a will, the presumption is that a transfer of property is a gift, but the whole provision will be considered to see if there is a trust obligation intended. Thus trust instruments and especially wills must be drafted with great care to ensure that intentions are clear.

There is one last strange exception to the principle that precatory words do not create a trust obligation and this is the case of **Re Steele's WT**.[19] In this case the testatrix left a diamond necklace to her son in her will with the phrase: 'I request my said son to do all in his power by this will or otherwise to give effect to my wish'. The wish was to make the necklace a family heirloom for her son to hold on trust for the next generation of the family. The words 'request' and 'wish' are undoubtedly precatory and not mandatory but the court held the provision created a trust because the clause was copied from an earlier case where the exact same clause had been held to create a trust. This may be considered an exception that succeeded purely because of the precedent and not a general principle. It is submitted that such reliance on precedent should be avoided today in favour of clear simple mandatory words.

---

18   [1905] AC 84.
19   [1948] Ch 603.

There may be clear simple mandatory words but no real intention to create a trust. In such cases the transferor's intent may be to pretend to create a trust to protect assets from creditors. These cases are known as 'shams'.

Midland Bank plc v Wyatt[20]

Mr and Mrs Wyatt were joint owners of the family home, subject to mortgage. They both signed a declaration of trust of the beneficial interest of the house in favour of Mrs Wyatt and their daughters. At this point, if the trust were in existence, Mr Wyatt held only bare legal title and no beneficial interest. Mr Wyatt took out loans with his bank on the understanding that he still had a beneficial interest in the property. His business went into receivership and the bank attempted to effect security against the house. Mr Wyatt claimed that he was only a trustee of the house for his wife and daughters and therefore it could not be used to satisfy his creditors.

Judgment: Although Mr Wyatt had signed a declaration of trust, the court held that the arrangement was purely a sham; Mr Wyatt had never intended to create a trust. He had never intended to give his beneficial interest in the property to his wife and daughters he had merely set up the arrangement to defeat his creditors. Therefore the trust did not exist and the bank could take action against the house.

6.1.2 Lack of clear certainty of intention

Generally a disposition of property in a will is under the presumption that an absolute gift is intended unless there is clear evidence to the contrary. This principle was originally known as the rule in *Lassence v Tierney*.[21] Thus a testamentary provision which may have been intended as a trust

---

20   [1995] 3 FCR 11.
21   (1849) 1 Mac & Cr 551; 41 ER 1379: the rule is a rule of interpretation: the rule prescribes that if a testator leaves a legacy absolutely, but restricts the mode of the legatee's enjoyment of it to secure certain objects for the benefit of the legatee, on the failure of those objects the absolute gift prevails, but, if there be no absolute gift as between the legatee and the estate, but particular modes of enjoyment are prescribed, and those modes of enjoyment fail, the legacy forms part of the testator's estate. In the latter case the gift is only for a particular purpose; in the former, the purpose is the benefit of the legatee as to the whole amount of the legacy, and the directions and restrictions are to be considered as applicable to a sum no longer part of the testator's estate, but already the property of the legatee. In every case, therefore, the question must he one of construction, and on construction the intention that the gift should be absolute as between the legatee and the estate is to be collected from the whole of the will, and not from there being words which, standing alone, would constitute an absolute gift.

but does not show clear evidence of that intention will be an absolute gift to the legatee. For an *intervivos* gratuitous transfer of property if there is no clear certainty of intention to create a trust or give a gift then the property will be held on resulting trust by the transferee for the transferor. Situations involving clear certainty of intention to create a trust but failure of one or more of the other certainties will be discussed subsequently.

6.1.3 Trust or power?

A power of appointment is another mechanism of equity which allows others to distribute our property. A power is the authority to deal with property in a certain way.

The person who gives someone else a power is the donor of the power; the person who receives it is the donee. The persons who receive the property when the power is exercised are the appointees.

There are different types of powers and they may be classified by the donee's relationship to the property (or his office), or by the class of potential appointees. We will first consider the donee's relationship to the trust property. This may result in either a bare power or a fiduciary power. Although other terms are used for these powers the use of different terms for the same power has caused confusion. Therefore we will follow the classification of bare or fiduciary powers in line with the practitioners' text *"Thomas on Powers"*.[22]

Bare and fiduciary powers
A bare or personal power is a power given to a donee who is not a trustee of the property and so does not have legal title to it. For example, Sam owns shares in China Oil. In his will he gives Tim a power of appointment over his (Sam's) property: 'Tim may select which of my grandchildren is to receive my shares in China Oil or the proceeds of sale from these shares after my death.' Sam is the donor of the power, Tim is the donee of the power, and Sam's grandchildren are the potential appointees of the power.

Donor (Sam) $\longrightarrow$ Donee (Tim)
Appointees (Grandchildren)

This is a bare power of appointment. Tim does not have to have legal title transferred to him as he is not the trustee of the property. He has only a power to appoint (that is- to choose) whichever of Sam's grandchildren he wishes to receive the shares or the proceeds of their sale. He does not have to do anything because a power is discretionary it is not mandatory like a trust As this is a bare power he is not a trustee and so Tim is not under a fiduciary duty. As this is a bare power the potential appointees, the

---

22   G. Thomas, *Thomas on Powers*, 2nd edition (London: Sweet & Maxwell, 1998).

grandchildren, can do nothing whatsoever to compel Tim to exercise his power. The only obligation is to consider exercising the discretion from time to time.[23] If Tim chooses not to appoint, the property will either devolve in accordance with any alternative provisions (*i.e.* a gift over) or it will go on resulting trust back to the donor. The court will of course intervene if the donee exceeds or abuses the power given to him. The donee of a bare power exercises it by instructing the legal owner of the property, often a trustee, who to give the property to.

Powers are often found in association with trusts. If the donee is not the trustee, he does not have legal title to the property, it is bare power. For example, 'I leave my estate to Paul to hold on trust for my children until they reach 25 years of age. Whilst Paul is holding the estate on trust, my wife may give the income from the property to any charity she wishes.' Here the testator's wife has a power of appointment, she is the donee of the power, she does not hold the legal title to the property, and she merely has the authority to tell the trustee who to give the interest to. The potential appointees are any charity of my wife's choice.

The main difference between a power and a trust is that a power is discretionary, it does not have to be carried out, and a trust is mandatory, it must be performed. In the example above, the testator's wife does not have to pick any charity; she has discretion whether to exercise her power, she 'may' give the money to any charity but does not have to. If she does not appoint a charity then the income from the fund is usually added to the capital unless specified otherwise. The trustee, Paul, must hold the property on trust and give it to the children when they reach a certain age. His obligations are mandatory; he must perform his trust duties.

A fiduciary power is where a trustee is given a power of appointment over the trust property. Because the donee is already under a fiduciary obligation to protect the trust property and carry out the trust, the donee/trustee is then under a fiduciary duty with regard to the power. However, this does not mean the donee can be compelled to exercise the power. For example, 'I give my estate to Paul to hold on trust for my grandchildren when they reach 18 years. Before this Paul may distribute any income from the estate to any of my children as he thinks fit.' Paul is here a trustee and also has a power of appointment. This power is therefore a fiduciary power because he is a trustee. As all powers are discretionary

---

23 *Re Hay's ST* [1981] 3 All ER 786. The limits of the obligation of the donee were considered by Sir Robert Megarry V.C.: 'A mere power is very different [from a discretionary trust]. Normally the trustee is not bound to exercise it, and the court will not compel him to do so. That, however, does not mean that he can simply fold his hands and ignore it, for normally he must from time to time consider whether or not to exercise his power, and the court may direct him to do this ...'

the fiduciary power does not have to be exercised by the donee. Of course, the trustee is under a mandatory obligation and so the beneficiaries can go to court to ask the court to make him carry out his trust obligations.

General, special or hybrid powers

Powers are also classified by potential donees. They may be general, special, or hybrid/intermediate powers. The general power of appointment does not specify any class of appointee or restrict the class of appointee. Thus a general power of appointment may be in favour of anyone, including the donee. For example, I leave my house to Hannah for life with power to appoint to the remainder any such persons as she may at her absolute discretion choose. Hannah has the power to pick anyone she wishes to receive the house when she dies. However, this is a power and so she does not have to choose anyone. If she does not choose then any relevant provision in the testator's will takes effect or it will fall to the residual legatee. If there is no residual legatee then the house will be distributed on the rules of intestacy.

A special power of appointment specifies the class of appointees from which the donee must choose. For example, I leave my house to Hannah for life with power to appoint to the remainder any of my grandchildren as she may at her absolute discretion choose. Here the donee, Hannah, must choose one of the donor's grandchildren, if she does exercise her discretion. In **Re Combe**,[24] the son was given a special power of appointment as the trustees were directed to hold property, 'on trust for such person or persons as my said son … shall by will appoint, but I direct that such appointment must be confined to any relation or relations of mine of the whole blood.' Thus the trustees held the property in trust until the son exercised his bare (because he was not a trustee) special power of appointment in favour of a blood relative.

A hybrid/intermediate power of appointment forbids certain persons from being in the potential class of appointees. For example, I leave my house to Hannah for life with power to appoint to the remainder any such persons as she may at her absolute discretion choose except supporters of Chelsea Football Club. Thus Hannah can select anyone to be her successor to the house except a supporter of Chelsea Football Club.

Trust powers

There is also a type of power which is very confusingly called a 'trust power'. This is a power which is coupled with a trust-like obligation. These powers would normally only occur when the potential appointees are members of a very small class of the donor's family members and there is

---

24   [1925] Ch 210.

no direction for the property to go elsewhere if the power is not exercised. The obligation here arises because if the power is not exercised the property would result back to the donor's estate and this is not what the donor intended. If a trust power is not exercised then the property is usually divided equally among the class of appointees.[25] Courts do not always find in favour of trust powers and good drafting should avoid the necessity for such deliberations. Thus, in **Re Weekes' Settlement**,[26] the husband was left property for life with the provision 'and I give to him power to dispose of all said property amongst our children'. The husband failed to appoint. Romer J. held that the husband had a mere power and not a trust power. The property resulted back to the wife's estate.

Differentiating between a trust and a power
It is very important to differentiate between a trust and a power because a trust must be carried out, the trustees are under a fiduciary duty with regard to the trust property and the beneficiaries, who in turn have rights as against the trustees and the trust property. However, it can be very difficult to distinguish, as, in the same way that trusts may be created without the use of the word 'trust', powers may be created without the use of the word 'power'. The courts distinguish by considering the words used by the settlor/ donor and the construction of the provision. If the words are mandatory, for example 'must' or 'shall' then the provision is probably a trust , if the words used are discretionary, for example 'may', then the provision is likely to be a power. For example, in **Re Coates**,[27] the provision read:

'if my wife feels that I have forgotten any friend I direct my executors to pay to such friends as are nominated by my wife a sum not exceeding GBP25 per friend with maximum aggregate payment of GBP250 so that such friends may buy a small memento of our friendship.'

There was no mandatory obligation on the wife to distribute, she could decide to if she 'feels' it necessary, this was construed as a power.

Very similar provisions may be construed in different ways because of one word. For example, in both **Re Sayer**,[28] and **Re Saxone Ltd's Trust Deed**,[29] the directors of two companies were able to distribute funds to employees of the respective companies and their dependents. However, in *Re Sayer* the directors were 'empowered to make payments', whereas in *Re Saxone* the clause provided that the fund 'shall in the discretion of the

---

25 Trust powers are often said to come from the case of *Burrough v. Philcox* (1840) 5 My&Cr 72.
26 [1897] Ch 289.
27 (*Coates v Brittlebank*) (1881) 30 WR 99.
28 [1956] 3 All ER 600.
29 [1962] 2 All ER 904.

directors' be distributed. In *Re Sayer* the court held the clause was a power, whereas in *Re Saxone* the use of 'shall' meant that the directors had to distribute the fund and so it was a discretionary trust.

McPhail v Doulton[30] is the most celebrated case in distinguishing between a power and a trust and will be considered again when the tests used by the courts to decide if there is sufficient certainty of subject matter of the trust are discussed below. The House of Lords considered the relevant provisions of Bertram Baden's will to decide if they created a trust or power:

'trustees shall apply the net income of the fund in making at their absolute discretion grants to or for the benefit of any of the officers and employees or ex-officers or ex-employees or to any relatives or dependants of such persons in such amounts or at such times and on such conditions (if any) as they think fit'.

The Court of Appeal held that the provision was merely a power of appointment and thus discretionary. However, following *Re Saxone*, Lord Wilberforce held the use of the imperative word 'shall' meant that the instruction was mandatory; it had to be carried out. It was a trust.

The difference of opinion between the Court of Appeal and the House of Lords highlights how difficult it may be to distinguish between a trust and a power. However, there is one clear rule for distinguishing and that is where the property is subject to a gift over it cannot be a trust obligation. This is because the person selected to decide who is to receive the property does not have to select as the property has an alternative destination if there is no selection. As there is no mandatory obligation, it is purely discretionary and so is a power;[31] of course the fact that there is no gift over does not mean that the provision is always a trust.[32] For example, Donald leaves the following provision in his will: 'I leave my shares in British Petroleum to my wife; she may distribute the income from the shares to any animal sanctuary for 10 years. After 10 years she shall give the shares to my son, Ben.' There are two parts to this provision; the ultimate gift of the shares and the ability to distribute the income from the shares before that ultimate gift. Here, the wife is under a mandatory obligation, she 'shall' give the shares to the son after 10 years, but she 'may' give the income before then to any animal sanctuary. Therefore, there is a 'gift over', the shares will be given ultimately to the son. This is a trust obligation. The ability to give the income to the animal sanctuary in the meantime is purely discretionary; she 'may'. This is a power because it cannot be mandatory as there is an ultimate destination for the shares and the income if she does not distribute the income.[33]

---

30 (*Re Baden's DT No. 1*) [1971] AC 424.
31 *Re Mills* [1930] 1 Ch 654.
32 *Re Weekes' Settlement* [1897] Ch 289.
33 See Lord Wilberforce in *McPhail v. Doulton* [1971] AC 424.

Just to add to the confusion discretionary trusts may be exhaustive or non-exhaustive. An exhaustive discretionary trust places the trustees under an obligation to distribute the income from the trust as it arises. However, a non-exhaustive discretionary trust provides that the trustees *may* accumulate income until the terms of the trust say it must finally be distributed. The non-exhaustive discretionary trust then appears to be a power of appointment with a gift over.

Therefore it is not always easy to distinguish between a power and a trust but it is important because of the different obligations and rights of the parties. The usual method is to note if there is a gift over, which indicates a power, if there is not then the words and construction of the relevant provision must be construed.

Trusts and powers will be discussed again when we consider the tests used to decide certainty of objects.

6.2 Certainty of Subject Matter

The settlor must specify what property is to form the subject matter of the trust and the quantum (amount) of the beneficiary's interest in this trust property, unless it is a discretionary trust and the interest is left to the discretion of the trustees. The trustees must know this so that they can protect the property and distribute it in accordance with the trust. The court must be able to ascertain what property forms the subject matter of the trust and the beneficial interest in that property in order to make the trustee carry out the trust. Therefore the subject matter must be identifiable or distinguishable.

Problems occur when:

1   the description of the property has been too vague; or
2   the property is a share or portion of a larger stock and it is not clear which item or items are to be the trust property; or
3   the description of the quantum of the purported beneficiary's interest is uncertain (and there is no provision which will allow that to be made certain).

To be ascertainable the subject matter of a trust must be identifiable; if it is in chattels they must be identifiable or segregated, if it is in specie, i.e. money, then it must be quantifiable. A trust is possible over the residuary estate of a testator because it is quantifiable; it can be 'worked out'. [34] Thus a provision in a will that reads, 'I leave the residue of my estate to my brother Tim to hold on trust for my children in equal shares until they reach 25 years', would be a valid fixed trust of whatever was left of the

---

34   *T Choitheram International SA v Pagarani* [2001] 1 WLR 1

testator's estate after the debts of the estate, the costs of administration and every other provision had been paid. However, problems occur when attempts are made to create trusts over the residue of a gift, e.g. 'I leave my case of wine to my brother Tim, he must hold whatever he does not drink himself on trust for my brother Robert'. As we shall see this would fail as a trust and take effect as an absolute gift as the amount forming the subject matter of the trust, 'whatever he does not drink' is uncertain.

6.2.1 Segregation: chattels and intangibles

The subject matter of a trust must be ascertainable; that is it must be possible to discover with certainty what it is. [35] For example, the income from a fund is certain as it can be ascertained; if the fund is invested in a bank account then the income is the interest which is paid on the account, even though this may vary over time, the income will always be whatever the bank pay and so is certain.

For chattels to form the subject matter of a trust they must be clearly identified or, if they are part of a group of items, they must be segregated, that is separated or isolated from others or from the main body or group. An item may also be ascertained if it is appropriated, that is set apart for a specific use. The idea of certainty of subject matter for chattels is that all chattels are slightly different, to use the example of a trust over six of twelve Han Dynasty vases- the six must be ascertainable; this may be achieved by segregating them, separating them from the other vases and identifying this six as the vases subject to the trust obligation. They may also be identified for use as the trust property by appropriating them, again setting them aside for use as the trust property. The six must be identified or segregated because no two Han vases are absolutely identical. This principle holds true even for items which we might consider identical, for example mobile phones of the same make, model and date of manufacture, and even the micro-chips that make up those phones. However much the manufacturers may claim they are identical there will be minute differences, no two are exactly identical and so they must be identified or segregated if they are to form the subject matter of a trust. If trust property forms part of a larger whole then it is usually necessary to segregate it or identify it in a way that segregates it, e.g. by marking boxes or bottles etc. This seems particularly relevant when the subject matter is chattels, movable tangible personal property. The situation with intangible property is less settled.

---

35 Identification or Segregation of trust property is necessary for trusts: *In the Matter of Lehman Brothers International (Europe) (In Administration) and In the matte of the Insolvency Act 1986* [2012] UKSC 6.

Re London Wine Co. Ltd.[36]

The company sold wine to customers, but the wine was held in the company's cellars and stores awaiting delivery. There was some evidence that there had been an intention that the wine was to be held on trust for the customers to avoid the wine being part of the general assets on an insolvent liquidation, but the wine had not been segregated or marked so that it could be identified as being the trust property of any particular customer.

Judgment: the court held that there was no trust as it was impossible to say which bottle belonged to whom. According to Lord Oliver J, 'as it seems to me, to create a trust it must be possible to ascertain with certainty not only what the interest of the beneficiary is to be but to what property it is to attach.'

This may be contrasted with the previously considered case of **Re Kayford Ltd**,[37] where the company had intended the money to be on trust for the customers' and had paid the customers' money into a special account. The money was segregated from the company's and thus identifiable. The point is further illustrated by **Re Stapylton Fletcher**,[38] which followed **Re London Wine Co. Ltd**. [39]In this case customers had paid a wine merchant to store wine in segregated bottles, or for '*en primeur*' wines (wine still in the cask and not yet bottled). The court held that there were trusts in favour of the customers who had paid for the segregated bottled wine but no trusts for the customers who had paid for the wine still in casks, as it was not segregated and identifiable. The court placed much emphasis on the concept of 'ascertained goods' in the Sale of Goods Act 1979. Thus the goods which were identified as the customers were ascertained for the purposes of the legislation. The issue in *Re London Wine* and *Stapylton* has been dealt with in as far as it involves purchasers from an insolvent seller by the Sale of Goods (Amendment) Act 1995.[40] This provides that purchasers who have paid for unascertained goods which are held as part of an identified whole should be treated as tenants in common of the whole, thus having a proprietary interest and ranking ahead of general creditors on insolvency.

Shortly after this the Privy Council considered the issue of certainty of subject matter with regard to tangible chattels

Re Goldcorp Exchange Ltd.[41]

Purchasers of bullion paid for the bullion, but it was stored by the company. Some bullion was segregated for certain customers, but most

36   [1986] PCC 121.
37   [1975] 1 WLR 279.
38   [1994] 1 WLR 1181.
39   [1986] PCC 121.
40   Inserting S20A into the Sale of Goods Act 1979
41   [1995] 1 AC 74.

remained together. Some customers had specified the purchase of a particular type of gold coin, but these had not been segregated. Goldcorp became insolvent and a dispute ensued over whether the gold was held on trust.

Judgment: the Privy Council held that the unsegregated bullion was not subject to a trust. Only the bullion that was segregated was subject to a trust. Those customers whose gold was segregated held the beneficial interest in the bullion and so could defeat the claims of Goldcorp's secured creditors. Although the Council expressed sympathy for the customers who had paid for unsegregated gold, it was keen to point out that a legal or equitable right in property cannot exist in the air, floating over an unidentified mass of property. Thus it can only exist in relation to property which is specifically ascertained. As this was a matter of property rights, the Council noted that equity should not develop its own flexible notion of certainty of subject matter just in order to provide the sympathetic result in a particular case.

The decision in *Goldcorp* was made despite the fact that individual bars of bullion carry registration numbers and can be identified, and the customers who had specified the purchase of the particular gold coins came very close to having an identifiable interest. Again the most important factor in this decision seems to be the insolvency of the company; if a trust were declared over all the gold then the priority of insolvent distribution would be disturbed and this would harm commercial certainty although it might provide individual justice.[42]

Thus the general principle is that tangible chattels that form the subject matter of trust must be segregated or identifiable. As noted above, however much chattels may seem to be identical the law does not usually treat them as such because they may vary in minute detail. However, an exception to this principle has arisen for intangible property or *choses in action*.[43] In the case of **Hunter v. Moss**,[44] the Court of Appeal declined to follow *Re London Wine Co.*, preferring instead to distinguish the case.

Hunter v. Moss[45]

Moss held 950 shares in Moss Ltd absolutely. Hunter worked for Moss Ltd and Moss made an oral declaration of trust of 50 of his 950 shares in favour of Hunter. Moss and Hunter then argued and Moss refused to honour the

---

42   See Gerard McCormack, 'The Remedial Constructive Trusts and Commercial Transactions' [1996] 17(1) *Comp Law* 3-11.
43   A *chose in action* is literally a right to take action whether at law or in equity. The term is now applied to intangible personal property, e.g. the benefit of a debt, as the person who has the benefit of a debt may sue (claim) upon the debt.
44   [1994] 1 WLR 452.
45   [1994] 1 WLR 452.

trust. Moss argued there was no certainty of subject matter as the shares were not identified or segregated. Thus there was no valid trust.

Judgment: the Court of Appeal distinguished and so did not follow *Re London Wine Co.*. The Court upheld the trust because the shares were in a company which was clearly identifiable and all the shares in this company were identical. *Choses in action* (and ownership of a share gives a *chose in action*) were not the same as chattels such as bottles of wine because *choses in action* are identical. The Court stressed that even bottles of wine of the same type and vintage may not be identical: some of them may be 'corked' *etc*. But the shares were identical because they merely served as evidence of a right against the company. Thus it did not matter which fifty shares were held on trust and therefore the trust was valid.

There has been some academic debate over the decision in *Hunter v Moss*, with some support but much criticism[46], although in particular Professor Hudson notes the context of the decisions. In *Re London Wine Company*, there was an insolvent liquidation and not enough assets to settle the obligations to every creditor, someone had to lose, and the court's decision upholds the normal principles on insolvent liquidation that all the assets go into the pot to be distributed between the creditors according to the recognised priority in liquidation. To recognise a trust over certain of the assets would upset the priority. In *Hunter v Moss*, the purported settlor was not in an insolvent state and was merely trying to avoid his promise. Hudson says the Court was here free to prevent the settlor acting unconscionably without affecting the established rules on property distribution.

Although there has been some judicial support for *Hunter v. Moss*,[47] this has not been without some caution. Thus in **Re Harvard Securities Ltd,**[48] Neuberger J had to consider whether there were trusts involving English and Australian shares. Neuberger J. followed *Hunter v. Moss* and found a trust of the English shares, but no trust for those which were subject to the different principles of Australian law.

Some commentators have concluded that *Hunter v Moss* has identified that intangible property is subject to different principles from tangible property, as intangible property is fungible or interchangeable,[49] which

---

46   Penner simply states that the Court of Appeal's decision in Hunter threw this area of law into 'turmoil': J. Penner, *The Law of Trusts* (Oxford: Oxford University Press,2008), 189. It should be remembered that Penner also questioned the decision in *Re Kayford* because it upset the normal priorities on an insolvent liquidation.

47   See for example *Re Clowes (No.2)* [1994] 2 All ER 316

48   [1997] 2 BCLC 369.

49   Property is said to be fungible in nature if it is composed of legally equivalent units so that the units are interchangeable and can be divided and owned separately: Sir Roy Goode, 'Are Intangible Assets Fungibles?' (2003) *LMCLQ* 379 at 383.

means that segregation is not necessary. However, this does not account for earlier judgments such as ***Mac-Jordan v. Brookmount***,[50] where it was held there could be no trust of an unsegregated amount of money. In *Mac-Jordan*, an employer had the contractual right to retain 3% of the contract price as trustee for the builder until the work was deemed satisfactory. The money was not segregated, but kept by the employer with the employer's other money. The employer became insolvent and the builder claimed the 3% as a beneficiary. The court held that the money that formed the subject matter of the trust was not ascertainable. The trust failed for certainty of subject matter.

In ***Re Lehman Brothers International (Europe) (In Administration)***,[51] the Supreme Court noted that, 'Under English law the mere segregation of money into separate bank accounts is not sufficient to establish a proprietary interest in those funds for anyone other than the account holder.' Thus if a claimant wishes to establish a proprietary interest in the fund because the account holder is insolvent there must have been a declaration of trust over the fund in the account. As the Supreme Court noted neither segregation nor a declaration of trust on their own is enough for the claimant to establish a proprietary interest: 'When both elements are present they work together to give the complete protection against the risk of the [defendant's] insolvency that the [claimant] requires.' [52]

Of course the issue of segregation for money is not always a problem. For example if a trust is created in a will for a certain amount of money this does not have to be segregated as the executors are under a duty to realise the assets of the estate, pay the debts and then if they can, distribute in accordance with the will. They would therefore pass the required amount to the trustee. Thus the money would be ascertained.

The issue of segregation of assets for a trust has been dealt with in a different way by the Australian courts as they have accepted that a trust could be created over a group of assets with the trustees given the power to divide the group into shares for the designated beneficiaries.[53]

6.2.2 Attempts to create a trust over part of a gift

As mentioned above although it is possible to have a trust over the residuary estate, as the term residuary estate is certain because it may be worked out, it may be a problem if a trust is declared over the residue or whatever is left of a gift. For example, in ***Palmer v. Simmonds***,[54] the

---

50   [1992] BCLC

51   [2010] UKSC 6.

52   [2010] UKSC 6 at 2 per Lord Hope.

53   *White v Shortall* [2006] NSWSC 1379.

54   (1854) 2 Drew 221.

testatrix left her estate to Mr Harrison, but added that 'the bulk of my said residuary estate' should be held on trust. As Vice-Chancellor Sir R.T. Kindersley noted:

'what she there meant could not be her residuary estate, which she had already in clear terms given; but the bulk of it... What is the meaning then of bulk ? ...When a person is said to have given the bulk of his property, what is meant is not the whole but the greater part ... When, therefore, the testatrix uses that term, can I say she has used a term expressing a definite, clear, certain part of her estate, or the whole of her estate?[55]

The Court held that it was not possible to identify and quantify what 'the bulk of' was; therefore there was no trust and Harrison took absolutely.[56]

In *Sprange v. Barnard*,[57] it was held that it was impossible to quantify 'the remaining part of what is left' and so there was no trust. Similarly in the *Estate of Last*,[58] a trust of 'anything that is left' failed. In *Re Jones*,[59] the testator left his property to his wife for the use and benefit during her lifetime and "such parts of my estate as she shall not have sold" would pass by her will to other persons, the Court ruled that the trust was not valid and the wife took an absolute interest of the estate. In these cases a failure to create a trust over part of a gift results in the donee of the gift receiving everything as an absolute gift. This is known as the rule in *Hancock v. Watson*,[60] and operates because as we do not know what property is the subject matter of the express trust, we also cannot identify what subject matter should be held on resulting trust for the settlor or the testator's estate. Therefore all the property is an absolute gift. For example, 'I leave all of the money in my savings account to Donald. Whatever he does not use he shall leave in his will to Brian.' This provision gives a gift of the money to Donald, but then purports to create a trust over whatever 'he does not use' in favour of Brian. The subject matter of the purported trust is uncertain; Donald may spend all of the money. Thus the purported trust is void for uncertainty. Therefore Donald takes the gift of all of the money absolutely with no trust obligation. Brian has no interest.

6.2.3 Beneficial interest

The property to be held on trust may be quite certain, but the extent of each beneficiary's interest might not be. If a testator creates a discretionary trust giving his trustees discretion to decide the beneficial interest then

---

55 *Palmer v. Simmonds* (1854) 2 Drew 221, at 225-227.
56 There was also an issue with the testatrix's use of the phrase 'in full confidence' with regard to certainty of intention to create a trust.
57 (1789) 2 Bro CC 585.
58 [1958] P 137.

there should be no issue with the validity of the trust. However, if the trust is a fixed trust and the extent of the beneficiary's interest is not certain, then the trust will fail for uncertainty and the property result back to the settlor or the testator's estate.

Boyce v. Boyce[61]

Two houses were left on trust for two sisters, Maria and Charlotte. The trustees were to convey to Maria 'whichever she may think proper to choose or select'. Charlotte was to have the other. Maria died before the testator and so before she could make her choice. The will was not rewritten. The court had to decide if there was a trust.

Judgment: there was no trust in Charlotte's favour because, although it was certain that the two houses were the subject matter of the trust, it was not certain which Maria would have picked and so it was not certain which was held for Charlotte's benefit. The trustees held the property on resulting trust for the testator's estate.

Many commentators have noted that Boyce v Boyce represents a harsh interpretation of the rule that the beneficial interest must be certain. There have been other cases where it seems the courts will try to validate a trust if it is capable of enforcement.

Re Knapton[62]

By will the testatrix bequeathed 'one house each to each of my nephews and nieces and one to Nellie Hind. One to Florence Knapton. One to my Sister. One to my Brother'. The testatrix did not specify which house was to go to which beneficiary or who was to have first choice of a house. A declaration was sought as to whether the gifts failed for uncertainty and, if not, seeking directions as to the manner in which they should take effect. Applying Boyce v Boyce strictly the gifts should have failed as it was uncertain which house each beneficiary was to get.

Judgment: Simonds J. held that the gifts did not fail for uncertainty, as the beneficiaries could choose which house they wanted in the order named. With regard to the initial gifts, which did not list the beneficiaries but just referred to nephews and nieces, Simonds J. held that civil law and in particular an analogy from Roman law should apply. Thus the nephews and nieces could agree on the choice of house or, if they could not agree, they could draw lots.

---

59   [1898] 1 Ch 438
60   [1902] AC 14 explained by Lord Davey at 22. Although the rule is often referred to as the rule in *Lassence v Tierney* (1849) 1 Mac & G 551, it is a different rule.
61   (1894) 16 Sim 476.
62   *(Knapton v Hindle)* [1941] Ch 428.

In similar vein, uncertainty in the extent of the beneficiary's interest was removed by the use of common sense in *Re Golay's WT.*[63]

Re Golay's WT[64]

The testator directed his executors to let Totty, 'enjoy one of my flats during her lifetime and to receive a reasonable income from my other properties'. There were two issues of uncertainty: first, which flat should Totty live in? and what did the testator mean by 'reasonable income'?

Judgment: a trust had been created. The executors could select the flat, and they could decide what constitutes a reasonable income in the circumstances, bearing in mind such objective factors as Totty's previous standard of living etc. If the executors were not able to do this, the court could decide the matter.

Of course the decision in *Re Knapton* and *Re Golay's* depended on the interpretation of the wording of the trust instruments by the courts. It is likely that a court faced with exactly the situation in *Boyce v Boyce* would feel bound by that decision.

Thus to create an express trust there must be certainty of subject. The actual subject matter of the trust must be certain so that the trustees know what property they are to manage. If the subject matter is uncertain then the trust will fail and the property will return to (or perhaps has never left) the settlor's estate. However, if an attempt to create a trust over part of a gift fails then the transfer becomes an absolute gift of all the property to the transferee. Chattels must be identifiable or segregated to make them ascertainable. There is an exception for intangible property, in particular shares. If the issue is one of the beneficial interests, that is what property is held for each beneficiary, then failure to identify the beneficial interest will cause the trust to fail and the property will result back to the settlor or testator's estate.

6.3 Certainty of Object

There must be certainty of object because the trustees have to know in whose favour they are to perform the trust and the court has to know in whose favour to decree performance of the trust.[65] The beneficiaries must either have been identified by the settlor or the trustees must have the means to identify them.[66] The nature of private trusts varies according to the powers and discretion given to the trustees. The number of beneficiaries of a trust may vary considerably, from a fixed trust identifying

---

63   [1965] 1 WLR 969
64   [1965] 1 WLR 969
65   See the beneficiary principle in the next chapter.
66   From the maxim *certum est quod certum reddi potest* (that is certain which can be made certain).

one named beneficiary to a discretionary trust identifying classes of potential beneficiaries that may number in the hundreds or thousands. If the identification of the beneficiaries is uncertain then the trust fails and the property results back to the settlor or testator's estate. To decide if there is sufficient certainty of objects the courts have developed tests. These tests vary according to whether there is a fixed trust, a discretionary trust or a power of appointment.

As considered before the terms used to describe trusts and powers have been many and varied, and their application has not been uniform. In fact some decisions have categorised what would today be considered a power as a trust and vice versa. This has not helped in the distinction of what certainty is required for a trust or power to be upheld and what test should be applied. The test for powers has traditionally been the most relaxed and we will start by considering it along with the test for trust, the most rigorous.

6.3.1 Certainty of objects for powers and trusts

The donee of a power of appointment does not have to exercise his power, it is discretionary, he can almost ignore it, just being required to consider exercising it from time to time.[67] Whereas the trustee of a trust must carry out the trust obligation, it is mandatory. Therefore a trustee must know the identity of his beneficiaries, but this is not so important for the donee of a power of appointment. The courts have therefore developed different tests to decide whether there is certainty of objects for powers separately from trusts.

Re Gestetner Settlement[68]
Sigmund Gestetner 'settled' property for members of a specified class. However, the class was enormous, including five charitable bodies, any employee or former employee of Gestetner Ltd., or their spouses, widows or widowers. The trustees had discretion as to the distribution of the fund, and there was a gift over in default of appointment in favour of the settlor's children. Although today this would obviously be classified as a power because of the gift over, Harman J considered it to be a discretionary trust with the trustee's duty carried out when they considered distribution.[69]

---

67   *Re Hay's Settlement Trusts* [1981] 3 All ER 786

68   [1953] Ch 672.

69   According to *Harman J.*, where a power does not impose a trust on the donee's conscience, it is not necessary to know all the objects in order to appoint Watt, G., *Todd & Watt's Cases & Materials on Equity and Trusts*, 7th edition (Oxford University Press, 2009) ,58

As a discretionary trust the question arose whether the trust was void for uncertainty of objects because the possible class of beneficiaries was so large.

Harman J: 'I cannot see here that there is such a duty as makes it essential for these trustees to survey the whole field and to consider whether A is more deserving of bounty than B. That is a task which was and which must have been known to the settlor to be impossible, having regard to the ramifications of the persons who might become members of this class... There is no uncertainty in so far as it is quite certain whether particular individuals are objects of the power. What is not certain is how many objects there are; and it does not seem to me that such uncertainty will invalidate a trust worded in this way. I accordingly declare this trust valid.'

As Harman J. held the trust valid because, 'it can be postulated easily enough whether (someone) is or is not eligible to receive the settlor's bounty', the test for certainty of objects was called the 'any given postulant test'. [70] The only issue with the test was whether the class of potential beneficiaries or appointees had been identified with sufficient certainty for the trustee/donee to carry out the trust or power, this was referred to as conceptual certainty. The issue of evidential certainty, whether there was evidence that someone came within the class, could always be answered, if not by the trustee/donee then by the court. The courts subsequently had to decide if this test was to apply to all powers or even be extended to trusts.

Inland Revenue Commissioners v. Broadway Cottages Trust[71]
£80,000 was placed in trust with the income to be applied for the benefit of anybody in a very wide class of beneficiaries, which included a charity, the Broadway Cottages Trust. Direction was sought on whether this was a valid trust and whether the *Re Gestetner* test applied. At first instance the trust was held to be void because the objects were uncertain.

Judgment: in the Court of Appeal Jenkins LJ stated that the test to be applied for a trust is the 'list certainty' test.[72] The whole range of potential objects should be ascertained or capable of being ascertained in order for the trustees to consider those eligible. The trustee had to be able to literally list all of the potential beneficiaries. Thus, although the trust in the present case was quite workable and it would have been valid under *Re Gestetner* principles as a power, it was an attempt to create a trust and so was invalid for uncertainty of objects.

---

70 A postulant, from the Latin *postulare*, 'to ask', one who makes a request or demand; hence, a candidate

71 [1955] Ch 20.

72 As proposed by Lord Eldon in *Morice v. Bishop of Durham* (1805) 10 Ves 522.

Thus the *Re Gestetner* test applied only to powers and the 'list certainty' test was to be used for trusts. It has been suggested that the decision in *Broadway Cottages* is a misinterpretation and misapplication of the beneficiary principle as espoused in **Morice v. Bishop of Durham.** [73] This states that there must be somebody in whose favour the court can decree performance of the trust, and so there must be identifiable human beneficiaries for there to be a valid trust. The Court of Appeal seem to have interpreted the beneficiary principle as requiring that all beneficiaries of a trust must be identified. The House of Lords had an opportunity to consider the tests in *Re Gulbenkian's ST*.[74]

Re Gulbenkian's ST[75]
Calouste Gulbenkian's settlement contained amongst its objects 'persons with whom Nubar Gulbenkian may from time to time be employed or residing.' A declaration was sought of the validity of the provision as a similar power had been declared void for uncertainty in *Re Gresham's Settlement*.[76]

Judgment: the Court of Appeal re-affirmed the *Re Gestetner* test, and criticised the 'list certainty' test for discretionary trusts, suggesting that the test should be the same as that for powers.[77] The House of Lords applied the Re Gestetner test and held that the power was valid, also directed that the 'list certainty' test should be used for discretionary trusts. Lord Upjohn explained that the test for powers is: 'whether it can be said with certainty that any given individual is or is not a member of the class.' The House noted that the test should not be used for trust powers,[78] because of the obligation and lack of freedom of choice of the donee of a trust power.

Therefore powers were subject to Lord Upjohn's test, and trusts including trust powers, were subject to the list certainty test. There was still some confusion regarding the nature of trusts and powers and the tests for certainty of objects applicable to each, and the House of Lords had to consider these issues again.

---

73   (1805) 10 Ves 522.
74   [1970] AC 108.
75   [1970] AC 108.
76   [1956] 1 WLR 563.
77   *Re Gulbenkian's ST* [1968] Ch 126 (CA) mainly per Lord Denning.
78   As explained above, this is a power which is coupled with a trust-like obligation. These powers would normally only occur when the potential appointees are members of a very small class of the donor's family members and there is no direction for the property to go elsewhere if the power is not exercised. The obligation here arises because if the power is not exercised the property would result back to the donor's estate and this is not what the donor intended.

McPhail v. Doulton[79]

Bertram Baden created a fund to be held upon certain trusts in favour of the staff and ex-staff of Matthew Hall & Co. Ltd., and their relatives and dependants. The trustees could accumulate the income, so the question arose, as they could defer distribution, was this a trust or a power? The provision purported to identify a wide class of potential beneficiaries: 'to or for the benefit of any officers and employees or ex-officers or ex-employees of the company or to any relations or dependents of any such persons in such amounts at such times and on such conditions (if any) as they think fit ...' Thus a second question arose, was there certainty of objects? In particular the use of the term 'relatives' was questioned for conceptual certainty and the size of the potential class raised the issue of which test for certainty should be used.

Judgment: at first instance and in the Court of Appeal the provision was held to create a valid power. However, the House of Lords held by a 3/2 majority that the provision attempted to create a trust because of the imperative language used ('shall').[80] The trust was valid because the list certainty test should only apply to fixed trusts and this was a discretionary trust. The test to be applied to discretionary trusts is similar to that for mere powers, *i.e.* Lord Upjohn's test in *Re Gulbenkian*.[81] The reasoning behind the majority decision was explained by Lord Wilberforce:

' a trustee with a duty to distribute, particularly among a potentially very large class, would surely never require the preparation of a complete list of names, which anyhow would tell him little that he needs to know. He would examine the field, by class and category; might indeed make diligent and careful enquiries, depending on how much money he had to give away and the means at his disposal, as to the composition and needs of particular categories and of individuals within them; decide upon certain priorities or proportions, and then select individuals according to their needs and qualifications. If he acts in this manner, can it really be said that he is not carrying out the trust?'

Lord Wilberforce then stressed the inappropriateness of the list certainty

---

79 *(Re Baden's DT No. 1)* [1971] AC 424.

80 The trustees had no choice; they had to distribute the money although they had discretion as to whom they could distribute it to. As has already been mentioned the distinction between a discretionary trust and a fiduciary power is not always easy to make, as Lord Wilberforce noted: 'what to one mind may appear as a power of distribution coupled with a trust to dispose of the undistributed surplus ... may to another appear as a trust for distribution coupled with a power to withhold a portion and accumulate or otherwise dispose of it.'

81 The case was sent back to the Chancery Division for application of the correct test.

test to ensure equal division for discretionary trusts: '... it does not follow that execution is impossible unless there can be equal division ... Equal division is surely the last thing the settlor ever intended: equal division among all may, probably would, produce a result beneficial to none.' Lord Wilberforce then considered the usefulness of the *Re Gulbenkian* test (Lord Upjohn's 'is/is not' test) when ascertaining the objects of a discretionary trust:

'A second look at [*Re Gulbenkian*] ... suggests to me that it does not discourage the application of a similar test for the validity of trusts as to the question of certainty, I desire to emphasise the distinction clearly made between linguistic or semantic uncertainty which, if unresolved by the court, renders the gift void, and the difficulty of ascertaining the existence or whereabouts of members of the class, a matter with which the court can appropriately deal on an application for directions. There may be a third case where the meaning of the words used is clear but the definition of beneficiaries is so hopelessly wide as not to form "anything like a class" so that the trust is administratively unworkable ... I hesitate to give examples ... but perhaps "all the residents of Greater London" will serve. I do not think that a discretionary trust for 'relatives' even of a living person falls within this category.'

Therefore the trustees of a discretionary trust do not have to be able to list all of the beneficiaries because equal division is unnecessary, and in fact probably contrary to the intention of the settlor. Therefore Lord Upjohn's 'is/is not' test may be applied to both powers and discretionary trust with the only important difference between the application being the issue of administrative unworkability (which will be considered subsequently). The 'list certainty' test is only used for fixed trusts.[82]

Different tests are required because of the different obligations on trustees of a fixed trust and a discretionary trust. A trustee under a fixed trust by its very nature has no discretion; therefore he must know all of the beneficiaries and the extent of their beneficial interests. The list certainty is exemplified by *OT Computers Ltd v First National Tricity Finance Ltd*.[83] When OTC, trading as Tiny Computers, began to make substantial losses the company instructed its bank to open two separate trust accounts: one for customer deposits; and the other for money due to 'urgent suppliers'. The company created two schedules: one with the names of its customers; and the other with the names of some of its suppliers. The court held that the trust for customers was valid, but the trust in favour of 'urgent suppliers' failed because it was impossible to say who was an 'urgent supplier'. It was impossible to write a list of 'urgent' suppliers as it was

---

82   It was mentioned that it might be appropriate for small 'family-type' discretionary trusts.

83   [2003] EWHC 1010.

conceptually uncertain what an "urgent" supplier was. This also illustrates that the class of beneficiaries under a fixed trust must be, as with a discretionary trust, conceptually certain.

6.3.2 Limits of the is/is not test

Both discretionary trusts and powers of appointment are subject to the Lord Upjohn's 'is/is not' test. The only difference being that a discretionary trust may be void for administrative unworkability. However, some general limits have been set for this test for powers and discretionary trusts. In *McPhail v Doulton*,[84] Lord Wilberforce distinguished between three types of uncertainty of object:

'Two final points: first, as to the question of certainty, I desire to emphasise the distinction clearly made and explained by Lord Upjohn between linguistic or semantic uncertainty which, if unresolved by the court, renders the gift void, and the difficulty of ascertaining the existence or whereabouts of members of the class, a matter with which the court can appropriately deal on an application for directions. There may be a third case where the meaning of the words used is clear but the definition of beneficiaries is so wide as not to form 'anything like a class' so that the trust is administratively unworkable .... I hesitate to give examples, for they may prejudice future cases, but perhaps 'all the residents of Greater London' will serve.'

The possible issues were therefore uncertainty of the language used to identify the class (conceptual uncertainty), uncertainty as to an individual being within the class (evidential uncertainty), and, for discretionary trusts, the possibility that the potential class of beneficiaries was so large that the trustees could not effectively carry out their duties (administrative unworkability). In addition to these factors as with all attempts to create trusts capriciousness must not play a major part, thus the identification of objects must not be by some whimsical or nonsensical factor.

Conceptual uncertainty
Sometimes referred to as linguistic certainty, conceptual certainty refers to the words used to identify the class of beneficiaries and must be such that the trustees can identify them. If the words used do not clearly identify the possible beneficiaries then there is no certainty of objects and the trust will fail. This applies to fixed trust as well as discretionary trusts and powers. The most obvious example is the word 'friends'. In *Brown v Gould*,[85] Megarry J stated that 'old friends' was conceptually uncertain as:

'If there is a trust for "my old friends", all concerned are faced with uncertainty as to the concept or idea enshrined in these words. It may not

---

84 *(Re Baden's DT No. 1)* [1971] AC 424.

be difficult to resolve that "old" "means not "aged' but "of long standing"; but then there is the question how long is "long." Friendship, too, is a concept with almost infinite shades of meaning. Where the concept is uncertain, the gift is void. Where the concept is certain, then mere difficulty in tracing and discovering those who are entitled normally does not invalidate the gift.'

Again Megarry J. stressed that once the concept was certain evidential problems could be dealt with.

Certain other everyday terms may also cause problems, for example the term 'customers' was held conceptually uncertain because it was not clear whether customers were those who purchased or just visitors to the shop.[86] In *Re Baden's Deed Trusts (No.2)*,[87] the return of *McPhail v Doulton* to the High Court to apply the judgment of the House of Lords on the relevant points of law, the terms 'relatives' and 'dependents' were held conceptually certain. The executors wanted the trust to fail and the property to result back to the estate, thus they appealed on the conceptual certainty of these terms and the application of the 'is/is not' test. The Court of Appeal held unanimously that the test applied and the terms were conceptually certain; [88] however, the three Lord Justices differed in their reasoning.

If there is a problem with the words used and the conceptual certainty of the possible class of beneficiaries/appointees then the uncertainty can be removed by the provision requiring the opinion of a third party, especially if the third party is an expert.

Thus, in *Clayton v. Ramsden*,[89] a condition was struck down for uncertainty when it purported to cause the donee to forfeit a gift if he should marry a person 'not of Jewish parentage and not of the Jewish faith'. The problem being, what is meant by 'Jewish faith'? However, in *Re Tuck's Settlement Trusts*,[90] the settlor wished to ensure that successors to his baronetcy were of the Jewish blood and faith. Thus money was left on trust for male issue so long as he should be of the Jewish faith 'and shall be married to an approved wife'. The settlement defined an 'approved wife' as 'a wife of Jewish blood by one or both of her parents and who has been brought up in and has never departed from and at the date of her marriage continues to worship according to the Jewish faith'. The settlement went on to provide that in case of dispute or doubt whether a person qualified as an approved wife, the decision of the chief rabbi in London of either the Portuguese or the Anglo-German community was to

---

85 [1972] Ch 53.
86 *Spafax (1965) Ltd v Dommett* (1972) 116 Sol Jo 711.
87 [1972] Ch 607 (EWHC).
88 *Re Baden's DT (No.2)*, [1973] Ch 9 (EWCA).
89 [1943] AC 320.
90 *(Public Trustee v Tuck)* [1978] Ch 49.

be conclusive. The court held that the concept was certain enough and if there had been any uncertainty the settlor had provided the means of removing it by the appointment of an expert adjudicator.

Trustees can also be given the position of adjudicator providing it is within their knowledge to make the decision. However, the settlor must take care that the terms used are not too uncertain. Thus it seems that, for instruments giving such discretion to a third party or a trustee to be effective, the criteria for the trustee/third party's decision must be very clear.

It should also be noted that conceptual certainty is required for fixed trusts. Thus a trust which provides, 'I leave $100,000 to be held on trust by my executors until the first Christmas after my death when they must divide the money equally between my five best friends,' would fail for conceptual uncertainty. However, this could be resolved by further clarification, e.g. '...my five best friends, Percy, Barry, Kylie, Ben and Brandon.'

Evidential uncertainty

The practical difficulty encountered in attempting to ascertain whether a postulant is within a class is referred to as Evidential uncertainty. This type of uncertainty will not render the gift void. As Sachs LJ stated in *Re Baden's DT (No.2)*:[91]

'The court is never defeated by evidential uncertainty ...Once the class of persons to be benefited is conceptually certain it then becomes a question of fact to be determined on evidence whether any postulant has on inquiry been proved to be within it; if he is not so proved then he is not in it.'

Similarly Megarry J. stressed, in **Brown v Gould**,[92] that once the concept was certain evidential problems could be dealt with. Thus once the class of beneficiaries has been identified with sufficient certainty then proving that a person is/is not in the class will not be a problem for the trustees, and ultimately the court, as it is a question of fact. This pragmatic approach does allow the court to deal with any issue and may be linked to Lord Wilberforce's administrative workability point; if the trust is workable it is valid.[93] 'A trust should be upheld if there is sufficient practical certainty in its definition for it to be carried out... according to the expressed intention of the settlor.'

Administrative unworkability

The idea of 'administrative unworkability' was raised by Lord Wilberforce in *McPhail v Doulton* when considering the usefulness of the *Re Gulbenkian* test (the 'is/ is not' test) for ascertaining the objects of a

---

91   *Re Baden's DT (No.2)*, [1973] Ch 9 (EWCA).
92   [1972] Ch 53.
93   *McPhail v Doulton (Re Baden's DT No. 1)* [1971] AC 424.

discretionary trust. Lord Wilberforce suggested this was the only difference between the application of the test for powers and discretionary trusts.

Lord Wilberforce explained this concept as,

'the meaning of the words used is clear but the definition of beneficiaries is so hopelessly wide as not to form "anything like a class" so that the trust is administratively unworkable ... I hesitate to give examples ... but perhaps "all the residents of Greater London" will serve. I do not think that a discretionary trust for 'relatives' even of a living person falls within this category.'

Thus a trust may be void if there are too many beneficiaries because it is literally impossible for the trustees to administer it effectively. This principle is sometimes linked to the idea that such a large class would be capricious, nonsensical, and so the provision would be invalid. The principle was applied in *R v. District Auditor ex parte West Yorkshire Metropolitan County Council*.[94] In this case, the Council was being disbanded because of local government re-organisation, it purported to dispose of surplus funds by leaving a trust fund 'for the benefit of any or all or some of the inhabitants of West Yorkshire'. The local authority was clearly not acting capriciously; it had good reason to want to benefit the inhabitants of the area. The only question was whether the trust was administratively unworkable. The court held that the trust was not for charitable purposes and so not a charitable trust. Lloyd LJ considered that the term 'inhabitants' was conceptually certain, but the class of 2,500,000 was too large and it was therefore administratively unworkable. As the proposed class was so wide as to be unascertainable in practical terms, the trust was a non-charitable purpose trust and thus void.

Administrative unworkability will invalidate a trust but not a power, as a power is discretionary and does not have to be carried out. Therefore the same degree of administrative workability is not required. Thus in *Re Hay's Settlement Trusts*,[95] a power of appointment was created which allowed appointment of anyone except for the settlor, her husband and the trustees. The court held that the power was not void because of its size, as apart from the duties to periodically consider appointing and to only appoint within the limits provided, the donees were not under a mandatory obligation.

Thus administrative unworkability applies only to trusts, and not to powers, and is the only difference in the application of the 'is/is not' test between deciding certainty of objects for powers and discretionary trusts.[96]

---

94   [1986] RVR 24.
95   [1981] 3 All ER 786.
96   Administrative unworkability could also invalidate a fixed trust, for example a large fund to be divided equally between all the residents of a city would be a fixed trust, it might be possible to list all the inhabitants but also might be administratively unworkable.

There have been some attempts to link administrative unworkability to capriciousness, that the appointing of a large class is whimsical or nonsensical; however, the courts have tried to maintain capriciousness as a separate invalidating element.

Capriciousness

A trust or power which identifies its beneficiaries/appointees by some capricious factor, for example a trust for anybody with red hair or green eyes, will usually be invalid because it displays no sensible intention on the part of the settlor.[97] In **Re Manisty's Settlement,**[98] the settlement gave trustees a discretionary power to apply the trust fund for the benefit of a small class of the settlor's near relations, excepting a smaller excluded class. The trustees were also given power at their absolute discretion to declare that any person, corporation, or charity should benefit. The question was whether the power was void for uncertainty. The court held that the power, despite being very wide, was not capricious and therefore valid. Templeman J. discussed capriciousness in relation to trusts and powers:

'The court may also be persuaded to intervene if the trustees act "capriciously", that is to say, act for reasons which I apprehend could be said to be irrational, perverse or irrelevant to any sensible expectation of the settlor; for example, if they chose a beneficiary by height or complexion or by the irrelevant fact that he was a resident of Greater London…The objection to the capricious exercise of a power may well extend to the creation of a capricious power. A power to benefit "residents of Greater London" is capricious because the terms of the power negates any sensible intention on the part of the settlor. If the settlor intended and expected the trustees would have regard to persons with some claim on his bounty or some interest in an institution favoured by the settlor, or if the settlor had any other sensible intention or expectation, he would not have required the trustees to consider only an accidental conglomeration of persons who have no discernible link with the settlor or with any institution. A capricious power negatives a sensible consideration by the trustees of the exercise of the power. But a wide power, be it special or intermediate, does not negative or prohibit a sensible approach by the trustees to the consideration and exercise of their powers.'

Thus trustees and donees cannot exercise a trust or power capriciously and the objects of a trust or power cannot be identified by capricious factors. Any attempt to exercise or create such a trust or power will usually be void.

---

97   *Re Manisty's Settlement* [1974] Ch 17 per Templeman J.
98   *Re Manisty's Settlement* [1974] Ch 17.

The confusion that has surrounded the ideas of administrative unworkability and capriciousness may stem from an unfortunate choice of example by Templeman J. The identification a power in favour of the residents of Greater London being invalidated as capricious was similar to the identification of a trust in favour of the residents of Greater London being invalidated for administrative unworkability. However, Templeman J. was highlighting such a power might be invalid because it might be considered capricious as the identification of the appointees was by a whimsical factor, not because the number of potential appointees was administratively unworkable. Powers will not be void because of the size of the class of potential appointees. As Megarry VC noted in *Re **Hay's** Settlement Trusts*,[99] a trust or power in favour of all the residents of Greater London would not be capricious if it was made by a settlor or donor with a sensible reason for benefitting the residents of Greater London. In such circumstances both the trust and the power would be valid, but the trust would be subject to the further requirement that it was administratively workable.

6.4 Gifts Subject to a Condition Precedent

This section deals with a strange and very small group of cases which are referred to as gifts subject to a condition precedent. These cases have benefitted from the 'any given postulant test' as applied in *Re Allen*:[100] the gift is valid if it is possible to say that one or more persons qualify.

Re **Barlow's** WT[101]

The testatrix left a large estate that included a collection of valuable paintings. She directed her executors to have the paintings valued and then, 'to allow any member of my family and any friends of mine who may wish to do so', to purchase the paintings at well below the valuation. Of course the issue was whether 'family' and 'friends' were conceptually uncertain. Family was similar to relatives and dependants which had been held to be conceptually certain in *Re Baden (No. 2)* and so was not a too much of a problem, but friends was a difficult term. Browne-Wilkinson J held that it was up to anybody wishing to purchase the paintings to prove that they were friends of the deceased. As the executors were not directed to give a painting to each of the testatrix's friends they did not need to ascertain the whole class, i.e. all of the testatrix's friends. The executors could therefore exercise the power, thus it was valid.

---

99   [1981] 3 All ER 786.
100 [1953] Ch 810.
101 [1979] 1 WLR 278.

Therefore a gift subject to a condition precedent will be upheld if one person can come forward to satisfy the condition. It is not construed as a trust in favour of a class so the concept of the class does not have to be certain. Whether the instrument can be construed in this way is a matter of construction. It is only likely to be construed in this way if the subject matter is a small number of items as in *Barlow's*.

6 .5 Summary

Therefore to create a valid express trust the three certainties must be present, these are the certainties of intention, subject matter and object. To create an express trust the declaration of trust and the surrounding circumstances must evidence an intention to place the transferee of property under a trust obligation and nothing else. If there is no evidence of an intention to give a gift or create a trust obligation *intervivos* then the property will be held on resulting trust for the settlor. If there is no evidence of an intention to create a trust obligation in a testamentary provision then the property will be an absolute gift. The use of precatory words, such as 'wish' and 'hope', will not create a trust on their own, but their use is not fatal to a trust intention being found. The whole of the instrument must be considered. The word 'trust' does not have to be used and a trust can be construed from actions. An attempt to use a trust as a 'sham' or façade for other purposes is not a true intention to create a trust.

The subject matter of the trust obligation must also be certain. Any confusion over the subject matter can be fatal to the trust. Thus if there has been an attempt to create a trust over part of a gift, as in 'the remaining part of', then the result will be an absolute gift. Tangible chattels must be identifiable or segregated from a group. Otherwise the property will result back to the putative settlor/testator's estate. However, this may be better expressed as that it has never been subject to the trust obligation and so has never left the estate. Intangible property, choses in actions, does not seem to require the same segregation or identification from a group. The beneficial interest must be certain otherwise the property will result back, although in a discretionary trust the trustees may have discretion to decide the extent of beneficial interest.

The objects of a trust and power must be certain so that the trustees or donees know in whose favour they must or may exercise them. For a fixed trust the trustees must be able to literally list the beneficiaries and their beneficial interests so that they can carry out their duties as required. For a discretionary trust or a power the trustees or donees do not need to have such certainty because of their discretion, they must therefore merely be able to say if a person 'is or is not' in the class of potential beneficiaries. The words used to describe the potential class must be conceptually certain, although an expert can be appointed by the settlor to resolve any difficulties. Evidential certainty will not defeat a trust because it is a question of fact that the trustees or court can decide. The objects of a trust or power must not be identified by any capricious factor. The only difference between the use of the 'is/ is not' test for discretionary trusts and powers is that for a discretionary trust to be valid the class of objects must not be so large as to be administratively unworkable.

An exception to the requirement for conceptual certainty is the gift subject to a condition precedent. Here, even though the class of potential beneficiaries may be identified by a word that is not conceptually certain, such as 'friends', as the trustees do not have to identify all the members of this dubious class, the provision is construed as a series of gifts subject to the condition that at least one person can come forward and prove to the satisfaction of the trustees that they are a member of the designated class. It seems that this will be limited to provisions that relate to relatively few items.

The requirements for these certainties and what happens if they are not present can be expressed as follows:

Three Certainties	Why is it necessary?	How is this decided?	Effect of failure
Certainty of intention	To ensure that a trust was intended and no other relationship or transaction	Precatory words are not enough (*Lambe v Eames*) Words used and construction of whole instrument (Re Adams and the Kensington Vestry & Comisky v. Bowring–Hanbury) Do not have to use word 'trust' and may be construed from actions (Paul v Constance). A sham is not a valid intention (*Midland Bank plc v Wyatt*)	Intervivos- if no evidence of gift or trust then resulting trust. Testamentary-absolute gift to transferee
Certainty of subject matter: subject matter and beneficial interest	To identify the property the trustee protects for the trust and in which the beneficiaries have an interest. Thus the certainty includes the certainty of beneficial interests.	Identification or segregation of chattels as subject matter (Re London Wine). Unless intangible (Hunter v Moss) Beneficial interest must be certain (Boyce v Boyce). In a discretionary trust the trustees have discretion to decide beneficial interest.	Failure of trust over part of gift is an absolute gift to transferee (Hancock v Watson). Otherwise resulting trust for settlor/testator's estate (Boyce v Boyce).
Certainty of objects	To identify the beneficiaries who the trustees hold the trust property for.	For a fixed trust it must be possible to list the beneficiaries. For a discretionary trust it must be possible to say who is or is not within the potential class of beneficiaries.	Resulting trust for settlor/testator's estate.

The tests used for certainty of objects can be further clarified as follows:

Type	Obligation	Test	Limits
Fixed trust	Mandatory	List certainty (*IRC v Broadway Cottages*)	Evidential and conceptual certainty, capriciousness, administrative unworkability
Discretionary trust	Mandatory	Is / is not (*McPhail v Doulton*)	Evidential and conceptual certainty, capriciousness (*Re Manisty's*), administrative unworkability (*McPhail v Doulton & West Yorkshire Council*
Power	Discretionary But cannot act outside power Donee must consider exercising that power from time to time (Re Hay's)	Is / is not (*Re Gulbenkian*)	Evidential and conceptual certainty, capriciousness (*Re Manisty's*), **But not** administrative unworkability.
Gift subject to condition precedent	Discretionary	Any given postulant (*Re Allen*)	Evidential: can one person satisfy donees that they are as specified (*Re Barlow's*).

CHAPTER 7
THE BENEFICIARY PRINCIPLE: TRUSTS OF IMPERFECT OBLIGATION AND UNINCORPORATED ASSOCIATIONS

7.1 The Beneficiary Principle

We have considered the three certainties, that, in order for a trust to be valid, there must be certainty that a settlor intended to place the trustee under a trust obligation when he transferred property to him, that the property must be clearly identified or capable of being identified and the beneficiaries must be identified. The certainty of subject matter and objects are necessary so a trustee knows what property he is holding on trust and for whom. Linked to this is the beneficiary principle.

Once a trust is constituted the only people who may enforce that trust are the beneficiaries. The settlor, unless he has made himself a beneficiary or trustee, or reserved some other right for himself in the trust instrument, loses all interest in the trust. If the settlor has retained no interest in the trust the only action that may be possible for him against a trustee not performing his duties to the trust is one of breach of contract, resulting, if successful, in damages not the enforcement of the trust.

The beneficiaries have an interest in the trust property. The beneficiaries should know whether the trustees are performing their obligations because they stand to lose if those duties are neglected or abused and can call the trustees to account for the subject matter of the trust. They can take action against a trustee to enforce the trust. If there is no beneficiary, there is nobody to keep check on the trustees. For this reason, Sir William Grant MR, in *Morice v. Bishop of Durham*,[1] espoused what has become known as the beneficiary principle: 'there must be somebody in whose favour the court can decree performance.'

There must be an identifiable beneficiary in order for there to be a valid trust. The trustee must know for whose benefit he holds the trust property and in whose favour he must distribute it. A court must be able to identify the beneficiaries so that it can order the trustee to perform the trust in their

---

1 (1805) 10 Ves 522.

favour. The beneficiary, or somebody acting on their behalf, must be capable of coming to the court to ask for its help. Thus the beneficiary must be a legal person, usually a human being, but a corporate body such as a registered company, will satisfy the beneficiary principle because it is a non-living legal entity.

As the beneficiary must usually be human, trusts for purposes are void. For example, in *Re Astor's Settlement Trusts*,[2] a trust for the 'maintenance of good understanding between nations' and 'the preservation of the independence and integrity of newspapers' was held to be void because there was no human beneficiary who could ask the court to enforce the trust. Similarly, the testator, in *Re Endacott*,[3] was unable to give his residuary estate, 'to North Tawton Devon Parish Council for the purpose of providing some useful memorial to myself'.

An exception is made for charitable purposes, those which provide public benefit, but only if the purpose comes within the accepted categories of charity. Thus, in *Morice v. Bishop of Durham*,[4] a bequest to the Bishop of Durham 'for such objects of benevolence and liberality as the Bishop of Durham in his own discretion shall most approve', was construed as a private purpose and so void. The bequest was not a gift to the Bishop himself and was possible to construe as outside the accepted charitable purposes. Similarly, in *Re Shaw*,[5] the playwright, George Bernard Shaw was not able to establish a trust of the residue of his estate to research the development of a 40-letter alphabet, 'investigate the time and labour wasted by our lack of at least 14 unequivocal single symbols', and to translate his play '*Androcles and the Lion*' into the new alphabet. The trust would benefit purposes and not identifiable beneficiaries, and as the purposes were not considered charitable, the trust was void for offending the beneficiary principle.

7.2 Exceptions to the Beneficiary Principle

As with any rule of equity there are exceptions that have been developed because of custom. These exceptions relate to:
1   Charitable trusts;
2   Trusts of imperfect obligation;
3   The *Re Denley* exception;
4   Gifts or trusts in favour of unincorporated associations.

Charitable trusts are dealt with in detail in the next chapter. They are valid whether or not there is an identifiable beneficiary because they are of

2   (*Astor v Scholfield*) [1952] Ch 534.
3   (*Corpe v Endacott*) [1960] Ch 232.
4   (1805) 10 Ves 522.
5   [1957] 1 WLR 729.

public benefit, so in a way we are all beneficiaries and the Attorney General may enforce the trust on behalf of the public. For this reason charitable trusts may be pure purpose trusts as long as their purposes come within, or are analogous to, the recognised classifications of charity.

The other exceptions will be considered in turn.

7.3 Non-charitable Purpose Trusts or Trusts of Imperfect Obligation

There is a small group of non-charitable purpose trusts which are accepted as valid. These are sometimes referred to as trusts of imperfect obligation because, although they are valid and the trustee may carry them out without fear of challenge, the trustee cannot be forced to carry out the obligations of the trust. This is because these are purpose trusts and no human beneficiaries can come before the court to ask it to enforce the obligations on the trustee. For example, I leave £10,000 to my executors to care for my pet goldfish for as long as the law allows. Obviously the goldfish cannot come to court to make the executors carry out the trust (no matter how clever it may be). However, the executors can choose to carry out this trust as it is valid, and if they do my residuary legatees or next of kin cannot say they are in breach of their fiduciary duties to my estate and make them account for any money they have spent. If the executors choose not to look after the goldfish someone else might be found or the money would result back to the estate. When the goldfish dies any money left should result back to my estate unless another destination has been specified.

Non-charitable purpose trusts have developed as recognised exceptions to the beneficiary principle because, although not of public benefit and so not charitable, their purposes were accepted as beneficial to society because the purposes are customary practice. Testators have traditionally made provision in their wills for the erection and/or maintenance of a tomb or monument, for the saying of prayers for their souls, and for the upkeep of their favourite animals. Thus, these have developed as recognised exceptions to the beneficiary principle. However, they are not enforceable, because there is no human beneficiary and are thus only carried out if the trustee wants to. They are subject to an imperfect obligation.

7.3.1 The anomalous categories

In **Re Endacott**,[6] Harman J held that the testator's attempt to give his residuary estate, 'to North Tawton Devon Parish Council for the purpose of providing some useful memorial to myself' was an attempt to create a non-charitable purpose trust and so void. It was of 'too wide and uncertain

---

6   (*Corpe v Endacott*) [1960] Ch 232.

a nature to fall within the anomalous class of cases in which trusts, although not charitable, were upheld as being of a public character.' Harman J. then clarified what non-charitable purposes would be permitted. These are:

1   The erection and/or maintenance of tombs and monuments;
2   The saying of masses in private;
3   The maintenance of specific animals.

Harman J also clarified that the categories of non-charitable purpose trusts will not be extended, if anything they could be reduced.[7] Thus to be recognised as a valid non-charitable purpose trust, the trust must fall within one of the recognised categories. (As explained subsequently the trust must also not offend the rule against perpetuities and must not be capricious.)

Trusts for the erection and/or maintenance of tombs and monuments have been held valid trusts of imperfect obligation, even though they are private purpose trusts, because of the respect for, and the need to commemorate, the dead.[8]

In the context of trusts of imperfect obligation, masses are prayer services said for the benefit of the dead. Traditionally people would leave sums in their wills for priests or monks to say prayers for their souls. Trusts for saying masses in public are generally held to be charitable because they are open to anyone to attend and so gain benefit.[9] Trusts for saying masses in private are not charitable because they fail the public benefit requirement, but may be upheld as trusts of imperfect obligation if they do not exceed the perpetuity period.[10]

Trusts or gifts to benefit animals in general, or a particular type of animal, are usually charitable.[11] However, gifts to benefit a specific animal or specific animals cannot be charitable because of the lack of public benefit, but may be trusts of imperfect obligation. They are permitted because of the special affection that people can have for their animals, which may manifest itself in the bequest of sums of money in the deceased's will for the maintenance and upkeep of their pet. For example, an American heiress Leona Helmsley

---

7   There is also one other strange case where a non-charitable purpose trust was upheld which is included in every equity text as an example of the sometimes bizarre judgments of the English judiciary. In *Re Thompson* [1934] Ch 342, a gift in support of foxhunting was allowed. This could be attributed to the English aristocracy's (of which the judiciary were and still are a part) love of foxhunting at that time. It is unlikely that a similar trust would be upheld today because of legislation in England which bans hunting with dogs.
8   *Re Hooper* [1932] 1 Ch 38; *Pirbright v Salwey* [1896] WN 86.
9   *Re Hetherington* [1990] Ch 1.
10   *Bourne v. Keane* [1919] AC 815.
11   *Re Wedgwood* [1915] 1 Ch 113.

left her Maltese terrier 'Trouble,' $12 million (US) when she died. The dog was looked after by the General Manager of one of the heiress' family hotels until it died at the age of 12, some four years after its mistress, when the remaining fund reverted to The Leona M. and Harry B. Helmsley Charitable Trust for charitable purposes.

The principle has been accepted in various cases such as *Mitford v. Reynolds,*[12] where a gift was upheld for the upkeep of the testator's horses and for the erection of a monument. Similarly in *Pettingall v. Pettingall,*[13] the testator left £50 per year for his executor to use to maintain the testator's favourite black mare. After the death of the horse the excess funds were to be taken absolutely by the executor. The residuary legatees argued that the trust was invalid and they should therefore take the property. The court held there was a valid trust of imperfect obligation. The executor could not be made to carry out the testator's wishes but, as he wanted to carry out the trust, he could.

This is typical of the litigation which surrounds these cases as they are usually challenged by residuary legatees or next of kin who hope that the trust will be declared invalid so that the fund will fall into residue or be distributed on the rules of intestacy in their favour.

Even though these trusts may come within one of the anomalous exceptions to the rule against private purpose trusts they must still comply with the rule against perpetuities and the purpose must not be capricious. If the trust does fail then the money will result back to the testator's estate. If the trust is subject to a subsequent trust or gift then its failure will not fail the subsequent trust or gift. If the subsequent provision is valid then its interest will be accelerated, thus on the failure of the non-charitable purpose trust the fund will be accelerated to the subsequent provision.

7.3.2 Non-charitable purpose trusts and perpetuities

Non-charitable purpose trusts must comply with the rule against perpetuities and the rule against inalienability (or excessive duration). Thus the trust must vest or begin within the perpetuity period and not continue for longer than the perpetuity period. As there is generally no life in being associated with these trusts the relevant perpetuity period is just 21 years. These trusts are excluded from the Perpetuities and Accumulations Act 2009 by s.18 which provides 'This Act does not affect the rule of law which limits the duration of non-charitable purpose trusts'. Therefore the statutory perpetuity period and the wait and see provision do not apply directly to non-charitable purpose trusts. Of course a will may specify a trust in favour of human beneficiaries with a gift over to a

---

12 (1848) 16 Sim 105.
13 (1842) 11 LJ Ch 176.

non-charitable purpose trust, in which case the operation of the first trust could be subject to the statutory provisions and so the statute indirectly affects the non-charitable purpose trust.

Thus a non-charitable purpose trust must vest within 21 years of the testator's death and must not be carried on for longer than 21 years. As these two limbs are subject to the common law the trust will be void if there is the slightest chance the rule against perpetuities or the rule against excessive duration will be offended.

Thus a trust for the saying of masses in private must begin within 21 years of the testator's death and must not continue for longer than 21 years after the testator's death. To be valid such a trust must provide for the exhaustion of the fund within this period, or for the fund to be applied to a human beneficiary before the 21 year period is up, or for the trust to be brought to an end at this point.

Trusts for the erection of a tomb or monument are usually not a problem because the law presumes the tomb or monument will be built within 21 years of the testator's death and so it is vested within the period. More problematic is a provision for the maintenance of a tomb or monument as that may continue for longer than 21 years and so offend the rule against excessive duration. For example, in *Mussett v. Bingle*,[14] the testator's will provided for the building of a monument and its maintenance. This was a private purpose trust and should have been void, but it came within one of the recognised exceptions to the beneficiary principle. However, although it was accepted that the monument could be built within 21 years the second part of the legacy for the maintenance of the monument could have continued for longer than 21 years and so offended the rule against excessive duration. The court held the first part for the erection of the monument was a valid trust of imperfect obligation and could be carried out, but the second part for maintenance was void. Thus the fund left after erection of the monument, which would have been used for the maintenance, fell into residue.

It is quite simple to save these provisions with a simple 'saving clause' which provides that the maintenance element of the provision cannot continue for longer than the perpetuity period. Thus in *Pirbright v Salwey*,[15] a trust was set up to build and maintain a burial enclosure. As the burial enclosure could be built within 21 years it did not offend the rule against perpetuities. The second part of the provision for maintenance was also valid as it contained the clause "as long as the law allows". Thus the maintenance could not be for longer than 21 years and so it did not fall foul of the rule against excessive duration.

---

14   [1876] WN 170 (HC).
15   [1896] WN 86.

Similarly, in *Re Hooper*[16], the gift for the upkeep of the family graves and monuments was valid because they were to be maintained only "so far as the trustees could legally do so."

Non-charitable purpose trusts involving animals are subject to the same problems. Trusts for the upkeep of specific animals will usually vest within 21 years of the testator's death, and so not offend the rule against perpetuities, but they if there is a chance they may continue for longer than 21 years after the death of the testator then they should be void. However, judges have tended to be quite generous in their interpretation of the maintenance of animals. Thus, in *Re Dean*,[17] the trust was upheld even though it provided for the maintenance of the testator's horses and hounds for 50 years and should have been void for offending the rule against excessive duration. In *Re Haines*,[18] judicial notice was taken that cats cannot live beyond 21 years.

7.3.3 Capricious purposes

The purpose of a non-charitable purpose trust must not be capricious. Thus it must not be whimsical or nonsensical. Thus, in *M'Caig v University of Glasgow*,[19] a gift for the erection of 'artistic towers' was held invalid. Similarly, in **Brown v Burdett**,[20] the testatrix devised a freehold house, yard, garden, and outbuildings to trustees and their heirs, upon trust to 'blockade' the house for 20 years. This involved bricking up and covering with zinc and iron all doors and windows (and fireplaces) to the rooms. All contents of the rooms not specified in the will were to remain in the bricked up rooms, especially her clock! This was to be done 'as far as is practicable' on the day of my funeral. Only four rooms were to be left open for the housekeeper and his wife to live in. The housekeeper's duties involved ensuring that the rooms remained blockaded. Furthermore the trustees were to visit every three months to check the testatrix's instructions were being complied with. The court held this was an attempt to create a non-charitable purpose trust which had attempted to comply with the rule against excessive duration, as it was to be maintained for 20 years, but whose purpose was capricious. As Vice-Chancellor Bacon stated, 'The Court will disregard a direction the effect of which is to make this property useless…'[21] thus the Vice-Chancellor declared:

'I think I must "unseal" this useless, undisposed of property.' Thus this provision in the will failed and the property was treated as intestacy.

---

16   [1932] 1 Ch 38.
17   (1889) 41 Ch D 552.
18   1952 WL 12533, The Times (November 7).
19   (1907) 44 SLR 198.
20   (1882) 21 Ch D 667 at 673.
21   (1882) 21 Ch D 667.

As the trend of the modern age is to sing one's own praises it is worth noting that the courts have traditionally taken a dim view of attempts at self-aggrandisement in trusts and have deemed them capricious. Thus, in *M'Caig's Trustees v Kirk-Session of United Free Church of Lismore*,[22] a trust to erect bronze statues of the testatrix and her parents was declared invalid because it was 'a sheer waste of money'. Similarly, the nature of the gift in *Re Endacott*,[23] 'for the purpose of providing some useful memorial to myself', could be seen as contrary to natural modesty and thus capricious. In contrast it may be seen that the trust to erect a monument to the testator's wife's first husband that was upheld in *Mussett v. Bingle*,[24] was particularly unusual and should be commended.

7.3.4 The "new" non-charitable purpose trusts

We have already mentioned the development of non-charitable purpose trusts which have been developed in some jurisdictions, mostly associated with tax avoidance.[25] They do not require identification of human beneficiaries and so can confuse issues of beneficial ownership thus avoiding or delaying taxation. These trusts are statutory and cannot be created in common law jurisdictions that do not have the relevant enabling legislation as they offend the beneficiary principle. [26] However, jurisdictions which are parties to the Hague Convention on the Law Applicable to Trusts and their Recognition, 1985, may have to recognise them.

7.4 Unincorporated Associations

In *Conservative and Unionist Central Office v. Burrell*,[27] Lawton LJ. defined an unincorporated association as:

'two or more persons bound together for one or more common purposes, not being business purposes, by mutual undertakings, each having mutual duties and obligations, in an organisation which has rules which identify in whom control of it and its funds rests and on what terms and which can be joined or left at will.'

---

22 (1915) 52 SLR 347.
23 [1960] Ch 232.
24 [1876] WN 170.
25 For example, the STAR (Special Trusts Alternative Regime) trusts of the Cayman Islands.
26 see Matthews, 'Shooting STAR' (1997) 11 *TLI* 67; Duckworth, 'STAR WARS: The colony strikes back' (1998) 12 *TLI* 16; Matthews, 'STAR: Big Bang or Red Dwarf?' (1998) 12 *TLI* 98; Duckworth, 'STAR WARS: Smiting the bull' (1999) 13 *TLI* 158.
27 *(Inspector of Taxes)* [1982] 1 WLR 522 at 525; [1982] 2 All ER 1 at 4.

Unincorporated associations exist for many different purposes often to allow groups of like-minded individuals to pursue a hobby or sporting pastime. Unincorporated associations have no separate legal existence from their members, they are not corporate bodies like a registered company, and therefore they are unable to hold property in their own right. However unincorporated associations do exist and their members do leave money in their wills to the association to continue its purposes. Often the members of the association will appoint a member as treasurer to hold the associations' funds and to receive gifts on its behalf. Of course the treasurer will then hold the gift on trust, but the beneficiary cannot be the association as it has no legal personality and if it is for the purposes of the association, which are often not charitable,[28] this will be a private purpose trust, which should be void. If the treasurer holds the fund on trust for the members of the association then there are problems identifying the members as it may include future members or even members who leave the association. This may cause perpetuity problems as unincorporated associations may continue indefinitely. Therefore new members may join outside the perpetuity period and so a trust which was to benefit them would vest outside the perpetuity period (usually 21 years because human lives are not associated with the association's purpose) and fail because of the rule against perpetuities. If the trust continued indefinitely it would offend the rule against excessive duration. In all these instances the gift should fail and result back to the testator's estate, thus these gifts are often challenged by residuary legatees or next of kin hoping to make such gifts fail for their own benefit.

The problems with gifts to unincorporated associations were exemplified in *Leahy v A-G for New South Wales*.[29]

Leahy v A-G for New South Wales[30]

The testator left a large estate including an Australian sheep station to be held on trust 'for such order of nuns of the Catholic Church or the Christian Brothers as my executors . . . shall select . . .' The construction of the will made it clear this was not a gift to the present members of such orders as it was intended to benefit future members as well and so was a trust. The trust was in favour of a large group of people who were not easily identifiable. Some of these orders were closed orders, they had no contact with the public, and so they failed the public benefit requirement of charitable trusts.

Judgment: the trust was void as it did not exclude future members and so offended perpetuity. If it were a trust for the purposes of the associations

---

28   If the unincorporated association is a charity then it can be the beneficiary of a trust because the Attorney–General enforces it.

29   [1959] AC 457.

30   [1959] AC 457; [1959] 2 All ER 300.

it was void as a private purpose trust which infringed the beneficiary principle.

However, these associations are popular and, although not charitable, are seen as beneficial to society. Thus the law has to deal with: 'the artificial and anomalous conception of an unincorporated society which, though it is not a separate entity in law, is yet for many purposes regarded as a continuing entity and, however inaccurately, as something other than an aggregate of its members.'[31] The courts have therefore tried to construe gifts in favour of unincorporated associations as benignantly as possible to ensure they are valid. In so doing the courts have stopped short of a legal fiction and just bent the rules a little construing a trust as not incurring the mischief of the beneficiary principle because the members can enforce the trust (*Re Denley's* exception), or as a gift to present members of the association (*Neville Estates'* interpretation). Thus the validity of such a gift will fall to the construction of the wording of the gift and such trusts and gifts may still fail.

7.4.1 The *Re Denley's* exception

The *Re Denley's* exception is not a true exception to the beneficiary principle but a method of construing a private purpose trust to find beneficiaries who can enforce the trust so that the principle is satisfied.

In *Re Denley's TD*,[32] land was transferred to trustees to be used as a sports field for the benefit of the employees of a company, and for 'the benefit of such other persons as the trustees may allow to use the same'. The persons entitled to use the sports facilities had no corporate form. The gift did not infringe the perpetuity rules because it was expressly confined to the perpetuity period with a gift over of the property to a hospital. However, this was a trust for a purpose, the provision of sports facilities for the employees, and so should have been void as a private purpose trust. It also could not be charitable because trusts for amateur sports were not charitable at this time and the identification of beneficiaries as employees of the company meant there was a personal nexus and so defeated the public nature of a charitable trust. Goff J adopted a novel interpretation of the trust: 'Where, then, the trust, though expressed as a purpose, is directly or indirectly for the benefit of an individual or individuals, it seems to me

---

31 *Leahy v. A-G of New South Wales* [1959] AC 457, 477; [1959] 2 All ER 300 at 307 *per* Viscount Simonds. Confusingly the term 'company' has been used at times to refer to unincorporated associations and also to partnerships. Today it is more commonly used to refer to companies registered under the Companies Acts.

32 *Re Denley's Trust Deed, Holman v HH Martyn & Co Ltd* [1969] 1 Ch 373; [1968] 3 All ER 65; [1968] 3 WLR 457; 112 Sol Jo 673.

that it is in general outside the mischief of the beneficiary principle.'[33] Thus Goff J. held that, although the trust was expressed to be for a purpose, the individual employees of the company were beneficiaries and so could enforce the trust.

This reasoning focuses not on the identification of beneficiaries but the prevention of the mischief that the beneficiary principle was adopted to deal with, that is whether there is someone who can ask the court to make the trustees perform the trust. As with trusts in favour of unincorporated associations generally the courts try to enforce these trusts if they can by adopting a benignant interpretation. The *Re Denley's* approach was used in *Re Lipinski's WT*,[34] to construe the gift to construct or improve buildings for the Hull Judaeans (Maccabi) Association as valid even though it was an unincorporated association and should have been void. The court held that the gift did not infringe the perpetuity period because the members had the right to terminate the trust for their own benefit. The judgment in *Re Lipinski's* is not clear and seems to confuse *Re Denley's* with the contractual approach in *Neville Estates* discussed below. The *Re Denley's* justification should apply only to trusts which are expressly limited to the perpetuity period, whereas the second interpretation in *Neville Estates* is a gift to present members subject to the rules of the association, which means that they can end the association and take the fund so it does not offend perpetuity.

The *Re Denley's* interpretation is useful but will not save all gifts in favour of unincorporated associations as this was definitely a trust with a gift over in favour of the hospital when the agreed term of the trust had ended.

7.4.2 The contractual approach

The decision in *Leahy v. A-G for New South Wales*,[35] attracted some criticism and so judges tried to think how they could construe such gifts as being valid. The most important judicial consideration of this problem was by Cross J. in *Neville Estates v. Madden*.[36] Neville claimed specific performance of a contract for the sale of land owned by the Catford Synagogue, an unincorporated association. The Synagogue trustees claimed that the consent of the Charity Commissioners was required as the gift of land was a charitable purpose trust and Cross J. upheld the charitable status. However, more importantly for us, he discussed *obiter* the possible ways that an unincorporated association could receive a gift.

---

33   [1969] 1 Ch. 373 at 383-384.
34   [1976] Ch 235.
35   [1959] AC 457.
36   [1962] Ch 832.

Cross J identified three ways in which unincorporated associations may receive and hold property:

- As a gift to present members as joint tenants/tenants in common; or,
- As a gift to present members to hold in accordance with the contractual rules and obligations of the association; or,
- As a gift on trust for present and future members.

Cross J. considered the second method the most useful:

' it may be a gift to the existing members not as joint tenants, but subject to their respective contractual rights and liabilities towards one another as members of the association. In such a case a member cannot sever his share. It will accrue to the other members on his death or resignation, even though such members include persons who became members after the gift took effect. If this is the effect of the gift, it will not be open to objection on the score of perpetuity or uncertainty.'

Subsequent judgments have confirmed this is the best approach. Thus, in *Re Recher's WT*,[37] the testatrix left a share of her residuary estate to the London and Provincial Anti-Vivisection Society, an unincorporated association. Brightman J had to determine whether the gift was valid and considered four possible ways to allow a gift to an unincorporated association, incorporating the possibilities from both *Neville Estates* and *Re Denley's*:

1 *A gift to the trustees for the purposes of the association*: such a gift would be held on trust as a pure purpose trust and would fail for offending the beneficiary principle, unless the association was charitable.

2 *A gift to the present individual members of the association*: this may be held as joint tenants or as tenants in common. If they hold as joint tenants, the principle of survivorship will mean that the last surviving member of the association will eventually hold all of the funds unless other members choose to sever their share before they die. If severance occurs then the member would take his share and it would not be used for the purposes of the association. If the members hold as tenants in common then they have identifiable shares which they can take and again the purposes of the association would not be furthered.

3 *A gift to present and future members under the *Re Denley's* exception*: this would only work if the beneficiaries are clearly identifiable and so can ask the court to enforce the trust. The trust must be limited to the perpetuity period, as in *Re Denley's* itself, otherwise it will fail.

4 *A gift to the present members of the association subject to their contractual rights and obligations*: this is Cross J.'s second suggestion and is the most practical. It avoids perpetuity problems because the gift vests in the present members and the rules of the association should provide for

---

37 [1972] Ch 526.

the members to bring it to an end so it will not carry on indefinitely. However, usually the members will need to vote as a majority to bring the association to an end and take the fund therefore the association will continue with the use of the fund for its purposes. Thus the wishes of the testator are furthered.

Brightman J. justified the last method as the most effective construction based on Cross J.'s second suggestion, as he held that an unincorporated association could represent, 'an organization of individuals bound together by a contract under which their subscriptions became, as it were mandated towards a certain type of expenditure.' Therefore any gift was 'an accretion to the funds which are the subject matter of the contract which the members have made inter se'. Thus in this situation the members have a contractual relationship based upon the rules of the association and any gift to the association is just an addition to their funds. The rules or contract should provide for the ending of the association and allow the members to decide what to do with the association's funds. If that is so the association may be brought to an end at anytime so there is no trust in favour of the association preventing them doing this. Thus this is a gift to individuals and so would be valid. Brightman J. applied this to the case before him and said:

'In my judgment the legacy in the present case to the London and Provincial Society ought to be construed as a legacy of that type, that is to say, a legacy to the members beneficially as an accretion to the funds subject to the contract which they have made *inter se*. Of course, the testatrix did not intend the members of the society to divide her bounty between themselves, and doubtless she was ignorant of that remote but theoretical possibility. Her knowledge or absence of knowledge of the true legal analysis of the gift is irrelevant. The legacy is accordingly in my view valid, subject only to the effect of the events of January 1st, 1957.'

Unfortunately those events were fatal to the gift, as Mrs Recher's will was dated 23/5/57 and the Association had ceased to exist on 1/1/57. Therefore the gift had already lapsed when the testatrix made her will.

Today if a gift in favour of an unincorporated association can be construed in accordance with the 'contractual approach', it should be. In effect any such gift is a gift to the present members of the association subject to the agreement/contract between them, this is not a trust, although the fund is usually added to the association's funds, held by a human treasurer on the associations' behalf, and is used for the association's purposes as intended by the testator.

7.4.3 Problems with the contractual approach

The contractual approach will only apply if the association has a set of rules which are in effect a contract between the members.[38] If the association does not have a set of rules then the gift to the association must be to hold on trust and perpetuity problems arise. There will also be problems if the members are not in control of their association's funds. Thus, in *Re Grant's WT*,[39] Vinelott J held that a gift to 'the Labour Party Property Committee for the benefit of the Chertsey Headquarters of the Chertsey and Walton constituency Labour Party' could not be construed as a gift to the members of the local constituency party. The local association's funds were under the control of the national Labour Party and so, although the local association had its own rules, the members could not use their rules to divide the funds amongst themselves. It was also not possible to construe this as a *Re Denley's* exception purpose trust as it was not restricted to the perpetuity period and therefore the gift was void.

7.4.4 Gifts to unincorporated associations with purposes attached

In *Re Lipinski's Will Trusts*,[40] Harry Lipinski left a gift of half his residuary estate in his will, 'for the Hull Judaeans Association in memory of my late wife to be used solely in the work of constructing the new buildings for the association and/or improvements in the said buildings'. The residuary legatees disputed validity of the gift. This was not just a gift to the present members that they could decide to distribute as it had a purpose attached.

Oliver J upheld the gift giving two possible solutions:

That it was valid on the contractual (*Neville* and *Recher* analysis) as the purpose was not binding on the members because they could alter the rules; or, It was valid as a trust for the members under the *Re Denley's* exception. There were no perpetuity problems as the association could spend both the capital and the income from the gift.

More recently, in *Re Horley Town Football Club*,[41] the settlor settled land on trust 'for the primary purpose of securing a permanent ground for the Horley Football Club...' This was a gift to the association with a purpose attached. Lawrence Collins J. held that it was valid as 'a gift to the Club, as a "contract holding" gift to the club and its members for the time being within category (2) in Neville Estates v Madden'.

---

38   Conservative and Unionist Central Office v. Burrell [1982] 1 WLR 522

39   [1980] 1 WLR 360

40   *(Gosschalk v Levy)* [1976] Ch 235.

41   [2006] EWHC 2386.

The attitude of the courts has changed since the decision in *Leahy* and it now seems a court will strive to interpret a gift to an unincorporated association as a gift to its present members subject to the rules of the association. This interpretation allows that the members can end the association and take the gift as individuals and so does not offend perpetuity. This will occur even if the gift has a purpose attached. However, the association must have rules and the gift must be under the control of the association and its members.

7.5 What happens when the Association Ends?

Another problem that arises with such associations is what to do with funds when the association ends. The association may be ended because the members no longer wish to pursue the common activity, membership has been reduced to a level which is not sustainable, a court has ordered the end of the association or the association has achieved its purpose, for example if the association is an appeal for funds for a particular purpose and the required amount has been raised.

If there are surplus finds when an unincorporated association is wound up then there may be a problem in deciding what to do with them. The answer to this problem will depend upon: how the fund is held; the intention of the donors; and whether the fund was donated by the members themselves or by outsiders.

The main applicable principle will be considered in more detail in Chapter 10 when resulting trusts are considered, but in general, if the donor intended the money to be used for a purpose and it cannot be achieved then he has retained an interest in the fund and it should be returned to him (or his estate if deceased), this is an automatic resulting trust. However, this may not always be possible as donors may not be identifiable, perhaps because money has been collected by street collection. In such cases the money may go to the Crown on the principle of *bona vacantia*, that the property is to the good of no one, (literally there is no owner), or divided on a contractual basis amongst the members of the association. The latter solution will usually occur if the association's rules provide for the disposal of surplus funds. When no such rules exist, there are a number of possibilities.

In deciding which disposal to make the court will consider where the funds have come from. If the funds were contributed by the members themselves they may be distributed in the following ways:

On resulting trust for members in proportion to their contributions; this will only apply if the funds were subject to a **Re Denley**'s exception purpose trust. This will only be possible if the trust has not infringed the perpetuity period. Thus, in **Re Hobourn Aero-Components Ltd's Air Raid**

Distress Fund's Trusts,[42] the members paid weekly contributions to a fund to help members whose homes had suffered air raid damage. When air raids ended in 1944 the fund was ended. The members wanted their unused contributions back, but the Charity Commissioners wanted to apply the fund to other charitable purposes by way of a *cy près* scheme. The court held that the fund was not charitable and therefore *cy près* could not apply. The fund was held on resulting trust for the members in proportion to their contributions.

To current members in accordance with contractual principles; this will follow any provision that is in the rules for such division. The modern approach is also to imply terms into the rules of the association to provide for such distribution of the members' own contributions. Usually this is to present members but may be to past members if the purpose of the association was to benefit all members present and future. If the fund was not intended to benefit the members themselves but to benefit third parties then there will be no implied term and the find may go *bona vacantia* to the Crown,[43] although there has been criticism of this approach with suggestion that such surplus finds should always be divided amongst present members.[44]

If the funds have been contributed by outsiders the courts have considered the intention of the donors. The funds may be returned to the donors by way of resulting trust in a manner similar to the *Quistclose* trust,[45] as a resulting trust will occur when funds are given for a particular purpose and that purpose is in some way frustrated. In *Re Gillingham Bus Disaster Fund,*[46] an appeal fund was established after 24 Royal Marine cadets were killed in a road accident. There was a considerable surplus when the appeal was wound up and the trustees sought directions as to what to do with the surplus. It is thought that people who give large gifts and are readily identifiable give for a purpose and, should the purpose fail, the gift goes on resulting trust. The problem in this case was that most

---

42 [1946] Ch 194.

43 *Re West Sussex Constabulary's Widows, Children & Benevolent Fund Trust* [1971] Ch 1.

44 See Walton J. in *Re Buckinghamshire Constabulary Widows' & Orphans' Fund Friendly Society* [1979] 1 WLR 936. See also *Davis v. Richards & Wallington Industries Ltd.* [1990] 1 WLR 1511, where surplus funds in a pension fund were returned by way of resulting trust to the employer and *bona vacantia* to the Crown. In *Air Jamaica Ltd. v. Charlton* [1999] 1 WLR 1399 PC, the pension fund surplus was returned by way of resulting trust to the company and the members.

45 *Barclays Bank v. Quistclose Investments Ltd* [1970] AC 567, discussed in Chapter 10.

46 [1958] Ch 300, affirmed [1959] Ch 62.

of the money had been raised by street collections *etc*. Harman J decided, quite surprisingly, that such contributions should also go on resulting trust, even though the donors were anonymous:

'I see no reason myself to suppose that the small giver who is anonymous has any wider intention -than the large giver who is named. They all give for the one object. If they can be found by inquiry the resulting trust can be executed in their favour. If they cannot I do not see how the money could then ... change its direction and become *bona vacantia*.'

Of course such a decision raises issues as to the intention of a person when they give money in a street collection and in identifying those who have made these donations. Thus, in *Re West Sussex Constabulary's Widows, Children and Benevolent Fund Trust*,[47] Goff J. directed the division of the surplus fund in a number of ways. Large donations should be returned by way of resulting trust, but money collected by way of street collections, entertainments and raffles should go to the Crown by way of *bona vacantia*. Goff J. justified the latter distribution because street collections were outright gifts so the donors had no interest by way of resulting trust and the money paid for entertainments etc. was a contractual payment which again negated any interest by way of resulting trust.

7.6 Summary

The beneficiary principle provides that there must be an ascertainable beneficiary in whose favour the court can decree performance. The beneficiary can be human or a non-living legal entity, such as a registered company. Trusts without beneficiaries are purpose trust and are void. There are recognised exceptions to this principle. These are charitable trusts, non-charitable purpose trusts (trusts of imperfect obligation), trusts for ascertainable beneficiaries (*Re Denley's exception*) and gifts to unincorporated associations subject to the *Neville Estates'* contractual interpretation.

Valid non-charitable purpose trusts are limited to three categories and there are unlikely to be any new exceptions created. The categories are the erection and maintenance of tombs and monuments, the saying of masses in private, and the maintenance of specific animals. All of these are subject to the rules against capriciousness and perpetuity. If a non-charitable purpose trust is set up with what the court considers a capricious purpose it will be void. If the trust will vest outside the perpetuity period, usually 21 years for these trusts because no human life is involved, it will be void. If the trust may continue for longer than 21 years it should also be void.

---

47   [1971] Ch 1.

The courts usually accept that the trust will vest within the period, so the problem is with maintenance which may exceed 21 years. If the trust specifies it will not carry on for longer than 21 years or has a saving provision, e.g. 'as long as the law allows' it should be valid. The courts have also been extremely generous in interpreting the lifespan of animals as not exceeding 21 years.

Unincorporated associations cause problems as they have no legal personality and cannot hold property in their own right. Therefore a gift to an unincorporated association can be seen as a gift for the purposes of the association and thus void as a purpose trust, for example *Leahy*. The problem with unincorporated associations being the subject of a trust may also involve perpetuity as they can last for longer than the perpetuity period. In *Re Denley's* an interpretation was made that the trust was for the benefit of the members of the association and so they could come forward to ensure it was performed. The beneficiary principle was thus not a problem. However, the *Re Denley's* exception will be limited to trusts which do not offend the perpetuity rules. In *Re Recher's* three other possibilities were considered to interpret gifts in favour of unincorporated associations. These were based upon Cross J's comments in Neville Estates. The second possibility identified in *Neville Estates* was followed in *Re Recher's* and is now considered the appropriate way to interpret gifts to unincorporated associations. This is the contractual approach; the gift is to present members subject to the contractual obligations (the rules) amongst them. This will be successful as long as the association has rules and the association retains control over the gift. If the gift has a purpose attached the members can choose to disregard the purpose using the rules of the association.

The contractual approach is generally applied to the distribution of funds on the dissolution of an unincorporated association unless the funds have been contributed by third parties for a purpose not to benefit the members. If this is the case then the funds will be held on resulting trust if the third parties can be traced or go *bona vacantia* to the state.

CHAPTER 8
CHARITABLE TRUSTS

8.1 What is Charity?

The legal concept of charity is quite different to the concept of charity in its everyday use. Until recently there was no clear statutory definition of charity but there were accepted judicial pronouncements on what charity consisted of: what purposes the law would uphold as charitable. The law restricted the categorisation of purposes as charitable because of the benefits which charitable status bestows on a trust, unincorporated association, or corporation. It is worth remembering that charitable trusts form only part of the general law of charities which is dealt with in many excellent specialist works.[1] However, charitable purposes for trusts are common to other methods of administering charity. The purposes considered charitable were developed in cases over centuries but always influenced by the origin of the law of charity in England.

The Anglo-American common law of charities came from the Church or Canon law.[2] Originally all matters to do with charity were under the ecclesiastical court's jurisdiction; however, this was taken over by the Court of Chancery in the sixteenth century, continuing with a religious theme because of the ecclesiastical background of most Chancellors. The Chancery jurisdiction encouraged the use of trusts to administer charities.[3]

The reformation of religion in England under Henry VIII resulted in the closure of the monasteries following allegations of corruption. These allegations may have been substantially true, but the abolition of the

---

1   Notably J. Warburton, *Tudor On Charities* (London, Sweet & Maxwell).
2   Charles P. Sherman, 'A Brief History of the Canon Law' (1918-1919) 7 *Cal. L. Rev.* 93, 94.
3   However, the ecclesiastical jurisdiction had recognised charitable trusts before this, for example the *pia causa* . Constantine the Great permitted bequests to the Church from 315 A.D. Donations to the Church were so successful that by 364 the Emperor Valentinian enacted a mortmain law. By the time of Justinian it became a settled principle of law that legacies for pious or charitable uses should receive special favour in the courts and be regarded as privileged. Similarly wills containing charitable dispositions of property became more liberally construed than other wills and would not fail for uncertainty of objects. Charles P. Sherman, 'A Brief History of the Canon Law' (1918-1919) 7 *Cal. L. Rev.* 93, 94-95. Quoting from Sherman, *Roman Law in the Modern World*, vol. I ss.379, 229.

monasteries left a gaping hole in the provision of charity. There was no longer a local religious house which could provide education for your children, healthcare for the sick, or alms for the poor. Henry's daughter Elizabeth I inherited a country with increasing social problems and, to avoid using her own money, she encouraged her wealthy citizens to provide charitable institutions by enacting the Charitable Uses Act 1601 (the Statute of Elizabeth), which gave examples of purposes that would be considered charitable in its Preamble or introduction. Although the Statute's Preamble was repealed some time ago,[4] it remained the guiding spirit of modern charitable purposes until the Charities Act 2006. These purposes were clarified by Lord Macnaghten, in *Income Tax Special Purposes Commissioners v. Pemsel*,[5] in four heads as: the relief of poverty, the advancement of education, the advancement of religion, and other purposes beneficial to the community. Until the Charities Act 2006 these were the only legal definitions of charity. Now the classification of charitable purposes is contained in the Charities Act 2011.

8.2 The Benefits of Charitable Status

Charities are seen to be good for society as a whole, thus charitable trusts are referred to as public purpose trusts as they benefit the public as a whole. Because of this public benefit charities are given legal and fiscal privileges which are intended to encourage people to donate to charity.[6] These privileges mean that charities are big business, in the UK in 2009 there were 189,143 registered charities with a combined income of £48 billion a year. In the United States of America the figure is even higher. Most of this money is held on trust.

The benefits of charitable status are:

- That the objects of a charitable trust do not have to be certain;
- That the trust may be for "pure" purposes (it does not have to comply with the beneficiary principle);
- Administrative benefits for trustees;
- That the perpetuity rule against remote vesting is relaxed;
- That the rule against inalienability does not apply and charities may continue indefinitely;

---

4   By the Mortmain and Charitable Uses Act 1888.
5   [1891] AC 531.
6   Gary Watt (2008) writes that charitable trusts are treated advantageously because they save the state money. Charitable purposes are those that the state would have to provide if charity did not, and so the state encourages private individuals to use their money for public purposes. Watt also notes that the advancement of religion is unique in the heads of charity as a purpose which the state would not have to support.

- Cy-près
- Fiscal advantages.

Certainty of objects: if a trust is for a charitable purpose then the trustees do not have to be able to identify the beneficiaries or even to be able to ascertain the class of potential beneficiaries. As Grant MR said in **Morice v Bishop of Durham**:[7] '…it is now settled, upon authority, which it is too late to controvert, that where a charitable purpose is expressed, however general, the bequest shall not fail on account of the uncertainty of the object…' As the trustees do not have to be certain of the identity of the class of beneficiaries then the rules regarding administrative unworkability do not apply to charities. It does not matter how many potential beneficiaries there may be for a charitable trust it will not fail. A gift for the relief of poverty in England would therefore be a valid charitable gift.

Pure purpose trusts: a charitable trust is by definition a purpose trust, and they may be pure purpose trusts. Thus trusts 'for the welfare of animals' may be valid, as may a trust 'for charitable purposes.' Of course to be valid the purpose must be a recognised charitable purpose. As noted in the discussion of the beneficiary principle, charitable trusts will not fail for non-compliance with the beneficiary principle as the Attorney-General will enforce the trust on behalf of us all in the name of the Crown. Actions to enforce a charitable trust can be brought by almost anyone, but they must join the Attorney-General to the action, although he may decline to take part if he is in doubt the purpose is charitable.

The Attorney-General acts on behalf of the Crown as *parens patriae*, and enforces charitable trusts in the courts.

Administrative benefits: charitable trusts also enjoy administrative advantages in that there is no limit upon the number of people who may act as trustees of a charity,[8] and charitable trustees may act upon a majority vote, whereas non-charitable trustees must act unanimously. Trustees of a charitable trust must perform their role to the same standard as trustees of a private trust.[9] However, Courts have acted leniently to trustees of charitable trusts where the trustees have acted honestly and loss has

---

7   (1804) 9 Ves Jr 399. As noted before Roman law did not fail wills containing charitable dispositions of property for uncertainty of objects: Charles P. Sherman, 'A Brief History of the Canon Law' (1918-1919) 7 *Cal. L. Rev.* 93, 94-95

8   See J. Warburton, *Tudor On Charities* (London, Sweet & Maxwell: 2003, 9th edition), p. 215 [5-022].

9   Peter Luxton, *The Law of Charities* (Oxford, Oxford University Press: 2001), p.361 [9.75]. Because of the public nature of charitable trusts, the decisions of trustees may be amenable to judicial review: *R (Beer (trading as Hammer trout farm) v Hampshire Farmers Markets Ltd* [2003] EWCA Civ 1056.

occurred to the charity by a mistake.[10] As Lord Eldon stated: 'To act on any other principle would be to deter all prudent persons from becoming trustees of charities.'[11]

Rule against perpetuities: the rule against remote vesting applies to charitable trust but is usually relaxed. Thus a gift over from one charity to another is valid even if it takes effect outside of the perpetuity period.[12]

The rule against inalienability: charities are exempt from the rule against inalienability (the rule against excessive duration) and may therefore continue indefinitely.[13] In fact as charities are for public benefit it may be considered desirable that they do continue for as long as possible, even in perpetuity! [14]

Cy-Près: any gift that is given to charity is treated as having been given to charity as a whole and remains forever dedicated to charity. Even if the donor specifies a particular charity or type of charity, if that particular charitable body fails after the gift is made then the gift will be given to another similar charity, cy-près or 'as near as possible' to the original intention of the testator. Similarly if a charitable organisation fails then any excess fund is usually applied for other charitable purposes. Cy-près may also apply if the organisation has ceased to exist before the testator's death but the testator has failed to change the provision in his will. In these circumstances the Attorney-General will aid the trustees (if any exist) and the court by drawing up a *cy-près* scheme or scheme of distribution for the fund to other charities.

Fiscal advantages: tax breaks are the most common reason for organisations to seek charitable status. The major fiscal advantages enjoyed by charities are to do with income tax and corporation tax,[15] estate duty,[16] and taxes on capital gains,[17] Stamp Duty[18] and local taxes. In addition some charities are exempt from charging Value Added Tax (VAT) for their goods and services.

---

10 Peter Luxton, *The Law of Charities* (Oxford, Oxford University Press: 2001), p.364 [9.83] referring to *A-G v Exeter Corporation* (1826) 2 Russ 45, 54 (Lord Eldon L.C.).

11 *A-G v Exeter Corporation* (1826) 2 Russ 45, 54 (Lord Eldon L.C.).

12 *Re Tyler* [1891] 3 Ch 252.

13 *Henry Goodman & ors v The Mayor and Free Burgesses of the Borough of Saltash* (1882) 7 App Cas 633, at 651-652.

14 See the case regarding Shakespeare's house: *Thompson v Shakespeare* [1859] Johnson's Reports 612; [1860] 1 De G.F. & J. 399.

15 Income and Corporation Taxes Act 1988, s505.

16 Inheritance Tax Act 1984, s23.

17 Taxation of Chargeable Gains Act 1992, s256.

18 Finance Act 1982, s129.

Many of the cases we shall consider have involved the Inland Revenue challenging the charitable status of trusts because of concerns that they are being used to avoid tax. Of course the remainder will be directions sought by trustees concerned that they may attract some personal liability if they distribute a fund which is not a valid charitable trust and challenges by residuary legatees and next of kin to try to invalidate provisions for their personal benefit.

8.3 The Definition of Charity for Public Purpose Trusts

To determine that a trust has charitable status it must conform to the legal understanding of the term charity. At common law it was noted by Sachs L.J. in *Incorporated Council of Law Reporting for England and Wales v. Attorney-General*, the word charity is 'wide, elastic', and '...has an admirable breadth and flexibility which enables it to be reasonably applied from generation to generation to meet changing circumstances'. However, the UK now has statutory classifications of charitable purposes in the Charities Act 2011, which is a consolidating act bringing previous charities legislation and the developments of the Charities Act 2006, largely unchanged, into one statute. It is interesting to note, however, that charitable purposes are still largely dependent on the earlier decided cases.

A guide to charitable purposes was first given in the Preamble to the Charitable Uses Act 1601 (the Statute of Elizabeth). The purposes identified as charitable in the Preamble, with modern spelling, punctuation and grammar, were:

'...the relief of aged, impotent and poor people; the maintenance of sick and maimed soldiers and mariners; schools of learning, free schools, and scholars in universities; the repair of bridges, ports, havens, causeways, churches, sea banks and highways; the education and preferment of orphans; the relief, stock, or maintenance for houses of correction; the marriage of poor maids; the support, aid and help of young tradesmen, handicraftsmen and persons decayed; the relief and redemption of prisoners or captives; the aid and ease of poor inhabitants concerning payment of fifteens, setting out of soldiers and other taxes...'[19]

---

19   Original: 'some for Releife of aged impotent and poore people, some for Maintenance of sicke and maymed Souldiers and Marriners, Schooles of Learninge, Free Schooles and Schollers in Universities, some for Repaire of Bridges Portes Havens Causwaies Churches Seabankes and Highwaies, some for Educacion and prefermente of Orphans, some for or towardes Reliefe Stocke or Maintenance of Howses of Correccion, some for Mariages of poore Maides, some for Supportacion Ayde and Helpe of younge tradesmen Handicraftesmen and persons decayed, and others for reliefe or redemption of Prisoners or Captives, and for aide or ease of any poore Inhabitantes concerninge paymente of Fifteenes, setting out of Souldiers and other Taxes...' 'Fifteens' were a tax. Source   see   http://www.hks.harvard.edu/fs/phall/01.%20Charitable%20uses.pdf

The common law of charitable purposes developed by analogy to the purposes within the Preamble; thus to be charitable any trust must be within the 'spirit and intendment' of the statute.[20] In *Income Tax Special Purposes Commissioners v. Pemsel,*[21] Lord Macnaghten noted that charity has a technical legal meaning:[22]

'"Charity" in its legal sense comprises four principal divisions: trusts for the relief of poverty; trusts for the advancement of education; trusts for the advancement of religion; and trusts for other purposes beneficial to the community, not falling under any of the preceding heads.'

The Pemsel heads were intended to help identify charitable purposes rather than delineate what was charitable. As Lord Wilberforce noted in *Scottish Burial Reform & Cremation Society v Glasgow Corporation*:[23]

'… it is a classification of convenience, there may well be purposes which do not fit neatly into one or other of the headings; … the words used must not be given the force of statute to be construed; … the law of charity is a moving subject and may well have evolved since 1891'.

The Pemsel heads have now been displaced by the statutory classification of charitable purposes in the Charities Act 2011. Similarly the 2011 Act now displaces the Preamble and any reference to the Preamble in any document relating to a charitable trust or company should now be read as referring to the Charities Act 2011.[24]

The Charities Act 2011 provides a statutory definition of charity in s.1(1): an institution, whether company or trust, is a charity 'which is established for charitable purposes only' and 'falls to be subject to the control of the High Court in the exercise of its jurisdiction with respect to charities'. The thirteen purposes which are considered charitable are set out in s3(1):

1 The prevention or relief of poverty.
2 The advancement of education;
3 The advancement of religion;
4 The advancement of health or the saving of lives;
5 The advancement of citizenship or community development;
6 The advancement of the arts, culture, heritage or science;
7 The advancement of amateur sport;
8 The advancement of human rights, conflict resolution, or reconciliation or the promotion of religious or racial harmony or equality and diversity;
9 The advancement of environmental protection or improvement;

---

20 *Morice v. Bishop of Durham* (1805) 9 Ves 399.
21 [1891] AC 531.
22 [1891] AC 531, 583.
23 [1968] AC 138.
24 Charities Act 2011, s.1(2).

10 The relief of those in need by reason of youth, age, ill-health, disability, financial hardship or other disadvantage;
11 The advancement of animal welfare;
12 The promotion of the efficiency of the armed forces of the Crown, or of the efficiency of the police, fire and rescue services or ambulance services;
13 Any other purposes within subsection 4 [categories of charitable purpose which are already accepted as charitable under existing case law].

The first three categories are almost the same as the first three Pemsel heads and the relevant case law will still apply to identifying these categories. Furthermore the Charities Act 2011, s.3(1)(m)(iii), provides that categories of charity that have been accepted in the old case law will continue to be valid under the 2011 Act.

Thus to be charitable a trust must:

1 belong to an accepted category of charitable purposes;
2 be for the benefit of a section of the public (although this requirement does not apply to charities for the relief of poverty);[25] and,
3 be exclusively charitable (if the fund could be applied for non-charitable purposes at the discretion of the trustees then it is not charitable).[26]

8.3.1 The Prevention or Relief of Poverty

It has been said that property ownership brings with it duties, and one of these historically has been to support the poor.[27] This has traditionally been the most important head of charity and has been construed widely as the relief of any poverty, has been widely considered of such importance to us all. The statute has added the prevention of poverty to the head thus allowing that provision may be made to prevent the need for relief. Just as there is no clear definition of charity, there is also no clear definition of poverty. The Preamble referred to 'the relief of aged, impotent and poor people' and 'the marriages of poor maids'. The judiciary have attempted to give some guidance. Thus Sir Raymond Evershed MR, in *Re Coulthurst*,[28] stated, '...poverty does not mean destitution; it may not unfairly be paraphrased for present purposes as meaning persons who have to "go short" in the ordinary acceptance of that term.' In *Re*

---

25 Charities Act s.2(1)(b).
26 Charities Act 2011, s.1(1).
27 David Kennedy, 'Some Caution about Property Rights as a Recipe for Economic Development' (2011) 1(1) *Accounting, Economics, and Law* article 3, p 34.
28 [1951] Ch 661.

Scarisbrick's WT,[29] 'needy' persons were considered to come within the category of poverty. In ***Dingle v Turner***,[30] Lord Cross stated that poverty referred to, 'people who can fairly be said to be, according to current standards, "poor persons"'.

Generally the judicial interpretation of poverty has been wide. Thus provision for ladies in reduced circumstances,[31] ladies of limited means,[32] and for the aid of distressed gentlefolk have all been held to be charitable under the poverty head.[33] It is also accepted that trusts for the benefit of the old come within this head. Therefore, in *Re Lucas*,[34] a testator left in remainder a trust to provide for 'the oldest respectable inhabitants in Gunvile to the amount of 5s per week each'. It was held that this was a valid charitable trust as the amount of the gift implied poverty and coupled with use of the word 'oldest,' implying age, was sufficient to render the gift a good charitable bequest.

Problems have only arisen if the provision is not exclusively for the poor and those who are not in need may take advantage of it. Thus in *Re Gwyon*,[35] a gift to provide knickers (short trousers) to the boys of Farnham failed because it did not exclude affluent children, indeed it excluded those already in receipt of charitable funds. It should be noted that the testator had provided that 'Gwyon's Present' should be embroidered across the waistband of the knickers, which may have prevented any affluent child from wishing to wear the knickers, although this was not taken into account by the court! The trust failed and the property devolved as on intestacy.

There has been some concern over the term 'working class'. In *Re Sanders' WT*,[36] a gift for the provision of housing for the working classes was held not to be charitable, because it would be quite possible for somebody to benefit who was working class but not poor. However, in *Re Niyazi's WT*,[37] a gift for the construction of a working men's hostel in Cyprus was held valid as the beneficiaries would be poor.

8.3.2 The Advancement of Education

The courts have again adopted a very wide interpretation of the education head. The Statute of Elizabeth referred to 'schools of learning, free schools and scholars in universities'; 'the education and preferment of orphans' and 'the supportation, aid and help of young tradesmen, handicraftmen,

29 [1951] Ch. 622.
30 [1972] AC 601.
31 *Shaw v. Halifax Corporation* [1915] 2 KB 170.
32 *Re Gardom (Le Page v Gardom)* [1915] WN 216.
33 *Re Young* [1951] Ch 344.
34 *(Rhys v A-G)* [1922] 2 Ch 52.
35 *Sub nom Public Trustee v A-G* [1930] 1 Ch. 255.
36 [1954] Ch 265.
37 [1978] 1 WLR 910.

and persons decayed.' However, the courts have accepted all forms of education and training provided that there is some benefit to the public. Even research carried out with no direct teaching will be charitable if it is useful and of public benefit. In *Re Hopkins WT*,[38] the court stated that in order that a gift for research should be charitable the research either must be of educational value to the researcher or must be so directed as to lead to something which will pass into the store of educational material, or so as to improve the sum of communicable knowledge in an area which education (including in this last context the formation of literary taste and appreciation) may cover. Thus the trust to finance the search for the missing manuscripts which would prove that Francis Bacon wrote the plays attributed to William Shakespeare was held to come under the education head and be validly charitable. This was educational as it involved research into England's greatest dramatist although such manuscripts may no longer exist, indeed they may never have existed. Thus for research to be charitable under this head it must be useful, disseminated and of public benefit.[39] Thus, in *Incorporated Council of Law Reporting for England and Wales v. A-G*,[40] Buckley LJ stated that the ICLR was fulfilling a charitable purpose under the education head as its work was, 'to the improvement of a useful branch of human knowledge and its public dissemination.' Although the council was carrying on a business, profits, if any, could not be distributed to its members but had to be applied in the further pursuit of its objects. Pure research is not charitable because it confers no public benefit. Thus, as mentioned in the last chapter, George Bernard Shaw's attempt to finance a trust to develop a 40-letter alphabet and translate his plays into it was held not charitable and therefore void as a pure purpose trust because it was not possible to say it was of public benefit. [41]

Trusts for the promotion of the arts and culture are generally charitable under the education head. In *Re Delius*,[42] a trust for the promotion of the music of Delius was held valid under the education head. Museums and art galleries may also be charitable under the education head.[43]

Student unions are usually considered to be charitable under the education head as long as their purpose is seen to aid the education and welfare of the students and is not invalidated by political purposes.[44]

---

38 (*Naish v Francis Bacon Society Inc*) [1965] Ch 669.
39 *McGovern v Attorney-General* [1982] Ch 321.
40 [1972] Ch 73.
41 *Re Shaw* [1957] 1 WLR 729.
42 [1957] Ch 299.
43 *British Museum v White* [1826] 2 Sim & St 594; *Thompson v Shakespeare* [1859] Johnson's Reports 612; [1860] 1 De G.F. & J. 399.
44 *London Hospital Medical College v IRC* [1976] 1 W.L.R. 613; *A-G v. Ross* [1986] 1 WLR 252.

One of the most benign interpretations of the education head by the judiciary has been the inclusion of some trusts for the promotion of sport or recreation. Before the statutory inclusion of a head for amateur sports such trusts were generally not charitable and so void. Thus, in *Re Nottage*,[45] a trust to purchase an annual trophy for yacht racing was held not to be charitable. The only exception appeared to be when the game itself is of an educational nature, for example chess in *Re Dupree's DT*.[46] The courts, however, adopted the interpretation that if the sports or recreational facilities were linked to an educational establishment then the trust came within the second head. Thus, in *Re Marriette*,[47] a gift to provide squash and Eton fives courts for Aldenham School was held to be charitable because of the benefits of physical education. The House of Lords, in *IRC v. McMullen*,[48] held that a trust to promote the playing of football and other sports in schools and universities was charitable under the education head as part of a balanced education. Similarly gifts to provide sport and recreation facilities for the armed services will be charitable.[49] The provision of an amateur sports head in the 2011 Act gives further scope for the validation of charitable sports trusts, although the previous case law remains good law and it may still be possible to validate a trust for the promotion of sport in a school under the second head.

8.3.3 The Advancement of Religion

The third Pemsel head is unusual as the Preamble did not refer to religion apart from the repair of churches. However, by the time of the Pemsel decision it was widely accepted that gifts for the advancement of religious beliefs were charitable. Gary Watt has also noted that the advancement of religion is unique amongst the heads as it is a purpose which would not have to be fulfilled by the state if it were not charitable.

The religious purposes which would originally have been considered charitable would have been those of the established Church of England. This was developed to include other Christian beliefs and more recently other recognised religions. In *Thornton v. Howe*,[50] Romilly MR made some much quoted observations on religion including, 'the Court of Chancery makes no distinction between one religion and another',[51] which might sound very modern and anti-discriminatory. He followed this with the

---

45   [1895] 2 Ch 649.
46   [1945] 16.
47   [1915] 2 Ch 284.
48   [1981] AC 1.
49   *Re Gray* [1925] Ch 362.
50   (1862) 31 Beav 14; 54 ER 1042.
51   (1862) 31 Beav 14, 19.

comment that, 'although this Court might consider the opinions sought to be propagated foolish or even devoid of foundation', the trust will be charitable unless the beliefs are 'adverse to the very foundations of all religion and that they are subversive of all morality.'[52] Again this might sound very permissive, as this was a trust for 'printing, publishing and propagating the sacred writings' of Joanna Southcott who claimed to have been impregnated by the Holy Ghost and to have been about to give birth to a second Messiah. Her heir in law brought the case to have the trust declared void and so the property would pass to her. The Master of the Rolls had to read Joanna's writings to make his judgment and declared her a 'foolish, ignorant woman'. However, he held the gift charitable, which meant that the property would usually have been applied as a charitable trust. Unfortunately the gift included land and so fell foul of the Statute of Mortmain,[53] and thus went to the Crown.

Of more import for modern permissive attitudes are the comment of Cross J in **Neville Estates Ltd v Madden**,[54] "As between different religions the law stands neutral, but it assumes that any religion is at least likely to be better than none." One of the by-products of this neutral attitude to religions is that a court cannot decide if any religion is better than another and so cannot accept that a trust which has a main purpose of converting non-believers to that religion is of public benefit. Thus charities for proselytising (conversion) should not be charitable.[55]

Generally to be charitable religion should involve the belief in a divine being.[56] Thus, in **Re South Place Ethical Society**,[57] the agnostic Ethical Society was not charitable as it was concerned with the 'study and dissemination of ethical principles' and was not concerned with religion, which is man's relations with God not man's relations with man. However, the Society was charitable under the education and fourth heads.

The need for a religion to be monotheistic, the belief in one God, had been raised by Lord Parker in **Bowman v Secular Society**.[58] This would include Islam but exclude Hinduism and Buddhism. Modern cases have accepted that mainstream religions, including Hinduism[59] and Buddhism,[60] are also charitable. Other beliefs such as spiritualism and humanism have traditionally been excluded from charitable status.[61]

---

52   (1862) 31 Beav 14, 20.
53   9 Geo. 2, C.36.
54   [1962] Ch 832.
55   *Income Tax Special Purposes Commissioners v. Pemsel* [1891] AC 531.
56   *Bowman v. Secular Society* [1917] AC 406.
57   *(Barralet v. Attorney-General)* [1980] 1 WLR 1565.
58   *Bowman v. Secular Society* [1917] AC 406.
59   *Varsani v. Jesani* [1999] Ch 219.
60   *Muman v.Nagasena* [2000] 1 WLR 299.
61   *Re Hummeltenberg* [1923] 1 Ch 237.

The recognition of some religious or belief groups has caused concern when they are viewed as cults or with purposes that are not of public benefit. Of particular concern in the UK has been the Church of Scientology. In *R. v. Registrar General ex parte Segerdal*,[62] the Scientologists were again refused charitable status because there is no belief in a divine being.[63] Guidance was given as to what was required for a religion to be considered charitable: there must be a belief in a supreme being; the organisation must involve worship of that being; and the advancement of the religion must be of public benefit. However, with the inclusion of Buddhism as a recognised religion, [64] this guidance may be doubted and public policy remains the chief reason that the Church of Scientology has been refused charitable status.

The statutory provision for the advancement of religion now also provides, in s.3(2)(a)(i), that religion 'will include a religion which does not involve belief in a god'. This gives statutory recognition that Hinduism and Buddhism should be recognised as religions for the purposes of charity. Of more interesting effect, however, is s.3(2)(a)(i), which provides that religion includes 'a religion which does not involve a belief in a god.' Although this provision was obviously intended to cover such belief system religions as Buddhism, it may make it much harder to deny the Church of Scientology charitable status.

Once the religion is acknowledged then the purposes of the gift may be very wide. For example gifts have been held charitable for the building and repair of churches and church property, the support of the clergy, and sometimes for missionary work (although, as noted above, conversion may not be charitable).[65] A trust to promote faith healing has been accepted as charitable.[66] Ancillary organisations, such as the Salvation Army, may also be charitable. Provision for the repose of the souls of the dead is charitable.[67]

One of the main problems with religious charities is closed religious orders as they do not confer public benefit. This is discussed with public benefit subsequently.

8.3.4 Other Categories of Charitable Purposes

Outside the first three heads the Preamble referred to 'the relief of aged,

---

62 [1970] 2 QB 697.
63 The Church of Scientology has been held charitable in both Australia and New Zealand.
64 *Muman v.Nagasena* [2000] 1 WLR 299.
65 *Income Tax Special Purposes Commissioners v. Pemsel* [1891] AC 531.
66 *Funnell v. Stewart* [1996] 1 WLR 288.
67 *Re Hetherington* [1990] Ch 1.

impotent people; the maintenance of sick and maimed soldiers and mariners; the repair of bridges, ports, havens, causeways sea banks and highways; the relief, stock or maintenance for houses of correction; the relief or redemption of prisoners or captives; and the aid or ease of any poor inhabitants concerning payments of fifteens, setting out of soldiers and other taxes.'

Many of these functions have since been taken over by the state, and some are now obsolete. Lord Macnaghten's fourth head included all the examples in the Preamble that did not come under the other heads, and others that were developed by the courts, but was not such a wide 'catch-all' provision as it might first appear. The law has been wary of admitting new charitable trusts under this heading. The Charities Act 2011 s.3(1) provides new categories of charitable purpose, although some cover purposes usually included in the fourth Pemsel head, most are self-explanatory and many cover overlapping purposes:

d) The advancement of health or the saving of lives: s.3(2)(b) also provides that this head includes 'the prevention or relief of sickness, disease or human suffering'. Medical trusts have usually been charitable and medical trusts devoted to research will usually be charitable under the education head;

e) The advancement of citizenship or community development: s.3(2)(c) further provides that this head includes rural or urban regeneration and the promotion of civic responsibility, volunteering, the voluntary sector or the effectiveness, or efficiency of charities. Trusts for local amenities are mentioned in the Preamble and would include the building of bridges and providing public water supplies.[68] Trusts for localities have included provision for people within an area, such as *Re Lewis*,[69] where a gift of £100 each to 10 blind boys and 10 blind girls in Tottenham was valid. However, the courts have been wary of accepting a trust in favour of a class within a class, as discussed below.[70]

f) The advancement of the arts, culture, heritage or science: these purposes have usually been covered under the education head,[71] but now will have a specific category;

g) The advancement of amateur sport: s.3(2)(d) further clarifies that 'sport' 'means sports or games which promote health by involving physical or mental skill or exertion'. These trusts have traditionally not

---

68 Given as example by the Lord Chancellor in *Jones v Williams* (1767) Amb 651
69 [1955] Ch. 104.
70 See Lord Simonds in *Williams v. IRC* [1947] AC 447 and *IRC v. Baddeley* [1955] AC 572.
71 For example *Re Delius* [1957] Ch 299, *Re Hopkins WT* [1965] Ch 669, *Re Shakespeare Memorial Trust* [1923] 2 Ch. 398.

been charitable unless they were linked to an educational institution, when they could be brought under the education Pemsel head, or as a trust for a locality under the fourth head if the provision of sports facilities was to benefit the locality not the sport;[72]

h) The advancement of human rights, conflict resolution or reconciliation, or the promotion of religious or racial harmony or equality and diversity: this head may see organisations such as Amnesty International gaining charitable status;

i) The advancement of environmental protection or improvement: the fourth head had previously recognised some environmental groups as charitable, for example the National Trust;[73]

j) The relief of those in need by reason of youth, age, ill-health, disability, financial hardship or other disadvantage: s.3(2)(e) provides that relief includes the provision of accommodation or care to these persons. The Preamble merely referred to the 'aged' and 'impotent';

k) The advancement of animal welfare: trusts for the welfare of animals generally have been charitable under the fourth Pemsel head as long as they confer a benefit upon mankind, which may include improving public morality.[74] However, the animals have to be cared for, thus a trust for an animal sanctuary for 'all animals birds or other creatures not human', where the animals could live free from 'molestation or destruction by man' was not charitable as it excluded humans and so was of no public benefit and the animals were free to kill each other;[75]

l) The promotion of the efficiency of the armed forces of the Crown, or of the efficiency of the police, fire and rescue services or ambulance services: s.3(2)(f) further provides that "fire and rescue services" means services provided by the fire and rescue authorities under Part 2 of the Fire and Rescue Services Act 2004. The Preamble referred to purposes and trusts in favour of the armed services and by analogy the police force and fire and ambulance services have usually been held to be charitable under the fourth Pemsel head.

m) The final category provides that purposes may be charitable if they are 'any other purposes:

(i) that are not within paragraphs (a) to (l) but are recognised as charitable purposes by virtue of section 5 (recreational and similar trusts etc.) or under the old law,

(ii) that may reasonably be regarded as analogous to, or within the

---

72 *Guild v IRC* [1992] 2 AC 310.

73 *Re Verrall* [1916] 1 Ch. 100.

74 *Re Wedgwood* [1915] 1 Ch 113. Trusts for the care of individual animals are not charitable but may be valid non-charitable purpose trusts (trusts of imperfect obligation).

75 *Re Grove Grady*[1929] 1 Ch. 557.

      spirit of, any purposes falling within any of paragraphs (a) to (l) or subparagraph (i) or,

(iii) that may reasonably be regarded as analogous to, or within the spirit of, any purposes which have been recognised under the law relating to charities in England and Wales, as falling within subparagraph (ii) or this subparagraph.'

This may allow for newly arising purposes to be considered charitable, if appropriate.

It is worth noting that a trust may have a purpose or purposes which are charitable under more than one head. For example the Incorporated Council of Law Reporting was held charitable under the fourth head and the education head.[76] As the statutory heads overlap it will still be possible for a purpose to be charitable under more than one head.

There may also be general charitable trusts, for example in *Moggridge v Thackwell*,[77] the will provided that property might be used for 'such charities as the trustees sees fit'. This would be a general charitable trust and valid as the trustees are restricted to using the fund for recognised charitable purposes. Similar provision might be for 'charitable purposes'.

8.8 The Public Benefit Requirement

Charitable trusts are public purpose trusts and so it makes sense they should confer a public benefit. In order to be charitable a trust must be, 'For the benefit of the community or an appreciably important class of the community'.[78] Traditionally the courts have adopted a negative approach to deciding if a trust is of public benefit. In *Oppenheim v. Tobacco Securities Trust Co.*,[79] the House of Lords adopted the 'personal nexus' test. In *Oppenheim* the trust fund was to provide education for the children of employees and former employees of the British-American Tobacco Co. Ltd. [BAT]. The House of Lords held that, even though the potential beneficiaries numbered over 100,000, they were 'neither a community nor a section of the community for charitable purposes.' These beneficiaries were to be identified merely on the basis of a relationship with the testator, they were children of employees of his company. There was a personal nexus and as Lord Simonds noted, to be charitable the beneficiaries must be identified on no such basis: 'the quality which distinguishes them from members of the community must be a quality which does not depend

---

76   *Incorporated Council of Law Reporting for England and Wales v. A-G* [1972] Ch 73.

77   (1807) 13 Ves 416.

78   *Verge v. Somerville* [1924] AC 496. The Charities Act 2011, s.2(1)(b) now provides that all charities must be for public benefit.

79   [1951] AC 297. Originally used in *Re Compton* [1945] Ch 123

upon their relationship to a particular individual [or company]'. The personal nexus negated the public benefit of the trust and meant the trust could never be charitable.

Although the personal nexus test has been criticised, it has remained the test for the public benefit requirement.[80] The *Oppenheim* personal nexus test is in two parts. To be of public benefit a trust's beneficiaries:

- must not be numerically negligible; and
- must be distinguished from other members of the public by a quality which does not depend on their relationship with a particular individual.

The idea of what is numerically negligible has never been clearly identified. Thus the first limb of the test may have been intended to be a judicial safeguard to be used to invalidate trusts which are for so few people there is little or no public benefit but there is no personal nexus.

The test was applied in **IRC v. Educational Grants Association Ltd,**[81] when a similar trust for the education of the children of the employees of the Metal Box Co. Ltd was invalidated because of the identification of the beneficiaries by a personal nexus to the company. It may seem strange that trusts which will provide education for potentially thousands of children are not of public benefit but the reasoning behind these decisions is not the numbers involved but the personal nexus and the use of public money. As we have noted, charities receive fiscal benefits, generally in the form of tax breaks, and these are in effect a subsidy from other tax payers. Thus as Harman LJ noted, 'It is an admirable thing that the children of employees should have a higher education, but I do not see why that should be at the expense of the taxpayer.'

At common law the public benefit requirement differs between the four heads of charity. It is presumed for the poverty, education and religion heads, but must be established for the fourth head. In effect, although public benefit is presumed for the first three heads the court will usually consider if there is a personal nexus in its judgment and, if there is not, establish public benefit.

- *The relief of poverty*

Trusts for the relief of poverty do not need to confer public benefit as long as they relieve the poverty of poor persons.[82] The relief of any poverty is

---

80 Although the Charity Commission has now provided guidance on public benefit in Charities and Public Benefits (January 2008) which provides that public benefit involves two key principles: there must be an identifiable benefit or benefits; and, benefit must be to the public or a section of the public. Existing case law remains important.

81 [1967] Ch 993.

82 *Isaac v Defriez* (1754) Amb 595.

believed to be of public benefit in itself. Thus Evershed MR stated, in *Re Scarisbrick WT*,[83] 'the relief of poverty is of so altruistic a character that the public benefit may necessarily be inferred'. Thus a personal nexus will not invalidate a trust for the relief of poverty(comma) and trusts for 'poor relations' have been recognised as charitable for over 200 years. In *Re Cohen*,[84] a trust, 'for or towards the maintenance and benefit of any relatives of mine whom my trustees shall consider to be in special need', was held to be valid. In *Re Segelman*,[85] a gift for the 'poor and needy' among a class that consisted of only six of the testator's relatives and their issue at the time of the testator's death was held to be charitable. Similar trusts have been set up for 'poor employees'. Thus in *Dingle v. Turner*,[86] the trust instructed the trustees: 'to apply the income thereof in paying pensions to poor employees of E. Dingle & Co Ltd who are of the age of 60 years at least or who being of the age of 45 years at least are incapacitated from earning their living by reason of some physical or mental infirmity.' The House of Lords held the trust was validly charitable because the personal nexus test did not apply to trusts for the relief of poverty. The only limit of the exemption of trust for the relief of poverty from the personal nexus test is that the trust cannot simply be in favour of named individuals but must be in favour of a class. For example a trust for the relief of poverty of Bill and Ben might not be charitable, but a trust for the relief of poverty of my children and their children when the testator only has two sons, Bill and Ben, would probably be charitable.

- *The advancement of education*

The common law presumes public benefit for the second Pemsel head, but the personal nexus does apply. That is why the trust for education in *Oppenheim v. Tobacco Securities Trust Co.*,[87] which was for the education of employees' children, was not charitable. The product of the educational trust must also be of public benefit. Thus any research must provide public benefit. Pure research will usually not be considered of public benefit. That was the reasoning behind the decision in *Re Shaw*,[88] where the playwright George Bernard Shaw's attempt to create a research trust of his residuary estate to research the utility of the development of a new 40 letter phonetic alphabet was held to confer no public benefit. The public benefit requirement for education also gives rise to the interesting concept of quality as regards the purpose of the trust. For education quality definitely

---

83 [1951] Ch. 622.
84 [1973] 1 All ER 889.
85 [1996] Ch 171.
86 [1972] AC 601.
87 [1951] AC 297. Originally used in *Re Compton* [1945] Ch 123.
88 [1957] 1 WLR 729.

does matter. Thus in **Re Pinion**,[89] the testator directed his executors to give his studio and its contents to the National Trust for the benefit of the English nation. The National Trust refused the gift and in default the executors were to set up a museum to house the objects. The Court of Appeal considered whether the establishment of the museum for the collection would be charitable under the second head. Unusually the Court called expert opinion to decide on the worthiness of the paintings and furniture which the testator wanted to be housed in the museum. One expert commented that he was astounded that 'so voracious a collector should not by hazard have picked up even one meritorious object'. In holding that the purpose did not come under the second head because of the lack of public benefit, Harman LJ commented, 'I can conceive of no useful object to be served in foisting upon the public this mass of junk. It has neither public utility nor educational value'.

- *The advancement of religion*

Public benefit is presumed for the third head but the personal nexus test applies. Generally trusts for the advancement of religion will be charitable provided that there is some contact with the public. Thus gifts for the saying of masses in public are charitable, [90]but masses said in private are not.[91] If there is no public contact, for example if the gift is to a closed order then it will not be charitable. Thus in **Gilmour v. Coats**,[92] the gift to the Carmelite priory was not charitable because this was a closed order devoted to prayer and contemplation. However, it should be noted that Cross J did note, in **Neville Estates v Madden**,[93] that: 'the members for the time being of the Catford Synagogue are no more a section of the public than the members for the time being of the Carmelite Priory... But the court is, I think, entitled to assume that some benefit accrues to the public from the attendance at places of worship of persons who live in the world and mix with their fellow citizens.'

Thus private worship was considered to confer a public benefit. It may be possible by analogy to the circumstances in Neville to argue that practice of a religious observance in private could confer some public benefit and be charitable.

Other purposes beneficial to the community
The fourth Pemsel head does not have presumed public benefit and so

89 (*Westminster Bank Ltd v Pinion*) [1965] Ch 85 EWCA.
90 *Re Hetherington* [1990] Ch 1.
91 They may still be valid non-charitable purpose trusts (trusts of imperfect obligation).
92 [1949] AC 426.
93 [1962] Ch 832, 853.

public benefit must always be established for this head. Any personal nexus will invalidate the charitable nature of these purposes. Many of the purposes covered here will automatically confer benefit on a wide section of the community (e.g. trusts to build roads, bridges and supply water). Such trusts may be confined to a particular locality, for example the building of a bridge or road, but should be available to anyone. The trust may even benefit an area outside the jurisdiction.[94] However, the restriction of those who are to benefit to a group within the locality may negate public benefit and invalidate the charitable nature of the trust. These trusts have been seen to benefit a 'class within a class'. In *Williams v. IRC*,[95] a trust for the benefit of 'Welsh people in London' was held not to be charitable, as this was a 'class within a class'. Similarly in *IRC v. Baddeley*,[96] land was conveyed for the benefit of the Stratford and Newtown Methodist Mission for the provision of religious and recreational facilities for the residents of West Ham and Leyton who 'for the time being are members or likely to become members of the Methodist Church and of insufficient means otherwise to enjoy the advantages provided by these presents ' Thus the gift was limited to those who were Methodists or likely to become Methodists within the locality. This was a class within a class and evoked a famous quote from Lord Simonds highlighting the ridiculous nature of such gifts: 'Who ever heard of a bridge to be crossed only by impecunious Methodists?'[97]

The Charities Act 2006 removed the presumption of public benefit for all heads of charitable purpose.[98] Public benefit must now be established for all heads. However, the existing case law will still be relevant for establishing public benefit.[99] The guidance given by the Charity Commission is that the exemption of trusts for the relief of poverty from the personal nexus test remains good law.

8.9 The Trust must be Exclusively Charitable

A charitable trust must have purely charitable purposes. It cannot have non-charitable purposes unless they are ancillary to its main charitable purposes. Similarly gifts for 'charitable' purposes must be exclusively for

---

94   For example, in *Mitford v Reynolds* (1848) 16 Sim 105, a trust for the benefit of indigenous inhabitants of a certain town in India was held charitable.

95   [1947] AC 447.

96   [1955] AC 572.

97   It should be noted that Lord Reid delivered a powerful dissenting judgment as he could see no special reason for considering this group not a section of the community.

98   Now the Charities Act 2011, s.2(1)(b) & s.4(2).

99   Charities Act 2011, s.3(3).

charitable purposes. If the trust or gift has mixed charitable and non-charitable objectives, the whole fund might be regarded as non-charitable. The courts distinguish charitable or non-charitable purposes on the construction of the provision. In doing so a 'benignant construction should be given if possible' to deal with any ambiguity to interpret the provision as charitable.[100] This is because charitable trusts and gifts are to the benefit of us all. Although the justification is usually given as 'there must be a certain bias in the mind of the court in favour of doing what the testator or testatrix obviously wanted to be done'.[101]

However, if there is a chance that the trustees may use the funds for non-charitable purposes the trust should not be a valid charitable trust.[102]

Some of the factors that need to be considered in determining whether the trust or gift is exclusively charitable are:

- The use of the words 'and' and 'or';
- Gifts to those in public office;
- Charging for charitable services.

The significance of the construction of a provision is shown most obviously in the 'and/or' cases. The general rule is that the word 'or' is to be interpreted disjunctively and the word 'and' conjunctively. Thus a gift 'for charitable or benevolent purposes' will generally not be construed as a charitable gift because it is possible for the gift to be applied for objects which are benevolent but not charitable.[103] Similarly, instruments which provided 'such charitable or public purposes as my trustee thinks proper',[104] and 'public, benevolent or charitable purposes'[105] as my trustees think fit were read as being capable of separating the purposes and so allowing the funds to be used for non-charitable purposes. Thus they failed as charitable trusts.

The word 'and' is usually read conjunctively. Therefore a gift 'for charitable and benevolent purposes' will generally be charitable, as any purposes of the trust must be both charitable and benevolent.[106] Similarly in *Re Sutton*,[107] 'charitable and deserving objects' was held conjunctive and any purposes of the trust had to be both charitable and deserving.

---

100 *IRC v McMullen* [1981] AC 1, per Lord Hailsham. See also Lord Loreburn L.C. in *Weir v. Crum-Brown* [1908] AC 162, 167: 'Now there is no better rule than that a benignant construction will be placed upon charitable bequests.'

101 *In re Bradbury, Deceased-Needham v. Reekie* [1951] 1 T.L.R. 130.

102 *Chichester Diocesan Fund v Simpson* [1944] AC 341.

103 *Chichester Diocesan Board of Finance v. Simpson* [1944] AC 341.

104 *Blair v Duncan* [1902] AC 37.

105 *Houston v Burns* [1918] AC 337.

106 *Re Best* [1904] 2 Ch 354.

107 [1901] 2 Ch 640.

However, in **Re Eades**,[108] the phrase 'such religious, charitable and philanthropic objects' was interpreted as being capable of being read disjunctively and so failed. Similarly in **Attorney-General of the Bahamas v Royal Trust Co**,[109] a gift for the 'education and welfare' of children in the Bahamas was void.

There may also be problems with the purpose behind gifts to people who hold a particular office, as it may be a gift for them in their official capacity or to use generally for non-charitable purposes. A gift to the vicars and churchwardens of two named churches 'for parochial work' was held not to be charitable in **Farley v. Westminster Bank Ltd**.[110] It seems this was because 'parochial work' might involve work which was not charitable. This should be contrasted with a gift to a vicar 'to be used for his work in the parish', which was held to be charitable.[111] Similarly a gift to the vicar and churchwardens of a particular church 'for any purpose in connection with the said church which they may select' was held to be validly charitable.[112] This is an area where the construction of the particular provision is particularly important. The gift must be to the office holder to use only for charitable purposes.

Charging for services may also be seen as conferring private benefit and accordingly as being non-charitable. However, a charitable organisation may charge for its services as long as the money raised is restricted to being used for the charitable purposes of the organisation and it does not make commercial profits which are distributed to private individuals (or exclude the public and so affect the public benefit requirement). Thus in **Scottish Burial Reform and Cremation Society Ltd v Glasgow City Corpn**,[113] the company was non-profit making and its main object was to promote inexpensive and sanitary methods of disposal of the dead, in particular to promote cremation. For many years the company had carried on a crematorium in Glasgow, charging fees, but the fees were not intended to yield a profit. The House of Lords held that the company was a charity because its purpose came under the fourth head, it was of public benefit and it was exclusively charitable. Similarly in **Re Resch's WT**,[114] a gift was left to a private hospital which charged high fees. The Hospital was held charitable as it gave care and treatment that the local National Health Service hospital did not give and gave concessions including free treatment to the poor. However, it should be noted that a charitable body's exemption

---

108 [1920] 2 Ch 353.
109 [1986] 3 All ER 423.
110 [1939] AC 430.
111 *Re Simpson* [1946] Ch 299.
112 *Re Eastes* [1948] Ch 257.
113 [1968] AC 138, HL.
114 [1969] 1 AC 514.

from taxation may be lifted if the proceeds are not used for charitable purposes or the main purpose of the organisation becomes commercial.

If a charitable trust has non-charitable purposes which are *de minimis* or ancillary to the charitable purposes then the trust's charitable status may be upheld. In **Re Coxen**,[115] a substantial gift to charity was made which included provision for an annual dinner for the trustees. The gift was held to be charitable because of the minimal nature of the provision compared to the gift, and the consideration that the provision of the dinner might reward the trustees for their work and so aid the better administration of the charity.

If a trust or gift has mixed charitable and non-charitable purposes it may be possible to sever the charitable portion to save it. If there is no direction as to portions then 'equity is equality'.[116] However, if the trustees can choose non-charitable instead of charitable purposes then the gift or trust will not be charitable.[117]

8.10 Political Purposes

The modern approach of the courts to political purposes has been that they may not be charitable. As we shall see this is linked to the idea that a political purpose implies changing the law and a court could not be satisfied that a change in the law would be for the benefit of the public so would fail the public benefit requirement. Political purposes are dealt with as separate from public benefit as it has been such an important and controversial topic.

Political purposes have not always been considered as non-charitable as long as the donor/testator believed the purposes were of public benefit then they would be upheld as charitable. Thus, in **Re Scowcroft**,[118] a gift 'for the furtherance of Conservative principles and religious and mental improvement' was held to be charitable. Similarly gifts to change the law regarding vivisection, the live dissection of animals, have been held charitable; for example, in **Armstrong v. Reeves**,[119] a gift to change the law to stop all vivisection was held to be charitable. In **Re Foveaux**,[120] a gift to the International Society for the Total Suppression of Vivisection was held to be charitable.

However, this interpretation of political purposes changed in the twentieth century. Trusts which were obviously for political purposes were

---

115 [1948] Ch 747.
116 *Salusbury v Denton* (1857) 21 JP 726.
117 *Chichester Diocesan Fund v Simpson* [1944] AC 341.
118 [1898] 2 Ch 638.
119 (1890) 25 LR 235.
120 [1895] 2 Ch 501.

refused charitable status. Thus trusts for the advancement of the cause of the Conservative,[121] Labour[122] and Liberal[123] parties in England were held not to be charitable. Similarly, although we have noted that university students' unions may be charitable, they may lose charitable status if they donate funds for political purposes,[124] or use funds for political campaigning.[125]

Trusts whose purposes were less obviously political were harder to deal with and the courts adopted the test of whether the purpose was to change the law. As has been noted, judges have used this test as they claim that they are not in a position to decide if the proposed change in the law is of public benefit and so it cannot be charitable. In *National Anti-Vivisection Society v. IRC*,[126] Lord Parker said:

'A trust for the attainment of political objects has always been held invalid, not because it is illegal, for everyone is at liberty to advocate or promote by any lawful means a change in the law, but because the court has no means of judging whether a proposed change in the law will or will not be for the public benefit, and therefore cannot say that a gift to secure the change is a charitable gift.'

Thus in *Re Bushnell*,[127] there was an attempt to create a trust for 'the advancement and propagation of the teaching of socialised medicine.' The testator died before the National Health Service had been established din the UK and so any such 'socialised medicine' would have involved changing the law. Therefore the trust was not charitable.

The most controversial cases have involved purposes which many people would consider 'good' causes which are not overtly political. For example, in *National Anti-Vivisection Society v. IRC*,[128] it was argued that the National Anti-Vivisection Society had mixed purposes, one of which was to change the law on vivisection. We have already considered Lord Parker's comment on changing the law being a political purpose; however, it may surprise that he was in favour of the Society being considered charitable as he did not consider the change of the law its main purpose. The Society was held not to be charitable because, as Lord Simonds said:

'Lord Parker uses slightly different language but means the same thing

---

121 *Bonar Law Memorial Trust v. IRC* (1933) 49 TLR 220.
122 A trust to promote socialism: *Re Hopkinson* [1949] 1 All ER 246.
123 *Re Ogden* [1933] Ch 678.
124 *Baldry v. Feintuck* [1972] 1 WLR 552.
125 *A-G v. Ross* [1986] 1 WLR 252. In *Webb v. O'Doherty* (1991) 3 Admin LR 731 (Ch.D.) an injunction was granted to prevent a students' union from campaigning against the Gulf War.
126 [1948] AC 31 HL.
127 [1975] 1 WLR 1596.
128 [1948] AC 31 HL.

when he says that the court has no means of judging whether a proposed change in the law will or will not be for the public benefit. It is not for the court to judge and the court has no means of judging. I conclude that the main object of the society is political and for that reason the society is not established for charitable purposes only.'

The leading case in this area is *McGovern v. A-G*.[129] The case involved Amnesty International, an international organisation which campaigns for human rights generally but notably the freedom from torture of political prisoners and securing the release of prisoners of conscience. These were clearly political purposes but Amnesty claimed its UK organisation would not campaign on these matters to change the law in the UK. In holding that the trust was not charitable, Slade J noted:[130]

'The mere fact that the trust was intended to be carried out abroad would not by itself necessarily deprive it of charitable status. [but] the court will have no adequate means of judging whether a proposed change in the law of a foreign country will or will not be for the public benefit. Furthermore the court would also, I conceive be bound to consider the consequences for this country as a matter of public policy. In a number of such cases there would arise a substantial prima facie risk that such a trust, if enforced, could prejudice the relations of this country with the foreign country concerned '

Slade J identified five purposes which would be considered political:

* to further the interests of a particular political party;
* to procure changes in the laws of this country;
* to bring about changes in the laws of a foreign country;
* to bring about a reversal of government policy;
* to bring about a reversal of government policy in a foreign country.

These purposes will invalidate any attempt at charitable status.

The main problem for charities is that they may have mixed purposes and wish to engage in some political campaigning. If they do they risk losing the benefits of charitable status.

The inclusion of specific heads of charity which may involve campaigning for a change in the law, in particular the advancement of human rights, conflict resolution or reconciliation or the promotion of religious or racial harmony or equality and diversity,[131] and the advancement of environmental protection or improvement,[132] has meant

---

129 [1982] Ch 321.
130 Amnesty International was confirmed to have a political purpose in *R. v. Radio Authority ex parte Bull* [1997] 3 WLR 1094.
131 The Charities Act 2011, s.3(1)(h).
132 The Charities Act 2011, s.3(1)(i).

that some of these organisations may now be able to maintain their charitable status whilst being actively political, and some organisations, such as Amnesty, may attain charitable status whilst continuing their political purposes..

8.11 *Cy-près* - Saving Charity

One of the benefits extended to charity is the power of the courts to pass funds dedicated to charity to other similar charitable purposes if the original charitable purpose is no longer possible. Generally, when a private trust fails the property results back to the settlor or the testator's estate, the settlor is free to resettle the property if he so wishes whereas the testamentary failure results in the property passing to the residual legatee or the testator's next of kin. Similarly, if an attempt to create an *intervivos* charitable trust fails the settlor is free to resettle the property. However, most charitable trusts are testamentary and if they fail the testator's wishes may be thwarted. On failure of a testamentary charitable trust the court has the inherent power to apply the property *cy-près*, a Norman French phrase meaning 'as near as possible', for other charitable purposes which are as near as possible to those the testator intended. The court will only do this if it can detect a general charitable intent in the gift or trust, or if the gift or trust has already been dedicated to charity. This is justified by the principle that after property is dedicated to charity it, or its substitutions, will remain dedicated to charitable purposes.

The term *cy-près* is often used for any scheme which applies property from one charitable purpose to another although strictly speaking these schemes are not all *cy-près*, for example gifts which appear to be for a charitable purpose but which have been left to a non-existent organisation may be subject to an order under the *Sign Manual* (literally the Royal signature), which orders the deceased's personal representatives to donate the gift in favour of a particular charity. Originally the *Sign Manual* was the signature of the monarch, but is more likely today to be the Attorney General.

8.12 Summary

The law of charitable purposes has developed from the initial purposes indicated in the Preamble to the Statute of Elizabeth, through the categorisation of the Pemsel heads into the thirteen statutory purposes recognised as charitable in the Charities Act 2011. To be charitable a trust has to be for one of these recognised purposes, or analogous to them, be of public benefit and be wholly and exclusively charitable. Public benefit is still determined by a negative test to determine that the class of potential beneficiaries is not numerically negligible and the beneficiaries are not identified by some characteristic linking them to the testator. The presumption of public benefit no longer applies to any head of charity and must be established for all. However, it seems that the relief of poverty will still be exempt from the personal nexus test. A trust or gift which has mixed charitable and non-charitable purposes should not be charitable. Problems arise when testators use 'or' and 'and', separating or linking purposes which may be both charitable and non-charitable. If the interpretation of these provisions is that the property may be used for non-charitable purposes then the trust or gift will not be charitable. It may sometimes be possible to sever or apportion property between the charitable and non-charitable purposes.

If a charitable gift or trust fails it may be possible to save the property for charity using the ancient doctrine of *cy-près* or another scheme of distribution. This will usually depend on the general charitable intent of the testator or whether the trust or gift was already vested in charity.

CHAPTER 9
CONSTITUTION OF TRUSTS & PERFECTION OF GIFTS

9.1 Why is it Important to Know When a Trust is Constituted and a Gift is Perfected?

In the seminal case of ***Milroy v Lord***,[1] Turner L.J. noted

'...I take the law of this court to be well settled, that, in order to render a voluntary settlement valid and effectual, the settler must have done everything which, according to the nature of the property comprised in the settlement, was necessary to be done in order to transfer the property and render the settlement binding upon him. He may, of course, do this by actually transferring the property to the persons for whom he intends to provide, and the provision will then be effectual, and it will be equally effectual if he transfers the property to a trustee for the purposes of the settlement, or declares that he himself holds in trust for those purposes;... but, in order to render the settlement binding, one or other of these modes must...be resorted to, for there is no equity in this court to perfect an imperfect gift. The cases I think go further to this extent, that if the settlement is intended to be effectuated by one of the modes to which I have referred, the court will not give effect to it by applying another of those modes. If it is intended to take effect by transfer; the court will not hold the intended transfer to operate as a declaration of trust, for then every imperfect instrument would be converted into a perfect trust...'

Thus Turner L.J. identified three methods by which you can allow another to enjoy your property without giving you something in return:

- You may give it to them: a gift (and Turner LJ states equity will not perfect an imperfect gift, or construe a trust from a failed gift);
- You may create a trust by transferring the property to the trustee; or
- You may create a trust by declaring yourself (the settlor) trustee- that you hold the property on trust for the beneficiary.

The last comment of Turner L.J. also clarifies that equity will not construe a valid trust from a failed gift. Equity tries not to confuse gifts and trusts

---

1   (1862) 4 De GF & J 264.

but there are overlaps between the two; trusts may be viewed as gifts over time. For example if David is suffering from a terminal illness and wants to give his infant son a flat, he may transfer the property to Michael to give to his son when he becomes an adult. David is giving the flat to his son, but is doing so by way of a trust. The trust is constituted when David transfers the property to Michael with the intention that Michael is to hold it on trust and give it to David's son when he is an adult. Michael will be trustee of the flat until David's son is an reaches majority when he will transfer the property, thus perfecting the gift.

When a trust comes into being there are important consequences; it is usually irrevocable, the settlor cannot call for the property back and has usually lost all interest in the trust property;[2] the trustee is under trust obligations, he must carry out the trust until its purpose is over and he distributes the trust property in accordance with the trust instructions;[3] and the beneficiaries have enforceable rights.

When a gift is made there are also important consequences; the donor loses all interest in the property and the donee can do as he wishes with the property.[4] The common law does not recognise a 'gift for a second', you can lend property but you cannot give property and then make the donee return the property. The principle that the donee may do as he wishes with the property is enforced by the rule against inalienability- the common law does not like restrictions on the ability of the donee to deal with the property absolutely.

A trust is constituted when it is established. This is usually when the trust property has been transferred to the trustee by the settlor (or by executors of the testator's estate) under a binding trust obligation. A trust may also be constituted by a settlor declaring himself trustee of his own property. A gift is perfected when the property has been transferred to the donee by the donor with the intent that the donee is to receive the beneficial interest in the property as well as legal title.

If the trust property is not transferred to the trustees then the trust is not constituted and there is no trust. If the property of a gift is not

---

2   *Re Bowden* [1936] Ch 71; a settlor may reserve express powers of revocation in the trust instrument: see Patrick O'Hagan 'The reluctant settlor—property, powers and pretences' Trusts & Trustees (2011) 17 (10): 905-919.

3   A trust may be brought to an early end by a court or by the beneficiaries using the rule in *Saunders v Vautier*.

4   To set aside gifts for mistake the donor or settler must have been operating 'under some mistake of so serious a character as to render it unjust on the part of the donee to retain the property given to him by the donor.' *Ogilvie v Littleboy* (1897) 13 TLR 399 at 400, per Lindley LJ. For recent developments in other jurisdictions see David Hayton. 'Setting gifts aside for mistake' (2011) *Trusts & Trustees* 17 (10): 937-944.

transferred to the donee then the trust is not perfected and there is no gift. Similarly, if the trust property is transferred to the trustee but the trust intention is not communicated then the trustee is not under the trust obligation and the trust does not exist. If property is transferred to another but there is no intent of the transferee to give the beneficial interest in the property to that other then there is no gift.

As we have noted, formality is not usually as important in equity as it is at common law. However, the important consequences of the constitution of a trust and the perfection of a gift mean that equity will look closely at the circumstances of a transfer of property to see that it has been transferred to the trustee or donee ensuring that the trust is constituted or the gift perfected and all the consequent rights and obligations have come into effect.

The effort involved in transferring property and sometimes the consequent delay are important, as they give the settlor / donor the chance to think about the consequences of his actions and to be sure he intends to part with his interest in such property by way of trust or gift.

Two of the maxims of equity are extremely important in considering the requirements in the constitution of a trust or the perfection of a gift in equity:

- *Equity will not assist a volunteer;*
- *Equity will not perfect an imperfect gift.*

A volunteer is someone who has not given consideration, *e.g.*, the donee of a gift. In this maxim equity follows the law; (usually) equity will not enforce a bargain unless consideration has been given. If consideration has passed then equity follows the law in enforcing and protecting the rights of those who have given consideration; this is the basis for the concept of equity's darling,[5] the bona fide purchaser without notice of an equitable interest. If property has not been transferred to the donee the gift is imperfect. A donee is by nature a volunteer, thus he has no contractual rights and so cannot sue at common law to perfect the gift. Here *equity follows the law* and will not assist the donee to perfect the gift. The principle that equity will not step in to perfect a gift may also be extended to *equity will not constitute an incompletely constituted trust*. The only volunteer equity will assist is the beneficiary of a trust, most beneficiaries have not given consideration for their beneficial interests,[6] but if a trust is validly constituted then equity will enforce the beneficiary's rights against the

---

5   Along with the concept of conscience.
6   Sometimes a trust is intended for which the proposed settlor has received some consideration or for which binding promises, covenants, are made. These are known as covenants to settle and may sometimes be enforceable even though the trust has not been constituted.

trustee and others who receive trust property with notice of a breach of trust. However, equity will only assist this volunteer when the trust has been constituted. If a trust is not constituted there is no trust and the intended beneficiaries have no rights in equity. We now consider the requirements of equity for the constitution of trusts and the perfection of gifts and the exceptions or relaxations of the rule.

9.2 Formalities in the Transferring of Property

To constitute a valid trust the settlor must transfer the property to the trustees. To perfect a valid gift the donor must transfer the property to the donee with the intent that the donee is to receive the beneficial interest in the property. The method of transferring property depends on the nature of that property. Legal title to a chattel will generally be transferred by delivery of the chattel. If the chattel is too big to hand over, transfer of some indication of title will be required (*e.g.* the keys to a car etc.). Passing of the registration document to a car may be evidence of the gift, but it may not be conclusive; the registration document shows the car's keeper, not it's owner.

A transfer of shares has to comply with requirements in the Companies Act 2006 and any requirements in the company's articles of association. Generally, a transfer of shares should be made by the transferor signing the share transfer form, delivering the form and the share certificates to the transferee; the transferee then has to deliver the share transfer form to the company to have the transfer registered in the company's share register. The directors (applying any criteria contained in the company's constitution[7]) decide whether or not to accept the transfer into the new name, and, if they do, the company alters its register of members to reflect the transfer, issues a new certificate to the new owner and cancels the share certificate of the previous owner. If appropriate the new owner also has to pay stamp duty.

There are also formalities required in the transfer of a cheque. As a cheque is merely an instruction to pay, a volunteer cannot cash a cheque if the donor changes his mind or dies before the cheque has been paid.[8] A cheque is a special form of bill of exchange and so may usually be negotiated, meaning it may be sold or given away. If a cheque has been made out in your favour, i.e. your name is on it as a payee, then to pass it to someone else you need to endorse it. This is usually done by signing the

---

7   For example the articles may contain a provision such as- '(1) The directors may, in their absolute discretion and without assigning any reason therefore, approve or refuse to approve any transfer of any share, whether or not it is a fully paid share.'

8   *Curnock v IRC* [2003] WTLR 955.

back of the cheque, which allows the bearer to pay the cheque into their account. Banks have tried to restrict the negotiability of cheques which is why they are usually crossed 'a/c payee only' which should make them non-negotiable. However, cheques may still be negotiated regardless of such crossing; crossing may be 'crossed out' or signed through, although the banks frown on this practice and try to exclude it contractually. Today the practice of negotiating a cheque is rare.

We have already noted the formality requirements for a valid declaration of trust of land as provided by statute. The Law of Property Act 1925 s53(1)(b) provides that a declaration of trust of land must be manifested and proved in writing. There are also formality requirements for the transfer of land. Legal title in land must be conveyed by deed.[9] Thus an enforceable trust of land requires transfer of legal title to the land by deed, unless the settlor is declaring a trust with himself as trustee, and written proof of the declaration of trust. For the settlor declaring himself trustee of his own land the requirement would just be for written proof of the declaration of trust. We have also seen that there are written formality requirements for the disposition of an equitable interest in land. The Law of Property Act 1925, s.53(1)(c), states that any disposition of the equitable interest in a trust may only be made in writing. Thus a gift of the equitable interest must be in writing.

Thus the method of transfer of the property to be the subject matter of a trust or gift depends on the nature of the property and the legal requirements for transfer of that type of property. The formality requirements are said to give the donor/settlor the time to change his mind and to stress the impact of his actions. However, in enforcing formalities equity has to consider balancing the need for formality against the wishes of the donor/settlor. Let us now look at what is required for a valid declaration of the settlor as trustee, before we go on to consider the rules of equity regarding the transfer of property for the constitution of a trust or the perfection of a gift.

9.3 Declaration of Settlor as Trustee

A settlor may create a trust by declaring himself a trustee. Obviously the settlor already has legal title to the property and so does not have to transfer it to another. Thus there are no problems with constitution of the trust to do with the transfer of the property. The most important factor is therefore a valid declaration of trust. There must be a clear declaration of trust and the cases we have already considered regarding the certainty of

---

9   Section 52 Law of Property Act 1925, the deed must comply with s1 of the Law of Property (Miscellaneous Provisions) Act 1989, s1, which requires that a deed must be signed, delivered and witnessed by at least one person.

intention to create a trust are important for evidencing this clear intention to place oneself under a trust obligation. The word 'trust' does not have to be used, but there must be words and/or actions which evidence this intention to place oneself under a trust obligation. Thus, in **Paul v. Constance**[10] the Court held that Mr Constance's words 'this money is as much yours as mine' and the couple's actions in depositing their joint winnings in the bank account were evidence of Mr Constance's intention to make himself trustee of the account for them both. The Court of Appeal noted that Mr Constance probably would not have understood the legal concept of a trust but held that his words and actions evidenced his intention to place himself under the equivalent of a trust obligation.

A self-declaration of trust may arise impliedly from the actions of the settlor: for example a company may impliedly declare itself to be a trustee of money on behalf of its customers;[11] and a company may impliedly declare itself trustee of money loaned for a specific purpose on behalf of the lender.[12] There are no formality requirements for a self-declaration of a trust of personal property; however, a self-declaration of a trust of land will need to comply with the Law of Property Act 1925, s53(1)(b), it will need to be manifested and proved in writing to be enforceable.

One of the important principles of equity which was confirmed in **Milroy v Lord**,[13] is that *equity will not construe a valid trust from a failed gift*. Often when the donor of an attempted gift has failed to transfer the property as required to the donee, perhaps because the donor has died before they can perfect the gift, then the donee, or someone acting on his behalf, will attempt to argue that the donor's intention to give the property has placed them under an obligation to give the property and so they must have been holding it on trust for the purported donee. Of course this cannot be the case as there must be a certainty of intention to create a trust to establish a valid trust and here there is a clear certainty to give a gift, not to place oneself under a trust obligation.[14] However, this has not prevented disappointed donee's from arguing this and even one Court of Appeal decision accepting such argument. There are numerous examples of equity refusing to construe a valid trust from a failed gift.

---

10   [1977] 1 WLR 527.
11   *Re Kayford* [1975] 1 WLR 279.
12   *Barclay's Bank Ltd. v. Quistclose Investments Ltd.* [1970] AC 567 HL
13   (1862) 4 De GF & J 264.
14   E.g. Romer J, in *Re Fry* [1946] Ch 312, noted that the intention of the donor to give the property, which he failed to do, could not constitute an intention to hold the property on trust.

Jones v. Lock[15]

Mr. Jones returned from a business trip. His baby's nurse complained that he had not brought anything back for his baby son. Mr. Jones then produced a cheque for £900 and said, in the presence of his wife and the baby's nurse: 'Look you here, I give this to baby.' He then placed the cheque into the baby's hand, before placing it in a safe for safekeeping. He died a few days later. The gift was not perfected as he had not endorsed the back of the cheque in his son's favour. It was argued on behalf of the son that Mr. Jones had declared himself a trustee of the cheque in his son's favour. However, the Court was clear that the failure of the gift was not enough to evidence a self-declaration of trust. Mr. Jones' words were merely 'loose conversation' and not enough to evidence the certainty of intention to place him under a trust obligation.

Richards v. Delbridge[16]

Mr. Delbridge wanted to give the lease he had over business premises, which he used for his successful bone manure business, to his grandson, Edward Benetto Richards. He endorsed on the lease 'this deed and all thereto belonging I give to Edward Benetto Richards from this time forth with all stock-in-trade'. He then gave the lease to Richards' mother to hold for Richards, but died before it was delivered to Richards himself. There was no transfer of the lease as, at this time, statute required leases to be assigned by deed only. Thus the intended gift did not comply with the formalities required. The grandson argued that Delbridge had declared himself trustee to hold the lease on trust for grandson. The Court held that there was no self-declaration of trust. To declare a valid trust it was not necessary to use words such as 'I declare myself trustee', but it was necessary to do or to say something equivalent to it. As the grandfather had not there was no trust.

When there is a self-declaration of trust there may be some confusion over whether constitution has occurred. This was the case in *T. Choithram International SA v. Paragani*,[17] the settlor had repeatedly declared that he would give his property, mostly shares, to a charitable company which he had set up and of which he was one of the trustees. He died declaring that all his property now belonged to the trust. However, the necessary formalities for share transfer had not been complied with and his next of kin argued that there was no valid constitution of the trust and so it fell into residue and should be divided amongst them. The Privy Council, overturning a decision of the High Court of the British Virgin Islands, held

---

15   (1865) LR 1 Ch App 25.
16   (1874) LR 18 Eq 11.
17   [2001] 1 WLR 1; [2001] 2 All ER 492.

that the trust was constituted at the moment the settlor declared his property belonged to the trust as he was one of the trustees.

9.4 The Rules for Transferring Property to Constitute a Trust and Perfect a Gift

The principles applicable to the transfer of property to constitute a trust when the trustee is not the settlor and to perfect a gift are the same. Both require the transfer of legal title to property to another; the trustee or the donor. When equity has to consider whether there has been a transfer of property sufficient to constitute a trust or perfect a gift it has taken a quite strict approach because of the consequences of constitution of a trust and perfection of a gift. The principle to be applied was identified in Milroy v. Lord.[18] The settlor attempted to create a trust by transferring shares to Lord to be held for Milroy. However, the share transfer was never registered in the company records by the settlor. Lord had powers of attorney and could have registered the transfer but did not. Milroy asked the Court to enforce the trust as there was clear evidence that the settlor had intended to create a trust. The Court held that there had been no transfer of property thus there was no trust because it remained unconstituted. For the constitution of a trust or the perfection of a gift, equity required that 'the settlor must have done everything which, according to the nature of the property comprised in the settlement, was necessary to be done in order to transfer the property and render the settlement binding upon him.' The settlor should have transferred the shares in the required manner to the trustee, Lord, for the trust to be constituted. Milroy was a volunteer and equity would not assist a volunteer. This may seem harsh and ignore other equitable maxims, such as equity looks to the intent not the form, but reflects the important consequences of the constitution of a trust and the perfection of a gift.

Thus the principle of equity which is applied by courts when considering whether there has been the constitution of a trust or the perfection of a gift is whether the settlor or donor has done 'everything necessary' to transfer the property to the trustee or donee according to the nature of the property. This principle was applied in *Re Fry*.[19]

Mr. Fry was a resident of Florida in the United States of America. Fry wished to transfer shares in a private company to his son. Fry signed the share transfer form and gave it and the share certificates to his son, who then sent the transfer to the company to be registered. As this was during the Second World War, the consent of the British Treasury was required for transfers of shares involving those not resident in the UK. Fry did not

18   (1862) 4 De G.F. & J 264.
19   [1946] Ch 312.

apply for treasury consent and died before it could be obtained.

Judgment: it was held that the donor had not done all that he was required to do for the transfer of the shares to the donee; therefore the gift was not perfected. Romer J. reasoned thus:

'Now I should have thought it was difficult to say that the testator had done everything that was required to be done by him at the time of his death, for it was necessary for him to obtain permission from the Treasury for the assignment and he had not obtained it. Moreover, the Treasury might in any case have required further information of the kind referred to in the questionnaire which was submitted to him, or answers supplemental to those which he had given in reply to it; and, if so approached, he might have refused to concern himself with the matter further, in which case I do not know how anyone could have compelled him to do so… [Treasury] sanction was never in fact obtained; it might indeed (although the probabilities are certainly otherwise) never have been forthcoming at all.' [20]

Romer J also held that the intended transfer as a gift did not create a trust:

'As the testator intended the gifts now in question "to take effect by transfer," it follows from these observations of Turner L.J. [in Milroy v Lord] that no question as to the creation of a trust in favour of the donees can arise, and indeed, no argument so based was advanced on their behalf.' [21] There was some criticism that the decision in **Re Fry** was too harsh and that there should be some flexibility in the principle regarding what a settlor or donor had to do to constitute a trust or perfect a gift, especially in the light of settlors'/donors' intentions and reliance on third parties to complete the transfer. The Court of Appeal considered this in **Re Rose**.[22]

Rose wanted to transfer shares in a private company to trustees. In March 1943 Rose executed a deed transferring the shares to the trustees; all other formalities that Rose could attend to were completed. However, the directors of the company had the power to refuse to register transfers of shares; thus they had to approve registration of the new share holders. The directors did not approve registration of the trustees as the owners of the shares until June 1943. The trustees were duly entered in the register of members. Rose died within five years of the transfer being registered by the directors, but more than five years after he had completed all that was within his power to transfer the shares. The time of transfer was very important as, if the trust had been constituted within five years of his death, the shares would have formed part of his estate for taxation purposes, if he had divested himself of title to the shares more than five years before his death then the shares would not form part of his estate and were not liable

---

20   [1946] Ch 312 at 317.
21   [1946] Ch 312 at 316.
22   [1952] Ch 499.

to taxation. Thus the court had to consider whether the trust was constituted when Rose had done everything within his power to transfer the shares, or was it constituted two months later, when the directors approved the transfer to the trustees. The latter would follow the principle in *Milroy v Lord* and *Re Fry*, as Rose had not done everything necessary to transfer the shares as he had not obtained the consent of the directors.

Judgment: the Court held that March 1943 was the effective date for the transfer of the equitable ownership of the shares. Rose was a trustee from that date. The Court was not upholding an express trust but recognising Rose had done everything within his power to transfer the shares to his trustees when the deed was executed. He had divested himself of the beneficial ownership in favour of the beneficiaries of the express trust and held legal title purely on constructive trust to be passed to the trustees for the benefit of the beneficiaries.

The principle from *Re Rose* is that a trust will be constituted and a gift perfected when the settlor or donor has done all that is in his power to transfer title to the property to the trustees or the donees. This principle was applied by the Court of Appeal in **Mascall v. Mascall**.[23]

A father wanted to give registered land to his son, Mascall. The Father sent the necessary form to the Inland Revenue for the payment of Stamp Duty and gave the Land Certificate to his son. Legal title to registered land only passes when the Land Registry registers the transfer. It is usually the responsibility of the transferee to register the transfer at the Land Registry. Before the son could register the transfer he quarrelled with his father. The father attempted to prevent the gift by seeking a declaration that the transfer had not taken place and so the gift was not perfected.

Judgment: the Court of Appeal applied *Re Rose* and held that as the father had done all within his power to effect the transfer the gift was perfected. The father held the land on trust for his son until his son registered the transfer in legal title.

The relaxation of the rule for effective transfer of property in *Milroy v Lord*, that a transferor must have done everything necessary according to the nature of the property to transfer it to the transferee, to the rule in *Re Rose*, that a transferor must have done everything within his power to transfer the property to the transferee, was subjected to a strange development by the Court of Appeal in **Pennington v. Waine**.[24]

Ada Crampton wanted to make her nephew, Harold Crampton, a director of a private company in which she held 1,500 shares. Directors were required to have a share ownership, thus Ada wanted to give Harold 400 of her shares to enable him to become a director. She also intended to

---

23   (1984) 50 P&CR 119.
24   [2002] EWCA Civ 227; [2002] 1 WLR 2075.

leave Harold more shares in her will so that he could take control of the company. Ada signed the share transfer form and sent it to Pennington, her accountant. Pennington arranged for Harold to be appointed director of the company, but Ada died before Pennington completed the share transfer to Harold. Ada's will left Harold more shares which would, together with the 400 she had tried to give to him, have given Harold a 51% controlling interest in the company. Ada's residuary beneficiaries claimed that the transfer was invalid and that the shares should fall into residue for them. Ada had not done all that was necessary to perfect the gift and so failed the rule in *Milroy v Lord*. She had also not done all within her power, as Pennington was her agent and seen as an extension of her, thus as he had not done all within his power to transfer the shares this failed the rule in *Re Rose*.

Judgment: the Court of Appeal held that there had been a valid transfer of the shares.

The reasoning behind the decision seems a little unclear. Clarke L.J. seemed to view this as an extension of the *Re Rose* principle, although unlike *Re Rose* and *Mascall v Mascall* there had not been delivery of the subject matter or means of registering title to the subject matter to the transferee. Arden L.J. seemed to approve the perfecting to the gift on the basis of unconscionability, because, if Ada had been alive, it would have been "unconscionable" for her to go back on her promise. This seems to be a variety of estoppel with the signing of the share transfer form and delivery of this to her agent, together with Harold's knowledge that he was to receive the shares as consideration for him taking over the running of the company,[25] being viewed as putting Ada in a position where she could not have instructed Pennington to stop the transfer to Harold. This seems to ignore previous authorities such as *Re Fry*, where Fry had delivered signed share transfer forms and share certificates to the transferee but not obtained Treasury consent for the transfer. Romer J. noted that Fry could have changed his mind and could not have been compelled to transfer the property. There also seems to be some consideration that either Ada or Pennington had become trustees of the shares when the gift was not perfected.

There has been much criticism of the decision in *Pennington*, as there is always a concern over the use of 'unconscionability' as the basis for judicial decisions, especially in an area which has traditionally emphasised the need for certainty.[26] The decision seems to have been based on a misunderstanding of the decision by the Privy Council in *T. Choithram*

---

25   Sarah Worthington , *Equity* (2nd edition, 2006, Clarendon Law Series: Oxford).
26   J. Garton, 'The Role of the Trust Mechanism in the Rule in Re. Rose' (2003) 67 Conv 364.

International SA v. Paragani,[27] where a settlor was a trustee of a charitable trust and on his death bed made a declaration that all his property now belonged to the trust. The majority of the property was shares and there had been no execution of share transfer forms etc. The Privy Council held that, if the settlor had recovered, it would have been unconscionable for him to have gone back on his declaration. The difference in circumstances is important, in *Choitram* the settlor was a trustee and gave his property to the trust, he already had legal title and was a trustee, he was in a dual position in relation to the property, so a trustee had legal title to the property. In *Pennington*, Ada was transferring shares to Harold. The decision seems to undermine the equitable principles that *Equity will not assist volunteer,* and *Equity will not perfect an imperfect gift.*

In *Zeital v Kaye*,[28] the Court of Appeal distinguished *Pennington v Waine* and followed *Re Rose*, holding the signing of a share transfer certificate without the addition of the donees name was not a transfer of the share because the donor had not done all within his power to effect the transfer.

It is submitted that the *Pennington* principle in which equity will perfect an imperfect gift if it would be unconscionable for the donor to go back on his promise is unlikely to be followed. The estoppel argument may be followed but was not the clear reasoning for the decision in Pennington and needs to be considered with other forms of estoppel. Thus the equitable principle guiding effective transfer of property for the constitution of a trust or the perfection of a gift is still that from **Milroy v Lord,** the settlor/donor must do all that is necessary to effect the transfer, but may exceptionally be relaxed to the rule in **Re Rose,** that he must do all within his power if he then has to rely on a third party to perfect the gift or constitute the trust.

9.5 Exceptions to the Rules of Transfer

As with any rule there are exceptions to the rules that equity will not perfect an imperfect gift and equity will not assist a volunteer.29 The exceptions to the rules of constitution and perfection involve any circumstance where, although the transferor has not done everything necessary, or within his power, to transfer the property to the transferee the property coincidentally ends up in the hands of the donee or trustee,

---

27   [2001] 1 WLR 1.
28   [2010] W.T.L.R. 913.
29   If the donees of a purported gift or the beneficiaries of a purported trust have acted to their detriment on a promise or representation made by the donor or settlor, they may be able to force him to perfect the gift or constitute the trust under the doctrine of proprietary estoppel. This topic is covered in more detail in the chapter on equity and the family home.

this includes the rule in Strong v Bird, and the principle of donationes mortis causa (DMC), 'gifts made in contemplation of death'.[30]

9.5.1 Coincidental or fortuitous receipt of trust property

There is a principle that equity will uphold a gift or trust if the property was intended to be transferred to the donee or trustee and legal title to the property has coincidentally ended up in the hands of the donee or trustee even though the donor or settlor has not done everything within his power to effect the transfer.

Re Ralli's WT[31]

Ambrose Ralli left his residuary estate to his wife for life, then to his two daughters, Helen and Irene absolutely. Helen, by a marriage settlement, covenanted to settle all other present and after acquired property on Irene's children. Irene's husband was trustee under Helen's marriage settlement and was also a trustee under Helen's father's will. Helen died in 1956 but the property did not fall into her estate until after her mother died in 1961. Irene's husband brought an action to determine whether he held the property on the trusts of Helen's marriage settlement of 1924 or under the terms of her father's will of 1892.

Judgment: the court held that the settlement trust was constituted and that Irene's husband held the property on trust for his children. It was purely coincidental that he was trustee of both trusts, but that meant he held legal title as trustee for the father's will trust until that trust determined, at which point he held legal title for Helen's trust, even though she had not expressly transferred the property to him. As Buckley J noted: 'in my judgment the circumstance that the plaintiff holds the fund because he was appointed a trustee of the will is irrelevant. He is at law the owner of the fund, and the means by which he became so have no effect upon the quality of his legal ownership.'

The rationale behind this case seems to be that Helen had declared herself trustee of her interest under the Will Trust, or it would have been unconscionable for Helen to require the trustee to transfer the remainder interest to her. If either were the case her personal representative could be in no better position than her. Thus it did not matter how the trustee acquired legal title to the property, as soon as he did the trust was constituted.

---

30 It has been claimed that only *Strong v Bird* is a true exception to the rules on constitution or perfection as *donationes mortis causa* may be explained by the exigencies of the situation, and the doctrine of *Re Rose* relies on actions outside the donor's control: Joseph Jaconelli, 'Problems in the rule in Strong v Bird' (2006) (Sep-Oct) *Conveyancer and Property Lawyer* 432, 433.

31 [1964] Ch 288 Ch D.

This principle of coincidental receipt was used in the previously mentioned ***T Choithram International SA v Pagarani***.[32] Here the settlor executed a deed of trust to set up a charitable organization of which he was one of the trustees. He was ill for some time and made repeated declarations that after providing for his family all his wealth would go the charity. He instructed his accountants to 'transfer all my wealth with the companies to the Trust'. However, by the time of his death he had not executed any share transfers. On his deathbed he orally declared that all of his wealth now belonged to the charity. On the face of it he had tried to make a gift to the charity but had carried out none of the formalities required to effect the transfer. If *Milroy v Lord* and *Re Rose* were applied it would seem that there was no gift and that the failed gift could not be interpreted as a trust. The Privy Council held the settlor's oral declaration was properly to be construed as a declaration of trust. He was one of the trustees and so the constitution problem was overcome; he had declared himself trustee of the shares. It only remained for him to transfer the shares from his sole name and into the names of his co-trustees but this was a tidying-up exercise in the context of a trust that had already been established. It did not matter that only one of the trustees had legal title the trust was constituted. If he had lived he would have had to transfer title to his fellow trustees. It would have been unconscionable for him to go back on his declaration. The Council stressed that: 'Although equity would not aid a volunteer, it would not strive officiously to defeat a gift'.[33]

9.5.2 The rule in *Strong v Bird*

In this instance the rule is linked to the coincidental receipt principle and relies on a donor appointing the purported donee as executor of his will or failing to prevent the purported donee from being appointed administrator of his estate. The modern development of the rule states that when an imperfect gift is made during the donor's lifetime, and the purported donee is appointed executor by will or becomes an administrator under the rules of intestacy the vesting of the property in the donee as executor or administrator perfects the gift.

Strong v. Bird[34]
Bird borrowed £1,100 from his stepmother, Mrs Bird, who lived in his house as a paying lodger. It was agreed that the debt should be paid off by

---

32   [2001] 2 All ER 492.
33   As already noted the principles in this case were relied upon by Arden LJ in her judgment in *Pennington v Waine*, although there are significant differences in the circumstances of the cases.
34   (1874) LR 18 Eq 315.

a deduction of £100 from each quarter's payment of rent by Mrs Bird. Deductions were made for the first two quarters but thereafter Mrs Bird paid the full amount. This was at Christmas 1866, when Mrs Bird told her stepson that he did not owe her the money anymore, she was releasing him from the debt. Mrs Bird died four years later in December 1870. However, at the time the statement of gift was not enough to release the stepson from the debt at law as this needed consideration for the release in the form of a deed. Bird was appointed Mrs Bird's sole executor and proved the will. Mrs Bird's next of kin claimed against Mr Bird for £900, being the balance of the debt.

Judgment: the court held that Mrs Bird had continued to intend to release her stepson from his debt until she died, she had merely failed to comply with the formalities required for the release of the debt and the perfection of the gift. As an executor receives legal title to the deceased's property to allow him to administer the deceased's estate, the appointment of Bird as executor perfected the gift and released the debt.

The rule in **Strong v Bird** is that if a donor fails to comply with the formalities required for transfer of the gift property during his lifetime, and continues to intend the gift until his death, if the donee later becomes executor of the donor and has the gift property transferred to him in that capacity, then the original gift is perfected. This may be viewed as coincidental receipt or the appointment of the purported donee as executor may be seen as an intention to vest legal title in the purported donee and so perfect the gift.[35]

Although **Strong v. Bird** applied to a debt the rule has been extended to perfect imperfect gifts.[36] As administrators also receive legal title to the deceased's estate the principle has also been extended, somewhat more controversially, as these are not selected by the deceased, to personal representatives generally.

Re James[37]
Sarah was unpaid housekeeper for Mr James James for 19 years. However, he promised his house was Sarah's when he died. The house was never actually transferred to Sarah. Mr James James died. His son, John James inherited the property and promised to honour his father's promise. John James handed over the furniture and title deeds of the house and premises,

---

35   The wider rule has been said to rest upon "somewhat shaky foundations", as Frances Bird lived for 11 quarters after her declaration of gift and for 9 of these it could be interpreted that she gave her stepson £100 as a gift: Joseph Jaconelli, 'Problems in the rule in Strong v Bird' (2006) (Sep-Oct) *Conveyancer and Property Lawyer* 432, 433.

36   *Re Stewart* [1908] 2 Ch 251.

37   [1935] Ch 449.

forming part of his father's estate, to Sarah and allowed her to occupy the house rent free. However, the house still had not been conveyed to her when John James died intestate. Sarah applied for and was granted letters of administration. There had been no conveyance of the house to her, the gift was, applying the rule in *Milroy v Lord* and the more relaxed rule later developed in *Re Rose*, imperfect.

Judgment: the court held that there was a continuing intention on the part of the donor up to the time of his death to give the property to Sarah, and by her appointment as administratrix she had acquired the legal estate. The rule in *Strong v Bird* applied. The vesting of property in her as the administratrix perfected the imperfect gift. Thus, the legal estate acquired by an administrator is no less effectual than that of an executor appointed by will to perfect an imperfect gift made by the deceased owner of the estate to the administrator.

The importance of the continuing intention to give the property up to the time of death is shown in the unfortunate case of *Re Gonin*.[38]

The plaintiff, Lucy Gonin, and the two defendants were sisters. They were born out of wedlock, but their parents subsequently married. The first defendant left home in 1926, the second defendant in 1936, but the plaintiff, Lucy, stayed at home until 1940, when she obtained an appointment with the Air Ministry. However the parents were getting on in years and needed someone to look after them. Accordingly in 1944 they asked Lucy to return home to look after them. It was Lucy's understanding that, in consideration of her going to live with them and looking after them for the rest of their lives, they would make a gift of the house in which they lived and its contents to her. Apart from some pocket money in the early years Lucy received no payment from the parents. The father died in 1957. The mother owned the freehold of the property comprising the house and adjoining land and wanted to leave the house to Lucy, but worried that, as Lucy had been born illegitimately, she could not leave property to her illegitimate children by will (a mistaken belief) and that, if she attempted to do so, the only effect would be that she would be held to have died intestate and her estate would go to other relatives. Accordingly, on 9 March 1962, unknown to Lucy, the mother signed a cheque in Lucy's favour for £33,000 which Lucy was to have on the mother's death. Over the years the mother made gifts of specific items of furniture to Lucy. In 1963 the mother sold part of the house for £7,000 and placed the proceeds of the sale in her bank account. Some time later, she sold three building plots which formed part of the property for £12,000. She offered that money to Lucy as a gift, but Lucy did not take up the offer. The mother died intestate in November 1968. Lucy then discovered the envelope with

---

38   [1979] Ch 16.

the cheque but was unable to cash the cheque because, being merely a mandate to pay and Lucy being a volunteer, its effect terminates upon death and she had no cause of action to recover from the estate. In September 1970 Lucy obtained letters of administration to the mother's estate and in September 1973 commenced two actions. She claimed the house under the rule in **Strong v Bird** putting forward the cheque as proof that her mother had intended her to have the house. She also claimed the furniture which had been given to her by her mother during her lifetime.

Judgment: the court held that she could not rely upon *Strong v, Bird* because in order to do so she would have to prove that her mother intended an immediate *inter vivos* gift of the house and a continuing intention to benefit Lucy until she died. The signing of the cheque indicated that there was no such intention as the cheque was a substitute for the house. Similarly her mother's dealing with the house and land had shown that she considered it to be still her own property and not Lucy's. However, Lucy's claim in respect of the furniture succeeded since there was sufficient evidence that it had been the mother's intention that there should be an immediate gift of the furniture.

The rule is based upon the maxim that *equity imputes an intention to fulfil an obligation*, as receipt of the property by the person promised release from a debt or promised a gift in their role as executor or administrator is seen to fulfil the promise made by the deceased.

The rule requires these factors:

- There must have been an intention on the part of the donor to make an immediate *inter vivos* gift or to release a debt;
- The intention must have continued until the death of the donor;
- The person so promised must become the executor or administrator and so receive legal title to the deceased's property; and,
- The rule will not apply if there is any evidence to the contrary (**Re Gonin**).

There has been some criticism of the extension of the rule to administrators, as this does not evidence an intention by the deceased to pass legal title to the purported transferee, but may be the result of tactical legal advice to the purported transferee. Of course it may be argued that the deceased should have executed a will and appointed another as executor if they did not intend the purported transferee to take the legal title and so perfect the gift.

9.5.3 *Donationes mortis causa*

A *donatio mortis causa* (DMC), plural *donationes mortis causa*, is a lifetime gift which is conditional upon, and takes effect upon, death. *Donationes mortis causa* do not have to comply either with the requirements for *inter vivos* or testamentary gifts. The principle is borrowed directly from Roman law.[39] The three requirements for a valid DMC were stated in *Cain v Moon*:[40]

i) the gift must be made in contemplation of death;
ii) the gift must be conditional on death; and
iii) the donor must have parted with dominion over the subject matter.

There used to be some confusion over whether the nature of the property was important for upholding *donationes mortis causa*, with particular concern regarding purported gifts of land in contemplation of death.[41] However, it now seems that the subject matter is unimportant and almost any property can be the subject of a valid *donatio mortis causa* as long as the indicia of title are sufficient to illustrate the intent of the deceased to part with dominion over the property. Thus even land may be the subject of a *donatio mortis causa*.

Sen v. Headley [42]

On his deathbed Mr. Hewett, aged 86, said to Mrs. Sen, 'The house is yours, Margaret. You have the keys. They are in your bag. The deeds are in the steel box.' Mrs. Sen went to the house and took the deeds out of the box. Mr. Hewett's family contested the gift. *Judgment*: the Court held that the house had been given to Mrs. S by way of a valid *donatio mortis causa*.

There is an exception with cheques and promissory notes because they are merely mandates to pay. If the payee of a cheque is a volunteer he cannot enforce payment of the donor's own cheque because he has no claim on the estate.[43] However, a donor may give a third party cheque by way of DMC if he endorses it.[44]

The requirements for a valid *donatio mortis causa* need to be considered separately:

The gift must be in contemplation of death

The donor must make the gift in contemplation of death. More is needed than a general reflection that we will all die one day. This will usually occur close to death during his last illness, or when someone is undertaking a hazardous journey or active military service.[45] It does not matter if death occurs some time after the contemplation of death or that it occurs as a

---

39 Montague Crackanthorpe, 'The Uses of Legal History' (1896) 19 *Annu. Rep. A.B.A.* 343, 355.
40 [1896] 2 QB 283: confirmed in *Re Craven's Estate* [1937] Ch 426.
41 Following Lord Eldon's decision in *Duffield v Elwes* (1827) 1 Bli (NS) 497.
42 [1991] Ch 425 (EWCA).
43 *Re Beaumont* [1902] 1 Ch 886; *Re Leaper* [1916] 1 Ch 579.
44 *Jones v. Lock* (1865) LR 1 Ch App 25; *Re Mead* (1880) 15 Ch D 651).
45 *Agnew v Belfast Banking Co* [1896] 2 IR 204.

result of a cause which was not in contemplation when the gift was made.[46] For example, if the donor made conditional gifts in contemplation of death from a terminal illness and then died in a road accident the DMC may still be valid.

The gift must be conditional on death

The gift will not take effect until death, and, it is revocable if the donor does not die. Thus the gift must be on terms that if the donor does not die the property will revert to him.[47] However, this is usually implied. A donor can revoke his gift anytime before he dies but not after death by his will.[48] Although it has been argued that it may be possible to prevent the gift being revoked using the doctrine of estoppel.[49]

The donor must part with dominion over the subject matter

If the subject matter of the property concerned is a chattel the donor should part with dominion by physical delivery of the chattel to the donee, unless the chattel is too large to hand over, or the subject matter is the contents of bank accounts, *choses in action*, or land. In these cases the donor should give the donee some indicia of title. For example: the bankbook to transfer a bank account;[50] the keys to give a car;[51] and the deeds to give land.[52] If the donor does not part with dominion over the property or indication of title to the property then there can be no valid *donatio mortis causa*.

An issue has arisen over whether the donor must part with complete control and whether parting with an item which controls another item designates parting with dominion. For example, when items are stored in a box and the donor gives the box to somebody; has he given the items inside? Questions have also arisen over the giving of keys to such a box. Generally it has been accepted that this gives the box and its contents to the donee, even if the contents are other boxes or keys to other boxes or indicia of title such as deeds to property, as 'it does not matter in how many boxes the subject matter of a gift may be contained or that each, except the last, contains a key which opens the next, so long as the scope of the gift is made clear'.[53]

---

46 *Wilkes v Allington* [1931] 2 Ch 104.
47 *Re Lillingston* [1952] 2 All ER 184.
48 *Jones v Selby* (1710) 2 Eq Cas Abr 573.
49 See Mark Pawlowski, 'Revocable gifts and estoppel' (2012) 18(1) (January) *Trusts & Trustees* 64-67.
50 *Birch v. Treasury Solicitor* [1951] Ch 298.
51 *Woodard v. Woodard* [1995] 3 All ER 980.
52 *Sen v. Headley*[1991] 1 Ch 425.
53 *Re Lillingston* [1952] 2 All ER 184 *per* Wynn-Parry LJ.

If there is more than one key to the box then the donor must usually part with all of the keys otherwise he has not surrendered dominion.[54] However, in **Woodard v. Woodard**,[55] it was thought that the donor had retained a set of car keys, but the car was still deemed to be a valid *donatio mortis causa*. Mr Woodard was terminally ill in hospital and gave the keys to his car to his son so that the son could bring his mother to visit him. Mr Woodward said many times that, as he had no need for the car any more, his son could keep it. When Mr Woodard died his wife took action to recover the car for the estate, but the court held that there had been an *inter vivos* gift. Mrs. Woodard appealed, and the son changed his claim to one by way of *donatio mortis causa*. The logbook of the car was never handed over and the issue of the spare set of car keys was also raised. The Court of Appeal held that the car was the subject matter of a valid *donatio mortis causa*.

Therefore, a DMC is a lifetime gift that is conditional upon, and only takes effect upon, death. It does not have to comply with any formality requirements and is not a normal lifetime gift as title only passes upon the donor's death. It is not a testamentary gift and does not take effect under the terms of a will and so, as it takes effect upon death, a donee of a *donatio mortis causa* takes in precedence to beneficiaries under a will.

Example
Stephen is involved in a car crash and is pulled from the wreckage by Freddie. Freddie calls an ambulance but Stephen is seriously injured and believes he is dying. He takes his Rolex watch from his wrist and gives it to Freddie saying, 'I want you to have my watch.' Stephen dies shortly after. Stephen's will provides for the watch to be given to his son, Mark. However, the gift is a gift made in contemplation of death, conditional upon death and Stephen has parted with dominion over the watch by giving it to Freddie. Therefore, it is a valid DMC and Freddie will take precedence over any testamentary disposition of the watch.

Donationes mortis causa are important because they operate as an exception to the usual rules on intervivos gifts; they are dependent on death; if the donor does not die they can reclaim them. Also they do not need to comply with the usual formality requirements such as the Law of Property Act 1925 and the Wills Act 1837, s.5, as they are a form of constructive trust (on some interpretations).

---

54   *Re Craven's Estate* [1937] Ch 423.
55   [1995] 3 All ER 980, EWCA.

9.6 Covenants to Settle

At times a person will make a promise to create a trust in the future, perhaps because they have not yet received the property they want to be the subject matter of the trust. Usually these promises are unenforceable but sometimes the purported-settlor will covenant to settle. This is a promise in the form of a deed and may be enforceable. For example, Freddie knows that his good friend, Stephen, intends to leave him some money in his will and Freddie would like to settle this property on trust for his children, Ben and Alex. Freddie may make a covenant with Lisa (his purported-trustee) that he will transfer the property to her on trust for his children when Freddie receives the legacy.

Covenants to settle are made because you cannot have a trust of future property.[56] You can have a trust of the future income from a bank account or the future dividend of shares because that subject matter will be certain; it is whatever the interest paid or the dividend declared. However, a yet to be given benefit is not certain as the donor may change his mind. For example, Freddie may never receive his legacy from Stephen for a number of reasons: Stephen could change his mind before death and revoke his will; Freddie could die before Stephen and the gift will lapse; Stephen's estate may not be large enough to satisfy the legacy; or he could spend the fund from which the legacy is to be paid. Therefore Freddie cannot declare a trust of the future property, but he can covenant to settle it. Similarly, if there is a valid trust deed, but the property is never given to the trustees, the deed of covenant may be construed as a covenant to settle.

The important question is whether the covenant to settle may be enforced by either the purported-trustees or by the purported-beneficiaries if the purported-settlor does not transfer the property to constitute the trust. In other words, what happens if Freddie receives his legacy from Stephen and does not transfer the property to Lisa? As there is a deed we have to consider whether the covenant may be enforced at common law or in equity.

9.6.1 Enforcing covenants to settle at common law

Here we have to consider what will happen depending on who tries to enforce the covenant.

Can the purported-trustees sue to enforce the contract? The purported-trustees do not usually provide consideration for the promise, but the common law does recognise the deed and therefore the trustees (*e.g.* Lisa) are able to sue at common law. However, the common law remedy is

---

56   *Re Ellenborough* [1903] 1 Ch 697. However, see the discussion and application in *Re Bowden* [1936] Ch 71.

damages, and, because the trustees have suffered no loss, any damages awarded would be nominal. As this is an action based upon contract then the six-year limitation period would apply.

Can the purported-beneficiaries sue to enforce the contract? As they are not parties to the contract then the doctrine of privity means that the beneficiaries cannot usually sue to enforce the contract. Of course, if the beneficiaries are parties to the contract then they can enforce it. For example in *Cannon v. Hartley*,[57] a father promised as part of a separation agreement to settle money on his daughter when he received it under the will of his parents. When he received the money he refused to settle it as agreed. The agreement was a covenant under seal. The court held that although the daughter was a volunteer, as she had provided no consideration and this was not a marriage settlement, she could not enforce the agreement as a beneficiary. However, she was a party to the covenant under seal and therefore she could sue for damages at common law.

Can the purported-trustees sue on behalf of the purported-beneficiaries? There is confusing authority for the answer to this question, as the focus seems to have been not on whether the purported-trustees *may* sue on behalf of the purported beneficiaries but on whether the purported-trustees may be *compelled* to sue on behalf of the purported-beneficiaries. Thus, in *Re Pryce*,[58] it was held that the trustees should not be compelled to take action on the covenant; in *Re Kay's Settlement*[59] the trustees were directed not to sue; and in *Re Cook's ST*,[60] Buckley J held that the trustees were not obliged to sue. This may suggest that if the purported-trustees are privy to the contract they may sue on behalf of the beneficiaries but they may not be compelled by the purported-beneficiaries. Of course the justification for this is that there is still no enforceable trust in equity and the fiduciary obligations may therefore have not arisen.

9.6.2 Enforcing covenants to settle in equity

The question of whether the covenant may be enforced in equity again focuses on which party is attempting to enforce the covenant.

Can the purported-trustees sue in equity? The purported-trustee is viewed as a volunteer in equity, as the deed is not recognised as consideration, and so has no standing to sue.

Can the purported-beneficiaries sue in equity? Although most purported-beneficiaries have not given consideration as usually understood at common law, equity recognises 'marriage consideration.'

---

57   [1949] Ch 213
58   [1917] 1 Ch 234.
59   [1939] Ch 329.
60   [1965] 902.

Therefore going through with the marriage will be regarded as the husband and wife giving consideration. Furthermore the children and grandchildren of the marriage, the marriage 'issue', are also regarded as having given consideration because of these ties of the blood. However, any party not tied by blood and the legitimate marriage, for example illegitimate children, children by a former marriage, and remoter relatives cannot sue.[61] Thus any marriage settlement covenant may be enforced in equity by the parties to the marriage and their issue if they were intended to benefit.[62]

Re Plumptre's Marriage Settlement[63]
The marriage settlement provided that a father would settle monies on his daughter for life and then in remainder to her next-of-kin. The settlement contained a standard 'after acquired' property clause. However, the next-of-kin were not given the 'after acquired' property and sued to enforce the covenant.
Judgment: although the next-of-kin were party to the covenant, their action was time barred at common law. They could not pursue an action in equity because they were volunteers, they had not given any consideration, and were not within the marriage consideration.

Pullan v. Koe[64]
A marriage settlement which settled property on trusts for life in favour of a husband and wife and then in remainder to their children contained a covenant whereby the wife promised to settle after acquired property on the children. When the husband died his estate retained bonds which were after acquired property for the purposes of the covenant. The trustees of the marriage settlement trust sought a declaration as to whether the executors of the husband's estate could be forced to transfer the bonds to them for the marriage settlement trust.
Judgment: as the trustees were party to the covenant they could have enforced the covenant at common law but this action was now time barred. However, although the deed of covenant was not recognised as consideration in equity, the wife and children of the marriage were within the marriage consideration and so could enforce the agreement as beneficiaries in equity.

Can there be a trust of a promise? As a trust can have virtually any property as its subject matter, there is no reason why a promise to benefit by way of covenant cannot be the subject matter of a trust, as it is an enforceable promise, a right to take action, a *chose in action*. An example of

---

61   *Re Plumptre's Marriage Settlement* [1910] 1 Ch 609.
62   *Pullan v. Koe* [1913] 1 Ch 9.
63   [1910] 1 Ch 609.
64   [1913] 1 Ch 9.

this is *Fletcher v. Fletcher*:[65] Fletcher covenanted by deed with trustees to settle property on them for the benefit of his illegitimate sons. The sons could not enforce the promise at common law as they were not parties to the covenant. The sons could not enforce the promise in equity as, even though there were ties of blood, they were not within any marriage consideration. However, Wigram V-C upheld the surviving son's claim on the grounds that the covenant, the promise, was held on a fully constituted trust. Thus the son was a beneficiary of a constituted trust and could enforce the trust in equity as any other beneficiary.

Therefore it is possible to have a trust of a promise, although these may be limited to trusts of a promise to pay money, as if the promise is made by covenant it gives rise to a right to take action and this chose in action is certain subject matter for a valid enforceable trust. However, the courts have been reluctant to extend this principle and have even been cautious in following *Fletcher v Fletcher* unless there is clear intention to create a trust of the promise. Thus Parcq LJ in *Re Schebsman* noted that:[66]

'Unless an intention to create a trust is clearly to be collected from the language used and the circumstances of the case, I think that the court ought not to be astute to discover indications of such intention.'

Thus it seems unlikely that *Fletcher v Fletcher* would be followed today and it must be remembered that even if it were used as authority it is restricted to promises to pay money and would be unlikely to be authority for enforcing other promises. This may not seem to be a particularly important issue as, in response to social changes, there has been a decline in the incidence of marriage settlements throughout the twentieth century. However, it seems that recent developments in advice for wealth management have included succession planning which may involve marriage settlements. These settlements may involve the new statutory private purpose trusts available in offshore jurisdictions such as the Cayman Islands. If there is a renewed interest in the marriage settlement then issues as to the enforceability of promises to provide property for the trust may regain importance.

9.7 Summary

There are three methods by which we may allow others to enjoy our property without receiving anything in return. We may give the property to them, we may transfer property to another to hold on trust for them and we may declare ourselves to be trustee of our own property for the benefit of the other. For a trust to be valid and enforceable it must be completely constituted or supported by valuable consideration. For a self-declaration

---

65   (1844) 4 Hare 67.
66   [1944] Ch 83 at 104.

of trust no property needs to be transferred as the trustee already has legal title. All that is required is a valid declaration of trust; if the trust is of land then it must comply with the formality requirements in statute. A trust with another as trustee is constituted when legal title passes to the trustee and once constituted the trust is enforceable and the settlor loses all rights to the trust property. For a gift to be perfected then legal title to the gift property must be transferred to the donee. Two maxims are relevant to the rules on constitution. These are *Equity will not assist a volunteer*, and *Equity will not perfect an imperfect gift*. To transfer property to trustees then legal title must be transferred, the general rule used to be that a settlor had to have done all that was necessary for the particular trust property to transfer legal title to the trustee (*Milroy v Lord*). This rule was mitigated somewhat in *Re Rose* when it was expressed as the settlor must have done all within his power to transfer the legal title of the property to the trustee. A failed gift will not be construed as a trust (**Richards v Delbridge**). There are three exceptions to the rule on constitution; these are the rule in **Strong v Bird**, the principle of coincidental receipt from **Railli's WT** and *donationes mortis causa*.

CHAPTER 10
IMPLIED, RESULTING AND CONSTRUCTIVE TRUSTS

10.1 What is an Implied Trust?

In the nineteenth century lawyers identified implied, resulting and constructive trusts as distinct categories of trust from express trusts.[1] The title of this chapter paraphrases s.53(2) of the Law of Property Act 1925, where the implied trust is referred to as a separate category of trust from the resulting and constructive trust. More recently Lord Reid referred to these trusts as separate categories: 'It is not disputed that a man can become a trustee without making a declaration of trust or evincing any intention to become a trustee. The facts may impose on him an implied, constructive or resulting trust.'[2]

Although these comments seem to classify the resulting and constructive trust as distinct from the implied trust it is usually accepted that resulting and constructive trust are implied trusts because the parties do not expressly create them. These trusts arise because, in certain circumstances, a court will declare the legal owner of property to hold it on trust for another or for themselves and others although there may have been no enforceable express declaration of trust. The court presumes the resulting trust from the circumstances, automatically returns the property to a legal owner who has not disposed of their beneficial interest, or infers the constructive trust from the circumstances as representing the intentions of the parties. The trustee may have no idea that they hold the property

---

1   Paul Mathews, 'The Words Which Are Not There: A Partial History of the Constructive Trust', in Charles Mitchell (ed), *Constructive and Resulting Trusts* (Hart Publishing, 2009), 13.

2   [1971] AC 886, per Lord Reid at 896. The implied trust was also referred to by Lord Browne Wilkinson in *Westdeutsche Landesbank v Islington LBC* [1996] AC 669. Thomas and Hudson suggest the term "implied trust" refers to trusts created unknowingly by a settlor as in *Paul v Constance* [1977] 1 WLR 527: G.W. Thomas and A.S. Hudson, *The Law of Trusts*, (2004, Oxford: Oxford University Press), para. 1.20. However, as the traditional interpretation of *Paul v Constance* is that Mr. Constance intended to hold the property for the benefit of Miss Paul and himself this is usually interpreted as being an intention to create an express trust.

on trust and the trust may arise without any of the requirements or formalities necessary for an express trust, indeed the very absence of formalities may be the reason the court recognises a trust. Thus resulting and constructive trusts are declared by the court and may not have been created expressly by the parties. However, resulting and constructive trusts may also be used to enforce an express trust which has not been created in accordance with the usual requirements for a valid express trust. For example the trust may not have complied with the statutory formalities required for a trust of land,[3] in which case the court may infer a constructive trust, as in *Bannister v Bannister*,[4] or the presumption of a resulting trust arises, as in *Hodgson v Marks*.[5] An automatic resulting trust may also arise when there has been an intention to create an express trust and there is no certainty as to the beneficiaries or their interests, as in *Boyce v Boyce*,[6] thus the property automatically results back to the settlor.

Trusts may also arise without the express intent of any of the parties to the trust because of statutory provisions, for example the rules of intestacy can provide for assets to be held in a 'statutory trust' (a 'trust for sale') if assets exceed a fixed sum.[7] Thus some academics prefer to refer to implied trusts as trusts arising by operation of law, to distinguish them from expressly created trusts.[8] For clarity the term implied trust will be used to refer to any trust created by statute, and to resulting and constructive trusts. Thus, it may be considered that an implied trust is quite simply, a trust which is enforced but is not an enforceable express trust; it has not been expressly created or it has been expressly created but not in accordance with the requirements for a valid enforceable trust.[9]

Definition
An implied trust is:

1 any trust which is enforced but has not been expressly created by a settlor; or
2 any trust which is enforced that has been expressly created but does not comply with the requirements for a valid express trust.

---

3 s.53(1)(b) LPA 1925, for; WN 261,
4 [1948] 2 All ER 133.
5 [1971] Ch 892.
6 (1894) 16 Sim 476.
7 Administration of Estates Act 1925.
8 E.g. J.E. Penner, *The Law of Trusts*, Oxford, Oxford University Press, 2008, at 87.
9 Maitland considered the difficulties with these terms and possible meanings settling on express trusts being distinct from 'trusts that are not Express'. FW Maitland, *Equity: A Course of Lectures*, J Brunyate (ed), rev edn (Cambridge, Cambridge University press, 1936) 74.

This definition may be disputed, but arguably it serves to cover as a general definition dealing with most of the problems students encounter attempting, to compromise between trusts arising under these different circumstances and given many different labels. It is also supported by the words of Lord Nottingham, the father of equity and modern trusts: 'All trusts are either, first, express trusts, which are raised and created by act of the parties, or implied trusts, which are raised or created by act or construction of law'.[10]

The courts will sometimes claim that the resulting trust is recognised because the court presumes that the parties intended a trust to arise from their conduct, a "presumed resulting trust", or circumstances have automatically given rise to the trust, an "automatic resulting trust". The constructive trust is recognised by the court because the conscience of the legal owner is so affected that it would be unconscionable for them to deny that they hold the property on trust. Sometimes similar circumstances have been recognised as giving rise to a resulting trust in one case and a constructive trust in another.[11] There are many overlaps between the circumstances giving rise to these 'bedfellows'.[12] Indeed, in Hong Kong, one judge when considering family cases giving rise to possible resulting or constructive trusts commented: "…it hardly matters what label one uses. What the court is concerned with is a trust implied by law…"[13]

10.2 The Remedial Resulting or Constructive Trust

There has been some debate over the 'remedial' nature of constructive trusts, and to a lesser extent resulting trusts. It might be considered that all resulting and constructive trusts are remedial as they are not expressly created by the parties, but are applied by the courts as a remedy at the instigation of the claimant. Usually a claim is brought against the legal owner of property for the court to declare that the legal owner holds legal title subject to the claimant's beneficial interest. If the court recognises an implied trust it is interfering with the defendant's property rights and remedying a wrong done to the claimant. This may seem to be a remedy

---

10   Cook v Fountain (1676) 3 Swans 585, 591-592. per Lord Nottingham
11   For example the previously mentioned *Hodgson v Marks* and *Bannister v Bannister* can both be interpreted as resulting trusts or constructive trusts, but *Hodgson* was declared to give rise to a resulting trust and *Bannister* to a constructive trust.
12   Paul Matthews, 'The Words Which Are Not There: A Partial History of the Constructive Trust', in Charles Mitchell (ed), *Constructive and Resulting Trusts* (Hart Publishing, 2009), 4.
13   *Lui Kam Lau v Leung Ming Fai* [1994] 3 HKC 477 per Tong DJ

available to the court to effect justice. However, the traditional English law viewpoint is that these trusts are institutional and not remedial. They are institutional because they arise only in certain accepted circumstances. The claim that these trusts are remedial has been supported by the overlapping circumstances and inconsistent categorisation of these trusts. However, English judges have, for the most part, consistently claimed that they do not create resulting or constructive trusts; they merely infer them from accepted circumstances. This is to reinforce the idea that equity is not arbitrary and there is certainty in the law. The concern over the use of implied trusts may be traced back to Lord Nottingham:

'.... express trusts are declared either by word or writing; and these declarations appear either by direct and manifest proof, or violent and necessary presumption. These last are commonly called presumptive trusts; and that is, when the Court, upon consideration of all circumstances presumes there was a declaration, either by word or writing, though the plain and direct proof thereof be not extant... so the trust, if there be any, must either be implied by the law, or presumed by the Court. There is one good, general, and infallible rule that goes to both these kinds of trusts; it is such a general rule as never deceives; a general rule to which there is no exception, and that is this; the law never implies, the Court never presumes a trust, but in case of absolute necessity. The reason of this rule is sacred; for if the Chancery do once take liberty to construe a trust by implication of law, or to presume a trust, unnecessarily, a way is opened to the *Lord Chancellor* to construe or presume any man in *England* out of his estate; and so at last every case in court will become *casus pro amico.'*[14]

Thus the importance of not interfering with property rights has prevented the arbitrary use of implied trusts. However, there have been occasions when equity has recognised an implied trust and the judge concerned struggled to justify his decision.

Wassell v Leggatt[15]

The wife was given a legacy during her marriage that her husband 'forcibly deprived her of'. The appropriation occurred before the Married Women's Property Act 1882. The wife asked her husband to return the legacy many times but only took action to recover after his death. The legacy was held by the husband's estate. In deciding whether the wife was entitled to the legacy Romer J. considered how the husband held the property. The husband was not an intermeddler in a trust because the money was the wife's absolutely, there was no separation of title and therefore no trust in being, at the time he took the legacy from her. The

---

14   Cook v Fountain (1676) 3 Swans 585, 591-592. per Lord Nottingham
15   [1896] 1 Ch 554

husband believed he was entitled to the legacy so there was no question he regarded himself as a trustee, this made it difficult to consider him a constructive trustee. It was unlikely that a resulting trust had arisen. However, Romer J. held the husband held the legacy on trust for the wife:

'The plaintiff took the legacy before the coming into operation of the Married Women's Property Act, 1882, and the husband, when he got hold of the money, became a trustee of it for his wife. That he became a trustee is clear upon consideration of what her remedies were. She was entitled to recover the money: but how could she then do so? She had no right to the money at common law. In equity he could be sued, but that must have been because he was a trustee for her, and she was beneficially entitled; for I do not know how her right in equity could have been described except as one arising from the position of trustee on his part and *cestui que trust* on hers.'[16]

Although Romer J. referred to the husband's conscience being affected this did not fall within any accepted category of constructive trust. Thus Romer J. enforced a trust because there was no other way of protecting the wife's property right even though the right was one not previously recognised by equity.

More recently the debate regarding the remedial implied trust centred on Lord Denning's campaign to adopt a "new model constructive trust". This was an attempt by Lord Denning to use the constructive trust as a panacea for wrongs that arose from circumstances that equity would not traditionally remedy. Lord Denning's campaign followed on the creation of the common intention constructive trust, which was adopted by English law to deal with situations where a cohabitating couple in a domestic relationship had ended the relationship and there was a dispute over the domestic property which could not be settled by traditional land or trust law.[17] Lord Denning proposed the new model constructive trust in *Hussey v Palmer*:[18]

'It is a trust imposed by law whenever justice and good conscience require it. It is a liberal process, founded on large principles of equity, to be applied in cases where the defendant cannot conscientiously keep the property for himself alone, but ought to allow another to have the property or a share in it. The trust may arise at the outset when the property is acquired, or later on, as the circumstances may require. It is an equitable remedy by which the court can enable an aggrieved party to obtain restitution.'[19]

---

16   [1896] 1 Ch 554, at p.558.
17   *Gissing v Gissing* [1971] AC 886 (HL). The common intention constructive trust will be considered in more detail in chapter 11, Equity and the Family Home.
18   [1972] 3 All ER 744.

However, Lord Denning's ideas were firmly rejected by other members of the judiciary. For example Dillon L.J. commented that: 'The court does not as yet sit, as under a palm tree, to exercise a general discretion to do what the man in the street, on a general overview of the case, might regard as fair.'[20] Thus the use of the constructive trust has since been restricted to strict institutional principles.

When we consider the restrictive interpretation of the English common intention constructive trust in the next chapter it may be considered that this was a reaction to Lord Denning's attempt to use the constructive trust whenever justice required. However, some jurisdictions have accepted the idea of the remedial constructive or resulting trust.[21] In England recent judicial comment has favoured a less restrictive use of the constructive trust with 'unconscionability' a criterion for imposing a constructive trust.[22] As Lord Browne-Wilkinson stated in **Westdeutsche Landesbank Girozentrale v Islington London Borough Council**:[23]

'Equity operates on the conscience of the owner of the legal interest ... [and in the case of a constructive trust] ... the conscience of the legal owner requires him to carry out the purposes ... which the law imposes on him by reason of his unconscionable conduct.'

Whether resulting and constructive trusts are remedial in nature or not, their great value as a remedy lies in the fact that they may arise without any of the requirements of an express trust. Of particular importance is their express exemption from the formalities required for the creation of a trust of land or the disposition of an equitable interest.

Note
Section 53(2) of the Law of Property Act 1925 expressly excludes implied, resulting and constructive trusts from the formality requirements for the enforcement of trusts of land and the disposition of an equitable interest proscribed in the preceding ss.53(1)(b) & 53(1)(c).[24]

---

19 *Hussey v. Palmer* [1972]] 3 All ER 744.
20 *Springette v Defoe* [1992] FLR 388 at 393.
21 Australia bases the common intention constructive trust upon the unconscionability of the legal owner's assertion of full ownership as against the other party's interest: *Muschinski v Dodds* (1985) 160 C.L.R. 583. In Canada the focus has been to prevent the unjust enrichment of the legal owner at the expense of the other party: *Pettkus v Becker* (1980) 117 D.L.R. (3d) 257. In New Zealand the courts have tried to give effect to 'the reasonable expectations' of the parties to share the property: *Gillies v Keogh* [1989] 2 N.Z.L.R. 327.
22 See *Stack v Dowden* [2007] UKHL 17, and *Jones v Kernott* [2011] UKSC 53, discussed in chapter 13 Equity and the Family Home
23 [1996] AC 669.
24 LPA 1925, section 53(1)(b): 'a declaration of trust respecting land or any interest therein must be manifested and proved by some writing signed by

10.3 Resulting Trusts

The word 'resulting' derives from the Latin *resultare* meaning to spring or leap back.[25] As we have seen, if the owner of property gratuitously disposes of it without clear indication that a gift or other purpose was intended, or if the owner of property fails to completely dispose of their interest in that property, then equity decrees that he still retains the beneficial interest in the property. Ownership springs back.

In *Vandervell (No 2)*,[26] Megarry J. categorized resulting trusts as either presumed or automatic. Lord Browne Wilkinson specified in *Westdeutsche Landesbank Girozentrale v Islington London Borough Council*,[27] that resulting trusts arose in two situations: first, with the contribution to purchase price of property (a presumption only); second, where the beneficial owner of property has failed to dispose of the property. However, with the greatest respect to his Lordship, it seems that, apart from ignoring gratuitous transfers of property, it seems that this leaves us with the two situations which are reflected in Megarry J.'s categorisations of presumed and automatic resulting trusts and so it is still useful to use these terms.

The theoretical basis behind resulting trusts has also attracted much academic and judicial debate. Lord Browne Wilkinson stated in *Westdeutsche Landesbank Girozentrale v Islington LBC*:[28]

'Both types of resulting trust are traditionally regarded as examples of trusts giving effect to the common intention of the parties. A resulting trust is not imposed by law against the intention of the trustee (as is a constructive trust) but gives effect to his presumed intention.'

However, it is not just the presumed intention of the parties that is considered as the absence of intention has also been focused upon. In *Air Jamaica v Charlton*,[29] Lord Millett commented that:

'[A] resulting trust arises by operation of law ... But it arises whether or not the transferor intended to retain a beneficial interest – he almost always does not – since it responds to the absence of any intention on his part to pass a beneficial interest to the recipient. It may arise even when the transferor positively wished to part with the beneficial interest.'

---

some person who is able to declare such a trust or by his will.' Section 53(1)(c): 'a disposition of an equitable interest or trust subsisting at the time of the disposition, must be in writing signed by the person disposing of the same, or by his agent thereto lawfully authorised in writing or by will.'

25 John Mee, ' "Automatic" Resulting Trusts: Retention, Restitution, or Reposing Trust?', in Charles Mitchell (ed), *Constructive and Resulting Trusts* (Hart Publishing, 2009), 230.

26 [1974] Ch 269, 294; [1974] 1 All ER 47, 64.

27 See *Westdeutsche Landesbank v Islington LBC* [1996] AC 669 at 708.

28 [1996] AC 669.

29 [1999] 1 WLR 1399 PC.

This point was developed in *Twinsectra Ltd v Yardley*,[30] where the nature of the resulting trust was considered:

'Express trusts are fundamentally dependent upon the intention of the parties whereas the role of intention in resulting trusts is a negative one, the essential question being whether or not the provider intended to benefit the recipient and not whether he or she intended to create a trust. The latter question is relevant to whether the provider succeeded in creating an express trust, but its relevance to the resulting trust is only an indication of lack of intention to benefit the recipient.'

However, as noted above, Megarry J's categorisation of presumed and automatic resulting trusts is still useful in considering the circumstances giving rise to the resulting trust.

10.4 Presumed Resulting Trusts

The presumption of resulting trust is an old presumption and together with its counterpart, the presumption of advancement, has been claimed to have been "… part of the law of trusts for perhaps as long as we have had a law of trusts." [31] A presumption is a conclusion or inference as to a fact in issue drawn from other facts accepted as true. Thus in some circumstances the court will presume from the actions of the parties that a resulting trust was intended. These circumstances are the *intervivos* voluntary conveyance of property to another and the purchase of property in the name of another.[32]

Note
A disposition in a will, for example "£100,000 to Michael", is presumed to be a gift unless there is clear evidence that another purpose was intended.[33]

Thus merely by establishing that a party has transferred property *intervivos* for no consideration or has contributed to the purchase price of property the presumption of resulting trust arises. However, it is important to remember that the presumption of resulting trust is merely a presumption. It is an aid to the court when there is little or no evidence of the intent behind a transfer or contribution or the evidence is unreliable and tainted with self-interest. The presumption will not arise if there is evidence that property was transferred or a contribution made as a loan or gift or for some other reason. Furthermore the presumption may be rebutted by evidence of the intention behind the transfer or contribution to purchase price.

---

30   [2002] All ER 377.
31   Robert Chambers, 'Is There a presumption of Resulting Trust?', in Charles Mitchell (ed), *Constructive and Resulting Trusts* (Hart Publishing, 2009), 267.
32   FW Maitland, *Equity: A Course of Lectures*, J Brunyate (ed), rev edn (Cambridge, Cambridge University press, 1936) 78.
33   FW Maitland, *Equity: A Course of Lectures*, J Brunyate (ed), rev edn (Cambridge, Cambridge University press, 1936) 77.

A voluntary conveyance is the transfer of property from the legal owner to another without any consideration.

When one party transfers property into the name of another for no consideration it is presumed that the transferee holds the property on resulting trust for the donor unless there is clear evidence of a different intent. This presumption has already been considered in the case of *Hodgson v. Marks*,[34] and is further exemplified in the case of *Re Vinogradoff*.[35]

Hodgson v. Marks.[36]

Mrs. Hodgson had transferred her house to her lodger for no consideration. She always intended it should be returned to her or that she should retain an interest. When the lodger subsequently sold the house to Mr Marks the court had to decide if there was an enforceable trust. It was clear this was not a gift but a trust; however, it could not be enforced as an express trust because the formality requirements for the creation of a trust of land, that it be evidenced in writing,[37] had not been complied with. Although the court could not enforce an express trust, declining to follow *Rochefoucauld v Boustead*,[38] the court accepted the evidence of Mrs Hodgson's transfer of the property for no consideration as giving rise to the presumption of a resulting trust. This could have been rebutted by evidence that a gift was intended, but of course this evidence could not be provided as no gift was intended. As this was a resulting trust it did not have to comply with the requirement in s.53(1)(b) of the Law of Property Act 1925 because implied trusts, resulting and constructive trusts are expressly excluded from this requirement by s.53(2) LPA.[39] The court could enforce the resulting trust.

Re Vinogradoff [40]

Mrs. Vinogradoff had transferred £800 of War Loan into the names of herself and her granddaughter but continued to receive the dividends from the loan herself until her death. After Mrs. Vinogradoff died it was held that the granddaughter, even though a child, held her half of the Loan on resulting trust for Mrs. Vinogradoff's estate. There was no evidence to rebut the presumption of resulting trust.

34   [1971] Ch 892.
35   [1935] WN 68
36   [1971] Ch 892.
37   S.53(1)(b) LPA 1925.
38   [1897] 1 Ch 196.
39   However, the usefulness of the presumption of resulting trust has declined in the UK in recent years. In *Lohia v Lohia* [2001] WTLR 101 it was concluded that s.60(3) of the Law of Property Act 1925 removes the presumption of resulting trust for voluntary conveyances of property. See note subsequently.
40   [1935] WN 68

Note

The presumption of resulting trust is said today to no longer arise on the gratuitous transfer of land into the name of another.

In *Lohia v Lohia*,[41] it was suggested that s.60(3) of the Law of Property Act 1925 might remove the presumption of resulting trust for voluntary conveyances of land. Section 60(3) Law of Property Act 1925 provides: 'In a voluntary conveyance a resulting trust for the grantor shall not be implied merely by reason that the property is not expressed to be conveyed for the use or benefit of the grantee.' However, even if the presumption is removed for real property it would still apply for the voluntary transfer of personal property, and is apparently still available to the court in the circumstances of *Hodgson v Marks*[42] where there was express intention to create a trust of land but the formalities were not complied with and not to enforce the trust would be to aid a fraud.[43]

The presumption of resulting trust also arises if a party provides the money for a purchase or makes a contribution to the purchase of property which is held in the name of another. The presumption is that the property is held by the transferee on resulting trust for the person who provided the money or for the transferee and the person who provided the money.[44] This presumption was explained in *Dyer v Dyer*:[45]

'the trust of a legal estate ...; whether taken in the names of the purchasers and others jointly or in the names of others without that of the purchasers; whether in one name or several ... results to the one who advances the purchase money.'

Note

The proportion of interest in the property held on resulting trust is usually directly proportionate to the contribution.[46]

---

41   [2001] WTLR 101.
42   [1971] Ch 892.
43   Although today it might be more appropriate to remedy the wrong by applying a constructive trust as in *Bannister v Bannister* [1948] 2 All ER 133.
44   *Williams & Glyn's Bank v. Boland* [1981] AC 487; *Springette v. Defoe* (1992) 24 HLR 552.
45   (1788) 2 Cox Eq Cas 92, per Eyre CB
46   However, the proportionate interest is no longer applicable for property conveyed into joint names in a familial situation: see *Stack v Dowden* [2007] 2 AC 432 and chapter 13 Equity and the Family Home. This has led to claims that the usefulness of the presumption of resulting trust has waned in the familial context a claim further supported by the increased use of the doctrine of the common intention constructive trust.

Example

Alex buys a flat in London. Rachel has provided the entire purchase price for the flat but the flat is bought in Alex's sole name. The presumption is that Alex holds the flat on resulting trust for Rachel. Alternatively, if Alex has contributed 25% of the purchase price and Rachel 75% then Alex will be presumed to hold the flat on trust for himself and Rachel in proportion to their contributions, i.e. 25% for Alex, 75% for Rachel.

This presumption has much to do with commercial reality and the expectation that a person will always want their money back unless they intended the contribution to be a gift. As the Court of Chancery developed this presumption it was apparent that such a presumption was not always appropriate for familial situations. Thus the presumption of advancement was developed to counter the presumption of resulting trust. The presumption of advancement is a presumption that a gratuitous transferor or contribution will be presumed to be a gift to the transferee if they are within certain recognised family relationships of the transferor.

Note

The presumption of resulting trust is rebuttable.

10.4.1 Rebutting the presumption of resulting trust

The presumption of resulting trust is merely an aid for the court to decide who is the owner of property when there is no clear evidence as to the intention behind a transfer or contribution to the purchase of property. Thus it is a rebuttable presumption and may be rebutted by evidence that the transfer/contribution was:

- a loan,
- a gift, or
- made to a family member subject to the contrary presumption of advancement.

It is important to distinguish between a loan and a contribution giving rise to a resulting trust as a loan will be repayable based on the original loan and interest, whereas a trust is a proprietary interest. The purchased property may have increased in value to such an extent that its value is far more than the loan and interest, in which case the lender may try to argue they have an interest by way of resulting trust. The converse may also be true.

Vajpeyi v Yusaf[47]

The female claimant had provided the male defendant with £10,000 in 1980 to purchase a house that the defendant rented out as an investment

---

47 [2003] EWHC 2339 (Ch), 147 Sol Jo LB 1120.

property. The claimant subsequently sold the defendant a second house in 1994. The defendant married another woman, and, after several years had elapsed, the claimant brought proceedings arguing that the defendant held the first house on trust for her and himself because the £10,000 had been an investment in that property. The defendant argued that the £10,000 had been a loan and thus there could be no resulting trust concerning the first house. The defendant further submitted that both loans had been repaid. The court held that in all the circumstances, the money advanced had been a loan and not an investment in the house; the presumption of resulting trust was not strong and easily rebutted by the evidence of the circumstances surrounding the contribution.

The presumption can also be rebutted by evidence that the money advanced was a gift.

Fowkes v Pascoe[48]

The testatrix had bought stock using her own money, which she placed in the names of herself and the son of her daughter-in-law. There was evidence the first purchase had been a gift and the court concluded that the subsequent purchases had also been gifts. The presumption of resulting trust was rebutted. This case can be contrasted with the case of *Re Vinogradoff* above.

Aroso v Coutts and Co[49]

The deceased transferred money into the joint names of himself and his nephew. He also gave the bank a mandate which instructed the bank to hold the account on trust for them both with the survivor to take all. The court held that the terms of the mandate rebutted the presumption of a resulting trust.

The presumption of resulting trust will not arise if the presumption of advancement applies to the transfer or contribution.

10.4.2 The presumption of advancement

The presumption of advancement is an inference based upon society's expectations as to the intention behind a transfer of property between those in a close family relationship. As such, the presumption of advancement has been criticised around the common law world as anachronistic and discriminatory. In some jurisdictions it has been restricted. In the United Kingdom it will be abolished when the Equality Act 2010, s.199 is implemented. Section 199 provides:

---

48 (1875) 10 Ch App 343.
49 [2001] 1 All ER (Comm) 241.

(1) The presumption of advancement (by which, for example, a husband is presumed to be making a gift to his wife if he transfers property to her, or purchases property in her name) is abolished.
(2) The abolition by subsection (1) of the presumption of advancement does not have effect in relation to—
  (a) anything done before the commencement of this section, or
  (b) anything done pursuant to any obligation incurred before the commencement of this section.

As the abolition is not retrospective, the presumption of advancement may still be encountered in the UK for some years to come with regard to transfers or contributions made prior to the implementation date of the Act.[50]

The presumption of advancement works in the opposite direction to the presumption of resulting trust. Strictly speaking it does not rebut the presumption of advancement but prevents it from arising. However, it is now often categorized as a 'sub-rule' of the general presumption of resulting trust. The presumption of advancement is based upon the assumption that a transfer of property between some recognised categories of family relationship will give rise to a presumption that a gift was intended: equity will presume that the transfer or contribution was a gift intended to advance the recipient in life because of 'the natural consideration of blood and affection'.[51] The traditional categories of family relationship giving rise to a presumption of advancement are transfers of property or contributions from:

- a father to his children;[52]
- a man to those to whom he is *in loco parentis*;[53]
- a husband to his wife;[54] and,
- an engaged man to his fiancée.[55]

The presumption of advancement does not apply to transfers or contributions from:

- a mother to her children;[56]
- a child to their parent;[57]

---

50 The presumption is still applicable in some other common law jurisdictions such as Hong Kong. See below on other jurisdictions.
51 *Grey v Grey* (1677) 2 Swans 594, at 598, per Lord Nottingham.
52 *Grey v Grey* (1677) 2 Swans 594.
53 *Ebrand v Dancer* (1680) 2 Chan Cas 26.
54 *Kingdon v Bridges* (1688) 2 Vern 68.
55 *Moate v Moate* [1948] 2 All ER 486. In *Mossop v Mossop* [1989] Fam 77, the Law Reform (Miscellaneous Provisions) Act 1970, s2(1), was interpreted as confirming the presumption of advancement operates as between fiancé and fiancée.
56 *Re De Visme* (1863) 2 De G J & S 17.
57 *Grey v Grey* (1677) 2 Swans 594.

- a wife to her husband;[58]
- one cohabitee to another.[59]

The presumption does not apply to a transfer between a mother and her child as the presumptions derive from a time when a married woman had little or no right to own property in her own right, and, as Jessel MR stated in **Bennet v Bennet**,[60] 'no moral legal obligation…no obligation according to the rules of equity…to provide for her child…' Similarly, the presumption did not apply as between wife and husband because the wife was under no obligation to support the husband. Similarly it did not apply as between children and parent because, 'fathers are bound to provide for their children, but children do not provide for their fathers'.[61] The possibility of a presumption of advancement between cohabitees was raised in *Rider v Kidder*.[62] However, Lord Eldon was quick to dismiss this as the couple 'standing in no relation to each other' no question of advancement could arise. More recently, in **Windeler v Whitehall**,[63] Millett J, as he then was, stated:

'English law recognises neither the term nor the obligation to which [cohabitation] gives effect. In [England], a husband has a legal obligation to support his wife even if they were living apart. A man has no legal obligation to support his mistress even if they are living together.'

Note
The presumption of advancement is itself rebuttable by evidence that a gift was not intended.

10.4.3 Rebutting the presumption of advancement

Even before the statutory abolition of the presumption of advancement the strength of the presumption of advancement in England had diminished. It exists, but is easy to rebut by evidence of contrary intention,[64] and its effectiveness when the property concerned is land is even more questionable. As Lord Diplock stated in **Pettitt v. Pettitt**,[65] 'It would in my view, be an abuse of the legal technique for ascertaining or imputing intention to apply to transactions between the post-war generation of married couples 'presumptions' which are based upon inferences of fact

---

58   *Re Young, Trye v Sullivan* (1885) 28 ChD 705.
59   *Rider v Kidder* (1805) 10 Ves 360.
60   (1879) 10 Ch. D. 474, 477-478.
61   *Grey v Grey* (1677) 2 Swans 594, 598-599.
62   (1805) 10 Ves 360.
63   [1989] FCT 268.
64   *Tribe v. Tribe* [1996] Ch 107.
65   [1970] AC 777.

which an earlier generation of judges drew as the most likely intentions of earlier generations of spouses belonging to the propertied classes of a different social era.'

Thus the presumption may be rebutted by evidence that a gift was not intended but there are issues to do with the evidence that may be admitted and the burden of proof in this evidential battle.

10.4.4 The evidential battle

In deciding whether to apply the presumptions of resulting trust or advancement the court first looks at all the evidence to try to seek the intent of the transferor or contributor at the time of transfer. If there is clear evidence of intent then the presumptions will not arise. In deciding whether there is evidence of intent behind a transfer or contribution the courts will use the 'rule' in *Shephard v Cartwright*:[66]

Acts or declarations of the parties before or at the time of the purchase, or so immediately after it as to constitute a part of the transaction, are admissible in evidence, either for or against the party who did the act or made the declaration; but subsequent acts and declarations are only admissible in evidence against the party who made them.

The presumptions of resulting trust and advancement only arise if there is no clear evidence and are therefore "longstops". The presumptions have usually only been applied when one or all of the parties to the transaction have died, when there is no acceptable evidence because the evidence is tainted with illegality, or the witnesses are all plainly self-serving and unreliable. In such cases gratuitous transfers or contributions involving close family members may result in 'a battle of competing presumptions',[67] although it is really a battle of evidence or the lack of it. In this battle the standard of proof required is the civil standard, the balance of probabilities. Therefore the court will decide if it is more probable than not that the presumption is rebutted. The burden of proof in this battle follows the general principle that he who asserts must prove. The legal burden is therefore upon the party seeking to show that beneficial ownership is not the same as legal ownership, usually the claimant. However, the claimant need only bring evidence of voluntary transfer or contribution to establish the presumption of resulting trust. As *equity will not assist a volunteer*, the legal owner, usually the defendant, then faces an evidential burden to rebut the presumption. This may be done by adducing evidence that

---

66 *Shephard v Cartwright* [1955] AC 431. The rule has been clarified as not excluding testimony before the court as the court may weigh the credibility of this testimony: *Ip Man Shan, Henry v Ching Hing Construction Company Ltd (No 2)* [2003] 1 HKC 256, [181].

67 *Cheung, Lily v Commissioner of Estate Duty* [1987] 3 HKC 307.

consideration was paid, that a gift was intended, that there was another purpose to the transfer (for example an express trust in favour of other beneficiaries), or that the transferee is within the recognised categories of advancement. If the presumption of resulting trust is rebutted by the presumption of advancement then the burden is on the claimant to displace the presumption of advancement with an evidential burden to adduce evidence to support this, for example evidence that the transfer was a loan or a trust.

Warren v Gurney[68]

A father purchased a house in his daughter's name but he retained the title deeds. Before he died he wrote a document entitled, "my wish", in which he expressed the desire that the property be divided between his three daughters. The Court of Appeal held that the presumption of advancement was rebutted as it was clear from the evidence of the retention of title deeds and the letter of wishes that there was no intention of a gift. The daughter held the property on resulting trust for her father's estate.

10.4.5 Illegality and the presumptions

Traditionally a trust could never be recognised as arising from illegal motives as it is a creature of equity and so of conscience. As *he who comes to equity must come with clean hands,* so no claimant could found his cause upon 'an immoral or an illegal act.'[69] In these circumstances the principle the court applied was, 'Let the estate lie where it falls':[70] thus the owner at common law was the absolute owner. However, in more recent cases the courts have relaxed these rules to allow that a resulting trust may arise if the claimant may establish it without relying on their illegal motive.

Tinsley v Milligan[71]

The defendant Milligan had purchased a property with another woman, the claimant Tinsley, but had registered the property in Tinsley's sole name so that Milligan could fraudulently claim state benefits. Tinsley moved out and took action against Milligan claiming an absolute interest in the property. When Milligan attempted to defend the claim on the basis of a beneficial interest by way of contribution to purchase price Tinsley claimed Milligan could not rely on her illegal motives to establish the resulting trust. The House of Lords held that Milligan had an interest by way of resulting trust. She did not have to rely on her illegal motives to establish this; merely that she had contributed to the purchase price.

---

68 [1944] 2 All ER 472.
69 *Holman v Johnson* (1775) 1 Cowp 341, 343, per Lord Mansfield C.J.
70 *Muckleston v Brown* (1801) 6 Ves 52, 68-69, per Lord Eldon L.C.
71 [1994] 1 AC 340.

The justification for this approach may be that to support Tinsley's claim would have given her absolute title to the property even though she had conspired in the fraud. Thus the modern approach of the courts is to allow the presumption of resulting trust to arise even when a motive for a transfer is illegal, as all the court considers is whether there is a gratuitous transfer or contribution. However, the court will not allow either party to lead evidence of an illegal motive to rebut the presumption of resulting trust. No party can rely on their illegal motives to establish an interest. Thus, if property is purchased in, or transferred into, the name of another for an illegal purpose, then the provider is not prevented from asserting an interest by way of resulting trust. The plaintiff only pleads the presumption and does not have to rely on the illegal purpose to establish this. The burden is then on the legal owner to rebut this. However, if the legal owner raises the presumption of advancement then the provider will not be able to rely on the illegal purpose to rebut this: this is referred to as the 'reliance principle'.[72] Again if the presumption of advancement arises to rebut the presumption of resulting trust then illegal motives behind the transfer or contribution cannot be relied on to rebut the advancement.

Gascoigne v Gascoigne[73]
The husband took a lease of land in his wife's name as he was in debt and wished to avoid his creditors. This was done with the wife's full knowledge and they built a house upon the land. When the couple separated he attempted to claim that the wife held the house on resulting trust for him. However, the court would not hear evidence of the illegal motive in the transfer to rebut the presumption of advancement in the wife's favour.

In *Tinker v Tinker*,[74] a husband had conveyed the property into his wife's name on the advice of his solicitor when he began a business venture. Lord Denning, in accepting that the husband had acted honestly on this advice said:

'But, whether the solicitor gave that advice or not, I am quite clear that the husband cannot have it both ways. So he is on the horns of a dilemma. He cannot say that the house is his own and, at one and the same time, say that it is his wife's. As against his wife, he wants to say that it belongs to *him*. As against his creditors, that it belongs to *her*. That simply will not do. Either it was conveyed to her for her own use absolutely; or it was conveyed to her as trustee for her husband. It must be one or other. The

---

72   James Brightwell, 'Good riddance to the presumption of advancement?' (2010) 16(8) (September) *Trusts & Trustees* 627, 630.
73   [1918] 1 KB 223, 87 LJKB 333, 118 LT 347, 34 TLR 168, [1916-17] All ER Rep Ext 1143.
74   [1970] 1 All ER 540.

presumption is that it was conveyed to her for her own use; and he does not rebut that presumption by saying that he only did it to defeat his creditors. I think that it belongs to her.'[75]

Equity has also developed the principle to allow evidence of illegal or improper motives behind a transfer to be used to rebut the presumption of advancement if the illegal purposes were not carried out or were retreated from.

Tribe v. Tribe[76]

A father transferred shares into his son's name to keep his business out of the reach of his potential creditors. However, the liability never arose and so the father never had to deceive his creditors. The son refused to return the shares relying on the presumption of advancement. The father was allowed to give evidence as to his real intention for the transfer to rebut the presumption. The Court held that the son held the shares on resulting trust because the father was not relying on an illegal motive that had been carried out. Millet LJ opined:

'In my opinion the weight of the authorities supports the view that a person who seeks to recover property transferred by him for an illegal purpose can lead evidence of his dishonest intention whenever it is necessary for him to do so provided that he has withdrawn from the transaction before the illegal purpose has been carried out.'

Ali v Khan[77]

A father transferred property to his daughter for one third of its value. This was in order to allow her to borrow against the property to finance the weddings of his daughters. The daughter claimed that the presumption of advancement meant that the discount in price had been a gift to her. However, evidence was brought to show that the house was the family home and the father had never intended the transfer to be a gift; it was merely to facilitate the loan. The daughter argued that this was an illegal purpose and thus could not be used to rebut the presumption of advancement and give rise to a resulting trust. The Court of Appeal held that this was merely a financial arrangement and not an illegal purpose, therefore the daughter held the property on resulting trust in proportion to the amount of contribution for her father.

Note

Any attempt to place an asset beyond the reach of your creditors may be set aside by s.423 of the Insolvency Act 1986. This is known as the 'avoidance' provision as it relies on an intention by the transferor to avoid

---

75   [1970] 1 All ER 540 at 542.
76   [1996] Ch 107.
77   [2002] EWCA Civ 974, 5 ITELR 232.

his liabilities. Thus a sale at an undervalue or a gratuitous transfer will be set aside under the provision and the property treated as the property of the transferor for the purposes of insolvency. An attempt to create a trust to avoid liability will be a sham as in *Midland Bank v Wyatt*,[78] and thus void.

10.4.6 The demise of the presumption of advancement in the UK

The recent statutory attempt to abolish the presumption of advancement is the result of sustained criticism over its appropriateness in modern Britain. Criticism has focused on three main issues: the presumption is anachronistic; the presumption is discriminatory; and the application of the reliance principle when illegal motives are associated with transactions produces arbitrary results.[79]

The presumption of advancement is undoubtedly a product of a bygone age, as the presumption may be traced to Lord Nottingham's decision in *Grey v Grey*,[80] itself based upon an earlier common law principle. However, there is no need for the presumption to be considered anachronistic as in some jurisdictions the categories recognised as giving rise to the presumption have been restricted or enlarged to reflect changing socio-economic realities, ensuring the presumption reflects modern needs.[81]

It is hard to deny that the traditional categories of advancement are discriminatory as they all concern transfers from, or contribution by, men. Thus, the UK legislated to abolish the presumption because the government believed it did not comply with its obligations under the European Convention on Human Rights.[82] However, Glister has argued that the presumption does not breach the protocol, as the Article only provides for equality of rights and responsibilities in the context of marriage and the parental presumption of advancement depends on parenthood rather than marriage. Similarly the presumption from fiancé to fiancée would also be outside the scope of the Article. Glister also argues that the presumption is not a 'right' but merely an evidential tool or presumption of a state of affairs and thus the marital presumption also falls outside the Article.[83]

---

78   [1995] 1 FLR 697.
79   James Brightwell, 'Good riddance to the presumption of advancement?' (2010) 16(8) (September) *Trusts & Trustees* 627, 630.
80   (1677) 2 Swans 594.
81   For example Hong Kong: see Steven Gallagher, 'The Presumption of Advancement in Hong Kong', *The Hong Kong Lawyer*, November 2011, 14-25.
82   Article 5 of the Seventh Protocol.
83   See Jamie Glister, 'Section 199 of the Equality Act 2010: How Not to Abolish the Presumption of Advancement' [2010] 73(5) *Modern Law Review* 807, 813. Glister cites the fact that Ireland ratified the protocol in August 2001 but still maintains the presumptions although acknowledging they are anachronistic.

Furthermore, use of the spousal presumption had already decreased because of the wide powers of the court to reorder property rights on divorce under the Matrimonial Causes Act 1973.[84] Of course if the spousal presumption had been made reciprocal then it would not be discriminatory and the extension of the presumption to mothers and their children would have eliminated discrimination against fathers.

The reliance principle, as expounded in *Tinsley v Milligan*,[85] has been criticised as making beneficial ownership arbitrarily dependent on familial relationship.[86] However, Glister has argued that the original position with regard to the application of the presumptions was that the presumption of advancement would prevent the presumption of resulting trust from ever arising,[87] and so all the legal owner had to do was establish the required relationship to raise the presumption of advancement, thus placing an evidential burden on the plaintiff to rebut this.[88] Glister refers to this as the absence of the presumption of resulting trust and has argued for a return to this state of affairs, as it would be a fairer tactical burden for the parties.

Another criticism of the presumption is that the parent child presumption should not apply to adult offspring. Interestingly, in *Grey v Grey*,[89] Lord Nottingham noted that a married son who had already received a marriage settlement and so 'appears to be fully advanced' and 'emancipated' would not be the donee of further purchases by his father in his name. In Canada this has been the justification for the presumption only applying to infant children.[90]

Thus it seems that most criticisms of the presumption of advancement can be rebutted and some jurisdictions have decided to modify it rather

---

DPP v B [2009] IEHC 196 at [50 & [54]. Jamie Glister, 'Section 199 of the Equality Act 2010: How Not to Abolish the Presumption of Advancement' [2010] 73(5) *Modern Law Review* 807, 816.

84 The powers available to the court on divorce may also be available on separation of engaged couples: Law Reform (Miscellaneous Provisions) Act 1970, s2(1).

85 [1994] 1 AC 340.

86 The possibility of such arbitrary results was one of the criticisms of the Law Commission of England and Wales which led to the recommendation to abolish the presumption of advancement. Law Commission, 'The Presumption of Advancement: Does it have any Effect in Practice?' (Law Com, 2006). Law Commission, 'The Illegality Defence' (Law Com No 320, 2010) s.1.23.

87 Referring to Lord Nottingham's comments in *Grey v Grey* (1677) 2 Swans 594, 597–8; 36 ER 742, 743; and the report in DEC Yale (ed), *Lord Nottingham's Chancery Cases* (Selden Society, vol i, 1957; vol ii, 1961), case 643.

88 Jamie Glister, 'Is There a Presumption of Advancement?'(2011) 33(39) *Sydney Law Review,* 39-66.

89 (1677) 2 Swans 594 at pp. 600-601.

90 *Pecore v Pecore* [2007] 1 SCR 795.

than discard it altogether. Canada has removed the presumption as between husband and wife or parent to an adult child,[91] and New Zealand has abolished the presumption for spouses.[92] In Australia and Hong Kong the presumption has been acknowledged as operating between mother and child,[93] and in Hong Kong the presumption has even been extended to a man's concubine or de facto wife.[94]

The presumption of resulting trust was a development of equity in recognition of commercial transactions because equity is suspicious of gifts and tries to seek bargains.[95] Therefore, it was presumed that a businessman would always intend to have his property returned or retain an interest in it. Similarly, equity prefers the tenancy in common for commercial transactions as a vindication of initial property rights rather than joint tenancy and the 'gamble of the tontine'[96] Thus equity adopted the presumption of advancement to avoid the presumption of resulting trust in recognition of the special nature of family relationships as opposed to commercial arrangements. However, it may now be too late to save this useful evidential tool in the UK.

---

91   *Pecore v Pecore* [2007] 1 SCR 795.
92   Property (Relationships) Act 1976, s.4.
93   For Australia see *Brown v Brown* (1993) 31 NSWLR 582 & *Nelson v Nelson* (1995) 184 CLR 538. In Hong Kong see *Lee Tso Fong v Kwok Wai Sun* [2008] 4 HKC 36. see also the Supreme Court of Prince Edward Island, Canada, *Dagle v Dagle Estate (1990) 70 DLR (4th) 201.*
94   *Li Hung Chan v Wong Woon Heung (alias Wong Yuen)* (1950) 34 HKLR 213; *Cheung Pui Yuen v Worldcup Investments Inc.* [2008] HKEC 1808 (Court of Final Appeal). The political and social history of Hong Kong has given rise to some confusion over relationships that can categorise a 'wife'. The Chinese customary status of concubine is defined in s 14 of the Legitimacy Ordinance (Cap 184) as a union of concubinage, entered by a male partner and a female partner before 7 October 1971, under which union the female partner has, during the lifetime of the male partner, been accepted by his wife as his concubine and recognized as such by the family generally.
95   *Pecore v Pecore* (2007) SCC 17 at 24.
96   See *Stack v Dowden* [2007] UKHL 17; 2 AC 432, at [60] per Baroness Hale. The 'gamble of the tontine' refers to an arrangement whereby investors pay into a fund which is held by all investors as joint tenants, thus all own the whole of the fund and do not have separate shares in the fund. As each investor dies the others benefit from survivorship- the deceased's 'share' of the fund is not taken from the fund but remains as part of the whole owned by the survivors. This continues until there is one surviving investor who takes the whole absolutely. Equity presumes that co-owners of property own as tenants in common and have divisible shares in the property rather than owning as joint tenants when survivorship operates.

290 The Law of Trusts

10.5 Automatic Resulting Trusts

Resulting trusts are also said to arise automatically because of circumstances surrounding the transfer. Automatic resulting trusts are more controversial than presumed resulting trusts. Commentators and courts alike have had difficulties in explaining what the basis and justification is for the recognition of such trusts. It has been claimed that the automatic resulting trust is an instrument of restitution to reverse the unjust enrichment of the trustee, or that the beneficial interest in the property has been, ' "retained" by the settlor; in other words, "it is never drawn out of him"'.[97]

The circumstances giving rise to an automatic resulting trust are:

- The failure of an express trust or gift;
- A failure to dispose of the beneficial interest in property;
- When property is given for a purpose and the purpose fails; for example, the *Quistclose* trust and surplus funds.

If there is a failure of a trust or gift the property is held on resulting trust for the settlor or donor. Thus if there is certainty of intent to place the transferee under a trust obligation but there is uncertainty of the subject matter,[98] the beneficial interest,[99] or the beneficiaries or objects of the trust,[100] then the property will be held on resulting trust for the settlor or the testator's estate.[101] Maitland justified this by saying: 'I have made A a trustee for somebody, and a trustee he must be- if for no one else then for me or my representatives.'[102] Thus an attempt has been made to create a trust and the trustee knows this, therefore he must hold it on trust and cannot take it himself. He must hold it on trust for the settlor or testator's estate. Similarly if the settlor fails to observe the requirements of law, such

---

97 John Mee, ' "Automatic" Resulting Trusts: Retention, Restitution, or Reposing Trust?', in Charles Mitchell (ed), *Constructive and Resulting Trusts* (Hart Publishing, 2009), 207 & 208. see also Birke Hacker, 'Proprietary restitution after impaired consent transfers: a generalized power model' (2009) 68(2) *Cambridge Law Journal* 324-360.

98 *Palmer v Simmonds* (1854) 2 Drew 221.

99 *Boyce v Boyce*(1894) 16 Sim 476.

100 *Re Astor's Settlement Trusts (Astor v Scholfield)* [1952] Ch 534

101 As noted above, a disposition in a will is presumed to be a gift unless there is clear evidence that another purpose was intended: FW Maitland, Equity: A Course of Lectures, J Brunyate (ed), rev edn (Cambridge, Cambridge University press, 1936) 77. Thus if there is no clear intention to place the recipient under a trust obligation the disposition in a will is a gift.

102 FW Maitland, *Equity: A Course of Lectures*, J Brunyate (ed), rev edn (Cambridge, Cambridge University press, 1936) 77. Cited by John Mee, ' "Automatic" Resulting Trusts: Retention, Restitution, or Reposing Trust?', in Charles Mitchell (ed), *Constructive and Resulting Trusts* (Hart Publishing, 2009), 209.

as the perpetuity period,[103] then the trust will fail and the property result back.

A resulting trust can also occur if there is a failure to dispose of the beneficial interest in property.

Vandervell v. IRC[104]

Mr. Vandervell had been trying to minimise his and his estate's liability to tax. He also wished to make a gift to the Royal College of Surgeons. Vandervell transferred shares to the Royal College of Surgeons subject to an option to purchase in favour of his trustees. He did not stipulate for whose benefit the trustees held the option. The court held that the option must be held for Mr. Vandervell because, in Lord Wilberforce's words: 'the option was vested in the trustee company as a trustee on trusts, not defined at the time, possibly to be defined later. but the equitable or beneficial interest cannot remain in the air; the consequence in law must be that it remains in the settlor'. As Lord Diplock observed, 'equity abhors a beneficial vacuum'.[105] Mr. Vandervell had not divested himself of all of his interest in the shares and so was liable to tax.

The circumstances giving rise to a resulting trust and constructive trust were considered in *Westdeutsche Landesbank Girozentrale v Islington LBC*,[106] where the House of Lords had to consider whether a trust had arisen on the failure of a financial transaction.

Westdeutsche Landesbank Girozentrale v Islington London Borough Council [107]

Islington London Borough Council entered into an interest rate swap agreement with the Bank to raise funds. The Bank passed £2.5 million to the Council and the Council made some interest payments. In a separate action not involving the parties such swap deals by public authorities were held to be *ultra vires*. The contract was thus void for mistake. It was apparent that the Council had to repay the money but the nature of their holding of the money and so the action available to the Bank to recover it was important as it could affect the type of interest awarded on the money. If the Council held the money on trust then compound interest might be awarded, if this were a simple common law action for money had and received then only simple interest could be awarded. The bank subsequently brought an action against the Council for repayment of £1,145,525.93. At first instance the judge held that the bank was entitled to recover the principal sum plus compound interest from 1 April 1990. The

---

103   Air Jamaica v Charlton [1999] 1 WLR 1399.
104   [1967] 2 AC 291 HL.
105   *Vandervell v. IRC* [1966] Ch 261 CA.
106   [1996] AC 669, *HL*
107   [1996] AC 669, *HL*

Court of Appeal dismissed the Council's appeal and allowed the Bank's cross-appeal from the judge's decision that the interest should run from April 1990. The local authority appealed to the House of Lords against the award of compound interest. The House of Lords held that this was a common law action for money had and received and so the Bank was entitled to recover only simple interest. The House also noted that, in the absence of fraud, the courts of equity had never awarded compound interest except against a trustee or other person owing fiduciary duties who had made an improper account of profits. As the money was passed under a contract later found void for mistake the Council was not holding the money on resulting trust. It was simply a debtor creditor relationship which was later found void and so no fiduciary duty was owed by the Council to the Bank.

The House of Lords identified fundamental propositions for the law of trusts:

- equity acts on the legal owner's conscience
- there must be clearly identifiable trust property.

Thus a trustee will only be a trustee if he knows, or should have known, he holds clearly identifiable property for the benefit of someone else. In this case there was no resulting trust because by the time the Council became aware of the invalidity of the contract its account was overdrawn. Therefore there was no time when there was both knowledge affecting the Council's conscience and a trust fund.

An automatic resulting trust will also arise when property is given for a purpose but that purpose cannot be carried out. This principle contains resulting trusts for surplus funds and the *Quistclose* trust.

10.5.1 Surplus funds

We have already considered the position of surplus funds when a charitable purpose for which they were donated is completed or cannot be completed. If there is evidence of a general charitable intent behind the donation then the funds may be applied *cy-près* for other charitable purposes. However, if there is no general charitable intent or the purpose was not charitable and the donor is identifiable they may automatically be held on resulting trust for the donor.

Re Trusts of the Abbott Trust[108]

Donations were made to a fund to support two sisters who had fallen on hard times. They died and the court had to decide what to do with the surplus funds. The court held that the donations were to maintain the

---

108 [1900] 2 Ch. 326.

sisters and were not an outright gift to them. Therefore they were held on resulting trust for the donors.

If the nature of the donation makes it almost impossible to trace the donor, perhaps donations made by collection in the street, then the property will go *bona vacantia* to the Crown.

If there are surplus funds remaining after the ending of a non-charitable unincorporated association there are problems in deciding what to do with the funds. As considered earlier the ownership of funds for an unincorporated association causes problems because the association cannot hold property in its own right. The fund cannot be held on trust for the association as this would be a trust for the purposes of the association and so a non-charitable purpose trust which should be void.[109] Any trust for the members raises issues of perpetuity because of remote vesting.[110] Thus as we have seen any gift in favour of an unincorporated association is construed, if it can be, as a gift to the present members of the association subject to the rules of the association.[111] If there have been donations from non-members and it is accepted that they intended their donations to be used for a particular purpose then they should be returned to the donor by way of resulting trust. However, if it would be impossible or impracticable to trace the donees, again perhaps if the fund was raised by street collection, then the donation should go *bona vacantia* to the Crown.[112]

Traditionally funds that were contributed by members were considered held on resulting trust for the members in proportion to their contributions to the fund.[113] If a donation from a member can be traced to the donee then it was held on resulting trust unless the donor was considered to have relinquished beneficial interest in the property. More recently the courts have considered the contractual nature of property holding for unincorporated associations and applied this contractual analysis in deciding how surplus funds should be distributed. Thus, today, if it is accepted that the donor has parted with their beneficial interest in the donation, it is more likely that the fund will be distributed amongst the present members of the association as directed in the rules of the association.[114]

---

109 *Leahy v. A-G of New South Wales* [1959] AC 457; Re *Astor's Settlement Trusts (Astor v Scholfield)* [1952] Ch 534

110 *Neville Estates v. Madden* [1962] Ch 832; *Re Recher's WT* [1972] Ch 526.

111 *Neville Estates v. Madden* [1962] Ch 832, per Cross J's second constrcution; *Re Recher's WT* [1972] Ch 526.

112 Confirmed in *Westdeutsche Landesbank v Islington LBC* [1996] AC 669.

113 *Re West Sussex Constabulary's Widows, Children and Benevolent (1930)Fund Trusts* [1971] Ch 1.

114 *Re Bucks Constabulary Benevolent Fund* [1978] 1 WLR 641; [1979] 1 All ER 623; *Re Bucks Constabulary Widows and Orphans Fund Friendly Society (No 2)* [1979] 1 WLR 936

10.5.2 The *Quistclose* trust

The *Quistclose* trust is named after **Barclays Bank v. Quistclose Investments Ltd**,[115] and has been described as 'the single most important application of equitable principles in commercial life'.[116] A *Quistclose* trust may arise when the lender loans money to a borrower on condition that it will be used for a specified purpose but the money is not used or is used for another purpose.

Note
This is an important innovation in equity as loans are usually just debts at common law and not trusts. Therefore loan money becomes an asset of the borrower subject purely to a debt obligation. If the borrower becomes insolvent the lender has no proprietary claim on the money. However, the *Quistclose* trust gives the lender a proprietary claim and priority in liquidation.

Barclays Bank v. Quistclose Investments Ltd[117]
Quistclose loaned money to Rolls Razors to allow it to pay a declared dividend to its shareholders. The money was paid into a separate account at Barclays Bank. Barclays knew of the arrangement. Rolls Razors went into liquidation. The dividend could not be paid and Barclays sought to keep the money in the account as set-off against Rolls Razors' overdraft. The House of Lords held that the bank could not do this because Rolls Razors held the money on trust for *Quistclose*. Thus it could not be used to set-off Barclays' debt or for distribution in Rolls Razors' liquidation.

The justification for this decision was quite complicated. The House of Lords held that Rolls Razors held the money initially on a trust for the shareholders to pay the dividend and then, if that trust was not carried out, Rolls Razors held the money on a secondary trust for the lender *Quistclose*. The secondary trust was a resulting trust. There was mention that the two trusts were part of a single express trust and that the beneficial interest never left the lender. The latter comment seems more comprehensible with the borrower just having a power to use the money for the agreed purpose.

The *Quistclose* trust has been further developed and applied in circumstances which are significantly different to those of *Quistclose* itself.

---

115 [1970] AC 567.
116 Lord Millett writing extra-judicially in the preface to Swadling, *The Quistclose Trusts: Critical Essays* (Hart Publishing, Oxford and Portland, Oregon: 2004).
117 [1970] AC 567.

Carreras Rothmans Ltd v Freeman Mathews Treasure Ltd[118]

The claimant company was a cigarette manufacturer which employed Freeman to handle its advertising. Freeman had entered into contracts with production agencies and the media as the principal, although the contracts were for Carreras advertising. Freeman was in financial difficulty and so Carreras paid money into a special account for the sole purpose of settling debts with the agencies and media working on the Carreras' account. This was not a loan. The debts were not paid and the money remained in the account. A few months later Freeman went into liquidation. The agencies and media organisations called on Carreras to settle the debts, which it did, taking assignment of the creditors' rights of action against Freeman. Carreras then called upon Freeman's liquidator to pay it the money in the account. The liquidator refused. The court held that the monies in the account were held on resulting trust for Carreras and not part of Freeman's assets to be distributed among its creditors. Thus the *Quistclose* principle was extended to situations not just involving straightforward loans, as here there was an antecedent debt owed by the lender.

Lord Millet attempted to clarify the justification of *Quistclose* trusts in **Twinsectra v Yardley**.[119] Lord Millet noted 'formidable difficulties' with the primary and secondary trust justification.[120] He held that a borrower who borrows money for a purpose agreed with the lender holds the fund on resulting trust from the beginning for the lender subject only to a power or duty to use the fund for the specific purpose.[121] Thus the *Quistclose* trust is a resulting trust:

'Like all resulting trusts, the trust in favour of the lender arises when the lender parts with money on terms which do not exhaust the beneficial interest ... It is a default trust which fills the gap when some part of the beneficial interest is undisposed of and prevents it from being "in suspense".'[122]

The test to decide whether the money is a straightforward loan or subject to the *Quistclose* principle is, 'whether the parties intended the money to be at the free disposal of the recipient.'[123] Therefore if a loan is

---

118 [1985] Ch 207.
119 [2002] UKHL 12; 2 AC 164.
120 [2002] UKHL 12, at [79].
121 [2002] UKHL 12, at [100].
122 [2002] UKHL 12, at [102]. This approach has not been without criticism, see Michael Smolyansky, 'Reigning in the Quistclose Trusts: A Response to Twinsectra v Yardley' (2010) 16(7) *Trusts & Trustees* 558-568, but has been defended by Lord Millett writing extra-judicially, 'The Quistclose Trust- a reply' (2011) 17(1) *Trusts & Trustees* 7-16.
123 *Twinsectra v Yardley* [2002] UKHL 12, at [74], per Lord Millett referring to Lord Mustill in *re Goldcorp Exchange Ltd* [1995] 1 AC 74, 100.

made to a borrower for a specific purpose and the borrower is not free to apply the money for any other purpose, that arrangement gives rise to fiduciary obligations on the part of the borrower, which a court of equity will enforce by way of *Quistclose* trust.[124]

It has also been debated whether the loan fund need be placed in a separate account and so segregated from the trustee's own funds. Lord Millett noted this was not a requirement in his obiter comments in *Twinsectra v Yardley*,[125] when he emphasised that the duty to keep money separate for the trust fund arose from the trust and was not a pre-condition for the existence of the trust. Subsequent decisions have now supported this view. [126]

Cooper v Liquidator of PRG Powerhouse Group Ltd[127]

Cooper was Managing Director of Powerhouse and was provided with a car. Powerhouse entered the finance agreement and paid the payments from Cooper's wages. Cooper resigned but wanted to keep the car and so agreed to pay the finance company the balance owing on the car. Cooper paid a cheque to Powerhouse for it to discharge the finance. Powerhouse did not pay the finance company until the day before Powerhouse went into administration. The cheque was thus returned dishonoured. Cooper's cheque was paid into Powerhouse's main account and mixed with other funds. If he were merely a creditor he would receive only a proportion of the money. The High Court held that there was a *Quistclose* trust even though the fund had not been kept separate.

The High Court relied on the principle stated by Watkins L.J. in *R v Clowes (No 2)*:[128] 'where a trustee mixes trust money with his own…the beneficiaries are entitled to a first charge on the mixed fund.' The principle thus seems to be that if money is advanced for a purpose, it does not matter that it is mixed with the borrower's own as he is under a duty to keep it separate,[129] and the trust will not be defeated by his actions.[130] This

---

124 *Twinsectra v Yardley* [2002] UKHL 12, at [68], per Lord Millett.

125 [2002] UKHL 12, at [83], per Lord Millett.

126 In *re Farepak Food and Gifts Ltd* [2006] All ER (D) 265 (Dec), Mann J held that the mixing of money is not itself inconsistent with the Quistclose trust.

127 [2008] EWHC 498; All ER (D) 211 (Mar) (Ch).

128 [1994] 2 All ER 316.

129 *Twinsectra v Yardley* [2002] UKHL 12, at [83], per Lord Millet.

130 But note that if funds obtained on an ordinary purchase were designated for a company's client account but were not placed there, in consequence of a breach of trust by the company, the client had no proprietary right in the misplaced funds and so no right to trace: *Moriarty v Atkinson* [2008] EWCA Civ 1604; [2010] 1 BCLC 142; (2009) The Times, January 12.

principle has been followed in Bermuda[131] and Hong Kong.[132]

It has been noted that retention of title, or *Romalpa* clauses, and *Quistclose* trusts share the same purpose, that is all the cases involve an attempt:

'by a person who has paid money or supplied goods to an insolvent company to escape from the normally fruitless position of unsecured creditor by claiming a beneficial interest in the money or goods supplied or in assets which in some way represent them.'[133]

However, there is some inconsistency in the readiness of the courts to recognise the two forms of security, as where the *Quistclose* trust has thrived the *Romalpa* clause has been severely restricted.[134]

10.6 Constructive Trusts

Maitland cited *Lewin on Trusts* as giving 'one grand rule' for constructive trust that 'wherever a person clothed with a fiduciary character gains some personal advantage by availing himself of his situation as a trustee, he becomes a trustee of the advantage so gained.'[135] Although it is very attractive to reduce the requirements for a constructive trust to this level, Maitland noted that the constructive trust was not restricted in such a way.[136] Since the late 19th century the development of the constructive trust has been such that today it is very difficult to provide a simple definition of a constructive trust.[137] This may in part be that the judiciary, whilst

---

131 *Kingate Global Fund Ltd v Knightsbridge (USD) Fund Limited et al* [2010] WTLR 1201 (CA); see Keith Robinson, 'Madoff meets Quistclose' (2011) 17(7) *Trusts & Trustees* 668-676.

132 *Typhoon 8 Research Ltd v Seapower Resources International Ltd* [2002] 2 HKLRD 660, where a *Quistclose* trust was controversially applied to a rental deposit; see Rebecca Wing Chi Lee, 'Rental Deposits as (*Quistclose*) Trusts' (2003) 33 *Hong Kong Law Journal* 27.

133 Goodhart & Jones, 'The Infiltration of Equitable Doctrine into English Commercial Law' (1980) 43 *MLR* 489, 511.

134 Lusina Ho, and P. St J. Smart, 'Quistclose and Romalpa: Ambivalence and Contradiction' (2009) 39 *Hong Kong L. J.* 37. Kelry C. F. Loi, 'Revisiting Quistclose Trusts, Romalpa Clauses and Registrable Charges: A Reply to Ho and Smart' (2011) 41 *Hong Kong L. J.* 343.

135 FW Maitland, *Equity: A Course of Lectures*, J Brunyate (ed), rev edn (Cambridge, Cambridge University press, 1936) 80. Maitland then referred to the leading case as *Keech v Sandford* (1726) Sel Cas Ch 1, considered later in the chapter on fiduciaries.

136 FW Maitland, *Equity: A Course of Lectures*, J Brunyate (ed), rev edn (Cambridge, Cambridge University press, 1936) 81-85.

137 In fact the 'constructive trust' has been described as a 'fiction' as it is not a trust but courts orders to pay a sum of money or convey an interest in property: William Swadling, 'The Fiction of the Constructive Trust' (2011) (64) *Current Legal Problems* 399-433.

wishing to avoid the tag 'remedial' for the constructive trust, have also not wished to limit its application by a precise definition.[138] Previously we noted that traditionally the courts refer to constructive trusts as institutional. Thus the courts should only impose a constructive trust in certain prescribed situations. To support this institutional claim it has frequently been stated that a constructive trust arises by operation of the law, and not by reason of the intention of the parties.[139] However, this ignores the common intention constructive trust. As it is so difficult to define the constructive trust it may be easier to examine the circumstances in which a constructive trust may arise. It is important to remember that the constructive trustee is in many ways not really a trustee at all in the usual sense as he has trusteeship imposed upon him because of past conduct. Therefore the constructive trustee may not even be aware that he is a trustee until the court declares him such. Millett LJ, as he then was, attempted to clarify the use of the terms constructive trust and constructive trustee in *Paragon Finance plc v DB Thakerar (a firm)*.[140] The distinction is made according to when the legal owner is under the trust obligation. Millett L.J. said that the expressions constructive trust and constructive trustee 'have been used by equity lawyers to describe two entirely different situations.' The constructive trust 'covers those cases... where the defendant, though not expressly appointed as trustee, has assumed the duties of a trustee by a lawful transaction which was independent of and preceded the breach of trust and is not impeached by the plaintiff.' The constructive trustee is such 'as a direct consequence of the unlawful transaction that is impeached by the plaintiff.'[141] Thus the constructive trust arose when it would be unconscionable for the legal owner of property to ignore the beneficial interests of another whereas the constructive trustee,

'...is not in fact a trustee at all, even though he may be liable to account as if he were. He never assumes the position of a trustee, and if he receives the trust property at all it is adversely to the plaintiff by an unlawful transaction which is impugned by the plaintiff. In such a case the expressions 'constructive trust' and 'constructive trustee' are misleading for there is no trust and usually no chance of a proprietary remedy; they are nothing more than a formula of equitable relief.'[142]

---

138 See the comments of Edmund-Davies L.J. in *Carl Zeiss Stiftung v Herbert Smith & Co.* [1969] 2 Ch 276, 300.

139 For example, "...express trusts are created by the will of the parties, whereas constructive trusts are imposed by law." Paul Mathews, 'The Words Which Are Not There: A Partial History of the Constructive Trust', in Charles Mitchell (ed), *Constructive and Resulting Trusts* (Hart Publishing, 2009), 4.

140 [1999] 1 ITELR 735 (CA).

141 [1999] 1 ITELR 735 at 749.

142 [1999] 1 ITELR 735 at 749-750.

The constructive trust has most often been used to combat fraud. Here, of course, fraud is not used in the same sense as deceit at common law. This is the more general concept described by Viscount Haldane LC in *Nocton v Lord Ashburton*:[143] 'any breach of the sort of obligation which is enforced by a court that from the beginning regarded itself as a court of conscience.' Thus unconscionable behaviour is the basis of equitable fraud as equity, 'correct men's consciences for frauds, breach of trusts, wrongs and oppressions.'[144] Thus the court imposes or recognises a 'constructive trust' that protects a beneficial interest in property in favour of a claimant and that is then held on trust by the legal owner.

The importance of the constructive trust is, of course the proprietary rights that the beneficiaries have in the trust property. If the court declares that property is held on constructive trust then the beneficiaries may assert their proprietary interest. If the court declares that someone is accountable as a constructive trustee then the remedy available to the beneficiary is purely personal, that is they may make the defendant account for any loss to the trust but this is equivalent to common law damages, as the defendant will provide money as compensation.[145]

Example

If a defendant receives property knowing that it has been obtained in breach of trust (knowing receipt/recipient liability) he will hold that property on constructive trust for the beneficiaries. If a defendant aids in the misappropriation of trust property in breach of trust he will be liable for the breach as if he were a trustee, perhaps more correctly as an accessory to the breach. He has traditionally, although perhaps incorrectly, been termed a 'constructive trustee' and held to account for the loss to the trust. He cannot hold the property on constructive trust as he does not hold the property now and may never have held it. A proprietary remedy would be pointless.

There has been some debate over whether the trustee or fiduciary who makes a profit from their position is a constructive trustee of the profit. Some have claimed that as the principal never had the profit the trustee or fiduciary is merely accountable as a constructive trustee. The Privy Council's reasoning in *A.G. v Reid*,[146] was creative, but to many it seemed reasonable to adopt the general approach that if the trustee or fiduciary has received something that they should not have received, in Reid's case as we shall consider later it was a bribe, the principal has a greater claim

---

143   [1914] AC 932, 954.
144   *Earl of Oxford's Case* (1615) 1 Ch Rep 1, *per* Lord Ellesmere.
145   For example, see the liability of an accessory to a breach of trust in chapter 19 Liability of Strangers to the Trust.
146   [1994] 1 AC 324.

to the profit and so the trustee or fiduciary holds that property on constructive trust for their principal. This is a proprietary interest. However, in ***Sinclair Investments (UK) Ltd v Versailles Trade Finance Ltd (in administrative receivership)***, [147] the Court of Appeal noted that it was bound by its own previous decisions and declined to follow *A-G v Reid*, holding where there was a bribe the principal had never had the property and so there was no proprietary interest merely a personal remedy for the principal against the agent. The Court of Appeal also confirmed that the UK does not have a remedial constructive trust.

The debate over the remedial or institutional nature of the constructive trust and the uses to which it is put, has led Swadling to argue that the constructive trust is not actually a trust but a remedy of equity.[148] However, this has been countered by Wright who argues that the constructive trust is a trust however much it may differ from the express private trust, but that is to be expected as there are many types of trust and many have only limited similarity to the express private trust.[149] With such confusion surrounding the nature of the constructive trust it is best to simply consider the situations in which a constructive trust may arise.

10.7 The Accepted Categories of Constructive Trust

Below are some categories of constructive trust; once again academic opinions vary on categorisation of these circumstances as constructive trusts. These are by no means exhaustive.

Constructive trusts may be imposed or recognised by the court:

1   When a trustee or fiduciary in breach of trust or their fiduciary duty makes a profit from their fiduciary position;
2   When strangers to the trust have damaged the trust;
3   To prevent fraud
4   When there has been unlawful killing;
5   To help parties under a specifically enforceable contract;
6   To enforce "special" testamentary trusts;
7   To give effect to common intentions- the common intention constructive trust.

---

147   [2011] EWCA Civ 347.
148   William Swadling, 'The Fiction of the Constructive Trust' (2011) 64 *Current Legal Problems* 399-433.
149   David Wright, 'How much of a trust is a constructive trust?' (2012) 18(3) *Trusts & Trustees* 264-272.

10.7.1 Trustee in breach of trust or fiduciary in breach of their fiduciary duty

As we shall see the trustee has onerous duties and is prohibited from benefiting from the trust or his position as trustee. If he does he may be liable to account to the trust for any benefit he receives, even if the trust has not made a corresponding loss. He will hold any benefit on constructive trust for the trust.[150] The trustee is a special type of fiduciary.

A fiduciary is someone in a special relationship of good faith with another party and has strict duties of loyalty and good faith. For example company directors are fiduciaries of the company and owe duties of good faith to the company as a whole. They must not allow their interests to conflict with their duties to the company, make secret profits from their position, and must always act in the best interests of the company. If they benefit from their position they will hold any benefit on trust for their principal.[151]

10.7.2 When strangers to the trust have damaged the trust

A constructive trust may be imposed upon somebody who intermeddles with trust property; or somebody who dishonestly assists in a breach of trust; or somebody who knowingly receives trust property. These parties are known as strangers to the trust and will be discussed later.

10.7.3 To prevent fraud

As we have previously noted the equity jurisdiction has existed to prevent fraud; thus constructive trusts are often imposed to prevent fraud or unconscionable conduct.

Peffer v. Rigg[152]
Mr and Mrs Rigg purchased a house jointly with Mr and Mrs Peffer, legal title being conveyed into Mr Rigg's sole name. Mr Rigg sold the house to

---

150 *Boardman v. Phipps* [1967] 2 AC 46.

151 For example if they receive a bribe: *AG V Reid* [1994] 1 AC 324. However, the use of a constructive trust in these situations is not without criticism, see Andrew D. Hicks, 'The Remedial Principle of *Keech v Samford* Reconsidered' (2010) 69(2) *Cambridge Law Journal* 287-320. In *Sinclair Investments (UK) Ltd v Versailles Trade Finance Ltd (in administrative receivership)*[2011] EWCA Civ 347, the Court of Appeal decided that Reid had been wrongly decided and that there was no proprietary interest merely a personal remedy for the principal against the agent. The Court of Appeal also confirmed that the UK does not have a remedial constructive trust.

152 [1977] 1 WLR 285.

his wife for £1 as part of his divorce settlement. Mr and Mrs Peffer had not entered their interest at the Land Registry but it was held that Mrs Rigg held the property on constructive trust for herself and the Peffers.

Binions v. Evans[153]

Binions purchased a house at a discounted price subject to an express agreement to permit Mrs Evans to live in the property. When Binions sought to evict Mrs Evans, who was merely a contractual licensee, the court held that she had a life interest by way of constructive trust.

10.7.4 When there has been unlawful killing[154]

If a beneficiary under a will or intestacy kills the testator or intestate and thereby acquires legal title to the property a constructive trust will be imposed in order to prevent the killer from benefiting from his crime.[155]

Re Crippen's Estate[156]

Crippen murdered his wife. She died intestate so Crippen was the beneficiary of her estate. Crippen was convicted of his wife's murder and hanged. Crippen had executed a will leaving all his estate to his mistress. In an action for probate Crippen's personal representative was passed over in favour of administration to the wife's next of kin. Sir Samuel Evans commented: 'It is clear that the law is, that no person can obtain, or enforce, any rights resulting to him from his own crime…The human mind revolts at the very idea that any other doctrine could be possible…'[157]

Scotching v Birch[158]

Parents of a boy had separated. The mother killed the son in what she claimed was a suicide pact and was awaiting trial for murder. A dispute arose between the parents over the burial of the son. The son had died intestate and so the parents were entitled equally to his estate and also to

---

153 [1972] Ch 359.
154 Equity has used the constructive trust or constructive trusteeship to combat may types of illegal gain for example in *AG V Reid* [1994] 1 AC 324 a constructive trust was applied to prevent Reid from benefiting from bribes he had received as the Director of Public Prosecutions in Hong Kong.
155 A similar rule of public policy applies if a joint tenant unlawfully kills a fellow joint tenant. The rule of survivorship in the killers favour is disapplied. This is now s.1 of the Forfeiture Act 1982. See John Wilson, 'Death, Severance and Survivorship' [2007] *Fam Law* 1082.
156 [1911] P 108; Sub nom *In the Estate of Cunigunda (Otherwise Cora) Crippen, deceased.*
157 [1911] P 108, at 112, per Sir Samuel Evans.
158 [2008] EWHC 844 (Ch), [2008] All ER (D) 265 (Mar).

his corpse. The father argued that the mother was not entitled because it was a rule of public policy that a person who unlawfully kills another is prohibited from taking a benefit under the will or intestacy of the victim. The court upheld this principle. If any property had passed to the mother she would hold it on constructive trust for her son's estate.

The Forfeiture Act 1982 provides that the rule of public policy preventing anyone from gaining from unlawful killing may be disapplied if the circumstances are such that it would be unjust to enforce the rule. For example, a wife who had been subject to repeated domestic violence and abuse shot her husband dead and was allowed to take the property she inherited from him absolutely and not on constructive trust.[159]

10.7.5 To help parties under a specifically enforceable contract

Because equity considers as done that which ought to be done, the interest of the purchaser of property under a specifically enforceable contract for sale is deemed to arise in equity from the moment that the contract is made. A constructive trust is imposed upon the vendor. Between exchange of contracts and completion the vendor holds the property on trust for the purchaser. It was said in *Lysaght v Edwards*,[160] 'the vendor is a constructive trustee for the purchaser of the estate from the moment the contract is entered into'.

10.7.6 To enforce "special" testamentary trusts

There is some controversy over these examples but it may be that mutual wills, secret trusts and *donationes mortis causa* are enforced by way of constructive trust. Although mutual wills do not comply with the usual principles applicable to the doctrine of wills they are enforced in equity. There is some dispute over how these mutual wills are enforced, some authorities have referred to a contractual basis for enforcing the obligations and other to a 'floating' constructive trust. Similarly, there has been academic debate as to whether a secret trust is an express or implied trust. As enforcement of secret trusts requires communication of the trust obligation to the trustee it may be that they are express trusts; however, if they are express trusts they do not comply with the formalities required in the Wills Act and so should not be valid. Thus they may be enforced by way of the constructive trust. The *Donatio mortis causa* may be considered a constructive trust, as it is a gift made in contemplation of death that is only perfected on the death of the donor and may be recalled at any time before death. Thus the constructive trust crystallises on the death of the donor.

---

159 *Re K (Deceased)* [1986] Fam 180.
160 (1876) 2 Ch D 499, 506.

10.7.7 To give effect to common intentions- the common intention constructive trust

These trusts are used to uphold informal trusts of land which could not be enforced because they lack the formality required for a declaration of such a trust,[161] or for a binding contract.[162] The former situations usually involve domestic homes and the latter commercial relationships. Informal interests in land may arise by way of resulting trust, constructive trust or as a remedy imposed through proprietary estoppel.

For a domestic constructive trust to be declared a common intention to create a trust must be found from the evidence of the parties; this can be either an express agreement or inferred from the facts. When deciding the share held on constructive trust the question that the court must ask is; what proportion is needed fulfil the intention and to address the unconscionability of the legal owner? The use of the common intention constructive trust to settle disputes over ownership of the family home will be considered in detail in chapter 11 **Equity and the Family Home.**

The commercial use of the common intention constructive trust is often referred to as the '*Pallant v Morgan* equity' after the case of **Pallant v Morgan.**[163] These constructive trusts arise because the parties have agreed to enter into a transaction whereby one of them acquires a property and they then exploit it together. The parties have not entered into a binding contract or complied with the requirements of s.2 of the Law of Property (Miscellaneous Provisions) Act 1989, which provides that a contract for the sale or other disposition of an interest in land can only be made in writing. One party acquires the land and then exploits it without the other. Equity will hold that the legal owner of the property holds it on constructive trust for both parties. The constructive trust is effective because s.2(5) of the 1989 Act expressly excludes resulting, implied and constructive trusts from the writing requirements.[164]

The constructive trust is awarded based upon the defendant's unconscionable behaviour in an agreement 'keeping out of the market' the claimant. The agreement has been described as a joint venture and usually involves protracted negotiations but not a binding contract.[165] The main

---

161 S.53(1)(b) LPA 1925.
162 S.2 of the Law of Property (Miscellaneous Provisions) Act 1989.
163 [1953] Ch 43.
164 Similarly it has been held that this requirement does not apply to an interest in land by way of proprietary estoppel. See *Alvina Whittaker v Anthony David Kinnear* [2011] EWHC 1479, at [25], where it is noted that an argument based upon s.2 was rejected in allowing proprietary estoppel in *Thorner v Major* [2009] UKHL 18; [2009] 1 WLR 776 (HL).
165 *Banner Homes Group plc v Luff Development Ltd* [2000] Ch 372; [2000] 2 WLR 772.

problem for a claimant trying to establish that the defendant has acted unconscionably is in establishing that the agreement was a joint venture.

If the parties have negotiated 'subject to contract' and such clauses have been inserted into the negotiation correspondence then there will be no joint venture. In *Kilcarne Holdings Ltd v Targetfollow (Birmingham) Ltd*,[166] the court at first instance found that there was no joint venture because of such clauses. This was upheld by the Court of Appeal which, following *Banner Homes*,[167] clarified that what was required for a successful claim for a constructive trust was:[168]

1   an arrangement or understanding between the parties; and,
2   the claimant must act (usually to their detriment in not taking advantage of a commercial opportunity) in reliance upon this understanding.

In these circumstances it will be unconscionable for the defendant to ignore the understanding and equity will enforce a constructive trust. There is a marked similarity between the commercial common intention constructive trust and proprietary estoppel, a similarity that is echoed in its domestic counterpart and discussed in the next chapter. Thus actions may be based on both.[169] Interestingly, although traditionally categorised as a constructive trust,[170] there has been recent judicial indication, although in a minority, that the better way to consider the equity in *Pallant v Morgan* is by way of holding the defendant to account in equity.[171]

10.8 Summary

In certain circumstances equity will imply that the legal owner of property holds that property subject to a trust in favour of someone else. These implied trusts are usually categorised as either resulting or constructive. A resulting trust may arise in the following circumstances: (i) where an owner transfers their property to another without receiving consideration for the transfer;(ii) where an owner contributes towards the purchase of property that is held in the name of another; (iii) where property is transferred to another to be held on an express trust but the trust fails for

---

166 [2004] EWHC 2547 (Ch).
167 *Banner Homes Group plc v Luff Development Ltd* [2000] Ch 372; [2000] 2 WLR 772.
168 *Kilcarne Holdings Ltd v Targetfollow (Birmingham) Ltd* [2005] EWCA Civ 1355.
169 See *Cobbe v Yeoman's Row* [2008] 1 WLR 1752, where the house of Lords declined to find the claimant had an interest by way of constructive trust or proprietary estoppel.
170 For example Lord Millett was quite clear that this interest is by way of a constructive trust: *Paragon Finance plc v Thakerar* [1999] 1 ITLER 735 at 750.
171 *Crossco No.4 Unlimited v Jolan Ltd* [2011] EWCA Civ 1619 at [88] per Etherton L.J.

some reason; (iv) a failure by the beneficial owner of property to completely dispose of his beneficial interest in the property; and (v) where property is transferred to another for a purpose and the purpose cannot be carried out (this type of resulting trust includes the *Quistclose* trust). In these circumstances the new legal owner will sometimes be regarded as holding the property on trust for the transferor. Resulting trusts of type (i) and (ii) are typically categorised as presumed resulting trusts, whereas type (iii), (iv) and (v) are usually automatic resulting trusts.

The presumption of resulting trust ((i) and (ii) above) is merely a presumption to aid the court when there is no clear or admissible evidence of the intention of the transferor or contributor, perhaps because one or both of the parties involved have died, or where the evidence of the parties may not be relied upon because it is clearly self-serving. The presumption of resulting trust may be rebutted by evidence that the transfer was intended as a gift or loan, or that the transferor and transferee are within recognised categories of family relationship when the presumption of advancement arises and displaces the presumption of resulting trust so that the transfer is regarded as a gift to the transferee. The presumption of advancement may itself be rebutted by evidence that a loan or trust was intended. However, the presumptions of resulting trust and advancement cannot be rebutted by evidence of illegal purposes behind the transfer.

Constructive trusts are difficult to define and classify. There are accepted circumstances when a constructive trust will be imposed on a legal owner. A constructive trust may also be imposed if it would be unconscionable to allow the legal owner of property to assert his legal rights and ignore the beneficial interest of the non-legal owner. Thus most constructive trusts arise when the legal owner of property has received property as a consequence of equitable fraud. However, constructive trusts in England are not available to the courts merely for the sake of justice. Thus they are not remedial but institutional, that is their recognition and enforcement by the court is dependent on accepted circumstances.

PART 3
RIGHTING WRONGS

CHAPTER 11
EQUITY AND THE FAMILY HOME

11.1 Equity and women's property rights

The common law has, until relatively recently, largely ignored the independent property rights of women, especially a married woman who was regarded as a 'shadow of her husband'.[1] The Chancellor has from the early years of the separate equity jurisdiction intervened to protect women's property rights with the trust. In the last chapter we considered the case of **Wassell v Leggatt,**[2] where a husband had forcibly deprived his wife of a legacy she received during her marriage. The woman had no right to property independent of her husband; this right only arose after the Married Women's Property Act 1882 was implemented. However, equity was able to recognise and protect her interest in the legacy by way of the constructive trust. We have also seen that equity presumed any transfer of property into a wife's name or contribution towards property purchased in a wife's name by a husband did not give rise to the presumption of resulting trust but was presumed advancement.[3]

It may seem strange that even today, after legislation designed to promote equality has been passed in almost all areas of the law, property rights for some women are still only protected by way of the law of trusts, a law which has become more suited to commercial purposes than disputes over the family home.[4]

---

1   A relatively recent judicial pronouncement: *Caunce v Caunce* [1969] 1 WLR 286.
2   [1896] 1 Ch 554
3   See for example *Kingdon v Bridges* (1688) 2 Vern 68; *Bennet v Bennet* (1879) 10 Ch. D. 474.
4   Anne Barlow & Craig Lind, 'A matter of trust: the allocation of rights in the family home' (1999) 19 *Legal Studies* 468-488.

11.2 The problems with cohabiting

When a couple decide to live together, whether they marry or decide to cohabit without marrying, they often do not consider what will happen to the property they live in if their relationship ends. Cohabiting may involve one partner moving into a property already owned by the other party, or the purchase of a property together. Traditionally the marital home was held in the name of the husband alone and even today married and unmarried couples may decide to hold the family home in the name of one partner only because of mortgage requirements or other financial obligations. However the property is held, both parties may contribute to its purchase through contributions to the deposit, paying legal fees and mortgage payments. Once the property has been bought one income may be used for mortgage payments and the other used for general household expenses such as food and utility bills. Unfortunately there is a chance that the relationship will break down. Relationships of love and affection are often based upon implied trust not express trust, therefore there is rarely an express agreement that the sole legal owner of the family home holds the property on trust for both, if there is an agreement it will usually have been expressed orally, not in writing. If the relationship breaks down then there will often be dispute over the ownership of the most valuable family asset; the family home. The most bitter of disputes usually occur on the break-up of a relationship and may be exacerbated by financial difficulties which may have contributed to the end of the relationship and involve claims against one or both of the parties by a third party, usually a bank or building society, for possession and sale of the domestic home.[5] If the couple are married or in a civil partnership the Matrimonial Causes Act 1973, ss. 23-25A, gives the court 'almost limitless' discretionary power on divorce to decide the division of the property between the parties.[6] However, if the couple are unmarried there may be problems ensuring both parties get their 'fair' share of the family home as the law is only interested in enforcing ownership by reference to the principles of land law and the law of trusts.[7]

---

5   See Simone Wong, 'Constructive trusts over the family home: lessons to be learned from other commonwealth jurisdictions?' (1998) 18(3) *Legal Studies* 369-390.

6   *Thomas v Thomas* [1995] 2 FLR 668 (EWCA), per Waite L.J. However, the ability of the court to 'encourage' the trustee of a discretionary trust to select one of the parties to a divorce to receive benefits for distribution in the divorce suggested in *Thomas v Thomas* has been doubted in *TL v ML (Ancillary Relief: Claim Against Assets of Extended Family)* [2005] EWHC 2860 (Fam), at [85], by Nicholas Mostyn Q.C. Reference to marriage in this chapter should also be considered to include a civil partnership recognised under the Civil Partnership Act 2004.

7   See the comments of Lord Diplock in *Gissing v Gissing* [1971] AC 866 at 905-906, quoted below at text to footnote 25.

There may also be problems if the legal owner of the family home dies intestate. The court has power under the Inheritance (Provision for Family and Dependants) Act 1975 to order provision for the survivor but will only order this if it is satisfied the survivor was dependant on the deceased and the deceased failed to provide adequate provision for the survivor in his will. Often a claim under the Inheritance (Provision for Family and Dependants) Act 1975 will include linked or alternative claims that there was a trust of the cohabited property.

Re Estate of David John Evans, Deceased[8]

The deceased's partner claimed an interest in a property registered in the sole name of the deceased by way of constructive trust, and the bulk of his estate under the Act. The court rejected the constructive trust claim but allowed the survivor a cash sum from the estate to be used to purchase a property for her to reside in for life. The property was then to go to the deceased's sons.

Confusion over property rights is not helped by the term 'common-law marriage', which has no analogous legal recognition in England and most common law jurisdictions.[9] It has been suggested that unmarried cohabiting couples should be given the same protection and rights as married couples. However, this has not been effected in England yet as marriage and now civil partnerships are seen as important institutions for social cohesion and so generally beneficial to society, and thus accorded a special status at law. In fact if the parties are not married or in a civil partnership then the court may infer that strict separation of finances was intended.[10]

Many of the cases in this chapter are from the 1970s and 1980s in England as this was the time of the development of this area of the law. The cases often involve married couples, as the Matrimonial Causes Act was not enacted until 1973 and the courts have continued to consider the law of trusts when dividing the family home on divorce.

11.3 How does equity decide to divide?

The courts have approached the division of the family home on a different basis from commercial property, as persons 'engaged in business can be

---

8   [2011] EWHC 945 (Ch).
9   Although see de facto wife according to custom and the presumption of advancement: *Cheung Pui Yuen v Worldcup Investments Inc* [2008] HKCU 1669 (CFA).
10 For example, in Hong Kong Tong D.J. noted: "But the fact that the parties are not married, may well be a pointer that their respective independent separate interests should be recognised." *Lui Kam Lau v Leung Ming Fai* [1994] 3 HKC 477, 488.

regarded as capable of looking after themselves'.[11] The leading case on informal trusts of the family is the House of Lords decision in *Stack v Dowden*.[12] The House of Lords attempted to clarify how a court should approach the problem of division of the family home.[13] Recently the Supreme Court has revisited this area in *Jones v Kernott*,[14] and approved and clarified much of the guidance in *Stack v Dowden*.

Note
In *Stack v Dowden* the House of Lords emphasised that these principles apply only to non-commercial family arrangements.

Although in *Jones v Kernott*,[15] Lord Walker and Lady Hale gave a joint judgment in which they emphasised the different approach that should be taken for properties held in joint or single names, it is submitted that in all these cases the court is faced with two questions:

1 Is there an interest? And, if there is,
2 How much should each party get?

If there has been a written declaration of trust which complies with s.53(1)(b) of the Law of Property Act 1925, specifically it is manifested and proved in writing, then the court will enforce this even though it does not conform to the legal title, unless a party can prove that this does not represent the parties intentions or that these intentions changed and the court should give effect to the change.

Goodman v Gallant [16]
A husband and wife purchased a house in the husband's sole name. They then divorced and the husband sold the house to his ex-wife and her new boyfriend at a discount to reflect the divorce settlement to the ex-wife. The unmarried couple bought the house with an express clause in the conveyance that they purchased as joint tenants. When the couple later separated the wife tried to claim more of a share in the property to reflect her ex-husband's discount of the price. The court held that the express declaration should be followed and the property divided equally.

---

11 *Royal Bank of Scotland v Etridge (No 2)* [202] 2 AC 773 at 88, per Lord Nicholls of Birkenhead.
12 [2007] UKHL 17; 1 FLR 1858.
13 However there has been some academic debate about the value of the judgment in Stack in clarifying this area of the law, see for example Martin Dixon, 'The never-ending story: co-ownership after *Stack v Dowden*' [2007] 71 *Conv.* 456, and Mathew Harding, 'Defending *Stack v Dowden*' [2009] *Conv* 309.
14 [2011] UKSC 53.
15 [2011] UKSC 53, at [52] per Lord Walker and Lady Hale.
16 [1986] Fam 106.

In recent years it has become popular, especially amongst the wealthy, to draw up a pre-nuptial agreement. This is an agreement made between the parties as to the division of property on the eventual break-up of the marriage. The traditional position of the English courts was to disregard these agreements, as, whilst they might not constitute an encouragement to divorce, they were not seen as in-line with the traditional English belief that marriage was forever. In fact they might be regarded as similar to trusts which contain provision for the couple on separation which have been traditionally declared void for offending public policy.[17] However, recent judicial direction is that the courts may take account of these agreements, as long as they are freely entered into and there is no evidence of duress, fraud or misrepresentation, but they are not binding on the courts.[18] It has been suggested that an post-nuptial agreement, an agreement after marriage would be even more persuasive for a court as the parties have the rights of the married couple on marriage and have subsequently agreed to vary these rights.[19]

If there is no express declaration of trust the court will consider how the legal title to the property is held. If it is in joint names then section 1 of the Law of Property Act 1925 provides that it must be held as joint tenants. Although the parties can hold the beneficial interest as joint tenants or tenants in common, there is a strong presumption that equity follows the law and thus there is a presumption that the beneficial interest is held jointly with the consequent right of survivorship.[20] It is up to the party disputing such equal beneficial ownership to bring evidence to support this and rebut the presumption.

Note
The burden of proof is on the party seeking to establish an interest or a change in beneficial interest from the legal interest, as he who asserts must

---

17 For example, in *Westmeath (Earl) v Countess of Westmeath* (1821) Jac 126, Lord Eldon queried an agreement to pay an annuity to a wife whilst the couple was separated as it might prevent the future reconciliation of the couple.

18 *Radmacher (formerly Granatino) v Granatino* [2010] UKSC 42: the Supreme Court advocated following a prenuptial agreement unless it would be unfair to do so.

19 The author is grateful for these suggestions to the noted English family law practitioner Mr Frederick Cosgrove-Gibson. For an example of a post-nuptial agreement which was not freely entered into and was subject to misrepresentation and so not binding see *Jenna Kremen v Boris Agrest* [2012] EWHC 45 (Fam).

20 The right of survivorship or *ius accresendi* provides that on the death of any joint tenant the other joint tenants automatically own all of the interest in the property between them. The deceased has no devisable separate interest and so his 'share' is subsumed into the overall interest of his joint tenants.

prove. As these cases are civil then the burden of proof is the balance of probabilities, the party seeking to establish an interest or a change in interest will have to prove to the court that it was more likely than not that the interest was held as they claim.

Goodman v Carlton[21]

Mr. Goodman purchased his house which was conveyed into his name and that of Mrs Carlton, whose name was necessary to secure mortgage finance. Mr. Goodman told Mrs Carlton that her name would be taken off the legal title after one year. Mr. Goodman made all of the mortgage repayments and lived alone in the house. Mr. Goodman died intestate and the question arose as to whether Mrs Carlton had acquired the property beneficially by survivorship,[22] or whether she held the property on resulting trust for Mr. Goodman's estate. The Court of Appeal held that she held the property on resulting trust for the estate as Mr. Goodman had purchased the property himself, and Mrs Carlton's assistance was only temporary and nominal.

If the property is in a single name then equity will again follow the law and presume that the property is held beneficially in line with legal title.

Note

The most problematic cases involve property held in a single name when the couple are unmarried.

In a single name case it is up to the party disputing beneficial interest following legal title to establish they have an interest. Thus the court must again consider the two questions:[23]

1   Does the party asserting an interest have an interest? And, if he or she does then
2   What is that interest?

In considering the first question, if there is an express declaration of trust proved in writing then it will be enforced.[24] If there is no written evidence of an express trust then equity will only recognise and enforce interests if they can be established using recognised trust principles. As Lord Diplock stated in *Gissing v Gissing*:[25]

---

21   [2002] EWCA Civ; 5452 FLR 259.
22   In the UK legal title to property can only be held as joint tenants, s.1 of the Law of Property Act 1925, thus survivorship applies. However, the beneficial interest may be held as tenants in common.
23   *Jones v Kernott* [2011] UKSC 53, at [52] per Lord Walker and Lady Hale.
24   Complying with the formality requirements of s.53(1)(b) of the Law of Property Act 1925.
25   [1971] AC 886 UKHL

'Any claim to a beneficial interest in land by a person, whether spouse or stranger, in whom the legal estate in the land is not vested must be based upon the proposition that the person in whom the legal estate is vested holds it as a trustee upon trust to give effect to the beneficial interest of the claimant as *cestui que trust*. The legal principles applicable to the claim are those of the English law of trusts and in particular, in the kind of dispute between spouses that comes before the courts, the law relating to the creation and operation of "resulting, implied or constructive trusts".'[26]

Thus, if the couple are unmarried the law does not provide for the division of their home except by recognised property law principles. The beneficial interest will follow the legal estate unless the non-legal 'owner' can rely on the following principles:

1　The resulting trust;
2　The constructive trust;
3　Proprietary estoppel.

As most couples do not write down the private agreements that they have reached, then any agreement is unenforceable unless these three principles can apply.

Note
Equity is able to enforce these informal interests because s.53(2) of the Law of Property Act 1925 provides that implied, resulting and constructive trusts do not have to comply with the formality requirements in s.53(1)(b) and so do not have to be evidenced in writing.

Note
Section 2 of the Law of Property (Miscellaneous Provisions) Act 1989 provides that a contract for the sale or other disposition of an interest in land can only be made in writing. However, s.2(5) expressly excludes resulting, implied and constructive trusts. Similarly it has been held that this requirement does not apply to an interest in land by way of proprietary estoppel.[27]

So the problems are that couples often do not formally agree that the property they are to live in is to be held on trust and, even if they do agree on this, they do not agree on how much each party is to get if the relationship breaks down. These are questions that equity can resolve

---

26　[1971] AC 886, per Lord Diplock at 905-906. See also Lord Morris of Borth-y-Gest comments confirming this at 900.

27　See *Alvina Whittaker v Anthony David Kinnear* [2011] EWHC 1479, at [25], where it is noted that an argument based upon s.2 was rejected in allowing proprietary estoppel in *Thorner v Major* [2009] UKHL 18; [2009] 1 WLR 776 (HL).

through the use of resulting trust, constructive trust, or proprietary estoppel.

Note

There is a simple solution to this problem as noted by Lord Ward:[28]

"Perhaps conveyancers do not read the law reports. I will try one more time: always try to agree on and then record how the beneficial interest is to be held. It is not very difficult to do."

In defence of conveyancers it should be noted that trying to tell a couple who are embarking on a romantic undertaking, which involves the purchase of property or letting one party move into the other's property, that they should plan for their eventual break-up probably requires an enormous amount of tact and would often result in very unhappy clients. The addition of a box to clarify the beneficial interest in the property on the form for registration of transfers of land may have helped reduce the incidence of these disputes,[29] but of course this will not help where a party is moving into a property already owned by their new partner.

Therefore, informal interest in the family home may arise by way of resulting trust, constructive trust, or as a remedy imposed through proprietary estoppel.

11.4 Resulting trust

An interest in a family home by way of resulting trust will be a presumption of resulting trust and thus rebuttable. We have already considered resulting trusts and the presumption that a party who contributes money to the purchase price of a property will intend to retain an interest in that property.[30] Therefore, a resulting trust arises in favour of a contributor to the purchase price of property but only by direct contributions to the purchase price. Thus the only question that concerns the court is - what proportion of the purchase price did the claimant contributed? Under the traditional principles of equity and the resulting trust the contribution gave rise to a proportionate share in the property. A contribution of 10% of purchase price would give rise to a 10% beneficial interest in the property.

There has been some confusion over what contributions would constitute a contribution giving rise to an interest by way of resulting trust. In *Curley v Parkes*[31] Peter Gibson L.J. stated that only direct contributions

---

28   *Goodman v Carlton* [2002] EWCA Civ; 5452 FLR 259.

29   This box is in the official Land Registry application form (TR1). See the comments in *Jones v Kernott* [2011] UKSC 53, at [18], Lord Walker and Lady Hale, and Moran, 'Anything to Declare? Express Declarations of Trust in *Stack v Dowden*' [2007] 74 *Conv* 364.

30   *Dyer v Dyer* (1788) 2 Cox Eq Cas 92.

31   [2004] EWCA Civ 1515; [2004] All ER (D) 344 (Oct).

to purchase price would give rise to such an interest.

Curley v Parkes[32]

Ms Parkes purchased a house in which to cohabit with Mr Curley. She contributed approximately 10% of the purchase price by way of sale of her previous property and savings. The remaining 90% was financed by way of mortgage in her sole name. From the beginning of their residence in the house the couple contributed similar amounts to a joint bank account from which household expenses including the mortgage payments were paid. Within a year Mr Curley's employer asked him to relocate and agreed to finance the relocation. The employer purchased the property from Ms Parkes and paid relocation expenses including removal expenses, solicitors fees and a contribution to increased mortgage payments consequent on buying a new house. Ms Parkes purchased the new more expensive property in her sole name with an increased mortgage which again represented nearly 90% of the purchase price. Mr Curley received £8,500 from his employers as part of the relocation scheme and a further £260 monthly for the increased mortgage. Mr Curley did not pay anything to the purchase price but did pay £9,000 into Ms Parke's bank account afterwards which he later claimed was to repay the deposit. Mr Curley also paid £8,000 into the joint account. Within a year the relationship had ended and Mr Curley claimed an interest in the property and an order that it should be sold. Mr Curley claimed an interest by way of resulting trust as he had contributed £9,000 to Ms Parkes' bank account, paid the legal fees and stamp duty of £2,800 and the removal costs of £1,500, some 9% of the purchase price. Peter Gibson LJ found all these payments to have been made subsequent to purchase of the property and so not giving rise to a resulting trust.[33]

It should be noted that Peter Gibson L.J. did note that these contributions might give rise to an interest by way of constructive trust if there was an express agreement that Ms Parkes held the property on trust or might be circumstances from which a court could infer or imply a constructive trust.[34] Furthermore if there were an interest by way of constructive trust then these contributions would be relevant in quantifying that interest.

Thus it seems that only direct contributions to the purchase price of the property will be enough to give rise to an interest by way of resulting trust, thus contributions to the deposit or taking out the mortgage in your name at the time of purchase. Payment of consequent or associated costs of purchase or payment of the subsequent mortgage payments will not be enough to raise the presumption. This is because when considering an

32   [2004] EWCA Civ 1515; [2004] All ER (D) 344 (Oct).
33   [2004] EWCA Civ 1515 at paras [21]–[21].
34   [2004] EWCA Civ 1515 at paras [14]–[15].

interest by way of resulting trust the court has traditionally considered that the interest of the parties crystallizes at the time of purchase. However, as we have already noted, the resulting trust was originally an instrument of equity created for commercial relationships and reflected the presumptions of equity as to men of business investing their money in property and always wishing to retain an interest. The proportionate share was therefore a presumption for commercial relationships. In **Stack v Dowden,**[35] it was stated that if a property is purchased in joint names for cohabitation as a family home there is a strong presumption that the beneficial interest is held on trust jointly, that is in equal shares.[36] This has been more firmly stated by the Supreme Court in **Jones v Kernott:**[37]

'The time has come to make it clear…that in the case of the purchase of a house or a flat in *joint names* [emphasis added] for joint occupation by a married or unmarried couple, where both are responsible for any mortgage, there is no presumption of a resulting trust arising from their having contributed to the deposit (or indeed the rest of the purchase) in unequal shares. The presumption is that the parties intended a joint tenancy both in law and equity. But that intention can of course be rebutted by evidence of a contrary intention, which may more readily be shown where the parties did not share their financial resources.'

Example
In 2008 Peter and Mary buy a flat in Leeds for £200,000. Peter contributes £50,000 and Mary £100,000. The balance is paid by mortgage to which they contribute equally. The couple has now separated and sold the flat. After settling the outstanding mortgage there is a balance remaining of £300,000. If the presumption of resulting trust is applied then the sale price should be divided, after repaying the mortgage, in the ratio 1:2 for Peter and Mary, i.e. Peter will receive £100,000 and Mary £200,000. This would seem to fairly reflect a commercial arrangement unless contrary express terms had been included. However, if **Stack v Dowden** is followed the sale price should be divided equally and both will receive £150,000.

Thus the presumption of resulting trust no longer applies to a property

---

35   [2007] UKHL 17; 1 FLR 1858.
36   [2009] UKHL 18; [2009] 1 WLR 776 (HL). It is worth noting however, that, although *Stack v Dowden* is considered highly persuasive in all common law jurisdictions, this rebuttal of the proportionate nature of the resulting trust for a domestic home may not apply everywhere, for example, s.9 of the Conveyancing and Property Ordinance in Hong Kong provides a statutory presumption that a tenancy in common arises in the conveyance of property into two or more names without contrary indication.
37   [2011] UKSC 53, at [25], per Lord Walker and Lady Hale.

bought for domestic use and conveyed into joint names.[38] In these circumstances a joint beneficial interest will be presumed resulting in equal beneficial interests. This presumption of joint beneficial interest is justified by claims that the decision to put the property into joint names would almost always have been a conscious decision and so must be given different consideration from the single name cases. Also it seemed unfair to adopt a stricter approach for joint name cases when single name cases, as we shall see, have been decided using the more flexible common intention constructive trust, taking note of all contributions to family life, even though the circumstances also gave rise to a presumption of resulting trust. Thus joint name cases immediately give both parties an interest in the property. After this the questions to be asked in joint name cases were not simply, 'what is the extent of the parties' beneficial interests?' but, 'did the parties intend their beneficial interests to be different from their legal interests?' and 'if they did, in what way and to what extent?' When considering this the court was 'seeking to ascertain the parties' shared intentions, actual, inferred or imputed, with respect to the property, in the light of their whole course of conduct in relation to it. This could be done by 'undertaking a survey of the whole course of dealing between the parties and taking account of all conduct which threw light on the question what shares were intended'. Thus the court could take 'a wide view of what contributions were to be taken into account, while remaining sceptical of the value of alleged improvements that were really insignificant, or elaborate arguments, suggestive of creative accounting, as to how the family finances were arranged'. This is very similar to the approach a court takes in quantifying interest in the family home once an interest by way of common intention constructive trust has been established. However, the House of Lords noted that, ultimately, cases in which joint legal owners would be taken to have intended that their beneficial interests should be different from their legal interests would be very unusual.

Of course this presumption of joint beneficial interest is again merely a presumption and may be rebutted; however, the burden of displacing the presumption of equal beneficial interest would be upon the person seeking to show that the parties had intended their beneficial interests to be different from their legal interests. In the ordinary domestic case it would be difficult to establish to the court's satisfaction that an intention to keep a sort of balance sheet of contributions existed, or should be inferred or imputed to joint-owners. Thus the presumption of joint beneficial interest would be rebutted only in 'very unusual' circumstances which are exemplified in the facts of *Stack v Dowden* itself.

---

38 This approach had been considered in earlier family cases and noted as an 'old' approach by Lord Denning in *Bernard v Josephs* [1982] Ch 391 at p397.

Stack v Dowden[39]

The unmarried couple had cohabited for over 20 years and had four children. Their first home had been purchased in the woman's sole name, using funds from an account in her sole name plus a mortgage in her name and had been offered to her at a favourable price under the terms of a will. The couple did a great deal of work together on improvements to the property. After 10 years the property was sold and the new home was conveyed into joint names. The purchase price was made up of the proceeds from the first property, plus the woman's substantial savings, plus a mortgage in the couple's joint names. Over time, the mortgage loan was repaid by a series of lump sum payments, to which both contributed, although the woman made more than half the contributions. Throughout the period of the cohabitation, the couple kept separate bank accounts and made separate investments and savings. After the couple separated the man sought an order for sale and equal division of the property; the woman claimed that she was entitled to 65% of the property, having contributed far more than the man. Their Lordships noted that to establish that a jointly owned property is not also owned jointly in equity the party seeking to establish this must bring highly cogent evidence that this was not the parties' intention. This case was a very unusual one, as, although the couple had cohabited for a long time and had four children together, they had kept their financial affairs rigidly separate. This was strongly indicative that they did not intend their share to be held equally. The woman was awarded 65% of the house.

Thus the presumption of resulting trust will arise if a party has contributed to the purchase price of the property. If the property is in a single name then the extent of the interest will be proportionate to the contribution to purchase price.[40] If the property is in joint names then the presumption of resulting trust does not arise as it is displaced by the legal title which is considered an indication of an intent to share the property. Thus registration of the property in joint names, even if the parties have contributed unequally to purchase or one party has not contributed at all, will result in a presumption of joint beneficial ownership.

11.5 Constructive trust

An interest in the family home can also arise by way of constructive trust. We have already considered constructive trusts and their enforcement to prevent unconscionable behaviour. In this area of the law the constructive trust has been enforced to uphold the common intentions of the parties.

---

39   [2007] UKHL 17; 1 FLR 1858.
40   This will apply even if the parties intended to purchase in joint names but were advised not to: *Thomas v Hurst* (CA) 30 March 2012.

The concept of the common intention constructive trust may be traced back to the comments of the House of Lords in *Gissing v. Gissing:*[41]

'Where there was a common intention at the time of the acquisition of the house that the beneficial interest should be shared. It would be a breach of faith by the spouse in whose name the legal estate was vested to fail to give effect to that intention and the other spouse will be held entitled to a share in the beneficial interest.'[42]

The common intention constructive trust is usually enforced in single name cases when the legal and non-legal owner have agreed a common intention that the property will be held by the legal owner for the benefit of them both, and the legal owner is now refusing to honour this common intention and recognise the non-legal owner's interest. So either one party has moved into a property owned by their partner and a promise has been made that the legal owner holds the property on trust for them both, or the couple purchase a house together but register title only in the name of one of them. Equity will enforce the agreement through the constructive trust because the legal owner is acting unconscionably.

The express common intention constructive trust applies only to land, as it is only necessary to infer a constructive trust in order to avoid the formality requirements for an enforceable trust of land in s.53(1)(b) LPA.[43]

Rowe v. Prance[44]

Miss Rowe and Mr Prance enjoyed a close relationship for 14 years, during which time Prance made numerous promises that he would live with and marry Miss Rowe. Mr Prance purchased a boat with his own money, registered in his name, and with the intention that the parties would live on it and sail the world. Mr Prance told Miss Rowe that the boat could not be registered in her name because she did not have the requisite sailing certificate. Miss Rowe negotiated the purchase of the boat and gave up her rented accommodation to live on it. Mr Prance often referred to the boat as "ours". Two years later the relationship broke down and Miss Rowe

---

41 [1971] AC 886. However, the term common intention constructive trust was first used in 1988 in English academic writing and 1999 in an English judicial decision, *Mollo v Mollo*, 8 October 1999, Chancery Division, cited by Paul Matthews, 'The Words Which Are Not There: A Partial History of the Constructive Trust', in Charles Mitchell (ed), *Constructive and Resulting Trusts*, Hart Publishing, Oxford, 2009, p. 24. Matthews' chapter discusses the development of proprietary estoppel and the common intention constructive trust.

42 [1971] AC 886, at 900, per Lord Morris of Borth-y-Gest agreeing with Lord Diplock.

43 *Rowe v. Prance* [1999] 2 F.L.R. 787; [2000] W.T.L.R. 249.

44 [1999] 2 F.L.R. 787; [2000] W.T.L.R. 249; [1999] Fam. Law 623; [1999] E.G. 75 (C.S.); (1999) 96(21) L.S.G. 41.

claimed an interest in the boat by way of either express trust or common intention constructive trust. Mr Nicholas Warren QC held, following Paul v Constance,[45] that Mr Prance had effectively declared himself a trustee of the boat for them both in equal shares. Mr Warren did not have to consider the issue of the constructive trust argument as the express trust was not subject to any formalities associated with land.

11.6 Requirements for a common intention constructive trust

In *Lloyds Bank plc v Rosset*,[46] Lord Bridge of Harwich outlined the three elements required for the claimant to establish that she had an interest by way of common intention constructive trust. The claimant must establish:

1 that there was a common intention that the legal owner held the property on trust for the couple;
2 That the claimant relied on this bargain to her detriment; and,
3 That the legal owner's assertion of his legal interest ignoring the claimant's interest was unconscionable.

We will consider these factors individually although it should be noted that they often overlap, for example the circumstances giving rise to the common intention will also establish detrimental reliance and unconscionability. In fact once the claimant has established a common intention and detrimental reliance upon this then unconscionability on the part of the legal owner will normally follow.

11.6.1 Common intention: the bargain

The obvious first factor for the claimant to establish is the common intention that the legal owner held the property for the benefit of them both. As Lord Bridge stated in *Lloyds Bank plc v Rosset* this could be by way of:[47]

1 An express bargain; or,
2 An implied bargain;

The express bargain common intention constructive trust
Lord Bridge identified the express bargain in the following terms:

'The first and fundamental question which must always be resolved is whether, independently of any inference to be drawn from the conduct of the parties in the course of sharing the house as their home and managing their joint affairs, there has at any time prior to acquisition, or exceptionally at some later date, been any agreement, arrangement or understanding reached between them that the property is to be shared beneficially. The

45   [1977] 1 WLR 527
46   [1991] 1 AC 107.
47   [1991] 1 AC 107, at 132.

finding of an agreement or arrangement to share in this sense can only, I think, be based on evidence of express discussions between the partners, however imperfectly remembered and however imprecise their terms may have been. Once a finding to this effect is made it will only be necessary for the partner asserting a claim to a beneficial interest against the partner entitled to the legal estate to show that he or she has acted to his or her detriment or significantly altered his or her position in reliance on the agreement in order to give rise to a constructive trust or a proprietary estoppel.'[48]

Therefore, express agreement must be just that, express. There must be express discussion between the parties, as was subsequently clarified by Dillon L.J.:

'It is not enough to establish a common intention which is sufficient to found an implied or constructive trust of land that each of them happened at the same time to have been thinking on the same lines in his or her uncommunicated thoughts while neither had any knowledge of the thinking of the other.'[49]

Thus there must be an express discussion between the parties, although it has been noted by academic writers that the reality of cohabiting relationships is that silence is often taken as indicating positive assent.[50] Furthermore, the discussion that forms the basis of the agreement will usually occur prior to the parties acquiring the property and only unusually will it occur subsequently, for example when a party moves into the property already owned by the other party. The agreement does not have to include specification of the size of the parties' respective interests.[51]

Strangely the express discussion does not actually have to conclude with an express agreement that the legal owner holds the home on trust but may be as to why one of the parties cannot be on the legal title to the property.

Grant v Edwards[52]

The woman was involved in divorce proceedings relating to a previous failed relationship. In discussions between the parties in respect of the woman's beneficial interest in the property with her new partner he said she should not be on the legal title as it might reduce the amount she would receive in the active divorce proceedings. The property was

---

48 [1991] 1 AC 107 at p.132.
49 *Springette v Defoe* (1992) 65 P & CR 1; (1992) 24 H.L.R. 552, at 557 per Dillon L.J.
50 A. Bottomley, 'Self and Subjectivities: Language of Claim in Property' (1993) 20(1) (Spring) *Journal of Law & Society* 63, 64.
51 *Drake v Whipp* [1996] 1 FLR 826.
52 [1986] Ch 638.

conveyed into the man's sole name. When the couple separated the court held the woman was entitled to a share in the home, as there was a clear inference from their discussions that they had a common intention that she would have a share.

Note
It seems that the court may infer an agreement to share from an excuse not to do so.

Eves v Eves[53]
The property was registered in the man's sole name. The woman made no financial contribution to the property but contributed to its renovation including breaking up ground with a 14lb sledgehammer. The couple discussed the possibility of the woman having a share of the property but the man told her she was under 21 and thus too young to be on the title deeds. The court held the discussions were evidence of an express common intention that she was to have a share and her renovation work acts to her detriment in reliance upon the belief that she had an interest in the property. Therefore she was entitled to a share in the property.'

Hammond v Mitchell[54]
The title to the property was conveyed to the man's sole name on his assurance that the woman need not 'fear for the future because when we are married [the house] will be half yours anyway…' The court held this statement to express the common intention that she had an interest.

Recently, in **Stack v Dowden**,[55] Lord Neuberger, in his dissenting judgment, referred to the court's ability to infer an intention from objective deduction, this would represent the subjective intention of the parties, and also the court's ability to impute an intention from the evidence which may attribute an intention to the parties even though they had no such intention.[56] This may explain the cases where the courts have taken an excuse not to agree, probably indicating the party's intention not to share the property, as evidence of an express agreement. However, this 'lurking

---

53   [1975] 3 All ER 768.
54   [1991] 1 WLR 1127.
55   *Stack v Dowden* [2007] 2 AC 432.
56   *Stack v Dowden* [2007] 2 AC 432, at 472 para [126]. Of course Nick Piska in 'Intention, Fairness and the Presumption of Resulting Trust after *Stack v Dowden*' (2008) 71 MLR 120, has noted that, 'Subjective intentions can never be accessed directly, so the court must always direct itself to a consideration of the parties' objective intentions through a careful consideration of the relevant facts.' As noted by the Supreme Court in *Jones v Kernott*[2011] UKSC 53, at [34], per Lord Walker and Lady Hale.

imprecision' does not make it any easier to apply,[57] and the ability to discern an express agreement to beneficially share property from an express agreement not to have joint legal ownership has been criticised.[58] Lord Bridge's first category of common intention constructive trust thus relies on an express discussion between the parties.

The implied bargain common intention constructive trust
Lord Bridge's second category is the implied common intention constructive trust. This relies on an implied bargain between the parties based upon the circumstances of the cohabitation and was founded upon Lord Diplock's comments in *Gissing v. Gissing*:[59]

'But parties to a transaction in connection with the acquisition of land may well have formed a common intention that the beneficial interest in the land shall be vested in them jointly without having used express words to communicate this intention to one another; or their recollections of the words used may be imperfect or conflicting by the time any dispute arises. In such The court can use that conduct to infer a common intention to share the equitable interest. This has led to judicial and academic debate on what contributions the court can take into account to infer a common intention. The debate has centred upon indirect financial contributions to the upkeep of the household, especially a wife or partner using her income to meet household expenses when the husband or other partner's income is used to pay the mortgage. This debate originated with Lord Diplock's comment in *Gissing v Gissing*,[61] that if a wife used her income to meet household expenses:

'...this would be consistent with and might be corroborative of an original common intention that she should share in the beneficial interest in the matrimonial home and that her payment of other household expenses were intended by both spouses to be treated as including a contribution by the wife to the purchase price of the matrimonial home '

---

57 Simon Gardner, 'Family property today' (2008) 124 *L.Q.R.* 422.
58 See P. Clarke, 'The Family Home: Intention and Agreement' [1992] 22 *Fam Law* 724; Simon Gardner, 'Rethinking Family Property' (1993) 109 *L.Q.R.* 263. Although some commentators have defended this approach arguing that the test for finding the relevant joint intention of the parties should be objective and not subjective, thus it should not matter what the party making the statement thought: see John Mee, *Property rights of Cohabitees*, Hart Publishing, Oxford, 1999; Nicola Glover & Paul Todd, 'The myth of common intention' (1996) 16 *Legal Studies* 325. Of course this ignores the requirement that the intention must be 'common' to the parties.
59 [1971] AC 886.
60 [1971] AC 886, at 906 per Lord Diplock.
61 [1971] AC 866.

Such comments might be taken to imply that the court has a wide power to construe from the conduct of the parties that they intended the property to be held beneficially for them both. This was the basis for Lord Denning's 'New Model' constructive trust referred to in the last chapter. Lord Denning was of the view that the constructive trust should be applied whenever 'justice and good conscience require',[62] thus, in the previously mentioned *Eves v Eves*,[63] Lord Denning's judgment focused on the woman's contributions to renovating the property, in particular the wielding of a 14lb sledgehammer. However, the new model constructive trust was criticised for importing 'palm-tree justice' into the law,[64] conjuring to the mind 'the image of a potentate stretched out under a palm-tree, dispensing justice to his subjects upon the whim of the moment.[65] The House of Lords rejected the remedial constructive trust in favour of the traditional institutional approach.[66]

There have been cases where the courts have inferred a bargain from the circumstances of the relationship but these have usually focused on the joint maintenance of the property.[67] Judicial discussion of implied bargains has reiterated that contributions from which the court may infer a bargain must be directly referable to the property.

Burns v Burns[68]

The unmarried couple had lived together for 19 years. The woman had stayed at home to care for their two children. When the relationship ended the woman claimed a share of the property based on her indirect contributions to their living expenses. The court held that they were not entitled to take domestic duties and later contributions to household expenses into account. May LJ said:

'When the house is taken in the man's name alone, if the woman makes no "real" or "substantial" financial contribution towards either the purchase price, deposit or mortgage instalments by the means of which the family home was acquired, then she is not entitled to any share in the beneficial interest in that home even though over a very substantial number of years she may have worked just as hard as the man in maintaining the family.'[69]

---

62 *Hussey v Palmer* [1972] 3 All ER 744.
63 [1975] 3 All ER 768.
64 *Springette v Defoe* [1992] 2 FLR 388 (EWCA), per Dillon L.J.
65 John Mee, 'Property rights of Cohabitees' (Hart Publishing: 1999).
66 In fact Lord Diplock's common intention constructive trust has been criticised as being contrary ot the principles of English trust law: see Lord Browne-Wilkinson 'Constructive Trusts and Unjust Enrichment' [1996] 10 *TLI* 98 – 101.
67 *Grant v Edwards* [1986] Ch 638.
68 [1984] Ch 317.
69 [1984] Ch 317, 345.

In *Lloyds Bank plc v Rosset*,[70] Lord Bridge attempted to clarify the circumstances and contributions from which the court could infer a common intention:[71]

'Where the court must rely entirely on the conduct of the parties…to infer a common intention to share the property beneficially and…to give rise to a constructive trust. In this situation direct contributions to the purchase price by the [claimant], whether initially or by payment of mortgage instalments, will readily justify the inference necessary to the creation of a constructive trust. But…it is extremely doubtful whether anything else will do.'[72]

Lord Bridge then noted the judgments in *Gissing v Gissing*,[73] and *Pettitt v Pettitt*,[74] in support of his statement.

Gissing v Gissing[75]

The husband had paid the deposit for the property and the mortgage. The wife claimed an interest in the property because of her indirect contributions to the household such as clothes for herself and their child, housekeeping, gardening and buying furniture. The court held that this was not evidence from which it could be inferred that the parties had a common intention and the conduct was not referable to the house.

Pettitt v Pettitt[76]

The house was in the sole name of the wife. The husband claimed a share in the sale proceeds because he had redecorated and improved the property. He claimed to have increased its value. The House of Lords held that this was not evidence of a common intention that he should have a share in the property

Lloyds Bank plc v Rosset[77]

The married couple purchased a house that was in a state of disrepair. It was conveyed into the name of Mr Rosset alone and he fully financed the

---

70   [1991] 1 AC 107.
71   It has been claimed that Lord Bridge did not really clarify this area with his comments but that may be because Lord Bridge did not declare the law to be such as academic commentators had suggested. See for example C. Rotherham, 'The property rights of unmarried cohabitees- the case for reform' [2004] *Conv* 268.
72   [1991] 1 AC 107, 133.
73   [1971] AC 866.
74   [1970] AC 777.
75   [1971] AC 866.
76   [1970] AC 777.
77   [1991] 1 AC 107.

purchase by way of mortgage. Mrs Rosset supervised the building work and undertook most of the decorating. The relationship broke down and Mr Rosset defaulted on the mortgage. Mrs Rosset claimed a beneficial interest in the house. The House of Lords held that there was no evidence of a common intention that she had an interest by way of constructive trust. The type of work carried out was the work any partner would carry out in the circumstances. Lord Bridge commented that if the judge views a wife's conduct as 'the most natural thing in the world for any wife' she would fail.[78]

Thus, although these decisions have been criticised as failing to take account of 'the economic inequality between men and women' and 'the effects of sexual division of labour in these relationships',[79] at present evidence that will establish an implied bargain common intention constructive trust is restricted to the 'solid tug of money',[80] that is contributions to the purchase price of the property or possibly by the payment of mortgage instalments, usually from the time of acquisition of the property.[81] Subsequent payment of the mortgage may not be evidence of an intention to share the property but merely financial convenience.[82] The emphasis on direct contributions to the purchase price supports the claim that the common intention constructive trust is not a remedial constructive trust but is institutional based on accepted circumstances and property rights.

Other jurisdictions have adopted more flexible approaches to considering interests in the family home attempting a fairer distribution of property in consequence of the relationship rather than focusing purely on property law principles.[83] Australia bases the common intention constructive trust upon the unconscionability of the legal owner's assertion of full ownership as against the other party's interest.[84] In Canada the focus has been to prevent the unjust enrichment of the legal owner at the expense of the other party.[85] In New Zealand the courts have tried to give effect to 'the reasonable expectations' of the parties to share the property.[86]

Note

There may be scope for future English decisions to take account of indirect contributions to infer a bargain after obiter comments in **Stack v Dowden**

---

78 [1991] 1 AC 107, 131. Strangely this echoed Lord Denning in *Cooke v Head* [1972] 2 All ER 38, 'for a female non-legal owner to succeed she must show that she did much more than most women would do.'

79 Simone Wong, 'Constructive trusts over the family home: lessons to be learned from other commonwealth jurisdictions?' (1998) 18(3) *Legal Studies* 369-390.

80 Simone Wong, 'Constructive trusts over the family home: lessons to be learned from other commonwealth jurisdictions?' (1998) 18(3) *Legal Studies* 369, at 372.

81 For further discussion of indirect contributions see Mark Pawlowski, 'Beneficial Entitlement- Do indirect contributions suffice? [2002] 32 *Fam Law* 190-194.

but at present it seems that only contributions to the purchase price will evidence an implied bargain common intention constructive trust.

Note
If there is an express agreement to share the beneficial interest then the court will not have to consider whether to infer a common intention from the circumstances.

Note
The strict adherence to the requirement for contributions to the purchase price is because equity is being asked to vary property interests.

The reluctance of the court to accept indirect contributions as giving rise to a property interest is because the court is being asked to depart from the legal title in apportioning beneficial interests. Lord Diplock stated in *Gissing v Gissing*:[87]

'In drawing such an inference, what spouses said and did which led up to the acquisition of a matrimonial home and what they said and did while the acquisition was being carried through is on a different footing from what they said and did after the acquisition was completed. Unless it is alleged that there was some subsequent fresh agreement, acted upon by the parties, to vary the original beneficial interests created when the matrimonial home was acquired, what they said and did after the acquisition was completed is relevant if it is explicable only upon the basis of their having manifested to one another at the time of the acquisition some particular common intention as to how the beneficial interests should be held.'[88]

---

82 see facts of *James v Thomas* [2007] EWCA Civ 1212, discussed below.
83 See Simone Wong, 'Constructive trusts over the family home: lessons to be learned from other commonwealth jurisdictions?' (1998) 18(3) *Legal Studies* 369-390.
84 See *Muschinski v Dodds* (1985) 160 C.L.R. 583. The court may also focus on the idea of a joint venture with a pooling of funds see *Baumgartner v Baumgartner* (1987) 164 C.L.R. 137: Tory v Jones (1990) DFC 1195-905. See Anthony Mason, 'The place of equity and equitable remedies in the contemporary common law world' (1994) 110 *L.Q.R.* 238.
85 *Pettkus v Becker* (1980) 117 D.L.R. (3d) 257; [1980] 2 S.C.R. 834: *Peter v Beblow* [1993] 1 SCR 980: see also Mary Welstead, 'Domestic Contributions and Constructive Trusts: The Canadian Perspective' (1987) *Denning Law Journal* 151-161.
86 *Gillies v Keogh* [1989] 2 N.Z.L.R. 327: *McMahon v McMahon* [1996] 3 N.Z.L.R. 334.
87 [1971] AC 886.
88 [1971] AC 886, at 906

James v Thomas[89]

Mr Thomas was the sole owner of a property some years before he met Miss James. She moved in with him and began helping him in his business. The profits of the business were used to pay the mortgage of the property. Eventually she became a partner in the business. When the relationship broke down James sought an order that Thomas held the property on trust for the two of them in equal shares because of the contributions the business had made to the property. The Court of Appeal dismissed her appeal upholding the trial judge's findings that there was no express agreement and the payments to the mortgage would represent nothing more than payment of the couple's outgoings. They were not enough to represent an understanding that Thomas had accepted she had an interest in the property.

Thus pre- or post-acquisition discussion, or contributions to purchase price (usually pre-acquisition) are more likely to give rise to an interest than post-acquisition contributions.

This is because there is a conceptual distinction between pre-acquisition common intention and post-acquisition common intention. If the common intention was pre-acquisition then beneficial ownership had not yet crystallised, whereas if post-acquisition this implied a change of ownership. Thus, '[i]n the absence of express post-acquisition agreement, compelling evidence was required.'[90] That evidence it seems will only be provided by direct contributions to the purchase price.

The problem with varying property interests also arises if the relationship between the parties changes after they have agreed on their interests. Generally the court should respect property interests when they have crystallised. However, if there is express agreement to vary the interest the court will usually respect this. More controversial was the question of whether the court may infer from a change of circumstances that crystallised interests should be varied. The Supreme Court has recently considered this question.

Jones v Kernott[91]

An unmarried couple cohabited in a property purchased in joint names. The woman, a hairdresser, had paid the deposit and had bought the property at a reduced price from the estate of a deceased client. There was some evidence that the man, a seasonally employed ice-cream salesman had contributed to the mortgage. The couple had two children. After eight years the man left and subsequently purchased his own property. The

89   [2007] EWCA Civ 1212; [2008] 1 F.L.R. 1598.
90   *Chan Chui Mee v Mak Chi Choi* [2009] 1 HKLRD 343, per Johnson Lam J.
91   [2011] UKSC 53.

woman continued to pay the mortgage and bills on the first house. The man ceased to contribute, even for the children's upkeep. After fourteen and a half years of separation the man claimed his half interest in the property. At first instance this was refused and the court divided the property 80% to the woman and 20% to the man inferring an agreement to vary the beneficial interest from the original 50:50 because of the man's ceasing to contribute. The Court of Appeal allowed the man's appeal believing that they could not infer such a variation from the conduct of the parties. The Supreme Court restored the first instance decision holding that the conduct was such as to evidence an agreement to vary the interests.

Note
In *Jones v Kernott* the parties had already agreed to share the beneficial interest, as they were joint tenants. Thus the decision did not imply a right in the property because of the conduct of the parties but varied those rights because of the conduct.

Thus *Jones v Kernott* is an important decision and may be a sign that courts will imply a bargain from conduct more readily in the future.

It may be considered that equity has failed to develop this remedy to adequately reflect the needs of modern society, particularly with regard to the implied bargain common intention constructive trust. However, although it has been equity's role to adapt the common law to the changing needs of society, there is reluctance on the part of the judiciary to be seen to arbitrarily reorder property rights and a feeling that if there is a problem with the law and society the legislature should address this. Lord Diplock himself was realistic about the limits of the implied bargain common intention constructive trust:[92]

'How, then, does the court ascertain the "common intention" of spouses as to their respective proprietary interests in a family asset when at the time it was acquired or improved as a result of contributions in money or money's worth by each of them they failed to formulate it themselves? It may be possible to infer from their conduct that they did in fact form an actual common intention as to their respective proprietary interests and where this is possible the courts should give effect to it. But in the case of transactions between husband and wife relating to family assets their actual common contemplation at the time of its acquisition or improvement probably goes no further than its common use and enjoyment by themselves and their children, and while that use continues their respective proprietary interests in it are of no practical importance to them. They only become of importance if the asset ceases to be used and

---

92   Pettitt v Pettitt, [1970] AC 777 at 822.

enjoyed by them in common and they do not think of the possibility of this happening. In many cases, and most of those which come before the courts, the true inference from the evidence is that at the time of its acquisition or improvement the spouses formed no common intention as to their proprietary rights in the family asset. They gave no thought to the subject of proprietary rights at all.'

The truth of the matter is that couples often do not consider the nature or extent of their property rights in the family home.

Note
It will be apparent that direct contributions to the purchase price can give rise to a resulting trust as well. Today when the resulting trust and the constructive trust overlap in familial circumstances then 'there is no room for the operation of a resulting trust'.[93] This may be important as the quantification of interest varies according to the type of interest recognised.[94]

Limits on the bargain
An interest is not automatic on proof of contributions to the purchase price as, in line with the rebuttable nature of the presumption of resulting trust, the contribution may evidence the common intention but may be rebutted by evidence that there never was an intention to share the property.[95] If there is clear evidence that the parties had not agreed that the property was to be held on trust by the legal owner for the cohabitee, for instance that another financial arrangement had been made, then there will be no common intention constructive trust.[96]

Note
For both the express bargain and implied bargain constructive trust there must also be detrimental reliance on the bargain by the claimant and an element of unconscionability in the legal owner's conduct.

Thus to establish a common intention constructive trust there must be evidence of an agreement between the parties that both parties are to have a share in the property. This agreement can be express or implied from the conduct of the parties, such inferences usually being restricted to direct contributions to the purchase price. The non-legal owner must have relied to their detriment upon this agreement and it must be unconscionable for the legal owner to ignore the non-legal owner's interest.

---

93   *Drake v Whipp* [1996] 1 FLR 826.
94   Although *Stack v Dowden* [2007] UKHL 17 may have reduced the differences in quantification when the property is in joint names as discussed above.
95   Thomas v. Fuller Brown [1988] 1 FLR 237.
96   *Re Estate of David John Evans, Deceased* [2011] EWHC 945 (Ch).

11.6.2 Detrimental reliance for constructive trusts

In addition to the bargain, whether express or implied the claimant must also prove that they have relied to their detriment on the bargain, as 'mere common intention is not by itself enough: the claimant has also to prove that by so acting they was acquiring a beneficial interest.'[97] Thus there are two distinct elements to this requirement: the claimant must have acted to their detriment and the claimant must have done so because they relied on the agreement to share the property.[98] If there has been an express bargain then detrimental reliance may be minimal as it is seen as unconscionable for the legal owner to have gone back on his express assurance.

Example
Barry promises Maria that he will share his flat with her. Because of this she gives up her flat which is subsidised by the local authority to move in with him. She also assists in the construction of a roof building and garden. Such activities would be seen as detrimental to Maria and, if the activities were carried out because Maria believed Barry's promise that she had an interest in the property, would support her claim for an interest in the property. Thus any act performed to the detriment of the claimant relying on a belief that they have an interest in a property may be 'detrimental reliance'. Note that detrimental reliance is not enough without an express or implied bargain to establish an interest in a property by way of common intention constructive trust

Examples of detrimental reliance include: contributions to the running of the house;[99] financing and building an extension;[100] and indirect financial support allowing mortgage repayments to be kept up.[101]

Note
The acts or detriment that will constitute detrimental reliance may not constitute evidence of an implied bargain constructive trust. Actions that may be considered much less detrimental than direct contributions to the purchase price suffice for detrimental reliance.

---

97   *Midland v Dobson* [1986] 1 FLR 171
98   For discussion of the possible discriminatory nature of this requirement see A. Lawson, 'The things we do for love: detrimental reliance in the family home' (1996) *Legal Studies* 218-231
99   *Grant v Edwards* [1986] Ch 638.
100 *Mollo v Mollo* [2000] WTLR 227. N.b. this section merely considers what would be considered detrimental reliance not what would evidence an implied bargain e.g. *Thomas v Fuller-Brown* [1988] 1 FLR 237.
101 *Hammond v Mitchell* [1991] 1 WLR 1127.

11.6.3 Unconscionability for constructive trusts

Equity will not always impose a constructive trust to fulfil an agreement, as equity will not assist a volunteer, it must also be unconscionable for the legal owner of property to ignore the agreement. Although unconscionability is not always referred to in judgments it must be remembered that the constructive trust is based upon conscience, and so before the court will declare there is a constructive trust it must be satisfied there is an element of unconscionability or equitable fraud in the behaviour of the defendant. Thus the bargain and the detrimental reliance of the claimant must make it unconscionable for the legal owner to deny the claimant's interest in the property. This will be seen as similar to the approach required for proprietary estoppel and indicates the similar principles underlying the doctrines.[102]

Note
Although the courts note the three elements necessary to impose a common intention constructive trust, these elements often overlap. For example a contribution to purchase price will imply a common intention and may be considered detrimental reliance.

11.6.4 How much? Quantification of interests under a constructive trust

Once the claimant has established they have an interest in the property by way of constructive trust the court must then decide how much of an interest the claimant has. If the amount of beneficial interest has been expressly agreed or the court may infer from clear evidence an intention as to the shares of the interest then the court may honour this agreement.[103] However, where the court can define no clear intention as to the shares in the property then the court may take a 'broad-brush approach' to quantification of the shares.[104] The court will try to give effect to the bargain and may take into account all circumstances of the relationship in doing this, for example housework. Therefore, once a bargain is established, whether express or implied, the court may consider all the factors that it could not consider to infer a bargain in deciding how much of a bargain there is, for example mortgage contributions that would not themselves give rise to an interest by way of constructive trust may be taken into account when deciding how much of an interest there is.[105]

---

102 D. Hayton, 'Constructive Trusts of Homes- A Bold Approach' (1993) 109 LQR 485.
103 *Drake v Whipp* [1996] 1 FLR 826.
104 *Drake v Whipp* [1996] 1 FLR 826.
105 *Springette v Defoe* (1992) 65 P & CR 1.

Note

These matters are still NOT relevant in ascertaining whether a constructive trust exists. They are only relevant once the constructive trust has been established in deciding what is the amount of the share by way of constructive trust.

Once an interest has been established and there is no agreed quantification of this interest, the court is under a duty to consider the 'whole course of dealing' between the parties.[106] Thus the claimant's share is not necessarily limited to the precise value of their financial contributions to the relationship. When considering the parties' interests the court should ask: "What would be a fair share for each party having regard to the whole course of dealing between them in relation to the property?"[107]

This is particularly important when quantifying an interest that arises in circumstances that would also give rise to a resulting trust.

Midland Bank v Cooke[108]

The husband and wife purchased the property using in part a wedding gift from the groom's family, a cheque for £1100. The wife thus held a share by resulting trust (half the cheque), which would have represented 6.7% of the property's value. However, the court held she also had an interest by way of common intention constructive trust. The court quantified that interest based on the whole course of dealings between the husband and wife. Waite L.J. attributed to the parties, 'an intention to share beneficial ownership equally, explicitly, because such a conclusion was mirrored in the past pattern of their shared endeavour, their family life and their mutual commitment'. Therefore the wife was entitled to 50% of the value of the house.

Oxley v Hiscock[109]

Title to the property was in the name of the man alone. There was no express agreement regarding beneficial interests. Both parties had made contributions. A resulting trust for the woman would give her 20% of the value of the property. The Court held that once the necessary common intention to share the beneficial interest has been established the presumption of a resulting trust arising from contribution to the purchase price is rebutted and the parties then move into the greater freedom of the constructive trust. Chadwick L.J. said the court should decide the interest

---

106 *Midland Bank v Cooke* [1995] 4 All ER 562, 574, *per* Waite LJ, approved in *Stack v Dowden*[2007] UKHL 17.
107 *Oxley v Hiscock* [2004] 3 All ER 703, at 739 para [73], per Chadwick LJ

108 [1995] 4 All ER 562.
109 [2004] EWCA Civ 546; 3 All ER 703; [2005] Fam 211.

by asking: 'What would be a fair share for each party having regard to the whole course of dealing between them in relation to the property?'[110] The Court rejected the presumption that the parties should have equal interests because of the circumstances of their relationship but awarded the woman 40% of the value of the property.

Note
Although the court may consider an intention to share the property should result in equal division of the property, on the basis that equality is equity, the duty to consider the whole course of dealings may rebut equal division.

Today, if circumstances give rise to a resulting trust and a common intention constructive trust the court should impose the constructive trust in the interests of fairness between the parties.

11.7 Proprietary estoppel

If the claimant cannot establish an interest by way of resulting or constructive trust then she may be able to establish an interest by way of proprietary estoppel. Often this is the only way for a claimant to establish an interest if she has made no substantial contribution to the purchase price and there is no express common intention. Estoppel is an equitable principle applied to stop a legal owner asserting his legal rights unconscionably. The use of the term proprietary estoppel is relatively recent.[111] Equity recognises rights in property arising by way of the 'conduct and relationship of the parties.'[112] In *Taylor's Fashions Ltd v Liverpool Victoria Trustees Co Ltd*,[113] Oliver J. described proprietary estoppel as,

'a very much broader approach which is directed to ascertaining whether, in particular individual circumstances, it would be unconscionable for a party to be permitted to deny that which, knowingly or unknowingly, he has allowed or encouraged another to assume to his detriment rather than by inquiring whether the circumstances can be fitted within the confines of some preconceived formula serving as a universal yardstick for every form of unconscionable behaviour.'[114]

Therefore proprietary estoppel may have a wider application than the constructive trust.

110　[2005] Fam 211, para [69].
111　Paul Matthews dates the use of the term to 1966, 'The Words Which Are Not There: A Partial History of the Constructive Trust', in Charles Mitchell (ed), *Constructive and Resulting Trusts*, Hart Publishing, Oxford, 2009, p.24.
112　*Crabb v Arun District Council*: [1976] 1 Ch 179 at p.192, per Scarman L.J.
113　[1982] 1 QB 133; [1981]1 All ER 897.
114　[1981]1 All ER 897, at 915-916.

11.8 Requirements for proprietary estoppel

Although many judges have attempted to establish the factors or elements necessary for a successful claim for proprietary estoppel,[115] it is submitted that one of the most useful questions that the court must ask itself is that formulated by Oliver J. in *Taylor's Fashions Ltd v Liverpool Victoria Trustees Co Ltd*:[116] '...simply whether, in all the circumstances of the case, it was unconscionable for the defendants to seek to take advantage of the mistake which, at the material time, everybody shared...' [117]

Oliver J. developed this into a two-part test:

1 Has the party asserting their legal rights allowed the claimant to act to his detriment in reliance on a mistaken assumption?
And, if yes,
2 Would it be unconscionable for the defendant to assert those legal rights?

More recently, in *Thorner v Major*,[118] the House of Lords clarified the elements necessary for proprietary estoppel. Thus to establish a claim based on proprietary estoppel the claimant must prove a promise, representation or assurance made to him or her, reliance on that promise by the claimant and detriment in consequence of his/her reasonable reliance.[119] The effect of these elements being present is to make it unconscionable for the legal owner to assert his legal interests.[120] Thus, ultimately the question becomes, 'whether looked at in the round, in the circumstances that have happened, it would be unconscionable for the promise not to be kept even if there was not initially a legally binding contract.'[121]

To express this in terms similar to that used for the common intention constructive trust there are three elements necessary for proprietary estoppel:

---

115 For example, in *Matharu v Matharu* [1994] 2 FLR 597, Roch LJ stated that the elements of proprietary estoppel were: A has made a mistake as to his or her legal rights; A has spent money / acted on the belief; B knows of legal rights inconsistent with the equity; B knows of A's mistaken belief; B encourages A directly or by not asserting rights. If this is the case then B will be stopped from asserting his legal rights.
116 [1981]1 All ER 897.
117 [1981]1 All ER 897, at 918.
118 [2009] UKHL 18; [2009] 1 WLR 776 (HL).
119 *Thorner v Major* [2009] UKHL 18; [2009] 1 WLR 776, at [29] per Lord Wlker.
120 *Taylor's Fashions Ltd v Liverpool Victoria Trustees Co Ltd* [1981]1 All ER 897, at 912.
121 *Suggitt v Suggitt* [2011] EWHC 903. at 43 per Roger Kaye Q.C..

1   A belief;
2   Detrimental reliance; and,
3   Unconscionability.

However, the separation and identification of elements in proprietary estoppel should not be rigid. As Robert Walker L.J. stated in *Gillett v Holt*:[122]

'...the doctrine of proprietary estoppel cannot be treated as subdivided into three or four watertight compartments. Both sides are agreed on that, and in the course of the oral argument in this court it repeatedly became apparent that the quality of the relevant assurances may influence the issue of reliance, that reliance and detriment are often intertwined, and that whether there is a distinct need for a "mutual understanding" may depend on how the other elements are formulated and understood. Moreover the fundamental principle that equity is concerned to prevent unconscionable conduct permeates all the elements of the doctrine. In the end the court must look at the matter in the round...The overwhelming weight of authority shows that detriment is required. But the authorities also show that it is not a narrow or technical concept. The detriment need not consist of the expenditure of money or other quantifiable financial detriment, so long as it is something substantial. The requirement must be approached as part of a broad inquiry as to whether repudiation of an assurance is or is not unconscionable in all the circumstances.'

Thus although we refer to the elements necessary to establish a claim, it may be that the behaviour of the parties is such that it would be hard to isolate and identify the elements but equity should remedy the situation. This may also apply to the elements of the common intention constructive trust.

Note
In contrast to other forms of estoppel, such as promissory estoppel, proprietary estoppel may be, and often is, used as a sword as well as a shield. Thus it may be used to bring an action.

The importance of proprietary estoppel is that it has been used to prevent the legal owner of property from refusing to honour a promise to a future interest in property.[123]

---

122   [2001] Ch 210.
123   *Re Basham (Deceased)* [1986] 1 W.L.R. 1498; [1987] 1 All ER 405 (Ch. D.). A principle confirmed by the House of Lords in *Thorner v Major* [2009] UKHL 18; [2009] W.T.L.R. 713; [2009] 1 W.L.R. 1752. See Penelope Reed, 'Proprietary estoppel: the law after *Cobbe v Thorner* amd its impact on inheritance tax' (2010) *Private Client Business* 49.

11.8.1 The belief

Many of the cases involve family or near family situations, many involve agricultural properties and workers. There must have been a belief or expectation as to the interests of the parties. This can be by way of an express promise or assurance by the legal owner to the other party that the other party will have an interest in the property, or by way of a mistaken belief on the part of the party asserting an interest. The use of the term 'mistaken' may also be misleading as often there is a clear belief because of express promises by the legal owner that he intends to keep but then changes his mind.

Gillett v Holt[124]

Holt was a very wealthy 38 year-old farmer. He met Gillett, who was only 12 years old, in 1952. Gillett used to help out at Holt's farm and caddy for him on the golf course. When Gillett was 15, Holt proposed that he should leave school and work full-time for him. Against the wishes of both his parents and his headmaster he did so. For almost 40 years Holt was very close to Gillett, his wife, and his children, giving them expensive birthday presents and paying for the education of one of the children. He stated on at least seven occasions that he would leave the bulk of his considerable estate, including the farm of which Gillett became the manager, to him. He made wills to this effect but his attitude changed when he met a young solicitor. He subsequently removed Gillett from his will. Gillett claimed an interest in Holt's farm on the basis of Holt's assurances and Gillett's detrimental reliance upon those assurances. He claimed to have worked for years for much less than he was entitled. The Court of Appeal ordered that Gillett should receive the farm of which he was the manager and £100,000 to compensate him for the years of work.

Thorner v Major[125]

David Thorner was the second cousin of Peter Thorner, a farmer. David began visiting Peter and working on his farm without pay. Peter never said that he intended to leave the farm to David but in 1990 handed a notice regarding two life insurance policies on his life to David saying they were for his death duties. David claimed that he then believed Peter would leave the farm to him but nothing was ever said. Peter did make a will leaving the residue of his estate to David but this was destroyed in 1997 in unknown circumstances. Peter died intestate and David claimed an interest on the property. David was awarded the farm subject to inheritance tax.

---

124 [2001] Ch 210.
125 [2009] UKHL 18; [2009] 1 WLR 776 (HL).

Thus there may be no express promise just a belief purely on the part of the claimant encouraged by the circumstances. In this circumstance the legal owner must know of the mistaken belief and not correct it. If the other party then acts to their detriment the legal owner may be accountable in equity for his conduct.

Example

Michael works on Peter's farm for a low wage. Peter has never told Michael that he will have an interest in the property. Michael tells Peter that he does not need to be paid any wage from now on, as he knows he will inherit the farm from Peter. Peter allows Michael to continue working for him without a wage. Although Peter has not made any representation to Michael he has allowed Michael to act to his detriment in reliance on a mistaken belief. Peter dies and Michael discovers he has not been left the farm in Peter's will. Michael may have a claim in equity, as Peter should have told Michael he would not be leaving the property to him and not have allowed him to act to his detriment in this mistaken belief.

11.8.2 Detrimental reliance for proprietary estoppel

Similarly to the detriment required for the common intention constructive trust the detriment complained of for proprietary estoppel must have been suffered in reliance upon the mistaken belief. [126]

Coombes v Smith[127]

A woman left her husband and moved into a house provided by her lover. She lived in the house with their child while he continued to live with his wife and family. She asked him to put the house into joint names and he said there was no need to worry, as she would always have a roof over her head. The relationship ended and she claimed an interest in the property. The court held there had been a promise or representation but that she had not acted to her detriment even though she had left her husband, had her lover's child, neglected her career, and decorated the property. She left her husband because she was unhappy, had the child because she wanted to, and gave up her job because she was pregnant.

The circumstances of the relationship giving rise to a successful claim do not have to be one where the claimant has suffered detriment at all times. In the previously discussed case of *Gillett v Holt*,[128] Holt's counsel claimed that Gillett had not suffered any detriment because he had lived with his family at one of Holt's farms and had received gifts and the

---

126 [2011] EWHC 903, at [59] per Roger Kaye Q.C.
127 [1986] 1 WLR 808.
128 [2001] Ch 210.

education of his son. Robert Walker LJ considered this and stated:

'The detriment need not consist of the expenditure of money or other quantifiable financial detriment, so long as it is something substantial. The requirement must be approached as part of a broad inquiry as to whether repudiation of an assurance is or is not unconscionable in all the circumstances.'[129]

Other examples of detrimental reliance include giving up an opportunity,[130] and time and effort in obtaining planning permission.[131]

11.8.3 Unconscionability for proprietary estoppel

Unconscionability is also a factor that is necessary for establishing proprietary estoppel. This requirement was explained in *Suggitt v Suggitt*:[132] 'ultimately the question becomes one viewed at the moment of crystallisation, namely, whether, looked at in the round, in the circumstances that have happened, it would be unconscionable for the promise not to be kept even if there was not initially a legally binding contract.'[133]

John Michael Suggitt v Caroline Ann Suggitt[134]

The case involved a brother and sister. The father, Frank, died in 2009, the son, John, brought a claim against his sister, Caroline, who had inherited the entire estate of the father, under a will executed in 1997. John claimed all farms and properties of his father and all monies, asking that the court grant Caroline and her child a life interest only in one bungalow. John had worked for his father on the farm at various times for many years and had attended agricultural college to learn how to run the farm when it was his. John had often grumbled and complained 'that his father gave him nothing: no wage, no share, nothing.'[135] However, the judge, Roger Kaye Q.C., noted that John received food, board, lodging, college fees, living expenses and a share of the grain harvest, which John referred to as 'the sweepings but which amounted to about £4,700, and a share of the sheep sales, about £5,000. John was also allowed to set up his own herd of beef cattle on the farm.

The judge accepted the will reflected Frank's wishes as it gave all the property to Caroline.[136] However, the judge noted various statements by Frank that amounted to a promise that John would receive the farm.[137] For

---

129   [2001] Ch 210, at 232.
130   *Lloyd v Dugdale* [2002] 2 P & CR 13.
131   *Cobbe v Yeomans Row Management Ltd* [2005] EWHC 266.
132   [2011] EWHC 903 (Ch).
133   [2011] EWHC 903, at [43] per Roger Kaye Q.C.
134   [2011] EWHC 903 (Ch).
135   [2011] EWHC 903, at [15] per Roger Kaye Q.C.
136   [2011] EWHC 903, at [27].

example, Frank ignored John's suggestions for the farm saying that "you can do what you want when the farm is yours." Frank also said, "no farmer pays their son, as it will all be theirs one day." And that John was sent to agricultural college to learn skills "to run the farms in the future."

Although evidence of John's reliance on this promise was weak, it existed, and this reliance was to his detriment although he had also benefited from working for his father.[138] Thus there was detrimental reliance.

From this Roger Kaye Q.C. stated: 'I am satisfied that it would be unconscionable to deprive John of his reasonable expectations based upon his father's repeated assurances and indications that the farm or farmland would be his when he was gone.' [139] The Judge continued, "I am not however at all satisfied he promised him everything as John suggested." [140] Thus John was to receive the farmland and one of the houses and the sister would receive the other property and the personal monies of the father to achieve a clear division between brother and sister. The sister appealed but the appeal was dismissed by the Court of Appeal.[141]

It is submitted that if the claimant can establish they have acted to their detriment in reliance upon a mistaken belief encouraged by the legal owner then it will usually follow that the legal owner would be considered to be acting unconscionably if he asserts his legal interests.

11.8.4 How much? The remedies available for proprietary estoppel

Once the claimant has established she should be awarded a remedy against the defendant by way of proprietary estoppel the next question the court must consider is how to effect that remedy. As proprietary estoppel is linked to preventing unconscionable conduct by the legal owner of property 'the task of the court is to do justice- to do what is necessary to avoid an unconscionable result.' [142] The court will consider the mistaken belief and the extent of the detriment suffered and decide what the minimum equity is to do justice.

In **Stack v Dowden**,[143] Lord Walker referred with approval to the comments of Scarman LJ in *Crabb v Arun District Council:*[144]

---

137 [2011] EWHC 903, at [47] per Roger Kaye Q.C.
138 [2011] EWHC 903, at [57] per Roger Kaye Q.C.
139 [2011] EWHC 903, at [60] per Roger Kaye Q.C.
140 [2011] EWHC 903, at [60] per Roger Kaye Q.C.
141 *Suggitt v Suggitt* [2012] EWCA Civ 1140.
142 *Suggitt v Suggitt* [2011] EWHC 903, at [44] per Roger Kaye Q.C.
143 [2007] 2 AC 432 at p.448, para. [37].
144 [1976] 1 Ch 179 at p.199.

'... there can be no doubt that since Ramsden v Dyson (1865) LR 1 HL 129 the courts have acted upon the basis that they have to determine not only the extent of the equity, but also the conditions necessary to satisfy it, and they have done so in a great number and variety of cases.'

The court aims to grant the relief required 'to enable the claimant to have the benefit of the equitable right which he is held to have'. Thus the court does not grant relief beyond the minimum necessary to do justice, although this 'does not require the court to be constitutionally parsimonious' but 'it does implicitly recognise that the court must also do justice to the defendant'.[145] Thus the court is not limited to a proprietary remedy but may be creative in doing justice.[146] If there is a clear-cut promise which gives rise to the estoppel then, 'the court's natural response is to fulfil the claimant's expectations.' However, the court has to consider what it is trying to achieve. The court will seek to address the detriment in a way which will satisfy the equity but not adversely effect the defendant to such an extent that its effect would be disproportionate to the detriment it is trying to avoid.[147] The aim is not just to compensate the claimant for their detriment but also to satisfy the equity considering all the circumstances including the claimant's expectation and detriment.[148] The court must consider practical matters such as 'the administrative feasibility and cost of the measures ordered; their fiscal consequences; the need in some cases for a 'clean break' between antagonistic parties, [149][150] and so forth...'

Thus, although the use of the word 'minimum' may imply that the court has limited powers, the court has wide power and has used this creatively to remedy unconscionable conduct by legal owners. This is discussed below in contrast to the remedy available by way of constructive trust.

11.9 Resulting trust, constructive trust or proprietary estoppel?

In the previous chapter it was noted that the resulting trust and the constructive trust are 'bedfellows' and may arise in similar circumstances.[151] In deciding whether to award an interest in the family home the courts have seemingly brought the doctrines of resulting trust,

---

145 *Jennings v Rice* [2002] EWCA Civ 159; [2003] 1 P & CR 8 (p.100) at p.113, *per* Walker LJ. See also *Pascoe v Turner* [1979] 1 WLR 431.

146 Gardner, 'Wives' guarantees of their husbands' debts' (1999) *L.Q.R.* 115.

147 See *Jennings v Rice* at p.111 *per* Aldous LJ and at pp.114-116 *per* Walker LJ; also the Hog Kong case of *Luo Xing Juan v Estate of Hui Shui See (Deceased)* [2008] HKCU 918, at [70], *per* Mr Justice Ribeiro PJ.

148 *Jennings v Rice* [2002] EWCA Civ 159; [2003] 1 P & CR 8.

149 (1987-1988) 164 CLR 387 at p.419.

150 (1987-1988) 164 CLR 387 at p.419

constructive trust and proprietary estoppel closer together so that similar facts may give rise to each as a cause of action.[152] For example, contributions to purchase price may give rise to an interest by way of resulting trust, an implied bargain constructive trust, or proprietary estoppel because of the assurances and conduct of the legal owner.

Therefore we have to consider which cause of action is most appropriate or likely to be upheld by the court. If the circumstances give rise to both a resulting trust and a constructive trust then there is 'no room' for the operation of the resulting trust in a domestic case.[153] The presumption of resulting trust was originally devised for commercial relationships to assert individual interests whereas the common intention constructive trust is more suited to do justice among cohabitees. Thus the court is free to move into the 'greater freedom' of the constructive trust when deciding the extent of the parties' interests.

The requirements for an action by way of constructive trust or proprietary estoppel are drawing together in many ways. As Sir Nicholas Browne Wilkinson V.C., as he then was, noted 'The two principles have been developed separately without cross-fertilisation between them: but they rest on the same foundation and have on all matters reached the same conclusions'.[154] The main difference is that the constructive trust is, or should be, based upon a bargain whereas proprietary estoppel relies on a reasonable belief. It might be noted that the constructive trust is based upon a present interest whereas proprietary estoppel may be based upon a hope of an interest in the future. This distinction may have little real effect as circumstances may give rise to both actions and these are often pleaded in the alternative.[155] It might be thought that the claimant would prefer the 'broad-brush' approach of the constructive trust as a remedy rather then

---

151 Paul Matthews, 'The Words Which Are Not There: A Partial History of the Constructive Trust', in Charles Mitchell (ed), *Constructive and Resulting Trusts* (Hart Publishing, 2009), 4.

152 In Hong Kong an informal interest in a property may also arise by way of promissory estoppel: see the Court of Final Appeal decision in *Luo Xing Juan v Estate of Hui Shui See (Deceased)* [2008] HKCU 918. Although this devlopment has attracted some academic critcism, see Kelvin F.K. Low, 'Case Comment *Luo Xing Juan Angela v Estate of Hui Shui See Willy, Deceased*: family property & interposed companies' (2009) (6) *Conv* 524-532. For developments in the doctrine of promissory estoppel in Australia see *Waltons Stores (Interstate) Ltd v Maher* (1988) 164 CLR 387; 62 ALJR 110; 76 ALR 513.

153 *Drake v Whipp* [1996] 1 FLR 826; *Oxley v Hiscock* [2004] EWCA Civ 546.

154 *Grant v Edwards* [1986] Ch 638, at per Sir Nicholas Browne Wilkinson V.C. See also P. Ferguson, 'Constructive trusts- a note of caution' (1993) 109 (Jan) *L.Q.R.* 114.

155 See for example *Mollo v Mollo* [2000] WTLR 227.

the 'minimum to do equity'. In **Stack v Dowden,**[156] Lord Walker contrasted the consequences of a proprietary estoppel with the consequences of a common intention constructive trust:

'Proprietary estoppel typically consists of asserting an equitable claim against the conscience of the "true" owner. The claim is a "mere equity". It is to be satisfied by the minimum award necessary to do justice,[157] which may sometimes lead to no more than a monetary award. A "common intention" constructive trust, by contrast, is identifying the true beneficial owner or owners, and the size of their beneficial interests.' [158]

Although the 'disparaging-sounding epithet' 'mere' is used this does not mean the relief which may be granted is insignificant.[159] The courts have been creative in their remedies when faced with rectifying unconscionable conduct giving rise to proprietary estoppel. Thus the court may convey the fee simple and award compensation,[160] a life interest in property,[161] or a monetary payment equivalent to a life interest.[162]

11. 10 Problems with informal interests in land

One of the main problems with informal trusts of land is that they are not apparent to third parties. Thus a third party dealing with a legal owner, who may himself not be aware he holds the property on trust, although perhaps he should, will have no warning of the informal interest. This may be particularly true of the institutional constructive trust as Lord Browne Wilkinson noted in **Westdeutsche Landesbank Girozentrale v Islington London Borough Council:**[163]

'Under an institutional constructive trust, the trust arises by operation of law as from the date of the circumstances which give rise to it: the function of the court is merely to declare that such a trust has arisen in the past. The consequences that flow from such a trust having arisen (including the possibly unfair consequences to third parties who in the interim have received the trust property) are also determined by rules of law, not under a discretion. A remedial constructive trust, as I understand it, is different. It is a judicial remedy giving rise to an enforceable equitable obligation: the extent to which it operates retrospectively to the prejudice

---

156 [2007] 2 AC 432 at p.448, [37]
157 *Crabb v Arun District Council* [1976] Ch 179, p.198.
158 [2007] 2 AC 432 at p.448, [37]
159 Luo Xing Juan v Estate of Hui Shui See (Deceased) [2008] HKCU 918, at [67], per Ribeiro PJ.
160 *Gillett v Holt* [2001] Ch 210.
161 *Inwards v Baker* [1965] 2 QB 29.
162 *Baker v Baker* (1993) 25 HLR 408.
163 [1996] AC 669, at 714-715.

of third parties lies in the discretion of the court.'

Thus an interest by way of constructive trust in England will arise from the date of the detrimental reliance,[164] and so may adversely affect secured and unsecured creditors or those who have purchased the trust property.

The interest that is awarded as a remedy for proprietary estoppel arises from the date of judgment. The court will consider third party interests in declaring an appropriate remedy. It has also been claimed that an estoppel interest may not be capable of binding third parties,[165] although, of course, if they are parties to an act designed to defeat an interest then they may be bound.[166]

11.11 Summary

The approach of the courts to disputes over the family home depends on the nature of the relationship. If the parties are married or in a civil partnership then the court has wide statutory powers to distribute property; however, if the parties are not married then property law principles apply.

The approach of the courts is to ask if the parties have an interest and if so what the extent of that interest is. This will depend on the legal title to the property and whether it is in joint names or a single name. If legal title to a domestic property is in joint names then equity will presume the beneficial interest is owned jointly as well unless there is strong evidence to the contrary. If a party is not registered as a legal owner of a property then an interest by way of trust in the property should comply with s53(1)(b) LPA and be proved in writing. If there is such evidence a court may follow this. However, the court may declare there to be an interest by way of resulting or constructive trust which do not have to comply with the writing requirements because they are expressly excluded in s.53(2) LPA. The most troublesome cases to come before the courts are those where a couple has cohabited and the home is registered in one name alone. Here, the party claiming the beneficial interests depart from the legal interest must establish an interest by way of resulting trust, constructive trust or proprietary estoppel.

The resulting trust for a family home is a presumption of resulting trust and so may be rebutted by evidence that a trust was not intended. It arises only by way of contributions to the purchase price. The interest that accrues by way of resulting trust is in proportion to the contribution made to the purchase price.

---

164 See also P. Ferguson, 'Constructive trusts- a note of caution' (1993) 109 (Jan) L.Q.R. 114.
165 D. Hayton, 'Equitable rights of cohabitees' (1990) *Conv* 370.
166 See for example *Gillett v Holt* [2001] Ch 210.

The constructive trust used in domestic circumstances is based upon common intention. To establish such a trust the claimant must show there was a bargain, either express or implied, they relied to their detriment upon this bargain, and that it would be unconscionable for the legal owner to ignore their interest. An implied bargain will usually only be inferred from direct contributions to purchase price of the property, as in a resulting trust. The interest that the claimant will obtain by way of the common intention constructive trust is designed to give effect to the bargain and the court may consider the whole course of dealing between the parties in determining this. If the circumstances of a resulting trust overlap with a constructive trust then the court should move into the freedom of the constructive trust to give effect to the bargain between the parties.

A claimant may alternatively claim an interest by way of proprietary estoppel. This claim relies on a belief by the claimant that is known to the legal owner, detrimental reliance on this belief, and unconscionability on the part of the legal owner in ignoring the claimant's belief and detriment. The court will award the successful claimant the minimum to do equity in rectifying or avoiding the detriment.

CHAPTER 12
MUTUAL WILLS AND SECRET TRUSTS

This chapter will discuss the doctrines of mutual will and secret trusts. It should be noted that there is some conflict over the usefulness of both doctrines amongst practitioners and academics. Most academic texts consider the doctrines but there is some evidence that practitioners who work with trusts and wills are rarely asked to create mutual wills or secret trusts,[1] furthermore if they are asked to do so it is often perceived good practice to attempt to dissuade the testator from such constructions because of the problems associated with drafting and evidence.[2]

12.1 The Will

Today it is taken for granted that anyone has the right to make a will in which, after the deduction of expenses for the disposal of their body and the settlement of their debts, they may distribute their estate to whoever they wish; however, this testamentary capability is of relatively recent date and 'far from being a natural right, testamentary disposition is a novelty in the history of law.'[3]

The word 'testament' is derived from the Latin for 'witness' and refers to the witnessed wishes of the deceased as to the disposal of his property after his death. The Romans did not at first recognise testamentary dispositions of land and when eventually they were recognised it was subject to approval of the state. The refusal to recognise the right to testamentary disposition of land was probably because of primitive concepts of common property and belief that the transfer of land was a matter of public interest, which created fears that testamentary dispositions

---

1   See Rowena Meagher, 'Secret trusts- do they have a future?' (2003) *Conveyancer and Property Lawyer, 203.* Meager's research noted that 35% of lawyers responding to her survey had been asked for advice on "secret" testamentary dispositions during their careers.

2   See David Rowell, (2003) *TELJ* January/February, 14-16. In New Zealand legislation has been introduced to clarify the use of mutual wills: see Nicky Richardson, 'Legislation for mutual wills in New Zealand' (2010) 24(2) *Trust Law International* 99-109.

3   Quoted from De Laveleye, *Primitive Property*, p. 157 by Henry E. Davis, Paper before the American Bar Association (1898) 6 *American Lawyer* 205, 209.

of land would restrict the community's use of land. The refusal to allow wills of land was rather like the restrictions on mortmain and restraints on alienation and perpetuities.[4]

At common law such testamentary disposition of the property of the deceased as was allowed was limited to personal property. Land devolved according to local custom, usually to the eldest son or to be divided in fixed proportions between the heirs.[5] As we have seen, one of the reasons for the development of the law of trusts was the ability of the trust to circumvent the common law restrictions on testamentary disposal of land. Thus a settlor would convey his land *intervivos* to trustees to hold on trust for himself and his chosen heirs. On his death the trustees would convey the land to the heirs. The Statute of Uses[6] severely restricted this right and, in the face of an uprising in the north of England, Henry VIII was forced to concede a limited right of testamentary disposition of land in the Statute of Wills in 1540.[7]

A will is an instrument complying with the formalities provided in the Wills Act 1837 by which the person making it (the testator) provides for the distribution or administration of property after his death. A will is a public document and may be inspected at the public records office. The public nature of the will is to ensure that no fraud has been committed with regard to the testator's estate. The Wills Act provides that the will must be in writing, signed by the testator or by someone in his presence under his direction and witnessed by two or more witnesses.[8] Generally a witness should not be a beneficiary under the will because of the obvious risk of fraud.[9] When a will complies with these formalities it is 'executed' and is enforceable on the death of the testator. The testator may, however, revoke his will at any time before death by destroying it, or ordering it destroyed, or by executing a new will or by marrying.[10] Alterations or additions to the will may be made by a codicil, which must also comply with the formalities in the Wills Act.[11] If a codicil is executed it will confirm the earlier will subject to the changes in the codicil and the will is now

---

4   Henry E. Davis, Paper before the American Bar Association (1898) 6 *American Lawyer* 205, 208.

5   There were of course local variations in the rules governing the inheritance of land.

6   27 Hen VIII cap 10, 1535.

7   32 Hen VIII cap 1, 1540.

8   Section 9.

9   Section 15. See however *Re Young* [1951] Ch 344, discussed below, where a witness to a will was allowed to benefit as he was a beneficiary under a secret trust and did not know that that he was benefiting.

10   Wills Act 1837 ss. 18 & 20.

11   Wills Act 1837 ss 20 &21.

considered to date from the date of execution of the codicil, thus it postdates and supersedes any other will. Any purported disposition of property after the death of the testator that does not comply with the formalities required by the Wills Act will be void.[12]

If a person dies with a validly executed will they are said to die testate, if they have no validly executed will they are said to die intestate. The personal representatives of the deceased administer and distribute the estate of the deceased; they are termed "executors" for those dying testate and "administrators" for those intestate. A will should identify the executors of the deceased who are under a fiduciary duty to gather in the assets of the deceased, pay for the lawful disposal of the deceased's body,[13] settle the debts of the estate and then distribute the remains of the estate in accordance with the will.

If the deceased dies intestate then someone may apply to the High Court for letters of administration to become the administrator of the deceased's estate. The administrator has similar duties and powers to those of the executor except that he will distribute the remains of the estate according to the rules of intestacy.[14] A person can die partly testate, leaving a will that only deals with part of his estate in which case the will is followed and then the rules of intestacy apply to any property not disposed of in the will.

A will is said to be 'ambulatory in nature', as it 'walks around with' the testator until his death: a will is revocable until the death of the testator and is only effective upon the death of the testator;[15] it 'speaks only from the death.'[16] Thus *donationes mortis causa* take precedence to dispositions in a will because the *donationo mortis causa* is a lifetime gift which is completed or crystallised by the death of the donor, and he is free to revoke it at any time up to his death; however, the donor's will, if it provides for the subject matter of the gift to be given to someone else, only takes effect after the death upon the administration of his estate. It is a later disposition of the property and so does not take effect.

---

12   An attempt to dispose of property not in the written form required by the Wills Act is referred to as 'nuncupative' and may only be enforced in rare accepted circumstances for example for members of the armed forces in a battle situation: Wills Act 1837 s.11.

13   Although they only have a duty to lawfully dispose of the deceased's body and not to carry out his wishes as to the means of disposal: *Williams v Williams* (1882) 20 Ch D 659.

14   See the Administration of estates Act 1925 (as amended see Intestate's Estates Act 1952).

15   Although it may be possible to enforce a provision in an earlier will by way of estoppel e.g. *Gillett v Holt* [2000] 1 WLR 195, CA, considered in the chapter on equity and the family home. See Mark Pawlowski, 'Revocable gifts and estoppel' (2012) 18(1) (January) *Trusts & Trustees* 64-67.

The revocable nature of the will and the requirements in the Wills Act for a valid will are aspects of the law of will which should invalidate mutual wills and secret trusts. Mutual wills are executed by parties who wish to prevent each other from being able to revoke their wills, and secret trusts are arrangements whereby the testator places the recipient under an obligation to dispose of property after his death although this obligation is not written in the will. Mutual wills do not comply with the nature of wills, and secret trusts do not comply with the formalities of the Wills Act. Both should be invalid but both may be enforced by equity if certain requirements are complied with.

12.2 Mutual wills

Mutual wills have been described as 'anomalous and unprincipled',[17] as the doctrine of mutual wills conflicts with some of the basic principles of the law of succession. Mutual wills occur when two parties come to an agreement about the disposition of their property on their death. Usually a husband and wife create mutual wills. They will make a single joint will or wills in identical terms,[18] which refer to the mutual obligation on both parties to ensure that the property of the first to die is left to the survivor who must then dispose of the property according to the terms they have agreed.[19] It is even possible that the survivor obtains no benefit under the will of the first to die.[20]

12.2.1 The agreement

To be enforceable mutual wills the agreement between the parties must be certain and, in effect, a contract between the parties not to revoke the will and to be binding on the parties.[21] Thus there are two requirements:

- There must be a definite and unequivocal agreement not to revoke the wills;[22] and,
- It must be clear from the words and actions of parties that they intended to be bound upon death.[23]

The agreement not to revoke should usually be contained in the wills; however, evidence from outside of the will may be admitted to confirm

---

16   *Re Crippen's Estate* [1911] P 108; Sub nom In the Estate of Cunigunda (Otherwise Cora) Crippen, deceased. Wills Act 1837 s.24.
17   *Re Walters (Deceased)* [2007] EWHC 3060 (Ch); [2008] WTLR, per Rimer L.J.
18   For an example of a single jont will see *In the Goods of Piazzi-Smyth* [1898] P.7.
19   *Duffour v. Pereira* (1769) Dick 419.
20   *Re Dale* [1994] Ch 31.
21   *Re Dale* [1994] Ch 31.
22   *Re Green* [1951] Ch 158; *Re Cleaver* [1981] 1 WLR 939; [1981] 2 All ER 1018
23   *Re Goodchild (Deceased)* [1996] 1 WLR 694; [1997] 3 All ER 63.

the existence of the agreement when the agreement has not been included in the will.[24] It must be clear from the words and actions of the parties that they intended to be bound by the agreement, which usually should be contained in the will; however, again, evidence from outside of the will may be admitted to confirm the existence of the agreement when the agreement has not been included in the will.[25]

Re Cleaver[26]

The husband and wife made wills in each other's favour with remainders to their children. After the husband's death the wife made one will which was consistent with the mutual wills and then made two more which were inconsistent with it. Parol evidence was admitted to show that the wife had regarded herself as under an obligation to leave her estate in accordance with the mutual will.

The mere fact that the wills have been executed at the same time and in the same form,[27] though possibly evidence of an agreement, will not be conclusive: there must be "a contract at law between the two testators".[28]

Re Goodchild (Deceased)[29]

The husband and wife executed simultaneous wills in identical form, leaving their estates to the survivor, who was then to leave the property to their children. After the wife died the husband remarried and made another will in favour of his new wife.

Judgment: the identical wills were not mutual wills because there was no evidence of an agreement that the survivor should not be able to revoke his will. It was also stated that, had the wills been mutual, the revocation effected by the subsequent marriage of the survivor would have had no effect upon the property subject to the mutual wills.

This approach was followed in **Birch v. Curtis,**[30] where it was held that the mere execution of corresponding wills at the same time and in an agreed form did not create mutual wills - it imposed merely a moral obligation upon the survivor.

In effect the agreement is 'a contract at law between the two testators',[31]

---

24   *Re Cleaver* [1981] 1 WLR 939; [1981] 2 All ER 1018.
25   *Re Cleaver* [1981] 2 All ER 1018.
26   [1981] 2 All ER 1018.
27   *In re Oldham (Hadwen v Myles)* [1925] Ch. 75; *Gray v Perpetual Trust Company [on appeal from the High Court of Australia]* [1928] AC 391 (PC).
28   *Re Goodchild (Deceased)* [1996] 1 WLR 694; [1997] 3 All ER 63.
29   [1996] 1 WLR 694; [1997] 3 All ER 63.
30   [2002] EWHC (Ch) 1158.
31   *Re Goodchild (Deceased)* [1996] 1 WLR 694; see also *Duffour v. Pereira* (1769) Dick 419; *Re Dale* [1994] Ch 31.

although the basis of equity's enforcement of the agreement, whether contract or trust, will be discussed below. Mutual wills usually create a life interest for the survivor;[32] however, the gift to the survivor may be expressed as an absolute gift, subject to an obligation to dispose of the residue. The survivor does not have to receive any benefit under the first to die's will for it to be enforced.[33]

Re Dale[34]

A husband and wife made mutual wills by which they agreed to leave their estates to their son and daughter equally. When the husband died his estate devolved in accordance with the mutual wills, but his wife purported to change her will, leaving only a small legacy to her daughter and the residue to her son. It was argued that she was not bound by the mutual wills because she took no benefit from the estate of her late husband.

Judgment: the widow was bound by the original agreement and so was the son.

12.2.2 Revocation of mutual wills

As a will is revocable until the death of the testator it is necessary to consider what will happen if either party revokes their will. Changes to the wills that do not affect the agreement may have no effect on the binding nature of the wills. If the parties wish to effect changes to their mutual agreement then subsequent mutual changes should be effected by new mutual wills or codicils and such will become binding on the death of the first party.

If a party to mutual wills revokes their will before the death of the other party then both are no longer bound by the agreement and the mutual wills are not enforceable.[35] As Lord Camden noted with regard to the joint will of the husband and wife in *Dufour v Pereira*:[36]

'It might have been revoked by both jointly; it might have been revoked separately, provided the party intending it, had given notice to the other of such revocation. But I cannot be of the opinion that either of them could, during their joint lives, do it secretly; or that after the death of either, it could be done by the survivor by another will.'

If the first to die changes his will without the knowledge and approval of the other party the wills will cease to be mutual and the survivor is not

---

32 *Duffour v. Pereira* (1769) Dick 419.
33 *Re Dale* [1994] Ch 31.
34 [1993] 4 All ER 129; [1994] Ch 31.
35 *Ip Man Shan, Henry v Ching Hing Construction Company Ltd (No 2)* [2003] 1 HKC 256.
36 *Dufour v. Pereira* (1769) Dick 419 at 420-421.

bound by the agreement.[37] The survivor may be able to claim damages for breach of the contract from the estate of the deceased if they have not received the property they were expecting.[38]

If the survivor changes his will in breach of the agreement, or destroys his will and so dies intestate then the survivor's personal representatives will hold the property on constructive trust for the purposes agreed.

12.2.3 Why are mutual wills enforced?

As testators are accepted to have freedom to revoke their wills until death, the survivor to mutual wills should have freedom to make a new will. The question then arises; how are mutual wills enforced? The discussion of this question has centred upon whether mutual wills are enforced in the law of contract or of trusts.

If we accept that there must in effect be a contract between the parties it might appear logical for there to be a contractual solution, *i.e.* that the obligation is contractual. In one of the earliest mutual wills cases, *Dufour v. Pereira*, Lord Camden explained the basis of the obligation and its enforcement: '[I]t is a contract between the parties, which cannot be rescinded, but by the consent of both. The first that dies, carries his part of the contract into execution. Will the Court afterwards permit the other to break the contract? Certainly not.'[39]

The contractual approach is supported by the recognition that if the first party to die breaches the agreement his estate will be liable in damages to the survivor.[40]

The problem with the contractual approach is that it does not explain other aspects of enforcement.[41] For example, if the survivor decides not to carry out the obligations under the mutual wills the estate of the deceased would not be able to sue on the contract as it has lost nothing. It might be thought that the estate of the first to die has the right to pursue a contractual remedy for specific performance of the contractual obligations but this was rejected in *Re Dale*.[42] Furthermore, the ultimate beneficiaries under the mutual wills would not be able to sue as there is no privity of contract between them and the survivor.[43]

---

37 *Re Hobley* (1997) Times, 16 June.
38 *Robinson v. Ommanney* (1883) 23 Ch D 285
39 *Dufour v. Pereira* (1769) Dick 419 at 421 per Lord Camden C.
40 *Robinson v. Ommanney* (1883) 23 Ch D 285.
41 Although the contractual approach may still be the basis for enforcement in the United States of America: see John M. Mowrer, 'Joint and Mutual Wills – Effect of Contract Not to Revoke' (1976) 41 *Missouri Law Review* 127-132.
42 [1994] Ch 31.
43 Although they might now be able to rely on the Contracts (Rights of Third Parties) Act 1999.

Mutual wills are enforced on the basis of conscience; equity will prevent the surviving party going back on the agreement if it would be unconscionable to do so. The basis of the doctrine is therefore the constructive trust in order to prevent fraud by the survivor as against the first to die.[44] Thus Lord Camden also said in *Dufour v Pereira*:[45] '…he that dies first, does by his death carry the agreement on his part into execution. If the other then refuses, he is guilty of a fraud, can never unbind himself, and becomes a trustee of course. For no man shall deceive another to his prejudice.'

Equity will construct a trust against the conscience of the survivor to carry out the obligations agreed with the first to die because otherwise the first to die would not have made a will in the way they did; a similar justification is made below for the enforcement of secret trusts. Thus, in *Re Dale*,[46] it was held that the wife had held the property on constructive trust from the moment of the husband's death and then the son held the estate as executor on constructive trust for himself and his sister in equal shares.

Healey v. Brown[47]

The husband and wife made mutual wills. The London flat in which they lived was to go to the husband's niece after the death of the second testator, and the rest of their property was to go to the husband's son by a previous marriage. After the wife died, the husband transferred the flat into the joint names of himself and his son. When the husband died the flat accordingly passed to his son by survivorship. The husband's niece appealed, claiming that the property should not have been disposed of contrary to the terms of the mutual will.

Judgment: the son held one half of the flat on trust for the niece. [48]

This decision casts doubt on the contractual approach as the son was not a party to the agreement but was held to hold the property for him and his cousin, also the division of the property bears no relation to the agreement.

It may be easier to think of mutual wills as a contract to perform the obligations and not to revoke the mutual wills which is subject to a trust from the death of the first party against the conscience of the survivor. Therefore mutual wills are enforced on the basis of conscience and the law of trusts;[49] however, there may be problems with identifying what property is subject to the trust obligation.

---

44   *Re Dale* [1994] Ch 32. see Patrick O'Hagan, 'Mutual Wills' (1994) 144 (Sept) *New Law Journal* 1272.
45   (1769) 1 Dick 419.
46   [1994] Ch 31.
47   [2002] 19 EG 147 (CS).
48   Following *Re Goodchild (Deceased)* [1996] 1 WLR 694.
49   Shovelar v Lane [2011] EWCA Civ 802; (2011) The Times, August 24.

12.2.4 What property forms the subject matter of the constructive trust?

It might be thought that it is only the property the survivor inherits from the first to die; however, we have already seen that the survivor does not need to inherit any property to be under the obligation.[50] It might also be thought that it is all the property that the survivor inherits and owned themselves at the time of the death of the first party; however, this raises the question of the freedom of the survivor to use the property until they die. It might be that the trust attaches to all the property the survivor owns at the time of their death; however, this raises issues about the freedom of the survivor to dispose of *after acquired property*.

If the mutual wills clearly refer to property and what is to be done with it then this should be enforced. For example if the first to die has specified that the survivor is to enjoy their jointly owned flat for life and then pass it to their son, this would be enforced. If the wills do not clearly identify the property subject to the obligation or, as is usually the case refer to the parties whole estate or residue after specified bequests then the approach of the courts has varied over time. It used to be thought that the trust covered the whole of the estate of the survivor at the time of the death of the first party.[51] As already noted this may cause some problems because it may restrict the survivor's ability to sell such property and enjoy it during their lifetime. More recent discussion of this issue has identified the survivor's interest as analogous to a life tenant in all of the property he owns at the time of the death of the first party.[52] The survivor may do what he wishes with the property during his lifetime as long as he does nothing 'deliberately to defeat the compact',[53] in a similar manner to the common law concept of waste. The constructive trust is 'a floating obligation, suspended during the lifetime of the survivor' which can then 'descend upon the assets at his death and crystallise into a trust.'[54] The constructive trust arises on the death of the first party,[55] but crystallises as to subject matter on the death of the survivor. Thus the survivor is entitled to the full use and enjoyment of the subject matter during their lifetime as long as they do nothing inconsistent with the agreement.[56] Therefore they

---

50 *Re Dale* [1994] Ch 31.
51 *Re Hagger* [1930] 2 Ch 190.
52 *Re Cleaver* [1981] 2 All ER 1018
53 See *Re Goodchild (Deceased)* [1996] 1 WLR 694; *Healey v. Brown* [2002] 19 EG 147 (CS).
54 *Birmingham v. Renfrew* (1936) 57 CLR 666 *per* Dixon J; confirmed in *Re Goodchild (Deceased)* [1996] 1 WLR 694.
55 *Re Dale* [1994] Ch 32. see Patrick O'Hagan, 'Mutual Wills' (1994) 144 (Sept) *New Law Journal* 1272.
56 *Ng Jack Fong v Ng Chan Ning* [2008] 2 HKC 527 (HKCA).

may sell the property if it is necessary for their maintenance as long as the sale is not solely to defeat the agreement, for example the survivor might sell the family home to fund care in a residential home if that were necessary. The intended beneficiary may bring action to prevent the survivor dissipating the trust property to defeat the agreement.[57]

There is still some dispute over whether the obligation covers *after acquired property*. For example, husband and wife execute mutual wills leaving all their property to each other for life and then to their son. If the wife dies first and the husband inherits her property but later wins the lottery; is the husband free to leave the money from the lottery to whomsoever he wishes or must he leave it to the son? There is some authority that the survivor is free to decide whatever he likes as to the *after acquired property* but this will depend on the wording of the obligation.[58]

12.3 Secret Trusts

To some extent all trusts are secret. One of the reasons for the development of the law of trusts was the public nature of conveyancing of property. Feudal transfers of property required 'notoriety', that is publicity, mainly because the parties might not be literate and public transfers of property ensured that transfers of ownership were witnessed. Of course some people did not wish their business to be known, perhaps they were in debt and wished to transfer property without the requisite publicity, or they wished to transfer property to a child in preference to others. In these circumstances they could convey property to other parties on trust for the ultimate beneficiary and hide the true purpose.

It has often been conjectured that secret trusts were originally created because of the public nature of a will. If a testator wished to benefit a mistress or illegitimate child the legacy would become public and offend the testator's family; however, a legacy could be made in favour of a trusted friend or solicitor which on the face of the will looked simply to be a gift but was in effect subject to the agreed obligation to be used for the mistress and child. It seems more likely that the true reasons for secret trusts were more prosaic. The idea that a testator would be so ashamed of his conduct as to risk a secret trust arrangement is to project Victorian morals back into time. Secret trusts have been known since the fifteenth and sixteenth centuries when English society accepted that gentlemen

---

57   see *Re Walters (Walters v Olin)* [2008] EWCA Civ 782; [2009] Ch. 212 (CA). See also Peter Luxton, *Walters v Olin*: uncertainty of subject matter- an insoluble problem in mutual wills?' [2009] 6 *Conv* 498-505, and Christine Davis, 'Mutual wills; formalities, constructive trusts' [2003] (May/June) *Conv* 238-247.

58   *In Re Green, Deceased, Lindner v Green* [1951] Ch. 148.

would have illegitimate children and so illegitimacy was not a stigma.[59] Indeed illegitimate children had for centuries been openly provided for in wills and given names witnessing their patrimonial link, for example Fitzwilliam, son of William, and even to the king, Fitzroy. In the twelfth century there had even been an illegitimate son of Henry II, known as 'Geoffrey the Bastard', who rose to become Chancellor. The more likely reasons for the creation of secret trusts were to avoid restrictions on property transfer because of political and/or religious oppression. For example, *The Duchess of Suffolk v Herenden*,[60] involved a secret trust established to avoid restrictions on Roman Catholics owning property; however, there are issues with this theory, as it would involve judges ignoring statutory prohibitions and political factors to enforce the testator's wishes. The secret trust may have further developed because of protestant restrictions in the seventeenth century on provisions to the church for the saying of masses for the testator's soul after death; the mortuary gift, as, "when we die our thoughts turn to our souls, however those we leave behind are more concerned with the deceased's property and may not want to follow out his wishes." [61] It has also been speculated that secret trusts were used by testators who were unable to make up their minds about exactly who should receive what. At a time when life expectancy was much shorter than today a testator might inherit his property at a young age and still be encouraged to write a will just in case he died young. At that point he could create a will leaving property to trusted friends hoping to inform them subsequently who he wanted to benefit from the provision.[62]

Today we use the term 'secret trust' to refer to testamentary dispositions of property that do not comply with the formalities required in the Wills Act.[63] These are trusts agreed between the trustee and the testator during the testator's life but only constituted by the transfer of property to the trustee in the testator's will. The trust may be fully secret and so, on the face of the will it may not be evident there is a trust at all, or half-secret

---

59 Lawrence Stone, *Road to divorce : England 1530-1987*, Oxford, Oxford University Press: 1990.
60 *Bartie v Herenden* (1560) unreported, reprinted in Sir John Baker, *Baker & Milsom sources of English legal history: private law to 1750*, Oxford University Press, 2nd edition, 2010.
61 Philippe Ariès, *Western Attitudes Towards Death*, Marion Boyars Publishers Limited, London & New York, 1976. Philippe Ariès, *The Hour of Our Death*, Peregrine Books, London 1983 (reprinted 1987).
62 For a more recent example of an uncertain testatrix and equity's response see *Re Snowden, (Smith v Spowage)* [1979] Ch 528.
63 A secret or half-secret trust may also be constituted by a transaction inter vivos: *Nichols v IRC* [1973] 3 All ER 632, 637. A fully secret trust may also arise on intestacy: *Sellack v Harris* (1708) 2 Eq Ca Ab 46.

when it is apparent there is a trust but the terms are not disclosed. In both cases the disposition should be void for failing to comply with the Wills Act. All the information to create a testamentary disposition such as a trust should be contained in the validly executed will and parol evidence, evidence not contained in the will, should not be admitted unless it is necessary to resolve an ambiguity, or in the event of fraud. However, in certain circumstances equity will admit parol evidence to establish secret trusts.[64] Equity has chosen to enforce these trusts because when there is evidence of a secret trust the law is 'on the horns of a dilemma',[65] as it has to choose between strict compliance with the formality requirements of the Wills Act and giving effect to the wishes of the testator.

12.3.1 Fully secret trusts

In a fully secret trust the testator leaves property to a legatee on the understanding that it is to be held on trust for the secret beneficiary. There is no mention of the existence or the terms of the trust in the will. Thus it should be void and the property an absolute gift to the legatee under the will or held on resulting trust for the testator's estate. However, if it complies with certain requirements of equity the secret trust will be enforced and the legatee will hold the property subject to the secret trust obligations.

Note
One of the main problems with secret trusts is finding evidence of the testator's true intent and the secret trustee's obligations to rebut the gift in the will.

In *Ottaway v Norman*,[66] Brightman J stated that the basic requirements for the establishment of a fully secret trust were:

1   Certainty of intention of the testator to subject the transferee (the secret trustee) to a trust obligation in favour of the secret beneficiary;
2   Communication of that intention to the transferee-including the existence and details of the trust;
3   Acceptance of the obligation by the transferee expressly or implicitly.[67]

These elements can precede or succeed the execution of the will (the drawing up, signing and witnessing of the will). Therefore they can occur at any time up to the death of the testator.

---

64   *Blackwell v Blackwell* [1929] AC 318 (HL). Indeed a fully secret trust cannot be established without parol evidence.
65   Bryn Perrins, 'Secret trusts: the key to the dehors?' [1985] *Conveyancer and Property Lawyer* 248
66   [1972] Ch 698.
67   Silence will be deemed acceptance of the obligation- see *Moss v Cooper* (1861) 1 J&H 352 discussed below.

The requirement of certainty of intention to subject the transferee to a trust obligation is very similar to the certainty of intention required for the creation of an express trust and the cases which were discussed to evidence such certainty are relevant here.[68]

Re Snowden, (Smith v Spowage)[69]

The testatrix, 86 year old Ethel Snowden, wrote a will which left her entire residuary estate to her brother, Bert, as she did not know how to distribute the estate among her nephews and nieces. There was evidence from a solicitor that she wanted to be "fair to everybody" and that she had said shortly before her death that her brother would "know what to do" with the property. Bert apparently agreed with this plan. She died. Six days later her brother died, having inherited the residuary estate. Bert had left everything to his own son (obviously one of Ethel's nephews). The other nephews and nieces argued that the testatrix had created a secret trust in favour of all of them equally.

Judgement: Ethel had not demonstrated sufficient intention to impose a trust obligation on her brother merely a moral obligation. There must be an intention by the testatrix to subject the transferee to trust obligations, i.e. a mandatory obligation on the secret trustee to hold the property as trustee. A moral obligation on the transferee is insufficient to create a trust.

This had been considered in the earlier case of ***McCormick v Grogan.***[70]

McCormick v Grogan[71]

The testator executed a very short will in 1851. He had cholera and knew he had only a short time left to live and so he called for Grogan. When Grogan arrived the testator told Grogan that there was a will in the desk drawer and a letter instructing Grogan as to certain bequests. The letter stated: "I do not wish you to act strictly to the foregoing instructions, but leave it entirely to your own good judgment to do as you think I would if living, and as the parties are deserving." After the testator died Grogan distributed some of the property. McCormick claimed against Grogan as he considered that Grogan was under a secret trust obligation and that he was deserving and had been overlooked by Grogan.

Judgment: the House of Lords held that the words used did not evidence an intention to place Grogan under a trust obligation. Therefore Grogan held the property subject only to a moral obligation to provide for the people mentioned in the letter. There was no secret trust.

---

68   E.g. *Re Adams and the Kensington Vestry [1884] 27 ChD 394, Comisky v. Bowring–Hanbury* [1905] AC 84, etc.
69   [1979] Ch 528.
70   (1869) LR 4 HL 82.
71   (1869) LR 4 HL 82.

A secret trustee of a fully secret trust must be aware that he is receiving property subject to a trust obligation and must accept this obligation before the death of the testator, otherwise the gift will be construed as an absolute gift.

Wallgrave v. Tebbs[72]

A testator left property to two individuals, the testator whilst contemplating who should be the ultimate beneficiaries of the property, did not, during his lifetime, notify the transferees of his intention to create a secret trust or of the identity of the secret beneficiaries. When the testator died, the absolute gift to the transferees was perfected; they still knew nothing of any secret trust. Some time later notes were discovered left by the testator that identified the intended beneficiaries. The question for the court became; was there a secret trust?

Judgment: the court held there was no secret trust and that the transferees took absolutely. Once a gift has been perfected an obligation cannot then be added to that gift.

Thus a testator must communicate the existence of the trust to the secret trustee before he dies, but in contrast to a half secret trust, as discussed below, communication may be made after the will has been executed. If the testator communicates both the existence of the trust and its terms to the secret trustee before his death equity will enforce the trust.

If the testator communicates the intention to create a trust to the secret trustee but not its terms, the secret trustee will hold the property on resulting trust for the testator's estate.

Re Boyes[73]

The testator transferred property to his solicitor by will, which the solicitor had agreed to hold on trust for purposes to be disclosed to him later by the testator. The testator died before telling the solicitor the terms of the trust. Later an unattested piece of paper was found naming a beneficiary of the property.

Judgment: The court held there was no secret trust, as the terms of the trust had not been communicated to the solicitor. However, as the solicitor had agreed to hold the property on trust, he could not take the property absolutely and held the property on resulting trust for the testator's estate.

There is some uncertainty about exactly what must be communicated to the secret trustee by the testator before his death for the trust to be binding. It seems that the trustee must be told of the transfer of the property in the will and that it is not as a gift but under a trust obligation. The trustee must be given enough details of the trust to allow him to make

---

72   (1855) 20 JP 84, 2 K & J 313.
73   *Re Boyes (Boyes v Carritt)* (1884) 26 Ch D 531.

a decision to accept or refuse the obligation. Thus the general terms to allow him to perform the trust rather than every detail.[74] However, it has been speculated that some of the details of the trust may be communicated after the death of the testator, for example in a sealed letter. The idea of sealed instructions was considered in *McCormick v Grogan*,[75] where the secret trust failed not because instructions were left in a letter for the recipient, but the instructions in the letter were held to be merely providing a moral obligation not a trust. In *Re Keen*,[76] Lord Wright M.R. noted:

'To take a parallel, a ship which sails under sealed orders, is sailing under orders though the exact terms are not ascertained by the captain till later. I note that the case of a trust put into writing which is placed in the trustees' hands in a sealed envelope, was hypothetically treated by Kay J. as possibly constituting a communication in a case of this nature: [citing *In re Boyes*[77]]…The trustees had the means of knowledge available whenever it became necessary and proper to open the envelope.'[78]

Thus details of the trust may be communicated to the trustee after the death of the testator but the trustee must accept the obligation before the death of the testator for the trust to be binding. If the trust is communicated to the trustee and he does not expressly accept it his silence will be presumed acceptance.

Moss v. Cooper[79]

John Hill left property to three persons. He had communicated to all three that the property should be used for certain charities. Two of them said they accepted, but the third remained silent.

Judgment: Page Wood V-C held that all three had accepted the obligations:

"If they, by their silence, bid him to believe they would so apply it, I apprehend it is quite clear that a trust would be created and that it is altogether immaterial whether the promise is made before or after the execution of the will, that being a reasonable instrument".

Once the obligation has been accepted then the testator must communicate any changes in the arrangements to the trustees otherwise the changes will not be effective.

---

74 He must be certain of the subject matter of the trust, see the Hong Kong case of *Leung Chi Man v Mok Sau Lim* [2005] HKCU 761.
75 (1869) LR 4 HL 82.
76 *Re Keen (Evershed v Griffiths)* [1937] Ch 236, [1937] 1 All ER 452.
77 (1884) 26 Ch D 531.
78 [1937] Ch 236 at 242.
79 (1861) 1 J&H 352.

Re Cooper[80]

Having previously communicated the terms of a secret trust to the secret trustees the testator left £5,000 by will to them. However, after communication he had added a codicil to the will, increasing the amount to be held on secret trust to £10,000. However, he did not communicate this alteration to the secret trustees. The court held that only the original £5,000 was subject to the secret trust obligations, the later £5,000 was held for the testator's estate on resulting trust. The secret trustees could not keep the extra £5,000 because they were aware of the trust obligation; they could not carry the change in the trust obligation out because the changes had not been communicated to them to be accepted.

If there is more than one secret trustee then all must accept the obligation for it to be binding on them all if the property is transferred to them as tenants in common. Those who do not accept the obligation will take their share absolutely.

Re Stead[81]

Mrs Stead left property in her will to Mrs Witham and Mrs Andrews as tenants in common. Mrs Stead informed Mrs Witham that the £2,000 was to be held on trust for Joan Collett. However, no communication was made to Mrs Andrews.

Judgement: Mrs Witham was bound by the secret trust, but Mrs Andrews took her share absolutely.

However, if the secret trustees are joint tenants of the property different principles are applied. If the obligation is only communicated to one of them before the execution of the will then all will be bound by the obligation. If the obligation is communicated after the execution of the will then only those who have accepted are bound. This strange difference, similar to that applied for the requirements of communication of a half-secret trust, is justified on the basis that where the testator does not communicate the obligation until after the execution of the will, those who have not accepted may keep the beneficial interest in the property because they have not encouraged the testator to make his will in their favour. In the case where the testator communicates to one of the trustees before the execution of the will it may be that the trustees could be seen to encourage the making of the will in their favour and so should not be allowed to benefit.

If the secret trustee revokes his acceptance of the obligation whilst the testator is alive, then he will take the property absolutely.[82] The testator should ensure that the will is changed to prevent the trustee taking the

---

80   [1939] Ch 811.
81   [1900] 1 Ch 237.
82   *Whitton v Russell* (1739) 1 Atk 539.

property. However, it is possible that the nature of the revocation could affect this old rule though, for example if a secret trustee gained admittance to the bedside of the dying testator and whispered into his ear a revocation of his acceptance when there was no opportunity for the testator to change his will any evidence of this conduct might be considered unconscionable and so the trust enforced or the property returned to the testator's estate. If the secret trustee revokes acceptance after the death of the testator then the trust is already constituted and a new trustee will be found as equity will not allow a trust to fail for want of a trustee.[83] Similarly, if the secret trustee dies after the death of the testator but before the trust is carried out then the trust is constituted and a new trustee will be found. Of course the carrying out of the trust by new trustees requires knowledge of the existence and details of the trust. However, if the secret trustee dies before the testator the trust should fail as the gift to the trustee will lapse.[84]

Failure of a fully secret trust will result in the legatee taking absolutely,[85] unless there is evidence that the recipient knew of the trust obligation when he will hold the property on resulting trust for the testator's estate.[86] A secret trustee can benefit from a secret trust for example by retaining surplus funds if the testator has so directed.[87] However, there are, of course, as with all matters to do with secret trusts, evidential problems and consequent danger of fraud.

12.3.2 Half-secret trusts

A half-secret trust is apparent on the face of the will, for example 'I leave £10,000 to Michael for the trusts we have agreed'. However, although it is apparent there is a trust, the terms of the trust are not in the will and again this should make the trust void because it does not comply with the requirements of the Wills Act. However, if the creation of the half-secret trust complies with the requirements equity has developed then it will be enforced and the legatee will hold subject to the secret trust obligations. The requirements are similar to those for a fully secret trust but for one important difference. The requirements were explained in **Blackwell v Blackwell**:[88]

1 intention;
2 communication;
3 acquiescence (acceptance).

---

83 Supported by *obiter* comments in *Maddock* [1902] 2 Ch 220.
84 *Re Maddock* [1902] 2 Ch 220.
85 *Wallgrave v Tebbs* (1855) 20 JP 84, 2 K & J 313.
86 *Re Boyes* (1884) 26 Ch D 531.
87 *Irvine v Sullivan* (1869) LR 8 Eq 673.
88 [1929] AC 318.

So these are the same basic requirements as for a fully secret trust and the same principles and cases apply. Thus acceptance will be deemed from silence as in **Moss v Cooper**.[89] The major difference is the requirement of communication. For a valid half-secret trust to be created the communication of the trust obligation by the testator to the trustee must be before or at the time of execution of the will. This added requirement is based upon obiter comments by Viscount Sumner in *Blackwell* that if the communication is made after execution of the will then there will not be a valid half-secret trust. Thus to create a fully secret trust the testator may communicate the obligation to the secret trustee anytime before he dies but to create a half secret trust the obligation must be communicated to the secret trustee before or at the time of the execution of the will. If the communication of the trust obligation is made after the execution of the will the trust will not be enforceable. This requirement seems strange as it penalises the testator for partially complying with the Wills Act, whereas a fully secret trust completely disregards the requirements in the Wills Act. Viscount Sumner justified this because:[90]

'A testator cannot reserve to himself a power of making future unwitnessed dispositions by merely naming a trustee and leaving the purposes of the trust to be supplied afterwards, nor can a legatee give testamentary validity to an unexecuted codicil by accepting an indefinite trust, never communicated to him in the testator's lifetime... To hold otherwise would indeed be to enable the testator to "give the go-by" to the Wills Act, because he did not choose to comply with them.'

Although there is some debate over the reasoning of Viscount Sumner this requirement has been upheld as necessary for the creation of half-secret trusts.[91]

The benefits of the half-secret trust are that they are not as susceptible to fraud or failure as the fully secret trust because there is obviously a trust obligation. A secret trustee under a half-secret trust can never take the property absolutely as it is obvious he was meant to be under a trust obligation. If the exact terms of the trust are not known then the secret trustee holds the property on resulting trust for the testator's estate. If the attempted half-secret trust was over the residuary estate, the trustee will hold the residuary on resulting trust for the next of kin.[92] If the secret trustee revokes acceptance of the obligations before the testator's death, then, when the testator dies, the intended trust property will be held on resulting trust for the testator's estate (unlike the position with fully secret trusts). Similarly, if the half-secret trustee predeceases the testator

---

89   (1861) 1 J&H 352.
90   *Blackwell v. Blackwell* [1929] AC 318 at 339.
91   E.g. *Re Keen* [1937] Ch 236; *Re Bateman's WT* [1970] 1 WLR 1463.
92   *Re Cooper* [1939] Ch 811.

depending on the knowledge of the details of the trust, a new trustee will be appointed or, if there is not enough information available to fulfil the trust obligation, the property will result back to the testator's estate.

12.4 Why are secret trusts enforced?

As Perrins has said the law is "on the horns of a dilemma" because we have the clear wishes of the testator but there are also the requirements of a statute which are not being complied with.[93] The justification for the enforcement of fully secret and half-secret trusts has received much academic and judicial consideration. At times theories have been propounded which seek to justify both types of secret trusts, at others theories have been advanced which only justify one type. These theories have also at times sought to justify the difference in communication requirements. The main general theories for the enforcement of secret trusts are the fraud theory and the '*dehors* the will' theory.

12.4.1. The fraud theory

The most widely accepted theory is that secret trusts are enforced because equity will not permit a statute to be used as an instrument of fraud. If the terms of the Wills Act were strictly enforced then the secret trustee takes the subject matter beneficially and the testator would have been thwarted in his wishes. Equity will not allow the Wills Act, a statute intended to prevent fraud, to be used to permit this fraud. Lord Eldon said, in *Muckleston v Brown*,[94] that secret trusts are enforced, "...on the ground, that the testator would not have devised the estate to him [the secret trustee], unless he had undertaken to pay that sum... The principle is, that the statute shall not be used to cover a fraud".

In *McCormick v. Grogan*,[95] the House of Lords did not hold the testator's instructions to Grogan sufficiently certain to create a secret trust but explained:

'...it is only in clear cases of fraud that this doctrine has been applied - cases in which the court has been persuaded that there has been a fraudulent inducement held out on the part of the apparent beneficiary in order to lead the testator to confide to him the duty which he so undertook to perform.'[96]

Thus the secret trust is enforced to prevent the trustee fraudulently inducing the testator into leaving the property to the trustee in his will.

---

93   Bryn Perrins, 'Secret trusts: the key to the dehors?' [1985] *Conveyancer and Property Lawyer* 248
94   (1801) 6 Ves 52, at 69.
95   (1869) LR 4 HL 82.
96   (1869) LR 4 HL 82 per Lord Hatherley LC.

Lord Westbury stated that:

'The court of equity has, from a very early period, decided that even an Act of Parliament shall not be used as an instrument of fraud; and if in the machinery of perpetrating a fraud an Act of Parliament intervenes, the court of equity does not set aside the Act of Parliament, but it fastens on the individual who gets a title under that Act, and imposes upon him a personal obligation, because he applies the Act as an instrument for accomplishing a fraud.'[97]

Lord Hatherly continued:

'If a legatee states to testator that upon testator's confiding his property, apparently disposing of it, to him, the legatee, by a regular and formal instrument, he will carry into effect all such intentions as testator shall confide to him, then that legatee ... shall have fastened upon his conscience the trust of carrying into full effect those instructions which he received upon such representations'.

Thus equity does not ignore the statute but enforces the personal obligation of the trustee because the trustee acted '*malo animo*', knowing 'the testator or intestate was beguiled and deceived by his conduct.'[98]

There has been some criticism of this view of the fraud theory, as it might be thought that equity could simply counteract the fraud by considering the trustee to hold the property on resulting trust for the testator's estate. However, it has been argued that the resulting trust is not an adequate remedy, as it does not fulfil the purpose intended by the testator.[99] This is supported by Viscount Sumner's comments in *Blackwell v. Blackwell*,[100]

'For the prevention of fraud equity fastens on the conscience of the legatee a trust, a trust, that is, which otherwise would be inoperative; in other words it makes him do what the will in itself has nothing to do with; it lets him take what the will gives him and then makes him apply it, as the Court of conscience directs, and it does so in order to give effect to wishes of the testator, which would not otherwise be effectual.'

Therefore equity will enforce a secret trust because it will not allow a statute to be used to perpetrate a fraud on the testator by not having his wishes carried out. This is supported by early judicial comment such as Lord Hardwicke in *Drakeford v Wilks*:[101]

"if the testatrix has a conversation with a legatee, and the legatee promises that, in consideration of the testator's disposition in favour of

---

97   (1869) LR 4 HL 82.
98   (1869) LR 4 HL 82 per Lord Westbury.
99   David Hodge, 'Secret Trusts: the fraud theory revisited' [1980] *Conveyancer and Property Lawyer* 341-350.
100 [1929] A.C. 318 at 335.
101 (1747) 3 ATK 539, at 540-541.

her, she will do an act in favour of a third person, and the testator lets the will stand, it is very proper the person who undertook to do the act should perform, because, I must take it, if (the secret trustee) had not so promised, the testatrix would have altered her will."

The fraud theory is also regarded as the justification for the half-secret trust, although there is much less chance of fraud with a half-secret trust as the trust is apparent in the will, but parol evidence will be admitted to ensure the half-secret trustee carries out his obligations.[102]

12.4.2 The *dehors* the will theory

There has been some speculation that a secret trust is *dehors* the will; that the trust takes effect outside the will and so is not governed by testamentary legislation. This is based upon a consideration that the trust is created from the moment the obligation is assumed, it is therefore an *intervivos* trust which is fully constituted by the property being transferred to the trustee by the will. This is a form of 'floating trust'. There is some judicial support for this view, for example Megarry V-C in *Re Snowden*:[103]

'…the whole basis of secret trusts, as I understand it, is that they operate outside the will, changing nothing that is written in it, and allowing it to operate according to its tenor, but then fastening a trust on to the property in the hands of the recipient'.

There are also some references to secret trusts operating outside the Wills Act in *Blackwell v Blackwell*,[104] and *Cullen v A.G. for Ireland*.[105] However, there are problems with the *dehors* theory, as a trust is not constituted until the property is transferred to the trustee and so is not enforceable until the death of the testator.[106] Also the testator is free to revoke his will at any point until death, so the obligation is easily avoided. There is also the problem with an *intervivos* secret trust dealing with land. Such a trust should comply with the formality requirements in the Law of Property Act 1925, s 53(1)(b). However, in *Ottaway v, Norman*,[107] an oral secret trust of land was enforced.

Greg Allan has recently suggested that secret trusts are enforced both

---

102 Bryn Perrins, 'Secret trusts: the key to the dehors?' [1985] *Conveyancer and Property Lawyer* 248
103 [1979] Ch 528.
104 [1929] AC 318.
105 (1866) LR 1 HL 190.
106 For academic criticism see for example Patricia Critchley, 'Instruments of Fraud, Testamentary Dispositions, And the Doctrine of Secret Trusts' (1999) 115 (Oct) *Law Quarterly Review* 631; Patricia Critchley, 'Privileged Wills and testamentary Formalities: A time to Die?' (1999) 58(1) *Cambridge Law Journal*, 49-58.
107 [1972] Ch 698.

to prevent fraud and because they operate *dehors* the will. The formalities are not a problem as this is not a testamentary disposition but a testamentary intention.

12.4.3 Why are secret trusts enforced?

It is submitted that attempting to reconcile modern attitudes to the formalities required by statute and secret trusts is to ignore the original legal context of their enforcement. Lord Nottingham drafted the Statute of Frauds which was enacted in 1677. It contained provisions which have now become the formality provisions for the declaration of trusts of land in the Law of Property Act 1925, s.53(1)(b), and for testamentary dispositions in the Wills Act, s.9. However, at around the same time that he would have been drafting this legislation insisting on formalities, Nottingham also gave his famous judgment on when the court may imply a trust in *Cook v Fountain*.[108] Nottingham could have introduced an exception for secret trusts into the legislation but he did not. Instead he introduced the exception for the formality requirements for a declaration of a trust of land which became the Law of Property Act 1925 s.53(2). Thus he either considered the secret trust an *intervivos* trust which was implied by the court and so exempt from the formality requirements or he did not consider the Statute of Frauds to affect the power of equity to enforce a secret trust. At this point it may be appropriate to consider the reason for the Statute of Frauds; it has often been claimed that the Statute was introduced, and its successors also, to ensure that fraud was not committed on the settlor or beneficiaries of a trust. However, this is not the mischief that the Statute was intended to prevent. The preamble to the Statute is quite clear that it is intended: 'For prevention of many fraudulent Practices which are commonly endeavoured to be upheld by Perjury and Subornation of Perjury.' Nottingham and his contemporaries had to deal with the mess of land title after the Civil War and Commonwealth. The mischief that the Statute of Frauds was intended to remedy was fraudulent claims to property; the legislature was trying to 'balance the hardship to a bona fide agreed purchaser of land, or of certain personal property, where there was a real agreement, with that to an owner which would result from the making of false claims of contract backed up by perjured testimony.' Thus secret trusts were generally outside the scope of the Statute and so subject to the usual principles of trusts. They would have been enforced on the basis that the court could imply an enforceable obligation on the trustee to fulfil the trust to prevent fraud on the testator. Today, although much confused by the attempts to justify their enforcement, it may be simpler to consider that the secret trust is an attempt to create an express

---

108   Cook v Fountain (1676) 3 Swans 585, 591-592. per Lord Nottingham

trust that is constituted on the death of the testator. Thus it may be revoked at any time before death.[109] However, it fails as an express trust because it does not comply with the formality requirements in the Wills Act and so may only be enforced as a constructive trust. Although the statutory provisions have changed to a certain extent over the centuries it may still be considered that the secret trust is outside the Wills Act because its enforcement does not involve the mischief the Statute of Frauds was intended to combat; thus there does not have to be fraud on the part of the trustee for it to be considered enforceable, this would also justify the enforcement of half-secret trusts.

12.5 The different requirements for half-secret trusts

The requirement that half-secret trusts must be communicated to the secret trustee before or at the time of the execution of the will is very hard to justify.[110] In some jurisdictions the difference has been abolished.[111] There are three main theories as to why it has been claimed there are different requirements, these are: incorporation by reference; the legal advice theory (or the 'naïve testator' theory); and, the mistaken interpretation theory.

12.5.1 Incorporation by reference

This is a probate doctrine which has been advanced as justification for the enforcement of half-secret trusts. The doctrine states that a document may be incorporated into a will if:

a) it is already in existence at the time of the execution of the will; and
b) it is identified in the will; and
c) it is referred to in the will as being already in existence.

It is not hard to see the similarities with the half-secret trust as it must be referred to in the will and it must have been communicated to the trustee before the will is executed. Paul Matthews has argued that this is the whole basis of half-secret trusts and that they are totally different from fully secret trusts.[112] However, Matthews' theory has been criticised as there seems to

---

109 Today of course an action for estoppel may be available to prevent a testator revoking the trust.
110 See Holdswoth, 'Secret Trusts' (1937) 53 *Law Quarterly Review* 501.
111 For example Ireland (see *Prendiville v Prendiville* [1989] No 597 Sp Ct 5) and New Zealand *(Ledgerwood v Perpetual Trustee* [1997] 41 NSWLR532); see John Mee, 'Half-secret trusts in England and Ireland.' (1992) (May/June) *Conveyancer and Property Lawyer,* 202-206; C.E.F. Rickett, 'Thoughts on Secret Trusts from New Zealand' (1996) (Jul/Aug) *The Conveyancer and Property Lawyer 302-308.*
112 Paul Matthews, 'The true basis of the half-secret trust?' [1979] *Conveyancer and Property Lawyer* 360.

have been no judicial acceptance of this theory, and the terms of the trust may be oral and so there is no document to incorporate into the will.

12.5.2 Legal advice and the naive testator

David Wilde has proposed a theory that would explain the separate communication requirements of fully secret and half-secret trusts.[113] Wilde claims that a testator who seeks legal advice as to the creation of an enforceable secret trust will most likely be advised to create a half-secret trust to minimise the risk of fraud. Equity will enforce a fully secret trust with less requirements as the testator is probably unadvised. However, the testator who attempts to create a half-secret trust has probably had the benefit of legal advice and so should not flagrantly disregard the requirements of the Wills Act.

Of course this is pure conjecture and there is no real evidence that this is the reason for the distinction. It seems that Viscount Sumner's requirement in *Blackwell v Blackwell* was purely to avoid 'unwitnessed dispositions' being made after the execution of the will in a manner similar to an unwitnessed codicil to a will.

12.5.3 The mistaken interpretation theory

Aaron Mak has persuasively argued that the distinction between the communication requirements for full and half secret trusts may just be the result of mistaken interpretation of the obiter statement of Parker V.C. in *Johnson v Ball*,[114] that a, 'testator cannot by his will prospectively create for himself a power to dispose of his property by an instrument not duly executed as a will or codicil.'[115] In clarifying this statement Viscount Sumner, in *Blackwell v Blackwell*,[116] noted that, 'A testator cannot reserve to himself a power of making future unattested dispositions by merely naming a trustee and leaving the purposes of the trust to be supplied afterwards' with the added comment, 'nor can a legatee give testamentary validity to an unexecuted codicil by accepting an indefinite trust, never communicated to him in the testator's lifetime'. Mak suggests this must mean the testator cannot communicate future dispositions after his death and submits this is confirmed by Viscount Sumner's following statement that, 'it is communication of the purpose to the legatee, coupled with

---

113 David Wilde, 'Secret and Semi-Secret Trusts: Justifying Distinctions Between The Two' (1995) (Sep/Oct) *Conveyancer and Property Lawyer* 366-378.
114 (1851) 5 De G & Sm 85 at 90.
115 Aaron Mak, 'Reconciling the Enforcement of Full and Half Secret Trusts: A Reinterpretation of Blackwell v Blackwell' (2013) 2 (Spring) *Hong Kong Student Law Gazette* 38-39.
116 (1929) AC 235.

acquiescence or promise on his part, that removes the matter from the Wills Act and brings it within the law of trust as applied in this instance to trustees'. However, subsequent misinterpretation of Viscount Sumner's dicta, for example, by Lord Wright MR in *Re Keen*,[117] has led to the distinction in communication requirements. Mak also notes that the dicta in *Johnson v Ball* and *Re Keen* led to the confusion that the reason for enforcing secret trusts was to prevent fraud by the trustee against the provisions of the Wills Act, not fraud against the testator.

12.6 Summary

Mutual wills are usually in the form of a life estate for the survivor in the joint property of the couple with agreed remainder beneficiaries, usually the couple's children. It is even possible that the survivor obtains no benefit under the will of the first to die. To be enforceable mutual wills there must be a definite and unequivocal agreement not to revoke the wills and an intention of both parties to be bound by the agreement upon death of the first party. The agreement not to revoke should usually be contained in the wills, but extrinsic evidence may be admitted to confirm the existence of the agreement. The mere fact that the wills have been executed at the same time and in the same form is not conclusive evidence that the wills are mutual.

If a party to mutual wills revokes their will before the death of the other party then both are no longer bound by the agreement and the mutual wills are not enforceable.

The survivor may be able to claim damages for breach of the contract from the estate of the deceased if they have not received the property they were expecting. If the survivor changes his will in breach of the agreement, or destroys his will and so dies intestate then the survivor's personal representatives will hold the property on constructive trust for the purposes agreed.

Mutual wills are enforced on the basis of conscience and the law of trusts. Thus a constructive trust arises on the first death. However, there may be problems with identifying what property is subject to the trust obligation. If the mutual wills clearly refer to property and what is to be done with it then this should be enforced. If the wills do not clearly identify the property subject to the obligation or, as is usually the case refer to the parties whole estate or residue after specified bequests then the survivor's interest is considered analogous to a life tenant in all of the property he owns at the time of the death of the first party. The survivor may do what he wishes with the property during his lifetime as long as he does nothing 'deliberately to defeat the compact'. The constructive trust arises on the

---

117 (1937) Ch 236 .

death of the first party, but crystallises as to subject matter on the death of the survivor.

Secret trusts are trusts that do not comply with the requirements of the Wills Act that all testamentary dispositions be in writing, signed by the testator and witnessed.

There are two types of secret trust, the fully secret trust which seems on the face of the will an absolute gift to the trustee, and the half-secret trust which is obviously a trust on the face of the will but does not provide details of the trust. Both should be void for not complying with the Wills Act. To be enforceable secret trusts must comply with certain requirements. These are almost the same for both fully secret and half-secret trusts: the testator must have intended to transfer the property to the secret trustee under a trust obligation; the testator must have communicated that intention to the trustee, and the trustee must have accepted that obligation. If the trustee is informed of the obligation but does not expressly accept it, it will be presumed he has accepted the obligation.

There is one important difference between secret trusts and that is that communication of the trust obligation to the secret trustee can be at any time before the death of the testator for a fully secret trust, but must be before or at the time of execution of the will for a half-secret trust.

If a fully secret trust fails then the legatee takes absolutely unless he knew he was under a trust obligation in which case he will hold the property on resulting trust for the testator's estate. A trustee under a fully secret trust may also disclaim the obligation, in which case he will take the property absolutely if the testator does not change his will. A half-secret trustee can never take the property as the obligation is obvious on the face of the will and the trust is constituted from the moment of the testator's death.

There are various theories as to why secret trusts are enforced and why there are different communication requirements. The orthodox view is that secret trusts are enforced because *equity will not allow a statute to be used for fraud*. Thus equity will not allow the statutory requirements to be used by the trustee to avoid his obligations in carrying out the trust. Another popular theory is the '*dehors* the will' theory, that secret trusts are *inter vivos* trusts which take effect outside the will but are constituted by the will. This has some judicial approval. There are problems with this view, however, as wills are ambulatory and may be revoked at any time before death, therefore if the secret trust was *inter vivos* it could not be revoked by changing the will.

It seems most likely that the secret trust, although created expressly, fails to comply with the requirements for an enforceable express trust and so is enforced as an implied trust, a constructive trust enforced against the conscience of the secret trustee to prevent statute being used as an instrument of fraud against the testator.

	Secret Trust	Half secret trust
Authority for creation requirements	*Ottaway v Norman* [1972]	*Blackwell v Blackwell* [1929]
Creation requirements	**Intention** of testator to subject transferee to trust obligation in favour of secret beneficiary **Communication** of the intention to transferee includes existence and details of the trust **Acceptance** of obligation by transferee expressly or implicitly	
Intention	Same as certainty of intention for creation of express trusts More than a moral obligation: *Re Snowden*	
Communication	Must be during life of testator BUT can be before or after the making of the will	Must be during life of testator but must be before or at the time of execution of the will: *Blackwell v Blackwell*
Acceptance	Obligation must be accepted by secret trustee Silence is deemed acceptance: *Moss v Cooper*	
Failure of trust- no communication of obligation to trustee	Trustee takes absolutely as conscience is not affected- *Walgrave v Tebbs*	Trustee holds on resulting trust for testator's estate. Half-secret trustee can never take property absolutely.
Failure of trust- communication of trust obligation but no communication of details	Trustee holds on resulting trust for testator's *estate Re Boyes* (1884)	
Failure of trust- trustee communicates revocation of acceptance of obligation to testator before testator's death	Trustee takes absolutely- it seems obligation is on testator to change will: *Whitton v Russell* (1739) 1 Atk 539	
Trustee revokes acceptance after death of testator	Trust constituted- equity will not allow a trust to fail for want of a trustee (*obiter Maddock*)	

CHAPTER 13
TRUSTEES

13.1 What is a Trustee?

A trustee is a body, whether human or a non-living entity, such as a registered company, which has legal title to property entrusted to it that it must administer in good faith for the benefit of others. There are many different types of trustee as there are many different types of trust. A trustee may not even know he is a trustee until a court informs him that the property which he considered his is actually held by him on constructive or resulting trust for another. As the nature of trusteeship varies depending on the type of trust so do the duties of the trustee. Of course today many trustees are professionals, for example banks, accountants and solicitors often act as trustees. However, there are still private and charitable trusts which are constituted with non-professional trustees, based purely on the original concept of a friend being entrusted with an obligation. In this chapter we will consider the various management duties of trustees generally and the concept of breach of trust and liability for breach of trust.

The trustee must act in good faith towards the trust and the beneficiaries of the trust; he is a fiduciary, but a special type of fiduciary. A trustee performs his functions in a fiduciary capacity: he is expected to act honestly and fairly in the best interests of the trust, which usually means acting in the best interests of the beneficiaries.[1] The next chapter will deal with fiduciaries and fiduciary duties generally and so will apply to trustees as well. The fiduciary obligations imposed by equity originate from the obligations imposed by the Court of Chancery on the trustee. However, it is submitted that the fiduciary nature of trusteeship is such that a trustee will often be held to a higher standard of behaviour than other fiduciaries. The fiduciary nature of trusteeship is exemplified by terms such as loyalty and good faith; and an overwhelming duty to put the interests of the trust before the trustee's own interests.

The trustee is in a position of power, as are other fiduciaries with regard to their principals. However, unlike most other fiduciaries, such as the company director or agent, the trustee has legal title to the trust property and administrative powers to deal with the trust property. As there is no requirement for the existence of a trust to be registered or declared, or the

---

1   *Armitage v Nurse* [1998] Ch. 241 at pp. 253E- 254 E per Millett L.J. Cited in *Spread Trustee Co Ltd v Hutcheson* [2011] UKPC 13 [46] per Lord Clarke.

extent of a trustee's powers to be communicated to outsiders to the trust, the trustee appears to outsiders to the trust to be the absolute owner of the trust property. Legal ownership of the trust property and the administrative powers of the trustee mean that the position of trustee is open to abuse. Therefore equity has developed a series of principles and rules to impose duties on the trustee, restrict the trustee's powers, and protect the trust and beneficiaries.

The fiduciary nature of trusteeship and the potential liability of the trustee for any losses to the trust make trusteeship an onerous task, a task made no easier as the general principle is that trustees should not be paid. The trust instrument may define precisely the extent of the trustee's powers and duties and it may limit the extent of the trustee's liability for any loss to the trust. In the absence of such directions from the settlor however, we must look to both the common law and (increasingly) to statute to ascertain the extent of the trustee's liability. The Trustee Acts 1925 and 2000 regulate trustees of trusts governed by the law of England and Wales.

13.2 Appointment of Trustees and Termination of Trusteeship

Any person who has the capacity to hold property has the capacity to be a trustee. At common law, a minor may not be a trustee, although there have been occasions when a court has declared that a minor is trustee of property held on resulting trust.[2] At common law there is no restriction on the number of trustees. Statutory limits have been placed on the number of trustees as this removes uncertainty for those dealing with the trustees. Thus although there may be any number of trustees of personalty, the settlor or his nominees should not appoint more than four.[3] Because of the particular problems of conveying land there cannot be more than four trustees of land.[4] This restriction does not apply to trusts for sale of land which are charitable, ecclesiastical or for public purposes.[5]

At common law a trust may be constituted with only one trustee, but it is submitted that at least two trustees should be appointed because, as legal title to trust property must vest in all trustees, this will ensure that no one trustee may deal with the trust property and prevent abuse of the trust. It is necessary to purchase trust land from at least two trustees or a trust corporation to overreach the interests of the beneficiaries.[6] A registered company may be a trustee, whether sole or in association with other trust

---

2   *Re Vinogradoff* [1935] WN 68.
3   **Trustee Act 1925** s36.
4   **Trustee Act 1925** s34(2).
5   Trustee Act 1925, s.34(3).
6   The Law of Property Act 1925, ss 2 & 27.

corporations or human trustees.

Trustees may be appointed by the settlor, those designated in the trust instrument, statute or the court. The first trustees are normally appointed by the settlor/ testator in the trust deed / will. If the trust is *inter vivos* they must be identified and capable of acting. The obligation must be accepted, this may be by express acceptance or implied from their beginning the duties of the trustee. Those selected may disclaim or refuse the trust obligation before acceptance. The trust obligation does not exist until the trustees accept the obligation and property is transferred to them. Once the trust is begun, it does not matter that they later disclaim the trust, they will continue in their role until they have been released from the obligation, by the methods considered below, and even when they have been removed from the trust obligation the trust will continue until its purpose is fulfilled or a court brings the trust to an end because it is a maxim of equity that *equity will not permit a trust to fail for want of a trustee.*

The trust instrument may provide the details of how a trustee is to be removed or how a trustee is to be appointed. The settlor may also reserve a power to appoint new trustees in the trust instrument. If there is no express power to create new trustees in the trust instrument the Trustee Act 1925, s.36, provides power to appoint new trustees. This section applies unless there is a contrary intention in the trust instrument. The section gives to the person nominated to appoint new trustees or, in default of such appointment the surviving or continuing trustees, or the personal representatives of the last surviving trustee the power to appoint new trustees in certain circumstances. Those circumstances are:

a) where a trustee is dead.;
b) where a trustee remains outside of the United Kingdom for more than 12 months;
c) where a trustee desires to be discharged from all or any of his duties;
d) where a trustee is unfit to act;
e) where a trustee is incapable of acting;
f) where the trustee is an infant;
g) where the trustee has been removed under a power contained in the trust instrument

The appointment must be in writing. Once appointed the new trustee has the same powers, authorities and discretions as an original trustee.

Beneficiaries of a trust may also now appoint trustees because of the Trusts of Land and Appointment of Trustees Act 1996, s19, which applies when there is nobody nominated to appoint new trustees and the beneficiaries are all *sui juris*, of full age and together beneficially entitled. In these circumstances the beneficiaries may give written direction to the trustees requiring them to appoint a specified person as trustee.

The court has authority to appoint a trustee by way of statute and its inherent jurisdiction.

The many statutory powers of the court to appoint a trustee include the Trustee Act 1925, s41, which provides:

'The court may, whenever it is expedient to appoint a new trustee or trustees, and it is found inexpedient, difficult or impracticable to do so without the assistance of the court, make an order appointing a new trustee or trustees, or although there is no existing trustee. In particular and without prejudice to the generality of the foregoing provision, the court may make an order appointing a new trustee in substitution for a trustee who is incapable by reason of a mental disorder within the meaning of the Mental Health Act 1983 of exercising his functions as trustee, or is a bankrupt, or is a corporation which is in liquidation or has been dissolved.'

This section gives the court the power to appoint a new trustee or trustees whenever it is difficult or impractical to do so without the assistance of the court. Section 42 of the Trustee Act 1925 provides, in similar words to s36(7), that any trustee(s) appointed by the court will have all powers etc of an original trustee.

The court also has jurisdiction under other statutes to replace trustees. These provisions may overlap with the general statutory powers of replacement.[7] For example the court may replace a trustee under the Trustee Act 1925, s.54, if the trustee is a patient under the Mental Health Act 1983. The court may also appoint a fit and proper person to be a judicial trustee under the Judicial Trustee Act 1896. This power is only used when the administration of a trust has broken down.

It is rarely necessary to invoke the court's inherent jurisdiction to remove or appoint trustees today because most instances are covered by the statutory powers, e.g. the trustee takes up residency abroad, refuses to act or is unfit to act, or becomes bankrupt. However, the power still exists. The principles to be applied by the court when considering appointing new trustees were considered in *Re Tempest*.[8] The court should:

- have regard to the wishes of the settlor;
- not appoint a person with a view to the interest of some of the beneficiaries, in opposition to the interests of others;
- have regard to the question whether appointment will promote or impede the execution of the trust;
- not appoint a person who would be in a position where there would be a conflict between his duty and interest.

---

7   See, for example, the Judicial Trustees Act 1896 and the Public Trustee Act 1906.

8   (1866) 1 Ch App 485.

The trust property must be vested in the new trustee in order for him to perform his duties. The deed of appointment can vest the trust property in the new trustees or the court can make an order vesting the property in the new body of trustees. Land must be conveyed to the new trustee.

Trusteeship may come to an end in a number of ways:

- Disclaimer;
- Death;
- Retirement;
- Removal.

A trustee may disclaim trusteeship at any time before constitution of the trust, but once he has accepted the office, whether expressly or impliedly, and the trust is constituted he may not disclaim it. When a trustee dies the surviving trustees assume his responsibilities as joint tenants. If the deceased trustee was a sole surviving trustee, his personal representatives may exercise his duties as trustee.[9]

The trustee may retire or be removed from trusteeship by:

- Express provision in the trust instrument;
- Statutory provision;
- Statutory power of the court;
- The court's inherent jurisdiction;
- Consent of the beneficiaries.

The trust instrument may expressly provide the circumstances in which a trustee may retire or be removed. Usually a new trustee must be appointed to replace the trustee. However, the Trustee Act 1925 s39, provides that a trustee may retire without any need to appoint another if he does so by deed and there are at least two trustees or a trust corporation remaining to administer the trust. The other trustees must also consent to this retirement by deed. A trustee may also pay the trust money into court under the Trustee Act 1925, s63. The trustee will remain a trustee, but he will effectively have ceased to act in relation to the trust property.

As noted above, the Trustee Act 1925, ss.36 and 41 also provide powers for the court to remove trustees and appoint new trustees in their place. Section 36 provides circumstances in which a trustee may be replaced by nominated persons, surviving trustees, or the personal representatives of the last surviving trustee, including a trustee's wish to retire from the role or unfitness to carry out the role. The court may remove a trustee under the Trustee Act 1925, s41, whenever it is expedient or necessary to do so, and appoint a new trustee to replace them.

---

9   Administration of Estates Act 1925 ss1-3

The court also has the inherent jurisdiction to remove a trustee.[10] The statutory powers of the court are mostly used in preference to the inherent jurisdiction today although there is one area where the inherent jurisdiction might still be useful. The court's inherent jurisdiction applies to trustees who have behaved improperly although not necessarily in breach of trust. This power may be exercised even though there is no evidence of actual misconduct; however, the court must be satisfied continuing in office would prejudice the trust.[11]

The beneficiaries may remove a trustee from office if there is express power for them to do so in the trust instrument, and a trustee may request the beneficiaries to allow him to retire, and his retirement will be effective if the beneficiaries, being all *sui juris* and together beneficially entitled, agree. The beneficiaries may also direct a trustee to retire under the Trusts of Land and Appointment of Trustees Act 1996, s19, if they are of full age, *sui juris*, and together beneficially entitled to all of the trust property. There must be at least two remaining trustees or a trust corporation. The trustee must either be replaced or the remaining trustees must consent to his retirement by deed.

Trusteeship also comes to an end when the trust has been fulfilled.

13.3 The Duty of Care to the Trust and the Standard of Care

In carrying out their duties to the trust the trustee is expected to act to a requisite standard of care. There is now a statutory standard of care specified in the Trustee Act 2000, s.1, which replaced the common law standard of care. However, the Trustee Act 2000 specifies that the statutory standard can be excluded from the trust by express instruction in the trust instrument.

The common law general standard of care expected of trustees when conducting the business of the trust and performing their duties to the trust was stated by Jessel MR in **Speight v Gaunt**:[12] 'a trustee ought to conduct the business of the trust in the same manner that an ordinary prudent man of business would conduct his own.'[13] In **Speight v Gaunt**,[14] the trustee had placed trust money into the hands of a broker who was a fraudster. In the judgment of the House of Lords there is consistent reference to the fact that

---

10   *Buchanan v Hamilton* (1801) 5 Ves 722.
11   *Moore v M'Glynn* (1894) 1 IR 74.
12   (1883) 22 Ch D 727.
13   Confirmed by Lord Blackburn in the House of Lords: "...as a general rule a trustee sufficiently discharges his duty if he takes in managing trust affairs all those precautions which an ordinary prudent man of business would take in managing similar affairs of his own." *Speight v Gaunt (1883) 9 App Cas, 1.*
14   *Speight v Gaunt* (1883) 9 App Cas, 1.

the trustee had no reason to distrust the fraudster. The House considered whether the trustee had been in wilful default of his duty because he did not take action against the fraudster when the securities were not forthcoming and fraud was first suspected. The Earl of Selborne L.C. commented that the trustee could not have done anything as the fraudster was insolvent at the time: the fraudster was '"irretrievably insolvent," so that nothing could by any diligence, have been recovered from him.'[15] Although in Speight the trustee was criticised for his 'looseness and seeming carelessness',[16] he was absolved from any liability for loss to the trust. Lord Fitzgerald was concerned about the lack of enquiries made by Gaunt after the broker had taken the fund but he could not link this to the loss the trust suffered which was from the initial fraudulent misappropriation of the funds. The later failure to inquire was not the cause of the loss and there was nothing more the trustee could have done after the loss to rectify the matter. [17] Emphasis was also placed upon the fact the trustee was unpaid and had accepted an onerous position.[18]One of the duties of the trustee, as considered below, is to invest the trust property so as to maintain the property for the beneficiaries. When exercising investments for the trust the trustee is expected to act to a slightly higher standard than when carrying out his general management duties – this is the standard of the ordinary prudent man of business in making investment decisions for the benefit of persons for whom he felt morally obliged to provide.[19]

It may be observed that the standard of care expected of trustees has traditionally not been very exacting. This may be because originally it was a voluntary, unpaid role, usually performed by gentlemen. However, it has become more usual to use professionals as trustees and to pay them for their services. Thus there has been recognition that the standard should be higher, especially for professional paid trustees. As Harman J stated in *Re Waterman's WT*,[20] 'a paid trustee is expected to exercise a higher standard of diligence and knowledge than an unpaid trustee and a bank which advertises itself largely in the public press as taking charge of administrations is under a special duty.'

The principle that a trustee who claimed to possess a particular skill for

---

15 *Speight v Gaunt (1883)* 9 App Cas, 1, 14. "He swears that he did not suspect, and that he had no grounds for suspecting, that anything was wrong, till Cooke's [the broker] insolvency became known, when it was too late to recover the money": *Speight v Gaunt* (1883) 9 App Cas, 1, 15, per the Earl of Selborne L.C.

16 *Speight v Gaunt* (1883) 9 App Cas, 1, 29, per Lord Fitzgerald.

17 *Speight v Gaunt* (1883) 9 App Cas, 1, 33, per Lord Fitzgerald.

18 *Speight v Gaunt* (1883) 9 App Cas, 1, 17, per Lord Blackburn.

19 *Re Whiteley* (1887) 12 App Cas 727.

20 [1952] 2 All ER 1054.

his role should be judged accordingly was considered in **Bartlett v. Barclays Bank Trust Co. Ltd,**[21] when Brightman J asserted that,

'the trust corporation holds itself out as capable of providing an expertise which it would be unrealistic to expect and unjust to demand from the ordinary prudent man or woman who accepts, probably unpaid and sometimes reluctantly from a sense of family duty, the burdens of a trusteeship so I think that a professional corporate trustee is liable for breach of trust if loss is caused to the trust fund because it neglects to exercise the special care and skill which it professes to have.'

The trustee bank had allowed the management company to invest in two development schemes which subsequently resulted in large losses for the fund. The bank tried to hide behind the corporate veil of the management company, but was held liable for the losses whether judged on the standard of a prudent man or a professional as the investments were, 'a gamble and not, on the evidence I have heard, a very good gamble.'[22]

Thus a professional trustee must perform his role with the particular care and skill to be expected of such a person.[23] The principle for unpaid trustees is still that, "[a] trustee who is honest and reasonably competent is not to be held responsible for a mere error of judgment, from which no businessman, however, prudent, can expect to be immune."[24] Thus, a trustee will not be liable for an innocent misapplication of funds and this would not even be grounds for removing the trustee from office.[25] Trustees of a charitable trust must perform their role to the same standard as trustees of a private trust.[26]

The statutory duty of care for trustees is similar to that of company directors. This was introduced in the Trustee Act 2000, s.1, and provides that trustees must perform their duties with, '… such care and skill as is reasonable in the circumstances, having regard in particular-to any special knowledge or experience that he has or holds himself out as having, and if he acts as a trustee in the conduct of his business or profession, to any special knowledge or experience that it is reasonable to expect of a person

---

21   [1980] Ch 515.

22   [1980] Ch 515, per Brightman J.

23   Bartlett v Barclays Bank Trust Co. Ltd (Nos 1 and 2) [1980] 1 All ER 139; 2 WLR 430. Confirmed in *Spread Trustee Co Ltd v Hutcheson* [2011] UKPC 13 [20].

24   The courts seem less willing to consider a professional trustee should not be held liable for errors of judgment: Peter Luxton, *The Law of Charities* (Oxford, Oxford University Press: 2001), p.361 [9.75]: Referring to Brightman J in *Bartlett v. Barclays Bank Trust Co. Ltd* [1980] Ch 515, at 534.

25   *Att-Gen v Caius College* (1837) 2 Keen 150 at 166. J. Warburton, *Tudor On Charities* (London, Sweet & Maxwell: 2003, 9th edition), p.225 [5-037].

26   Peter Luxton, *The Law of Charities* (Oxford, Oxford University Press: 2001), p.361 [9.75].

acting in the course of that kind of business or profession.'

The standard thus imparts a subjective element with a higher standard of care depending on the knowledge of the trustee and the role he is performing.

There have been claims that there is no need for a higher standard of care for professionals as all trustees should be judged to a high standard. Amateur unpaid trustees could then make use of the discretion afforded the court by the Trustee Act 1925, s.61, discussed below, to be exempted from all or partial liability for any loss if they have acted honestly and reasonably in the circumstances.[27]

13.4 Trustee Remuneration

This section could have been included with the fiduciary duties. However, it seems the rule against payment was always more specific to trustees than other fiduciaries and thus it is appropriate to include it in the section on management duties of trustees.

Trustees are under restrictions and duties because of the fiduciary nature of their role. Some fiduciary duties were at one time specific to trustees, for example the rule on fair dealing. However, the trustee's fiduciary duties are now common to all fiduciaries with the exception of the rule that trustees should not be paid. The main fiduciary duties are dealt with in the next chapter but all fiduciary duties derive from the principle that a fiduciary should not allow his interests to conflict with those of his principle and should not make a profit from his position. The application of these principles to the trustee has meant that a trustee should receive no payment for his role, however difficult and regardless of the potential personal cost to the trustee.

The general rule is that 'a trustee, executor, or administrator, shall have no allowance for his care and trouble'.[28] This derives from the concept of the trustee as a friend performing the role of trustee out of a sense of honour and loyalty and not for any reward. However, as today most people and corporations perform the role only for remuneration, the principle is now honoured more in the exception than the rule. The exceptions to the rule are; a trustee may be paid when:

1 There is authority in the trust instrument;
2 There is agreement of all the beneficiaries;
3 The court authorises payment;
4 The common law allows.
5 The Trustee Act 2000 s29.

---

27 Professional trustees usually make use of exemption clauses to attempt to avoid liability, as discussed below.
28 *Robinson v. Pett* (1734) 3 P.Wms 249.

Today, nearly every trust instrument provides a remuneration clause for the trustees. This may be the case even if the trustees are not professionals in case a professional is ever appointed as a trustee. Standard trust forms and contracts provided by trust corporations will always contain a remuneration clause (as well as exemption clauses). However, in upholding the principle of protecting the trust, any remuneration clause, as with an exemption clause, will be construed *contra proferentum* the trustee if it is ambiguous.

As the beneficiaries between them own the trust property, as in the rule in *Saunders v Vautier*, they may have the right to control its expenditure. If all the beneficiaries are of full age and absolutely entitled to the trust then they may authorise payment of the trustees.[29] Of course if there is any undue influence by the trustees of the beneficiaries to induce payment the provision may be avoided.

The court can authorise payment if it appoints a trust corporation as trustee. Of course it would be unlikely for a trust corporation to undertake the role if it were not paid. The court can also authorize payment under its inherent jurisdiction. For example, in *Re Duke of Norfolk's ST*,[30] a remuneration clause existed in the trust instrument, but the court increased the amount payable. New property had been added to the settlement and this had created extra work for the trustees. In *Boardman v Phipps*,[31] although the solicitor-trustee Boardman had to disgorge the profit he had made from his position as a fiduciary of the Phipps Family Trust, he was awarded a *quantum meruit* payment, a payment which reflected the amount of work he had undertaken for the trust.

The common law has also developed exceptions which allow for remuneration in certain circumstances. The rule in *Cradock v Piper*,[32] provides that a trustee who is also a solicitor may claim payment for work done in preparing and conducting litigation on behalf of the trust, as long as the trustees have unanimously authorised him to conduct this work. The rule in *Re Northcote*,[33] provides that if trust assets are in a foreign jurisdiction which permits remuneration then it will be allowed. In *Re Northcote*, the testator had died leaving assets in the UK and the USA. The executors were granted probate in England and also obtained a grant of probate in New York for the USA assets. The executors collected the assets in the USA, and gained commission, as entitled under local law. When this payment was challenged as being contrary to English law, which governed the estate, the court held that the executors were entitled to charge as

---

29   *Ayliffe v Murray* [1740] 2 Atk 58.
30   [1982] 1 Ch 61.
31   [1967] 2 AC 46.
32   (1850) 1 Mac & G 664.
33   [1949] 1 All ER 442.

permitted under the local jurisdiction.

The **Trustee Act 2000,** s29, provides a statutory charging clause for professional trustees to levy a reasonable charge for their services. This clause may be implied into all trusts and wills which do not have an express charging clause except charitable trust and pension trusts.

Although not payment as such, the common law has always permitted trustees to recover their legitimate expenses incurred in performing their duties to the trust.[34]

13.5 The Management Duties and Powers of Trustees

The management duties of the trustee will vary depending on the nature of the trust, for, as Millett J. noted, in *Lonrho plc v Fayed (No 2)*,[35] 'It is a mistake to suppose that in every situation in which a constructive trust arises the legal owner is necessarily subject to all the fiduciary obligations and disabilities of an express trustee.' This is because management of the trust may involve simply passing trust funds to the beneficiaries of a bare trust or may involve administering many different types of trust fund involving investment, selling and purchasing property and collecting rents for many years with ultimate distribution according to the instructions in the trust instrument. Thus the obligations, duties and powers of the trustee vary.

Professor Birks noted that rights and obligations relate to the same thing in substance,[36] by extension powers are a necessary corollary of duties. If a person is placed under a duty to perform some action then they must also have the power to perform that action. With trust obligations, the trust instrument, the common law, or statute will place the trustee under an obligation with regard to the trust. As the trustee will be in breach of trust and may face personal liability to the trust if he does not perform his duties, there must be a corresponding source of power for the trustee to perform those actions. Thus the duties of the trustee also give rise to powers.

The management duties of the trustee are:

- The duty to acquaint himself with the trust;
- The duty to carry out the trust (safeguard the trust);
- The duty to act unanimously;
- The duty to invest;
- The duty to act personally;
- The duty to deal fairly and equally with beneficiaries;
- The duty to distribute the trust property;

---

34 *Turner v. Hancock* 20 Ch D 303; *R. v. Beddoe* [1893]1 Ch 547.
35 [1991] 4 All ER 961.
36 P. Birks, 'Definition and Division: A Meditation on Institutes 3.13' in P Birks (ed) *The Classification of Obligations* (Clarendon Press Oxford 1997).

- The duty to account to the beneficiaries (this also extends to making good any unaccounted loss).

When a trustee is appointed he must acquaint himself with the terms of the trust instrument and the nature and extent of the trust property. If any trust property is in danger for any reason he must safeguard that property. This is sometimes referred to as the duty to collect in the trust assets. If the trustee is in any doubt concerning the construction of the trust instrument or how to administer the trust, the trustee should request directions from the court by an originating summons.

The trustee is also under a duty to carry out the trust. The instructions in the trust instrument must be followed. If the trust is a discretionary trust then the trustee must exercise that discretion within the limits set in the trust instrument. If the trustee acts outside these limits he has acted *ultra vires* and is in breach of trust. The trustee may be personally liable for any loss consequentially incurred by the trust.

The appointment of amateur trustees and the wish to protect the interests of the beneficiaries led to the development of the so-called rule in *Re Hastings-Bass*.[37] This rule has recently been doubted by the Court of Appeal.[38] The rule provided a protection for beneficiaries when the trustees had exercised their discretion taking into account considerations they should not have done or not taking into account considerations they should have done and the effect was not as intended. If the trustees had acted in this manner the transaction could be avoided at the instance of the trustees and so save the trust from loss and the trustees (and their advisors) from potential personal liability. For example, if a trustee made an investment without due regard to the nature of the trust or possible tax liability and the trust was likely to suffer as a result the trustees could apply to the court for the transaction to be declared void.

The Court of Appeal has attempted to clarify the rule in a number of cases. In *Sieff v Fox*,[39] Lloyd LJ restated the rule in *Re Hastings-Bass* as follows:

'I will, however, summarise the Re Hastings-Bass principle as I see it, as follows: (i) The best formulation of the principle seems to me to be this. Where trustees act under a discretion given to them by the terms of the trust, in circumstances in which they are free to decide whether or not to

---

37   [1975] Ch 25.
38   See *Sieff v Fox* [2005] 3 All ER 693, EWCA; *Pitt v Holt* [2011] 3 WLR 19, EWCA; *Futter* v *Futter* [2011] EWCA Civ 197. See also Lord Neuberger of Abbotsbury MR, 'Aspects of the Law of Mistake: Re Hastings-Bass' (2009) 15/4 *Trusts & Trustees* 189; and Tony Molloy and Toby Graham, 'Hard cases and bad law' (2011) 17 (9) *Trusts & Trustees* 803-806.
39   [2005] 3 All ER 693,728.

exercise that discretion, but the effect of the exercise is different from that which they intended, the court will interfere with their action if it is clear that they would not have acted as they did had they not failed to take into account considerations which they ought to have taken into account, or taken into account considerations which they ought not to have taken into account.'

Thus, if a trustee fails to consider matters which he ought to consider, or considers matters which he ought not to have considered, then the beneficiaries (or trustees) may seek a declaration that the exercise of discretion is void; provided that the decision might have been different but for the irregularity. The principle is meant to be simply a pragmatic rule which prevents technical breaches from being litigated. It has been noted that the test is similar to *Wednesbury* reasonableness, as applied in public law.[40]

However, recent Court of Appeal cases have effectively ended the rule and mean that the matter will now have to be solved by litigation between the beneficiaries and the trustees, and possibly their advisors. The rule may survive in other jurisdictions, for example Jersey.[41]

Trustees may be given absolute, uncontrolled discretion, in which case the court is generally loath to interfere in the management of the trustees and their exercise of their discretion unless they are defeating the object of the trust.[42]

In making decisions and carrying out any of the management duties trustees must act unanimously and not by majority vote (unless they are trustees of a charity or pension trust). In a private trust, should the trustees act in breach of trust, they will be jointly liable for that breach.[43]

13.6 The Duty to Invest

Trustees have a duty to protect the trust property. This involves a duty to invest the trust property. The traditional meaning of 'invest' for trust purposes is 'to employ money in the purchase of anything from which interest or profit is expected'.[44]

---

40   Gary Watt, *Trusts and Equity*, 3rd edition (Oxford: Oxford University Press, 2008).

41   See http://www.stepjournal.org/journal_archive/2011/step_journal_may_2011/the_end_of_the_rule_in_re.aspx

42   *Gisborne v Gisborne* (1877) 2 App Cas 300.

43   *Dubai Aluminium Co. Ltd. v. Salaam*, [2002] EWHL 48.

44   *Re Wragg* [1919] 2 Ch 58, adopting the definition in the *Oxford Shorter English Dictionary*.

13.6.1 The power to invest

In order to perform this duty, trustees need powers of investment. The trust instrument usually gives express powers of investment and these may be very wide. For example there may be clauses in the trust instrument which provide that a trustee may invest 'as he sees fit' or 'as if he were the beneficial owner of the trust property'. However, the trust instrument may also restrict investment, for example, the trust may only be allowed to accumulate income from trust property and buy land or shares. If the power of investment is restricted in the instrument then the trustee will generally be liable if he does not abide by these restrictions and the trust suffers consequential loss.

A trust instrument may specify that trustees must sell trust land and invest the proceeds in shares or bonds, or use trust capital to purchase land. If the trustees do not do as instructed then equity will still consider the trust property to be in the designated form because of the doctrine of conversion and the maxim *equity regards as done that which ought to be done*.

If powers of investment are not specified in the trust instrument then the Trustee Act 2000, s.3(1) grants a general power of investment: 'subject to the provisions of this Part, a trustee may make any kind of investment that he could make if he were absolutely entitled to the assets of the trust.' The trustee of a trust of land has 'all the powers of an absolute owner' with regard to the trust property.[45] The trust instrument may specify that the general power of investment will not apply.[46]

In addition trustees have statutory powers to purchase property. Trustees of land or the proceeds of sale of land may purchase land for occupation by a beneficiary, as an investment, or for any other reason. [47] Similarly, trustees of settled land also have the power to purchase freehold land or leasehold land for a term of more than 60 years.[48] Trustees of trust of personalty now have the power, under s.8 of the Trustee Act 2000, to purchase freehold or leasehold land as an investment, for occupation by a beneficiary, or for any other reason. Once the land is purchased the trustees will become trustees of land.

When making an investment the trustees must take note of the standard investment criteria which are specified in the Trustee Act 2000, s.4: a) the suitability to the trust of the type of investment; and b) the need for diversification. A trustee should also seek 'proper advice' before exercising

---

45 The Trusts of Land and Appointment of Trustee Act 1996, s6(1).
46 The Trustee Act 2000, s.6. Unless excluded by the instrument the general power of investment 'applies in relation to trusts whether created before or after' the commencement of the Act.
47 The Trusts of Land and Appointment of Trustee Act 1996, ss 6(3) & 17(1).
48 The Settled Land Act 1925, s.73.

any power of investment or reviewing investments unless 'he reasonably concludes that in all the circumstances it is unnecessary or inappropriate to do so.'[49] The Trustee Act 2000, s.5(4) defines 'Proper advice' as 'the advice of a person who is reasonably believed by the trustee to be qualified to give it by his ability in and practical experience of financial and other matters relating to the proposed investment.'

Note
When making an investment or reviewing investments the trustee will be judged by the statutory duty of care.[50]

When making an investment the trustee must consider the interests of all the beneficiaries of the trust and must not prefer the interests of any beneficiary over another. Thus if the trust is of a life interest then the trustee must take into account the interests of both the life tenant and remainder man when investing

If the trustees make unauthorised Investments they are liable for all loss incurred on the sale of the investment.[51] The investment belongs to the trustee personally and he has to repay the money used to the trust.[52] However, if all of the beneficiaries are *sui juris* they can adopt an unauthorised investment.[53] This ability to adopt the investment for the trust is probably most used when there has been a minor infringement by a non-professional trustee or the investment is doing well!

Trustees have been given wide powers of investment in the Trustee Act 2000 and the Trusts of Land and Appointment of Trustees Act 1996, with the latter now giving a trustee of land all the powers of an absolute owner.

13.6.2 Ethical investments

In recent times there have been growing concerns regarding ethical considerations for business and investment. Some trustees have been concerned that their duty to invest in the best interest of the trust should not preclude their considering ethical matters when choosing investments. The House of Lords considered this matter with regard to proposed trust investments nearly thirty years ago.

Cowan v. Scargill[54]
The pension fund of the National Coal Board (NCB) was administered by

---

49   The Trustee Act 2000, s.5.
50   The Trustee Act 2000 Schedule 1, para. 1.
51   *Knott v Cottee* (1852) 19 Beav 77.
52   *Wright v Morgan* [1926] AC 788.
53   *Re Patten and Edmonton Union Poor Guardians* (1883) 52 LJ Ch 787.
54   [1985] Ch 270.

trustees appointed equally by the NCB and the National Union of Mineworkers (NUM). The trustees appointed by the NCB proposed a portfolio of investment which involved foreign investments and companies which were in competition with the coal industry in the UK. The trustees appointed by the NUM, including Arthur Scargill, refused to approve of the proposals as they feared the investments would damage the domestic coal industry and affect the jobs of their members and the prospective beneficiaries of the pension fund. The NUM trustees put forward an alternative investment portfolio which they claimed offered similar prospects for return but would not involve investing in competing industries. The NCB trustees claimed the NUM's proposals would not provide similar returns and sought a declaration that the NUM trustees were in breach of their fiduciary duties to the pension fund.

Judgment: Sir Robert Megarry V-C stated that:

'...the starting point is the duty of the trustees to exercise their powers in the best interests of the present and future beneficiaries of the trust This duty of the trustees towards the beneficiaries is paramount. They must, of course, obey the law; but subject to that, they must put the interests of the beneficiaries first. When the purpose of the trust is to provide financial benefits for the beneficiaries, as is usually the case, the best interests of the beneficiaries are normally their best financial interests.'

Thus the NUM trustees could not consider any matter except the best financial interest of the pension fund beneficiaries and their proposal would be in breach of trust. The NUM trustees' arguments that the proposed investments would damage the beneficiaries because they might damage the domestic coal industry were rejected, as the pension scheme was fully funded and in no way dependent upon the fate of the NCB and the UK coal industry.

The Vice-Chancellor noted that 'Trustees may even have to act dishonourably (though not illegally) if the interests of their beneficiaries require it.'[55] As an example the Vice-Chancellor approved *Buttle v. Saunders*,[56] where the trustees were directed to 'gazump', that is accept a higher price for a property they had already agreed to sell, in order to obtain a better price for the beneficiaries.

Therefore trustees must not allow their personal views to interfere with their judgment:

'In the conduct of their own affairs they are free to abstain from making any such investments. Yet under a trust, if investments of this type would be more beneficial to the beneficiaries than other investments, the trustees must not refrain from making the investments by reasons of the views that they hold. Accordingly, although a trustee who takes advice on

---

55   *Cowan v Scargill* [1985] Ch 270, 288, per Megarry V-C.

investments is not bound to accept and act on that advice, he is not entitled to reject it merely because he sincerely disagrees with it, unless in addition to being sincere he is acting as a prudent man would act.'

The Vice-Chancellor noted that there might be circumstances where the trustees were entitled to take note of ethical considerations. For example, he accepted that 'the beneficiaries might well consider that it was far better to receive less than to receive more money from what they consider to be evil and tainted sources.' Although for such a consideration to be valid all of the beneficiaries must be adult and agree. The Vice-Chancellor also noted that the proposed investment may be contrary to the very objective of the trust; for example the trustees of a cancer charity might refuse to invest in the tobacco industry.

The decision in *Cowan v Scargill* has aroused some debate because it allows no room for trustees to consider any issue other than the best financial interests of the beneficiaries and even advocates trustees acting in what some may consider an immoral manner if it will benefit the beneficiaries. This may not seem very equitable.

The context of the decision is that Scargill was a very well-known political figure of the far left. The media had often demonised him for his views and this was a showdown with the NUM, a state run company under the control of the right-wing government of Prime Minister Margaret Thatcher. On top of this Scargill made the great mistake of representing himself, and seems to have annoyed the Vice-Chancellor in his representations, as Megarry V-C noted: 'some of the most sincere people are the most unreasonable.'

The matter of ethical investment was considered again in **Harries v. Church Commissioners for England.**[57] Here the plaintiff was the Bishop of Oxford who claimed that the Church Commissioners should not invest in anything which was contrary to Church of England doctrine, and he sought to limit their investment policy. The Church Commissioners already pursued an ethical investment policy by refusing to invest in armaments, gambling, tobacco, newspapers, and South Africa. The court approved *Cowan v. Scargill*, but Nicholls V-C upheld the Church Commissioners policy because trustees were free to exclude certain investments if they could do so without jeopardising the profitability of the portfolio. As the prohibited activities excluded only about 30% of the stock market there was scope for investment without a significant loss to the beneficiaries.

Therefore, at common law, ethical considerations of trustees will only be relevant for investment if:

---

56   [1950] 1 WLR 1097.
57   [1992] 1 WLR 1241.

- The settlor / trust instrument expressly provides;
- All the beneficiaries are of full age, *sui juris* and agree to the ethical considerations;
- The trust is a charitable trust and the investment may be contrary to the trust purpose, and alternative investment does not result in a significant loss to the beneficiaries.

A development in the recognition that ethical considerations may be important for the settlor, trustee or beneficiary but may not have been expressly provided for in the trust instrument is the Trustee Act 2000, s.4(3), which provides that ethical considerations may be taken into account as part of the standard investment criteria, thus, as long as ethical considerations are considered to fall within the standard investment criteria for a particular trust, the trustees may not be liable if an ethical investment is made and this causes loss to the trust.

13.7 The Duty to Act Personally and the Power to Delegate

A trustee has a duty to act personally. The general rule is *delegatus non potest delegare*; the trustee should not delegate his functions, as 'trustees who take on themselves the management of property for the benefit of others have no right to shift their duty on to other persons'.[58] However, this is another rule which has many exceptions both at common law and under statute and it has long been accepted that trustees may delegate their powers in certain circumstances. For example, it may be necessary to delegate certain specialist functions to professionals such as solicitors, bankers and stockbrokers. Thus it was accepted that trustees could delegate their administrative functions provided that delegation was reasonably necessary in the circumstances and that the trustees exercised the skill and care of 'an ordinary prudent man of business' in selecting and supervising an agent.[59] The modern rule was stated by Viscount Radcliffe in *Pilkington v IRC*:[60] 'The law is not that a trustee cannot delegate: it is that a trustee cannot delegate unless they have authority to do so'.

The accepted circumstances when a trustee may delegate his powers are:

- When the trust instrument so allows;
- When common usage allows;[61]
- When delegation of their administrative functions is reasonably necessary in the circumstances and the trustees have exercised the skill

---

58 *Turner v. Corney* (1841) 5 Beav 515, per Lord Langdale MR.
59 *Speight v. Gaunt* (1884) 9 App Cas 1.
60 [1964] AC 12.
61 *Ex parte Belchier* (1754) Amb 218.

and care of 'an ordinary prudent man of business' in selecting and supervising the agent;[62]

- When it is necessary to employ (and pay) agents to help in the execution of the trust;
- When it is necessary to delegate by power of attorney exercise of all trust powers for a period not exceeding 12 months.
- Statutory powers of delegation.

Generally trustees are not liable for the negligent acts of their agents, because, as Lord Hardwicke L.C. noted in *Ex parte Belchier*:[63] '[W]here trustees act by other hands, either from necessity, or conformable to the common usage of mankind, they are not answerable for losses.' However, they must exercise prudence and care in selecting the agents,[64] and they have a duty to supervise the agents and cannot leave them to their own devices.[65] If the trustee places the trust property in the agent's hands and the agent misappropriates that property then the trustee may be liable on the basis of wilful default. In *Re Vickery*[66], the executor of the deceased's estate placed the estate property in the hands of a solicitor who, unbeknownst to the executor, had at one time been suspended from practice. The solicitor absconded with the estate's assets. One of the beneficiaries under the will had informed the executor of the solicitor's suspension and asked him to retrieve the assets. The trustee had failed to do this. However, he was not held liable for the losses to the estate as he had acted honestly and reasonably in the circumstances. He had not been in wilful default by not getting the assets back as the solicitor had been promising to return the assets and he had believed him. Maugham J. justified this decision by stating: 'On the whole I have come to the conclusion that the defendant was on any view of the facts guilty only of an error of judgment, and this, in the case of loss occasioned by the defalcations of a solicitor, does not amount to wilful default on the part of the executor.' [67]

Wilful default involves a deliberate default with a particular consciousness, knowledge and state of mind.[68] For a trustee this means that he must have known he had a duty to act for the trust and has not done so.[69]

---

62 *Speight v. Gaunt* (1884) 9 App Cas 1.
63 (1754) Amb 218 at 219.
64 *Fry v Tapson* (1884) 28 Ch.D. 268.
65 *Att-Gen. V Leicester Corporation* (1844) 7 Beav. 176; *Re Lucking's WT* [1968] 1 WLR 866.
66 [1931] 1 Ch 572.
67 *Re Vickery* [1931] 1 Ch 572, 585, per Maugham J.
68 see Wolfe J's judgment in the Supreme Court case of *Wilkinson and Ors v Feldworth Financial Services Pty Ltd* (1998) 29 ACSR 642.
69 "a person is not guilty of willful neglect or default unless he is conscious that, in doing the act which is complained of or in omitting to do the act which it

The trustee must supervise the agent. Thus, in *Re Lucking's WT*,[70] there were two trustees, L and B of a family trust which held shares in a private family company. L had always been involved in running the family company, but B was appointed later to act as co-trustee. The manager of the business wrongfully withdrew £15,000 of company funds before being declared bankrupt. The court held L liable because of his failure to supervise the business; however, B was not liable because it was thought that he was entitled to rely upon L's experience of running the business.

Statutory powers of delegation were provided in the Trustee Act 1925 ss. 23 & 30. However, these were ambiguous as to the liability of the trustee and were replaced in the Trustee Act 2000. The Trustee Act 2000, s.11, provides that 'the trustees of a trust may authorise any person to exercise any or all of their delegable functions as their agent. Non-delegable functions are specified in s.11(2), which provides that a trustee of a private trust may delegate any functions apart from dispositive discretions, powers to appoint trustees, powers to delegate, or powers regarding the payment of fees. The delegable functions of a trustee of a charity are specified in s.11(3): functions which consist of a decision already taken by the trustees; investment functions; fund-raising functions; any other function authorised by the Secretary of State. Section 12 specifies that the persons who may be employed as an agent by the trustees includes one of the trustees themselves but excludes the beneficiaries, even if they are also trustees.

The Trustee Act 2002, s.15 provides special rules for the delegation of asset management functions: the delegation agreement must be evidenced in writing, and before trustees delegate such functions they should draw up a policy statement, which must also be evidenced in writing, and obtain the agent's agreement that he will act in accordance with it.

The Trustee Act 2000 specifies the duties of the trustee with regard to appointing and supervising the agent. Section.22 specifies the continuing duty of the trustee to review the arrangements with the agent. Section 23 (1) provides that 'a trustee is not liable for any act or default of the agent, nominee or custodian unless he has failed to comply with the duty of care applicable to him, under paragraph 3 of Schedule 1.' Schedule 1, Para. 3 provides that the statutory duty of care applies to the appointment of agent, nominees and custodians and to the process of the reviewing the arrangements. The statutory duty is that stated in section 1 of the Act

The Trusts of Land and Appointment of Trustees Act 1996, s.9, permits a trustee of a trust of land to delegate any of their functions to a beneficiary who is of full age and entitled to possession of the land.

---

is said he ought to have done, he is committing a breach of his duty, or is recklessly careless whether it is a breach of his duty or not."Re City Equitable Fire Insurance Co. [1925] Ch. 407, per Romer J. Confirmed in *Re Vickery* [1931] 1 Ch 572, 583, per Maugham J.

70   [1968] 1 WLR 866.

13.8 The Duty to Act Fairly and the Duty to Distribute

In running the trust a trustee has a duty to act fairly as between the beneficiaries and to take account of all their interests. Thus a trustee has no power to prefer one beneficiary to another,[71] unless he has been given such a power in the trust instrument, for example it is a discretionary trust. This means that trustee of a life interest trust must consider the interest of both the life tenant and the remainder-man; he cannot focus on achieving a high return of interest for the life-tenant while neglecting the capital, neither can he accumulate income for the remainder-man and neglect the return of interest.[72]

One of the duties of trustees is to distribute the interest and capital of the trust to the beneficiaries; this may be during the existence of trust and/or as the final act of the trust. They must do this as instructed in the trust instrument otherwise they are in breach of trust. In distributing the assets of the trust they must act fairly as between the beneficiaries unless they are instructed otherwise in the trust instrument or given discretion.

In cases where beneficiaries of a trust prove difficult to locate the trustees may also advertise for a period of not less than two months in the Gazette and in a local or foreign newspaper.[73] If no beneficiaries/creditors come forward after this time the trustees are free to distribute the property without the permission of the court. This absolves the trustees from liability for breach of trust. The missing beneficiaries may still be able to trace their property into the hands of other beneficiaries but not into the hands of a purchaser. Alternatively, if the trustees can identify the beneficiaries but are unable to find them after making reasonable enquiries they may apply to the court for a 'Benjamin Order',[74] which allows them to distribute the property as if the beneficiary was dead without fear of attracting liability for breach of trust. If the trustees continue having trouble identifying the beneficiaries then they may pay the money into court.[75]

13.9 The Duty to Account

Trustees have a duty to keep accounts and they must make those accounts available to the beneficiaries. The trust documents (the trust instrument, minutes of trustees' meetings etc.) are deemed to be trust property and as such they are the property of the beneficiaries, who have a right to see them. However, the trustees are under no duty to give reasons for the

---

71   *Lloyds Bank v Duker* [1987] 3 All ER 193.
72   This is known as the rule in *Howe v. Earl of Dartmouth* (1802) 7 Ves 137.
73   **Trustee Act 1925 s27.**
74   *Re Benjamin* [1902] 1 Ch 723.
75   *Re Gillingham Bus Disaster Fund* [1959] Ch 62.

exercise of their discretions,[76] and any information in the minutes concerning the exercise of those discretions may be withheld from the beneficiaries. In *Schmidt v. Rosewood Trust Ltd.*,[77] a case concerning a discretionary trust in the Isle of Man, the Privy Council doubted that the beneficiaries' right to see the trust documents was a proprietary right but stated that it was merely part of the inherent jurisdiction of the court to order disclosure. Recently, the High Court of Jersey has confirmed that letters of wishes, which are usually given by the settlor to his trustees in confidence, need not be disclosed to beneficiaries unless there is good reason for doing so.[78]

When a trust or estate has been administered the trustees/personal representatives must submit their final accounts to the beneficiaries, who will sign a deed of release. The deed discharges the trustees or personal representatives. If the beneficiaries are unwilling to sign a deed of release the trustee may apply for the accounts to be taken and approved by the court.

Linked to the duty to keep accounts is the duty to account and reconstitute the fund. If the accounts show a loss to the trust fund that is not explained or flows from a breach of trust then the trustees may have to make good that loss. In *Bartlett v Barclays Bank Trust Co Ltd (Nos. 1 & 2)*,[79] the nature of trustees' liability to beneficiaries was considered and said to include the duty:

- to account for the assets that ought to be in their hands;
- to reconstitute the fund; or if that were not possible,
- to compensate for any loss or account for any profit.

The duty to account thus may give rise to proprietary actions to return trust property or personal actions for equitable compensation although these will only be actionable if the loss to the trust is caused by the breach of trust.[80]

13.10 The Further Powers of the Trustee

Trustees may be given almost unlimited powers in the trust instrument. However, even if the trust instrument does not grant powers to the trustees, they may have powers which have been conferred either by the common law or by statute. The general rule is that these common law or statutory powers may be modified or excluded by the trust instrument, which remains the primary source of trustees' powers. It is highly unusual for the trustee to be able to exert a power which cannot be excluded or modified by the trust instrument.

---

76   *Re Londonderry's Settlement* [1965] Ch 918.
77   [2003] UKPC 26; [2003] 2 AC 709.
78   *Re Rabaiotti's Settlements* [2000] WTLR 953.
79   [1980] Ch 515.
80   See *Target Holdings Ltd v Redferns* [1996] 1 AC 421 discussed below.

As noted above, the powers are necessary for the trustee to perform his duties to the trust. Additional powers of the trustee include:

- The power of sale;
- The power to give receipts;
- The power to insure;
- The power of maintenance & advancement

Trustees hold the legal estate of the trust property and so, unless it is prohibited in the trust instrument,[81] may sell the trust property if they are acting in good conscience and as long as they obtain the best possible price.[82] For trust of land this is conformed in statute as they have 'all the powers of an absolute owner' subject to the restrictions regarding the purpose of the trust and consultation with the beneficiaries.[83] Trustees of land may also postpone sale indefinitely whether or not there is a term to the contrary in the trust instrument.[84]

Trustees have the power to give receipts for the sale of trust property.[85] This power is to safeguard purchasers of trust property from claims by the beneficiaries. The receipt will only be effective if the purchaser has no knowledge of any breach of trust involved in the transaction. Generally when trustees sell trust property all of the trustees must sign the receipt to ensure all of the trustees know of the sale and the buyer takes the property free from the beneficiaries' interests.[86] However, the sale of land is subject to the statutory provision that any receipt does not have to be signed by all of the trustees but must be signed by at least two trustees or an authorised representative of a trust corporation to ensure the buyer takes the property free from the beneficiaries' interests.[87] Upon a legitimate sale of trust property the beneficiaries' interests are transferred to the purchase monies, which are now subject to the trust.

Unless the trust instrument specifies otherwise there is no duty to insure the trust property, therefore if the property is destroyed the trustees are not liable for the loss. At common law there was no power to insure the

81 *Re Turner's WT* [1937] Ch 15.
82 *Buttle v. Saunders* [1950] 2 All ER 193.
83 The Trusts of Land and Trustees Act 1996, s.6(1). Land held under a strict settlement is subject to the tenant for life holding the legal estate and having the power of sale, subject to giving notice to the trustees: The Settled Land Act 1925, s38(1).
84 The Trusts of Land and Trustees Act 1996, s.4.
85 The Trustee Act 1925, s.14. Trustees of strict settlements have similar powers: The Settled Land Act 1925, s.95.
86 The Trustee Act 1925, s.14.
87 The Law of Property Act 1925, ss 2 & 27.

trust property unless specified in the trust instrument.[88] However, trustees now have statutory powers of insuring trust property. As trustees of land have 'all the powers of an absolute owner',[89] they may insure the property up to its full value.[90] Trustees of personalty may "insure any property which is subject to the trust against risks of loss or damage due to any event, and pay the premiums out of' income or capital.[91]

In addition the trustee may have the power to maintain the beneficiaries or advance capital to them.

13.11 The Power to Maintain and Advance

Although some trusts will provide income for the beneficiaries before the final distribution of the capital, trusts are often constituted which accumulate income and pay both the accumulated income and the capital to the beneficiaries at a certain date. For example, a trust may consist of shares in a company, the dividends from which are to be paid into a bank account and both shares and accumulated dividends paid to a beneficiary when he is 21 years old. However, what happens if the beneficiary needs some income or some of the capital before this time? Some trust instruments will specify a power of maintenance for the trustees to pay income to the beneficiaries in certain circumstances and some will specify a power of advancement for the trustees to pay capital to the beneficiaries in certain circumstances, otherwise the beneficiaries must wait however great their need.

The court has an inherent power to order maintenance and advancement, but this power is rarely used today because the Trustee Act 1925, ss.31 & 32, provides statutory powers, which are default powers unless prohibited by the trust instrument.[92] Today most trust instruments are drafted with express powers of maintenance and advancement; if not ss.31 & 32 may apply.

The Trustee Act 1925, s.31, relates to powers of maintenance and provides that:

(1) Where any property is held by trustees in trust for any person for any interest whatsoever, whether vested or contingent, then, subject to any prior interests or charges affecting that property-

(a) During the infancy of any such person, if his interest so long continues, the trustees may, at their sole discretion, pay to his parent or guardian, if any, or otherwise apply for or towards his maintenance, education,

---

88   *Re McEacharn* (1911) 103 LT 900.
89   The Trusts of Land and Appointment of Trustees Act 1996, s.6(1).
90   Trustees of a strict settlement have no powers to insure the settled land.
91   The Trustee Act 2000, s.34.
92   *Re Turner's WT* [1937] Ch 15.

or benefit, the whole or such part, if any, of the income of that property as may, in all the circumstances, be reasonable...

(b) If such person on attaining the age of [eighteen years] has not a vested interest in such income, the trustees shall thenceforth pay the income of that property and of any accretion thereto under subsection (2) of this subsection to him, until he either attains a vested interest therein or dies, or until failure of his interest

Provided that... the trustees shall have regard to the age of the infant and his requirements and generally to the circumstances of the case, and in particular to what other income, if any, is applicable for the same purposes...'

In exercising the statutory power to provide income the trustee must therefore first consider the age of the beneficiary. If the beneficiary is a child the decision to maintain the beneficiary from the income of the trust is solely a matter for the discretion of the trustees. The trustees must have sole regard for the interests of the child concerned, and whether such provision would be for their 'maintenance, education & benefit'. If the trustees are not satisfied that this is the case they may refuse to provide maintenance.

There is also a restriction on the provision of maintenance in the Trustee Act 1925, s.31(3), which provides that the beneficiary's interest must carry the intermediate income. This means that there must be no-one else with a prior interest in the income. Thus if there is a life-interest and the remainder-men ask for maintenance the trustees will not be able to provide maintenance using the statutory powers as the remainder-men's interests do not carry the intermediate income. The rules to do with intermediate income are very complicated but the general principle is that most beneficial interests carry the intermediate income unless there is an obvious prior interest entitled to the income, such as a life-interest, or they are contingent pecuniary interests; these are contingent interests of money. There are exceptions to the rule against contingent pecuniary interests carrying the intermediate income and these are that a contingent pecuniary interest will carry the intermediate income if:

- The gift is from a father or a person in loco parentis and the gift is contingent on the child reaching majority;[93]
- If the trust evidences an intention to maintain the beneficiary; or,
- If the testator has set aside a separate fund for the beneficiary.

The statute provides that if an adult beneficiary is contingently entitled to his interest, for example, property is held on trust dependent upon the beneficiary reaching the age of 25, then he will be entitled to the income

---

93   *Re Abrahams* [1969] 1 Ch 463.

upon attaining majority (18 years), unless there is a contrary intention in the trust instrument.[94]

The Trustee Act 1925, s.32, provides the power of advancement for trustees as it allows that they may advance capital, 'for the advancement or benefit' of a beneficiary "as they may, in their absolute discretion, think fit". This provision applies to adults or children. The amount advanced is limited to half the presumptive share. The presumptive share is the amount the beneficiary would get if the trust were brought to an end today and shares apportioned. When the contingency is reached and the share vests the beneficiaries must account to the other beneficiaries to the value of the advancement. These restrictions are best explained using an example:

Cheryl and Derek are both 16 years old and are beneficiaries of a trust of £400,000 contingent on them reaching 21 years old. Derek asks the trustees to advance him £100,000 using their powers under the Trustee Act 1925, s32. His presumptive share is £200,000, half of the fund, so the request is for half his presumptive share. The trustees may refuse to advance the capital but in this case decide to do so. Derek receives his £100,000. The trust now holds £300,000; this is held in the proportion 2:1 for Cheryl and Derek. Cheryl is now the beneficial owner of two thirds of the remainder and Derek only one third, as he has already taken half of his share. If the fund now grows to £600,000 Derek's presumptive share is one third of this, £200,000, but he cannot be advanced any more under the statutory power because he has had half of his original presumptive share already. Derek cannot receive any more funds until the contingency is reached; until he reaches 21 years when the trustees will give him the remains of his share. If Derek had taken less than half of his presumptive share, for example £80,000, this would have been 40% of his presumptive share. If two years later the fund increased to £600,000 Derek would be able to ask the trustees for the remaining 10% of his presumptive share; he has had 40% which is 20% of the whole fund. He would be able to ask for the remaining 10% of his presumptive share, which is 5% of the whole or £30,000; this would leave £570,000 in the fund. When Cheryl and Derek reached 21 years old the trustees would then distribute the remainder between them in the proportion 2:1; if the fund had remained at £570,000 then Cheryl would receive £380,000 and Derek £190,000. Derek would have received a total of £300,000 over the course of the trust. From this example it will be seen that it is good practice for trustees to advance less than half the beneficiary's presumptive share in case they need more capital in the future. If the contingency never occurs, for example Derek dies before reaching the age of 21 his estate does not have to repay the money to the trust. However, if the trustees had paid out more than half the presumptive share and Derek

---

94   *Re Sharp's ST* [1937] Ch 331.

died then the trustees might be personally liable to the trust for the overpayment, as they had acted in excess of the statutory power and would be in breach of trust.

If the beneficiary's interest is subject to a prior interest, for instance a prior life interest, then the prior interest's written consent must be obtained before capital may be advanced. For example, if property is left to Cheryl for life then to Derek and George absolutely on the contingency of their reaching 21, any advance to Derek and George will only be possible with the prior written consent of the life tenant.

The power to advance is purely discretionary and trustees may only advance capital if they consider it will be used for the 'advancement and benefit' of the beneficiary. The trustees must supervise the use of the fund to ensure it is only used for these purposes.[95] Generally financial benefits such as tax savings are construed as benefits for the purposes of the legislation,[96] but 'advancement and benefit' has received a wide interpretation; for example, in *Taylor v. Taylor*,[97] capital was advanced to pay the fees of the beneficiary to attend the Inns of Court in London, this was considered to confer a lasting benefit which would establish the beneficiary for life.

In *Re Clore's ST*,[98] funds were advanced to enable a beneficiary to make a donation to charity. The advancement may also benefit others if the primary purpose is to benefit the beneficiary; thus in *Re Kershaw's Trusts*,[99] an advancement was made from a wife's fund to her French husband to enable him to set up business in England, as this would benefit the wife by allowing the family to stay together and continue to live in England. Similarly, in *Re Pauling's ST*,[100] funds were advanced to provide furniture and a house for the parents of the beneficiaries as a family home.

13.12 Liability for Breach of Trust

If a trustee does not fulfil his duties to the trust then he is in breach of trust. This may be caused by not following the instructions in the trust instrument, making an unauthorised investment or acting outside the trustee's powers. The possible liability of the trustee for any loss occasioned by his breach of trust depends on the breach having caused the loss and the court being willing to apportion the liability to the trustee. Generally the courts are quite strict with trustees as they wish to encourage the highest standards of probity and good faith in an office which is open

---

95   *Re Pauling's ST* [1964] Ch 303.
96   *Pilkington v. IRC* [1964] AC 612.
97   (1875) LR 20 Eq 452.
98   [1966] 2 All ER 272.
99   (1868) L.R. 6 Eq. 322.
100 [1964] Ch 303.

to abuse. However, if there is a loss because of an error of judgement, for example in making an investment, then a court may not hold the trustee liable. The trustee's actions will be judged against the standard of care expected of trustees, which, as mentioned previously, is that 'a trustee ought to conduct the business of the trust in the same manner that an ordinary prudent man of business would conduct his own.'[101] If the matter is an investment then the slightly higher standard of the ordinary prudent man of business in making investment decisions for the benefit of persons for whom he felt morally obliged to provide would be used.[102]

In deciding whether a trustee is in breach of trust a trustee is to be judged 'not so much by success as by absence of proven default'.[103]

A trustee who commits a breach of trust by failing to fulfil his duties or by failing to adhere to the standards expected of a trustee may be personally liable to compensate the trust for any losses caused by his breach. He may also be liable to account for any profits which have been made in breach of trust. When there are two trustees the common law rule is that a trustee is only liable for his own breaches of trust, and not for those of his co-trustee, but mere inactivity or failure to supervise his co-trustee might be a breach of trust in itself. This is because trustees are meant to act unanimously; therefore their liability is joint and several.[104] Furthermore equity does not recognise the concept of a 'sleeping trustee' and therefore a trustee who merely leaves the administration of the trust to his co-trustees will be liable for their breaches of trust to the same extent as an active trustee.[105] In *Bahin v. Hughes*,[106] a trustee committed a breach of trust whilst the other remained inactive. Cotton LJ was of the opinion that: 'it would be laying down a wrong rule to hold that where one trustee acts honestly, though erroneously, the other trustee is to be held entitled to indemnity who by doing nothing neglects his duty more than the acting trustee.'

There have been instances where the court has relieved the innocent co-trustee of liability but these have been rare. For example, in the previously mentioned *Re Lucking's WT*,[107] where a newly appointed trustee was allowed to rely on his co-trustee's long-standing supervision of the family company and seeming superior knowledge of its running to exonerate him

---

101 *Speight v Gaunt* (1883) 22 Ch D 727, per Jessel M.R.
102 *Re Whiteley* (1887) 12 App Cas 727.
103 Peter Luxton, *The Law of Charities* (Oxford, Oxford University Press: 2001), p.361 [9.75]: referring to *Nestle v National Westmintsre Bank plc* [1993] 1 WLR 1260, 1284 (Leggatt LJ)..
104 *Dubai Aluminium Co. Ltd. v. Salaam*, [2002] EWHL 48.
105 *Bahin v. Hughes* (1886) 31 Ch D 390.
106 (1886) 31 Ch D 390.
107 [1968] 1 WLR 866.

from any negligence in not preventing the company's manager from absconding with company funds. The co-trustee was not so lucky and was held to account for the loss. Similarly, in *Re Partington*,[108] trustees reasonably relied upon the judgment of one of their number who was a solicitor, although it should be noted that the mere fact that the active trustee is a solicitor does not necessarily make it reasonable for the others to rely upon his judgment.[109] The passive trustee must genuinely and reasonably be deciding not to act because of one or more of the other trustees superior knowledge or skill, and he should continue to supervise his co-trustees as much as is reasonably possible.

Thus a trustee will be liable for any breach of trust except a fraudulent act by one of his co-trustees. Of course the trustees have the right to seek contribution from their negligent co-trustee for the compensation they pay to the trust,[110] although this may be of little value if the co-trustee is insolvent.

A trustee is not liable for breaches committed before his appointment,[111] or for those committed after his retirement. However, he remains liable for breaches committed during his period of office even after retirement. A trustee will be liable for breaches after his retirement if he has agreed to appoint new trustees who he believes might commit or allow a breach of trust.[112]

In a claim for breach of trust the plaintiff must establish a number of factors. Apart from establishing that there has been a breach of trust, the plaintiff must also establish that the trust has suffered a loss,[113] and that the loss was caused by the breach.[114] There must be a causal connection between the breach and the loss suffered.

Target Holdings Ltd v. Redferns[115]
A solicitor received the funds for a mortgage given by his client in favour of the plaintiff lender. The solicitor held the funds on trust. In breach of trust the solicitor paid the funds to a third party without authority before the mortgage security was complete. Subsequently the security required by the lender was completed. The mortgagor defaulted and the lender

---

108   (1887) 57 LT 654.
109   *Head v. Gould* [1898] 2 Ch 250.
110   *Ramskill v Edwards* (1885) 31 Ch D 10.
111   *Re Strahan* (1856) 8 De GM & G 291.
112   *Head v Gould* [1898] 2 Ch 250.
113   See *Nestlé v. National Westminster Bank plc* [1993] 1 WLR 1260.
114   *Target Holdings Ltd v. Redferns* [1996] 1 AC 421. See discussion in Geraint Thomas & Alastair Hudson, The Law of Trusts (Oxford, Oxford University Press: 2010, 2nd edition), p.945 [32.07].
115   [1996] 1 AC 421.

discovered the security was worth much less than its valuation. The plaintiff sued the solicitor for breach of trust and to account for the loss they suffered.

Judgment: the Court of Appeal held that the solicitor came under a duty to reinstate the fund as soon as he paid the funds out in breach of trust. However, on appeal to the House of Lords it was held that the solicitor was not liable. Although this was a case involving equitable compensation and so the common law rules of remoteness and causation did not apply, there must still be some causal connection between the breach of trust and the loss suffered. In the present case, although the defendant had acted in breach of trust, the plaintiff had received exactly what it bargained for. The security it received was as it had required, but it was not worth as much as the plaintiff had believed. This was the result of fraud on the part of the mortgagor. The plaintiff received the same security it would have received if the solicitor had not breached his trust. Therefore his breach did not cause the plaintiff's loss.

In order for there to be liability for breach of trust, the obligation which has been breached must have been a fiduciary obligation; not every obligation between a fiduciary and beneficiary will be fiduciary. In *Bristol & West Building Society v. Mothew*,[116] a solicitor held money in trust for Bristol & West pending completion of a purchase of land. Mothew negligently gave false information to Bristol & West who went ahead with the purchase in reliance upon that information. It was held that Mothew was liable in the tort of negligence, but that he was not liable for breach of trust merely because he was a fiduciary. He was not aware that the information was false, and had acted honestly and in accordance with his fiduciary duties.

An action for breach of trust is an action *in personam* against the trustee to restore the property to the trust. If it is not possible to trace the trust property for its return, the trustee is required to put the trust back into the position it would have been in had the breach not been committed.[117] The trustee must provide equitable compensation to account to the trust. The quantum of liability is generally to be assessed at the date of the judgment, [118] but the trustee may be liable to account for the highest intermediate value of the lost trust assets between the date of the breach and the date of judgment. The trustee is not entitled to deduct amounts of tax which would have been paid by the beneficiary, and he is required to pay interest, usually at 1% above bank rate, from the date of the breach. The interest

---

116 [1997] 2 WLR 436 M.
117 *Nocton v Lord Ashburton* [1914] AC 932, 952, per Lord Haldane L.C.. See discussion in Geraint Thomas & Alastair Hudson, The Law of Trusts (Oxford, Oxford University Press: 2010, 2nd edition), p.946 [32.11].
118 *Target Holdings Ltd v. Redferns* [1996] 1 AC 421.

charged will usually only be simple interest, but compound interest may be charged for fraudulent breaches of trust as equity assumes such misuse of the fund has been for profit.[119]

13.13 Avoiding Liability for Breach of Trust

There is a rebuttable presumption that trustees have faithfully discharged their duty.[120]

The High Court has an inherent jurisdiction inherited from the Court of Chancery to relieve a trustee from personal liability and is particularly sympathetic to trustees of a charitable trust because of the nature of their obligation.[121] This is especially the case for unpaid trustees. Courts have acted leniently to trustees of charitable trusts where the trustees have acted honestly and loss has occurred to the charity by a mistake,[122] as Lord Eldon stated: 'To act on any other principle would be to deter all prudent persons from becoming trustees of charities.'[123] In *A.G. v Pretyman* the court considered that prompt action by defaulting trustees was an important factor in deciding whether to exercise the court's discretion to absolve the trustee of liability for breach.[124]

The Limitation Act 1980 provides there is a six year limitation on actions for breach of trust, although there is no limit for fraudulent breach.[125] If the Limitation Act does not apply then the doctrine of laches will not allow an action to be taken after an undue delay.

Today the majority of trusts will be set up with professional trustees e.g., a bank's trust department, a solicitor or an accountant. People feel more confident in these professionals with their professional bodies monitoring them as well as the law of trusts. Also a bank is unlikely, even today, to be liquidated and so the trust fund is protected even more than by the law of trusts. Similarly solicitors and accountants firms will usually be formed as partnership with the other partners also liable for the

---

119 For the principles when equity will award compound interest see *Wallersteiner v Moir* (No 2) [1975] QB 373 at 388 C-D, per Lord Denning.

120 Hubert Picarda, *The Law and Practice Relating to Charities* (London, Butterworths: 1977), p.377. *A.G. v Earl of Stamford* (1843) 1 Ph 737 at 747.

121 Peter Luxton, *The Law of Charities* (Oxford, Oxford University Press: 2001), p.364 [9.83].

122 Peter Luxton, *The Law of Charities* (Oxford, Oxford University Press: 2001), p.364 [9.83] referring to *A-G v Exeter Corporation* (1826) 2 Russ 45, 54 (Lord Eldon L.C.).

123 *A-G v Exeter Corporation* (1826) 2 Russ 45, 54 (Lord Eldon L.C.).

124 *A.G. v Pretyman* (1841) 4 Beav 462, at 466, per Lord Langdale L.C.. Hubert Picarda, *The Law and Practice Relating to Charities* (London, Butterworths: 1977), p.378.

125 Section 21 of the Limitation Act 1980. Section 22 provides for a 12-year period for a claim to the estate of a deceased person.

professional trustee's losses. However, professional trustees will usually include exemption clauses in their standard form trust instruments or contracts for trusts. Exemption clauses are clauses written into the trust instrument which attempt to exempt liability. These clauses may exempt trustees from virtually all liability except for fraud. In *Armitage v. Nurse*,[126] a clause in the trust instrument stated that, 'no trustee shall be liable for any loss or damage which may happen to PA's fund or any part thereof at any time or from any cause whatsoever unless such loss shall be caused by his own actual fraud.' The Court of Appeal held that the words 'actual fraud' were equivalent to dishonesty and that therefore the trustees were not liable unless dishonesty could be established. Thus a trustee may exclude liability for their errors and negligence even if this includes 'gross negligence', [127] although any ambiguity in the clause will be construed against the trustee seeking to rely upon it.[128]

If a trustee is liable for a breach of trust he may seek contribution from his co-trustees[129] and indemnification from other parties. As we considered above a co-trustee who commits a fraudulent breach of trust may be solely liable. However, if more than one trustee is in breach but only one has profited from the breach then this trustee may be liable to indemnify the trustee who has not benefited. If trustees have relied in good faith upon the skill and knowledge of a solicitor co-trustee they may not be liable for his breach of trust or they may be able to claim indemnity from him,[130] as long as they have not participated in the breach.[131]

A trustee who is also a beneficiary who participates in a breach of trust must indemnify his co-trustees using his beneficial interest before liability is shared equally amongst the other beneficiaries.[132] The court also has the power to relieve a beneficiary of his beneficial interest if he has encouraged a breach the trust. Trustees are entitled to be indemnified from this interest if they have been made to account,[133] and the court may impound all or part of a beneficiary's interest if the trustee has committed the breach 'at the instigation or request or with the consent in writing of a beneficiary'. A beneficiary cannot sue the trustees for breach of trust if he has participated in or consented to the breach. Any other beneficiaries who

---

126 [1998] Ch 241.
127 Confirmed by the Privy Council: *Spread Trustee Co Ltd v Hutcheson* [2011] UKPC 13.
128 *Wight v Olswang (No 1)* (1999) *The Times* (18 May).
129 *Ramskill v Edwards* (1885) 31 Ch D 10; see also the Civil Liability (Contributions) Act 1978.
130 *Re Partington* (1887) 57 LT 654.
131 *Head v. Gould* [1898] 2 Ch 250.
132 This is known as the rule in *Chillingworth v. Chambers* [1896] 1 Ch 685.
133 *Re Pauling's ST* [1963] Ch 576.

have not participated or consented may sue. In order to consent or participate in a breach of the trust the beneficiary must be adult, *sui juris* and free from undue influence. The trustees may also be released from liability if the beneficiary has participated in or consented to the breach, or the beneficiaries release him from liability. The beneficiaries may release the trustees from liability for their breaches, provided that they are capable of granting release.

Finally a trustee may seek to be relieved from liability, either fully or partially, by virtue of s.61 of the Trustee Act 1925, which provides:[134]

'If it appears to the court that a trustee is or may be personally liable for any breach of trust but has acted honestly and reasonably, and ought fairly to be excused for the breach of trust and for omitting to obtain the directions of the court in the matter in which he committed such breach, then the court may relieve him either wholly or partly from personal liability for the same.'

The burden is on the trustee to prove he has acted honestly and reasonably, which is a question of fact, depending on the circumstances of the case. [135] There has been little guidance on the meaning of 'honestly', 'reasonably', and 'ought fairly to be excused'. However, in *Bartlett v. Barclays Bank Trust Co. Ltd,*[136] the bank attempted to rely upon the Trustee Act 1925, s.61. The court held that the bank had acted honestly but not reasonably. Therefore the court is usually reluctant to use this power to relieve a paid trustee from liability for breach of trust as it is not reasonable.[137] Of course they usually have exemption clauses designed to avoid liability.

13.14 Summary

Trustees are special types of fiduciaries who must always put the interests of the trust before their own interests. The trustee has many duties towards the trust but these vary depending on the nature of the trust. The general management duties of the trustee include the duty to acquaint himself with the trust instrument and the trust property, and the duty to perform the

---

134 The Companies Act 2006, s.1157, provides the court with similar power to relieve a company director either wholly or partially from liability for a breach of duty or trust to the company.

135 *Re Turner [1897] 1 Ch. 536.* (CA). *Tudor On Charities* (London, Sweet & Maxwell: 2003, 9th edition), p. 410 [10-060].

136 *(Nos 1 and 2)* [1980] 1 All ER 139; [1980] Ch 515.

137 *Bartlett v Barclays Bank Trust Co. Ltd (Nos 1 and 2)* [1980] 1 All ER 139: *Steel v Wellcome Custodian Trustees Ltd* [1988] 1 W.L.R. 167 at 174: J. Warburton, *Tudor On Charities* (London, Sweet & Maxwell: 2003, 9th edition), p. 274 [6-032]: Peter Luxton, *The Law of Charities* (Oxford, Oxford University Press: 2001), p.365 [9.85].

trust instructions. In performing the trust the trustee must act fairly as between the beneficiaries and this is particularly important when a trustee performs the duty of distributing trust assets. Trustees must invest the trust property to provide the best financial returns for the beneficiaries. Trustees may only delegate the trust duties when the trust instrument provides or when common usage or statute permits. A trustee has a duty to account to the beneficiaries for the trust property and to make good any losses to the trust caused by a breach of trust. Trustees are judged in their actions by the standards of a prudent man of business undertaking his own business. They are judged to a slightly higher standard when making investment decisions, as they must make such decisions as would a prudent man of business making investment decisions for someone he feels morally obliged towards. Trustees may make use of statutory powers of maintenance and advancement to provide income and capital to beneficiaries even though this is not expressly provided for in the trust instrument. If a trustee does not follow the trust instructions or acts below the standard of care expected of him he will be in breach of trust. If the breach of trust causes loss to the trust he may be liable to account for this loss. Trustees are jointly and severally liable for losses caused by breach of trust. A trustee may avoid liability if he honestly relied upon the superior knowledge of a co-trustee, or if his co-trustee acted fraudulently without his knowledge, or if he has included an exclusion clause in the trust instrument. A trustee may also be relieved from liability if a court feels that, even though he has been in breach of trust, he has acted honestly and reasonably and ought fairly to be relieved from liability in the circumstances.

CHAPTER 14
THE FIDUCIARY AND FIDUCIARY DUTIES

14.1 What is a Fiduciary?

We have already noted that the trustee is a special type of fiduciary, all trustees are fiduciaries but not all fiduciaries are trustees. The fiduciary nature of trusteeship is the duty of acting in good faith towards the trust and the beneficiaries. Other offices may also be fiduciary- the fiduciary owes a duty to act in good faith towards his principal. Traditionally there were certain offices that were automatically considered fiduciary: the trustee and beneficiary; the company director and the company; partners in a partnership to each other; the solicitor and his client; the agent and his principal; the guardian and his ward; a Crown servant and the Crown; an insolvency practitioner and creditors of the company they are liquidating; a personal representative and the deceased's estate. Thus an executor is expected to act according to the wishes of the testator in the best interests of the estate. Similarly, a company director is expected to act in the best interests of the company,[1] and a solicitor should act in the best interests of his clients. A non-living legal entity, such as a registered company, may be a fiduciary, for example a registered company may be a director of another registered company.

Today the relationships which give rise to a fiduciary duty and obligation are not limited to the traditional categories but also include many other relationships based upon trust and confidence.[2] The main identifying feature is of someone acting for another. In *Frame v Smith*,[3] it

---

1   This includes the best interests of the shareholders as a whole: *Re Smith and Fawcett Ltd* [1942] Ch 304; the duty is not to any individual shareholder: *Percival v Wright* [1902] 2 Ch 421.The interests of the company are not those of some particular section or sections of the company, but the interests of both present and future members of the company: *Gaiman v National Association for Mental Health* [1971] Ch 317. In cases of insolvency company directors may owe a duty to creditors as well: *West Mercia Safetyware Ltd v Dodd* [1988] BCLC 250, EWCA.

2   For example, in certain circumstances a doctor will be a fiduciary of his patient. The strange agency relationship of insurance brokers is that even though they receive commission from the insurance company, the insurer, they are the agent of the insured.

3   [1987] 2 SCR 99.

was proposed that a fiduciary relationship could be identified by considering the power and discretion that the person acting for another had. If the party undertaking to act for another has scope for the exercise of some discretion or power, which he can unilaterally exercise so as to affect the principal's legal or practical interests, and the principal is peculiarly vulnerable to or at the mercy of the party holding the discretion or power, then the relationship is fiduciary. A fiduciary relationship is therefore also characterised by the fiduciary being in a position of power with regard to the principal. A position that could be abused and so equity imposes the fiduciary duty, which is made up of various obligations, to ensure that this situation will never occur.

Lord Millett has given guidance on what constitutes a fiduciary relationship and when a fiduciary relationship will be recognised and enforced: a fiduciary is

'…someone who has undertaken to act for or on behalf of another in a particular matter in circumstances which give rise to a relationship of trust and confidence. The distinguishing obligation of a fiduciary is the obligation of loyalty. The principal is entitled to the single-minded loyalty of his fiduciary. This core liability has several facets. A fiduciary must act in good faith; he must not make a profit out of his trust; he must not place himself in a position where his duty and his interest may conflict; he may not act for his own benefit or the benefit of a third person without the informed consent of his principal. This is not intended to be an exhaustive list, but it is sufficient to indicate the nature of fiduciary obligations.' [4]

Lord Millett's identification of a fiduciary depends on someone undertaking to act for another in circumstances which give rise to a relationship of trust and confidence; this will usually involve power and the possibility that this power may be abused. To prevent the power of the fiduciary being abused Lord Millett noted the fiduciary relationship depended on loyalty, duty, trust and confidence. Breach of this loyalty, duty, trusts and confidence is treated very seriously by equity. The fiduciary may be liable for any breach of the fiduciary relationship which gives rise to loss to his principal. The remedy may be a personal action against the fiduciary or others who aid the fiduciary in the breach, or a proprietary action to recover by way of a constructive trust any assets the fiduciary misappropriates from his principal,[5] or that he obtains in breach of his fiduciary duties.[6] Thus as Jessel M.R. approved in *Re Hallett's Estate*, a

---

4   *Bristol & West Building Society v Mothew* [1998] 1 Ch 1, 18, per Millett L.J. as he then was.

5   See the chapters on tracing and strangers to the trust.

6   For example from a bribe: see *A.G. v Reid* [1994] 1 AC 324, although this has been doubted by the Court of Appeal, *Sinclair Investments (UK) Ltd v Versailles Trade Finance Ltd (in administrative receivership)* [2011] EWCA Civ 347. See the discussion in Chapter 10 on constructive trusts.

fiduciary relationship is one in which the fiduciary may be accountable as if he were a trustee:

'What is a fiduciary relationship? It is one in respect of which, if a wrong arise, the same remedy exists against the wrongdoer on behalf of the principal as would exist against a trustee on behalf of the cestui que trust.'[7]

Fiduciary duties are strictly enforced as a matter of public policy to ensure those in positions of trust and power carry out their duties. The imposition of fiduciary relationships in commercial settings and the remedies available for breach of fiduciary duties can help set higher standards in commerce. The duties of company directors are now prescribed in the Companies Act 2006, ss 171-177, but s.170(4) specifies that they are to be interpreted and applied in the same way as common law rules or equitable principles, and regard shall be had to the corresponding common law rules and equitable principles in interpreting and applying the general duties.

14.2 The Fiduciary Duty

The main fiduciary duty of loyalty and acting in good faith towards their principal has been developed into a number of overlapping obligations concerned to promote loyalty and faithfulness. It was originally developed in Chancery to restrain unconscionable abuse of legal power and position by trustees but now applies to all fiduciaries. As already noted, Lord Millett, in **Bristol and West BS v. Mothew**,[8] stated the principal obligations of the fiduciary are the duties to act in good faith, not to make a profit out of his trust, not to place himself in a position where his duty and his interest may conflict, and not to act for his own benefit or the benefit of a third person without the informed consent of his principal; although he stated this list of duties was not exhaustive.

The 'no-conflict' and the 'no-profit' rules are the two main rules which guide fiduciaries and from which all the other fiduciary rules have developed and are inextricably linked to each other and the duty of good faith. The importance of these rules and their interdependence was expressed by Lord Herschell, in **Bray v Ford**:[9] 'It is an inflexible rule of a Court of Equity that a person in a fiduciary position is not, unless otherwise expressly provided, entitled to make a profit; he is not entitled to put himself in a position where his duty and interest conflict.' If the fiduciary could make a profit from his position he might be tempted to place his own interests before those of his principal. Of course the rules

---

7   Jessell M.R. endorsed the logic of Fry J, which Fry J. had mistakenly believed he could not follow: *Re Hallett's Estate* (1880) 13 Ch D 696 at 712-713, per Jessel M.R.

8   [1998] Ch 1 at 18.

9   [1896] AC 44, HL.

have been relaxed for various situations, thus as Lord Millett noted above, a fiduciary must get the informed consent of his principal when he acts for his own benefit, thus a company director must inform the company and receive its consent if he has an interest in a venture in which the company is participating. Otherwise the fiduciary duties and rules are strictly enforced by the courts to ensure fiduciaries act to high standards of good faith.

14.3 The No-Conflict Rule

The no-conflict rule was expounded in *Aberdeen Railway Company v Blaikie Brothers*,[10] by Lord Cranworth:

'...it is a rule of universal application that no one, having such [fiduciary] duties to discharge, shall be allowed to enter into engagements in which he has, or can have, a personal interest conflicting, or which possibly may conflict, with the interests of those whom he is bound to protect.'

The rule that a fiduciary must not put himself in a position where his personal interest conflicts with his duty to the principal is strictly enforced. The leading case is still *Keech v. Sandford*.[11] A trustee held the lease of Romford market on trust for a minor. He asked the landlord to renew the lease, but the landlord refused because the remedy of distraint would not be available to him for default against a minor. The trustee then took the lease for himself. The court held that the trustee held the lease on constructive trust for the minor. Lord King LC remarked that:

'I very well see that if a trustee on the refusal to renew might have a lease to himself, few trust estates would be renewed to a *cestui que use*. This may seem hard that the trustee is the only person of all mankind who might not have the lease; but it is very proper that the rule should be strictly pursued, and not in the least relaxed; for it is very obvious what would be the consequences of letting trustees have the lease, on refusal to renew to the *cestui que use*.'

The point was very simple; if the trustee could make a profit from his position by taking the lease in his own name then trustees would act in their own interests not in the interests of their beneficiaries. Thus, in *Guinness plc v. Saunders*,[12] one of the directors of Guinness assisted in Guinness's takeover of Distillers Ltd. The director's fee was to be in proportion to the amount of the successful bid; thus the more that Guinness paid for the takeover the more the director would receive. On completion of the takeover the director received £5.5 million. This was an

---

10   (1854) 1 Macq. 461.
11   (1726) Sel Cas Ch 1. See FW Maitland, *Equity: A Course of Lectures*, J Brunyate (ed), rev edn (Cambridge, Cambridge University press, 1936) 80.
12   [1990] 2 AC 663.

obvious conflict between his personal interests and his duties to Guinness. When this was challenged the court held that the director held the £5.5 million on constructive trust for Guinness.

The no-conflict rule is reflected in the 'no-competition' rule; a fiduciary must not set himself up in competition with the principal.[13] If the fiduciary is in competition with his principal the principal may ask the court to stop the fiduciary from continuing in competition by way of an injunction and/ or account for any profit the fiduciary has made from such competition. The principal does not have to prove that the fiduciary has acted in bad faith or that the fiduciary stands to gain unfair advantage by virtue of knowledge of the principal's business. Thus, in *Re Thompson,*[14] an executor was restrained from carrying on his yacht-broking business in competition with the estate he was administering. Similarly, a fiduciary must not entice customers or clients away from the principal's business to his.

The test the courts apply to decide if the no-conflict rule has been breached is whether there is a 'real sensible possibility of conflict'.[15]

Boardman v. Phipps[16]
Boardman was a solicitor to the Phipps family trust and, together with one of the beneficiaries, Tom Phipps, attended meetings of a private company and obtained information about the company, in which the trust held a substantial although minority shareholding. Boardman and Tom Phipps realised that there was the potential to make a substantial profit for the trust if the trust purchased more shares in the company and reorganised the company. They informed the trustee of this but the trustee could not purchase more shares at that time. Boardman and Tom Phipps therefore decided to purchase shares themselves and effect the reorganisation. They informed the trustees and beneficiaries of the family trust. Boardman and Tom Phipps reorganised the company and realised substantial profits for themselves and for the trust. One of the beneficiaries challenged their actions.

Judgment: The House of Lords held, by a 3/2 majority, that Boardman and Tom Phipps should account to the trust for their profits. They had acted in good faith and they had made profits for the trust, but they had nevertheless made their profits purely as a result of information gained from their association with the trust. There was some discussion of Boardman and Phipps having made themselves *trustee de son tort, de facto* trustees because of their actions,[17] and thus they were in fiduciary positions to the trust when they received this information. They had allowed their

---

13   Bell v Lever Brothers Ltd [1932] AC 161.
14   [1930] 1 Ch 203.
15   *Boardman v. Phipps* [1967] 2 AC 46.
16   [1967] 2 AC 46.
17   See Chapter 17, Strangers to the Trust.

personal interests to conflict with their duties to the trust. However, they were allowed to claim payment on a *quantum meruit* basis for their services to the trust as they had undertaken so much work in the reorganisation.

The rule does not apply if the principal appoints a fiduciary knowing that the fiduciary has a pre-existing conflict of interest to his duty to the principal.[18] Similarly if the breach of duty does not occasion a profit for the fiduciary and the principal suffered no loss, the fiduciaries will not have any liability.

14.4 The No-Profit Rule

A fiduciary must not make a profit from his position. As noted previously this rule is linked to the no-competition rule as if the fiduciary could make a profit from his position he might prefer his interests to those of his principal. The cases discussed below may involve elements of both duties. This no-profit rule includes making a personal profit by dealing with the fiduciaries property, secret or incidental profits made because of the fiduciary position, taking bribes, taking advantage of business opportunities encountered because of the fiduciary position, not buying the principal's property, and not taking advantage of confidential information.

The test to be used to decide whether a fiduciary has made a profit from his position is whether he acquired the opportunity to make the profit by virtue of his fiduciary position. Thus, in *Re Macadam*,[19] trustees used their trusteeship and the trust's control of a private company to become directors of the company; thus they were held accountable to the trust for the fees they were paid as directors. If they had not exercised their votes and still been elected directors,[20] or if they had already been directors of the company which could be influenced by the trust before they became trustees they would not have been in breach of trust.[21]

As we have already seen when we considered Boardman v Phipps, the rule applies even when the principal profits from the fiduciaries actions.

Regal (Hastings) Ltd v. Gulliver[22]
Regal Ltd set up a subsidiary company, L Ltd, in order to acquire the leases of two cinemas. The lessor would not grant the leases unless the share capital in L Ltd was completely subscribed for. Regal Ltd was only able to subscribe for 40% of the share capital, and its directors agreed to subscribe for the other 60%. The consent of the shareholders was not sought. The company and the directors made a profit from their holdings in L Ltd.

---

18   *Sargeant v National Westminster Bank plc* (1990) 61 P & CR 518.
19   [1946] Ch 73.
20   *Re Gee* [1948] Ch 284.
21   *Re Dover Coalfield Extension Ltd* [1908] 1 Ch 65.
22   [1967] 2 AC 134, HL.

When Regal Ltd was sold the new controllers of the company sought an account of the profits made by the ex-directors.

Judgement: the House of Lords held that the ex-directors should account for their profits. They had acted *bona fide* and the company would not have been able to purchase the leases without their contributions, but, nevertheless, they had profited as a result of their position as fiduciaries, and they should be made to account.

The no-profit rule extends to bribes. In **Reading v. A-G**,[23] the House of Lords held that the Crown was entitled to confiscate £19,000 from a sergeant in the British Army who had taken bribes to travel in civilian trucks carrying contraband dressed in his military uniform in order to get through check points. It was held that he was in a fiduciary position to the Crown and held the bribes on constructive trust for the Crown. Similarly in **A-G for Hong Kong v Reid**,[24] Reid was the Director of the Commercial Crime Unit in Hong Kong and accepted bribes not to prosecute certain criminals. He had invested the money and it had increased. The Privy Council held that he was in a fiduciary position as a Crown employee and held the bribes on constructive trust for the Crown from the moment he accepted them. The fund therefore included any increase in value. The reasoning was that he ought to have handed the money to the Crown immediately it was given to him and, as *equity regards as done that which ought to be done*, he was presumed to hold the fund on constructive trust for the Crown. Any increase in value was therefore also the Crown's. However, as noted in Chapter 10, the use of a constructive trust in this situation has now been doubted by the Court of Appeal,[25] although the acceptance of a bribe by a fiduciary would always give rise to a personal action by the principal.

If the profit is not a bribe but is secret, concealed from the principal, the fiduciary will have to account. In **Industrial Development Consultants Ltd v. Cooley**,[26] Cooley was employed by Industrial Development Consultants Ltd to try to get the British Gas Board to employ the company as a development consultant. The Gas Board declined because they did not deal with development companies, but offered the contract to Cooley personally, who accepted it. Cooley was held liable to account for his profits to the company. Similarly, in **Crown Dilmun Ltd v Sutton**,[27] Sutton was a director of Crown Dilmun Ltd. Sutton declined the opportunity to bid for a contract to develop Fulham Football Stadium on behalf of Crown

---

23 [1951] AC 507.
24 [1994] 1 AC 324.
25 *Sinclair Investments (UK) Ltd v Versailles Trade Finance Ltd (in administrative receivership)* [2011] EWCA Civ 347.
26 [1972] 1 WLR 443
27 [2004] EWHC 52.

Dilmun. He then established his own company, appointing H, his solicitor, as its sole director and obtained the contract. Sutton's contract with Crown Dilmun contained a confidentiality clause. Crown Dilmun dismissed Sutton from his employment and the High Court found him liable to account for the profits. However, it should be noted that fiduciaries may make a profit from their position if they obtain the informed consent of their principal, for example a company director may obtain the informed consent of his company to take an opportunity.

Queensland Mines v Hudson[28]

Hudson was managing director, and thus a fiduciary, of Queensland Mines, a company that investigated mining opportunities. The company was interested in a particular mining operation and Hudson obtained the necessary licences for the company. The company ran into financial difficulties and could not undertake the mining operation. Hudson resigned as managing director of Queensland Mines and developed the mines himself. The company pursued an action to hold him to account for profits made.

Judgment: the Privy Council held he was not liable as Queensland Mines had not been able to afford to do the mining itself, this took the matter away from scope of Hudson's fiduciary duties. Hudson had not been dishonest as Queensland Mines' board of directors had full knowledge at all times of his activities.

This decision may seem hard to reconcile with the decision in *Boardman v Phipps*, where the House of Lords was clear that there had been no dishonesty on Boardman's part and he had disclosed this to the trustees, but still held him liable to account for the profit he had made from his position. However, the decision depends on the concept of informed consent and may be seen as more leniently applied to company directors than trustees.[29] It should be noted that the consent will not be effective if the director uses his voting power as a shareholder to secure the approval of the company in general meeting.[30]

Disclosure is important for insurance agents who are generally the agents of the insured not the insurer; therefore they owe fiduciary duties to the insured. The insurance agent is usually paid commission on the policy by the insurer. Therefore he is making a profit by reason of his position. However, it is accepted at common law that the agent may receive a commission on the policy as long as he discloses this to the insured, his principal, and that it is not excessive.

---

28   (1978) 18 ALR 1, PC.

29   Grantham, 'Can Directors Compete with the Company?' (2003) 66 *Modern Law Review* 109.

30   *Cook v Deeks* [1916] 1 AC 554, PC.

A fiduciary can be paid (although we have already seen how strictly the rule was applied against trustees), but should not make any unauthorised profit from his position. Thus a fiduciary must not make a profit out of property acquired by reason of his relationship with the principal. As we have seen, if the fiduciary does make profits from his position he will hold them on constructive trust for the principal. This is because he ought to have made them for the principal and *equity regards as done that which ought to be done*. He ought to have made them for the principal and so equity considers he did and holds them on trust for the principal.[31] The rule does not apply if the opportunity was available to the fiduciary from another source and not just obtained by reason of his fiduciary position, although the fiduciary may have the burden of establishing this was the case.

14.5 Not Purchasing the Principal's Property

A fiduciary must not purchase his principal's property. This principal is based upon the fiduciary being in a position of trust and power with regard to the principal's property. The principal has been developed into two rules, the rule against 'self-dealing' and the rule regulating 'fair dealing'.[32]

The rule against self-dealing is strictly applied. The rule is that a trustee must not buy trust property or sell his own property to the trust. If he does so the transaction may be voided at the instance of the beneficiaries.

The rule which regulates fair-dealing is that if a trustee purchases the beneficial interest in the trust from the beneficiary then the transaction may be set aside unless the trustee can show it was fair and honest.

The rule against self-dealing is strictly applied because if a trustee is allowed to purchase trust property there is a danger that he will abuse his position and buy at less than the best price obtainable. If he sells his own property to the trust there is a danger that he will demand too high a price. The rule applies to all fiduciaries not just trustees,[33] and sales to parties linked to the trustee/fiduciary. The rule against self-dealing applies even when the fiduciary makes a loss from the transaction or the principal makes a profit. There must be no possibility of the fiduciary abusing his position. If the fiduciary buys the principal's property or sells his own property to the principal the transaction is voidable at the instance of the principal when he discovers the transaction. If the fiduciary has bought

---

31   *A-G for Hong Kong v Reid* [1994] 1 AC 324.
32   See *Tito v Waddel* (No 2) [1977] 2 WLR 496, Ch.D.
33   In *Kane v. Radley-Kane* [1999] Ch 274 the rule was applied to a personal representative of a deceased estate who acquired shares for £50,000 from the estate when in fact they were worth over £1.1 million.

the principal's property and then sold it on to equity's darling, the principal can make the trustee account for any profit.[34]

When the principal discovers the transaction he may elect to affirm it; this would obviously be the case where the transaction is to the manifest advantage of the principal. The transaction will then no longer be voidable if the principal has had full knowledge of the circumstances of the transaction. The rule is only relaxed in exceptional circumstances.

Holder v. Holder[35]

The defendant was an executor of his father's will. He had tried to disclaim the office but, although he took no active part in the administration of his father's estate, he was too late. He was also tenant of one of his father's farms and announced to the other executors and beneficiaries of his father's will that he intended to buy this farm and another belonging to the estate at public auction. He did so. The plaintiff beneficiary claimed the son had breached the rule against self-dealing.

Judgment: the court held that the rule was not breached. Although the son was an executor and so in a fiduciary position, he had not taken an active part in the administration and had informed all concerned, including the plaintiff beneficiary, of his intentions. The plaintiff beneficiary had also accepted his share of the proceeds knowing what had happened. The property had been sold in a public auction and so there was no chance of the son influencing the other executors or beneficiaries and so gaining an unfair advantage from his fiduciary position.

The fair-dealing rule is not a prohibitive rule but a restriction on buying the beneficial interest of the beneficiaries. The rule is not as strict as self-dealing as the trustee must here deal with the beneficiary, thus the beneficiary has knowledge of the transaction. The rule is that if a trustee's purchase of the beneficial interest of a trust from a beneficiary is challenged the trustee bears the burden of establishing that the transaction was at arm's length, to the beneficiary's benefit and fair and honest. If the trustee cannot show this then the transaction may be set aside.

The rules may only be relied on if the actions are brought in a reasonable time and other equitable principles would apply. Thus both self-dealing and fair dealing transactions can only be set aside if *restitutio in integrum* is possible.[36] Otherwise the trustee (fiduciary) would hold any profits on constructive trust for the beneficiary (principal).

---

34   *Baker v Carter* (1835) 1 Y & C Ex 250.

35   [1968] Ch 353.

36   *Tate v Williamson* (1866) L.R. 2 Ch. App. 55.

14.6 No Profit from Confidential Information

Professionals must always take care that they do not represent clients with conflicting interest. They should also take care when undertaking work for new clients that they do not have confidential information from former clients that might lead to a conflict of duties. Professionals should ensure that information barriers, commonly referred to as 'Chinese Walls', are in place to ensure that no breach of duty occurs by a leak of confidential information.[37] If there is a high likelihood of conflict then the professional should decline to act for the new client.[38]

A fiduciary cannot make a profit from confidential information obtained by reason of his position because 'he who has received information in confidence shall not take unfair advantage of it.'[39] In *Seager v Copydex Ltd,* Copydex patented and manufactured an invention that Seager had informed them of whilst he was a client. Copydex had to pay compensation.

If a fiduciary is in possession of confidential information and makes a profit from its revelation then there is a duty to account for profits.[40]

14.7 Remedies for Breach of Fiduciary Duties

The remedies available for breach of the fiduciary duties are varied and depend on the circumstances. The principal is entitled to the most advantageous remedy and, if entitled in the alternative, must elect which he is to receive. As we have seen the remedies include: injunction to prevent the breach continuing; a proprietary remedy if property has been misappropriated; account and reconstitution of a trust fund; account of profits; equitable compensation or damages; and the constructive trust.

Often any profits made by a fiduciary from his position will be held on constructive trust. This allows the principal to benefit from any increase in the value of the profit since it was acquired as the constructive trust exists before the court declares it. As Lord Brown-Wilkinson stated in *Westdeutsche Landesbank Girozentrale v Islington LBC:*[41] 'Under an institutional constructive trust, the trust arises by operation of law as from the date of the circumstances which give rise to it: the function of the court is merely to declare that such trust has arisen in the past.'

Of course a breach of fiduciary duty will only be actionable if there is a loss to the principal or a gain to the fiduciary.

---

37 *Marks & Spencer plc v Freshfields Bruckhaus Deringer* [2004] EWCA Civ 741; 148 Sol Jo LB 788.
38 *Jefri Bolkiah v KPMG* [1999] 2 AC 222, HL.
39 *Seager v Copydex Ltd* [1967] 2 All ER 415, EWCA, per Lord Denning.
40 *A-G v. Guardian Newspapers Ltd* [1990] 1 AC 109, HL- the 'spycatcher' case.
41 [1996] AC 669.

14.8 Summary

Fiduciaries owe duties of good faith and loyalty to their principals. These duties have developed into two main rules: a fiduciary must not allow his personal interests to conflict with his duties to his principal, and; a fiduciary must not make a profit from his position. These two rules are linked and operate to ensure the fiduciary acts in good faith towards his principal. The fiduciary must not take advantage of a business opportunity he has obtained by reason of his position, or make a secret or incidental profit from his position. The rules are strictly enforced but may be relaxed if the fiduciary makes full disclosure of his conflicts or profits to his principal and his principal accepts these.

CHAPTER 15
BENEFICIARIES AND VARIATION OF TRUSTS

15.1 Beneficiaries

There are almost no restrictions on who may be a beneficiary. Whatever theory is accepted for the origin of the common law of trusts, trusts were originally created to provide for those who could not hold property in their own right, whether disqualified by law or disability, and this is still a principle use of the trust today. Trusts may be in favour of the many or few, natural persons or companies, public or private purposes, the ill, the young and even the unborn.

Once a trust is constituted the settler loses all interest in the property unless they have retained an interest for themselves.[1] The trust then becomes enforceable on its terms by the beneficiaries, or those acting on their behalf if they are incapable, against the trustees. The beneficiaries then have rights and powers with regard to the trust and the trust property dependent on the terms of the trust and based upon the fiduciary duty of the trustees.[2]

This may include a proprietary interest in the trust property enforceable against all except equity's darling.

The importance of the beneficiary's interest in the trust property was recognised early in the development of equity so that the beneficiaries were considered to have a proprietary interest in the trust property which could be enforced not just against the trustee but strangers to the trust who were not equity's darling. Thus if a third party received trust property from a trustee in breach of trust they were considered to hold it on (constructive) trust for the beneficiaries if they had not acted in good faith, had knowledge of the beneficiaries prior interest or if they had not given consideration for the property.[3]

The type of trust and the identification of the beneficiaries' interests will affect the rights and powers of the beneficiaries under the trust against the trustees and the trust property.

---

1   *Re Bowden* [1936] Ch 71
2   L. Smith, ' Trust and Patrimony' (2008) 38 *Revue General de Droit* 379.
3   Considered in the chapters on tracing and strangers to the trust.

15.2 Rights and powers of a beneficiary

When the trust is constituted the trustees are under an enforceable duty to perform the trust as instructed in the trust deed. This simply may be to distribute the trust property amongst identified beneficiaries in specified amounts, a bare trust, or to select at the trustees discretion amongst an identified class of beneficiaries, a discretionary trust. If the beneficiary may immediately enjoy the property it is described as 'held or vested in possession'. If the enjoyment of the property is deferred until the future it is known as a 'future interest'. Future interests may be remainders, reversions and executory interests. A remainder is an interest in property after a life interest. A reversion is an interest that reverts to the original owner after he has granted another use of it, typically a lease of land will revert possession of the land to the landlord at the end of the lease. An executory interest is an interest that is ended or created because of an event; they are said to 'shift' or 'spring up' because of an event. Thus a trust may provide that property is to be used by Anne for her life, but if she marries the property is to go to Mark. This is an example of a shifting interest, which is with Anne for her life unless and until she marries when it is shifted to Mark. An interest may also spring up, for example an interest for Anne when she reaches 21 years old, does not give Anne an interest until she reaches the designated age. Thus we may have present or future interests. To complicate matters further interest may also be vested or contingent. Here 'vested' does not mean vested in possession but vested in the sense that the interest will come to pass and cannot be stopped. Thus a future interest will be vested when the beneficiary is ascertained and the interest is only prevented from taking effect in possession because of the existence of a prior interest. For example, Gerald gives all his property to his wife Cheryl for life and in remainder to his son Anthony. Cheryl has a life interest and so has vested possession of the property. Anthony has a vested future interest, he is not entitled to possession, but he is identified and in existence and his possession is only prevented by his mother's prior interest which will come to an end. The future interest may be contingent, dependent upon a future event that may or may not happen, for example the beneficiary reaches the age of 21 years or is awarded a law degree. In our example if Gerald had left his property to Cheryl for life and then to his son Anthony when he attains the age of 21, the interest would be a contingent future interest because, although Anthony fulfils the first condition for a vested interest, he is ascertainable, his interest will not automatically follow his mother's prior interest as he must also fulfil the condition of reaching the age of 21 years. If he reaches the age of 21 before his mother's death then his interest will be a future vested interest. Thus there are many different types of beneficial interest and the powers and rights of the beneficiary are largely dependent on the type of interest they have. However, there are some general rights and powers that all beneficiaries have:

- To disclaim the interest: the beneficiary has the right to disclaim their interest under the trust. Thus a beneficiary can inform the settler or trustee that he does not wish to receive his share of the trust property at any time. If they do so then the trust may provide that the property is to go to another beneficiary or the property may result back to the settler or testator's estate.
- To dispose of their interest: a beneficiary may sell, give away or create a trust of their beneficial interests. If the trust property is land or an interest in land then they will have to comply with the formalities in S.53(1)(c) of the Law of Property Act 1925.[4]
- To take action against the trustee for a breach of trust: all potential trustees have the right to take action against trustees to prevent a breach of the trust or to make the trustee account for any breach which causes loss to the trust. They also have the right to take personal action against the trustee for any breach of trust which causes loss to them.[5]
- The right to information about the trust: this right has been the subject of some debate in recent judicial decisions[6] and academic articles.[7] It seems that the beneficiary has a right to information about the trust but that right may be limited in some circumstances, particularly with reference to the instructions from the settlor if they are not relevant to any breach of trust by the trustees. It seems there is no duty on the trustee of a discretionary trust to provide information to potential beneficiaries.[8]

15.3 Variations of Trusts

We have already considered what is required to create an enforceable private trust. The importance of complying with these requirements was that, once the private trust was constituted, a court would enforce the terms of the trust, ensuring that the trustee carried out the instructions of the settlor. Once the trust is constituted the first duty of the trustee is to

---

4   S.53(1)(c): 'a disposition of an equitable interest or trust subsisting at the time of the disposition, must be in writing signed by the person disposing of the same, or by his agent thereto lawfully authorised in writing or by will'.

5   A beneficiary may also have the right to trace property transferred in breach of trust.

6   See *Schmidt v Rosewood Trust Ltd* [2003] UKPC 26; [2003] 2 AC 709 (PC IoM):

7   Mary Ambrose, 'Disclosure to beneficiaries- wither confidentiality? (2006) (4) *Private Client Business* 236-244.

8   see Mahoney JA in *Hartigan Nominees Pty Ltd v Rydge* (1992) 29 NSWLR 405 at 432; *Tam Mei Kam v HSBC International Trustee Ltd* [2011] HKCU 964, [45], per Chan P.J. (CFA)

acquaint himself with the trust property and his instructions as a trustee. If a trustee does not follow his instructions he may be in breach of trust. Thus it may seem that the terms of a trust are sacred and not to be interfered with as they reflect the instructions of the settlor and will be enforced; however, in certain circumstances equity has provided for the terms of a trust to be changed, usually this has been because it is necessary to fulfil the trust's purpose, for example the use of *cy pres* to permit the general charitable purpose of a charitable trust, or in the best interests of the beneficiaries for a private trust. Equity's willingness to permit the variation of the terms of the trust reflects the pre-eminence of the beneficiaries' interests as opposed to the instructions of the settlor. Sometimes a trust may even be brought to an end at the instance of the beneficiaries and the trust property conveyed to them.[9]

The courts have usually approved variations of trust because circumstances have arisen which were not contemplated by the settlor and the interests of the beneficiaries will suffer if variation is not permitted. It may be possible to vary the terms of a trust using four authorities:

- express powers in the trust instrument;
- consent of the beneficiaries;
- a court using its inherent jurisdiction;[10] and,
- a court using statutory powers such as the Variation of Trusts Act 1958.

The first authority is found in the trust instrument itself as some settlors do provide express powers in the trust instrument for themselves or others to vary the terms of the trust, although it is almost impossible to provide for every eventuality.

15.4 Variation with beneficiaries' consent: the rule in *Saunders v Vautier*

Equity recognises the importance of the beneficiary's interest in the trust property to such an extent that: if all the beneficiaries who are together absolutely beneficially entitled to the whole of the trust property are recognised as legally competent (*sui juris*) and of full age they may call in unanimous agreement for the transfer of the trust property. This is known as the rule in *Saunders v Vautier*,[11] although it predates the case.

Saunders v Vautier[12]
A testator created a trust comprising stocks in favour of Vautier as sole

---

9   See the rule in *Saunders v Vautier* (1841) Cr & Ph 240 discussed below.
10   See *Chapman v Chapman* [1954] A.C. 429 discussed below.
11   (1841) Cr & Ph 240.
12   (1841) Cr & Ph 240.

beneficiary. The trustees were to hold the stock and accumulate the income until Vautier reached the age of 25. The trustees were then to transfer the stock and accumulated income to Vautier. When Vautier was 21 years old, the age of majority at the time, he applied to the court for a direction that the trustees transfer the trust property to him immediately. The court held that, as Vautier was of full age and had a vested interest in the whole of the beneficial interest of the fund, he was entitled to terminate the trust and take the fund.

It should be noted that the rule does not apply if an interest is merely contingent, that is, conditional on an event. In *Saunders v Vautier* an argument was made that Vautier's interest was contingent upon his reaching 25 years of age but the court rejected this, holding that the wording of the trust vested his interest immediately but attempted to delay his possession of the property. The rule reflects a vindication of the proprietary right of the beneficiary to the trust property and is consistent with the common law's hatred of restrictions on gifts.[13]

The rule has been developed so that if a beneficiary has an identifiable individual absolute interest he may call for this if it would not devalue the interest of the other beneficiaries.[14] The rule also applies to life interest trusts, as the life tenant and the remainder man own the whole beneficial interest between them. Therefore if they are *sui juris*, of full age and in agreement they may terminate the trust and divide the property amongst them.[15]

The rule has even been applied to discretionary trusts, even though members of a class of beneficiaries under a discretionary trust only have a *spes* (a hope) of an interest and the application of the rule defeats the protective nature of discretionary trusts. The rule has been applied to discretionary trusts because, even though not individually selected yet, as a group the potential beneficiaries will between them all own all of the beneficial interest in the trust property. Therefore, if they are all *sui juris*, of full age and in agreement they may call on the trustee to deliver the property to them and divide it as they wish.[16]

Example
Gerald sets up a trust of a £1 million with Omar as trustee in favour of those of his ten grandchildren who Omar at his absolute discretion will select. Even though he has not selected who is to receive the money his ten

---

13 This hatred of restrictions on gifts is matter of public policy similar to that to that in the rule against perpetuities and other attempts to prevent free use of property.
14 *Stephenson v Barclays Bank Trust Co Ltd* [1975] 1 ALL ER 626; [1975] 1 WLR 882.
15 *Brown v Pringle* (1845) 4 Hare 124, 14 LJ Ch 121, 8 Jur 1113; (1845) 67 ER 587.
16 *Re Smith* [1928] Ch 915.

grandchildren may, if they are all sui juris and of full age get together and call for their grandfather to transfer the money to them.

Of course the rule in *Saunders v Vautier* is not really variation of the trust but termination. Even if the beneficiaries have the property resettled this will be a new trust.

A settlor may introduce elements to prevent the rule's use. For example he may introduce a contingency,[17] for example only those of his grandchildren who become doctors may be eligible to be selected. However, the wording of a contingency must be very carefully considered because, as noted above, in *Saunders v Vautier* the representation that the age specification was a contingency was rejected and it was interpreted as just a delay for accumulation.

Example

Gerald sets up the following trust in his will: "I leave £1 million to Omar to hold on trust. Each of my ten grandchildren who becomes a solicitor before or at the age of 25 years old is to receive a proportionate share in this fund. If none of my grandchildren become a solicitor by the time they are 25 years old then the fund is to be given to the RSPCA."

The interests of the grandchildren are not vested unless they become a lawyer before or at the age of 25 years. If any do become a lawyer by this age their interest will vest but they will not be entitled to possession until all have reached the age of 25 years and it is known how many, if any, are lawyers and what amount each is to get. Thus until all have reached the age of 25 and it is known who has a vested interest they cannot get together to use the rule in *Saunders v Vautier* when they reach the age of majority.

A settlor may also prevent the use of the rule by including infants or those unborn as potential beneficiaries as they cannot consent to the use of the rule. A settlor could also include himself as one of the beneficiaries or someone else he could trust not to agree to the rule, as the call has to be unanimous.

15.5 Variation under the court's inherent jurisdiction

There may be circumstances where variation of the trust is necessary to protect the beneficiaries' interests and they are not able to take advantage of the rule in *Saunders v Vautier*. In those cases the court may be able to use its inherent jurisdiction to authorise variation of the terms of the trust, although the judiciary have not always been comfortable with this power. For example Farwell J noted, in *Re Walker*:[18] 'I decline to accept any suggestion that the Court has an inherent jurisdiction to alter a man's will

---

17   *Hiranand v Harilela* [2004] 4 HKC 231.
18   [1901] 1 Ch 879 at 885.

because it thinks it beneficial. It seems to me that is quite impossible.' Similarly Romer LJ stated, in *Re New*:[19] 'As a rule, the Court has no jurisdiction to give, and will not give, its sanction to the performance by trustees of acts with reference to the trust estate which are not, on the face of the instrument creating the trust, authorised by its terms.'

15.5.1 The inherent jurisdiction in *Re Downshire's Settled Estates*

The judicial flashpoint in the argument over the existence and extent of the inherent jurisdiction of the court to vary the terms of a trust came in *Re Downshire's Settled Estates*,[20] where, not very surprisingly, Lord Denning made the most fervent claim in favour of the court's inherent jurisdiction. The Court of Appeal heard three joined appeals which considered the power of the court to vary the terms of a trust under its inherent jurisdiction and statutory powers in s.64(1) of the Settled Land Act 1925 and s.57(1) of the Trustee Act 1925.

In *Re Downshire's Settled Estates* there was an alleged dispute amongst the beneficiaries and their representatives regarding resettlement and variation of the terms of a settlement trust involving life tenants and remainder-men. The variation would accelerate interests and release capital from discretionary trusts thus saving estate duty. At first instance Roxburgh J. held that the court could not authorise this under its inherent jurisdiction or under the Settled Land Act, 1925, s 64(1).[21]

Judgment: the Court of Appeal reversed the decision of Roxburgh J. and held that the court could authorise the scheme as a compromise between the beneficiaries under its inherent jurisdiction or under s 64(1).

In *Re Chapman's Settlement Trusts* a scheme was proposed that trustees should transfer the settled funds to a new settlement with similar terms except that discretionary powers of maintenance had been excluded. This would save estate duty. Harman J. had rejected the scheme on the grounds that the court had no power, either under its inherent jurisdiction or under the Trustee Act, 1925, s 57(1) to sanction it.

Judgment: the Court of Appeal held that the court had no jurisdiction under the Trustee Act, 1925, s 57(1), to sanction the scheme because it involved the alteration or re-moulding of the trusts. There were three instances where the court could use its inherent jurisdiction to alter the

---

19   [1901] 2 Ch 534 at 544.
20   A series of actions heard together by the Court of Appeal as *Downshire (Marquis) v Royal Bank of Scotland and Others; Re Chapman's Settlement Trusts; Chapman and Another v Chapman and Others; Re Blackwell's Settlement Trusts; Blackwell v Blackwell and Others* [1953] 1 All ER 103.
21   [1952] 2 All ER 603.

terms of a trust; these were when there was an emergency, when the beneficiaries required maintenance and when the court affected a compromise between the beneficiaries. This scheme did not come within these exceptions, although Lord Denning dissented on the grounds that the court should have used its compromise jurisdiction.

In *Re Blackwell's Settlement Trusts*, the plaintiff appealed from an order of Roxburgh J,[22] that a scheme involving the variation of the trusts of a settlement could not be authorised under the general jurisdiction of the court or under the Trustee Act, 1925, s 57(1), as this was restricted to administrative transactions.

Judgment: the Court of Appeal held the court had no jurisdiction to sanction the scheme under the Trustee Act, 1925, s 57(1), because it could not fairly be described as a disposition or transaction in the "management or administration of the property vested in the trustees", but reversed the decision of Roxburgh J as the scheme constituted a compromise the court could authorise under its inherent jurisdiction

Thus the Court of Appeal approved two of the variations citing the inherent jurisdiction of the court to authorise a compromise of a dispute between the beneficiaries. Sir Raymond Evershed M.R. gave the judgment of Romer LJ and himself identifying three well-established exceptions to the rule that a court should give effect to the intentions of the settlor:[23]

Variation for maintenance. This applied where there was a trust which accumulated income and did not provide for the maintenance of the beneficiaries the court would assume that the intention to provide for the family is so paramount that it will order maintenance in disregard of the trusts for accumulation.

Variation to affect a compromise between beneficiaries who cannot agree for themselves because they are under a disability (particularly infants) and persons who are beneficially interested or may become interested.[24] This power to 'compromise' was not to be construed narrowly so that it was just confined to 'compromises' of disputed rights.

Variation in an emergency to confer on the trustees administrative powers not expressed in the trust instrument. This applied when a situation arose in regard to the property creating what could fairly be called an emergency. The power did not extend to changes or re-arrangements of the beneficial interests but was restricted to administrative powers for the trustees with regard to the trust property itself.

The Court of Appeal also clarified that as the object of the Trustee Act, 1925, s 57, was to secure that trust property should be managed as advantageously as possible in the interests of the beneficiaries, the powers

---

22   [1952] 2 All ER 647.
23   [1953] 1 All ER 103 at 113.
24   Citing Re Trenchard [1902] 1 Ch 378 as authority.

of the court under this provision were restricted to authorising specific dealings with the property which were not possible under the court's inherent jurisdiction, either because no actual 'emergency' had arisen or because the situation was not one which the settlor could not have foreseen. The legislation was not intended 'to disturb the rule that the court will not re-write a trust or to add to such exceptions to that rule as had already found their way into the inherent jurisdiction.'[25]

Lord Evershed M.R. explained that:

'[t]he Court of Chancery has over many centuries evolved in relation to its peculiar or "extraordinary" jurisdiction many salutary powers including the "inherent jurisdiction" invoked in the present cases. It has not in general been the practice of the court to attempt precise definitions of such powers and thereby to run the risk of imposing undue fetters on their future application... In the present case we do not propose to depart from the well-established practice...[26]

...Just as the court has always insisted on the due and proper observance by trustees of the terms of their trusts, so also will it in its own orders depart as little as possible from the strict letter of the trust instrument... The general rule, as we have said, is that the court will give effect, as it requires the trustees themselves to do, to the intentions of a settlor as expressed in the trust instrument, and has not arrogated to itself any overriding power to disregard or re-write the trusts'.[27]

Thus although the court should usually give effect to the wishes of the settlor and the terms in the trust the court did have an inherent jurisdiction to vary the terms of the trust and this jurisdiction should not be delineated in too much detail as it might restrict the ability of the court to develop the jurisdiction. Lord Justice Denning dissented; raising issues to do with cases involving what he claimed were the conversion, emergency, maintenance and compromise jurisdictions of the court. He took a general jurisdiction from the authorities for the court to authorise variations of the terms of a trust when it was for the benefit of those who could not consent themselves.

15.5.2 The response of the House of Lords in *Chapman v Chapman*

The beneficiaries appealed the case of *Re Chapman's Settlement Trusts*, as *Chapman v Chapman*,[28] and the House of Lords took the opportunity to respond to the comments in the Court of Appeal, particularly Lord

25   [1953] 1 All ER 103 at 104.
26   [1953] 1 All ER 103 at 109.
27   [1953] 1 All ER 103 at 110 per Evershed M.R.
28   [1954] A.C. 429

Denning's wide claims for the inherent jurisdiction of the court to vary the terms of a trust. The House of Lords affirmed the Court of Appeal's decision and did not approve the scheme but commented:

'A judge of the Chancery Division has no inherent jurisdiction, in the execution of the trusts of a settlement, to sanction, on behalf of infant beneficiaries and unborn persons, a rearrangement of the trusts of that settlement for no other purpose than to secure an adventitious benefit (e.g., that estate duty payable in a certain event will, in consequence of the rearrangement, not be payable in respect of the trust funds).'

Lord Simmonds V.C. commented:

'My Lords, I am unable to accept as accurate this view of the origin, development and scope of the jurisdiction of the Court of Chancery. I do not propose to embark on the arduous task of tracing to its sources this peculiar jurisdiction. Many volumes have been devoted to it, and I have refreshed my memory by reference to some of them. Nowhere can I find any statement which would support the broad proposition for which the appellants contend… We are as little justified in saying that a court has a certain jurisdiction, merely because we think it ought to have it, as we should be in declaring that the substantive law is something different from what it has always been declared to be, merely because we think it ought to be so. It is even possible that we are not wiser than our ancestors. It is for the legislature, which does not rest under that disability, to determine whether there should be a change in the law and what that change should be.'[29]

Lord Morton of Henryton commented on the decisions in the Court of Appeal that the majority of the Court of Appeal were right in dismissing the Chapman appeal, which was before the House, but their decisions in *re Downshire Settled Estates*77 and in *re Blackwell's Settlement Trusts*77 went 'too far'.[30]

The House of Lords clarified that there was an inherent jurisdiction supported by authorities but it was restricted to four situations:[31]

- Conversion jurisdiction
- Maintenance jurisdiction
- Emergency or salvage jurisdiction
- Compromise jurisdiction

After Chapman the inherent jurisdiction of the court to vary the terms of a trust was therefore limited to the four categories and its powers under the inherent jurisdiction were severely limited.

---

29   [1954] A.C. 429 at 444. This restriction and these categories were confirmed in other Commonwealth jurisdictions e.g. Canada by the High Court of Ontario in Re Wright [1955] 1 DLR 213.

30   [1954] A.C. 429 at 444 at 462.

31   [1954] A.C. 429 at 445, per Lord Simmonds V.C.

Conversion jurisdiction

The conversion jurisdiction is the power of the court to authorise the change of trust property from real property (realty) to personal property (personalty) or vice versa. Thus even if the trust provided no express powers for trustees to convert property or specified that it should be maintained as a particular type of property the court could authorise the conversion. This had been important when the differences between the type of property was important for inheritance and settlement restrictions but is no longer as important today. Furthermore the court now has statutory powers to convert realty to personalty, s.6 of the Trusts of Land and Trustees Act 1996, and personalty to land, s.8 of the Trustee Act 2000. Section 57 of the Trustee Act 1925 may also be used as it gives the court authority to authorise administrative changes such as changes in investment when it is 'expedient' to do so.

Maintenance jurisdiction

If a trust instrument specifies that income be accumulated for the beneficiaries, the court may authorise the payment of income for their maintenance. Again this aspect of the inherent jurisdiction is less important today because of statutory powers of the court especially s.53 of the Trustee Act 1925 which provides for the provision of maintenance, education or benefit of an infant beneficiary. We have already discussed the statutory powers of the trustees to provide maintenance and advancement to the beneficiaries of a trust under s.31 & s.32 of the Trustee Act 1925, but these powers are not as important as the statutory (or inherent) powers of the court to authorise maintenance and advancement. This is because the statutory powers for trustees do not apply if there is a contrary intention in the trusts such as a direction to accumulate whereas, it seems, the court can override such express restrictions when it authorises such a variation under statute or its inherent jurisdiction.

Emergency jurisdiction

If circumstances arise threaten the very purpose of the trust which the settlor has not foreseen and the beneficiaries cannot agree to deal with because they are not competent, whether through infancy or another disability, the court may vary the terms of the trust to deal with this emergency. The emergency must be such that the variation is necessary to salvage the trust as to refuse to authorise the variation would 'make shipwreck of [the settlor's] intentions'.[32]

---

32   *Chapman v Chapman* [1954] A.C. 429 at 469, per Lord Asquith of Bishopstone

Re New[33]- **Court of Appeal**

The trust fund consisted of ordinary shares in a company. The company was being reorganised and it was proposed that the existing ordinary shares should be transferred to preference shares and debentures. The trust instrument did not authorise investment in these types of shares.

Judgment: the Court would authorise the change in the type of investment under its emergency jurisdiction.

In *Chapman v Chapman* Lord Morton clarified that the salvage jurisdiction applied only in relation 'to administrative acts by trustees and not to alteration of beneficial interests'.[34] The emergency jurisdiction is also less important today because fo the statutory powers in s.57 of the Trustee Act 1925 to authorise administrative changes when it is expedient to do so. The statutory authority is also more extensive than the inherent jurisdiction as it is not limited to situations where the beneficiaries are minors or under another incapacity.

Compromise jurisdiction

The court has an inherent jurisdiction to intervene in a genuine dispute between beneficiaries and those who represent beneficiaries who cannot consent for themselves to affect a compromise by consenting on behalf of the incapacitated. The problem with the compromise jurisdiction was that beneficiaries would collude in a false dispute to get the court to authorise a variation which would accelerate or vary their beneficial interests, as in *Re Downshire's Settled Estates* and *Chapman*. The House of Lords clarified in *Chapman* that the court did have an inherent jurisdiction to consent on behalf of the incapacitated to a variation to affect a compromise between beneficiaries; however, the dispute had to be 'genuine', involve those who could not consent for themselves and the court could only clarify beneficial interests, it could not vary the terms of the trust so as to reorganise or reapportion interests under the trust.[35]

15.5.3 The problems with *Chapman v Chapman*

The decision in Chapman v Chapman was intended to restrict the interpretation of the inherent jurisdiction as being a general power to vary the terms of the trust whenever it would benefit the beneficiaries. The effect of the judgment was in some ways quite restrictive and could result in a refusal by the court to authorise a variation which seemed necessary to continue the purpose of the trust.

---

33   [1901] 2 Ch 534.
34   [1954] A.C. 429 at 466, per Lord Morton.
35   *Chapman v Chapman* [1954] A.C. 429 at 444 at 471, per Lord Asquith of Bishopstone. See also comments of Lord Simonds L.C. and Lord Morton of Henryton.

Allen v Distillers Co (Biochemicals) Ltd [36]

The company had manufactured an anti-emetic drug for pregnant women called Thalidomide. The children born to mothers who had taken Thalidomide were severely disabled. A trust had been created to administer the compensation eventually paid by the company to the victims of its drug. The court was asked to approve a settlement deferring a beneficiary receiving his interest even though he had reached the age of majority to accumulate more income for other beneficiaries. There was a genuine dispute.

Judgment: the court had no inherent jurisdiction to vary the trust. Statutory variation was also not possible. Eventually it was discovered that the terms of the trust actually allowed for the vesting to take place when the children were older.

Mason v Fairbrother [37]

A pension fund was set up in 1929 for Co-operative Society employees with very limited powers of investment for the trustees in the Co-operative Society itself and a few other investments. By 1982 the fund contained £127m and the trustees wanted modern wide powers of investment appropriate for such a large fund. The beneficiaries of the trust were divided over whether the trustees should have these new wider powers. The trustees applied to court for variation of the terms of the trust arguing that it was unclear from the trust instrument whether all the fund had to be invested in the Co-operative Society or whether part should be invested under the Trustee Investment Act (TIA) 1961. As there was a genuine dispute the court could use its compromise jurisdiction to give the trustees wider powers than conferred by the TIA 1961.

Judgment: the court held there was a genuine dispute, but, in resolving the dispute, the court could not insert a whole new clause into the trust instrument; however, the court approved the variation under the expedient powers of s.57 of the Trustee Act 1925.

The Law Reform Committee voiced the possibility that the House of Lords had unduly restricted the jurisdiction of the court to come to the aid of beneficiaries who could not consent for themselves. The legislature responded with the Variation of Trust Act 1958.

15.6 Statutory variation: the Variation of Trusts Act 1958 [38]

The powers of the court to authorise variation of the terms of a trust under the Variation of Trusts Act 1958 are quite limited. They are designed to make good any adverse restriction on the inherent jurisdiction in the

---

36   [1974] QB 384.
37   [1983] 2 All ER 1078.
38   1958 Chapter 53, 6 & 7 Eliz 2, 23rd July, 1958.

decision of the House of Lords in *Chapman v Chapman*. Therefore the jurisdiction of the Act will usually apply in circumstances where other powers of the court do not. The Act gives the court the power to consent to variation on behalf of beneficiaries who are unable to consent themselves. Therefore it does not apply when the rule in *Saunders v Vautier* may be used.

The Act gives the court the power to approve variations that, except for one category, are for the benefit of beneficiaries who cannot consent for themselves. Those categories are:

- s1(1) (a): persons unable to consent for themselves due to infancy/incapacity;
- s1(1) (b): unascertained persons;
- s1(1) (c): persons unborn;
- s1(1) (d): persons contingently interested under a protective trust.

For the last category, s1(1)(d), the court does not have to be satisfied that the variation will be for the benefit of the beneficiary.

The first category is quite straightforward as it refers to infants or those incapacitated through other reasons such as illness whether mental or physical.

The second category refers to unascertained persons.

Example: unascertained persons

If Simon leaves property in trust for Benny (who is not married), then to any surviving spouse of Benny, and then to any children of Benny. Benny's future wife is unascertained; even if Benny is engaged to be married no one knows if he will marry, and so nobody knows whom Benny will marry. If a need arises to vary the terms of the trust Benny cannot authorise this variation using the rule in Saunders v Vautier as he is not the sole beneficiary. The court can approve a variation of the terms of the trust if Benny consents and the court believes the variation is in the best interests of the unascertained beneficiary, e.g. Benny's wife (if any), and those unborn (Benny and the possible wife's children, if any).

The second category does not give the court the power to consent on behalf of those who are ascertainable but hard to find. If the beneficiaries are ascertainable then their consent must be obtained unless they cannot consent for themselves, for example they are infants when the court may be able to use its powers under s.1(1)(a) to consent on their behalf. The third category, those unborn, covers the possible children of Benny and his possible wife.

The fourth category is persons contingently interested under a protective trust, which refers to persons whose interests are not vested and

---

39   See *Re Steed's WT* [1960] Ch 407 discussed below.

are at the discretion of a trustee.[39] This subsection differs from the previous categories as it does not require that the court has to be sure the variation is for the benefit of these beneficiaries; however, the interests of these beneficiaries cannot be disregarded altogether, but the court may approve a variation even though some interests suffer.[40]

15.6.1 Variation not resettlement

The power of the court is restricted to a variation of the terms of the trust but this must not amount to a resettlement of the trust. It may be very difficult at times to distinguish between a variation and resettlement. In *Re Ball's Settlement*,[41] Megarry J established a test to distinguish between variation and resettlement:

'If an arrangement changes the whole substratum of the trust, then it may well be that it cannot be regarded as merely varying the trust. But if an arrangement, while leaving the substratum, effectuates the purpose of the trust by other means, it may still be possible to regard that arrangement as merely varying the original trusts, even though the means employed are wholly different and even though the form is completely changed.'[42]

Therefore the dividing line is between variation of the terms of the trust which allows the trust purpose to be fulfilled but just changes how this is achieved, and variation which in effect changes the purpose of the trust.

Re T's Settlement Trust[43]

The beneficiary had an interest contingent on reaching the age of 21. As the beneficiary was thought by the trustees, including her mother, to be reckless, the trustees applied to the court 18 days before the beneficiary's 21st birthday to have the trust converted into a protective trust. The application was to vary the terms of the trust by either transferring her interest to new trustees to be held either on protective trust for her life, or to postpone the vesting of the interest until the beneficiary reached 25. It was accepted that the girl was immature and irresponsible in respect of financial matters.

Judgment: an arrangement that created a protective trust where none originally existed was an attempt at a resettlement and could not be authorised under the Act; however, changing the age of vesting was merely carrying out the trust purpose in a different manner and so a genuine variation in the best interests of the beneficiary. The age of vesting was raised to 25 years.

---

40   See *Re Burney's Settlement Trusts* [1961] 1 All ER 856; [1961] 1 WLR 545.
41   [1968] 1 WLR 899; [1968] 2 All ER 438.
42   [1968] 2 All ER 438 at 442.
43   [1964] Ch 158.

Re Holt's Settlement Trust[44]

Mrs Wilson had a life interest with remainder to her children who attained 21. Mrs Wilson proposed surrendering one half of her life interest in the income of the trust property in favour of the children in return for the children postponing their entitlement to the capital until attaining the age of 30.

Judgment: the variation was approved as it was merely deferring the childrens' interests and so a variation of the trust not a resettlement. It also gave the children more of the property and so was in their benefit.

The need for the variation to be for the benefit of the beneficiary on whose behalf the court is consenting has led to a wide interpretation of benefit.

15.6.2 What constitutes benefit?

Generally a variation of the terms of the trust that will result in a financial gain for the share of the beneficiary will be to their benefit. Thus variations which increase the financial share of the beneficiary,[45] and schemes to reduce the trust's liability to taxation will usually be approved.[46] The reality is, as Lord Denning noted, in **Re Weston's Settlement Trust**,[47] 'Nearly every variation that has come before the court has tax avoidance for its principal object: and no one has ever suggested that this is undesirable or contrary to public policy.' Although, as might be expected, the courts have been wary of approving variations which have had tax evasion as the primary motive. Thus in **Re Seale's Marriage Settlement**,[48] the court approved the movement of the trust to Canada as the family were emigrating and it was in the best interests of the infant beneficiaries to have their trust assets in their home jurisdiction. This may be contrasted with variation by relocation for 'illegitimate tax avoidance' as in Re Weston's Settlement Trusts.

Re Weston's Settlement Trusts[49]

The trustees sought the approval of the court on behalf of the infant beneficiaries for a transfer of the trust to Jersey. Jersey is a 'tax haven' and the trust fund, which amounted to some £400,000, would save approximately £163,000 in Capital Gains Tax if it were allowed to relocate.

---

44 [1969] 1 Ch 100.
45 *Re Holt's Settlement Trust* [1969] 1 Ch 100.
46 See comments in *Re Downshire's Settled Estates* [1953] 1 All ER 103 at 109 per Evershed M.R.
47 [1969] 1 Ch. 223 at 245.
48 *Re Seale's Marriage Settlement* [1961] Ch 574.
49 *In re Weston's Settlement (Weston v Weston)* [1969] 1 Ch. 223.

Judgement: the court held that the family's connection with Jersey was 'recent and tenuous' and the relocation should not be approved. Lord Justice Stamp commented that, 'I am not persuaded that this application represents more than a cheap exercise in tax avoidance which I ought not to sanction, as distinct from a legitimate avoidance of liability to taxation.'[50]

Lord Denning went a little further than his colleagues in asserting that there were benefits other than financial gain that should be considered for the infant beneficiaries.

'The court should not consider merely the financial benefits to the infants or unborn children, but also their educational and social benefit. There are many things in life more worthwhile than money. One of these things is to be brought up in this our England, which is still "the envy of less happier lands." I do not believe it is for the benefit of children to be uprooted from England and transported to another country simply to avoid tax.'[51]

Other benefits that may be considered are protecting an immature beneficiary from herself, as we have already seen in *Re T's Settlement Trust*,[52] and avoiding potential family disputes or personal conflict.

Re Remnant's Settlement Trusts [53]

The family trust instrument contained a forfeiture clause which provided that contingently entitled members who married a Roman Catholic would surrender their share. The trustees proposed variation of the terms of the trust by removing this forfeiture clause.

Judgment: the court approved the variation and the clause was removed as it was in the best interests of the children as they now had the free choice to marry whom they wished.

It will be seen from these cases that the intention of the settlor is disregarded if the variation does not change the nature of the trust and is in the best interests of the beneficiaries.

Goulding v. James[54]

The testatrix left property to her daughter for life with remainder to her grandson upon attaining the age of 40. If the grandson predeceased the daughter before attaining the age of 40, then his share was to be divided amongst his children. The testatrix had created the trust to ensure that her son-in-law did not get the trust property. She also wanted to restrict her grandson from receiving the property when he was young and reckless.

---

50   [1969] 1 Ch. 223 at 234.
51   [1969] 1 Ch. 223 at 245.
52   [1964] Ch 158.
53   *Re Remnant's Settlement Trusts (Hooper v Wenhaston)* [1970] Ch. 560.
54   [1997] 2 All ER 239.

The daughter and grandson proposed a variation of the terms of the trust so that 10% of the fund should be placed in trust for the grandson's children and the daughter and grandson should take the remaining amount immediately.

Judgment: the court consented to the variation on behalf of the unborn beneficiaries (the grandson's children) as it was to their financial benefit. It seems that the intention of the testatrix was of little importance.

The only circumstances when the intentions of the settlor seem important are when the trust is protective and the court is being asked to remove the protective element.[55]

15.6.3 When will the court not vary?

As already discussed the court will only approve a variation and not a resettlement of the trust. The variation must also be in the best interests of the beneficiaries for the first three categories of beneficiary on behalf of whom the court can consent.

The court will also not approve a variation which removes the protective element of a protective trust. A protective trust is intended to prevent a beneficiary squandering the trust property, thus it is usually a trust for the life or some lesser period of the beneficiary that is determinable upon some event, for example the bankruptcy of the beneficiary, at which point a discretionary trust arises in favour of the beneficiary or his family.[56]

Re Steed's Will Trusts [57]
Steed left property on protective trusts for his housekeeper for her life and then to whomever she appointed after her death. Steed had been concerned that the housekeeper's brother would take money from her and so the trustees had discretion to advance capital sums to the housekeeper as they should think fit. The trust provided that if the housekeeper should forfeit her interest the property was to be held on protective trusts for her children or her husband. The housekeeper purportedly exercised the power of advancement in favour of herself and then applied to the court for a variation of the trust to allow her to take the trust property. She argued that as she was unmarried and old it was unlikely she would have children and so it was unlikely there would be other beneficiaries.

Judgment: the court refused to authorise the variation because it would

---

55   *Re Steed's Will Trusts* [1960] Ch 407.
56   Trustee Act 1925, s.33. A protective trust cannot be created in favour of the settlor as beneficiary determinable upon his own bankruptcy as this would defeat his creditors.
57   [1960] Ch 407.

remove the protective element from the trust. Steed had intended that the housekeeper should be protected from her brother and no variation could be approved which removed this protection. The application was under s1(1)(d) and so the court did not have to consider whether there was benefit for the potential beneficiaries.

The court will also not approve a variation of the terms of a trust which amounts to a fraud on a power.

Example
Property is left to a life tenant with a power of appointment for the life tenant to select the beneficiaries in remainder. If the life tenant proposes a variation of the trust so that his life interest is terminated and the capital divided between himself and those he appoints in remainder, the variation could be proposed purely in order that the life tenant acquires a share of the capital. As he was not originally entitled to this capital, merely income, this would amount to a fraud on a power and the court will not approve it on behalf of beneficiaries who cannot consent for themselves.[58] It should be noted that if the life tenant and remaindermen are of full age and *sui juris* they may be able to take advantage of the rule in *Saunders v Vautier* and the court's sanction would be unnecessary.

Of course, if the variation is for a genuine reason then it may be approved. Fir example if the life tenant proposes a division of the property amongst himself and those in remainder because it will save inheritance tax and the life tenant only receives a similar amount to that he would have received under his life interest but those in remainder benefit by the saving it may be approved.[59]

15.7 Other statutory powers of variation

We have already considered circumstances in which a court will vary the terms of a trust, for example when a person is incapacitated because of mental illness[60] or a couple divorce, the court has the power to vary the terms of any trust interest they may have,[61] or if a settlor has not provided remuneration for trustees a court has statutory and common law powers to award remuneration to trustees.[62]

We have also considered some other important instances of statutory powers for the court to authorise variation including: the Trustee Act 1925 s57, which permits the court to approve variation of the terms of a trust which regulate the management of a trust when it is 'expedient' to do so;[63]

---

58   See *Re Brook's Settlement (Brooks v Brooks)* [1968] 3 All ER 416.
59   *Re Wallace's Settlements* [1968] 2 All ER 209
60   Mental Health Act 1983 s 96(1)(d).
61   Matrimonial Causes Act 1973, s24.
62   E.g. Boardman v Phipps [1967] 2 AC 46.

the Trustee Act 1925 s53, which permits the court to authorise provision of maintenance for infant beneficiaries when the trust provides for accumulation; and the Settled Land Act 1925 s64(1), which provides for the variation of the terms of a trust settlement when it is for the benefit of the beneficiaries or the settled land.[64]

15.8 Summary

Although a trustee is under a duty to carry out the terms of a trust once it is constituted, under certain circumstances equity permits the terms of a trust to be varied if it is in the best interests of the beneficiaries. Variation of the terms of a trust is permitted if the trust instrument provides for variation, if the beneficiaries agree to variation, under the court's inherent jurisdiction and under statutory provisions.

The focus on the interests of the beneficiaries' and the ignoring of the intent of the settlor exemplifies the pre-eminence of the beneficiaries' interests in the trust. This is reflected in the rule in *Saunders v Vautier* which provides that if all of the beneficiaries are of full age, *sui juris* and together beneficially entitled to the whole of the trust property they may call for the trustees to transfer it to them.

Other circumstances which may give rise to variation of the terms of a trust usually involve unforeseen circumstances, usually changes in the structure and incidence of taxation, which may threaten the interests of the beneficiaries. In these circumstances the court may rely on its inherent jurisdiction to vary the terms of the trust. The inherent jurisdiction was limited by the House of Lords in *Chapman v Chapman* to the power to consent to variations of the trust involving conversion of personalty to realty and vice versa, providing maintenance to infant beneficiaries when the trust did not or only provided for accumulation, varying the terms of a trust when there was an emergency or a situation of actual salvage of the trust, and to affect a compromise between beneficiaries in genuine dispute which did not affect the beneficial interests but merely clarified them. The inherent jurisdiction is not as important today as it was because the court has more statutory powers of variation.

The Variation of Trusts Act provides that the court may sanction a

---

63   *Re Downshire's Settled Estates* [1953] 1 All ER 103; *Anker-Peterson v Anker-Peterson* (1998) 12 TLI 166. An application may be made in chambers and so is less expensive than an application under the Variation of Trusts Act 1958. Foor a consideration of the extent of this power see *Sutton v England* [2009] EWHC 3270 (Ch) and the Court of Appeal decsion discussed in Robert Blower, 'The limits of section 57 Trustee Act 1925 after *Sutton v England*' (2012) 18(1) (Jan) *Trusts & Trustees* 11-16.

64   E.g. *Re Downshire's Settled Estates* [1953] 1 All ER 103; *Hambro v. Duke of Marlborough* [1994] Ch 158.

variation of the terms of a trust on behalf of infants or the incapacitated, unascertained person, those unborn and those contingently interested under a protective trust. For all but the last category the court must be sure the variation is in the best interests of those whom it is consenting for. The court can only approve variation of the trust and not resettlement. Thus a change in the terms which still permits the trust purpose to be fulfilled may be allowed but a change in the whole purpose of the trust, for example by introducing a protective element where none existed before, will not be allowed. The benefit to the beneficiaries has been widely construed but generally financial benefit will suffice. It seems the settlor's intentions are irrelevant unless the variation is to remove a protective element from a trust. The court will also not authorise a variation which will amount to a fraud on a power.

The court has many other statutory powers to authorise varying the terms of a trust.

CHAPTER 16
TRACING

16.1 What is Tracing?

We have already mentioned tracing when we have considered the possibility of the trust or the beneficiaries of the trust seeking the return of trust property when it has been disposed of in breach of the trust. Tracing exists at common law and in equity. Tracing involves identifying misappropriated property or substitutions for that property so that the property may be claimed. It will not be a surprise to discover that the common law has remained fixated on clear distinguishing of property interests when it traces, whereas equity has developed very flexible rules for tracing misappropriated property and its substitutions. Tracing is extremely important to protect the trust and consists of a series of principles or rules developed by equity to deal with those situations when assets of the trust have been misappropriated and the trustee is not in a position to compensate the trust, or money compensation would not be adequate because the property was too important to the trust. As tracing may identify property or its substitutions which have been misappropriated it is a useful anti-money laundering tool,[1] and may be used to identify assets which are the proceeds of crime or may be used to fund terror. Thus any restrictions on its use have been hotly contested and it is a topic that has attracted considerable judicial and academic debate over the last two decades.

One issue that has arisen with regard to tracing is the language used to describe the process. It has also been argued that tracing should be distinguished from the process of following property. Following property is where a court will identify the same property as it passes through the hands of subsequent holders, whereas tracing is the identification of substitutions for the property or its mixtures in the hands of subsequent holders.[2]

---

1   There are now many domestic and international laws trying to combat money laundering: see Saliou Bah, 'Recovery and return of proceeds of corruption in the international anti-corruption conventions' (2010) 1 *JBL* 15-34; Andrew Haynes, 'The international response to the Money laundering threat', in *A Practitioner's Guide to International Money laundering Law and regulation*, City & Financial Publications. 2003; Andrew Haynes, *The Law Relating to International Banking*, Bloomsbury Professional, 2010.
2   See *Foskett v. McKeown* [2001] 1 AC 102 at 128 per Lord Millett.

The most hotly contested topic in tracing is whether it is a process or a remedy; this is an important issue because, as argued by some academics and some judges,[3] if it is merely an evidential process, it seems unduly restrictive to preserve the distinction between common law tracing and tracing in equity and this would allow the more flexible rules that have been developed in equity to be available to any forensic investigation into misappropriated property. If following and tracing are merely evidentiary processes, then a cause of action is required to claim the identified property. Thus the following and tracing process becomes the first stage in the claiming of property:[4]

- Identification of the misappropriated property or its substitutions by following or tracing; and,
- A claim for the return of the property or its substitutions.

This argument has some attraction as it supports the evidentiary rules that are available for equitable tracing being available to the court in the identification stage for any action.

It benefits actions at common law for money had and received and conversion as they have traditionally been limited by the common law's inability to trace through mixed funds. Equity has no problem tracing through mixed funds as it has developed a series of evidential presumptions based on the simple premise that the trustee or fiduciary will always act in the best interests of the trust or his principal.

The value of tracing at common law and in equity is that identification of the property as the original misappropriated property or its substitutions opens the way for a proprietary claim; literally 'that is my property so return it.' Equity would usually enforce this by way of a constructive trust against the conscience of the legal owner.[5] However, equity required an initial fiduciary relationship for tracing in equity and this limits the use of the equitable rules of tracing. Of course the flexibility of the equitable tracing rules and the potential proprietary remedy has made them very attractive to those arguing for a unified law of restitution. Thus academics, such as Lionel Smith and Peter Birks,[6] have argued that as tracing is merely a process there is no need for an initial fiduciary relationship and the rules of tracing in equity should be available to identify any misappropriated property or its substitutions.

---

3   For example Peter Birks, Lionel Smith and Lord Millett- see below.
4   See Lionel Smith, 'Tracing into the Payment of a Debt' [1995] 54(2) *CLJ* 290.
5   See knowing receipt in the next chapter.
6   P. Birks, (ed), *Laundering and Tracing,* Clarendon Press: Oxford, 1995; P. Birks, 'Mixing and tracing: property and restitution'. (1992) 45 *CLP* 69-98; P. Birks, 'Property, Unjust Enrichment, and Tracing' (2001) 54 *Current Legal Problems* 231.

The ideas of Lionel Smith have been championed by English appellate judges,[7] both extra-judicially and most notably in the House of Lords in *Foskett v. McKeown*.[8] In *Foskett* it was noted that as tracing was merely a process there was no need for an initial fiduciary relationship, that was only necessary if the claim for the identified property was in equity; thus if the evidential rules of tracing in equity were used to identify the property it could then be claimed using other remedies including those available at common law.

It should be noted, however, that these comments were obiter and that the case of *Foskett v McKeown* involved what was described as, 'a textbook example of tracing through mixed substitutions.'[9] Funds were misappropriated in breach of trust, so there was an initial fiduciary relationship. Thus the comments on the future development of tracing were strictly obiter and it will be for future decisions to develop the law of tracing. Furthermore, although the issue in *Foskett* was straightforward,[10] the basis of the decisions of the judges in the Court of Appeal and the House of Lords, all of which evince some support for Smith's ideas, were not. The Court of Appeal approved of Lionel Smith's ideas, but came to a different decision than the House of Lords.[11] In the House of Lords, Lord Browne-Wilkinson and Lord Hoffmann agreed with Lord Millett, although the former admitted he had changed his mind after reading Lord Millett's judgment,[12] and Lords Steyn and Hope appeared to support Lord Millett's obiter comments but dissented upon the judgment.[13]

Although there is support for tracing being considered a process, tracing in equity is still being referred to as an '*in rem* remedy',[14] and there has also

---

7   See for example Smith, L., 'Unjust Enrichment, Property, and the structure of Trusts (2000) 116 Law Quarterly Review 412; Smith, Lionel, 'Tracing in Taylor v Plumer: Equity in the Court of King's Bench' [1995] Lloyd's Maritime and Commercial Law Quarterly 240.

8   [2000] 2 WLR 1299; [2001] 1 AC 102.

9   [2001] 1 AC 102, at 126.

10   See Lord Millett [2001] 1 AC 102, at 121; Lord Hoffman noted, at 115: 'I agree with [Lord Millett] that this is a straightforward case of mixed substitution (what the Roman lawyers, if they had had an economy which required tracing through bank accounts, would have called confusio).' But note Lord Hope, at 121, states that he had 'great difficulty in following this observation' as the relevant Roman Law texts differed on how they would treat mixed funds and were concerned with of corporeal property whereas this case dealt with the rights of ownership of incorporeal property.

11   [1997] 3 All ER 392.

12   [2001] 1 AC 102, at 108.

13   [2001] 1 AC 102.

14   See, for example, Delphine Pannatier Kessler, 'The recognition of tracing under the Hague Trusts Convention: an analysis of article 11 para 3 lit d for the perspective of Swiss law' (2012) 18(2) *Trusts & Trustees*, 149-158, at 149.

been some academic support for the retention of the fiduciary relationship as a prerequisite for tracing in equity because of the power of the tracing rules.[15] Thus although Lord Millett's comments are extremely persuasive we must wait for clear direction from the appellate courts to see if the law of tracing has been changed in any fundamental way.

Before considering the different processes and their rules, the nature of the remedies available if the process is successful should be discussed.

16.2 Personal or Proprietary Remedies?

Most actions at law or in equity are personal, for example suing for breach of contract or breach of trust. The main problem with a personal remedy occurs when the defendant is bankrupt; this will almost always make any personal action pointless, as any judgment awarded will simply be an unsecured debt and probably will not be satisfied. However, proprietary remedies give the claimant a right to recover a particular asset and so will defeat the claims of other creditors as the asset is not part of the bankrupt's estate.

Example
Tracey is holding £200,000 on trust for Brian and Bella in equal shares. Tracey takes the trust money for herself and puts it in her own personal bank account. Tracey is then declared bankrupt. Brian and Bella may sue Tracey for breach of trust but all of Tracey's assets will be vested in her trustee in bankruptcy and divided amongst her creditors. If the beneficiaries are awarded a judgment of £200,000 they will have to serve their judgment debt on Tracey's trustee in bankruptcy and it will rank with other unsecured creditors. There may be little or nothing left to satisfy their claim. However, if Brian and Bella can demonstrate that the £200,000 still belongs to them beneficially; thus they will be able to take the whole £200,000 ahead of Tracey's other creditors. This is a proprietary right, the £200,000 will not be passed to Tracey's trustee in bankruptcy because it does not belong to Tracey and has never belonged to her. Brian and Bella will have demonstrated that they owned the £200,000 beneficially.

The problem is that those who misappropriate assets seldom keep them in the same form.

Example
If Tracey had misappropriated the trust money and purchased £200,000 worth of shares before being declared bankrupt then a personal remedy against her would result in the same unsecured judgment debt. However,

---

15   See, for example, John Stevens, 'Vindicating the Proprietary Nature of Tracing' [2001] (Jan-Feb) *Conveyancer and Property Lawyer* 94-102.

if the beneficiaries could demonstrate that the shares were purchased using money belonging to them beneficially they could claim that the shares represent their property and were never owned by Tracey to join her assets on bankruptcy. If they can show that the shares, because they were purchased using their money, belong to them, this will bring them outside Tracey's assets for her bankruptcy and in effect defeat the claims of other creditors

The academic and judicial debate over tracing has focused upon traditional acceptance that common law tracing was merely a process to identify the defendant who was holding the property, after which a claim would be made, whereas equitable tracing was a proprietary remedy in itself, the property was identified as being trust property and so still subject to the trust. If the claimant has established that the defendant has his property, or something representing property in which he has a beneficial interest the claimant has a proprietary claim. The claimant may then elect either to recover the property plus any increase in value, or he may enforce an equitable lien over the defendant's property. If the claim is not proprietary there may be a claim for money had and received. This common law action has been subsumed into the nebulous law of restitution, perhaps more familiar to those from a civilian background.

Of course the benefits for the claimant asserting a proprietary interest is the priority on bankruptcy of the defendant and the possibility of the award of compound interest rather than simple interest, which is usually all that is available for restitution.[16]

Although there is support for the new terminology and abolishing the distinction, the common law and equitable rules are discussed below.

16.3 Following at Common Law

Following at common law is the process of tracking the same property as it passes through different hands. Tracing at common law is the process of identifying substitutions of the property. At common law, property taken from a legal owner will always be regarded as belonging to that owner. For example, if property is stolen the thief may sell the property to an innocent buyer but the buyer does not receive good title because of the principle *nemo dat quod non habet*, no one may give what they do not have. Thus the stolen property should always be recoverable by the original owner if it can be identified. Any recipient of property to which they did not have good title could be subject to an action for the tort of conversion. However, the common law has set up some limits on this principle to safeguard innocent purchasers. For example the principle of estoppel will prevent the original owner from insisting on his title if he has said or done

---

16   *Westdeutsche Landesbank Girozentrale v Islington L.B.C.* [1996] AC 669.

something which would make it unconscionable for him to deny the innocent buyer's right to the property. This doctrine usually applies when the owner has made it seem as if the person 'selling' the property without authority to sell did have authority to sell, e.g. the legal owner of property has told the buyer that the 'seller' is his agent.

The *nemo dat* principle is also subject to an exception if the seller is the actual or ostensible agent of the original owner. There are also some statutory exceptions in the Sale of Goods Act. Probably the most important exception to the *nemo dat* principle was the recognition that if a thief used stolen money to buy goods then the vendor of the goods received good title to the money. This principle was important as it encouraged faith in the acceptance of currency. However, if the recipient was a volunteer or had knowledge of the misappropriation of the funds then the money could be followed into his hands and a common law action, for money had and received, pursued.[17]

In some common law jurisdictions the principle of 'market overt' may also apply as a defence to an action for the recovery of property. Market overt is an ancient common law provision from England's mediaeval markets which provided that a buyer buying goods in good faith for a fair price in the hours of daylight at these markets would receive good title to the goods. The original justification for the rule of market overt was to balance the need for innocent buyers to get good title against the rights of original owners. The rule supposedly gave the original owner the chance to check the markets to see if his goods were being offered for sale;[18] however, the rule has been criticised as protecting those who purchase stolen property and so encouraging theft. The rule was repealed in England by the Sale of Goods (Amendment) Act 1994.

Thus following at common law relies on identifying the misappropriated specific asset or particular sum of money in the hands of the defendant. Of course if the original assets cannot be followed then the original owner is entitled to trace the substitutions for his property at common law.

16.4 Tracing at Common Law

Tracing is possible at common law and is available to any legal owner of property; however, it is restricted to clean substitutions for the misappropriated property.

---

17 See D.M. Fox, 'Identification of Money at Common Law' [2010] 69(1) *Cambridge Law Journal* 28-30.

18 *Harry Talbot v Mrs Lam* [1946] HKLR 17.

Taylor v. Plumer[19]

Sir Thomas Plumer, later Master of the Rolls, had given money to his stockbroker, Walsh, to purchase exchequer bonds on his behalf. Without authority Walsh used £22,500 to buy American investments and bullion instead, and attempted to flee with them. After a dramatic chase by Plumer's agents, Walsh was apprehended at Falmouth before he could leave the country in a boat bound for Lisbon from where he intended to go to America. Plumer's agents took the bullion and investments. Walsh was later declared bankrupt and his assignees in bankruptcy sought to recover the property

Judgment: the property belonged to Plumer because there had been a clean substitution of his misappropriated property for the bullion and investments. They represented his property. As Lord Ellenborough C.J. said:[20]

'It makes no difference in reason or law into what other form, different from the original, the change may have been made, whether it be into that of promissory notes for the security of the money which was produced by the sale of the goods of the principal... or into other merchandise...for the product of or substitute for the original thing still follows the nature of the thing itself, as long as it can be ascertained to be such, and the right only ceases when the means of ascertainment fail, which is the case when the subject is turned into money, and mixed and confounded in a general mass of the same description.'

Thus Lord Ellenborough noted that the limit on common law tracing would be when the property was mixed with other property.[21] As the property most commonly misappropriated is money and as it is common for this money to be paid into a bank account where it is mixed with funds of the wrongdoer or others, it is difficult for the common law to trace into this fund. The most restrictive limit on common law tracing is, however, the inability of the common law to trace through a mixed fund. Thus if money is misappropriated and mixed with funds of the wrongdoer or others in a bank account, it will not be possible to trace the misappropriated property into any property bought with this mixed fund at common law.

Example

If an accountant takes money from her principal and uses it to buy a car, common law tracing is possible; the claimant will be able to identify the car as the direct identifiable substitution for her property. However, If the accountant takes her client's money, pays it into her own bank account,

---

19   (1815) 3 M&S 562.
20   (1815) 3 M&S 562 at 575.
21   Confirmed by Jessel M.R. in *Re Hallet's Estate* (1879) 13 Ch D 696 at 717.

which already contains some of her own money and money belonging to other clients, and then uses money from the mixed fund in the account to buy a car, common law tracing is not possible; the funds of the claimant have been mixed with other money. It is not possible to say whose money has been used to buy the car and which bits of the car represent the original misappropriated funds.

The restriction on common law tracing through a mixed fund means that common law tracing through bank accounts is usually only available when the account contains only the misappropriated fund.

Banque Belge pour L'Etranger v. Hambrouck[22]

Hambrouck was the chief assistant accountant at an engineering works. He drew cheques from his employer's bank account and paid them into his own. The Bank credited his account with £6,000. Hambrouck then drew cheques from his account and paid them into the account of his mistress, Mlle. Spanoghe. When the fraud was detected the mistress' account contained £315 pounds. Evidence was presented that the mistress never paid any money into the account except the money that Hambrouck gave her.

Judgement: the majority of the Court of Appeal allowed common law tracing when the bank accounts were unmixed. Mlle Spanoghe had no defence as the only consideration she had given for the money was 'immoral consideration'.

The limits on common law tracing through bank accounts were highlighted in *Agip (Africa) Ltd v Jackson*.[23]

Agip (Africa) Ltd v Jackson[24]

One of Agip's employees had fraudulently misappropriated over US$500,000. The defendant, a firm of accountants, had arranged for the money to be taken from Agip by way of forged payment orders in favour of a series of dummy companies. The rogues intended to launder the money by using this series of shell companies and passing the money through a number of bank accounts in different jurisdictions. This is a standard money laundering process, rogues move money through different banks in different jurisdictions, change currencies, mix with other funds, change companies, at all times seeking to confuse the identity of the fund. Agip claimed the money was identifiable, after a series of convoluted transfers through banks in many countries, as being represented by a sum in Jackson's account. Agip sought to trace its money at common law.

Judgement: at first instance, Millett J. as he then was, held that it was not possible to trace funds through the clearing system of banks at common

22 [1921] 1 KB 321.
23 [1990] Ch. 265 (1st Instance); [1991] Ch 547 (CA).
24 [1990] Ch. 265 (1st Instance); [1991] Ch 547 (CA).

law, as the banking system relied on a series of banks using their own funds to pay the next bank in the chain subject to reimbursement from the ordering bank. All that passed between the banks was a 'stream of electrons'.[25] Thus the money in the bank account was not a direct substitution of the misappropriated money. However, it was possible to trace the money in the defendant's bank account in equity.

There are also defences to actions available once property has been traced at common law. The first we have already noted is when consideration has been given for misappropriated property. However, this is only available in limited circumstances for any property other than money. It may be possible to rely on a relatively new defence, the change of position defence, taken from the law of unjust enrichment.

Lipkin Gorman (a firm) v. Karpnale Ltd[26]

Cass was a solicitor working for the law firm of Lipkin Gorman. Cass made a number of withdrawals (amounting to £223,000) from the firm's client account which he lost gambling at the Playboy Club. The firm sought to recover the money from the club, by an action for knowing receipt or money had and received, or the bank by way of dishonest assistance (accessory liability), as the bank manager had known Cass was a gambler.

Judgment:[27] as we shall discuss later the firm could not recover against the club by way of knowing receipt or the bank by way of dishonest assistance, the firm did, however, succeed in a common law tracing action against the club and could recover the money by way of money had and received or unjust enrichment. The club had not given consideration for the money, as, although they had given gaming chips in exchange for the money, gaming contracts are void; 'binding in honour only.'[28] However, the Club was allowed to plead a change of position defence. The club had relied on the solicitor's right to gamble with the money and had taken the money believing this. In reliance upon this they had paid him on the rare occasions when he won. They had therefore changed their position in the honest belief that they could take the money. If they returned all the money they would be worse off than they had been before they received the money. Therefore they could offset the amounts they had paid the solicitor against the money they had to return to the firm. Lord Goff of Chieveley explained that the change of position defence was a defence to actions for restitution and explained the limits of the defence:[29]

---

25   [1990] Ch. 265 at 286.

26   [1991] 2 AC 548, [1992] 4 All ER 512 (HL).

27   See Lionel Smith, 'Simplifying claims to traceable proceeds' [2009] 125 (Apr) *Law Quarterly Review* 338-348.

28   Gaming Act 1845, s18, per Lord Goff [1991] 2 AC 548 at 575.

29   [1991] 2 AC 548 at 580, [1992] 4 All ER 512 at 534. Approved in *Abou-Ramah & Others v Abacha & Others* [2006] EWCA Civ 1492.

'It is, of course, plain that the defence is not open to one who has changed his position in bad faith, as where the defendant has paid away the money with knowledge of the facts entitling the plaintiff to restitution; and it is commonly accepted that the defence should not be open to a wrongdoer...At present I do not wish to state the principle any less broadly than this: that the defence is available to a person whose position has so changed that it would be inequitable in all the circumstances to require him to make restitution, or alternatively to make restitution in full. I wish to stress however that the mere fact that the defendant has spent the money, in whole or in part, does not of itself render it inequitable that he should be called upon to repay, because the expenditure might in any event have been incurred by him in the ordinary course of things. I fear that the mistaken assumption that mere expenditure of money may be regarded as amounting to a change of position for present purposes has led in the past to opposition by some to recognition of a defence which in fact is likely to be available only on comparatively rare occasions.'

The change of position defence is now sometimes referred to as the 'good faith' change of position defence, as it relies on the defendant having received funds in good faith, and then having used those funds in a manner in which it would now leave the defendant in a worse position in returning them than he was in before receipt of the disputed funds. For the purposes of this defence, relevant bad faith 'is capable of embracing a failure to act in a commercially acceptable way and sharp practice of a kind that falls short of outright dishonesty as well as dishonesty itself'.[30] The essential question for the court when considering the defence of change of position is 'whether on the facts of a particular case it would in all the circumstances be inequitable or unconscionable, and thus unjust, to allow the recipient of the money paid under a mistake of fact to deny restitution to the payer'.[31]

Common law tracing is only available in limited circumstances and is severely limited by its inability to trace through a mixed fund. This restriction does not limit tracing in equity.

16.5 Tracing in Equity

It is possible to trace misappropriated trust assets at common law but only the trustees may take such an action as they are the legal owners of the

---

30 *Niru Battery Manufacturing Co. v Milestone Trading Ltd* [2002] EWHC 1425; [2002] 2 All ER (Comm) 705 at [135] per Moore-Bick J); and see the discussion on appeal at [2003] EWCA Civ 1446; [2004] QB 985 at [143]-[165] per Clarke LJ. See also *Jeremy D Stone Consultants Ltd v National Westminster Bank Plc* [2013] EWHC 208 (Ch).

31 *Niru Battery Manufacturing Co. v Milestone Trading Ltd* [2003] EWCA Civ 1446; [2004] QB 985 at [162] per Clarke LJ endorsing Moore-Bick J's approach.

trust property. As the trust is not recognised at common law, the beneficiaries are not recognised as owners at common law and so have no cause of action.

It is possible to follow misappropriated trust property in equity as it passes from hand to hand. This is possible until the property reaches the hands of equity's darling, the bona fide purchaser for value without notice of the prior equitable interest. Equity will not follow the property into the hands of equity's darling. At this point equity will trace into the consideration given for the trust property and follow that substituted property until it reaches the hands of equity's darling or is dissipated, that is it is no longer in traceable form.[32]

Example

Tracey is a trustee of a flat for Brian and Bella. Tracey conveys the flat to her boyfriend Simon, who knows the flat is trust property. Simon conveys the flat to his brother Michael, who also knows the flat is trust property. At this point equity will follow the property into the hands of Michael even if he has paid for the flat as he has knowledge of the prior equitable interests of the trust. He will hold the flat on constructive trust for Brian and Bella. Michael sells the flat to Glynis for £2,000,000. Glynis has no knowledge that the flat is trust property. Therefore it is not possible to follow the property into her hands, as she is equity's darling. Equity will now trace into the consideration given by Glynis to Michael. Michael will hold the £2,000,000 on constructive trust for the trust. If he uses the money to buy other property equity will trace the original misappropriated property into this substituted property; that substituted property will now represent the trust property, and Michael will hold the substituted property on constructive trust for the trust, as his conscience is affected by his knowledge of the beneficial ownership of the flat and substituted property.

Traditionally to take advantage of the flexible rules of tracing in equity there have been three requirements:

1   There must be an initial fiduciary relationship;
2   The property must be in traceable form;

---

32   The vendor of property that is subject to later payment may insert a *Romalpa* clause into the contract of sale and retain beneficial ownership of the property. The vendor may then be able to trace the proceeds of any sub-sale of the property and recover them in priority to other creditors: *Aluminium Industrie Vaasen B.V. v. Romalpa Aluminium Ltd* [1976] 1 WLR 676. It may also be possible to trace substitutions for property which was subject to a Quistclose trust: see *Cooper v PRG Powerhouse Ltd (in creditors' voluntary liquidation)* [2008] EWHC 498 (Ch); Sandra Collins, 'Case Comment: Trusts: Tracing' (2008) 23(8) J.I.B.L.R. 89-91.

and,

3   It must be equitable to trace.

The most hotly contested of these requirements is the requirement for an initial fiduciary relationship between the parties, which stems from *Re Diplock*.[33] It may seem obvious that equitable tracing would require a fiduciary basis, but, as discussed above, it has been argued that if tracing is merely an evidential process it is not necessary. This was the basis of comments in *Foskett*, and it may be that a future appellate decision will remove this requirement but at present it seems still necessary in England.[34] Even if the initial fiduciary relationship is not necessary for the tracing process, an equitable interest will be necessary for a proprietary claim.[35] The requirement of an initial fiduciary relationship is not too burdensome, as Lord Millett himself noted some years before *Foskett*, in *Agip (Africa) Ltd v Jackson*,[36] as the courts often 'circumvent' it by finding the circumstances of the payment give rise to a fiduciary relationship on the basis of agency or the constructive trust.[37]

Equitable tracing is available into an unmixed fund and, if this is done, the beneficiary may elect either to assert a proprietary interest and take the property, or to have a charge on the property for the value of the misappropriated property.[38]

Tracing in equity is more flexible and more powerful than tracing at common law. Jessel M.R. noted in *Re Hallett's Estate*, that Lord Ellenborough had correctly identified the limits of tracing at common law in *Taylor v Plumer*,[39] as the common law could not trace into money which had been 'mixed and confounded in a general mess of the same description'. However, Jessel M.R. noted Lord Ellenborough's 'knowledge of the rules of Equity was not quite commensurate with his knowledge of the rules of the Common Law.' [40] Therefore the real value of tracing in equity is its ability to trace into and through mixed funds, whether in a

---

33   [1948] Ch 466.
34   See e.g. *Shalson v Russo*[2003] EWHC1637 (Ch).
35   *Westdeutsche Landesbank Girozentrale v. Islington L.B.C.* [1996] AC 669.
36   [1990] Ch. 265 at 290.
37   Lord Millett cited *Chase Manhattan Bank N.A. v Israel-British Bank (London) Ltd* [1981] Ch 105. Other instances include when the payment was induced by fraud e.g. *Bankers Trust Co v. Shapira* [1980] 1 WLR 1274, or was bribery of an employee e.g. *A-G for Hong Kong v. Reid* [1994] 1 AC 324. See Gerard McCormack, 'The Remedial Constructive Trusts and Commercial Transactions' [1996] 17(1) *Comp Law* 3-11.
38   *Re Hallett's Estate* (1879) 13 Ch D 696. See also *Foskett v. McKeown* [2001] 1 AC 102.
39   (1815) 3 M&S 562.
40   (1880) 13 Ch D 696 at 717, per Jessel M.R.

bank account or other property. Equity does this by following one main principle: the trustee or fiduciary is always presumed to have acted in the best interests of the trust or his principal.

16.5.1 Tracing into mixed funds

Equitable tracing derives from the case of *Re Hallett's Estate*.[41] The strength of tracing in equity is the panoply of rules that have been developed to allow property to be followed after it is mixed with other property. For example equity can trace when:

- The property has been mixed with the wrongdoer's property;
- The property has been mixed with innocent third parties' property;
- The mixed fund has reduced or increased in value.

As stated above, equity does this by following one main principle: the trustee or fiduciary is always presumed to have acted in the best interests of the trust or his principal. Thus, although at common law a mixture of funds is usually subject to co-ownership,[42] in equity, as a trustee should always keep trust funds separate from his own, if the trustee mixes trust funds with his own the mixed fund is regarded as belonging to the trust with the burden on the trustee to disprove this.[43] Tracing into a mixed fund outside of a bank account is best exemplified by the case of *Foskett v McKeown*.[44]

Foskett v McKeown[45]

Murphy and a partner, Mr Deasy, ran a fraudulent property development business. They purportedly held £2.6 million on trust which was fraudulently obtained from 220 people who wished to purchase properties in the Algarve, Portugal. The development never happened and Murphy and his partner used the money themselves. Murphy effected a whole life insurance policy in the sum of £1 million using some of the trust money to pay several annual premiums, each of over £10,000. There was some issue over which premiums were traceable to trust funds but the court eventually accepted that the first two annual premiums were paid out of Murphy's funds, it was unsure whose funds had been used to pay the third payment, but the fourth and fifth premiums were paid out of the trust's

---

41   (1879) 13 Ch D 696.
42   *Indian Oil Corpn v Greenstone Shipping SA* [1988] QB 345, [1987] 3 All ER 893.
43   *Re Tilley's WT* [1967] Ch 1179; *R v Clowes (No 2)* [1994] 2 All ER 316 per Watkins L.J.; *Sinclair Investments (UK) Ltd v Versailles Trade Finance Ltd (in administrative receivership)* [2011] EWCA Civ 347 at 138], per Lord Neuberger.
44   [2001] 1 AC 102.
45   [2001] 1 AC 102.

funds (£20,440). In 1991 Murphy committed suicide. The insurance company duly paid the sum assured to Murphy's wife and children, the named beneficiaries under the policy. The claimant sued the beneficiaries of the insurance policy as a representative of the investors for a *pro rata* share of the policy proceeds.

Judgment: at first instance the judge accepted that the investors had an interest in the policy because of the mixing of the premiums and awarded the investors 53% of the proceeds of the policy. Murphy's children appealed and the Court of Appeal, by a majority,[46] reversed the decision at first instance holding that the investors were only entitled to a lien representing their misappropriated money, thus only entitled to £20,440, because they had no interest in the policy. The House of Lords, by a majority,[47] reversed the Court of Appeal's decision and held the trustee had wrongly mixed the trust funds with his own by paying the fourth premium out of investors' funds. Therefore he had mixed the value of the premium with the value of the policy and thus the investors had a traceable interest in the policy.

It is interesting to consider the reasoning of these decisions. The Court of Appeal had decided, with Morritt L.J. dissenting, that the policy had been in force from the first payment so the children would have received the policy payout without the subsequent payments of the premiums using trust moneys. The children were the beneficial owners of the policy and the subsequent payments of the investors did not give rise to an interest by way of resulting or constructive trust. Thus the investors were only entitled to the return of their payments, which had unjustly enriched the children, not an interest in the policy. The analogy was made that the payments may have been regarded as improvements to the policy as improvements may be made to a house, in such circumstances a principal's funds used for the maintenance or improvement of a house would only be enforced by way of a charge against the property for the recovery of the misappropriated fund, not by recognition of a proprietary interest in the house.[48]

The majority of the House of Lords found the investors had a proprietary interest in the insurance payout. The analogy here was with the mixing of funds in a bank account by a wrongdoer and here equity would recognise a proprietary interest in proportion to the misappropriated funds in the account. Lord Millett explained:[49]

---

46   Sir Richard Scott V-C. and Hobhouse L.J.; Morritt L.J. dissenting.
47   Lord Browne-Wilkinson, Lord Hoffman and Lord Millett; Lord Steyn and Lord Hope of Craighead dissenting.
48   This was the analogy discussed by Sir Richard Scott V-C and by Hobhouse LJ [1998] Ch 265, 282 and 289-290.
49   [2001] 1 AC 102, 138.

'In my opinion there is no reason to differentiate between the first premium or premiums and later premiums. Such a distinction is not based on any principle. Why should the policy belong to the party who paid the first premium, without which there would have been no policy, rather than to the party who paid the last premium, without which it would normally have lapsed? Moreover, any such distinction would lead to the most capricious results.'

Lord Millett also dismissed the assumption that there was a principle that when tracing into a mixed fund a claimant was confined to a lien and could not elect to assert equitable ownership and to take a proportionate share:[50]

'In my view the time has come to state unequivocally that English law has no such rule. It conflicts with the rule that a trustee must not benefit from his trust…Accordingly, I would state the basic rule as follows. Where a trustee wrongfully uses trust money to provide part of the cost of acquiring an asset, the beneficiary is entitled *at his option* either to claim a proportionate share of the asset or to enforce a lien upon it to secure his personal claim against the trustee for the amount of the misapplied money. It does not matter whether the trustee mixed the trust money with his own in a single fund before using it to acquire the asset, or made separate payments (whether simultaneously or sequentially) out of the differently owned funds to acquire a single asset.'[51]

Murphy's children were innocent volunteers, the rule is that trust funds mixed with those of an innocent third party or another trust are shared *pari passu* (proportionately).[52] Thus, as the investors could trace their funds into two of the five payments they were entitled to a proportionate interest in the insurance payout, 40%.[53]

The situation in *Foskett v McKeown* was unusual as normally mixing takes place in bank accounts.

16.5.2 Tracing into bank accounts

Wrongdoers often misappropriate funds and attempt to hide them by passing them through bank accounts and mixing them with other funds. Equitable tracing allows these funds to be traced through different accounts even though they have been mixed with the wrongdoer's own

---

50   The assumption was based on Jessel MR's *obiter dicta* in *Re Hallett's Estate* (1879) 13 Ch D 696, 709.

51   [2001] 1 AC 102, 131. Followed in *Serious Fraud Office v Lexi Holdings plc* [2008] EWCA Crim 1443; [2009] 1 All ER 586.

52   *Re Diplock* [1948] Ch 465.

53   In fact there was some disagreement between the majority in the House of Lords on this division but this was eventually the accepted figure.

funds or those of other parties. Tracing into mixed bank accounts is subject to a series of evidentiary presumptions based upon the principles that the trustee is always presumed to act in the best interests of the trust and that the trustee must never benefit from his position as a trustee. At common law a mixture of property is usually subject to co-ownership.[54] However, as noted above, 'where a trustee mixes trust money with his own…the beneficiaries are entitled to a first charge on the mixed fund'.[55]

When the trustee has mixed money from the trust with money in his bank account equity has developed rules to decide whose money is used when payments are made from the account.

Example

Tracey is holding £20,000 on trust for Brian and Bella. She takes the £20,000, pays it into her own bank account, which already contains some of her own money. She then purchases certain items using the money in her account. Whose money has been used to purchase the items; the trust money or her money?

The general presumption is that the trustee has attempted to preserve the trust fund and so spends his own money first.

Re Hallett's Estate[56]

Hallett was allowed by the trustees of his marriage settlement trust in favour of his wife for life and then to himself and then to any issue of the marriage to take control of the trust fund. He used the funds to buy Russian bonds some of which were then passed to his bankers. Hallett was a solicitor and acted for Mrs Cotterill. He used some of her funds to buy Russian bonds and again deposited these with his bankers. Hallett directed his bankers to sell the bonds purchased with the trust's and Mrs Cotterill's monies. Hallett then made various payments in and out of the account. At time of his death the account had funds to meet the claim of the trust and Mrs Cotterill but not his general creditors. Hallett's personal representatives and the interested parties sought clarification of the status of the money in the account. They wanted to know if Hallett had spent the beneficiaries and Mrs Cotterill's money first.

Judgement: the Court of Appeal held that the withdrawals that had been made from the account were out of Hallett's own money and therefore the remaining money was the property of the trust and the client. The beneficiaries were entitled to a charge on the account to the extent of their claim. The Court of Appeal (notably Jessel MR) rejected the idea that

---

54 *Indian Oil Corpn v Greenstone Shipping SA* [1988] QB 345, [1987] 3 All ER 893.
55 *R v Clowes (No 2)* [1994] 2 All ER 316 per Watkins L.J. See also *Re Tilley's WT* [1967] Ch 1179.
56 *Re Hallett's Estate (Knatchbull v Hallett)* (1879) 13 ChD 696.

Hallett could have spent the trust money first on the grounds that it must be presumed he was acting honestly and would protect the funds of the trust and client.

So, returning to our example, if Tracey already has £20,000 in her account and she pays £20,000 of the trust money into her account, then she spends £20,000 on a holiday, there will be £20,000 left in her account. The beneficiaries will be entitled to trace this £20,000 because it will be presumed that Tracey spent her own money first and protected the trust fund, as was her duty.

The rigid application of the *Re Hallett's* principle might, however, cause hardship or injustice. For example, if the trustee mixes funds and then spends money from the mixed fund on an asset, such as shares, and then dissipates the rest, it would be inequitable to presume he spent his money first to buy the asset and then wasted trust money.

Re Oatway[57]

Oatway was a trustee who paid trust monies of £3,000 into his personal account containing his own monies. He then bought shares in Oceana Ltd for £2,137. After his drawing there was still more in the account than the amount of trust monies that had been paid in; Oatway paid further sums into the account but subsequently withdrew everything and it was dissipated. The shares were later sold for £2,474. Oatway died insolvent. The beneficiaries of the trust claimed the proceeds of the sale of the shares represented their monies. Oatway's personal representatives claimed that as Oatway had sufficient monies in his account to satisfy the claim of the beneficiaries at the time of the share purchase, the purchase must have been met by the Oatway's own funds. Thus the shares were his and he had dissipated the trust monies.

Judgment: the shares, and their subsequent sale monies, represented trust monies. Oatway could not withdraw and use the money free from the charge of the trust fund until he had satisfied that obligation.

Applying this to our example, if Tracey already has £20,000 in her account and pays £20,000 of the trust money into her account, then she spends £20,000 on shares, and dissipates the rest of the money, the beneficiaries will be able to trace into the shares.

The rule here is still based upon the principles that the trustee is presumed to act in the best interests of the trust and must not benefit from the trust. He is presumed to act honestly even when he is manifestly dishonest. If a trustee uses a mixed fund of trust money and his own money to buy shares then, although the total quantity of shares may be charged in favour of the trust if trust money is traceable to their purchase,

---

57   [1903] 2 Ch 356.

obviously only shares which could have been purchased with trust money are traceable. The shares will be held in proportion to the contributions. If the shares are trading at an increased price then the shares should still be allotted in proportion to initial contribution, for example if £10,000 of trust money and £10,000 of the trustee's money has been used to purchase £20,000 of shares and the value of the shares has now increased by 50% the £20,000 worth of shares are now worth £30,000, the trust does not just recover £10,000 worth of shares because this is a proprietary action and the property bought with trust money has increased in value. It is still trust money and the trust takes the profit rather than the trustee as discussed below in *Re Tilley' Will Trusts*,[58] and as held in *Foskett v McKeown*.[59] It may also be argued that the trustee has made £5,000 by his investment in the shares because of his position as a trustee, thus he would hold his profit on constructive trust for the trust.

As wrongdoing trustees and fiduciaries are often in positions of trust with regard to the assets of more than one party we need to consider what happens when the wrongdoer mixes innocent parties assets. We have already considered that when the wrongdoer mixes trust property with property of another trust or innocent party the mixed fund is divided proportionately between them.[60] However, there may be concerns when money of different trusts or innocent parties is mixed in a bank account and then payments are made from this mixed fund as to whose money has been used. Traditionally the banking law rule from *Clayton's Case*[61] applied to bank current accounts . This was the 'first in, first out' principle (FIFO).

Example

Tracey is a trustee of trust A and trust B. £30,000 of trust A's money is paid into a current account in March, then £10,000 of trust B's money is paid into the account in April. In May, Tracey takes £10,000 from the account and dissipates it. Applying FIFO, trust A will be presumed to bear the whole of the £10,000 loss. Therefore the remaining £30,000 will be distributed £20,000 to trust A and £10,000 to trust B.

This rule is obviously unfair and has been much criticised. In other situations the FIFO rule had been disapplied, for instance in *Re Hallett's Estate*,[62] the Court of Appeal had refused to apply the rule when a fiduciary had paid trust or money subject to another fiduciary obligation into a bank account, then paid his own funds into the account and then dissipated some of the mixed fund. The Court of Appeal held that the

---

58   [1967] Ch 1179.
59   [2001] 1 AC 102.
60   *Re Diplock* [1948] Ch 465.
61   *Clayton's Case, Devaynes v Noble* (1816) 1 Mer 529.
62   (1879) 13 Ch D 696.

fiduciary had dissipated his own funds first. The issue of the rules application to a mixed fund of innocent volunteers' monies was considered in *Sinclair v Brougham*.[63] The House of Lords held that in such situations the innocent parties were entitled to a proportionate share in the remaining mixed fund. Their interests in the fund, and in the loss, would be *pari passu*, on an equal footing to their contributions. There have been some doubts about this principle as *Sinclair v Brougham* was overruled in *Westdeutsche Landesbank Girozentrale v. Islington L.B.C.*[64] where Lord Browne-Wilkinson described it as 'a bewildering authority: no single *ratio decidendi* can be detected; all the reasoning is open to serious objection'.[65] However, the *pari passu* approach had been approved in *Barlow Clowes International Ltd v. Vaughan*,[66] where the trustees had mixed the investors' funds over many years and payments were made from the mixed fund. If the first in first out rule was applied those who had invested the longest would lose the most. Those who had invested most recently would get most of their money back. This seemed unfair and so the Court of Appeal proposed that the first in first out rule would apply unless a contrary intention was evident. In this case the investor's intention had been to pool their resources and share in gain proportionately. Thus they should also share in losses proportionately.[67] It was mentioned that the intent of the trustee was important, thus if the trustee intended to spend one trust's funds then that might preclude the pari passu approach.

Example
Tracey is a trustee of trust A and trust B. £30,000 of trust A's money is paid into a current account in March, then £10,000 of trust B's money is paid into the account in April. In May, Tracey takes £10,000 from the account and dissipates it. The remaining £30,000 will be distributed *pari passu* in the ration 3:1 thus trust A will receive £22,500 and trust B £7,500. They will share proportionately in the loss.

16.5.3 Increases in value

As equity is tracing the misappropriated property of the trusts or principal, and so the property represents the trust property, any increase in value of the substituted property is the trusts. If the trustee mixes funds of innocent

---

63   [1914] AC 398.
64   [1996] AC 669.
65   *Westdeutsche Landesbank Girozentrale v. Islington L.B.C.* [1996] AC 669, 713 per Lord Browne-Wilkinson. In re Diplock [1948] Ch 465 it was said that the FIFO rule would apply to the money of innocent parties mixed in a bank account.
66   [1992] 4 All ER 22.
67   Conformed in *Foskett v McKeown* [2001] 1 AC 102, at 132, per Lord Millet.

parties and uses some of the fund to purchase an asset, for example shares, which subsequently increases in value, then the claimants may claim a proportionate share in the asset as it has increased in value.

If the trustee mixes trust funds with his own funds and purchases an asset, which is held to represent the misappropriated trust money, then the trust is entitled to the asset and any increase in value.

Re Tilley' Will Trusts [68]

The testator had died in 1932 leaving property to his widow as sole trustee on trust to his widow for life with remainder to Charles and Mabel (his children by a former marriage) in equal shares. The trust properties were realised between 1933 and 1952 for a total of £2,237, which amount paid into the widow's account and mixed with her own funds. Until 1951, the widow's bank account was at various times substantially overdrawn, e.g.1945 - £25,536. Subsequently the widow purchased investments financed by her overdraft. In 1951 her account was in credit from her own personal contributions. In 1959 the widow died with her estate valued at £94,000. Mabel had predeceased the widow and her administrators sued the widow's personal representatives claiming that Mabel's estate was entitled to half of the proportion of the profits made by the widow.

Judgement: the trust monies were not used to purchase investments made by Mrs T but only used to reduce her overdraft, this is an application of the lowest intermediate balance rule discussed below. Thus the trust monies could not be traced into the widow's estate. Thus the trust was entitled only to a personal action against the estate, not a proprietary action, and so could only seek the return of the trust money. However, Ungoed-Thomas J did note that if the claimant had been entitled to trace into the assets they could have taken the increase in value.

We have already seen an application of this rule in *Foskett v McKeown*,[69] where the investors' funds had contributed £20,000 to the premiums for the policy but it was held their proprietary interest was reflected in approximately £400,000. This is again based upon the principles that the trustee is presumed to act in the best interests of the trust and also must not make a profit from his position as a trustee. Therefore if the asset increases in value then it is presumed the trustee wanted the trust to take the benefit and also the trustee cannot take the increase because he cannot profit from his position.

16.5.4 The limits of equitable tracing

It will not be possible to trace if the property does not represent the trust

68 [1967] Ch 1179.
69 [2001] 1 AC 102.

property, the trust property ceases to be identifiable or it is dissipated.

The Lowest intermediate balance rule

As this is a tracing action the claimant is seeking to establish the property in the defendant's hands represents their property. If this property has come from another source it will not represent the misappropriated property and so will not be subject to a proprietary action, just a personal action, as discussed above in *Re Tilley' Will Trusts*.[70]

Roscoe v Winder[71]

Mr Wigham purchased the goodwill of a business and agreed to collect a debt and pay it over to the company. Wigham collected the debt, £623, 8s, 5d, and paid £455, 18s, 1 d into his own bank account. The remainder of the debt was unaccounted for. Wigham drew out funds which were dissipated until the credit balance in his account was £25, 18s. Later he paid in more of his own monies and died. The balance in account was £358, 5s, 5d. The plaintiffs wanted to assert a charge over the account, as in *Re Hallett's*, for the balance.

Judgement: the plaintiffs could assert a charge, but only to £25, 18s. this represented the lowest intermediate balance after the money had been taken. The payments in afterwards were clearly not subject to the trust.

Example

If Tracey has £20,000 in her account, then she pays £20,000 of trust money into her account, then she spends £39,000, she will have £1000 left in her account. If she then receives her salary and the amount in her current account increases to £5,000, the beneficiaries will only be able to claim that £1000 represents the misappropriated trust money. The rest of the money in the account cannot possibly represent trust money. The beneficiaries will have a proprietary action against this £1,000, not the whole £5,000 in the account, but can maintain a personal action against Tracey for the missing £19,000.

It was noted in *Roscoe v. Winder*,[72] that the lowest intermediate balance rule would apply unless the trustee had evinced a contrary intent when paying the money into the account. Therefore, in our example, if Tracey had expressed an intention to reconstitute the trust fund when paying her wages into the account the trust could trace into the whole balance.

Property ceases to be identifiable

If the trust property is exchanged for other property which is not identifiable then the beneficiaries will not be able to trace. Thus, as we have

---

70   [1967] Ch 1179.
71   [1915] 1 Ch 62.
72   [1915] 1 Ch 62.

seen, in **Re Goldcorp Exchange Ltd**,[73] only the customers whose bullion had been segregated were able to trace and establish a trust.[74] Other customers whose money had not been used to buy identifiable gold could not trace. These latter customers had no proprietary action only a personal action in contract against the company. The money itself had been paid into an overdrawn bank account. Thus it could not be traced because it was no longer identifiable; this links to the principle that equitable tracing is not possible when the property is dissipated.[75]

Property is dissipated
If a fund is dissipated it is lost and so also ceases to be identifiable. Therefore, if the trustee spends trust money on a meal or a holiday, which he enjoys, then it will not be possible to trace the money into the meal or holiday because it has gone. It will not be possible to trace the trust money into the hands of the restaurant or travel agent unless they have knowledge of the breach of trust. Otherwise they are equity's darling and safe from any tracing. The beneficiaries may still pursue a personal action against the trustees, but if the trustee has misappropriated trust funds it is usually because he has no money of his own and so there may be little likelihood of success.

If trust money is used to pay a debt it is usually considered dissipated because the creditor's discharge of the debt is consideration for the money and so he is equity's darling. Thus money paid into an overdrawn bank account is dissipated, even if there is an agreed overdraft facility on the account which is subsequently used to purchase an asset.[76] It is not possible to trace into subsequent monies paid into the account if they do not represent trust money.[77]

It should be noted, however, that if trust money is used to pay off a legal charge upon property then the trust might be subrogated to the position of the chargee.[78]

---

73 [1995] 1 AC 74.
74 Identification or Segregation of trust property is necessary for trusts: *In the Matter of Lehman Brothers International (Europe) (In Administration) and In the matter of the Insolvency Act 1986* [2012] UKSC 6.
75 See Mark Pawlowski, 'Tracing into improvements, debts and, overdrawn accounts' (2011) 17(5) *Trusts & Trustees* 411-414.
76 *CY Foundation Group v Cheng Chee Tock* [2011] HKEC 1629; [2012] 1 HKLRD 532 at [21]-[27], per Barma J.
77 *Roscoe v. Winder* [1915] 1 Ch 62; *Re Diplock* [1948] Ch 465; *Re Tilley' Will Trusts* [1967] Ch 1179; *Bishopsgate Investment Management Ltd v. Homan* [1995] Ch 211.
78 *Boscawen v. Bajwa* [1996] 1 WLR 328. Subrogation is a doctrine which allows another to stand in the place of the holder of legal rights- for example an insurance company may sue in the name of the insured to recover money paid out under an insurance policy.

16.5.5 Defences to an equitable tracing claim

A defendant may seek to rely upon two defences to an equitable tracing claim:

1 That they are equity's darling (the bona fide purchaser); or,
2 that it is inequitable to trace against them.

Equity's darling- the bona fide purchaser for value without notice
As we have already considered, equity will not trace into the hands of a *bona fide* purchaser for value without notice of the breach of trust (equity's darling).[79] As Maitland said, 'Equity cannot touch him, because, to use the old phrase, his conscience is unaffected by the trust.' In such a case it may be possible to trace against the consideration given for the trust property. Alternatively the beneficiaries can take a personal action against the trustee.   Generally, no enquiry is made as to the adequacy of the consideration given.[80]

It should be noted that equity's darling may lose the protection of equity if they avoid the contract.

Independent Trustee Services Ltd v Susan Morris [81]
A fraudster had taken some £52 million in breach of trust from a number of occupational pension schemes he controlled. His wife had accepted £1.48 million, which represented traceable assets of the pension funds, as payment of an ancillary relief order. As the order had been discharged the wife was thus considered to have given consideration for the funds. Therefore she was equity's darling and the money could not be traced into her hands. However, she subsequently discovered that her husband was wealthier than he had disclosed and she had the order set aside on the grounds of fraud and non-disclosure. The trustees of the pension fund sought an order that the £1.48 million was now 'live' for tracing.

Judgement: the English Court of Appeal allowed that a tracing claim was 'live' against the £1.48 million that had been received by the wife. As she had successfully managed to have the order set aside she had no longer given value for the money; she was no longer equity's darling but merely an innocent volunteer. The money could be traced by the pension funds and she had to return it.[82]

79   *Leung Mui v Hong Kong and Shanghai Banking Corporation* (1923) 18 HKLR 56.
80   *Lipkin Gorman v. Karpnale Ltd.* [1991] 2 AC 548 at 581 per Lord Goff..
81   [2012] EWCA Civ 195.
82   See Jonathon Hilliard, 'Tracing into orders made on divorce: *Independent Trustee Services Ltd v Susan Morris'* [2012] EWCA Civ 195 (2012) 18(7) *Trusts & Trustees* 696-699.

Of course, if the recipient has knowledge of the breach of trust or has not given consideration then he is not equity's darling and it is possible to trace the property into his hands.[83] We shall consider the position of strangers to the trust who receive trust property knowing of a breach of trust in the next chapter, but it should be noted that as early as 1465 it was held that a person who bought land from a trustee with notice that the land was subject to the trust obligation was bound by the trust.[84] This was extended in 1595 to cover those who received trust property without knowledge but provided no consideration; volunteers.[85] Recent examples of tracing against innocent volunteers include *Foskett*, where the fraudster's children were innocent volunteers and could not defeat the claim. However, it will not always be possible to trace against volunteers.

It is inequitable to trace

In **Re Diplock**,[86] the Court of Appeal did not allow some of the tracing claims against the wrongly paid out charities because in some cases it would be inequitable to do so.

Re Diplock[87]

Caleb Diplock directed his executors in his will to apply the residue of his estate, some £263,000:

'for such charitable institution or institutions or other charitable or benevolent object or objects in England as my acting executors or executor may in their or his absolute discretion select and to be paid to or for such institutions and objects if more than one in such proportion as my executors or executor may think proper.'

His executors assumed the will created a valid charitable trust and distributed £203,000 among 139 different charities before the validity of the disposition was challenged. In **Chichester Diocesan Fund v Simpson**,[88] the House of Lords held that there was no charitable trust because of the uncertainty of the charitable objects and the possibility of the fund being used for non-charitable purposes. The trust failed and the funds should have fallen into residue for Diplock's next of kin. The next of kin sued the executors for breach of trust. The claim against the executors was eventually compromised. However, the claimants persisted in two actions against the wrongly paid charities; *in personam* against the recipient

---

83   *Chan Chun Chung v PBM (Hong Kong) Ltd* [2004] HKEC 630; [2005] 1 HKLRD 565, CFA.

84   YB 5 Ed IV, Mich pl 16, fo. 7.

85   Chudleigh's Case 1 Co Rep 113b, 122b.

86   [1948] Ch 465.

87   [1948] Ch 465.

88   [1944] AC 341.

institutions, and *in rem* against the assets held by the institutions as innocent volunteers.

   Judgement: the Court of Appeal explained the limits of the right to trace:

- An equitable remedy does not affect rights obtained by a bona fide transferee of the legal estate for value without notice (equity's darling); all equitable claims are extinguished against such persons.
- Tracing will not be permitted if it will produce inequity because ' He who comes to equity must do equity'.

Therefore, if an innocent volunteer spends money improving his land there can be no declaration of charge against the land because the way of enforcing the charge would be by ordering sale. Forcing the volunteer to convert his property would be inequitable and, as equity will do nothing in vain, equity would not grant a remedy in this situation.

   Thus it is possible to trace property held by an innocent volunteer if the property has not been used in such a way that it would be inequitable to order its return. The charities that had just put the money in their bank accounts had to return it. Those that had used it to improve their properties did not. Any personal action against the volunteers would rely on the claimants having sued the trustees first and not having been able to recover all the misappropriated fund.

Change of position defence

We have already considered the change of position defence when we considered common law tracing and the case of **Lipkin Gorman v. Karpnale Ltd**.[89] Lord Millett pointed out in **Foskett v McKeown**,[90] that the change of position defence applies only to claims where the defendant has legal and beneficial title to money and thus does not apply to claims in equity where the plaintiff is claiming that she still owns the equitable interest in the money.

16.6 Issues with Tracing

There has long been criticism of the different requirements and rules for tracing at common law and in equity. Denning J., as he then was, said of tracing in **Nelson v Larholt**:[91]

   'This principle has been evolved by the courts of law and equity side by side. In equity it took the form of an action to follow moneys impressed with an express trust, or with a constructive trust owing to a fiduciary relationship. In law it took the form of an action for money had and received or damages for conversion of a cheque. It is no longer appropriate,

89   [1991] 2 AC 548, [1992] 4 All ER 512.
90   [2001] 1 A.C. 101 at 129.
91   [1948] 1 K.B. 339

however, to draw a distinction between law and equity.'

Thus there has been criticism that is merely an evidential process and so there is no need for an initial fiduciary relationship and no need for a distinction between the evidential rules available at common law and in equity. Peter Birks and Lionel Smith led an academic debate about tracing which was summarised by Paul Matthews when he pointed to the purely practical nature of tracing:[92]

'Here is an area of the common law, argued by practitioners, made by judges, ignored by legislators...if you explain to foreign lawyers what are the rules of tracing in English Law, then at some point in the explanation, their confused expression changes to enlightenment, and they say "Ah you mean identifying property?"

Lord Millett attempted to settle the law of tracing in *Foskett v McKeown*. Lord Millett's obiter restatement of the law of tracing has been widely supported around the common law world.[93] There has been support in Australia and Hong Kong for Lord Millett's general approach that, 'Tracing is ... neither a claim nor a remedy',[94] and in Hong Kong tracing has been described as merely the discovery stage of an action.[95]

However, it is submitted that the law of tracing is far from settled. It is still unsure whether a fiduciary relationship is no longer required for tracing in equity, New Zealand having long abandoned the requirement,[96] but England and Hong Kong still requiring it.[97] A major decision accepting or rejecting Lord Millett's comments is necessary to clarify where the law stands.

Of course there is one simple principle which would support the continued separation of legal and equitable tracing rules and the necessity of a fiduciary relationship for tracing in equity. This is the presumption in all equitable tracing rules that the wrongdoer has acted as a fiduciary; he has always placed the best interests of the owner of the misappropriated property before his own. This is the justification for the rules of tracing in

---

92 Paul Matthews, 'Limits of Common Law Tracing', in Birks, P. (ed), *Laundering and Tracing*, Clarendon Press: Oxford, 1995.

93 See for example *Terkild Johan Terkildsen v Barber Asia Ltd* [2007] HKCU 399 (CFI).

94 *Foskett v McKeown* [2001] 1 AC 102 at 127-128. For Australia see *Evans v European Bank Ltd* [2004] NSWCA 82; for Hong Kong see *CY Foundation Group v Cheng Chee Tock* [2011] HKEC 1629; [2012] 1 HKLRD 532; *The Joint and Several Trustees of the Property of Karson Otto Fan, Karno (In Bankruptcy) v Kong Suk Chun* [2012] HKCU 324..

95 *Hang Seng Bank Ltd v Lau Ching Che* [2007] HKEC 2255 *per* Sakhrani J.

96 *Eiders Pastoral Ltdv Bank of New Zealand* (1989) 2 NZLR 180.

97 *First Laser Ltd v Fujian Enterprises (Holdings) Co Ltd* [2003] HKEC 7 *per* Lam D.J. Although this was doubted in *Hang Seng Bank Ltd v Lau Ching Che* [2007] HKEC 2255 *per* Sakhrani J

equity. As to the lack of express requirement of a fiduciary relationship in **Re Hallett's Estate**, Mr Hallett was a trustee and a solicitor, the assets belonged to a trust of which he was trustee and his client; Hallett was a fiduciary of the trust and his client; both fiduciary relationships so obvious there was no need to highlight them; however, the Court did. Jessel M.R. noted this case involved, 'one more instance of a solicitor betraying his trust'.[98] Then Jessel M.R. noted that Hallett's receipt of Mrs Cotterill's property and subsequent conversion was as an agent and bailee which made him a fiduciary; here it is best to consider the learned Judge's words:

'This receivership, of course, was the receivership of an agent - it was as bailee; therefore he was bailee of the bonds, and an agent to receive the dividends on the bonds. There is no doubt, therefore, that Mr. Hallett stood in a fiduciary position towards Mrs. Cotterill. Mr. Hallett, before his death, I regret to say, improperly sold the bonds and put the money to his general account at his bankers. It is not disputed that the money remained at his bankers mixed with his own money at the time of his death; that is, he had not drawn out that money from his bankers. In that position of matters Mrs. Cotterill claimed to be entitled to receive the proceeds, or the amount of the proceeds, of the bonds out of the money in the hands of Mr. Hallett's bankers at the time of his death, and that claim was allowed by the learned Judge of the Court below, and I think was properly so allowed. Indeed, as I understand the doctrines of Equity, it would have been too clear a case for argument, except for another decision of that learned Judge himself, Ex parte Dale & Co. (1). The modern doctrine of Equity as regards property disposed of by persons in a fiduciary position is a very clear and well-established doctrine. You can, if the sale was rightful, take the proceeds of the sale, if you can identify them. If the sale was wrongful, you can still take the proceeds of the sale, in a sense adopting the sale for the purpose of taking the proceeds, if you can identify them. There is no distinction, therefore, between a rightful and a wrongful disposition of the property, so far as regards the right of the beneficial owner to follow the proceeds. But it very often happens that you cannot identify the proceeds. The proceeds may have been invested together with money belonging to the person in a fiduciary position, in a purchase. He may have bought land with it, for instance, or he may have bought chattels with it. Now, what is the position of the beneficial owner as regards such purchases? I will, first of all, take his position when the purchase is clearly made with what I will call, for shortness, the trust money, although it is not confined, as I will shew presently, to express trusts. In that case, according to the now well-established doctrine of Equity, the beneficial owner has a right to elect either to take the property purchased, or to hold it as a security for the amount of the trust money laid out in the purchase; or, as we generally

---

98   (1880) 13 Ch D 696 at 706, per Jessel M.R.

express it, he is entitled at his election either to take the property, or to have a charge on the property for the amount of the trust money. But in the second case, where a trustee has mixed the money with his own, there is this distinction, that the cestui que trust, or beneficial owner, can no longer elect to take the property, because it is no longer bought with the trust-money simply and purely, but with a mixed fund. He is, however, still entitled to a charge on the property purchased, for the amount of the trust-money laid out in the purchase; and that charge is quite independent of the fact of the amount laid out by the trustee. The moment you get a substantial portion of it furnished by the trustee, using the word "trustee" in the sense I have mentioned, as including all persons in a fiduciary relation, the right to the charge follows. That is the modern doctrine of Equity. Has it ever been suggested, until very recently, that there is any distinction between an express trustee, or an agent, or a bailee, or a collector of rents, or anybody else in a fiduciary position? I have never heard, until quite recently, such a distinction suggested. It cannot, as far as I am aware (and since this Court sat last to hear this case, I have taken the trouble to look for authority), be found in any reported case even suggested, except in the recent decision of Mr. Justice Fry, to which I shall draw attention presently. It can have no foundation in principle, because the beneficial ownership is the same, wherever the legal ownership may be.'[99]

Thus Jessel M.R. based his judgment upon the fiduciary relationship and beneficial ownership of the property. Therefore equitable tracing has always required a fiduciary relationship; or perhaps it is better to say that the rules of equitable tracing have only ever been applied when there has been a breach of a fiduciary relationship, so that the principle that the fiduciary has always acted in the best interests of his principal may be applied.

There may be development of new rules of equity to assist those cases where to refuse to apply the rules of equity would be to allow the defendant to benefit from unconscionable behaviour because, as noted in *Re Diplock*,[100] equity comes in, 'not to destroy the common law but to fulfil it'; thus equity will step in when the common law cannot act, but this must be when there is 'an ancestry founded in history and in the practice and precedents of the courts administering equity jurisdiction'. This does not mean that equity cannot develop new remedies as Jessel M.R. noted in *Re Hallett's Estate*:[101]

'Therefore, the moment you establish the fiduciary relation, the modern rules of Equity, as regards following trust money, apply. I intentionally say

---

99   (1880) 13 Ch D 696 at 708-710, per Jessel M.R.
100 [1948] Ch. 465 at 481, quoting Maitland.
101 (1879) 13 Ch D 696.

modern rules, because it must not be forgotten that the rules of Courts of Equity are not, like the rules of the Common Law, supposed to have been established from time immemorial. It is perfectly well known that they have been established from time to time - altered, improved, and refined from time to time. In many cases we know the names of the Chancellors who invented them. No doubt they were invented for the purpose of securing the better administration of justice, but still they were invented. Take such things as these: the separate use of a married woman, the restraint on alienation, the modern rule against perpetuities, and the rules of equitable waste. We can name the Chancellors who first invented them, and state the date when they were first introduced into Equity jurisprudence; and, therefore, in cases of this kind, the older precedents in Equity are of very little value. The doctrines are progressive, refined, and improved; and if we want to know what the rules of Equity are, we must look, of course, rather to the more modern than the more ancient cases.' [102]

Therefore there may be developments in the law of equitable tracing which may expand its use, but as the principle behind the rules of equitable tracing is that the wrongdoer is always presumed to have acted to safeguard the misappropriated property because of his duty of good faith, it is hard to see how the requirement for a fiduciary relationship, a requirement that can often be engineered, may be dispensed with.

16.7 Summary

Tracing is the process of identifying property which is or represents misappropriated property. Tracing is available at common law but the common law cannot trace through a mixture of misappropriated property with other property. Tracing in equity is far more powerful than common law tracing because it has developed rules to deal with mixed funds. At present it seems that there needs to be an initial fiduciary relationship or interest for the rules of equitable tracing to be applied. This fiduciary relationship allows equity to develop principles from the fiduciary nature of trusteeship; every trustee is presumed to be acting honestly and in the best interests of the trust even if it is apparent he is not. Trustees are also not permitted to make a profit from their position. Thus if a trustee mixes trust funds with his own, equity will presume a first charge over the mixed fund in favour of the trust. If the trustee spends money from the mixed fund, equity will presume he has spent his own money first unless this would be unjust on the trust. If the trustee mixes funds of innocent parties, equity will presume the mixed fund is held *pari passu*, proportionate to the contributions. If payments are made from the mixed fund then assets purchased will be held *pari passu* and losses incurred will be suffered *pari passu*.

---

102   (1880) 13 Ch D 696 at 710, per Jessel M.R.

Equity will only trace into the lowest intermediate balance of an account as this is an identification process. Subsequent payments into an account will only be traced if they represent trust funds. Equity will not trace assets into the hands of equity's darling, but will trace into the hands of an innocent volunteer. Equity will trace into the consideration given by equity's darling. Equity will not trace when it is inequitable to do so.

When a proprietary action is no longer available it may be possible to take personal action against the trustee, this may also be preferable if the trustee has readily available assets and it is easier to sue the trustee. Of course usually the trustee has no assets, which is why we follow the property and trace its substitutions.

CHAPTER 17

LIABILITY OF STRANGERS TO THE TRUST

17.1 Who are Strangers to the Trust?

We have already considered that, when there is a breach of trust, the trustees may be liable for any loss caused by this breach.[1] The beneficiaries may take a personal action against the trustee but that will be of no use to the beneficiaries if the trustee is bankrupt or has absconded and cannot be found. In some circumstances it may be possible to make parties who have not been appointed as trustees of the trust liable for the loss caused by the breach of trust as if they were trustees. These parties have traditionally been referred to as 'strangers to the trust'.

Strangers to the trust are usually categorised from the judgment of Lord Selborne in *Barnes v. Addy*, to which the author has added emphasis where appropriate:[2]

'Those who create a trust clothe the trustee with a legal power and control over the trust property, imposing on him a corresponding responsibility. That responsibility may no doubt be extended in equity to others who are not properly trustees, if they are found either making themselves **trustees *de son tort***, or actually participating in any fraudulent conduct of the trustee to the injury of the *cestui que trust* [beneficiary]. But, on the other hand, strangers are not to be made constructive trustees merely because they act as the agents of trustees in transactions within their legal powers, transactions, perhaps of which a Court of Equity may disapprove, unless those agents **receive and become chargeable** with some part of the trust property, or unless they **assist with knowledge** in a dishonest and fraudulent design on the part of the trustees.'

Thus there are three traditional categories of stranger to the trust:

1 the trustee de son tort;
2 knowing receipt; and,
3 knowing assistance.

As these principles have been extended to property misappropriated in

---

1   *Target Holdings v. Redferns* [1996] 1 AC 421.
2   (1874) 9 Ch App 244 at 251-252.

breach of a fiduciary obligation,[3] they are extremely useful in combating financial fraud and money laundering in combination with the rules of tracing in equity.

17.2 Money Laundering

One of the biggest concerns for financial institutions and professionals today is that they may inadvertently be involved in money laundering. It has been said that 'criminally earned money is invariably transient in nature.'[4] However, with the international crackdown on organised crime and terrorism it has become apparent that some criminals and terrorists are so cash rich that their biggest problem is cleaning up their ill-gotten gains in order to enjoy it indefinitely. Money laundering is:

'...the process by which criminals attempt to conceal the true origin and ownership of their criminal activities. If undertaken successfully, it also allows them to maintain control over those proceeds and, ultimately, to provide a legitimate cover for their source of income.'[5]

The purpose of money laundering '...is to hide the proceeds of crime and get it to re-emerge in a different place and with an apparently honest source.'[6] There are three stages to the traditional money laundering process:[7]

1   Placement: the first stage and the most dangerous for the launderer. The aims 'are to take the cash from the location of acquisition and then to transform it into other asset forms, while avoiding detection from the authorities.'

2   Layering: which 'involves the creation of a complex web of transactions aimed at dissociating the illegal monies from their criminal origin.'

3   Integration: the final stage, which 'involves the introduction of the funds into the legitimate economic and financial system.'

In undertaking this process the registered company and the trust are very useful tools for the criminal. Movement of funds between companies, trusts and through their respective bank accounts in many different jurisdictions, in different currencies and using other financial tools, serves

---

3   For a consideration of knowing assistance and knowing receipt see Simon Gardner, 'Knowing assistance and knowing receipt: taking stock' (1996) 112 (Jan) *Law Quarterly Review* 56-94.

4   The Joint Money Laundering Steering Group's (a committee of trade associations run by the British Bankers Association) Guideline.

5   Andrew Haynes, *Butterworths Financial Services Law Guide*, Butterworths, London, 2nd edition, chapter 5, 'Money Laundering'.

6   Andrew Haynes, *Butterworths Financial Services Law Guide*, Butterworths, London, 2nd edition, chapter 5, 'Money Laundering'.

to confuse the trail back to the ill-gotten gains. Of course the process is slightly easier for terrorists as, contrary to some governments misinformation, their funds are usually considerably smaller and often come from legitimate sources. These funds must be laundered to protect the end source and the origin. For these transactions the criminal requires the help of financial institutions and professionals, and the more upright and honest these seem the more they are of use to the criminal. The criminal uses legitimate banks, solicitors, accountants and other businesses to give their transactions the veneer of respectability necessary to engender trust from other institutions, hoping to reduce checks and suspicion that would normally arise. Even before the international campaign to counter money laundering, equity's principles of tracing and stranger liability provided a means for beneficiaries to recover misappropriated assets from those who had received them, or assisted in the breach of trust if they had, or should have had, knowledge of the breach.

17.3 Trustees *de Son Tort* / Intermeddlers in the Trust

Smith L.J. noted, in **Mara v Browne**:[8]
'…it was said that he had made himself a constructive trustee, which, so far as I know, is the same thing as a trustee de son tort. Now, what constitutes a trustee de son tort? It appears to me if one, not being a trustee and not having authority from a trustee, takes upon himself to intermeddle with trust matters or to do acts characteristic of the office of trustee, he may thereby make himself what is called in law a trustee of his own wrong - i.e., a trustee de son tort, or, as it is also termed, a constructive trustee.'

Therefore a trustee *de son tort* is somebody who is not appointed a trustee but who intermeddles with the trust and by his actions, although not officially appointed a trustee, takes on the burden of trusteeship, and the potential liabilities of trusteeship for these actions. He may not necessarily do this for his own benefit, indeed he may be acting for the benefit of the beneficiaries, but if any losses are incurred as a result of his actions with regard to the trust, he may be liable for these losses as if he were an officially appointed trustee. This type of liability often occurs in the administration of a deceased estate, when the intermeddler is known as an executor *de son tort*.[9] The intermeddler may also be made to disgorge any profits he makes for himself associated with his role as a trustee de son tort; for example in **Boardman v Phipps**,[9] the solicitor, Boardman, and Tom Phipps believed they had the permission of all the beneficiaries to

---

7   R. Rhodes, & S. Palastrand, 'A Guide to Money Laundering Legislation' (2004) Vol. 8 No. 1 *JMLC* 9, 9.

8   [1896] 1 Ch 199 at 209.

9   [1967] 2 AC 46 (HL).

take over the company in which the trust had invested, however when it was established that such permission had not been received they were made to disgorge the profits they made to the Phipps family trust.

Note
The settlor of a trust can be a trustee *de son tort* if he interferes in the running of the trust and causes loss to the trust. Similarly a beneficiary who interferes in the running of the trust may also be a trustee *de son tort* and liable for any losses caused by his interference to his fellow beneficiaries.

An agent acting for the trustee will not normally be liable as a trustee de son tort, or any other form of stranger liability if he has acted honestly, even if the instructions he has followed have come from a dishonest trustee.[10]

Mara v Browne[11]
The first defendant, Hugh Browne, was a solicitor who advised the persons who were acting as trustees of a marriage settlement, though they were not yet formally appointed as such. Browne suggested a series of investments for the trust funds. They were not proper investments for trustees to make. The money was to be lent to fund building property of a speculative character and the margin was unsatisfactory. The investments were made and the money was lost. The claimants alleged that Hugh Browne had intermeddled with the trust and was liable as a trustee *de son tort*. They alleged that he had laid out the trust moneys at a time when there were no trustees, and therefore must be taken to have acted as a principal in the matter and not as a mere agent for the trustees. *Judgement*: the Court of Appeal held that it was incorrect to hold that at the relevant dates there were no trustees. But, even if there had been none, Hugh Browne would not have been liable. He did not intend or purport to act as a trustee and no one supposed that he was so acting. He purported to act throughout only as solicitor to the trustees and was understood by all concerned to be acting as such. It was noted that he would have been liable in contract for negligence if the action had not been time-barred.

17.4 Knowing Receipt/ Recipient Liability

We have already considered the position of equity's darling when he receives trust property. Equity will not trace property into the hands of equity's darling because as Maitland said, 'Equity cannot touch him, because, to use the old phrase, his conscience is unaffected by the trust.'

---

10   *Mara v Browne* [1896] 1 Ch 199.
11   [1896] 1 Ch 199.

Equity's darling has given consideration, so is not a volunteer, and has no knowledge of the breach of trust that has led to him receiving the trust property. However, a stranger who receives trust property and knows of the breach of trust which led to him receiving it will not be protected by equity. As early as 1465 it was held that a person who bought land from a trustee with notice that the land was subject to the trust obligation was bound by the trust.[12] Lord Selborne referred to this category of stranger to the trust as those who 'receive and become chargeable with some part of the trust property.'[13] The action of this category of stranger to the trust is traditionally referred to as 'knowing receipt', or, more recently, as 'recipient liability'.

The stranger in knowing receipt of trust property will hold that property subject to the trust obligation. The property may be traced into his hands and a proprietary action taken to recover the property. As he has knowledge of the breach of trust he is not equity's darling and will hold the property on constructive trust for the trust. If he has sold the property to equity's darling then the proprietary interest will shift to the money received for the property and he will hold this on constructive trust. If he has disposed of the property so that the property or its substitutions cannot be traced then a personal action may be taken against the stranger to account to the trust and he may be made to pay equitable compensation to the trust. This is a restitutionary action but the change of position defence will not be available, as he has not acted in good faith.

In *El Ajou v Dollar Land Holdings plc*,[14] Hoffmann LJ set out the requirements for a claimant to succeed in an action for knowing receipt:

1   a disposal of his assets in breach of fiduciary duty;[15]
2   the beneficial receipt by the defendant of assets which are traceable as representing the assets of the plaintiff; and
3   knowledge on the part of the defendant that the assets he received are traceable to a breach of fiduciary duty.

The receipt must be a direct consequence of the alleged breach of trust or fiduciary duty of which the recipient is said to have knowledge. The receipt must also be for the defendant's own use and benefit,[16] otherwise it would be more appropriate to consider an action for dishonest assistance.

Of course the main consideration apart from receipt of the trust property

---

12   YB 5 Ed IV, Mich pl 16, fo. 7.
13   *Barnes v Addy* (1874) 9 Ch App 244 at 251-252.
14   [1994] 1 BCLC 464, 478.
15   Assets may not include information, whether confidential or not: *Farah Constructions Pty Ltd v Say-Dee Pty Ltd* [2007] 10 ITELR 136.
16   The recipient must receive the property for his own benefit: *Agip (Africa) Ltd v Jackson* [1990] Ch. 265 at 291 *per* Millet J.

is that the defendant has knowledge of the breach of trust which led to his receipt.

17.5 Knowledge for Knowing Receipt

The knowledge that will constitute sufficient knowledge for knowing receipt has been the subject of some academic and judicial consideration and debate. Peter Gibson L.J. attempted to clarify the types of knowledge in *Baden Delvaux and Lecuit v. Société Général pour Favoriser le Dévélopment du Commerce et de l'Industrie en France SA*:[17]

1　actual knowledge;
2　wilfully shutting one's eyes to the obvious;
3　wilfully and recklessly failing to make such inquiries as an honest and reasonable man would make;
4　knowledge of circumstances which would indicate the facts to an honest and reasonable man
5　knowledge of circumstances which would put an honest and reasonable man on inquiry.

These are referred to as the *Baden* categories, and, as Peter Gibson L.J. noted,

'apart from actual knowledge, they are formulations of circumstances which may lead the court to impute knowledge of the facts to the alleged constructive trustee, even though he lacked actual knowledge of the facts.'

The usefulness of the categories is therefore in deciding the knowledge the defendant had and whether this would then be adequate to fix him with liability for the receipt. The first category of actual knowledge would obviously be enough but the remaining categories are not so clearly accepted as giving rise to liability. It has generally been thought that the second and third categories, because they require a degree of wilfulness or recklessness in accepting the property are sufficient to fix the recipient with liability, as their conscience has been affected by the knowledge and they will hold the property on constructive trust.

The knowledge in the fourth and fifth categories would usually not be considered enough to affect the conscience of the recipient to make them liable by way of a constructive trust.

Re Montagu's Settlement Trusts.[18]

The trustees, on advice from a firm of solicitors, settled chattels on the 10th Duke of Manchester, absolutely. This was in breach of trust but due to an honest mistake by the solicitors and the Duke. The Duke sold some of the

---

17　[1983] BCLC 325.
18　[1987] Ch 264.

assets while he was alive. When the 10th Duke died the 11th Duke claimed his predecessor was a constructive trustee of the mistakenly given chattels and liable to re-transfer the remaining assets and the traceable proceeds of sale of the disposed chattels. He also claimed the 10th Duke, and therefore his estate, should be personally liable for any loss because assets were disposed of and so untraceable.

Judgment: Megarry V-C held that the 10th Duke had not been in knowing receipt, as this would depend on the actual knowledge of the recipient. The 10th Duke had no knowledge of the terms of the trust, he had forgotten, and his solicitor's knowledge was not imputed to him. The breach resulted from an 'honest muddle'. Some 'want of probity' was required by the recipient to the extent that his conscience was affected by his knowledge to turn him into a constructive trustee. The question to be asked in these cases was: whether the conscience of the recipient is sufficiently affected to justify the imposition of a constructive trust? The Duke, and therefore his estate, was not liable as a constructive trustee because he did not have the subjective knowledge of the breach and therefore his conscience was not affected. However, his estate was liable to re-transfer undisposed trust assets and traceable proceeds as the Duke had been an innocent volunteer.

Thus *Re Montague's ST* seems to restrict the knowledge required to the first three Baden categories or just 'actual knowledge'. The fourth and fifth categories would never be enough to affect the conscience of the recipient so as to form a constructive trust.

The issue of knowledge was further considered in *Lipkin Gorman (a firm) v. Karpnale Ltd*,[19] a case we considered in the chapter on tracing. One of the claims the solicitors' firm made was for knowing receipt against the casino where their employee Cass had gambled away clients' funds. The claim failed as 'the court should be slow to assert that the club and their employees cannot assume that cash belongs to the person proffering it.'[20]

The Baden categories have fallen out of favour in recent years with more emphasis on the recipient having actual knowledge.

BCCI (Overseas) Ltd (in liquidation) v Akindele[21]

BCCI employees arranged an artificial loan arrangement with Akindele in 1985 for US$10m. The BCCI employees were in breach of their fiduciary duty as the arrangement was to facilitate a series of 'dummy' loans as a fraud on the bank. Akindele received US$16.7m in 1988 under the arrangement. Between 1985 and 1987, thus before he had received the

---

19 [1991] 2 AC 548 (HL).
20 [1992] 4 All ER 331 at 351 per Alliott J (the trial judge).
21 *Bank of Credit and Commerce International (Overseas) Ltd (in liquidation) v Akindele* [2001] Ch 436.

payment, but after he had entered the agreement, there was evidence that Akindele had knowledge of press rumours and warnings from business figures in Nigeria of the dubious nature of BCCI. Akindele was also aware of the arrest of BCCI officials in connection with money laundering. The liquidator of the bank took action to recover the money from Akindele for knowing receipt.

Judgement: The Court of Appeal held that Akindele was not in knowing receipt.

Nourse LJ doubted the usefulness of the *Baden* categories of knowledge, preferring to focus instead on adapting the question asked in *Re Montagu's ST*: '[J]ust as there is now a single test of dishonesty for knowing assistance, so ought there to be a single test of knowledge for knowing receipt. The recipient's state of knowledge must be such as to make it unconscionable for him to retain the benefit of the receipt.'[22]

Akindele's liability had to be based on actual or subjective knowledge which would make it unconscionable for him to retain the money. The Court held he was not liable, as he had no subjective knowledge of the frauds at the time of the transaction. The material date was 1985, when the transaction was entered into, and the later knowledge he acquired between 1985 and 1988 did not make it unconscionable for him to retain the money.

The courts have adopted this approach, thus the focus is now on whether the recipient's knowledge made it unconscionable for him to retain the property. There need not be actual dishonesty (although this is necessary for dishonest assistance/ accessory liability). Knowledge is a matter of fact and in determining whether the defendant knew of the breach the court can have regard to the attributes of the defendant.

Of course if the recipient has retained the property then it may be traced to him but the true strength of knowing receipt was clarified in *BCCI* when the Court of Appeal clarified that a restitutionary action could be maintained against the defendant if he had been in knowing receipt of the trust property and had then parted with it or lost it knowing it was trust property.[23] In such a case the defendant will be liable to account as if a trustee.

As many knowing receipt cases involve companies and their directors or other agents it has been necessary to consider whose knowledge will be relevant and if knowledge of an agent may be imputed to a principal.

---

22   *BCCI (Overseas) Ltd (in liquidation) v Akindele* [2001] Ch 436 at 455.
23   See Simon Gardner, 'Moment of truth for knowing receipt?' (2009) 125(Jan) *Law Quarterly Review* 20-24; Mathew Conaglen and Richard Nolan, 'Recipient Liability in Equity' (2001) 66 *Cambridge Law Journal* 515 Pauline Ridge, 'Justifying the Remedies for Dishonest Assistance' (2008) 124 *Law Quarterly Review* 455.

El Ajou v Dollar Land Holdings plc[24]

Three Canadians obtained money from *El Ajou* by bribing a manager to buy worthless shares with *El Ajou*'s money. The Canadians used the money to buy property from Dollar Land Holdings. Dollar Land Holdings knew that the Canadians were being investigated for some kind of fraud. One of Dollar Land Holdings' non-executive directors knew that the money came from a fraud.

Judgement: the Court of Appeal held that the non-executive director, who was responsible only for formal paperwork, but not for the business and who had played no part in business decisions, could be for certain purposes be the directing mind and will of the company. Therefore his knowledge was imputed to Dollar Land Holdings. Dollar Land Holdings were liable to *El Ajou* for the money they had received. It should be noted however, that the Court indicated that the knowledge of an agent would not automatically be imputed to his principal.

An alternative approach to knowing receipt was proposed by Lord Millett in his dissenting judgment in ***Twinsectra v Yardley***.[25] Lord Millett suggested that liability should be strict. That is the claimant need only prove receipt of property in breach of trust or fiduciary duty for the defendant to be liable for the loss, but subject to a change of position defence as with any restitutionary claim.

Gary Watt has proposed that a different approach could be the use of 'investigation norms'.[26] As most actions are against professionals, such as banks, the receipt should be subject to investigation as normal in that profession. Watt states that in the majority of commercial transactions the investigation into whether the vendor is entitled to sell is less than in a transaction involving land. He argues that a constructive notice doctrine should be introduced for all commercial transactions. Knowledge for recipient liability could then be subject to a two-part test:

1   What investigative techniques do reasonable and honest commercial transferees of certain assets normally employ to determine whether the transferor of those assets was entitled to transfer them?
2   Has the defendant complied with those investigative norms?
3   If the defendant has not complied with the investigation norms of their fellows they would have the requisite knowledge to be held liable if they had received property in breach of trust or fiduciary duty.

24   [1994] 2 All ER 685.
25   [2002] All ER 377.
26   Gary Watt, *Trusts and equity* (Oxford, Oxford University Press, 2008), 517.

17.6 Knowing Assistance/ Accessory Liability/ Dishonest Assistance

The extension of liability to strangers to the trust who have not received trust property for their own benefit but have aided in its misappropriation is probably the most important development of stranger liability for the modern financial and commercial world. Those involved in fraud try to hide the proceeds by moving the money through the banking system, changing currencies and banking jurisdictions, changing types of property and using corporations and trusts to disguise beneficial ownership.

When the proceeds have been laundered the fraudster and the laundered proceeds will often disappear and the beneficiaries will have no one to take action against. In these circumstances the beneficiaries may take action against those who have aided in the breach of trust. Any institution or professional involved in financial and commercial transactions must be wary that they will not be held to account as if they were a trustee for any breach of trust that their actions have aided.

This principle is known as knowing assistance, accessory liability or dishonest assistance.

The English Court of Appeal in *Abou-Rahmah v Abacha*,[27] confirmed that the essential elements of dishonest assistance are:[28]

1   that a third party has knowledge of the breach of trust or duty; and,
2   that, given that knowledge, the third party acts in a way which is contrary to normally acceptable standards of honest conduct (the objective test of honesty or dishonesty).

This remedy is enforced against somebody who has assisted in a breach of trust, or a fiduciary duty, they may have received the property but have passed it on and never obtained beneficial receipt of the property for themselves. The remedy has been called a constructive trust, although of course, unlike knowing receipt, the defendant is not being made a trustee of the trust property because he does not have it. It is better to think of the stranger as accounting to the trust for the loss as if he were a trustee,[29] or as 'accountable in equity'.[30]

---

27   [2006] EWCA Civ 1492.
28   See 'Case Report - Adnan Shaaban Abou-Rahmah, Khalid Al-Fulaij & Sons General Trading & Contracting Co v Al-Haji Abdul Kadir Abacha' (2007) 84(Mar) *Trusts and Estates Law & Tax Journal* 22.
29   In fact Lord Selborne's clearly states that the assistant is not a trustee: *Barnes v Addy* (1874) 9 Ch App 244 at 251-252.
30   *Dubai Aluminium Co Ltd v. Salaam* [2002] UKHL 48; [2003] 2 AC 366 at 404 per Lord Millett.

As the assistant may be considered similar to those who aid and abet in the criminal law,[31] the assistance does not have to cause the loss in order for the assistant to be liable. This is the most important aspect of potential liability for banks and other institutions as they may be liable if they have aided in the subsequent transfer of money obtained in breach of trust if they or their agents have the requisite knowledge.

17.7 Knowledge for Knowing Assistance, or Dishonesty?

There has been some issue over whether the defendant has merely to have knowledge of the breach or whether he must have acted dishonestly once he had this knowledge.[32] There has also been an issue over whether dishonesty should be judged on an objective or objective and subjective standard.

The confusion stems from Lord Selborne's original dictum in **Barnes v. Addy** with the authors' emphasis again added:[33]

'But, on the other hand, strangers are not to be made constructive trustees merely because they act as agents of trustees in transactions within their legal powers, transactions, perhaps of which the Court of Equity may disapprove, unless those agents ... *assist with knowledge* in a dishonest and fraudulent design on the part of the trustees ...'

Lord Selborne's dictum clarifies that an agent who merely acts at the order of a dishonest trustee will not be liable unless he has knowledge of the dishonest or fraudulent breach. This places the emphasis for dishonesty on the initial breach of trust and not the state of mind of the assistant. Thus in the previously considered case of **Lipkin Gorman v. Karpnale**,[34] the firm attempted to recover the misappropriated funds from the bank which had paid the money out of the firm's client account to the solicitor. The solicitor's actions were clearly a fraudulent breach of trust, he was certainly dishonest. However, even though the bank manager had known that the solicitor was a gambler, he had no reason to suspect that the solicitor was gambling the money away. Therefore, as the bank had not known of the breach of trust, it could not be liable for knowing assistance.

Today, the courts have moved away from a simple question of

---

31 Stephen B. Elliott and Charles Mitchell 'Remedies for Dishonest Assistance' [2004] 67 (1) *Modern Law Review* 16-47.

32 For a consideration of some Canadian cases see Patricia Steele and Cal D Johnson, 'Bankers as constructive trustees- liability for "knowing receipt" of trust property' (1998) 13 (12) *Journal of International Banking Law* 401-404; Sarah Collett, 'Constructive trusts- a glimmer of light? Part 1' (1998) 11(9) *Insolvency Intelligence* 65- 68.

33 (1874) 9 Ch App 244 at 251-252.

34 [1991] 2 AC 548.

knowledge for knowing assistance. The actions of the assistant have to be considered against his knowledge to decide whether he should be made to account in equity. This had been considered in the case of *Agip (Africa) Ltd v Jackson*,[35]a case considered in the previous chapter concerning tracing. Here the defendants' were liable even though they had no clear idea of what breach was occurring; however, they were suspicious that something was wrong and displayed a clear lack of probity. This idea of lack of probity has been developed so that the important factor is now the dishonesty of the assistant.

Royal Brunei Airlines v Tan (Kok Ming)[36]
Tan was the sole director and major shareholder of a company which Royal Brunei Airlines appointed as its agent. The money from the ticket sales was to be held by Tan's company on trust for Royal Brunei Airlines. However, the company was insolvent and Tan used the money in breach of trust to keep the company going. The company went into liquidation before Royal Brunei Airlines could recover the money. Royal Brunei Airlines then took action against Tan as a knowing assistant (direct action against Tan for the liability of the company would not be possible without piercing the corporate veil).

Judgement: at first instance Tan was not held liable for his actions. He had clearly assisted in the breach of trust, but, as the initial breach by the company was not fraudulent, the fact that Tan knew of the breach was irrelevant. On appeal the Privy Council held that Tan was liable for dishonest assistance. Lord Nicholls took the opportunity to clarify that dishonest assistance relied upon the actions of the assistant being dishonest because he knew of the breach of trust. It was irrelevant whether the initial breach by the trustee was dishonest or not. The dishonesty of the assistant should be considered by the objective standard of the ordinary honest person. Thus dishonesty was 'not acting as an honest person would in the circumstances'. The circumstances to be considered could take into account subjective elements such as the knowledge of the assistant. In considering the knowledge of the assistant the *Baden* categories were "best forgotten". Knowledge could be actual knowledge of the breach, or when the assistant deliberately closed his eyes to the circumstances or deliberately avoided asking questions.

Thus *Tan* confirmed that dishonesty on the part of the assistant was required to establish a claim for dishonest assistance,[37] but the possible

---

35   [1990] Ch. 265 (1st Instance); [1991] Ch 547 (CA).
36   [1995] 2 AC 378; 2 HKC 409. For a discussion of these issues see Jeremy Chan, 'Dishonesty and Knowledge' (2001) 31 *Hong Kong Law Journal* 283.
37   Confirmed by the Court of Appeal in *BCCI (Overseas) Ltd (in liquidation) v Akindele* [2001] Ch 436.

inclusion of a subjective element in the test for dishonesty was reminiscent of the *Ghosh* test, a test to establish dishonesty for theft,[38] which has caused some confusion in the criminal law. The House of Lords had the opportunity to clarify the nature of the dishonesty test for dishonest assistance in *Twinsectra Ltd. v. Yardley.*[39]

Twinsectra Ltd. v. Yardley[40]

Mr Leach, the 2nd defendant, was a solicitor acting for Mr Yardley, an entrepreneur. Twinsectra agreed to lend £1 million to Mr Yardley but only through another solicitor acting for Mr Yardley, Sims (this may have been their usual practice or they may already have been suspicious). Sims received the money on the undertaking that it would only be used for the purchase of a specified property. However, in breach of this undertaking, Sims paid the money to Leach who passed it to Yardley. Yardley used £375,000 used for purposes other than buying the specified property. The loan was not repaid and Twinsectra sued all parties, including Leach for knowing assistance.

Judgement: at first instance the trial judge made a significant finding of fact declaring that Leach was not dishonest simply misguided.

Appellate courts will rarely overturn a trial judge's finding of fact as he has access to the oral testimony of witnesses.

The judgment of the House of Lords should be considered with this in mind. The House of Lords held that, although Leach had been 'deliberately closing his eyes to facts which should have indicated a breach of trust', and adopting a 'blinkered approach to his role to his professional duties as a solicitor',[41] he was not liable because there was no evidence he had acted dishonestly. In deciding that Leach was not dishonest the majority interpreted Lord Nicholls' judgement in Tan as advocating a combined objective and subjective test for dishonesty in these situations, similar to the *Ghosh* test. The principle from the majority in *Twinsectra* was that to be liable it must be established that the defendant's conduct was dishonest by the standards of reasonable and honest people (objective) and that he himself realised that his conduct was dishonest by these standards (subjective).

Lord Millet dissented stating that the solicitor had been dishonest on the grounds that no reasonable solicitor could have failed to realise that

---

38   *R v Ghosh* [1999] 1 Cr App Rep (S) 225
39   [2002] UKHL 12; AC 164. See Alastair Speirs, 'Caught in the Tangled Web' [2000] 2 *Web Journal of Current Legal Issues*; Georgina Andrews, 'The redundancy of dishonest assistance' (2003) (Sep / Oct) *Conveyancer and Property Lawyer* 398- 410.
40   [2002] UKHL 12; 2 AC 164; 2 All ER 377.
41   [2002] 2 AC 164 at 174 per Lord Hoffman.

he was acting dishonestly in the circumstances.[42]

The judgment aroused more academic criticism, as it was claimed that a defendant could rely on his own claims that he did not know that what he did was dishonest by the standards of reasonable and honest people. However, it should be noted that Lord Hutton had referred to dishonesty requiring:

'...knowledge by the defendant that what he was doing would be regarded as dishonest by honest people, although he should not escape a finding of dishonesty because he sets his own standards of honesty and does not regard as dishonest what he knows would offend the normally accepted standards of honest conduct...'[43]

The Privy Council again considered the nature of dishonesty in *Barlow Clowes International Ltd (in liquidation) v Eurotrust International Ltd*.[44]

The claimant was a company registered in Gibraltar that was in liquidation. It had been operating a fraudulent offshore investment scheme offering high returns from investments in gilt-edged securities. The liquidator was attempting to recover some of the misappropriated funds from the defendant, Eurotrust, on the basis it had knowingly assisted in the fraudulent breach. The defendant was an Isle of Man company, and one of its principal directors Mr Henwood had administered bank accounts that had received money in breach of fiduciary duty from the claimant company.

Judgment: the trial judge, in the High Court of Gibraltar, found the defendant company liable. The judge held Henwood was strongly suspicious of the truth, that there was a breach of trust, as no honest person could have assisted in this arrangement. Henwood had consciously decided not to make inquiries to avoid the risk of discovering the truth. The judge imputed Henwood's knowledge to the defendant company and found it liable because of his suspicions. Eurotrust appealed on the basis that the evidence did not support the findings of the judge. Henwood claimed that he could not have been dishonest unless he was aware that what he was doing was dishonest by the ordinary standards of reasonable and honest people. He claimed he believed he had an overriding duty to his client and had not reflected on what ordinary standards of honesty required. The Privy Council upheld the trial judge's findings. In doing so the Council clarified that the test for dishonesty in these cases was behaviour which was contrary to the ordinary standards of honest behaviour. Lord Hoffman commented on Lord Hutton's test for dishonesty in *Twinsectra*:

'The reference to "what he knows would offend normally accepted

---

42 This approach had been favoured by the UK Court of Appeal in *Grupo Torras SA v Al-Sabah* [2001] Lloyd's Rep Bank 36.

43 [2002] 2 AC 164 at [36].

44 [2005] UKPC 37.

standards of conduct" meant only that his knowledge of the transaction had to be such as to render his participation contrary to normally acceptable standards of honest conduct. It did not require that he should have had reflections on what those normally acceptable standards were.'

Lord Hoffman continued that clear suspicion would be enough for consequent actions to be dishonest:

'...it was not necessary ... that Mr Henwood should have concluded that the disposals were of moneys held in trust. It was sufficient that he should have entertained clear suspicions that this was the case...someone can know, and can certainly suspect, that he is assisting in a misappropriation of money without knowing that the money is held on trust or what a trust means.'

Henwood had tried to hide behind the subjective element of the *Twinsectra* test but the Privy Council refused to allow this.

Therefore, after *Barlow Clowes*, to succeed in a claim for dishonest assistance the claimant does not have to prove that the defendant had actual knowledge of the breach of trust or fiduciary duty, but only that he had 'clear suspicions' that the transactions were a breach of trust and the assistance is consequently dishonest viewed by 'normally honest standards of conduct'. Therefore an employee who diverts money from his employer into the bank accounts of his own companies is acting dishonestly and will be liable for dishonest assistance.[45] Thus the dishonesty test is purely an objective test.

Starglade Properties Ltd v Nash[46]

Nash owned Larkstore Ltd which bought a development site from Starglade. Starglade had obtained a favourable soil engineer's report from Technograde Ltd. Nash saw this report on behalf of his company, but did not take assignment of Starglade's rights against Technograde in relation to the report. During the development there was a significant landslip. The neighbours to the development site sued Nash's company. Nash wanted to join (Part 20) proceedings against Technograde but in order to do this had to buy the assignment of the rights of the soil report from Starglade. Starglade's directors knew that Nash could not proceed without the assignment and so drove a very hard bargain. Nash agreed to give half of any damages recovered to Starglade. A document was produced which Nash signed recording the agreement and providing: 'we agree to hold all

---

45 *AAH Pharmaceuticals Ltd v Birdi* (Q.B. unreported 20 June 2011).

46 [2010] EWCA Civ 1314. For a discussion of this case see Don McCue, 'Dishonestly assisting in a breach of trust: further confirmation that Barlow Clowes will be followed in the Court of Appeal and a robust conclusion on the facts: *Starglade Properties Ltd v Nash* [2010] EWCA Civ 1312' (2011) 17(2) *Trusts & Trustees* 128-131.

monies received [from Technograde] on trust for division in accordance with the foregoing'.

Mr Nash was highly resentful of this agreement and Starglade's hard bargaining.

Three years later, January 2007, Mr Nash's company received £309,154.98 from Technograde in settlement of the claim. However, Mr Nash's company was now insolvent. It did not have enough funds, even with the settlement, to pay its joint venture partner, creditors and Starglade. Mr Nash asked his solicitor whether he could pay other creditors in priority to Starglade. The solicitor advised that it was arguable that as the joint venture partner had a charge over the site he had an 'arguable' case. Nash paid the joint venture partner £250,000 and gave £59,150 to other creditors. A few months later Nash dissolved his company. Starglade brought an action against Nash for assisting in a breach of trust. Nash argued that, as a layman, he did not know what a trust was.

Judgment: at first instance the trial judge accepted Nash was an 'honest and straightforward' witness who regarded Starglade as simply another commercial creditor which did not deserve payment as much because of the pressure it had used to get the agreement. The judge accepted that there was no doubt Nash had assisted in a breach of trust and that he could not have been wholly satisfied that what he was doing was lawful, but, on the other hand, he did not know that what he was doing was unlawful.[47] The test for dishonesty was that advised by the Privy Council in Barlow Clowes and so Nash was not dishonest in this respect as some members of the public would not think this dishonest.

Starglade appealed to the Court of Appeal. The Court of Appeal agreed that the correct test for dishonesty was that in Barlow Clowes. However, the trial judge had asked the wrong question. Nash was not seeking to prefer one creditor over others; he had acted purely to frustrate Starglade. Thus this was the deliberate removal of the assets of an insolvent company so as to entirely defeat the just claim of a creditor. This was not in accordance with ordinary standards of honest commercial behaviour, however much it might occur. It was therefore misleading to talk of conduct which some might think of as dishonest and others not. Just as the subjective understanding of the person that his conduct is dishonest is irrelevant, so also is it irrelevant that there may be a body of opinion which regards the ordinary standard of honest behaviour as being set too high. In civil proceedings it is for the court to determine what the standard is and apply it to the facts of the case. Therefore Starglade's appeal was allowed.

The issue of 'clear suspicion' was considered in ***Abou-Ramah & Others v Abacha & Others***.[48]

---

47 [2009] EWHC 148 (Ch); [2010] WTLR 1267.
48 [2006] EWCA Civ 1492.

Abou-Ramah & Others v Abacha & Others[49]

The claimants were a lawyer practicing in Kuwait and a Kuwaiti trading company. They were victims of a fraud in which they had been asked to administer an investment scheme consisting of $65 million. They were promised fees and a share in the scheme. However, the claimants first had to pay money into the scheme before the profits could be released. The claimants paid $625,000 which was allegedly for value added tax in Benin. The money was paid into the account of a Nigerian Bank, City Express Bank, at a branch of the Hong Kong and Shanghai Banking Corporation in London for onward transfer to a client, 'Trusty International' at its branch in Nigeria. The money disappeared shortly afterwards. The claimants claimed against the Nigerian Bank for knowing assistance.

Judgement: the trial judge ruled the bank's staff suspected that the fraudsters regularly assisted corrupt politicians to launder money, but concluded that knowledge of money laundering is not knowledge of breach of trust. He accepted that the Bank was not dishonest and accepted a change of position defence against a restitutionary claim. The claimants appealed to the Court of Appeal. The Court dismissed the appeal, as it was inappropriate to reverse the trial judge's finding of fact that the bank had not acted dishonestly. There was some discussion by the Court of the suspicions of the Bank's employees. The Court was again loath to overturn the trial judge's finding of fact that the Bank had not acted dishonestly. However, some justification of the finding was made on the basis that the Bank staff had suspicions, but had applied the required procedures under Nigerian law to settle these suspicions. However, Rix L.J. was quite critical of the bank's conduct.

The situation after *Abou-Ramah* seems to be that clear suspicions can impute knowledge of the breach but a professional who applies the required due diligence procedures to deal with these suspicions and is satisfied they have been dealt with will not be liable. This is obviously very significant for banks.

To decide if professionals like banks have allayed their suspicions by the appropriate procedure it is necessary to consider what enquiries they should make. This will usually depend on the jurisdictional requirements.

To establish a claim for knowing assistance after *Barlow Clowes* the claimant will have to prove that:

1   His assets were subject to a trust or fiduciary obligation;
2   There was a breach of this trust or fiduciary duty (although there is no need for the breach to be dishonest);[50]
3   The stranger (defendant) assisted in the breach;

---

49   [2006] EWCA Civ 1492.
50   *Royal Brunei Airlines v Tan (Kok Ming)* [1995] 2 AC 378; 2 HKC 409.

4   The stranger (defendant) had knowledge of the breach (or clear suspicions or should have made enquiries);
5   Given that knowledge, the stranger (defendant) acts in a way which is contrary to normally acceptable standards of honest conduct; and,
6   This conduct resulted in the claimant's loss.

17.8 Summary

A party who has no connection with a trust is referred to as a stranger to the trust. A stranger may be liable for a breach of trust if he intermeddles in the trust and by his actions the trust suffers loss. This will make him a trustee de son tort and he will be liable as if he were an officially appointed trustee. A stranger may also be liable for knowingly receiving trust property. The recipient must receive the trust property for his own benefit and have actual knowledge that he has received the property because of a breach of trust. If his knowledge makes it unconscionable for him to retain the benefit of the property he will be liable for knowing receipt. If he still has the property he will hold it on constructive trust for the trust. If he has disposed of or lost it knowing it to be trust property he will be liable to account for the loss to the trust as if he were a trustee.

A stranger may also be liable for a breach of trust if he has dishonestly assisted the person who has breached the trust. Here the assistant must have done something which helped in the breach of trust, this does not have to be the initial breach but may be subsequent disposal of the trust property. The stranger must also have knowledge of the breach of trust, but this does not have to be exact details of the breach and may be suspicions as to the nature of the transaction. The knowledge of the stranger must make his assistance dishonest by the standards of ordinary honest people. If there is a successful claim for dishonest assistance then the stranger is liable to account for the loss to the trust as if he were a trustee. However, he is not a trustee or a fiduciary.

Bibliography

Books and book chapters

Ariès, Philippe, *The Hour of Our Death*, Peregrine Books, London 1983 (reprinted 1987): 12.3

Ariès, Philippe, *Western Attitudes Towards Death*, Marion Boyars Publishers Limited, London & New York, 1976: 12.3

Aristotle *Nichomachean Ethics:* 1.2

Ashe, Thomas, *Epieikeia* (London, 1609): 1.2

Austin, "Fragments- On Contracts", in *2 Lectures on Jurisprudence* (4th edition, 1879): 5.2

Bacon, Francis, *Reading of the Statute of Uses,* in J. Spedding, R.L. Ellis and D.D. Heath (eds), *The Works of Francis Bacon* (14 vols, London, 1857-74): 1.5.3

Baker, Sir John, *Baker & Milsom sources of English legal history: private law to 1750,* Oxford University Press, 2nd edition, 2010: 12.3

Berman, Harold J., *Law and Revolution: The Formation of the Western Legal Tradition*(Harvard University Press, 1983): 1.5; 2.1

Birks, P. (ed), *Laundering and Tracing,* Clarendon Press: Oxford, 1995: 16.1; 16.6

Birks, P., 'Definition and Division: A Meditation on Institutes 3.13' in P Birks (ed) *The Classification of Obligations* (Clarendon Press Oxford 1997): 13.5

Burn, E.H., 'Cheshire & Burn's Modern Law of Real Property, 16th edition (London: Butterworths, 2000): 1.3; 4.2.2- 4.2.5

Chambers, Robert ,'Is There a presumption of Resulting Trust?', in Charles Mitchell (ed), *Constructive and Resulting Trusts* (Hart Publishing, 2009): 10.4

Denning, Alfred, *Landmarks in the Law* (LexisNexis UK: 1998): 1.8

Fitzgerald, P.J., *Salmon on Jurisprudence* (London : Sweet & Maxwell, 1966) 12th ed: 4.4

Gardner, Simon, *An introduction to the law of trusts* (Oxford ; New York : Oxford University Press, 2011) 3rd ed: 4.1

Germain, Christopher St., *Doctor and Student* 1528-31 (18th ed., Dublin, 1792): 1.4

Gilbert, *The Law of Uses* (London: W. Reed & P. Phelan, 3rd edn, 1811): 4.22

Gray, J.C., *The Rule Against Perpetuities,* also known as *Gray on Perpetuities* (4th ed. 1942): 5.6.3

Haley, M. & McMurtry, L. *Equity and Trusts,* 2nd edition (London: Sweet & Maxwell, 2009): 5.6.3

Hayton, D., (general editor) with Paul Matthews, Charles Mitchell, *Underhill and Hayton, law relating to trusts and trustees* (London : LexisNexis Butterworths, 2007) 17th ed: 4.1

Helmholz, Richard, & Zimmermann, Reinhard, (eds), *Itinera Fiduciae* (Dunker & Humblot: Berlin, 1998): 4.22

Ho, Lusina, *Trust Law in China* (Sweet & Maxwell Asia, Hong Kong 2003): 4.7

Jollowicz, H.F., *Roman Foundations of Modern Law* (Oxford, 1957): 1.2; 1.5.1

Law Commission of England and Wales, 'The Presumption of Advancement: Does it have any Effect in Practice?' (Law Com, 2006). Law Commission, 'The

Illegality Defence' (Law Com No 320, 2010): 10.4.6

Law Commission of England and Wales, Item 7 of the Sixth Programme of Law Reform: The Law of Trusts, *The Rules Against Perpetuities and Excessive Accumulations*: 5.6.2: 5.6.3

Lawson, A. 'The things we do for love: detrimental reliance in the family home' (1996) *Legal Studies* 218-231: 11.6.2

Luxton, Peter, *The Law of Charities* (Oxford, Oxford University Press: 2001): 8.2; 13.12; 13.13; 13.3

Ma, Lawrence, & Lower, Michael, *Principles of Equity & Trusts Law in Hong Kong* (Hong Kong: LexisNexis, 2009): 4.5.1

Ma, Lawrence, *Equity and Trusts Law in Hong Kong*, 2nd ed. (Hong Kong, Lexis Nexis, 2009): 5.6.3

Maitland, F. W., & Montague, F.C., *A Sketch of English Legal History*, 1850-1906. Charleston, SC : Bibliolife, 2010: 1.3; 1.5.1; 1.5.2; 1.5.5; 1.7; 4.2.3; 4.2.4

Maitland, F.W., *Equity* (Cambridge: Cambridge University Press, 1949 (first published 1909)); *Equity: A Course of Lectures*, J Brunyate (ed), rev edn (Cambridge, Cambridge University press, 1936): 1.6; 3.1; 3.2; 4.0; 4.2.2- 4.2.4; 10.1; 10.4- 10.6; 14.3

Maitland, S.R. ,*The Dark Ages; A Series of Essays, Intended to Illustrate the State of religion and Literature in the Ninth, Tenth, Eleventh and Twelfth Centuries*, (London: Francis & John Rivington, 3rd edition, 1853): 1.5.5; 4.2.5

Martin, Jill, *Modern Equity* (London: Sweet & Maxwell: 18th edition, 2009): 1.8

Matthews, P., 'Limits of Common Law Tracing', in Birks, P. (ed), *Laundering and Tracing*, Clarendon Press: Oxford, 1995: 16.6

Matthews, Paul, 'The Words Which Are Not There: A Partial History of the Constructive Trust', in Charles Mitchell (ed), *Constructive and Resulting Trusts* (Hart Publishing, 2009): 1.5.5; 2.3; 5.2; 10.1; 10.6; 11.7; 11.9

Maudsley, R.H., *The Modern Law of Perpetuities* (1979): 5.6.3

Meagher, R P, Heydon, J D, and Leeming, M J, *Meagher, Gummow and Lehane's Equity Doctrines & Remedies* (LexisNexis Butterworths, 4th ed, 2002): 5.2.1

Mee, John' "Automatic" Resulting Trusts: Retention, Restitution, or Reposing Trust?', in Charles Mitchell (ed), *Constructive and Resulting Trusts* (Hart Publishing, 2009): 10.3; 10.5

Milsom, S.F.C., *Historical Foundations of the Common Law* (London: Butterworths, 2nd edition, 1981): 1.1- 1.4; 2.1; 4.4

Mitchell, Charles (ed), *Constructive and Resulting Trusts* (Hart Publishing, 2009): 1.5.5; 2.3; 5.2; 10.1; 10.3; 10.5; 10.6; 11.5; 11.7; 11.9

Morey, William Carey, 'Outlines of Roman law: comprising its historical growth and general principles' (G.P. Putnam's Sons, 1896) (available on Google Books): 1.5.1

Oakley, A. J., *Parker and Mellows: the modern law of trusts*, 9th ed. (London: Sweet & Maxwell, 2009): 5.6.3

Penner, J. *The Law of Trusts* (Oxford: Oxford University Press,2008): 6.2.1; 10.1

Pettit, P.H., *Equity and the law of trusts* (Oxford ; New York : Oxford University Press, 2009) 11th ed.: 1.8; 3.6; 4.1

Roper, William, *The Life of Sir Thomas More*, in Richard S. Sylvester and Davis P. Harding (eds), *Two Early Tudor Lives* (New Haven, CT: Yale University Press, 1962): 1.5.4

Selden (sometimes Seldon), John, *Table Talk* (1689): 1.5.3; 2.1

Stone Lawrence & Stone, J.C. Fawtier, *An Open Elite? England 1540-1880* (Oxford: Clarendon Press 1986): 4.2.4; 4.2.5

Stone, Lawrence, *Road to divorce : England 1530-1987*, Oxford, Oxford University Press: 1990: 12.3

Swadling, *The Quistclose Trusts: Critical Essays* (Hart Publishing, Oxford and Portland, Oregon: 2004): 10.5.2

Swadling, William, 'A Hard Look at *Hodgson v Marks*' in Peter Birks and Francis Rose (eds), *Restitution and Equity Volume One: Resulting Trusts and Equitable Compensation* (Mansfield Press, 2000): 5.2.1

Thomas, G., *Thomas on Powers*, 2nd edition (London: Sweet & Maxwell, 1998): 6.1.3

Thomas, G.W., and Hudson, A.S., *The Law of Trusts*, (Oxford; Oxford University Press, 2004): 10.1; (Oxford, Oxford University Press: 2010, 2nd edition): 13.12

Warburton, J., *Tudor On Charities* (London, Sweet & Maxwell: 2003, 9th edition): 8.1; 8.2; 13.13; 13.3

Watt, G., *Todd & Watt's Cases & Materials on Equity and Trusts*, 7th edition (Oxford University Press, 2009): 6.3.1

Watt, Gary, *Trusts and Equity*, 3rd edition (Oxford: Oxford University Press, 2008): 13.5; 17.5

Woodley, Mick, *Osborne's Concise Law Dictionary* (London: Sweet & Maxwell, 2005).

Yale, D.E.C, (ed), *Lord Nottingham's Chancery Cases* (Selden Society, vol i, 1957; vol ii, 1961): 10.4.6

Journal articles

'Case Report - Adnan Shaaban Abou-Rahmah, Khalid Al-Fulaij & Sons General Trading & Contracting Co v Al-Haji Abdul Kadir Abacha' (2007) 84(Mar) *Trusts and Estates Law & Tax Journal* 22: 17.6

"Cestui Que Use': Cestui Que Trust' (1910) 26 *Law Quarterly Review* 196. 4.2; 4.2.3 7.1

Allan, Gregory, 'The Secret Is Out There: Searching for the Legal Justification for the Doctrine of Secret Trusts through Analysis of the Case Law' (2011) 40(1) *Common Law World Review* 311- 344: 12.4.2

Ambrose, Mary, 'Disclosure to beneficiaries- whither confidentiality? (2006) (4) *Private Client Business* 236-244: 15.2

Ames, James Barr, 'The Origin of Uses and Trusts', (1908) 21 *Harvard Law Review* 261-274: 4.2.5

Andrews, Georgina, 'The redundancy of dishonest assistance' (2003) (Sep/Oct) *Conveyancer and Property Lawyer* 398- 410: 17.7

Avery, Margaret E, 'Evaluation of the Effectiveness of the Court of Chancery under the Lancastrian Kings' (1970) 86 *Law Quarterly Review* 84: 4.2.4

Avini, Avisheh, 'The Origin of the Modern English Trust Revisited' (1995-1996) 70 *Tulane Law Review* 1139-1163: 4.22

Bah, Saliou, 'Recovery and return of proceeds of corruption in the international anti-corruption conventions' (2010) 1 *JBL* 15-34.   16.1

Barlow, Anne, & Lind, Craig, 'A matter of trust: the allocation of rights in the family home' (1999) 19 *Legal Studies* 468-488: 11.1

Birke Hacker, 'Proprietary restitution after impaired consent transfers: a generalized power model' (2009) 68(2) *Cambridge Law Journal* 324-360: 10.5

Birks, P., 'Mixing and tracing: property and restitution'. (1992) 45 *CLP* 69-98: 16.1

Birks, P., 'Property, Unjust Enrichment, and Tracing' (2001) 54 *Current Legal Problems* 231: 16.1

Blower, Robert, 'The limits of section 57 Trustee Act 1925 after *Sutton v England*' (2012) 18(1) (Jan) *Trusts & Trustees* 11-16: 15.7

Bordwell, Percy, 'The Repeal of the Statute of Uses' (1926) 39(4) *Harvard Law Review* 466: 4.2.4

Bottomley, A. 'Self and Subjectivities: Language of Claim in Property' (1993) 20(1) (Spring) *Journal of Law & Society* 63': 11.6.1

Brightwell, James 'Good riddance to the presumption of advancement?' (2010) 16(8) (September) *Trusts & Trustees* 627: 10.4.5; 10.4.6

Brown, Brendan F: 'The Ecclesiastical Origin of the Use', (1934-1935) 10 *Notre Dame Lawyer* 353- 366: 4.2.3

Browne-Wilkinson, Lord, 'Constructive Trusts and Unjust Enrichment' [1996] 10 *TLI* 98 – 101: 11.6.1

Burrows, Andrew, 'We do this in common law but that at equity', (2002) 22 *Oxford Journal of Legal Studies* 1: 1.7 ; 1.8

Carne, William Lindsay, 'A Sketch of the History of the High Court of Chancery from its Origin to the Chancellorship of Wolsey' (1927) 13(7) (Nov.) *The Virginia Law Review* 391: 1.3- 1.5.1; 1.6; 1.8; 3.7; 4.22

Chan, Jeremy, 'Dishonesty and Knowledge' (2001) 31 *Hong Kong Law Journal* 283: 17.7

Clarke, P., 'The Family Home: Intention and Agreement' [1992] 22 *Fam Law* 724 : 11.6.1

Collins, Sandra, 'Case Comment: Trusts: Tracing' (2008) 23(8) *J.I.B.L.R.* 89-91: 16.5

Conaglen, Mathew, and Nolan, Richard, 'Recipient Liability in Equity' (2001) 66 *Cambridge Law Journal* 515: 17.5

Crackanthorpe, Montague, 'The Uses of Legal History' (1896) 19 *Annu. Rep. A.B.A.* 343: 1.5.1; 4.2.2; 4.2.4; 9.5.3

Critchley, Patricia, 'Instruments of Fraud, Testamentary Dispositions, And the Doctrine of Secret Trusts' (1999) 115 (Oct) *Law Quarterly Review* 631: 12.4.2

Critchley, Patricia, 'Privileged Wills and testamentary Formalities: A time to Die?' (1999) 58(1) *Cambridge Law Journal*, 49-58: 12.4.2

Davis, Christine, 'Mutual wills; formalities, constructive trusts' [2003] (May / June) *Conv* 238-247: 12.2.4

Davis, Henry E., Paper before the American Bar Association (1898) 6 *American Lawyer* 205: 1.3; 4.2.2; 4.2.3; 12.1

Dixon, Martin, 'The never-ending story: co-ownership after *Stack v Dowden*' [2007] 71 *Conv.* 456: 11.3

Duckworth, 'STAR WARS: Smiting the bull' (1999) 13 TLI 158: 4.8; 7.3.4

Duckworth, 'STAR WARS: The colony strikes back' (1998) 12 TLI 16: 4.8; 7.3.4

Egerton, Thomas (Lord Ellesmere), *The Privileges and Prerogatives of the High Court of Chancery* (London 1641): 1.5.3

Elliott, Stephen B., and Mitchell, Charles, 'Remedies for Dishonest Assistance' [2004] 67 (1) *Modern Law Review* 16-47: 17.6

Emery, C., 'Do We Need a Rule Against Perpetuities?' (1994) 57 *MLR* 602: 5.6.3

Ferguson, P. 'Constructive trusts- a note of caution' (1993) 109 (Jan) *L.Q.R.* 114: 11.9; 11.10

Figueroa, Dante, 'Is the Lack of Trusts an Impediment for Expanding Business Opportunities in Latin America?' (January 26, 2007) *bepress Legal Series.* Working Paper 1962. http://law.bepress.com/expresso/eps/1962: 4.0

Fox, D.M. 'Identification of Money at Common Law' [2010] 69(1) *Cambridge Law Journal* 28-30: 16.3

Fratcher, William F., 'Uses of Uses', (1969) 34 *Missouri Law Review* 39-66: 4.2.3

Fuller, Lon L., 'Consideration and Form' (1941) 41 *Colum. L. Rev.* 799- 824: 4.5.1

Gallagher, Steven, 'The Presumption of Advancement in Hong Kong', *The Hong Kong Lawyer*, November 2011, 14-25: 10.4.6

Gardner, 'Wives' guarantees of their husbands' debts' (1999) *L.Q.R.* 115: 11.8.4

Gardner, Simon, 'Family property today' (2008) 124 *L.Q.R.* 422: 11.6.1

Gardner, Simon, 'Knowing assistance and knowing receipt: taking stock' (1996) 112 (Jan) *Law Quarterly Review* 56-94: 17.1

Gardner, Simon, 'Moment of truth for knowing receipt?' (2009) 125(Jan) *Law Quarterly Review* 20-24: 17.5

Garton, J., 'The Role of the Trust Mechanism in the Rule in Re. Rose' (2003) 67 Conv 364: 9.4

Gaudiosi, Monica M., 'The Influence of the Islamic law of WAQF on the Development of the Trust in England: The Case of Merton College', (1987-1988) 136 *University of Pennsylvania Law Review* 1231-1261: 4.22

Glister, Jamie 'Section 199 of the Equality Act 2010: How Not to Abolish the Presumption of Advancement' [2010] 73(5) *Modern Law Review* 807: 10.4.6

Glister, Jamie, 'Is There a Presumption of Advancement?'(2011) 33(39) *Sydney Law Review*, 39-66: 10.4.6

Glover, Nicola, & Todd, Paul, 'The myth of common intention' (1996) 16 *Legal Studies* 325: 11.6.1

Goode, Sir Roy, 'Are Intangible Assets Fungibles?' (2003) *LMCLQ* 379: 6.2.1

Goodhart & Jones, 'The Infiltration of Equitable Doctrine into English Commercial Law' *(1980)* 43 MLR *489:* 10.5.2

Grantham, 'Can Directors Compete with the Company?' (2003) 66 *Modern Law Review* 109: 14.4

Grantham, Ross, 'Doctrinal Bases for the Recognition of Proprietary Rights' (1996) Oxford Journal of Legal Studies 561- 585: 4.4

Hanbury, H.G., 'The Legislation of Richard III' (1962) 6(2) *The American Journal of Legal History* 95: 4.2.4

Harding, Mathew, 'Defending *Stack v Dowden*' [2009] *Conv* 309: 11.3

Haynes, Andrew, 'The international response to the Money laundering threat', in *A Practitioner's Guide to International Money laundering Law and regulation,* City & Financial Publications: 2003: 16.1

Haynes, Andrew, *Butterworths Financial Services Law Guide*, Butterworths, London, 2nd edition, chapter 5, 'Money Laundering': 17.2

Haynes, Andrew, *The Law Relating to International Banking*, Bloomsbury

Professional, 2010: 16.1

Hayton, D. 'Equitable rights of cohabitees' (1990) *Conv* 370: 11. 10

Hayton, D., 'Constructive Trusts of Homes- A Bold Approach' (1993) 109 LQR 485.

Hayton, D., 'The Development of the Trust Concept in Civil Law Jurisdictions' (2000) (Sep) *Journal of International Trust and Corporate Planning* 159: 4.7

Hayton. D. 'Setting gifts aside for mistake' (2011) *Trusts & Trustees* 17 (10): 937-944: 9.1

Helmholz, R.H., 'The Early Enforcement of Uses' [1979] 79 *Colum. Law Rev.* 1503-1513: 4.2.3

Herman, Shael, '*Utilitas Ecclesiae*: The Canonical Conception of the Trust (1995-1996) *Tul. L. Rev.* 2240-2278: 4.22

Hicks, Andrew D., 'The Remedial Principle of *Keech v Samford* Reconsidered' (2010) 69(2) *Cambridge Law Journal* 287-320: 10.7.1

Hilliard, Jonathon, 'Tracing into orders made on divorce: *Independent Trustee Services Ltd v Susan Morris'* [2012] EWCA Civ 195 (2012) 18(7) *Trusts & Trustees* 696-699: 16.5.5

Ho, Lusina, 'China: trust law and practice since 2001' (2010) 16 (3)(April) *Trusts & Trustees*, 124-127: 4.7

Ho, Lusina, 'The Reception of Trust in Asia: Emerging Asian Principles of Trust' (2004) *Singapore Journal of Legal Studies*, 287-304: 4.7

Ho, Lusina, and Smart, P. St J., 'Quistclose and Romalpa: Ambivalence and Contradiction' (2009) 39 *Hong Kong L. J.* 37: 10.5.2

Hodge, D., 'Secret Trusts: the fraud theory revisited' [1980] *Conveyancer and Property Lawyer* 341-350: 12.4.1

Holdsworth, S., 'Relation of the equity administered by the common law judges to the equity administered by the Chancellor' (1916) 26 *Yale Law Journal* 1: 1.7

Holdsworth, W.S., 'The Political Causes Which Shaped The Statute Of Uses' (1912-1913) 26 Harvard Law Review 108-127: 4.2.4

Holdswoth, 'Secret Trusts' (1937) 53 *Law Quarterly Review* 501: 12.5

Holmes, Oliver Wendell, 'Early English Equity' (1885) 1 *LQR* 162: 4.22

Holmes, Oliver Wendell, 'Law in Science and Science in Law' (1898-1899) 12 *Harv. L. Rev.* 443-463: 4.22

Hutchens, W., 'The PRC's First Trust Law: Trusts Without Chinese Characteristics' (2001) 15 *China Law & Practice*: 4.7

Ives, 'E.W. The Genesis of the Statute of Uses' (1967) 82 HER 676: 4.2.4

Jaconelli, Joseph, 'Problems in the rule in Strong v Bird' (2006) (Sep-Oct) *Conveyancer and Property Lawyer* 432: 9.5; 9.5.2

Jones, N.G., 'Trusts Litigation in Chancery after the Statute of Uses: the First Fifty Years': 4.2.5

Jones, N.G., 'Uses, Trusts and a Path to Privity', (1997) 56 *Cambridge Law Journal* 175-200: 4.2.4

Kennedy, D., 'Some Caution about Property Rights as a Recipe for Economic Development' (2011) 1(1) *Accounting, Economics, and Law* article 3: 8.4

Kessler, Delphine Pannatier, 'The recognition of tracing under the Hague Trusts Convention: an analysis of article 11 para 3 lit d for the perspective of Swiss law' (2012) 18(2) *Trusts & Trustees*, 149-158: 16.1

Kiralfy, A.K.R. 'Law Reform by Legal Fictions, Equity and Legislation in English Legal History' (1966) 10(1) (Jan.) *The American Journal of Legal History* 3: 3.2; 3.6; 3.7

Klinck, D.R., *Conscience, Equity and the Court of Chancery in Early Modern England*, Farnham: Ashgate Publishing Limited, 2010: 1.2; 1.5.3; 1.5.4

Langbein, J.H., 'Burn the Rembrandt? Trust Law's limits on the settlor's power to direct investments' (2010) *Boston University Law Review*: 5.6.2

Langbein, John H., 'The Contractarian Basis of the Law of Trusts', (1995-6) 105 *Yale Law Journal* 625-675: 4.5.1

Langbein, John H., 'The Secret Life of the Trust: The Trust as an Instrument of Commerce' (1997-1998) 107 *Yale Law Journal* 166-189: 4.8

Langlois, Charles V. 'The Comparative History of England and France during the Middles Ages' (1890) 5(18) (April) *The English Historical Review* 259: 4.22

Lapsley, Gaillard, 'Some Recent Advances in English Constitutional History (before 1485)' (1936) 5(2) *Cambridge Historical Journal* 119: 4.22

Leach, W. Barton, 'Perpetuities in a Nutshell', (1938) 51(4) *Harvard Law Review* 638: 5.6.3

Leach, W. Barton, 'Perpetuities in Perspective: Ending the Rule's Reign of Terror', (1952) 65(5) *Harvard Law Review* 721: 5.6.3

Lee, Rebecca Wing Chi, 'Rental Deposits as (*Quistclose*) Trusts' (2003) 33 *Hong Kong Law Journal* 27: 10.5.2

Lee, Rebecca, 'Conceptualizing the Chinese Trust' (2009) *International Comparative Law Quarterly* 58 (July), 665-669: 4.7

Loi, Kelry C. F., 'Revisiting Quistclose Trusts, Romalpa Clauses and Registrable Charges: A Reply to Ho and Smart' (2011) 41 *Hong Kong L. J.* 343: 10.5.2

Lord Neuberger of Abbotsbury MR, 'Aspects of the Law of Mistake: Re Hastings-Bass' (2009) 15/4 *Trusts & Trustees* 189: 13.5

Loughrey, Fiona, Hughes, Gareth, & Maurellet, Jose-Antonion, 'How to curb a headstart using the springboard doctrine', (2010) *Hong Kong Lawyer*, 24: 3.2

Low, Kelvin F.K., 'Case Comment *Luo Xing Juan Angela v Estate of Hui Shui See Willy, Deceased:* family property & interposed companies' (2009) (6) *Conv* 524-532: 11.9

Lupoi, Maurizio, 'The Civil Law Trust' (1999) 32 *Vanderbilt Journal of Transnational Law* 1-24: 4.7

Luxton, Peter, '*Walters v Olin*: uncertainty of subject matter- an insoluble problem in mutual wills?' [2009] 6 *Conv* 498-505: 12.2.4

Mak, Aaron 'Reconciling the Enforcement of Full and Half Secret Trusts: A Reinterpretation of Blackwell v Blackwell' (2013) 2 (Spring) *Hong Kong Student Law Gazette* 38-39: 12.5.3

Makdisi, George, 'Legal History of Islamic Law and the English Common Law: Origins and Metamorphoses', (1985-1986) 34 *Cleveland State Law Review* 3-18: 4.22

Markey, Maureen E., 'Ariadne's Thread: Leading Students into and out of the Labyrinth of the Rule Against Perpetuities' (2006) 54 *Cleveland State Law Review* 337: 5.6.3

Martin, J.'Fusion, fallacy and confusion: a comparative study', [1994] *Conveyancer and Property Lawyer* 13: 1.7

Mason, Anthony, 'The place of equity and equitable remedies in the contemporary common law world' (1994) 110 *L.Q.R.* 238: 11.6.1

Mason, Keith, 'Fusion: Fallacy, Future Or Finished?', 2004 (16 December) paper delivered at the Fusion Conference. Available at http://www.lawlink.nsw.gov.au/lawlink/Supreme_Court/ll_sc.nsf/pages/SCO_mason161204 : 1.7; 1.8

Matthews, P., 'Shooting STAR' (1997) 11 TLI 67: 4.8; 7.3.4

Matthews, P., 'STAR: Big Bang or Red Dwarf?' (1998) 12 TLI 98: 4.8; 7.3.4

Matthews, Paul, 'The Comparative Importance of the Rule in *Saunders v Vautier*' (2006) 122(APR) *Law Quarterly Review* 266-294: 5.6.3

Matthews, Paul, 'The true basis of the half-secret trust?' [1979] *Conveyancer and Property Lawyer* 360: 12.5.1

McCormack, Gerard, 'The Remedial Constructive Trusts and Commercial Transactions' [1996] 17(1) *Comp Law* 3-11: 6.2.1; 16.5

McCue, Don, 'Dishonestly assisting in a breach of trust: further confirmation that Barlow Clowes will be followed in the Court of Appeal and a robust conclusion on the facts: *Starglade Properties Ltd v Nash* [2010] EWCA Civ 1312' (2011) 17(2) *Trusts & Trustees* 128-131: 17.7

Mcnair, Mike, 'Equity and Conscience' (2007) 27(4) *Oxford Journal of Legal Studies* 659: 1.2; 1.4; 1.5.2- 1.5.5; 4.2.2

Meagher, Rowena, 'Secret trusts- do they have a future?' (2003) *Conveyancer and Property Lawyer, 203*: 12.0

Mee, John 'Half-secret trusts in England and Ireland.' (1992) (May/June) *Conveyancer and Property Lawyer*, 202-206: 12.5

Mee, John 'Property rights of Cohabitees' (Oxford: Hart Publishing, 1999): 11.6.1

Millett, P., 'The Quistclose Trust- a reply' (2011) 17(1) *Trusts & Trustees* 7-16: 10.5.2

Millett, Peter, 'Equity – the road ahead' (1995) 9 *TLI* 35: 1.8

Molloy, Tony, and Graham, Toby, 'Hard cases and bad law' (2011) **17 (9)** *Trusts & Trustees* 803-806: 13.5

Moran, 'Anything to Declare? Express Declarations of Trust in *Stack v Dowden*' [2007] 74 *Conv* 364: 11.3

Morray, Joseph P., 'The Rule Against Prolonged Indestructibility of Private Trusts' (1949-1950) 44 *Ill. L. Rev.* 467: 5.6.3

Mowrer, John M., 'Joint and Mutual Wills – Effect of Contract Not to Revoke' (1976) 41 *Missouri Law Review* 127-132: 12.2.3

Munby, Lord Justice, 'An unconscionable time a-dying: reports from a traveller in a foreign country' (2011) 17 (9) *Trusts & Trustees* 809-828: 1.8

Munger, Robert L. 'A Glance at Equity' (1915) 25(1) (Nov.) *The Yale Law Journal* 42: 1.4; 1.5; 1.5.1; 1.5.4: 1.7: 1.8: 2.1; 4.2.4: 4.2.5

Nelson, Stephen M., & Terry, Daniel L.F., 'New Trust Law in China' (2001) (September) *Trusts & Trustees* 12-14: 4.7

O'Hagan, Patrick, 'Mutual Wills' (1994) 144 (Sept) *New Law Journal* 1272: 12.2.3; 12.2.4

O'Hagan, Patrick, 'The reluctant settlor—property, powers and pretences' *Trusts & Trustees* (2011) **17 (10):** 905-919: 9.1

Pawlowski, Mark, 'Beneficial Entitlement- Do indirect contributions suffice? [2002] 32 *Fam Law* 190-194: 11.6.1

Pawlowski, Mark, 'Revocable gifts and estoppel' (2012) 18(1) (January) *Trusts & Trustees* 64-67: 9.5.3; 12.1

Pawlowski, Mark, 'Tracing into improvements, debts and, overdrawn accounts' (2011) 17(5) *Trusts & Trustees* 411-414: 16.5.4

Perrins, Bryn 'Secret trusts: the key to the dehors?' [1985] *Conveyancer and Property Lawyer* 248: 12.3; 12.4; 12.4.1

Picarda, Hubert, *The Law and Practice Relating to Charities* (London, Butterworths: 1977): 13.13

Piska, Nick, 'Intention, Fairness and the Presumption of Resulting Trust after *Stack v Dowden*' (2008) 71 MLR 120: 11.6.1

Prall, Stuart E., 'The Development of Equity in Tudor England' (1964) 8(1) The American Journal of Legal History 1: 1.2; 1.4; 1.5.1- 1.5.4; 1.6; 2.3; 3.2; 4.2.3; 4.2.4

Rappeport, Jack J., 'The Equitable Separate Estate and Restraints on Anticipation: its Modern Significance' (1956-1957) 11 *Miami Law Quarterly* 85: 5.6.3

Reed, Penelope, 'Proprietary estoppel: the law after *Cobbe v Thorner* amd its impact on inheritance tax' (2010) *Private Client Business* 49: 11.8

Reid, R.A., 'The Place of Trust in Jurisprudence' [1912] The Canadian Law Times 767-775: 4.4

Rhodes, R., & Palastrand, S., 'A Guide to Money Laundering Legislation' (2004) Vol. 8 No. 1 *JMLC* 9: 17.2

Richardson, Nicky, 'Legislation for mutual wills in New Zealand' (2010) 24(2) *Trust Law International* 99-109: 12.0

Rickett, C.E.F. 'Thoughts on Secret Trusts from New Zealand' (1996) (Jul/Aug) *The Conveyancer and Property Lawyer 302-308:* 12.5

Ridge, Pauline, 'Justifying the Remedies for Dishonest Assistance' (2008) 124 *Law Quarterly Review* 455: 17.5

Robinson, Keith, 'Madoff meets Quistclose' (2011) 17(7) *Trusts & Trustees* 668-676: 10.5.2

Rotherham, C., 'The property rights of unmarried cohabitees- the case for reform' [2004] *Conv* 268: 11.6.1

Sarah Collett, 'Constructive trusts- a glimmer of light? Part 1' (1998) 11(9) *Insolvency Intelligence*: 65- 68.

Schoeck, Richard J., 'The Place of Sir Thomas More in Legal History and Tradition: Some Notes and Observations' (1978) 23 *American Journal of Jurisprudence* 212: 1.5.2

Sheridan, 'English and Irish Secret Trusts.' [1951] 67 *Law Quarterly Review* 314: 12.5.1

Sherman, Charles P. 'A Brief History of the Canon Law' (1918-1919) 7 *Cal. L. Rev.* 93: 1.5.1; 8.1; 8.2

Simpson, A.W.B. "Entails and Perpetuities", (1979) 24 *Jur Rev* 1: 5.6.3

Smith, L., 'Tracing in Taylor v Plumer: Equity in the Court of King's Bench' [1995] Lloyd's Maritime and Commercial Law Quarterly 240: 16.1

Smith, L., 'Trust and Patrimony' (2008) 38 *Revue General de Droit* 379: 15.1

Smith, L., 'Unjust Enrichment, Property, and the structure of Trusts (2000) 116 Law Quarterly Review 412: 16.1

Smith, Lionel, 'Simplifying claims to traceable proceeds' [2009] 125 (Apr) *Law Quarterly Review* 338-348: 16.4

Smith, Lionel, 'Tracing into the Payment of a Debt' [1995] 54(2) *CLJ* 290: 16.1

Smolyansky, Michael, 'Reigning in the Quistclose Trusts: A Response to Twinsectra v Yardley' (2010) 16(7) *Trusts & Trustees* 558-568: 10.5.2

Speirs, Alastair 'Caught in the Tangled Web' [2000] 2 *Web Journal of Current Legal Issues:* 17.7

Steele, Patricia, and Johnson, Cal D, 'Bankers as constructive trustees- liability for "knowing receipt" of trust property' (1998) 13 (12) *Journal of International Banking Law* 401-404: 17.7

Stevens, John 'Vindicating the Proprietary Nature of Tracing' [2001] (Jan-Feb) *Conveyancer and Property Lawyer* 94-102: 16.1

Swadling, William, 'The Fiction of the Constructive Trust' (2011) 64 *Current Legal Problems* 399-433: 10.6

Tapsell, Grant, 'Laurence Hyde and the Politics of Religion in Later Stuart England' [2010] CXXV (517) *English Historical Review* 1414: 1.5.5

Thomas, Ann Van Wynen, 'Note on the Origin of Uses' (1949) 3 *S.W.L.J.* 162- 166: 4.22

Tudsbury, F., 'Equity and the common law", (1913) 29 *Law Quarterly Review* 154. 1.7

Van Caenegem, R.C., *The Birth of the English Common Law* (London: Cambridge University Press, 1973): 1.3

Van Tuyll, Frederik, 'The emergence of the Islamic trust' (2006) 12(9) Trusts & Trustees 7- 9: 4.22

Waters, Donovan, Q.C., 'The Future of the Trust from a Worldwide Perspective', in *The International Trust* (John Glasson, ed. 2002): 4.0

Welstead, Mary, 'Domestic Contributions and Constructive Trusts: The Canadian Perspective' (1987) *Denning Law Journal* 151-161: 11.6.1

Wilde, D. 'Secret and Semi-Secret Trusts: Justifying Distinctions Between The Two' (1995) (Sep/Oct) *Conveyancer and Property Lawyer* 366-378: 12.5.2

Wilson, John, 'Death, Severance and Survivorship' [2007] *Fam Law* 1082: 10.7.4

Wolff, Lutz-Christian, 'Law and Flexibility- Rule of Law Limits of a Rhetorical Silver Bullet' (2011) (11) (October) *The Journal Jurisprudence* 549-568: 1.5.3

Wong, Simone, 'Constructive trusts over the family home: lessons to be learned from other commonwealth jurisdictions?' (1998) 18(3) *Legal Studies* 369-390: 11.2; 11.6.1

Worthington , Sarah, *Equity* (2nd edition, 2006, Clarendon Law Series: Oxford): 9.4

Wright, D., 'How much of a trust is a constructive trust?' (2012) 18(3) *Trusts & Trustees* 264-272: 10.6

Yale, D.E.C., 'The Revival of Equitable Estates in the Seventeenth Century: An Explanation by Lord Nottingham' (1957) *Cambridge Law Journal* 72-86: 4.2.5

Websites

http://www.hks.harvard.edu/fs/phall/01.%20Charitable%20uses.pdf: 8.3

http://www.stepjournal.org/journal_archive/2011/step_journal_may_2011/the_end_of_the_rule_in_re.aspx: 13.5

http://www.britishempire.co.uk/: 1.1

Index